# Lecture Notes in Computer Science 2105

Edited by G. Goos, J. Hartmanis and J. van Leeuwen

D0988327

**Springer**
*Berlin*
*Heidelberg*
*New York*
*Barcelona*
*Hong Kong*
*London*
*Milan*
*Paris*
*Singapore*
*Tokyo*

Won Kim   Tok-Wang Ling
Yoon-Joon Lee   Seung-Soo Park (Eds.)

# The Human Society and the Internet

## Internet-Related Socio-Economic Issues

First International Conference, Human.Society@Internet 2001
Seoul, Korea, July 4-6, 2001
Proceedings

 Springer

Series Editors

Gerhard Goos, Karlsruhe University, Germany
Juris Hartmanis, Cornell University, NY, USA
Jan van Leeuwen, Utrecht University, The Netherlands

Volume Editors

Won Kim
Cyber Database Solutions, Inc.
3445 Executive Center Drive, Suite 256, Austin, TX 78731, USA
E-mail: won.kim@cyberdb.com

Tok-Wang Ling
National University of Singapore, Department of Computer Science
3 Science Drive 2, Singapore 117543
E-mail: lingtw@comp.nus.edu.sg

Yoon-Joon Lee
KAIST, Department of Computer Science
373-1 Yusung-Ku, Taejon, 305-701, Korea
E-mail: yjlee@cs.kaist.ac.kr

Seung-Soo Park
Ewha Womans University, Department of Computer Science and Engineering
Seodaemun-Ku, Seoul, 120-750, Korea
E-mail: sspark@ewha.ac.kr

Cataloging-in-Publication Data applied for

Die Deutsche Bibliothek - CIP-Einheitsaufnahme

The human society and the internet : internet related socio-economic issues ;
first international conference, human. society internet 2001, Seoul, Korea, July 4 - 6, 2001 ;
proceedings / Won Kim ... (ed.). - Berlin ; Heidelberg ; New York ; Barcelona ; Hong Kong ;
London ; Milan ; Paris ; Singapore ; Tokyo : Springer, 2001
  (Lecture notes in computer science ; Vol. 2105)
  ISBN 3-540-42313-3

CR Subject Classification (1998): K.4, K.5, K.6, K.8, C.2, H.5, H.4, J.1, J.3


ISSN 0302-9743
ISBN 3-540-42313-3 Springer-Verlag Berlin Heidelberg New York

This work is subject to copyright. All rights are reserved, whether the whole or part of the material is
concerned, specifically the rights of translation, reprinting, re-use of illustrations, recitation, broadcasting,
reproduction on microfilms or in any other way, and storage in data banks. Duplication of this publication
or parts thereof is permitted only under the provisions of the German Copyright Law of September 9, 1965,
in its current version, and permission for use must always be obtained from Springer-Verlag. Violations are
liable for prosecution under the German Copyright Law.

Springer-Verlag Berlin Heidelberg New York
a member of BertelsmannSpringer Science+Business Media GmbH

http://www.springer.de

© Springer-Verlag Berlin Heidelberg 2001
Printed in Germany

Typesetting: Camera-ready by author
Printed on acid-free paper      SPIN: 10839524      06/3142      5 4 3 2 1 0

# Foreword

During the past several years, the world has entered the first phase of the Internet Revolution. Investors showed confidence and faith in the prospects of the Internet-driven economy. In the US alone, some 30,000 dot com companies have sprung up to support electronic commerce with a wide variety of business models, technologies, and/or items or services to sell or even give away. Traditional businesses, so-called brick and mortar, or offline, businesses, have started to respond to challenges by Internet-based new competitors by augmenting their own businesses with Internet-based, or online, businesses and/or filing lawsuits against them. The initial business-to-consumer orientation of electronic commerce is giving way to business-to-business commerce, with large corporations forming electronic exchanges or consortia to conduct commerce among members.

Government, industry, and civic groups have started addressing social issues related to the Internet, such as taxation on electronic commerce, privacy, intellectual property rights, security, hacking, cyber crimes, digital divide, etc. Governments have started legitimizing electronic signatures and stepping up efforts to track down perpetrators of cyber crimes. The courts have started to wrestle with issues of privacy, intellectual property rights, crimes, and impediments to Internet-driven economy.

Although most of the innovations in Internet technology and business models are being created in the United States by hundreds of thousands of entrepreneurs funded by tens of billions of dollars of venture investment, both Europe and Pacific Asia have adopted these innovations remarkably fast, and have used them to fuel Internet-based economies.

With the above "Internet scenery" as backdrop, the First International Conference on Human.Society@Internet aims to provide a forum for meeting, holding discussions, and exchanging ideas and information for researchers, students, Internet-related business people, and government policy makers from Pacific Asia countries on the socio-economic issues and changes brought on by Internet technology. The conference technical sessions are organized around the following major themes: digital divide, law and regulations, contents control, culture, cyber education, digital governance, human computing, e-commerce/digital economy, and medical computing. The technical sessions include presentations of refereed research and position papers and invited talks by leading experts, tutorials, panel discussions, and product exhibits.

Total of 85 research papers were submitted from 14 countries and were reviewed through 11 country/regional program committees. Each paper was refereed by three experts chosen from the respective areas. Thirty-two papers were selected to be presented at the conference, based upon their technical quality and relevance to the conference. There were also 22 invited talks. Among the 54 contributions, 32 regular and 4 invited papers are included in the proceedings.

Many people deserve special thanks for their efforts to make the Human.Society@Internet 2001 a success. We express our appreciation to all the organizers and committee members of the participating countries for their tireless work. We are also grateful to all the sponsors for the financial support. Last not least, we thank Springer-Verlag for publishing the conference proceedings as a volume in its Lecture Notes in Computer Science series.

May 2001

**Won Kim**
**Tok-Wang Ling**
**Yoon-Joon Lee**
**Seung-Soo Park**

# Organizing Committee

## General Chair
Won Kim,     Cyber Database Solutions, MaxScan, USA
             Ewha Womans University, Korea

## Associate General Chair
Tok-Wang Ling, National University of Singapore, Singapore

## Country/Region General Chairs
Ron Saks-Davis, RMIT, Australia
Shan Wang, Renmin University of China, China
Tharam S. Dillon, Hong Kong Polytechnic University, Hong Kong
Nandlal L. Sarda, Indian Institute of Technology, India
F. Soesianto, Gadjah Mada University, Indonesia
Shinji Shimojo, Osaka University, Japan
Haruhisa Ishida, Keio University, ASCII Corporation, Japan
Kwan-Ho Song, Korea Network Information Center, Korea
Hwan-Seung Yong, Ewha Womans University, Korea
CheeSing Yap, Multimedia Development Corporation, Malaysia
Howard H. Frederick, New Zealand Center for Innovation &
             Enterpreneurship, UNITEC Faculty of Business, New Zealand
Tok-Wang Ling, National University of Singapore, Singapore
Chin-Chen Chang, National Chung Cheng University, Taiwan

## Advisory Committee (in Korea)
Whie-Kap Cho, Korea Information Security Agency
Sung-deuk Park,  National Computerization Agency
Chang-Bun Yoon, Korea Information Society Development Institute

## Global Function Chairs (in Korea)
**Global PC Chair**             Yoon-Joon Lee, KAIST
**Global Keynote Speech Chair** Young-Chul Kang, Maeil Business Newspaper
**Global Panels Chair**          Yong-Hak Kim, Yonsei University
**Global Publicity Chair**       Myung Kim, Ewha Womans University
**Global Tutorials Chair**       Chin-Wan Chung, KAIST
**Global Tutorials Co-chair**    Myung-Joon Kim, ETRI
**Global Exhibits Chair**        Chul-Yong Jung, Sangmyung University

## Country/Region Program Committee Chairs
James Thom, RMIT, Australia
Qiwen Wang, Beijing University, China
Francis Lau, Hong Kong University, Hong Kong
Hong Va Leong, Hong Kong Polytechnic University, Hong Kong
B.H. Jajoo, Indian Institute of Management, India

A. Susanto, Gadjah Mada University, Indonesia
Hisao Nojima, NTT LET Laboratories, Japan
Suguru Yamaguchi, Nara Institute of Science and Technology, Japan
Seung-Soo Park, Ewha Womans University, Korea
Kok-Meng Yew, HELP Institute, Malaysia
Donald Joyce, UNITEC Faculty of Business, New Zealand
Kian-Lee Tan, National University of Singapore, Singapore
Timothy K. Shih, Tamkang University, Taiwan

## Country/Region Publicity Chairs

M.D. Agrawal, Bharat Petroleum, India
J. B. Wahyu Agung, Atmajaya University, Indonesia
Shingo Ichii, University of Tokyo, Japan
Poh-Aun Lee, Multimedia University, Malaysia
Alison Young, UNITEC Faculty of Business, New Zealand
Suliman Al-Hawamdeh, Nanyang Technological University, Singapore
Tung-Shou Chen, National Taichung Institute of Technology, Taiwan

## The Rest of the Korea-Based Function Chairs

| | |
|---|---|
| **Finance Chair** | Ki-Joon Chae, Ewha Womans University |
| **Finance Co-chair** | Hee-Joon Song, Ewha Womans University |
| **Local Arrangements Chair** | Hune Cho, Kyungpook National University |
| **Local Arrangements Co-chair** | Yunmook Nah, Dankook University |
| **Proceedings Chair** | Suk-Doo Choi, Ewha Womans University |
| **Registrations Chair** | Eui-Kyeong Hong, University of Seoul |
| **Treasurer** | Miseon Kang , Ewha Womans University |
| **Secretary** | Soon Deok Kim, Ewha Womans University |

# Program Committee

**Hong Kong**

**Chair**        Francis Lau, Hong Kong University
**Vice Chair**   Hong Va Leong, Hong Kong Polytechnic University

**Members**
Henry Chan, The Hong Kong Polytechnic University
Ling Feng, Tilburg University, The Netherlands
James Kwok, Hong Kong University of Science and Technology
Ricky Y.K. Kwok, The University of Hong Kong
Wai Lam, The Chinese University of Hong Kong
Vincent K.N. Lau, The University of Hong Kong
Jianhua Ma, Hosei University, Japan
Kevin K.H. Pun, The University of Hong Kong
Clarence Tan, Bond University, Australia
Yu-Chee Tseng, National Chiao-Tung University, Taiwan
Cho-li Wang, The University of Hong Kong
Man Hon Wong, The Chinese University of Hong Kong
Man Leung Wong, Lingnan University
Chengzhong Xu, Wayne State University, USA


**Korea**

**Chair**        Seung Soo Park, Ewha Womans University

**Members**
Hune Cho, Kyungpook University
Hee Joon Song, Ewha Womans University
Pyung Joon Yoo, Yonsei University
Yong Mi Kim, Florida Atlantic University, USA
Hyoung-Joo Kim, Seoul National University
Kwang Yun Wohn, Korea Advanced Institute of Science
Won-Jun Lee, Ewha Womans University
Joong Ho Ahn, Seoul National University
Kyung Jun Lee, Korea University
Myung Hee Kang, Ewha Womans University
Hyun Mi Jung, Seoul National University
Soo Keun Oh, Ewha Womans University
Eui Sun Yoo, Ewha Womans University
Jung Ro Yoon, Korea Advanced Institute of Science
Yong Hak Kim, Yonsei University

## Malaysia

**Chair**    Yew Kok Meng, HELP Institute

**Members**
Yap Chee Sing, Multimedia Development Corporation
Lee Sai Peck, University of Malaysia
Lee Poh Aun, Multimedia University

## New Zealand

**Chair**        Donald Joyce, UNITEC

**Members**
Howard Frederick, UNITEC
Alison Young, UNITEC

## Singapore

**Chair**        Kian-Lee Tan, National University of Singapore

**Members**
Mong-Li Lee, National University of Singapore
Joseph Lee, Xplatform
Suliman Al-Hawamdeh, Nanyang Technological University
Ee-Peng Lim, Nanyang Technological University
Chun-Pong Yu, Sybase
Hwee-Hwa Pang, KRDL
Bonnie Cheuk, Arthur Andersen
Waltraut Ritter, Mindtheme Ltd.

## Taiwan

**Chair**        Timothy K. Shih, Tamkang University

**Members**
Han-Chieh Chao, National Dong Hwa University
Wen-Shyen Eric Chen, National Chung Hsing University
William C. Chu, TungHai University
Chyi-Ren Dow, Feng Chia University
Chung-Ming Huang, National Cheng Kung University
Wen-Shyong Hsieh, National Sun Yat-Sen University
Jonathan Lee, National Central University
Sheng-Tun Li, National Kaohsiung First University of Science and Technology
Yao-Nan Lien, National Chengchi University
An-Chi Liu, Feng Chia University

Yih-Jia Tsai, Tamkang University
Zsehong Tsai, National Taiwan University
Chun-Chia Wang, Kuang Wu Institute of Technology and Commerce
Shi-Nine Yang, National Tsing Hua University
Mark Liao, Academia Sinica
Jason Yi-Bing Lin, National Chiao Tung University
Wen-Hsiang Tsai, National Chiao Tung University
Simon Sheu, National Tsing Hua University

# Organization and Sponsorship

**Organized by**
*Human.Society@Internet* Organization Committee

**Managed by**
Ewha Institute of Science and Technology, Ewha Womans University, Korea
Korea Network Information Center, Korea

**Government Sponsor**
Korea Ministry of Information Communication

**Academic Societies**
Internet Technical Research Committee of Japan Science Promotion Society
Korea Cybercommunication Academic Society
Korea Medicine Information Society
Korea Multimedia Society
Korea Information Processing Society
Korea Information Science Society
Korea Patent Institute
Korea Society for Internet Information
Korea Society for Information Management
Korean Society for Journalism and Communication Studies
The Korean Society for Educational Technology
The Korea Society of Management Information Systems

**Industry Corporations**
Korea Telecom, Korea
Ehan Digitally, Korea
Ex-Em Inc., Korea

**Research Institutes**
Korea Information Society Development Institute
Korea Information Security Agency
Korea Electronics and Telecommunications Research Institute

# Table of Contents

## E-Commerce II

## Digital Divide II

## Virtual Enterprise

## Cyber Education I

## Digital Governance

## Human Computing

# Market Strategies in the Internet Content Business

Minzheong Song, Ph.D.
Senior researcher of Korea Telecom

Seochogu Woomyundong, R & D Center, Korea Telecom, Seoul, Korea.
Tel.: +82 2 526 5545
mzsong@kt.co.kr

**Abstract:** This project begins with introductory comments on the need for the market strategy for the Internet content business. This project deals with the market status globally and locally, and then set the strategies for the success of the Internet business, that is, strategies for increase of subscriber number & advertising revenue, strategic alliances for effective distribution, and pay service development.

## 1. Introduction

The Internet content business has some myths[1]: Bandwidth is increasing and cost is decreasing. Internet users demand rich audio-visual presentation and they want interaction with content providers. Community builds loyalty.

Digitized content is the key driver in the Internet business. The digital content means a targeted bundle of information, communication and transaction services in the paradigm of the convergence of the computer and telecommunications industries. However, strategies to create the attractive digital content will build on traditional media content and add communication and commerce facilities.

At the center of the Internet content business is the competence of companies to build communities of users, who need to address needs of highly specific groups by integrating content, communication and commerce services. This includes joining traditional contents with content-related advertising, information from other content providers and a wide range of new services, such as opportunities for customer interaction through chatting, discussion forums, bill-boards & consultation, governmental services & online financial transactions and so on. The Internet content provider needs satisfactory technical solutions in the area of media integration, secure transaction systems, user-oriented interfaces and high speed network access at reasonable prices.

On the other hand, companies have a strong interest in content distribution in several distribution channel or media. The importance of the cross-selling, i.e. repackaging content for distribution is increasing. The content is the most valuable asset for the Internet business. Therefore, the content competition in the value chain is increasing.

The purpose of this paper is to generate key strategies for the success of the Internet content business.

## 2. Types of the Internet content

The biggest change is likely to be in the advent of network-centric user interfaces. The Internet is global and defined as the network of networks that works to Internet-type protocols, not just the World Wide Web. This technology has reached surprising levels of relative maturity very quickly, but will continue to develop significantly over the next few years.

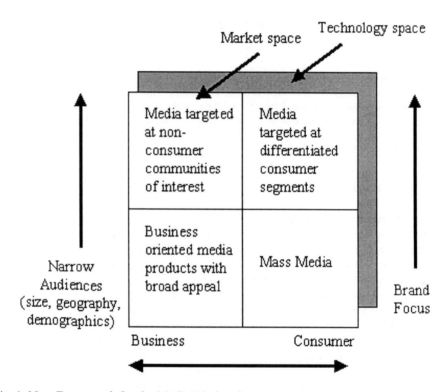

Fig. 1. New Framework for the Media Marketplace
Source: European Commission (DGXIII/E, 1997)

The new online landscape needs a new way of examining the market. The new market should not be considered in isolation from the technology space, but the two can be mapped onto each other (Figure 1). Recent studies and research have shown that there is a prevailing movement towards targeting products and services to clearly differentiated audiences, and the vertical axes therefore provide to illustrate this. The horizontal axis plots the customer focus of the products and services from business at one end, to consumer at the other.

There are two types of the media content in terms of user segmentation, consumer media and business media content. In addition, the type of the knowledge user could be added to those in the mezzo zone. Products and services that apply to each of these three types of use are extracted, and the general trend of movement is shown.

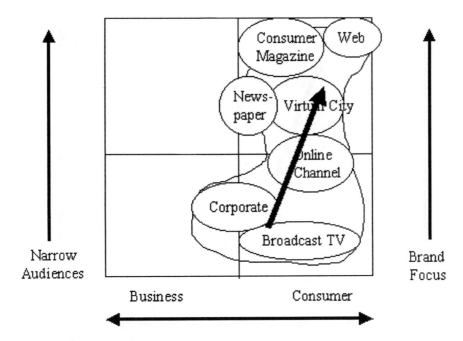

Fig. 2. Market Focus: Consumer
Source : European Commission(DGXIII/E, 1997)

## 2.1 Content for consumer

The movement within the consumer area is seen to be narrowing in terms of audience targeting and brand focus, as shown by the direction of the arrow (Figure 2).

The content for consumer includes broadcasting, film, online and offline communications platforms, traditional newspaper, book and magazine publishing.

The consumer media can be aimed at consumer segments of any size, in any place, and with interactivity. The difference will be the degree of interaction empowered, and the ability of consumers to become much more committed to an in-depth and long relationship with the media provider.

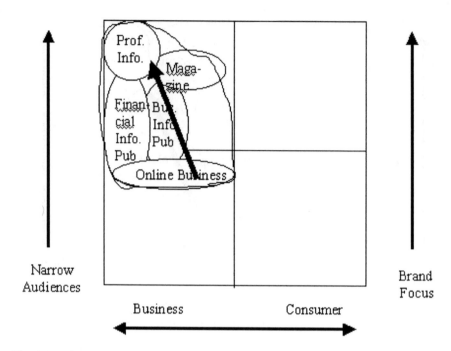

Fig. 3. Market Focus: Business
Source : European Commission(DGXIII/E, 1997)

## 2.2 Content for Business

In general, business media are those channels which are deployed directly by the corporation to enable communication - usually about a corporation's operations, goods and services - via print or online, with customers, suppliers and distributors. This can be business-to-business or business-to-consumer. It also includes any other media content which to inform decision making, such as online business information services, trade magazines.

The corporate media are driven by the business model and supply chain relationships of the particular vertical market in which that business operates. In the corporate business-to-business online service, it is somewhat easier to segment users into particular groups of customers who are seeking specific and defined products and services.

Companies access the Web's information to keep abreast of news affecting investments, currency obligations, transportation blockages and other events or trends that could affect their business on a daily or long-term basis.

Some Web businesses integrate news feeds, stock tickers, trusted third-party company ratings and analyses directly into products and services which they offer to their customers online as well as into their internal business processes.

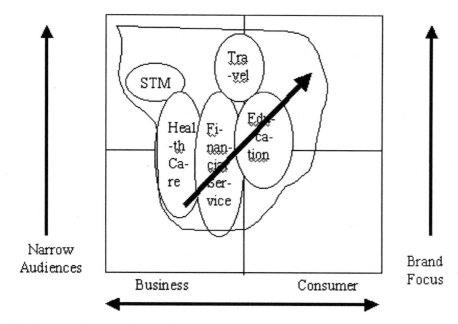

Fig.4. Market Focus: Knowledge
Source : European Commission(DGXIII/E, 1997)

## 2.3 Content for Knowledge

The knowledge media delivers information special to the education and research communities on consumer as well as corporate use. With the publishing technology and real-time methods of online distribution, the power-base moves towards the creation and editing community, away from the traditional media corporations that have played a powerful role in disseminating learning material and information.

The migration from business users (with largely pre-ordained budgets) to consumers (with discretionary, if smaller, budgets) within the knowledge media domain (See the figure 4) demands significant changes in packaging and pricing. Automation and personalization of use, where customers require ever more specific information, may alter the whole charging paradigm towards micro-transactions in this domain.

Packaging of content (which may embody search agents and other value-added features) becomes a strong differentiator. Users want to pay for what they deem to be of value, but may have trouble declaring this profile in advance.

Major business challenges for knowledge media organizations include finding ways to build customer loyalty. Building communities of interest will become critical.

Community owners will require billing and activity measurement technologies, enabling them to migrate from current flat-rate subscription models, to new business models in which content owners earn commission-based revenues by charging for metered access to specific content.

## 3. Economics of the Internet content business

There are two ways to make money in the Internet content business: Priced content through non-priced, advertising-backed content and paid one. The advertisers are still experimenting with new online media, and the percentage of their total advertising expenditure devoted to online media is still very small.

With the potential for fragmenting audiences, there is a need to investigate the dynamics of measuring response to interactive advertising on the Internet and to start actively profiling and managing the communication of messages to target groups. Advertisers on the Web are already demanding and receiving details of user behavior.[1]

The second source of the revenue is the payment management including pay-per-transaction. Technology for trading and payment management has a head-start due to the large infrastructures for clearance and settlement already constructed by many of the leading financial players.

However, few of these systems have to contend with the issues of real-time authorization and transaction execution across multiple networks. The issues of standard, security, multi-currency settlement, authentication, certification and authorization across multiple merchants and millions of users need to be resolved if Internet transaction is commercialized. A variety of techniques have emerged over the past few years but as yet there is no clear winner[2].

The content industry is an offspring of the converging telecommunications and media industries. Its development and growth have far reaching economic implications. The Internet content market is in a transition phase because of a gap in supply and demand. While technological development permits a fast progress in supplied services, households do not seem ready to integrate this new dimension.

Some aspects that are the main factors to promote the Internet content business are to consider in economic sense.

## 3.1 Price decrease for Internet access

For the B2B (business-to-business) communications, robust networks in the corporate environment (virtual private, Extranet, Intranet, etc), linking operations along the business supply chain, are becoming increasingly prevalent. The major global reduction in communications tariffs and expansion of bandwidth [3] is driving forward investment in high-performance processing platform technology at all points on the supply chain. Sufficient infrastructure to support all forms of advanced interactive corporate media comes to be taken for granted.

The price cuts lead to encourage development of a mass market. Competitive pressure leads a decrease in price of xDSL (x Digital Subscriber Line) and coaxial cable, while production rationalization and the development of cheaper displays enables the costs of services to be reduced.

Moreover, the progress of modem networks makes for lower costs in the use of cable network with two-way transmission. The xDSL prices profit from the competition in telecommunications resulting from deregulation. These price developments lead to Internet content services available to all households. The more people are using new information technologies, the greater prices are decreasing. It remains to be seen whether this trend will be sufficient to lead to the development of a mass market for the Internet content business.

Table 1. Price decrease to an acceptable level for consumers

| Average Price Decrease | Fiber to the Curb | DSL | Cable Modem | Adapter DVB | Modem | ISDN | Internet Adapter to TV | Internet -ready mobile phone |
|---|---|---|---|---|---|---|---|---|
| 1990-99 | 15% | 24% | 23% | 19% | 4% | 16% | 20% | 23% |
| 1999-2003 | 15% | 18% | 21% | 16% | 5% | 19% | 14% | 28% |

Source: Andersen Consulting, 1999

## 3.2 User demand: Convergence of reading and looking behavior

The use of the Internet publishing is "rational". The rational users can display an active attitude to Internet publishing services (they search actively for the information they want), or a passive one (which is comparable to passive consumption in front of the TV).

In considering different demand behaviors, we can identify four kinds of user: knowledge workers (professionals in information seeking); PC enthusiasts who use information technologies for private and professional interests; time constrained users such as consultants, lawyers, judges, etc.; and leisure seekers. Theoretically, for these four kinds of user, behavior can take the form of either active or passive consumption. But today, it is virtually always a case of active use.

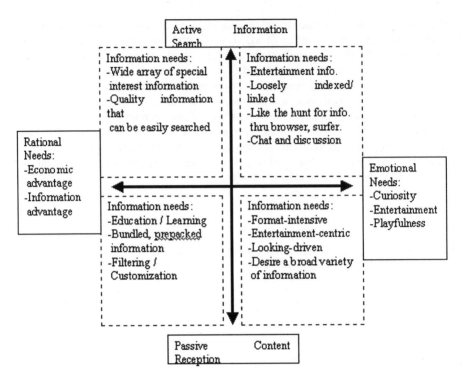

Fig.5. Content user's behavior
Source: Arthur Andersen, 1997; European Commission (DGXIII/E, 1997)

The paradigm shift that has occurred in the media and communication industries is not only a shift in terms of technical convergence. Although digitization technologies are the "enabler", they are not necessarily the main drivers within the digital media markets. The current market development shows, that the markets for digital information and communication services tend to be more and more demand driven. User demand can be encouraged, but not be pushed. This is a lesson that is still to be learned by many players in this industry.

People want content to affordable price. In order to exploit the market opportunities, the companies need new skills in producing high quality Internet content that meets exactly the requirement of users. The paradigm shift for suppliers in the transition towards an Internet economy is from a product oriented to a service oriented view.

Compared to the traditional media industries, the new information services are still only small businesses, and in many ways they are not operating in viable and profitable markets yet. Only when they succeed in offering a value added to the customer will the new markets become profitable.

Online services of newspaper publishers may illustrate this paradigm shift from "product" to "service". In the traditional print markets, publishing companies produce one or several "newspapers" or "magazines" and deliver these to their customers.

In the Internet content delivery, new concepts of readership community needs are emerging. Audiences are defining themselves as members of a group of individuals with similar interests who can interact online. This trend is already seen in the explosion of niche and lifestyle print magazines. But Internet content providers deliver a package of individual service offers rather than a mass product. These services fulfill the needs of such groups by integrating content, communication and commerce services.

A new stage has been reached in this development, and consumer demand determines the future development, rather than technology, as applications and content become more important.

While the use of the Internet content services is essentially active today, the most attractive market is on the side of passive applications: While the active user market is not expected to show any considerable growth over the next few years, most industrial players in Internet content business are concentrating their efforts on the progress of passive applications.

The market for passive services largely concerns leisure seekers, that is, a large part of the general public. The time-constrained users are also important target for passive applications. It is more likely, if the bandwidth capacity is better than now.

It appears that the rapid development of passive applications (resembling the TV context) will eventually be the only way to create a mass market. Inevitably, it has to be accompanied by a supply transfer from PC to TV.

Leisure seekers, who represent the major part of the general public interested in media technologies, are driven by entertainment, curiosity and playfulness. They constitute the principal gateway to the development of a mass market. To encourage these users to increase their consumption of the Internet content, providers of multimedia services have to supply cheap and very user-friendly applications. They also have to be very shrewd in terms of marketing.

The average public watch four hours a day in front of TV. Therefore, to ensure greater use of the Internet content by the general public, companies have to transfer their supply from the PC to the TV set. At present, the TV presents considerable advantages over the computer: easier to use, people are all in the habit of using this terminal (familiarity with TV should prevent psychological reluctance), and above all, there is already a wider installed base. Moreover, the history of information technologies should make companies remember that the success of mass market development depends on the size of the initial installed base.

## 3.3 Diversification, but strong economies of scope

To ensure a multitude of cheap services, firms have to realize important "economies of scope": The unstable character of the demand and its "zapping" behavior impose a policy of wide diversification on firms.

To be competitive, each firm has to be present wherever it is possible to capture a demand. Moreover, firms have to supply their services at low costs for the general public. To combine these two imperatives, companies have to try to obtain the largest possible economies of scope, by exploiting to the utmost the common point between different products and proliferating varieties. The target is to manage to offer products made to measure in appearance, but made in a production process that is very rationalized in reality.

It is also important to note that diversification has to be accompanied by growing interactivity of applications in order to reinforce the "zapping" possibilities.

## 3.4 The management of information overload

The problem is not the lack of information, but its excess. To have precise information on a subject, a seeker can find a multitude of documents and can feel lost, not knowing which is the best information. Sometimes, people want information on a subject but cannot find any studies on it, not knowing whether or not such studies actually exist.

One of the main expectations of Internet content business is to help people to find the essential part of what they want rapidly, to help them to select the best information in a short time. This management of information will be essential for Internet publishers, because all information existing today is not easily accessible for consumers.

# 4. Strategies for activating the Internet Content Business

## 4.1 From mass marketing to precision marketing

The precision marketing can be summarized by the capacity to supply a large range of personalized services, to ensure the customer loyalty. The issue in the Internet content market is to sell a multitude of products at different prices. Each company must have a profound knowledge of the market to develop its production and determine its price policy.

Therefore, it has to study a lot of data concerning consumer habits, such as time and frequency of access to servers, products sought, kind of network used. A detailed analysis of this data can help firms to perfect their methods of obtaining customer loyalty.

The problem for producers is that the demand on leisure is generally unstable. People seem to be ready for a large access to leisure applications, but only if these are constantly renewed. Today, leisure consumption by the general public is characterized by an important awareness effect that multimedia enterprises have to take into consideration.

To overcome this constraint, companies should supply a wide range of greatly differing leisure applications. Then, the most delicate operation for a company is to offer the consumer the possibility to move from one service to another, keeping him in the sphere of supply of this same company.

To succeed in this task, firms should build a strong brand name that can be recognized in the overabundance of information and applications. Creating this brand awareness will be one of their principal challenges.

A content provider's effort to specify interactive digital content for highly specific target markets is termed customization. It is demand side.

On the other hand, a user's interactive modification of a service for individual purposes is defined as personalization. In the Internet economy, new concepts of communities based on interests, needs and lifestyles are emerging. More than ever, audiences are defining themselves as members of a group of individuals with similar interests who can interact online.

The trend towards individualized lifestyles, together with the desire for personal independence and mobility, have already changed the parameters of traditional print media design.

The new media, the Internet provides media companies with the opportunity to join their traditional content with content-related advertising, information from other content providers and a whole range of entirely new services, such as opportunities for customer interaction through chat, discussion forums, free bill-boards, consultation, institutional and governmental services, and online financial transactions.

A major driver of the customization is advertisers and marketers. Internet is not yet a mass medium and cannot compete with traditional media in reach. But, the attractiveness of Internet services for advertisers is the quality of the audience and not the quantity. The development of a 1 to 1 marketing has been the talk of marketers for years. With its inherent feedback circle, the Internet medium could be the perfect environment for this approach.

While the service provider aims at customizing his offerings, he may also consider offering the user interactive tools to modify his services for his specific purposes. *PointCast* is an example of such a service that allows the user to determine what exactly he wants within a framework of content offered.

Although the personalization is a key word in the discussion of interactive content, there is some evidence to doubt the analytical idea behind that concept. At least, the personalization is not a value in all cases and by itself. It will certainly not be viable to improve low quality services or make them appear more attractive simply by giving the user an opportunity to "choose among the bad fruit".

It seems contradictory to expect from content providers to act as an information organizer in the vast amount of information available (i.e. provide targeted and pre-selected high quality content) and, at the same time, let the user actively generate his service. The problem with this idea is that this is exactly the service users expect from quality content providers; they are not interested in reshaping the content and services they get.

One way of viewing personalization in the sense of selecting content is to focus on giving the user the opportunity to quickly navigate within the service and to make intelligent queries. Classified ads are a good example. Electronic classifieds are no value added service if they do not include special query tools. It should be possible to make a database query for real estate classified ads, for example, according to categories such as <price>, <location> etc. This is the way how the personalization of service could be understood. The task in this example would be to provide the publisher with a tool that minimizes the effort of entering classified in a database and allows the user to make an online query according to his "personal" search criteria.

## 4.2 Marketing mix

The content [4]is the most important asset in the value chain of the interactive content industries. This holds true if some specifications are made in terms of what the concept of the content is. In particular, it is very important to understand the transition of the media industry from a product towards a service-oriented industry, since this transformation determines the concept of the content in the digital interactive services industry.

The term "content industry", which is becoming widely used, has rarely been defined in detail. While in the traditional media industries the content was usually media content, i.e. information (such as newspaper reports, broadcasts, etc.) and entertainment programs (such as features, movies, talk shows, etc.), in the digital media industries, the term of "content" has a broader reference.

The content, seen in terms of the new content industry, is more than the total of texts and images. Rather, the content is programmed and an integrated (information, entertainment, etc.) service package for a target group. It comprises communication services and transaction services.

The content industry comprises all businesses that are part of the value chain, beginning from content creation and ending with the devices the customers need in order to access and use the final product or service. This implies that the traditional media industries are involved in the content industry as well as independent digital studios, Internet access provider, telecom operators, cable TV network operators and hardware and software companies.

From a technical viewpoint, the content industry comprises each of three areas - content production, network distribution and information retrieval. Each segmented markets within the content industry has different drivers and impediments, requires different measures and initiatives to encourage market development and is at a different stage or level of market maturity.

Faced with a hesitant demand and a poor knowledge of potential users' needs, companies have to make important choices in terms of marketing positions in a very vague future. The consumption growth is characterized by several paradoxical trend which has to be taken into consideration by multimedia producers: Individualization but globalization of production and consumption standards, etc.

Therefore, producers have to direct their supply along different paths: very attractive and user-friendly services but also very targeted and personalized; multi-sensorial but easy to use services; access to an abundance of quick-to-find information. For companies, the greatest difficulty will be to combine the management of an ever-more efficient technological supply with the management of emotional values. In this situation, choices in terms of marketing-mix are particularly delicate.

## 4.3 Added value chain

The Internet content industry is moving towards vertical integration. Increasing variety of players have been attracted by this recent market, but only a few will be winners in the strong competition.

Now, it is still too early to know exactly what the future configuration of this production will be. As traditional media companies have to incorporate an electronic supply to stay competitive, they must face up to a new array of competitors from the communications, IT and financial services sectors.

Thus, while the use of Internet content is being developed on a large scale, the industrial organization of the supply is taking shape. Companies with different activities and especially of different sizes, which are now in mutual competition, often have strong input-output relations with each other.

Differences in size and in economic power could profit a few major players (such as telecommunications operators) and provoke a multitude of buy-outs.

Finally, the Internet content supplier is evolving on the basis of a vertical integration. Firms presenting the best marketing and technological skills, large-scale supply of services and strong experience in strategic competition will be in the best position to win huge market shares.

While large firms have a decisive role in the development of Internet content market, small companies will be in the front rank in terms of creativity: Internet content business is a capital-intensive activity. Investments in new products are ever higher because of technological progress and the fast development of standards.

Moreover, the strong competition leads to increasingly high minimum investments. Internet content business is an activity with great financial risks. To meet competition, companies have to be of a sufficient "critical size", to be able to spread their costs by achieving important 'economies of scale'.

Nevertheless, as in traditional media, large firms should work with smaller subcontractors to supply a very large range of products and to ensure a greater success potential. Furthermore, a multitude of subcontractors gives large firms a higher degree of adaptability and flexibility.

The subcontractors are small enterprises with a great deal of creative activity but without sufficient financial resources to develop and distribute their own products to the end user. The support of larger firms is indispensable for them. So, as an atomization of creations appears absolutely necessary to encourage the development of new products, the financial commitment of large firms is essential.

In these conditions, close-cooperation will be developed between majors and the most creative of small enterprises. This co-operation will enable transaction costs in Internet content production to be considerably reduced, each players concentrating on his own skills and using his partners' know-how to exploit his production.

The more Internet content market develops, the more the added value will move from infrastructure and services operators to content players. This added-value swing from the downstream of production chain to upstream will be the factor structuring future relations between big and small firms.

# 5. Conclusion

The convergence of telecommunications and media industries and the resulting paradigm shift in the media industries has been enabled by the rapid development in the area of digital technologies.

The new emerging markets have now reached a stage, in which these technologies as the enablers are no longer the main drivers. Case studies of success and failure show that markets for digital information and communication services tend to be more and more demand driven.

User demand may be encouraged, but cannot be pushed. This is a lesson that is still to be learned by many players in this industry. Information engineers move towards the center of value generation of the new media industries. Their skills are core competencies in the converging digital media and telecommunications industry. They provide solutions for all sectors of the value chain. The know-how in information engineering is needed to create attractive content, expand service function, develop script for self-executable content, improve interactive features and integrate them with e-commerce solutions. Information engineering is also required for content dissemination and delivery over networks, and it is essential for information retrieval, i.e. for the design of user interfaces and search and navigation tools.

If the content is the most valuable and important part of the interactive digital services industry, this should be properly reflected in the value chain.

Comparing the value chain of the converging industries with the value chain of the interactive services industry reveals that the share of content creation and content packaging has increased. In the traditional telecommunications industry, 80% of the value have been generated by network & service operator, and the rest by manufacturing equipment. It has been estimated that in traditional print markets (here: newspaper & magazine publishing), content creation and aggregation adds about 40% to the total value.

In the new digital services industry, the value added by content creation and processing will be more than 50%. Service integration, platform management and "byte transport" will each account for 10-15%, and end user technology about 10%.

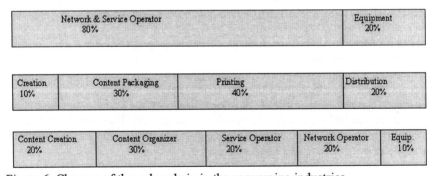

Figure 6. Changes of the value chain in the converging industries
Source: European Commission (1996); Jahrbuch Telekommunikation und Gesellschaft (1997)

Market of tomorrow requires a much broader skill and competency set than today. To occupy the strategic high ground, players will have to play new roles that will require combinations and extensions of current skill sets. They will be driven by market demand and by pressure from players entering the market from other industries.

The Internet congestion is a bottleneck for the development of commercially viable business applications. It will be a critical success factor for all Internet based services to solve this problem.

The cross-selling demands systematic guidelines for efficient interface management. One focus of research must be to establish standards for the multiple use of content and to invest in software improvement and quality process enhancement.

New servers and customer service functions, as well as high speed Internet applications, will enable a next generation online services whose offerings will be fully integrated with the Internet platform.

Strategic co-operations and outsourcing are gaining importance in the content industries.

As a consequence, "co-opetition" is the new market rule for big and small players: companies will have to compete in some areas, while co-operating at the same time in others. While big player concentration attracts much attention, numerous small businesses with a clear focus on specific aspects of the creation process are emerging and proving successful.

The value chain of the interactive digital services industry creates a paradoxical situation. On the one hand, the economies of digital technologies make it easier for all players to build new competencies. The content creators may develop into content deliverers, carriers think about entering the content creation sector.

On the other hand, it remains almost impossible for an individual player to control the whole value chain. Everybody needs partners. As a consequence, strategic alliances are critical for success and the business landscape is changing rapidly and continuously.

New companies are emerging, focusing on narrow aspects of the value chain and offering their special services to other companies. In this rapidly developing new market environment with alliances and co-operations changing everyday, companies must remain focused on their strategic objectives. The business model becomes more important than ever, i.e. the clear decision about which competencies to build in-house, and which competencies to outsource.

The game of playing around with alliances and co-operations is an opportunity for entrepreneurial activities, i.e. setting up small businesses and offering services to larger businesses, especially in the area of content creation and processing.

New media creation requires a combination of "publishing" skills (traditional skills of print media) and "programming" skills (skills of broadcasting companies). Motion is not just in pictures, but also in texts.

With regard to the digital content engineering, new content requires the combination of the "publishing" skills of producing in pages and chapters (space media skills) and with "programming" skills of producing in clips, sequences and episodes (time media skills). Multimedia adds animated graphics, images and video the text-based content, whilst giving the user control over the sequence of information consumption. User guidance and navigation charting become critical content features.

Multimedia thus transcends both print and TV, braking constraints on reading and looking. Hypertexts end linear reception processes. Improvement of compression technologies and the transmission rates for real video and audio transmission over narrow bandwidth networks are business critical.

In the long run, once bottlenecks such as low bandwidth no longer exist, services having the highest market potential will be combining "looking" and "reading" elements. As already mentioned, four sectors constitute major market segments for the digital interactive services industry from a demand side perspective. It is important to consider the user motives and the preferred way to interact with media according to the target audience.

# References

Bakos, J.Y. and Brynjolfsson, Erik: "Bundling Information Goods: Pricing, Profits and Efficiency." *Internet Publishing and Beyond: Economics of Digital Information and Intellectual Property,* Conference Paper (Jan. 23-25, 1997).

Blunden, Brian and Blunden, Margot (Ed.): *Advertising in a multimedia age.* Bruxelles: IEPRC/Pira International (1996).

Bruck, Peter A. and Selhofer, Hannes: *Oesterreichs Content Industry. Bestandsaufnahme und Marktstrategien.* Wien: Buchkultur (1997)

Bruck, Peter A. and Selhofer, Hannes: "The Ignored User. Critical Factors Determining User Demand for New Information Services." (Proceedings to the ENCIP European Communication Policy Research Conference 1997, Venice 23-25 March 1997). *Communications & Strategies,* Issue 26 (2nd quarter 1997) 277-302

Burgelmann, Jean-Claude and Verhoest, Pascale: "Trans-European Information Networks: Rhetoric and Practice." *Telematics and Informatics,* Vol. 13, No. 2/3 (Spring/Summer 1996) 67-80

Colombo, Massimo, Dang Nguyen, Godefroy, and Perucci, Antonio: "Multimedia, Paradigmatic Shift and Distinctive Competencies of Firms: an Empirical Analysis." *Communications & Strategies,* Issue 26 (2nd quarter 1997) 207- 254

Cox, Richard: "Drawing sea serpents: The publishing wars on personal computing and the Information age." *Firstmonday,* peer-reviewed journal on the Internet (1998).

Databank Consulting: "Review of Developments in Advanced Communication Markets." *FAIR Report Series Nr. 1* (Oct. 1996)

Diebold Deutschland GmbH, Telemedia GmbH: *Business Digital* (1996)

Do, Cuong V.: "Mergers, Acquisitions, and Alliances in the Internet Space." *M&A Strategies,* hosted by Digital Times (Mar. 16, 2000).

Dominick, J. R., Sherman, B. L., Messere, F.: *Broadcasting, cable, the Internet, and beyond,* McGrawHill, Boston (2000).

Dumort, Alain and Dryden, John: *The Economics of the Information Society.* Bruesel: Office for Official Publications of the European Communities (2000).

European Commission (EC): *ACTS 97.* Project Summaries, Annual technical report (1997).

EC: *ACTS - The Way Forward. Advanced Communication, Economic Growth and Social Development in Europe.* European Commission, DG XIII/B (1997)

EC, DG XIII: *Identification of influential technologies, impact assessment and recommendations for action.* Report by Meta_Generics Ltd. (November 1995).

EC, DG XIII/E: *Strategic Developments for the European Publishing Industry towards the Year 2000.* Report by Andersen Consulting and IENM / Techno-Z FH F&E. (September 1996).

EC, DG XIII: *The Markets for Electronic Information Services in the European Economic Area. Supply, Demand and Information.* IMO (October 1996).

EC: *Building the European Information Society for Us All.* Final Policy Report of the High Level Group of Experts (April 1997).

EITO (European Information Technology Observatory): *Annual Report.*

*The Emerging Digital Economy II. A Market-Entry Strategy Analysis for Media and Technology Ventures.* KPMG (1997).

Feifer, Richard and Tazbaz, Denise: Interface Design Principles for Interactive Multimedia. In: Telematics and Informatics, Vo. 14, No. 1 (February 1997). 51-66

Fontaine, Gilles: "Subscriber Control. What Impact on the European Electronic Communications Industry." *Communications & Strategies,* Issue 26 (2 nd quarter 1997). 255-274

Fuchs, Gerhard: "Interactive Television - a Shattered Dream?" *Communications & Strategies,* Issue 26 (2nd quarter 1997) 303-333

*(The) Future of the European Media Industry.* Financial Times Management Report (1996).

Grauer, Manfred and Merten, Udo: *Multimedia. Entwurf, Entwicklung und Einsatz in betrieblichen Informationssystemen.* Berlin/Heidelberg/ New York: Springer Verlag (1997).

Jahrbuch Telekommunikation und Gesellschaft 1997: *Die Ware Information* Ed. by Kubicek, Herbert et al. Heidelberg: R. v. Decker Verlag (1997)

Harnard, S.: *Post-Gutenberg Galaxy: The Fourth Revolution in the Means of Production of Knowledge.* Public-Access Computer Systems Review(electronic journal), 2(1) (1997) 35-93

Latzer, Michael: *Mediamatik - die Konvergenz von Telekommunikation, Computer und Rundfunk.* Opladen: Westdeutscher Verlag (1997).

OECD: *Science, Technology and Industry Outlook* (1996).

OECD: *Local Access Pricing and E-commerce* (2000).

FCC: *Availability of high-speed and advanced telecommunications services* (2000).

FCC: *Deployment of Advanced Telecommunications Capability.* Second Report (2000).

FCC: *High-Speed Services for Internet Access: Subscribership.* (2000).

Giese, Mark: "Self without body: Textual self-representation in an electronic community." *Firstmonday,* peer-reviewed journal on the Internet (1998).

Goldman Sachs: E-Commerce, Internet, B2B: 2B or not 2B, Version 1.1 (1999).

Goldman Sachs: Internet Korea (2000).

Kevin Werbach: "Syndication: The Emerging Model for Business in the Internet Era." *Harvard Business Review* (May-June 2000)

McKnight, Lee W., Boroumand, Jahangir: "Pricing Internet services: after flat rate." *Telecommunications Policy,* Vol. 24, Nr. 6/7 (July/August 2000) 565-590.

Miles, Peggy: *Internet World Guide to Webcasting,* John Wiley & Sons, Inc. (2000)

Morrison, Joline and Vogel, Doug: "The impact of presentation visuals on persuasion," *Information & Management* 33 (1998) 125-135.

Owen, Bruce M.: *The Internet Challenge to Television,* Harvard University Press, Cambridge et al. (1999)

Pierre, Samuel and Safa, Haidar: "Models for Storing and Presenting Multimedia Documents." *Telematics and Informatics.* Vol. 13, No. 4 (Fall 1996) 233-250

Rheingold, Howard: *The Virtual Community. Homesteading on the Electronic Frontier*. Addison-Wesely Publishing Company (1993).

Riefler, Katja: "Zeitungen online - Chance oder Risiko? Onlineaktivitaeten der Zeitungsverleger." *Media Perspektiven* (Oct. 1996) 537-549

Rojo, Alejandra and Ragsdale, Ronald G.: "Participation in Electronic Forums: Implications for the Design and Implementation of Collaborative Distributed Multimedia." *Telematics and Informatics*. Vol. 14, No. 1 (February 1997). 83- 96

Thiel, Shayla: "A Postmodern Medium," *The Journal of Electronic Publishing*. Vol. 4, Issue 1 (Sep. 1998).

Thurow, Lester C.: "An Era of Man-Made Brainpower Industries," *The Knowledge Economy*. Boston (1998) 199-217.

Varian, Hal R.: *Future of Electronic Journals, Presented at the Scholarly Communication and Technology Conference*. Emory University, April 1997. Published in Journal of Electronic Publishing (September 1998).

Varian, Hal R.: *How to Build an Economic Model in your Spare Time, part of a collection titled Passion and Craft: Economists at Work*. edited by Michael Szenberg, University of Michigan Press (1997).

Varian, Hal R. and Roehl, Richard: *Circulating Libraries and Video Rental Stores*. Working Paper (Dec. 1996). http://www.sims.berkeley.edu/

Varian, Hal R.: "Differential Pricing and Efficiency," *First Monday*, Vol.1 No.2 - August 5th.(1996).

Vogel, Andreas: "Fachverlage: Behutsame Schritte zum Electronic Publishing. Multimediaaktivitaeen von Fachbuch- und Fachzeitschriftenverlagen." *Media Perspektiven*. (Oct. 1996) 526-536

Zimmer, Jochen: "Pay TV: Durchbruch im digitalen Fernsehen? Bezahlfernsehen in Deutschland und im internationalen Vergleich." *Media Perspektiven* (July 1996) 386-401

---

1. Meyer, Eric K.: "The 10 Myths of Online Publishing." In: AJR (American Journalism Review) NewsLink (Aug. 4-10, 1998) http://www.newslink.org/emcol3.html

[2] The examples of first generation tools for targeting Web site advertising: Doubleclick (doubleclick.net); SmartClicks (smartclicks.com) at an individual user level, so that they can establish the most successful formats for presentation of their messages.

[3] In 1997, World Trade Organization (WTO) agreement creates a truly liberalized global telecommunication market from January 1998 (See http://www.wto.org)

[4] In the interactive digital services industry the term "content" refers to a wide range of information, entertainment, communication and transaction services that combine smart texts, intelligent graphics/simulations, motion in images and texts and are made available to an identifiable user group. The distinction does not matter whether these services are created to be sold (commercial services) or if they are available for free of end-user charges (e.g. corporate publishing and advertising).

# Government Initiatives and the Knowledge Economy: Case of Singapore

Chew Lay Lek and Suliman Al-Hawamdeh
Division of Information Studies, School of Applied Science, Nanyang
Technological University, Singapore 639798, Email:
assuliman@ntu.edu.sg

**Abstract.** With rapid technological changes, the global marketplace is becoming increasingly competitive. To survive the new millennium, economies need to be versatile and adapt rapidly to the changing environment in this highly interconnected world. The ability to harness the use of information to add value to existing processes is crucial. Singapore, without natural resources, will have to position itself as a preferred hub for the exchange of value-added information and knowledge if it is to carve a niche for itself in the new millennium. This paper focus on the role of science systems in a Knowledge-based economy; the initiatives adopted by the Singapore Government in gearing Singapore towards a Knowledge-based economy; and the challenges faced by the government in measuring the effectiveness of these initiatives

## 1 Introduction

To succeed in today's increasingly competitive global economy, a country has to leverage on whatever resources it has a comparative advantage to move ahead of its competitors. Thurow, in his book "The Future of Capitalism", stated that "Today, knowledge and skills now stand alone as the only source of comparative advantage"[32]. This certainly applies to Singapore, with its very limited natural resources. Singapore can only rely on its people to survive in the global market place. The challenge is to turn the population at large into skilled, knowledgeable and competent workers, that is, to nurture a knowledge-based economy. In his words, "Skilled people will become the only sustainable comparative advantage of a society."

Traditionally, the engine of economic growth depends on the availability of factors of production such as land, labor and capital. Although such production activities will still remain an important component of growth, the frogleap into the new millennium will be powered not by mere traditional production of goods and services but will focus on knowledge-based initiatives [1, 21]. The essence of a Knowledge-based economy, is the capacity to absorb, process and apply "knowledge" or "intellectual property" and translate it into a key source of competitive advantage together with the basic factors of production which continue to be important in the Knowledge-based economy. The emphasis is towards intellectual capital or knowledge as a source of value and wealth creation.

Thus, in a Knowledge-based economy, productivity and growth are largely determined by the rate of technical progress, the accumulation of knowledge and a network or systems that can efficiently distribute knowledge and information. In terms of labor or employment, there is also a shift in requirements. Workers need to be more creative and innovative with the use of acquired knowledge and be able to adapt to rapid technological changes. As such, learning on the part of both individuals and firms is crucial for realizing the productivity potential of new technologies and longer-term economic growth. In the world of Knowledge-based economy, the comparative advantage of an economy depends on how fast one can deliver the goods/services within the shortest time with the advent of changes in technology and the evolution of borderless economies [16, 33].

Government policies, in terms of science and technology, industry and education will need new emphasis in a Knowledge-based economy. Acknowledgment is needed of the central role of the firm, the importance of national innovation systems and the requirements for infrastructures and incentives, which encourage investments in research and training .

## 2    Role of Science and Technology in the Knowledge Economy

Science and technology will be the key driving forces in a knowledge-based economy. For example, in 1980, US Steel employed 120,000 people in steel making. In 1997, it turned out the same tonnage with 20,000 workers. According to the OECD reports, a country's science system takes on increased importance in a knowledge-based economy [17,18, 24]. Public research laboratories and institutions of higher education are at the core of the science system, which more broadly includes government science ministries and research councils, relevant enterprises and other private bodies, and supporting infrastructure. In the knowledge-based economy, the science system contributes to the key functions of:

**Knowledge production** – developing and providing new knowledge through research and innovation; (b) knowledge transmission – educating and developing human resources; The science system is a crucial element in knowledge transmission, particularly the education and training of scientists and engineers. In the knowledge-based economy, learning becomes extremely important in determining the fate of individuals, firms and national economies. Human capabilities for learning new skills and applying them are key to absorbing and using new technologies. Properly trained researchers and technicians are essential for producing and applying both scientific and technological knowledge. The science system, especially universities, is central to educating and training the workforce for the knowledge-based economy.

**Knowledge transfer** – disseminating knowledge and providing inputs to problem solving. The science system plays an important role in transferring and disseminating knowledge throughout the economy. One of the hallmarks of the knowledge-based economy is the recognition that the diffusion of knowledge is just as significant as its creation, leading to increased attention to *"knowledge distribution networks"* and *"national systems of innovation"*. These are the agents and structures, which support the advance and use of knowledge in the economy and the linkages between them. They are crucial to the capacity of a country to diffuse innovations and to absorb and maximize the contribution of technology to production processes and product development. In this environment, the science system has a major role in creating the enabling knowledge for technological progress and for developing a common cultural basis for the exchange of information [3, 5, 14, 18].

In a knowledge-based economy, the science system must balance not only its roles of knowledge production (research) and knowledge transmission (education and training) but also the third function of transferring knowledge to economic and social actors, especially enterprises, whose role is to exploit such knowledge .

## 3   Government Initiatives

In the highly connected Internet world today, we are witnessing dramatic changes in the way businesses and nations operate and compete. The global playing field is becoming more even and the barriers to entry are coming down. Small countries like Singapore can now plug into the global economy and become a global player.

To stay competitive, Singapore must remain relevant to the rest of the world, by adding value to the global economy, strengthening its capabilities as a manufacturing center for MNCs and as a regional services and information hub. It must upgrade its economy to one that is driven by knowledge-intensive industries amidst an environment that is teeming with innovative ideas if it will to succeed in its vision to build a knowledge-based economy.

In line with it, the Singapore Government developed IT2000 which aims to transform Singapore into an Intelligent Island, where the use of information technology is pervasive in every aspect of its society – at work , home and play. The 5 strategies thrusts are :
- develop Singapore into a global hub
- boost the economic engine
- enhance the potential of individuals
- link communities locally and globally
- improve the quality of life.

To advance quickly to a Knowledge-Based Economy, Singapore has to develop two key ingredients:

- a knowledge infrastructure; and
- human and intellectual capital.

The Government has rolled out various initiatives to develop these two key ingredients. In addition, the government also has to play a vital role in managing the science systems so as to promote the production, transmission and transfer of knowledge within the economy to be in line with its initiatives. The various initiatives that are set up by the government contributes to the production, transmission and transfer/diffusion of knowledge in one way or another.

## 3.1 National Infrastructures

One of the initiatives is the building of a comprehensive knowledge infrastructure to support the sharing and exchange of information and knowledge. This encompasses Singapore ONE, the legal and policy framework, introduced to support new ways of doing business such as e-commerce, as well as expanding the available resources for our network of educational and research institutes. This knowledge infrastructure will be linked to the major knowledge and business centers of the world. A knowledge infrastructure allows knowledge to be transmitted, shared and built upon among the masses, individuals in a company or organization, across companies in the same or different sector, and between countries. It consists of the physical networks and their interconnections with knowledge or 'thought' centers such as universities, research institutes, and business centers around the world. It started with the IT2000 Masterplan by the then National Computer Board (NCB), which was formerly the Technology authority of Singapore. Subsequently Singapore ONE came under the preview of Infocomm Development Authority (IDA) which was formed from the merger of NCB and Telecommunication Authority of Singapore (TAS).

Singapore ONE, Singapore's nation-wide broadband infrastructure for multimedia applications and services, based on the Automatic Switching Technology (ATM) was launched in June 1998 and is the result of Singapore's continuing effort to explore emerging technology trends and to exploit the opportunities early (http://www.s-one.gov.sg). The foundation is now well in place for the entire nation to use Singapore ONE. It has placed Singapore at the forefront of new broadband technology developments. Today, Singapore ONE is available for connections in 99% of all homes and is available in all schools, most tertiary institutions, almost all public libraries as well as many community centers throughout Singapore. There are also several hundreds information kiosks located along Orchard Road, in shopping malls, town centers and other public places, which are connected to Singapore ONE.

The number of users has grown steadily, from 106,900 as at end of 1999 to about 250,000 users today. To promote the use of Singapore ONE at the beginning, the then NCB and its partners conducted mass training events such as ONE Camp for students and parents and Surf @ Stadium for businesses and members of the public last year. Together, some 15,000 people were trained to use Singapore ONE. Building on the momentum, the then NCB with the support of the National Library Board (NLB) launched in May 1999, a permanent Singapore ONE training center called ONE Learning Place at the Toa Payoh Community Library.

To further expand market reach and consumer base, efforts are underway to link the ATM network to overseas network for broadband access to the rest of the world. Currently, Singapore ONE is offered over the @Home broadband network in the US which reaches out to 1 million north area subscribers. The number of new applications and services has also built up steadily. Today, many multinationals and local companies are already actively using Singapore ONE to deliver interactive, multimedia applications and services. There are about 180 applications on Singapore ONE. These cover many wide-ranging interests, from leisure and entertainment to health information, government and business services, shopping, banking and education.

To speed up the development of the broadband industry and market in Asia, IDA has taken proactive steps to forge partnerships with leading players in the region; such as Taiwan, China and Korea. The government has also provided a $150 million package for the setting up of the broadband Millennia (iBBMM industry) in Singapore. This is to support the development, hosting and delivery of broadband content in our industry and deployment of broadband services in the market [19,23].

IDA has also managed to get Microsoft to use Singapore as the launch site for its Asian Broadband Jump-start Initiative for the deployment of new broadband applications in Asia. IDA with the support of MOE has placed a Fast Track @ School Program, which allowed more than 50 schools to upgrade their broadband facilities and develop interactive broadband education content. For example, students from River Valley can film their won science experiments and put them online.

### 3.1.1 Manpower 21 Initiative

In the development of human and intellectual capital, which is the key competitive factor in our transition to a knowledge-based economy, the Government launched Manpower 21[21,25]. The Manpower 21 vision is for Singapore to become a Talent Capital, a center of ideas, innovation, knowledge and exchange. It is a hub of continuous learning for lifelong employability and a country where the Government, employers, unions, and community organizations work in unison to achieve the country's goals. In the plan, six core strategies were formulated to address all aspects of the manpower value chain, including manpower planning, lifelong learning, talent augmentation, manpower development, workplace transformation and partnership. They are:

- Integrated Manpower Planning
- Lifelong Learning for Lifelong Employability
- Augmenting Our Talent
- Transforming the Work Environment
- Developing a Vibrant Manpower Industry
- Redefining Partnerships

The vision of Singapore as a Talent Capital encapsulates the essence of the country's manpower transformation efforts. As Singaporean workers and international talent converge to work, learn, contribute and exchange, it will be able to tap knowledge to add value to Singapore, and transit it into a strong knowledge economy of the new millennium.

### 3.1.2 National Lifelong Learning

To help the workers to achieve the Lifelong Learning and the transfer of knowledge, a framework for continuously enhancing the workers' knowledge and skills had been established. The goal is to train and retrain workers so that they can continue to take on new jobs or enlarged duties, which is the essence of lifelong employability.

In one of his speeches, PM Goh Chok Tong mentioned that the lifelong learning system is based on five key principles. First, it will be easily accessible – so that everyone who wants to learn will have the full opportunity to upgrade his fullest potential. Second, it will be flexible – so that you can learn at your own time, place and pace alongside your family and work commitments. Third, it will lead to recognition – so that what you learn is nationally recognized and helps motivate continuously learn. Fourth, it will lead to employability – so that training and re-training will always be practical and employment driven. Fifth, it will be driven by partnerships – so as to promote shared responsibility and personal commitment among individuals, employers, unions, community groups and the Government [22].

In this respect, the government had established a dedicated Manpower Development Assistance Scheme or MDAS, with an initial funding of $200 million. It will focus on supporting strategic workforce development programmes under the School of Lifelong Learning. It will also support the Skills Redevelopment Program and the establishment of the National Skills Recognition System and industry training centers. Skill redevelopment is essential to help our economy, and workers to meet new challenges.

### 3.1.3 Promotion of Technopreneurship

Besides the physical infrastructure, the Government has also built a conducive environment that will nurture innovation and spur technological entrepreneurship, enabling knowledge production. Towards this end, there is a technopreneur committee chaired by DPM Dr. Tony Tan, which is looking at ways to create a business, and intellectual environment that will encourage the development and growth of start-up technology-based companies. One of the ongoing initiatives is to develop a Science Hub to attract high-tech entrepreneurship to Singapore and also the setting up of Technopreneurship 21.

Under Technopreneurship 21, a venture capital fund with US$1 billion was pumped in for start-ups in Singapore. Funding is not only opened to Singaporean entrepreneurs, but also foreigners who come to launch start-ups in Singapore. Since the launch of US$1b Technopreneurship Investment Fund (or TIF for short), to date it had been invested in 21 funds and committed US$443m (up to end of Feb 2000) from the 1 billion fund in less than 6 months. Out of these 21 funds, 8 funds are in partnership with the US based venture capitalists including Sequoia Capital, Doll Capital, Global
Catalyst Partners, Crystal Internet Ventures, J.H.Whitney, Origin Partners, Warburg Pincus and Walden International. Another partnership where the TIF will be committing US$100m is to the US $1billion ePlanet Fund with Draper Fisher Jurveston to connect the 2 regions of Asia and the US [9, 28].

Along this line, two initiatives that were launched in 1997 were: The first initiative is the establishment of the Institute of High Performance Computing (IHPC). IHPC is formed from the merger of the National Super-Computing Research Center and the NUS Center for Computational Mechanics. The potential impact of high performance computing to both the manufacturing and the services sectors of our economy is vast and growing. In the manufacturing, electronics and chemicals industries, high performance computing will enable companies to achieve better product quality, shorter time-to-market, reduced failure rates, and lower cost of design and production. For the financial services industries, the advantage of high performance computing can be very significant. High performance computing can analyze complex data relationship and identify hidden trends. The potential enhancement to a company's competitiveness can be enormous. One of the projects undertaken by IHPC is to assist Singapore industries in the use of high performance computing technology for solving all kinds of problems. This will enhance the competitiveness of Singapore.

The second initiative is the Technology Incubator Programs, which is to develop a more conducive environment for high technology start-ups. In the last few years, NSTB, together with other agencies, have gradually built up a support system for such start-ups, which makes it easier for individuals and companies to convert technological innovations into commercially viable business ventures. The Technology Incubator Program will further enhance this support system. Currently, scientists or engineers with good ideas often lack the ability or inclination to exploit such ideas for business. Also, they may not have the network or management experience. The Program will help to marry the technological expertise of innovators to the business expertise of investors and entrepreneurs. It also includes the financing, covering up to 85% of R&D costs and other business expenditures, for a period of two years. In return for up to 85% funding, the start-ups will allocate up to 30% stake to NSTB, out of which a percentage may be given to the Incubator Management Company.

### 3.1.4 Industry 21

In the arena of industries, a key vehicle in propelling Singapore towards a Knowledge-Based Economy is the EDB's Industry 21 launched in January 1999, a 10-year plan        for industry clusters. Industry 21 is a plan to operationalise the thrust to develop manufacturing and services as twin engines of growth and envisions Singapore as a vibrant and robust global hub of knowledge driven industries.

Under Industry 21, the emphasis will be on quality, high value-added and knowledge driven industries. Manpower capabilities and the ability to innovate will be key to developing such knowledge driven industries. Under the I21 blueprint, the EDB will grow and nurture the industry clusters and development programs in these areas: Electronics, Chemicals, Life Sciences, Engineering, Education and Healthcare, Logistics, Communications and Media Headquarters, World Class Companies/Promising Local Enterprises, Innovation, International Business, Resource Development Co-Investment [29].

The Government will be providing stronger support for manpower and innovation development through increased funding. For developing manpower capabilities in leading edge technologies, $800 million had been allocated to the Initiatives in New Technology (INTECH) grant scheme for manpower development.

One of the initiatives by PSB is the establishment of a national framework to help companies achieve People Excellence in a systematic way. The framework consists of three components which are: Information – A web-based online information system called Workforce One to help companies keep abreast of the latest developments such as the best global practices and latest trends. Capability development programs  - This brings together the various programs that are available to assist companies upgrade their workforce in an integrated way. People Excellence Awards – These awards will highlight the best organizational models and recognize companies that break new ground in human resource development.

### 3.2   Initiatives for Education

To move towards the Knowledge-based economy, initiatives are also adopted in the education of our future generations. One of the initiatives is the change in the curricula of the schools, which are revised to enable students to have more time and opportunities to explore and experiment. This will allow them to exercise and develop their thinking, information and creative capabilities and the incorporation of the IT subject into their curricula. One example is where the pupils of Radin Mas Primary School collaborated with pupils from Hawaii to create a virtual zoo. In Kranji Secondary School, every student is given an Internet account and school assignments and reading materials are delivered to students via the Internet.

In parallel, to promote a culture of entrepreneurship and innovation, the institutes of higher learning are developing a more holistic curriculum to instill not only technical skills, but skills that are needed for the students to operate effectively in an information economy [26, 30]. To expand the learning horizon of the students, another initiative by the government was the signing of an MOU between the Ministry of Education and Britain. This allows Singapore schools link those in Britain and collaborate on improving the standard of spoken and written English here -- by means of information technology. The MOU seeks to explore opportunities for cooperation in information and communications technology in education, to enhance teaching and learning at all levels and to identify common areas of interest [7].

To add to the intellectual vibrancy of our schools, and enrich the educational experience of Singaporean students, the government is also attracting bright foreign students to study in Singapore. To make Singapore, an education hub like Boston – a center of excellence for higher education, the government has also set out to attract top foreign universities to set up branches in Singapore. In this way, it enhances the creation and diffusion of ideas as there is an exchange of knowledge. Currently, the government had attracted INSEAD, the European institute of business administration based in France, and the University of Chicago Business School, to set up branch campuses in Singapore. Another top US business school, Wharton, is also collaborating with the new Singapore Management University to set up the Wharton-SMU Research Center [4].

In addition, MIT will be conducting engineering postgraduate courses in Singapore jointly with NUS and NTU. The Georgia Institute of Technology has also linked up with NUS to set up the Logistics Institute – Asia to undertake research, industry consulting, education and training. The medical school in Johns Hopkins University will also be setting up Johns Hopkins Singapore, a postgraduate medical research and education center at NUS. All these institutions will help us prepare Singapore for the knowledge-based economy.

### 3.3    Other Initiatives

Life sciences have emerged as another wave in scientific and technological innovations. Another initiative to propel towards the knowledge economy is the planning of Life Sciences industry . In line with this, the government has developed a S$1 billion corporate R&D fund to attract leading industry players to set up world-class corporate research centers in Singapore. This is complemented by a S$1 billion Life Sciences Investment Fund to co-invest in biotech start-ups and joint ventures [27]. To further boost the development of Life Sciences study and research, NTU will set-up the College of Life Sciences in two and a half years' time at a cost of $465 million.

An initiative by the Productivity and Standards Board (PSB) is the establishment of the National Best Practice Center, which will help small and medium local enterprises (LEs) to be globally competitive. It will help LEs raise their technological capability, efficiency and service quality and also encourage them to pool resources, exploit IT and modernize management PSB will also implement a Productivity Action 21 plan to prepare businesses and workers for the knowledge-based economy, paying special attention to raising productivity in the construction and retail sectors.

# 4    Challenges Faced by the Singapore Government

With the numerous initiatives undertaken to move towards a Knowledge-based economy, the Singapore Government is faced by the challenge of measuring their effectiveness.

## 4.1    Measurement of knowledge as an indicator of economic growth

Measuring the performance of the knowledge-based economy poses a great challenge. At the heart of the knowledge-based economy, knowledge itself is particularly hard to quantify and also to price. We have today only very indirect and partial indicators of growth in the knowledge base itself. An unknown proportion of knowledge is implicit, uncodified and stored only in the minds of individuals. Terrain such as knowledge stocks and flows, knowledge distribution and the relation between knowledge creation and economic performance is still virtually unmapped [17,18].

According to the OECD report, there are four principal reasons why knowledge indicators, however carefully constructed, cannot approximate the systematic comprehensiveness of traditional economic indicators. First, there are no stable formulae or "recipes" for translating inputs into knowledge creation into outputs of knowledge. Second, inputs into knowledge creation are hard to map because there are no knowledge accounts analogous to the traditional national accounts. Thirdly, knowledge lacks a systematic price system that would serve, as a basis for aggregating pieces of knowledge that is essentially unique. Finally, new knowledge creation is not necessarily a net addition to the stock of knowledge, and obsolescence of units of the knowledge stock is not documented.

To fully understand the workings of the knowledge-based economy, new economic concepts and measures are required which track phenomena beyond conventional market transactions. In general, improved indicators for the knowledge-based economy are needed:

**Knowledge stocks and flows** – Statistical techniques could be developed to estimate knowledge stocks based on current R&D input and flow measures. Development of knowledge flow indicators would yield better measures of the R&D and knowledge intensity of industries and economies. This includes more extensive and comparable indicators of the acquisition and use of different types of technology by industry, particularly information technologies. More creative analysis of existing patent data at the national and international levels could help trace flows of disembodied knowledge.

Knowledge rates of return – In order to assess knowledge outputs and evaluate the performance of knowledge-based economies, priority should be placed on developing improved indicators of the private and social rates of return to R&D and other knowledge inputs. This includes measuring returns to individuals, firms and societies in terms of employment, output, productivity and competitiveness, and could be based on both macro-level econometric analyses and firm-level surveys. One of the great challenges is to develop indicators and methodologies for gauging the impact of technology on productivity and economic growth.

**Knowledge networks** – Given the importance of tacit as well as codified knowledge, diffusion as well as creation of knowledge, and *know-how* and *know-who* in the knowledge-based economy, indicators of the knowledge distribution power and other characteristics of innovation systems are key. Firm-level innovation surveys, as well as other measurement approaches, need to be developed to better characterize innovation processes and interactions among firms and a range of institutional actors in the economy.

**Knowledge and learning** – Human capital indicators, particularly those relating to education and employment, are central measures for the knowledge-based economy. Measuring the private and social rates of return to investments in education and training will help point to means of enhancing the learning capacity of individuals and firms. Micro-level firm indicators on human resource requirements, employment and occupational mobility will help better match supply and demand for skills in the labor market [18,20,31].

## 5 Conclusion

The institution of the various initiatives by the Singapore Government in becoming a Knowledge-based economy can only be successful if it is accompanied by a cultural shift cutting across every level of society. Companies must be able to focus on their core competence and constantly innovate. They must be receptive to know-how, have the ability to see its commercial potential and have the flair in spotting new customer needs and fresh business opportunities. Employees too must shift their mindset from one of 'earning a living' to 'learning a living'. The industry and the government will have to work closely together to realize Singapore's vision to become an advanced and globally competitive knowledge economy. In its move to a Knowledge-based economy, the Singapore Government also has to ensure that appropriate measurements are established to measure the effectiveness of the implemented initiatives in advancing the knowledge in the economy to ensure that money is well spent. There is a need to develop our own performance measures as existing indicators have many shortcomings.

## References

1. Abramowitz, M. Thinking about Growth, Cambridge University Press, Cambridge, (1989).

2. Address by Dr. Lee Boon Yang at the Manpower 21: Singapore's National Manpower Plan Launch of the Manpower 21 Committees", (June 4 1999).

3. Baldwin, J., Diverty, B. and J. Johnson, J. Success, Innovation, Technology and Human Resource Strategies – An Interactive System, paper presented at the Conference on "The Effects of Technology and Innovation on Firm Performance and Employment", Washington, DC, 1-2 May, (1995).

4. Congratulatory Remarks by President S R Nathan at the Opening of University of Chicago's Graduate School of Business Asian Campus( September 14, 2000 )

5. David, P. and Foray, D. Accessing and Expanding the Science and Technology Knowledge Base, STI Review, No. 16, OECD, Paris, (1995).

6. Debresson, C. Breeding Innovation Clusters: A Source of Dynamic Development, World Development, Vol. 17, No. 1, (1989).

7. English Through IT Likely, Straits Times Article, Oct 9, (1999).

8. Gibbons, M., Limoge, C., Nowotny, H., Schwartzman, S. Scott, P. and Trow, M, The New Production of Knowledge: The Dynamics of Science and Research in Contemporary Societies, Sage Publications, London, (1994).

9. Jury, J. Singapore to foster Technopreneurship, European Venture Capital Journal, (1999).

10. Leontief, W. Input-Output Analysis of the Structure of Scientific Knowledge, paper presented at the Tenth International Conference on "Input-Output Techniques, Seville, (1993).

11. Lundvall, B. and Johnson, B. The Learning Economy, Journal of Industry Studies, Vol. 1, No. 2, (1994).

12. Machlup, F. The Production and Distribution of Knowledge in the United States, Princeton University Press, Princeton, NJ, (1962).

13. Mansfield, E., Rapoport, J. Romeo, A. Wagner, S. and Beardsley, G. Social and Private Rates of Return from Industrial Innovations, Quarterly Journal of Economics, Vol. 77, (1977).

14. OECD (1995a), *Industry and Technology: Scoreboard of Indicators*, Paris.

15. OECD (1995b), *Information Technology Outlook*, Paris.

16. OECD (1996a), *Employment and Growth in the Knowledge-based Economy*, Paris.

17. OECD (1996b), *Technology, Productivity and Job Creation*, Paris.

18. OECD (1996c), *Transitions to Learning Economies and Societies*, Paris.

19. Opening Address by Mr. Lim Swee Say, Minister for State, Ministry of Communications and Information Technology and Trade and Industry at Hooked on Broadband Seminar( September 18, 2000).

20. Porat, M. The Information Economy: Definition and Measurement, US Government Printing Office, Washington, DC, (1977).

21. Romer, P. The Origins of Endogenous Growth, The Journal of Economic Perspectives, Vol. 8, (1994).

22. PM Goh Chok Tong's National Day Rally Speech – 1999

23. Press release by NCB on Singapore Ready for Multimedia Age (June22, 1999) OECD Report (1996), Knowledge-Based Economy, Paris

24. Smith, K., Dietrichs, E. and Nas, S The Norwegian National Innovation System: A Pilot Study of Knowledge Creation, Distribution and Use, paper prepared at the OECD Workshop on National Innovation Systems, Vienna, 6 October, . (1995).

25. Speech by Deputy Prime Minister Lee Hsien Loong at Launch of Manpower21 (August 31, 1999 )

26. Speech by George Yeo, Minister for Trade & Industry at the People Excellence 2000 ( November 7, 2000 )

27. Speech by Radm(NS) Teo Chee Hean, Minister for Education at the Prize Presentation Ceremony of The Singapore Biology Olympiad ( December 2, 2000)

28. Speech by George Yeo, Minister for Information & the Arts and 2$^{nd}$ Minister for Trade & Industry at Launch of Techmonth (Sept 1 1998)

29. Speech by Mr Lee Yock Suan, Minister for Trade and Industry at the EDB Industry 21 Seminar (Jan 22 1999)

30. Speech by Prime Minister Goh Chok Tong at the Opening Ceremony of the Bukit Merah Skills Development Center (Feb11, 1999)

31. Tipping, J., Zeffren, E. and Fusfeld, A. Assessing the Value of Your Technology, Research Technology Management, September-October, (1995).

32. Thurow, Lester C. The Future of Capitalism. New York: William Morrow and Company, Inc., 1996.

33. US Department of Commerce The Information Economy, US Government Printing Office, Washington, DC, (1977).

34. World-Class Vision For Singapore, Straits Times Article, Oct 9, (1999).

# Impacts and Limitations of Intelligent Agents in Electronic Commerce

Dong Su Jin[1] and Kyoung Jun Lee[2]

[1] School of Business, Korea University
Anam-Dong, Sungbuk-Ku, Seoul 136-701, Korea
jinds@kuba.korea.ac.kr
[2] School of Business, Korea University
Anam-Dong, Sungbuk-Ku, Seoul 136-701, Korea
leekj@kuba.korea.ac.kr

**Abstract.** Agent-based economy or agent-based electronic commerce is the term for describing one of possible next steps of electronic commerce. The systematic understanding of the agent-based economy is important for researchers to develop practical intelligent agent systems, and for current electronic commerce industries to cope with the challenges of the intelligent agents. With these purposes, we conduct a comprehensive review of ongoing and future impacts of intelligent agents to electronic commerce from business model perspective. We classify intelligent agents by their functions and roles in electronic commerce and analyze the business model change by intelligent agents, based on Timmers's definition of business model. Changes in architecture of flows, responses of players, influences to revenue model and participant's benefits, and funding source are discussed with real world business examples and related researches. We also discuss the limitations of intelligent agents in electronic commerce.[1]

## 1 Introduction

One of terms representing changes of economy owing to the diffusion of Internet is *Reverse Market Economy* [16]. The term emphasizes the transformation of the existing economic structure into customer-driven economic structure as customers gain more bargaining power and information by connecting themselves with the Internet. However, although the number of participants that can be reached and the scope of product and raw materials they can deal with increase in the reverse market economy, its transaction process is still complicated. The actors using Internet now suffer from information overload rather than lack of information. They must analyze a lot of information, negotiate over multiple contracts, and execute a lot of complex transactions on Internet. Therefore, it has been asserted that it is necessary to develop marketplaces that control the increase of information overload [24].

---

[1] This work was supported by Korea Research Foundation Grant (KRF-99-041-C00328).

One of methods for solving the information overload problem is thought to be an intelligent agent. Many companies have been developing intelligent agents that can help Internet users reduce their information overload. Comparison-shopping agents and negotiation supporting agents are the representative examples. Kephart & Greenwald claim that within the next decade, the Internet could be populated with billions of agents exchanging information goods and services with one another and with people [21].

As such, advances in electronic commerce and agent technology are pushing the world rapidly toward ever-increasing e-business automation, where software agents act as autonomous (or semi-autonomous) businesses in their own right, buying and selling information goods and services online [17]. The situation may be called as 'agent-based economy' where the principal users of Internet are intelligent agents rather than human beings.

The difference of the 'agent-based economy' from the 'reverse market economy' depends on who are the principal users of Internet resources. When the human beings are the principal users, we may call this economy 'reverse market economy'. If the main users of Internet resources become agents, then we can say that we live in an agent based economy in Fig. 1.

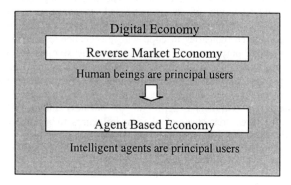

**Fig. 1.** Digital economy evolution from agent perspective

The systematic understanding of the agent-based economy is important for researchers to develop practical intelligent agent systems, and for current electronic commerce industries to cope with the challenges of the intelligent agents. With these purposes, we conduct a comprehensive review of ongoing and future impacts of intelligent agents to electronic commerce from business model perspective. The remainder of this paper is structured as follows. Section 2 we classify intelligent agents in electronic commerce by their roles and functions. Section 3 explains the changes of business model components and responses of electronic commerce entities confronting intelligent agents. Section 4 discusses the limitation of intelligent agents from business, social and technical perspective. Section 5 concludes with research and business implications.

# 2 Classification of intelligent agents in electronic commerce

An intelligent agent is a program that operates autonomously to retrieve and process information on a user's behalf. Tφ rissen defines an intelligent agent as a piece of software with an element of artificial intelligence, which can be used to support people in the use of computer applications [36]. Nwana defines agent as a component of software and/or hardware, which is capable of acting exactingly in order to accomplish tasks on behalf of its user [29].

Many studies have been made [13, 18] on what the characteristics of an intelligent agent should be to meet its goals. The most common qualities of them are independence, learning, autonomy, cooperation, responsiveness, pro-activity, sociality, and adoption. These qualities make intelligent agents differ from traditional software and well suited to the electronic commerce, which is inherently information intensive domain. Main functions of agents include search, compare, learn, negotiate, and collaboration [19]. Agents may also be classified as collaborative agents, interface agents, mobile agents, information agents, reactive agents, hybrid agents and smart agents [28].

The above researches have focused on classifying intelligent agents on the basis of intelligent agent's attributes. In this section, we classify intelligent agents in electronic commerce context. Table 1 summarizes the typical functions of intelligent agents in electronic commerce and the corresponding business examples or research projects.

**Table 1.** Main functions and examples of intelligent agent in electronic commerce

|    | Main functions or roles |
|----|--------------------------|
| 1  | Search information on products and merchants<br>Mysimon.com, Auctionwatch.com, Shopbinder.co.kr |
| 2  | Filter unimportant commercial messages<br>Adsubtract.com |
| 3  | Gather and Analyze information on customers and merchants<br>Ffly.com |
| 4  | Match qualified commerce party<br>Kasbah, Fastparts.com |
| 5  | Notify & Push event<br>Digitalimpact.com |
| 6  | Monitor & Report creation, change, and deletion of information<br>Netmind.com, Books.com |
| 7  | Support communication between business and customers<br>Artificiallife.com, Vperson.com |
| 8  | Personalize & recommend interface, contents, product, & services.<br>Personalogic.com, Technoagent.co.kr, My.yahoo.com |
| 9  | Make or Support a decision on bidding, pricing, and negotiation<br>AuctionBot, eMediator |
| 10 | Network among consumers, merchants, and manufacturers<br>Napster.com, OPEN4U.co.kr |

The major market players of electronic commerce are buyers, sellers, and intermediaries. Each market player can employ intelligent agent for its functional steps. Maes et al [25] presented agent applications based on CBB (Consumer Buying Behavior) model. Bailey& Bakos [3] suggested four roles of intermediary, which are aggregation, trust, matching, and facilitation. Nissen [27] proposed the relationship between buyers with sellers through so called Commerce Model. Fig.2 integrates the three models and the examples of intelligent agents mapped into the functional steps of the buyers, sellers and intermediaries.

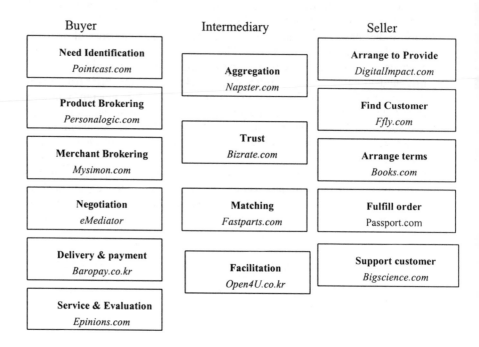

**Fig. 2.** Functional steps and their agent examples of market players.

# 3 Business model approach to Impacts of Intelligent Agent

Although technical researches on intelligent agents are abundant, yet there have not been many commercially successful cases of intelligent agents. One of reasons why the level of commercialization is low may be explained by the lack of understanding business aspects of intelligent agents. Related to this, there have been some researches on intelligent agents in the business point of view.

Maes et al [25] surveyed how agents are helping buyers and sellers combat information overload and reviewed the technologies involved in buying and selling agents and discussed several agent-mediated electronic commerce systems in the context of a general model of the consumer buying behavior model.

Jonkheer & Jansen [19] explore the boundaries of what might happen in markets when intelligent agents are introduced and used by market participants. They discuss existing commercial agent-like applications and models on how different functions of agents could affect different stages. Two types of markets - travel and bookselling - were examined, focusing on consumers' interests and the functionality of destination sites.

OECD [31] reports that the increasing presence of intelligent agents raises a number of user issues and policy considerations. As for electronic financial transactions, consumers must trust them if they are to grant them some autonomy and decision-making power. Issues of trust, privacy and consumer protection need to be addressed and there must be an appropriate legal and commercial environment for tackling the challenges that these non-human economic actors present on the Web.

Varian [37] point out that sellers discriminate price between the searchers and the non-searchers. He also explains that one of reasons why customers do not use intelligent agent is the loyalty program. If the customer stays with one merchant, he can receive benefits that cannot be offered by the low-price merchant. He also explains that agents are not always beneficial to consumer's benefits because they not only allow consumers easy access to other firms' prices, but they also allow the firms themselves to monitor each others price movements.

Crowston & Macinnes [10] present a simple framework for the decision of a vendor to block or accept a buyer's agent and provide empirical evidence to support the framework. Empirically, they found that agents seem to be accepted for differentiated goods, but resisted for more commoditized goods. An analysis of prices from one agent shows that a small number of sellers tended to have the lowest prices and while divergence in pricing remains, price dispersion declined over the period studied.

Kephart et al. [22] deal with Shopbot for buyer and Pricebot for seller. They present a theoretical analysis of a simple economic model, which is intended to capture some of essence of shopbots, and attempt to shed light on their potential impact on markets. They performed experimental simulations of an economy of agents, designed to model the dynamic interaction of electronic buyers, sellers, and shopbots.

Brynjolfsson & Smith [7] empirically analyzes consumer behavior at Internet shopbots sites that allow consumers to make one-click price comparisons for product offerings from multiple retailers. They found while shopbots substantially weaken the market positions of branded retailers, brand name and retailer loyalty still strongly influence consumer behavior at Internet shopbots.

Hanson [17] suggests some of the foreseeable developments and challenges in the growth of agent-based electronic commerce. He deals with emergence of a new type of agent-human hybrid firms, new business models and services tailored to agents, and a new forms of collective behavior that are agent-agent interactions.

Similar to the above researches, our paper also deals with intelligent agent from business perspective. Especially, we adopt a concept of business model to analyze the relationship between intelligent agents and electronic commerce. Using the Timmers's definition of business model, we will comprehensively discuss the impacts of intelligent agent to the business model components of electronic commerce business.

## 3.1 Impacts on business model components by intelligent agent

In the seminal paper, Business Models for Electronic Market, Timmers [35] defines the business model as follows:

    1) An architecture for the product, service and information flows,
    2) A description of the various business actors and their roles,
    3) A description of the potential benefits for the various business actors, and
    4) A description of the sources of revenues

If we add a funding component to his definition, then the impacts on the business model component by intelligent agents can be summarized as in Table 2.

**Table 2.** Impacts on business model components by Intelligent Agent.

| | Impacts of intelligent agent on business model component |
|---|---|
| Architecture of flow | Architectural change of the product, service and Information flows owing to agent |
| Actors and their roles | Changed role or response of the various business actors owing to agent |
| Source of Revenue | Threat to or creation of revenue sources owing to agent. |
| Potential Benefit | Change in potential benefits for the various business actors owing to agent. |
| Source of Funding | Funding source among main actors for developing, introducing, and maintaining the agent |

## 3.2 Architectural change in flows

### 3.2.1 Change in information flows: Change in navigation pattern

A recent research on the so-called 'diameter of the world wide web' shows that an HTML document on the web can be connected by, on average, 19 mouse clicks from any other HTML document [5]. This implies that, with a proper intelligent agent, we can find out a wanted web page by 19 clicks. However, current intelligent agents have only the level of intelligence of string matching capability, as pointed out in [33], so they cannot search or support the navigation of the documents effectively. However, if an intelligent agent is developed, which can exploit the knowledge of Internet structure and user's context beyond the simple string matching capability, then the navigation pattern of users will be changed. The representative examples of intelligent agents resulting in the users' navigation pattern are comparison shopping agents such as MySimon.com and peer-to-peer file sharing agents such as Napster.com.

To find out the best product, without agent, potential buyers had to navigate multiple Internet shopping sites sequentially. However, with the aid of comparison shopping agent, potential buyers do not have to navigate all the sites, but only visit the comparison shopping site. (In Fig. 3.) Such comparison shopping agent impacts the shopping site's business model, which has assumed that users will visit their sites for product search.

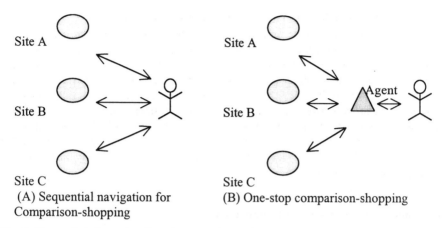

Site A

Site B

Site C

(A) Sequential navigation for
Comparison-shopping

Site A

Site B

Site C

(B) One-stop comparison-shopping

**Fig. 3.** Change in information flows between sites and users

Napster.com is a networking agent for MP3 file search, which is implemented by so called 'peer-to-peer' architecture rather than existing 'client-server' architecture. With the emergence of such agent, a user who wants to search and download a MP3 file from Internet does not visit any web pages, but uses a sort of agent program such as Napster and gets wanted MP3 files from the Internet. Napster has destroyed the business models of web-based music file service and even threatened the offline music industry. This is a typical example that an agent technology changes the information flows and impacts on the overall business model of existing business, which is online or offline.

### 3.2.2 Expected change in information organization: From eyeball to machine

Increase of software agent usages over human usage implies that there will be changes in current web design currently focused on human being's eyeball searching. As intelligent agents are emerging, web site design and promotion strategy should consider the new group of users and be changed to appeal to machine readability as well as human's eyeball readability. The gradual employment of XML (extensible markup language) as a machine-readable script language for web is interpreted as one of preparation for the emergence of agent.

However, as O'Leary pointed out, firms develop best practices knowledge bases with reuse in mind, yet different firms use different ontologies for these bases, making them difficult to share because of the many differences at the basic level of categories of processes. Therefore he concludes that there is no single optimal ontology for best practices [32] and expects that the standardization of ontologies across the various business entities will not come in the near future. Accordingly the change in information organization from eyeball to machine will take much time to be realized.

### 3.2.3 Expected change in pattern of consuming Internet resource

Unlike human beings who have limited time using Internet directly, intelligent agents can search and gather information without a rest. If such personal agents will become ubiquitous, it may be expected that unprotected Internet resources will become overwhelmed because of selfish users and their agent. To prevent such a tragedy of commons, it is claimed that the Internet would shift to a pay-as-you-go system where agents use e-cash as a bargaining chip [9]. Although there is no agreement on the possibility of the tragedy of the commons in the Internet [30], the abundance of software agents and the large consumption of Internet resource by them will affect the pricing of the Internet service and accordingly drive the advancement of micropayment technologies.

### 3.3 Changed role or response of related actors

### 3.3.1 Response of Sellers to Intelligent Agents

Confronting with the comparison shopping agents, some sellers with weak price competitiveness or branded vendor, which do not want a visit of the intelligent agents, have taken various actions to cope with the agents.

First, they use technical methods. In Bargain Finder case, sellers blocked the HTTP request from the IP address of Bargain Finder agent. In the case of Jango agent, sellers frequently changed text arrangement so that their user interface becomes incompatible with the agent's assumption. Some sites deploy a semantic barrier by presenting a common sense question that only average human being can answer. By doing so, they could block agent that cannot answer the easy question.

Second, they may use legal methods. eBay.com sued against the 'trespassing' of Bidder's edge's agent [20].

Third, they may adopt differentiation methods. Brynjolfsson & Smith [7] suggest several differential-pricing strategies for agent markets. They noted that sellers might adopt different pricing strategies for shipping cost between buyers' agent and other buyers who are not using agent. Bakos [4] also noted airlines offer many different prices and rules to make comparison difficult. Crowston & Macinnes [10] also presented similar results in their papers. Most of the current intelligent agents are known to be beneficial to buyers rather than sellers. But this is not so obvious since agents not only allow buyer easy access to other seller's prices, but they also allow sellers themselves to monitor each other's price movements [37]. In reality, buyer-owned shopbots and seller-owned pricebots try to maximize their owner's individual benefit. Rapidly increasing in number and sophistication, shopbots like comparison-shopping agent support to minimizing buyer's expenditure and maximizing benefits. In response to this trend, sellers may rely on their pricebots, which employ price-setting algorithms in an attempt to maximize benefits [22]. Some sites may charge lower prices, so called partitioned pricing, to price sensitive buyers using intelligent agent than buyers who visit their web site directly [7]. Examples of pricebots include Books.com's competitor monitoring agent, consumer information gathering agent, and data mining agent etc.

### 3.3.2 Changed role of Intermediary

With the emergence of the Internet, it has been anticipated that role of intermediaries may be reduced or eliminated, which is called, disintermediation hypothesis [14]. However, now it is agreed that although a certain type of intermediaries may extinct, a new types of electronic intermediaries will perform functions with such as aggregating information, matching buyers and sellers, managing physical channels, and providing trust etc. [3]. However, we may expect that the intelligent agent based marketplaces may replace role of the new intermediaries. The new disintermediation caused by intelligent agent may bring an emergence of agent based new intermediary, which is called facilitator [12].

### 3.4. Impacts on source of revenue

### 3.4.1 Direct threat to source of revenue: By impacting banner advertisement

One of the major revenue models of Internet content providers has been known to be banner advertisement model. Even an electronic shopping site such as buy.com has the revenue model from banner advertising rather than sales margin. However, if a software agent changes the large amount of current Internet navigation from human's eyeball navigation to agents' machinery navigation, the revenue model based on banner advertising would be threatened. Although navigation by agents may not reduce number of hits of the banner advertising, the effectiveness of the advertising will be damaged because intelligent agents will neither gather nor recognize the banner advertisements while they hit the banner advertisements. The lowered effectiveness of banner advertising will make advertisers invest less money on banner advertising. Moreover, some Internet users want a banner ad filtering functionality in their web browsers because banner advertisements tend to delay total download time of web pages. For instance, AdEater [23] and adsubtract.com automatically remove advertisement images from web pages during browsing. Vulkan also expected that the increasing usage of agent is likely to change the way revenues from advertising on the WWW are distributed and if most hits are from agents then this measurement is clearly no longer suitable [38]. As such, intelligent agents directly threaten the revenue model of existing electronic commerce.

### 3.4.2 Indirect threat to source of revenue: By impacting brand and reputation

As one of several economic factors reducing the chance of generating or sustaining monopoly profits in the digital marketplace, Choi & Whinston [8] points out the fact that rational consumers equipped with smart agents are less swayed by reputation. Intelligent agents are known to reduce the power of intangible assets, such as brand and reputation, of the existing electronic commerce businesses, which enables them to get much profits.

On the other hand, there are other opinions on the impacts of intelligent agents to brand or reputation effects. Brynjolfsson & Smith [7] demonstrates that while intelligent agents substantially weaken the market positions of branded name, brand name and seller loyalty still strongly influence buyer's behavior using intelligent agent's service. The reason may be derived from service quality differentiation, asymmetric market information regarding quality, or cognitive lock-in among buyers. OECD's report [31] claims that buyers will not use intelligent agent's advice because they do not trust information given by intelligent agent. Varian [37] points out that buyers may not use Shopbot because of existence of loyalty programs.

This issue depends on the capability of intelligent agents. If an agent has a capability enough to give a rational recommendation for its user, who suffers from bounded rationality, then businesses with brand and reputation may lose its power in market competition.

### 3.4.3 Creation of direct revenue

Although many people does not realize, but as Brown & Duguid [6] pointed out, without agents the Internet which has grown so dramatically in the past few years, would by now be unmanageable. The search-and-catalogue capability of agents transformed the sites such Lycos, Excite, and AltaVista etc from mere search engines into lucrative portals. It naturally means that the agents can become a direct source of revenue.

In addition, agents can create a new source of revenue for existing electronic commerce providers. The revenue model of auction sites is mainly based on commission from sellers. In auction, the more bidders participate, the more the final contract price increases and consequently the auction site acquires the more commission fee. Therefore, it is important for an auction site to develop a mechanism that motivates the participation of more bidders. Agent-based automated bidding will promote participation of bidders and create a direct revenue stream from bidders.

Agents exist for the benefit and convenience of users. If the benefit or the convenience is sufficient for the beneficiary willing to pay money for, it naturally creates direct revenue for the agent service provider.

### 3.4.4 Expansion of market size

According to Forester Research's recent survey, the 35 % of shopping mall visitors abandon shopping while inputting their subscription or payment information. This implies that reducing user's hassle in the subscription and payment process is very critical.

Form filling capability provided by Baropay.co.kr or Passport.com enables users to easily fill their information in the subscription or payment page. However, without a standard on the user information, it creates another hassle to users. In Korea, there has been an effort to establish industry standard in application of such intelligent agent. KECML (Korea Electronic Commerce Manipulation Language) derived from ECML was proposed as government-supported payment information standard for business-to-consumer electronic commerce and a form filling agent system based on the standard has been developed. Employing such a form filling agent is expected to contribute to increase of electronic commerce industry volumes.

Basically, agents exist for reducing transaction costs of electronic commerce; there fore the proper employment of agents have the impacts of expanding markets.

## 3.5 Change in benefit to participants

Although it is difficult to say that intelligent agents create much revenue, it is evident that they may increase or decrease benefit to related actors. Once an intelligent agent has been developed, its relative operation cost is very low and it can continue operating automatically in electronic commerce environment. Such an intelligent agent may benefit or damage related business actors without much cost. Napster.com in music industry is such a typical example.

If the increase of the entire market size can be achieved by intelligent agent like the form filling agents using KECML in the previous section, related actors will gain benefit in common. However, collusion among intelligent agents may do harm other market players. Jonkheer and Jansen [19] suggest a possibility of the emergence of so-called digital cartel. They call for an extensive ruling mechanism because agent mediated communication is hard to control and relatively easy to manipulate.

## 3.6 Source of Funding

To successfully introduce an intelligent agent to an industry, we should solve a problem who will pay the development and introduction costs. It means that an introduction of intelligent agent needs decision making on funding in the industry. Crowston [11] suggests three possible sources of funds to develop and employ intelligent agent: vendors, buyers, and third party. Table 3 summarizes the possible funding source among the actors.

**Table 3.** Funding source of intelligent agent in electronic commerce

| Funding Source | Comments |
| --- | --- |
| Funding From sellers | Commission for referral, Bundled into the cost of goods. |
| Funding From buyer | Charge the buyer fee, Sell agent software. |
| Funding From third party | Sell ads, Sell market information about clients. |
| No funding | Research Project. |

Based on the table 3, we may explain the case of intelligent agents in electronic auction. In auction, the more bidders participate, the higher bid price increases. Therefore, sellers may be willing to fund agents for inducing bidders using automated bidding agents. On the other hand, when an agent gives bidders some convenience in supporting functions of bidding process, monitoring and gathering prices of heterogeneous sources, then bidders may pay for such agents. If agent increases bidders' benefit larger than its costs, then bidders are willing to pay and get the agent software. Auctioneer may pay and use data mining agents for analyzing participant's bidding history.

# 4 Limitations of intelligent agents in electronic commerce

Though agent researches have been going on for more than a fifteen years and became a buzzword in the popular computing press [28], agents have not yet shown remarkable impacts. This may imply that agents have some limitations to be deployed in the real world business. In this section, we discuss the limitations of the intelligent agents in electronic commerce domains from the three points of view: technical, business, and social perspectives.

## 4.1 Technological Limitations

According to Maes [25] the impacts of intelligent agent may be occurring as agent technologies mature to better manage ambiguous content, personalized preferences, complex goals, changing environments, and disconnected parties. Since Internet environment is fundamentally open, a behavior of an agent is easy to be observed or imitated by its competitors. For example, if an agent's bidding patterns are too simple, then they may be easily disclosed by other parties, as the result users may not use the agents. Talukdar [34] mentioned that existing software agents tend to be rich in problem solving skills but poor in social and learning skills. For an instance, there exists considerable amount of researches in comparison shopping agent, these agents are not yet designed to learn about the customers and the changing marketplace or interrelations.

### 4.1.1 Limitation in processing of implicit knowledge and semantics

According to Afuah & Tucci [1] current Internet technologies have mainly two kinds of limitations: First, Internet cannot transfer tacit knowledge. Second, users of Internet, human beings, have a bounded rationality to process the vast amounts of information available on the Internet. While an intelligent agent supports augmenting the bounded rationality of human, it still has problems in understanding and transferring tacit knowledge [6]. Hanson [17] also pointed out that agents are faster at carrying out well-specified tasks and capable of employing sophisticated mathematical reasoning far beyond the typical human's ability, while human beings are vastly more able to learn from past behavior, to invent new approaches to problems, and employ what is usually called common sense. Recognizing the relative strength of human and agent, he proposed an agent-human hybrid firm in the marketplace.

In addition, current intelligent agents cannot process semantics involved in the exchanging of information. Therefore, actors, who do not want visit of agents, have employed a semantic barrier strategy.

### 4.1.2 Ontology Issues.

Ontology in intelligent agent is a language for the communication between agents. For independently developed agents to communicate seamlessly and even contract each other automatically, a standardized common ontology should be shared among the agents involved. For the electronic commerce area, there have been some efforts to develop agent ontology. One of them is the IBM's BRML(Business Rules Markup Languages)[15], which is an XML encoding of CLP (Courteous Logic Programs), a new knowledge representation formalism. Generalmagic.com also developed ontology named Telescript, but it is not widely used owing to incompatibility with other agents.

As such, commonly shared agent ontology in business domain has not been employed in real world applications. According to O'Leary [32], firms develop best practices knowledge bases with reuse in mind, but different firms use different ontologies for these bases, making them difficult to share. Applying Arrow's 'impossibility theorem [2]' to the problem of choosing optimal common language, he concludes that there is no single optimal ontology for best practices. His finding of the difficulty in developing common ontology for human reuse could be extended to the agent ontology area, which implies the more difficulty of developing a ontology standard for agent. In fact, the difficulty is one of important reasons why multiagent systems researches have not yet produced real world successful applications. Many researches have assumed a common ontology among the agents, but in reality it is not feasible. Therefore, deciding whether an agent system will depend on a common ontology or not, is very critical point for developing practically successful agent applications.

## 4.2 Limitation in business model and market based approach

Comparison shopping agent business started with the revenue model which makes money from banner advertising, referral fee, and listing payments. However, there has been fierce competition among so many similar comparison shopping businesses, therefore the revenue realized has been much smaller than expected. Even famous comparison shopping agents have not proved as an independent business model, so there were, as summarized in Table 4, finally acquired by the larger portals.

**Table 4.** Acquisition of comparison shopping agent by portals

| Comparison shopping agent sites | Recent their position |
| --- | --- |
| Mysimon.com | Acquired by Cnet.com |
| Jango.com | Acquired by Excite.com |
| Junglee.com | Acquired by Amazon.com |
| Personalogic.com | Acquired by AOL.com |

From the above cases, we learn that to develop and sustain successful agent based business, we should develop strong business model before its technical implementation. If we judge that an agent-based business will not sustain as an independent business entity, that we should consider product model, i.e., selling the agent product to electronic commerce providers, rather than service business itself.

For the practical use of agent in electronic commerce such as auction, bidding, and negotiation etc, the more investigation on the economic behavior of intelligent agents should be followed. So far most of technical studies on agent have focused only on improving the functionality of agents, but for the agents to be successfully applied to real-world electronic marketplace, then we should make effort to enhance the functionality of the agent based electronic marketplace. The key aspects of improving agent based electronic marketplace we suggest include interface between users and software agents, language for the communication between agents, trust between users and agents or among agents, security of agent behaviors and its internal codes, and market transaction mechanism synergistically operated with intelligent agent.

## 4.3 Social Limitations

Some researchers such as Odlykzo [30] do not have an optimistic view on the applicability of agents. He predicts that software agents will be used, but only to a limited extent. He pointed out that agents supposed to simplify life are not easy to master, and so are not as widespread as many people had hoped. He claims that even when software agents are used, they serve to encourage the growth of complexity that eats up any gain that had been achieved.

Brown & Duguid [6] pointed out that the human and the digital are significantly distinct and the distinction is rather useful. Human planning, coordinating, decision making, and negotiation are quite different from the capabilities or task characteristics of automated intelligent agent. Delegation to agent by human should be limited because rules and contracts rely on unspecifiable discretion and judgment on the part of the subject following those orders. Another problem is who will take responsibility for the agent decisions. Therefore, they claimed agent would be better to pursue not substitution but complimentarity.

Human beings are not only economically oriented, but also pursue enjoyment and affections. This fact is also applied to the Internet. Modahl classified the objectives of using Internet into three factors: career (money), enjoyment, and affections [26]. One of its implications to those who proclaim the occurrence of agent-based economy, where most of Internet users are agents rather than human beings, is that human users may mostly enjoy using the Internet rather than delegate their activities to agents.

As we see in the above, understanding the social limitation of agents, which has been neglected, gives a new insight to agent research and development. According to Wagner [39], a comprehensive underlying social theory for multi-agent environments is still missing, therefore the agent research should take into account not only particular problems (say the construction of a shopping agent) but also the consequences for society of these developments (such as the effects of agent-mediated commerce).

## 5. Conclusion

In the previous sections, we reviewed ongoing and future impacts of intelligent agents to electronic commerce as well as their limitations. We classified intelligent agents by their functions and typical roles in electronic commerce. Impacts on each component of business model are analyzed: changes in architecture of flows, responses of players, influences to revenue model and participant's benefits, and funding source.

The primary contribution of this research can be summarized as follows. First, we propose a digital economy development phase model from reverse market economy to agent-based economy with intelligent agent point of view. Second, we employ a business model framework to give a comprehensive review and preview of the impacts of intelligent agents. Third, we also deal with the technical, business, and social limitations of current phase of intelligent agent researches and real world implementations as well as their impacts to electronic commerce.

The systematic understanding of the agent-based economy will guide researchers to develop practical intelligent agent systems and help current electronic commerce industries cope with the challenges of the intelligent agents.

# References

1. Afuah, A., Tucci, C., Internet Business Models and Strategies, McGraw-Hill (2000)
2. Arrow, K., Social Choice and Individual Values, Yale Univ. Press, New Haven, Connecticut (1970)
3. Bailey, J., Bakos, Y.: An exploratory study of the emerging role of electronic intermediaries, International Journal of Electronic Commerce, 1(3): 7-20 (1997)
4. Bakos, Y., A Strategic Analysis of Electronic Marketplaces, MIS Quarterly, 15(3): 295-310 (1991)
5. Barabasi, A., Albert, R., Jeong, H. Scale-free characteristics of random networks: the topology of the worldwide web, Physica A 281: 69-77 (2000)
6. Brown, J., Duguid, P., Agents and Angels, Chapter 2 of The Social Life of Information, Harvard Business School Press (2000)
7. Brynjolfsson, E., Smith, D., The great equalizer? Consumer choice behavior at Internet shopbots, Working Paper, http://ebusiness.mit.edu/papers/tge/ (2001)
8. Choi, S., Winston, A., Is It Spring Time for Internet Tulips?, CREC Working Paper, University of Texas (1998).
9. Croft, D., The Agent Crisis and Resolution of 1999, http://alumnus.caltech.edu/ ~croft/research/ agent/crisis/ (1999)
10. Crowston, K., MacInnes, I., The effects of market-enabling Internet agents on competition and prices, Journal of Electronic Commerce Research 1(4) (2000)
11. Crowston, K., Market-making agents on the Internet", Proceedings of International Conferences on Information Systems (ICIS-96) (1996)
12. Finin, T., Labrou, Y., Mayfield, J., KQML as an Agent Communication Language, Software Agents (Eds. Jeff Bradshaw), MIT Press (1995)
13. Franklin, S., Graesser, A., Is it an agent, or just a Program: A Taxonomy for Autonomous Agents, Proceedings of the Third International Workshop on Agent Theories, Architectures, and Languages, Springer-Verlag (1996)
14. Gellman, R., Disintermediation and the Internet, Government Information Quarterly 13(1) (1998)
15. Grosof. B., Labrou. Y., Chan. H., Declarative Approach to Business Rules in Contracts: Courteous Logic Programs in XML, Proceedings of 1st ACM Conference on Electronic Commerce (EC-99) (1999)

16. Hagel, J., Armstrong, A., Net Gain: Expanding Markets Through Virtual Communities, McKinsey Quarterly, 1: 141-153 (1997)

17. Hanson, J., Cultivating the Agent Economy, Proceedings of the Fifth International Symposium on Autonomous Decentralized Systems (ISDAS-01), (2001)

18. Jennings, R., Wooldridge, M., Agent Technology, Foundations, Applications and Markets, Springer-Verlag (1998)

19. Jonkheer, K., Jansen, T., Intelligent agents, markets and competition, EIM. (1998)

20. Kaplan, C., Arguing Against Net Trespass, Cyber Law Journal, July 28, New York Times (2000)

21. Kephart, J., Greenwald, A., When Bots Collide, Harvard Business Review, July-August, (2000)

22. Kephart, J., Hanson, J., Greenwald, A., Dynamic Pricing by Software Agents, Computer Networks, 32(6):731-752 (2000)

23. Kushmerick, N., Learning to remove Internet advertisements, Proceedings of the Third Annual Conference on Autonomous Agents (1995)

24. Liang, T., Hung, J., A framework for applying intelligent agents to support electronic trading, Decision Support Systems 28: 305- 317 (2000)

25. Maes, P., Guttman, R., Moukas, A., Agents that buy and sell: Transforming Commerce as we know it, Communications of the ACM 42(3): 81-91 (1999)

26. Modahl, M., Now or Never: How Companies must change today to win the battle for Internet consumers, Harperbusiness (1999)

27. Nissen, M, The commerce model for electronic redesign, The Journal of Internet Purchasing (1997)

28. Nwana, H., Ndumu, D., A brief introduction to software agent technology, foundations, applications and markets, Springer-Verlag (1998)

29. Nwana, H., Software agents: an overview, Knowledge Engineering Review, 11(3): 205-204 (1996)

30. Odlyzko, A., The history of communications and its implications for the Internet, Working Paper, http://www.research.att.com/~amo (2000)

31. OECD, Electronic Commerce: Prices and consumer issues for three products: Books, Compact Discs, and Software (1998)

32. O'Leary, D., Different Firms, Different Ontologies, and No one best ontology, IEEE Intelligent Systems, September/October (2000)

33. Petrie, C., What an Agent And What So Intelligent About It, IEEE Internet Computing, July-August, (1997)

34. Talukdar, S., Collaboration rules for autonomous software agents, Decision Support Systems 24: 269-278 (1999)

35. Timmers, P., Business Models for Electronic Markets, Electronic Markets 8(2) (1998)

36. Tφ rissen, B., Intelligent Agents and Conceptual Modeling, http://www.pvv. org/~bct/sprithesis/iathesis.html (1996)

37. Varian, H., Market Structure in the Network Age, Prepared for Understanding the Digital Economy conference, Department of Commerce, Washington, D.C. (1999)

38. Vulkan, N., Economic Implications of Agent Technology and E-Commerce, The Economic Journal 453:67-90 (1999)

39. Wagner, D., Software Agents take the Internet as a Shortcut to Enter Society: A Survey of New Actors to Study for Social Theory, First Monday 5(7) (2000)

# Appling the AHP Techniques to Electronic Commerce in a Special Attention to Fashion Website Selection

## Nam Yong Lee[1] and Eun Hee Choi[1]

[1] Department of Computer at Graduate School, Soongsil University, Seoul, Korea
Nylee@Computing.Soongsil.ac.kr

**Abstract**-- Analytic Hierarchy Process has been recognized as one of the most important multiple criteria decision making(MCDM) techniques. Recently, it has gained substantial attention as a possible solution to the decision making problems in global electronic commerce environment. This study examined the issues related to the selection and evaluation of the fashion websites in Korea. In general, Websites are evaluated in terms of the purchaser. In order to select the best one of various fashion websites, evaluation criteria is essential. AHP is a mathematical decision-modeling tool for solving MCDM problems by decomposition, determination and synthesis. It provides the categorical and simple linear weighted average criteria ranking methods. The results of this study showed that a comprehensive list of selection criteria structured in a hierarchical framework is important for making better decision in electronic commerce. Also, this study provided good insights for the design of good fashion websites. **Index Terms**—Electronic commerce, Website Design, MCDM, AHP, Fashion Website

## 1   Introduction

Over the past two decades, numerous researchers have been concerned with multiple criteria decision making(MCDM) techniques[1][2][3]. Also, Analytic Hierarchy Process(AHP) has been recognized as one of the most important MCDM techniques. Recently, it has gained substantial attention as a possible solution to the decision making problems in global electronic commerce environment.

This study examined the issues related to the selection and evaluation of the domestic fashion websites in Korea. This study described the application of the AHP to evaluate various aspects of the domestic fashion sites. Domestic fashion site companies, in the face of fierce competition in the global market, generally strive to gain a competitive edge through high quality products with minimum costs. The success of this effort would depend largely upon how the products and service meet customer requirements, and how well those are realized through websites. In simple terms, AHP is a multi-criteria decision methodology that utilizes structured pair wise comparisons among similar aspects of alternatives to reach a scale of preference. As a powerful and robust decision analysis methodology for problem solving and decision-making in a complex environment, the AHP is very simple and appealing for solving large-scale real-world problems. It is especially powerful when a problem has many aspects that are hard to quantify. In the literature, most of the studies focused on comparing Internet Marketing Mix are based on tangible and measurable criteria such as products, prices, promotions and places.

The objective of this work is to provide criteria to evaluate various aspects of business-to-customer(B2C) electronic commerce, especially domestic fashion sites using the AHP technique and Marketing Mix.

## 2    Analytic Hierarchy Process

The AHP has been used by numerous researchers in various industrial applications[3][6][8]. AHP is a systematic procedure for representing the elements of any problem hierarchically. The essential steps in the application of the AHP involve decomposing a general decision problem in a hierarchical fashion into sub-problems that can be easily comprehended and evaluated, determining the priorities of the elements at each level of the decision hierarchy, and synthesizing the priorities to determine the overall priorities of the decision alternatives [6]. Karacal [3] summarizes the AHP procedure in terms of four steps:

*1) Break the decision problem into a hierarchy of interrelated problems:* top level being the macro decision objective such as selecting the best alternative. The lower levels contain attributes that contribute to the quality of this decision. The next lower levels represent the increased details of these attributes. The bottom of the hierarchy contains decision alternatives or selection of choices. Fig. 1 illustrates the standard format for an AHP decision model.

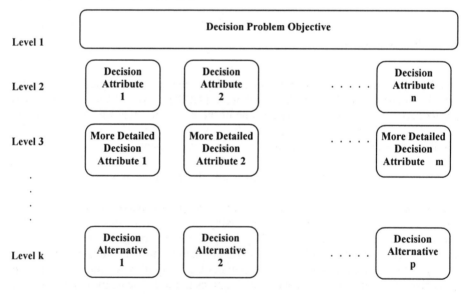

Fig. 1.    Standard Format of an AHP Decision Model

*2) Provide the matrix data for pairwise comparison of the decision elements:* to express judgments in pairwise comparisons, the following scale of absolute moderate; 5, strong; 7, very strong; 9, extreme; 2, 4, 6, 8, for compromise; reciprocals are used for the inverse comparisons.

Saaty suggests that you construct a matrix where each off-diagonal element is acquired by comparing the two factors in importance using a scale like that in Table 1[1]. For instance, if A is strongly more important than B, then A is 5 times as important as B, then B is 1/5 as important as A.

Table 1. Scale of Relative Importance for Pairwise Comparison

| Intensity of Relative Importance | Definition | Explanation |
|---|---|---|
| 1 | Equal importance | Two activities contribute equally to the objective. |
| 3 | Moderate importance of one over another | Experience and judgment slightly favor one activity over another. |
| 5 | Essential or strong | Experience and judgment strongly favor one activity over another. |
| 7 | Very strong importance | An activity is strongly favored and its dominance is demonstrated in practice. |
| 9 | Extreme importance | The evidence favoring one activity over another is the highest possible level of affirmation |
| 2,4,6,8 | Intermediate values between the two adjacent judgments | When compromise is needed. |

The elements in the next hierarchical level are arranged in the form of a matrix and pairwise judgmental values are assigned in satisfying the decision element of the present level for which the comparison matrix is built. Similarly, elements in the next level down are subjected to pairwise comparisons for a particular decision element in the previous level and values are assigned.

*3) Solve the pairwise comparison matrices for the eigen values and eigen vectors in order to estimate the relative weights of the decision elements:* The pairwise comparison values produce a ratio scale (a class of them multiplied by a constant) of weights of the relative importance. AHP assumes that the evaluator does not know the actual weights, represented with vector W. Therefore the observed pairwise relative weights matrix, A, contains inconsistencies. The matrix A has rank 1. $A.W = n.W$ where n is the eigenvalue and W is the eigen vector of A. $\hat{A}.\hat{W} = \lambda_{max}.\hat{W}$ where $\hat{A}$ is the observed pairwise comparisons matrix, $\lambda_{max}$ is the largest eigenvalue of A, and $\hat{W}$ is the estimation of W. $\lambda_{max}$ may be considered the estimaiton of n. The closer the value of computed $\lambda_{max}$ is to n, the more consistent are the observed values of $\hat{A}$. As a result, two measures called Consistency Index (CI) and Consistency Ratio (CR) are defined as follow: $CI = (\lambda_{max} - n) / (n - 1)$ and $CR = CI / ACI * 100$ where ACI is the average index of randomly generated weights for a matrix of similar size. A CR value of 0.10 or less is considered acceptable, otherwise to resolve the inconsistencies in pairwise comparisons, the values of matrix Â must be reassessed. Saaty recommends four different methods to estimate the values of W, one of which is normalizing each column by dividing the elements of each column by the sum of the column and adding the elements in each resulting row and dividing this sum by the number of elements in the row[1]. This is the process of averaging over the normalized columns.

*4) Aggregate the relative weights of the decision elements to obtain a rating for decision alternatives:* The last step of the process is the aggregation of the relative weights through the hierarchy by weighting relative values and summing the totals for each decision alternative and normalizing the results to equal 1.

The following methodologies are the main steps of using the AHP to the optimal fashion website's evaluation.
(1) Define the problem.
(2) Structure a hierarchy representing the problem.
(3) Perform pairwise comparison judgments on the fashion website's characteristics.
(4) Compute the local weights of the fashion website's characteristics in the hierarchy.
(5) Check the model and repeat any part as required.

# 3    Application

A case study of the use of the AHP in the selection of a candidate organizational sub-unit from traditional marketing mix elements will serve to illustrate the benefits of using such a tool as AHP. It will also serve to demonstrate how well AHP supports similar selection tasks.

For the sake of clarity, the case study will purposely be limited to four decision criteria and some decision alternatives (some candidate sub-units). Please note again that the criteria presented in this case study are intended to be prescriptive in nature rather than illustrative. While we have included decision criteria that are fairly common to the problem, firms that attempt to use the AHP for such decisions must identify the criteria, which are important and relevant with respect to their own particular element, and situation at the time the decision is to be made. Similarly, the pairwise preferences presented in the case study are intended only to facilitate the illustration of the AHP and are not meant to be prescriptive. Each organization must elicit its own expression of preferences from its decision makers at the time the model is applied.

Once the steps, the factors, the subfactors, and the alternatives were finalized in terms of a set of nodes, the definition of linkages between the nodes is accomplished through an iterative process. Next, the resulting preference matrices were formed and weighted by the group, again in an iterative manner. The following gives a summary of the resulting steps, the factors, the subfactors, and the alternatives and assessed weight matrices. The numbers before each factor/subfactor designate the node number. Fig. 2 shows the AHP hierarchical diagram. Table 2 through Table 6 will show the original pairwise weights of the AHP matrices.

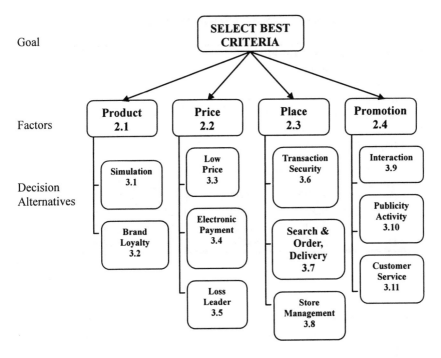

Fig. 2.  AHP Hierarchical Diagram

## 3.1    Definition of the Problem (Step 1)

### 3.1.1    Select Best Criterion

The problem on hand is the selection of the best criterion and the resulting model. The criterion in this context is interpreted as the whole process of conceptualizing and representing the fashion sites' characteristics. The objective of this study is to provide a criterion to evaluate various aspects of B2C electronic commerce, especially fashion sites using the marketing mix. Fashion sites' companies, in the face of fierce competition in the global market, generally strive to gain a competitive edge through high quality products with minimum costs. The success of this effort would depend largely upon how the products and service meet customer requirements, and how well those are realized through website. More detailed information on this approach can be obtained from references to the Internet Marketing; New Competition Method of the Global Information Age in 1997.

Table 2.    Node 1.1 Select Best Criterion

**Links from Lower Level:**
**Node 2.1 – product**
**Node 2.2 – price**
**Node 2.3 – place**
**Node 2.4 – promotion**

**Original Weights:**

|   | *A* | *B* | *c* | *D* |
|---|------|------|------|------|
| **A** | 1.000 | 2.667 | 1.667 | 0.333 |
| **B** | 0.375 | 1.000 | 0.625 | 0.125 |
| **C** | 0.600 | 1.600 | 1.000 | 0.200 |
| **D** | 3.000 | 8.000 | 5.000 | 1.000 |

## 3.2    Factors (Step 2)

### 3.2.1    Product

This is the principal part of the criterion being used as a popular website selection tool. That is to say, how closely the Internet product expresses the real fashion product that can be represented. Most Internet customers are hesitant about purchasing the clothing or are restricted to buying casuals. Therefore, companies are responsible for developing the most advanced simulation technology and creating the brand loyalty that the customer prefers and patronizes on the Internet. This node links to node 1.1.

Table 3.    Node 2.1 Product

**Links from Lower Level:**
**Node 3.1 – simulation**
**Node 3.2 – brand loyalty**

**Original Weights:**

|   | *A* | *B* |
|---|------|------|
| **A** | 1.000 | 0.200 |
| **B** | 5.000 | 1.000 |

### 3.2.2    Price

One of the Internet commerce's strongest points is that it is low in price, since Internet commerce cuts down on expenses in purchase/rent costs, operating costs, place costs, etc. In addition, by using the variable electronic payment systems it is possible to give service rapidly, conveniently and inexpensively. But the thing to be careful about is in deciding the product's price is how this price will include a delivery charge. That is to say, because the customer is given the real purchase price, to add the delivery charge to this price, the company must provide the customer with a variable delivery option and must select the cheaper delivery service. In addition, loss leader is a good opportunity to clear stored goods and sell other goods. This node also links to 1.1.

Table 4.   Node 2.2 Price

**Links from Lower Level:**
**Node 3.3 – low price**
**Node 3.4 – electronic payment**
**Node 3.5 – loss leader**

**Original Weights:**

|   | A | b | C |
|---|---|---|---|
| A | 1.000 | 1.800 | 0.200 |
| B | 0.556 | 1.000 | 0.111 |
| C | 5.000 | 9.000 | 1.000 |

### 3.2.3   Place

The highest merit of Internet shopping is in the concept of space. That is to say, the product exhibition space is infinite. So, the process from the product search to the order & the payment should be easy. Not only the product management but also the management in the virtual store - the memberships management, the order management, etc. - must be careful to offer convenient shopping. Finally, it is essential to use the technologies as SSL cryptographic algorithms or authenticity services efficiently. This node links to 1.1.

Table 5.   Node 2.3 Place

**Links from Lower Level:**
**Node 3.6 – transaction security**
**Node 3.7 – search & order, delivery**
**Node 3.8 – store management**

**Original Weights:**

|   | A | B | c |
|---|---|---|---|
| A | 1.000 | 0.600 | 0.600 |
| B | 1.667 | 1.000 | 1.000 |
| C | 1.667 | 1.000 | 1.000 |

### 3.2.4    Promotion

Internet promotion is to add an advertisement to sales promotion, publicity activity, customer protection, entertainment, a conversation room, etc. Contrary to the past's promotions, the promotion activity on the Internet is important to link the business with the customers. The promotion activity on the Internet supplies various information; it is remarkably more inexpensive than the other business services. This aspect is very important. Similar to the other nodes of the level, this node also links to 1.1 to allow the relations defined at lower levels to factor into the final result.

Table 6.    Node 2.4 Promotion

**Links from Lower Level:**
**Node 3.9 – interaction**
**Node 3.10 – publicity activity**
**Node 3.11 – customer service**

**Original Weights:**

|   | *A* | *B* | *C* |
|---|---|---|---|
| A | 1.000 | 0.333 | 1.000 |
| B | 3.000 | 1.000 | 3.000 |
| C | 1.000 | 0.333 | 1.000 |

## 3.3    Decision Alternatives (Step 3)

### 3.3.1    Simulation

In the case of fashion sites, the problem occurs because the customers can't feel or put on dresses directly. Although there are appropriate sizes and the customer can see the full product on a screen, the feel that the fit and the true style may differ from what is perceived on that screen. Also the sizes may differ a little form business to business. If the fashion site has developed the advanced simulation technology used in virtual reality, customers should be able to select dresses using a personal bodily index recorded in advance. After they identify them on the screen, they may decide whether to purchase or not. This node links to Product, which is in node 2.1.

### 3.3.2    Brand Loyalty

Brand loyalty is the consumer psychology that causes customers to patronize and prefer a specific brand. Brand loyalty on the Internet should be considered from two angles. The first uses a brand from the real market in the same way as before, the second creates a new brand on the Internet. Typically, most the businesses throughout the world use, on the Internet, a brand loyalty already established in the real market. But there are no business expecting great benefits from the Internet. On the other hand, venture businesses that use staff and capital on a small scale can create Internet related technologies or a proper brand on the Internet. In this case, Internet brand loyalty should gain a very important and strategic position regardless of the scale or reputation of the business. This node links to Product, which is in node 2.1.

### 3.3.3   Low Price

Internet commerce's strongest point is that it is low in price. The reasons that the costs must be lower than a real store are as follows. First, Internet commerce doesn't need to purchase or rent a physical store. Second, it cuts down on expenses for maintenance. Third, it is possible to go on working with a small number of employees efficiently. Fourth, since no broker is needed the place costs are sharply reduced. On the other hand, because customers think it's practical to add the product price to the delivery charge, it is important to offer various delivery options and select a good delivery service. This node links to Price, which is in node 2.2.

### 3.3.4   Electronic Payment

The electronic payment system on the Internet includes us of credit cards, cash receipts by an account, online remittance by Gyro, electronic money, etc. Although the Internet is convenient, quick and cheap, most customers are to use it because of worries about the security of electronic payment on the Internet. Therefore, The fashion sites should offer various electronic payment methods, and also provide security equipment in full. After this, the standard for electronic transactions can be standardized internationally. This node links to Price, which is in node 2.2.

### 3.3.5   Loss Leader

Loss leader strategy is to sell a part of products at a very low price or with a loss on cost. This pricing strategy lures new customers and increases the customer base after which customers can be persuaded to purchase products at the normal price. This can offer an opportunity to arouse customers' interest in the cheap price to clear the goods in stock. Also this can offer an opportunity to show or sell other products. This node links to Price, which is in node 2.2.

### 3.3.6   Transaction Security

Previously, I mentioned the security of electronic payment on the Internet. In addition to this, the fashion sites must introduce data cryptography or SSL cryptography to secure transactions. Also they must introduce technologies related to certification service and identify the transaction companion thoroughly. They require the security of business information on the internal local network and the security of the system maintenance information such as membership information and product information. Finally, they require that telephone network has an exclusive line secure from hacking. This node links to Place, which is in node 2.3.

### 3.3.7 Search & Order, Delivery

The fashion sites must have a simple procedure from the product search to the order & the delivery. They acquire from a manufacturing company, under a contract relationship, the product information and through the information must decide the range of the product information and the product price. Also they must manufacture and complement the product database to make it possible to search by subject, by individual product and by product groups. Finally, it is important to offer various delivery options and select a good delivery service. This node links to Place, which in node 2.3.

### 3.3.8 Store Management

Store management is largely divided into membership management, product management and order management. The membership management can check a transaction specification of the membership and service specification & credit standing by individual, by grouping and by class except managing memberships' elementary information. Through the product information acquired from a manufacturing company under a contract relationship, the product management can input and adjust & delete basic data. This also includes the product order and returned goods management and the product management in a campaign or sale. In addition, there is the order management including the order, delivery and the present condition of returned goods. Through this store management, the fashion sites can alter or change the resident enterprise or display products. Also they can offer various benefits or services to excellent members and can apply this information to marketing strategy. This node links to Place, which is in node 2.3.

### 3.3.9 Interaction

Internet commerce must be a two way street, in which the business offers information to the customer and the customer acquires a longing for information. This business must be entered into a specific homepage where the customer himself or herself can offer additional service-information of the product, the price, enjoyment, etc. – the buying. At the same time, they must be offered what they want - motivating of products or services. This node links to Promotion, which is in node 2.4.

### 3.3.10 Publicity Activity

By offering various kinds of business information to various customers internationally, the fashion sites will be used in the medium that conveys the publicity activity of the business. Typically, this consists of the business ideology - management policy, the vision or philosophy of the business, etc. -, the business news – new market or red-hot news, a matter of concern -, the principal product, simple information for services, research and development information, employment information, financial information, the communication window receiving the opinion about the business and etc. This node links to Promotion, which is in node 2.4.

### 3.3.11 Customer Service

Because customer service is a good medium to interact with the customer on the Internet, the fashion sites must be specially manufactured with the customer in mind. When the products have a defect, they may introduce information of the returned goods, simple services, a special service corner, planning business programs. Also they may open e-mail for customers' private use for customer contact with the person in charge of the customer service, or make Frequently Asked Questions(FAQ) beforehand for a problem that has occurred frequently. This node links to Promotion, which is in node 2.4.

## 4 Findings

The next step in the AHP procedure was the calculation of the relative weights of the decision alternatives. A set of spreadsheets is developed and is used to calculate the weights for each factor of the above matrices along with matrix consistencies. Then, after checking on the consistencies, and reassessing the assigned matrix values in an iterative manner, these relative weights are aggregated through a series of matrix calculations to yield a solution to the problem. Table 7 shows the output (weights) of matrix calculation.

The results of final weights obtained from the AHP clearly indicate that the low price and electronic payment are preferable to the others in terms of the factors and criteria considered in the AHP study.

Table 7.   The Weights of Matrix Calculation

| Factor | Weights | Decision Alternative | Weights |
|--------|---------|----------------------|---------|
| Product | 0.18 | Simulation | 0.83 |
| | | Brand Loyalty | 0.17 |
| Price | 0.47 | Low Price | 0.33 |
| | | Electronic Payment | 0.60 |
| | | Loss Leader | 0.07 |
| Place | 0.29 | Transaction Security | 0.46 |
| | | Search & Order, Delivery | 0.27 |
| | | Store Management | 0.27 |
| Promotion | 0.06 | Interaction | 0.43 |
| | | Publicity Activity | 0.14 |
| | | Customer Service | 0.43 |

# 5    Conclusion

The authors proposed criteria to evaluate various aspects of B2C electronic commerce, especially fashion sites. In fashion sites, the authors proposed the traditional marketing mix as the evaluation factors. The authors found, among these factors; that low price and electronic payment are important when a customer selects one of various fashion sites. In addition, transaction security, simulation and customer service are also important.

The AHP applied in this study is one of MCDM techniques that utilize structured pair wise comparisons among similar aspects of alternatives to reach a scale of preference. The AHP is a powerful and robust decision analysis methodology in problem solving and decision-making in electronic commerce environment. The authors still need to verify the decision alternatives by more practical cases. Also the authors want to generalize these decision alternatives and apply them to overall B2C in global electronic commerce environment.

# References

[1] Saaty, T.L. "The Analytic Hierarchy Process", 1980

[2] Zahedi, "The Analytic Hierarchy Process – A Survey of the Method and its Applications", Interfaces, Vol.16, Iss.4 1986, pp.96-108

[3] Karacal, S.C., Beaumariage, T.G. and Karacal, Z. A., "Comparison of simulation environments through analytic hierarchy process", Proceedings of the conference on Winter simulation, 1996, pp.740-747

[4] Karsten, R. and Garvin, T., "The use of the analytic hierarchy process in the selection of participants for a telecommuting pilot project", Proceedings of the 1996 conference on ACM SIGCPR/SIGMIS conference, 1996, pp.152-160

[5] Millet, I., "Ethical decision making using the analytic hierarchy process", Journal of Business Ethics, Vol.17, Iss.11, 1998, pp.421-430

[6] Wang, O., Xie, M. and Goh, T.N., "A comparative study of the prioritization matrix method and the analytic hierarchy process technique in quality function deployment", TOTAL QUALITY MANAGEMENT, Vol.9, No.6, 1998, pp.421-430

[7] Colin, A., "The analytic hierarchy process", Dr.Dobb's Journal, Vol.24, Iss.2, 1999, pp.123-127

[8] Dey, P.K., "Decision support system for pipeline route selection", Cost Engineering, Vol.41, Iss.10, 1999, pp.29-35

[9] Liu, D., Duan, G., Lei, N., and Wang, J.S., "Analytic Hierarchy Process Based Decision Modelling in CAPP Development Tools", The International Journal of Advanced Manufacturing Technology, Vol.15, 1999, pp.26-31

[10] Hoffman, D.L. and Novak, T.P., "HOW TO ACQUIRE CUSTOMERS ON THE WEB", HARVARD BUSINESS REVIEW, May-June 2000, 2000, pp.179-188

# Catalog Sharing through Catalog Interoperability

Jaewon Oh[1], Geunduk Park[1], Kapsoo Kim[2], Sang-goo Lee[3], and Chisu Wu[1]

[1] School of Computer Science and Engineering, Seoul National University,
Seoul, Korea, +82-2-880-6573
{jwoh, dean, wuchisu}@selab.snu.ac.kr
[2] Department of Computer Education, Seoul National University of Education,
Seoul, Korea, +82-2-3475-2503
kskim@ns.seoul-e.ac.kr
[3] School of Computer Science and Engineering, Seoul National University,
Seoul, Korea,+82-2-883-9235,
sglee@europa.snu.ac.kr

**Abstract.** Electronic catalogs (or e-catalogs), like their printed counterparts, hold information about the goods and services offered or requested by the market participants and, consequently, form the basis of the information phase of electronic commerce. As electronic malls as well as e-catalogs made by each of them rapidly increase in number, there are some emerging problems in dealing with e-catalogs such as the catalog heterogeneity and the redundant investment in the making of catalogs. In this paper, to achieve catalog interoperability and catalog sharing, we propose an extended catalog model of e-catalogs and present a view-integrated architecture for an electronic catalog library, named CatalogStop. The Live Catalog in CatalogStop is a virtual catalog that can be bound directly to the contents in the catalog repository or to a query that will retrieve the contents from possibly distributed and heterogeneous catalog sources using a standard protocol.

## 1 Introduction

The Internet is no longer an academic and research oriented network but an open public network with endless commercial opportunities. The exciting environment of electronic commerce (or e-commerce, for short) on this new mode of Internet encompasses a broad range of interaction processes among the various market participants; order, transport and delivery, mediation, invoice and payment, etc. These processes can be grouped into three basic phases of a commercial transaction: information, negotiation, and settlement [Schmid et al. 1998]. The information phase of a typical e-commerce transaction is where suppliers and consumers gather information and explore potential market partners for goods and services. Electronic catalogs, like their printed counterparts, hold information about the goods and services offered or requested by the participants and, consequently, form the basis of this phase of a transaction. Certain parts of the catalogs, such as pricing and terms and conditions, are important in the negotiation and settlement phases as well.

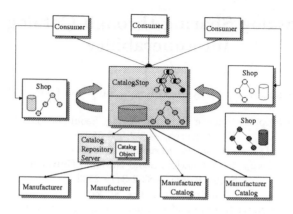

**Fig. 1.** The CatalogStop Business Model

The computerized nature of e-catalogs allows for opportunities to automate and streamline many of the processes involved in an e-commerce transaction. Catalog interoperability is essential in realizing these opportunities and will also provide for further benefits, including the abilities to compare products from different suppliers, to locate complementary products, and to customize catalogs for each individual user and situation [CommerceNet 1998]. Another potential benefit is in catalog sharing. Most Internet shops spend a significant amount of resources in building and maintaining their e-catalogs. The manufacturers of the products must send their product information to each and every shop that carries their products. The total process can be facilitated if certain parts of the efforts can be shared among the participants.

In January of 1998, we have launched a project to build a shared e-catalog repository, named CatalogStop.[4] The purpose is to provide a universal e-catalog repository with browsing, searching, and downloading capabilities in order to facilitate catalog sharing and interoperability. Figure 1 presents our business model showing the interactions around CatalogStop. The participants are classified into three types: manufacturers, Internet shops, and consumers.

– **Manufacturers**. A manufacturer can upload to CatalogStop the core catalogs of its products. A core catalog includes only basic product information that can be supplied by the manufacturer. For manufacturers, CatalogStop provides a low-overhead distribution channel for their product information.

---

[4] The project was funded by the Korean Ministry of Information and Communications and conducted jointly with Lotte.Com, Inc., Seoul, Korea, the operator of the largest (in terms of revenue) Internet shop in Korea, and Commerce Net Korea, Seoul, Korea, the Korean Chapter of the CommerceNet Global Partners.

Reduced promotional costs and extended reach are the principal benefits for the manufacturers.

- **Internet Shops.** An Internet shop is a distributor, wholesale or retail, who typically sets up a Web site of products and sells the products. Such a shop can download from CatalogStop the core catalogs of products it carries and customize them to meet its own particular style and requirements, instead of building them from scratch. Automated procedures can be set up to periodically poll CatalogStop for updated product information. Reduced catalog building costs and access to up-to-date product information are the principal benefits for these shops.

- **Consumers.** A consumer may be an individual purchasing personal items or the procurement department of a company ordering industrial supplies. Consumers will typically search and browse the shops for products and services they need. For those shops that conform to catalog exchange standards, one could query multiple shops concurrently and construct an integrated catalog or compare prices. Whether to conform to the standards and participate in such queries is a business decision that an individual shop has to make. However, should a shop decide to conform to the standards, CatalogStop can facilitate such conformance by providing the core catalogs in standard forms in the first place. In addition, consumers may query CatalogStop directly and be referred to the shops that have downloaded core catalogs of the resulting product(s), in which case, CatalogStop plays the role of a shopping directory. So, the benefit to the consumer is that CatalogStop facilitates catalog interoperability, which in turn will enable services for more effective decision making.

By the nature of its business model, CatalogStop must deal with catalogs from multiple sources that may be heterogeneous. There can be a spectrum of approaches to managing multi-source catalogs, where at one end of the spectrum is the fully materialized approach and at the other end is the virtual catalog approach. The fully materialized approach is somewhat of a brute-force approach where all catalogs are physically stored in one site using the catalog model provided by that site. As simple as it may seem, this is quite a practical approach where interoperability is not a big priority relative to other e-commerce functions such as order processing, billing, and customer management. Most of the commercial e-commerce software systems and hosting service providers, such as Open Market [Open Market 1999], take this approach. The virtual catalog approach provides some mechanism for catalog sources to respond to specific queries by mediators or agents, which will then restructure and combine the results for the customer. This approach is proposed in MEPC (Mediating Electronic Product Catalogs) [Lincke et al. 1997] and Virtual Catalogs [Keller 1997]. There are merits to having physical catalogs materialized in a repository and also to having the ability to dynamically query relevant sources and construct catalogs on the fly. A catalog object in CatalogStop is a virtual catalog that can be bound directly to the contents in the catalog repository or to a query that will retrieve the contents from possibly distributed and heterogeneous catalog sources using a standard protocol.

# 2 Live Catalogs: Extended Electronic Catalog

One of the interoperability issues not actively pursued in the literature is that of product classification (or categorization). Each participant dealing with e-catalogs has his/her own perspective of the whole product universe. This perspective, in most cases, takes the shape of a classification hierarchy. Without the consolidation of the classification hierarchies, we can only achieve partial catalog interoperability; only for the individual items that happen to sit on the lowest level of each of the hierarchies in concern. Thus, it is needed to extend the catalog model to include classification hierarchies as searchable and interoperable objects. In this section, we present the structure of a product catalog and a category catalog as well as the definition of a category, and finally describe our conceptual model of e-catalogs.

## 2.1 Product Catalogs

Physically, a product catalog is composed of a main web page to describe the essential characteristics of an item and some additional web pages to give more detailed information or a big image. From a logical view, it can be defined by three components - content, format, and presentation -, which are suggested, for catalog interoperability in PIX [CommerceNet 1998]. The content defines the data elements that the catalog has, the format defines how the different data elements in the catalog are identified, and the presentation defines the way the catalog is shown on the screen.

The content of a product catalog is represented by many attributes (or ontology) such as product ID, title, manufacturer, short description, and price. We have classified these attributes into three groups, i.e. core attributes, product-dependent attributes, and classification attributes. The core attributes are attributes that are common to all product families, such as product name, brand name, model ID, supplier, etc. and are composed of the Dublin core and commerce core [CommerceNet 1998]. The product dependent attributes are attributes that are specific to a certain family of products. For example, the size and the color are meaningful attributes for a skirt, while the power consumption and the capacity are so for a refrigerator. Additionally, in order to facilitate comparisons between products from different views, we categorize products by dimension, such as time, place, occasion, user type, and product family. This approach is similar to dimensional analysis in the Data Warehousing field. These attributes are called classification attributes. Being additional information, these attributes are important factors of the comparison and searching process.

Generally, these attributes that describe a product catalog are organized as a tree structure as shown in Figure 2 (a). To describe the structure of product catalogs, we use XML which is a data description language standardized by the World Wide Web Consortium (W3C). Since XML provides not only a flexible

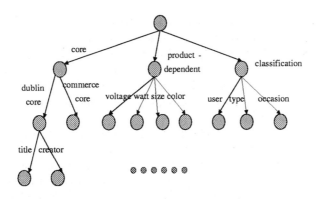

(a) A Sample Content Tree

```
<!ELEMENT p_catalog (common, dependent)>
<!ELEMENT common (dublin, commerce)>
<!ELEMENT dublin (title, creator, subject, date, identifier, sources,
publisher, type, format, language)>
<!ELEMENT commerce (brand, unit, price_unit, unit_price, sale_rate,
tax_rate, market_price, delivery_info, supplier_info)>
<!ELEMENT dependent (classification, product_depend)>
<!ELEMENT classification (user, time, place*, occasion*)>
<!ELEMENT product_depend (description, capacity, weight, voltage, watt,
size, color)>
<!ELEMENT description (point, sub_point*)*>
```

(b) A Sample DTD: Microwave Oven

**Fig. 2.** The Structure of a Product Catalog

approach to describing data structures but also a useful mechanism to exchange structured data, it is reasonable to use XML DTD as a tool for formatting product catalogs. Figure 2 (b) shows a sample XML DTD for a microwave oven.

## 2.2 Categories

Since numerous catalogs may be participating in CatalogStop, efficient searching methods should be provided for customers to access e-catalogs of products that best match their requirements. Generally, several searching methods can be provided such as hierarchical search, keyword search, and field search. However, as we are faced with the explosive increase in the numbers of documents, the results of field or keyword searches are so numerous that we are seldom satisfied with their precision. Thus, the hierarchical search based on well-organized categorization of products may be the most useful searching method in this situation. For the hierarchical search to make sense, it is essential to provide a mechanism that facilitates hierarchy management procedures such as inserting a new category, maintaining links between related categories, and giving different perspectives on the full hierarchy. To meet these requirements, we introduce a new method of category representation.

A category is a set of products that share a common property. Products can belong to several different categories, and some categories may contain other categories. There are many criteria to categorizing products, such as size, manufacturer, type of users, and time, and each product is grouped into some categories by the values of attributes corresponding to the criteria. Therefore, a category can be represented as conditions, which is called a rule, over the attributes of the products. For example, the rule of the category, tennis shoes, can be represented as follows:

$$Product\_Family = \text{``}AthleticShoes\text{''} \wedge Purpose = \text{``}Tennis\text{''} \ .$$

The subcategory of tennis shoes can be represented as a more specific condition, for example, the rule of Nike tennis shoes is as follows:

$$Product\_Family = \text{``}AthleticShoes\text{''} \wedge Purpose = \text{``}Tennis\text{''} \wedge$$

$$Manufacturer = \text{``}Nike\text{''} \ .$$

The benefit of this scheme is that it is not necessary to maintain the information on links between the product and the category it belongs to.

## 2.3 Category Catalogs

There exist some types of relationships between categories. The first type is a relationship between a category and its subcategory, which is called a partOf relationship. The second one is a relationship that can be used to link any two categories, which is called a relatedTo relationship. This is used to connect two matching products, or similar products. As shown in Figure 3, these relationships between categories can be represented using a DAG (Directed Acyclic Graph) in which nodes are categories and edges are relationships between categories.

The catalog that only holds information on categories and relationships between them is called a category catalog. When customers find product information using a hierarchical search, a category catalog may be a starting web page in their searching process.

The way category catalogs are defined seems to be similar to the way product catalogs are defined in that they are defined in terms of content, format, and presentation. However, the content of a category catalog is represented not by attributes but by categories that are expressed in the form of rules.

Using the concepts described above, the conceptual catalog model of CatalogStop will be expressed in Figure 4. Our conceptual model consists of three

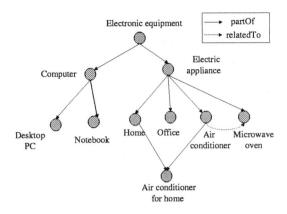

**Fig. 3.** A Sample DAG for Relationships between Categories

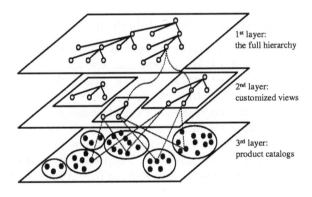

**Fig. 4.** The Conceptual Catalog Model of CatalogStop

layers. The uppermost rectangle represents the first layer, which means the full hierarchy of all products participating in CatalogStop. The small rectangles in the second layer represent customized views returned as results on queries issued by users of CatalogStop. In other words, this layer is a set of customized views dynamically constructed on the query time. The product information stored in XML documents constitutes the third layer, where a large circle represents the physical location of product catalogs.

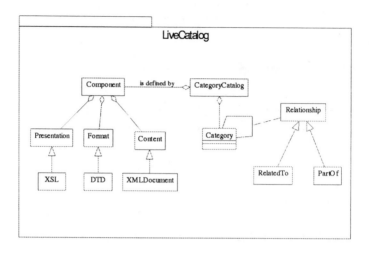

**Fig. 5.** The Live Catalog Component

## 2.4 Live Catalog Component in CatalogStop

In terms of data, a category catalog can provide a hierarchy of product information it covers in the form of a DAG. In addition, operations such as query and customize-view can be operated on that category catalog. So, a category catalog can be realized by a searchable object. Figure 5 presents the class diagram for the live catalog component that realizes a category catalog.

The live catalog component includes a Category Catalog object, which is defined by a Component object, and is composed of one or more Category objects as described in the previous subsection. There exist Relationships between Category objects, which are classified into RelatedTo and PartOf Relationships.

## 3 System Architecture

The goal of our research is to develop a common framework for interoperability among heterogeneous e-catalogs. As explained in the previous section, live catalogs are core components embodying product categorization in e-catalogs. Live catalogs concern directly the issue of semantics for interoperability. In this section, we present the principal components in CatalogStop, relationships among them, and its behavior.

To achieve interoperable catalogs, the following requirements were considered in terms of a system architecture.

- **Openness.** The catalog library system should be an open system that normally includes hardware and software from different vendors. For example,

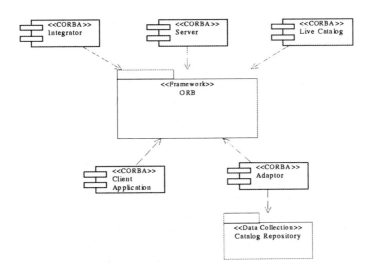

**Fig. 6.** The System Architecture

the system should be able to integrate heterogeneous catalogs from diverse catalog repositories.

- **Scalability.** The system should be scalable so that its capabilities can be increased by adding new resources to cope with new demands on the system.
- **Transparency.** Users should have completely transparent access to resources and have no need to know anything about the distribution of the system.
- **Dynamic reconfiguration.** The components in the system should be able to migrate or be redistributed to improve the performance of the system.

We propose a CORBA and XML-based architecture, which is called a view-integrated architecture, to meet these requirements. All the constituent components in the architecture have IDL-defined interfaces and exchange data in XML through these interfaces.

## 3.1 Components

Figure 6 presents the component diagram for our system architecture, which is a variation of the Model/View/Controller (MVC) paradigm [Gamma et al. 1995]. The model represents the application object and its encapsulated data, the view presents the object visually on the screen, and the controller defines the way the user interface reacts to user input and GUI events. Our architecture also consists of these three kinds of objects. We decompose the controller into three components, i.e. a Server, a Live Catalog, and an Integrator.

- A **Client application** presents e-catalogs visually to a user. Users can search for what they want, insert new catalogs, and delete catalogs.
- A **Server** encapsulates the business logic of the server side in our system. This business process object is entirely process-oriented and not associated with catalog-specific data or presentations. For example, long-lived processes such as load balancing and critical processes like authentication and authorization are handled by this component. In addition, it performs other jobs such as coordinating the creation of live catalog components. Client applications use this server component for entry into the global search space for product information.
- A **Live Catalog** encapsulates category information and provides interfaces through which other components can access it. Live catalog components are created on demand and do not store product data directly (except when caching for performance); instead they dynamically obtain current product data from an integrator to satisfy specific user requests. The detailed structure of a live catalog component was presented in the previous section. Users interact with live catalog components by using client applications. For example, after logging into the system successfully, a user is connected to the default live catalog component that provides the full hierarchy. For obtaining a customized view of the current catalog structure, the user can send a cutomize-view request to the default live catalog component.
- An **Integrator** stores and maintains the full hierarchies for all catalogs participating in our catalog framework. In addition, an integrator acts as a broker. It stores adaptor-provided advertisements of coverage in a central database along with relevant ontology. For example, an adaptor may advertise that it can respond to queries for shoes. The integrator uses these advertisements to determine which adaptors can support a particular request. A request for tennis shoes will be given to the above adaptor among others, and the integrator forwards this request to each responding adaptor and also composes the responses from them.
- An **Adaptor** provides interfaces through which an integrator can access product data stored in a catalog repository. The adaptor performs three roles: it advertises the coverage of a catalog repository; it understands queries received from an integrator and translate them into the language of the catalog repository; and it packages answers from the catalog repository into CEP (Catalog Exchange Protocol), our standard format for communication among components in CatalogStop.
- **Catalog Repositories** store and maintain product data directly, and can be on a single site or distributed across a network. Such data includes structured information, parameters, text, pictures, sound, etc. Each catalog repository communicates with an adaptor using its native language, such as SQL. Physical information related to product catalogs is hidden from all except the adjacent components (i.e. adaptors). So, an integrator does not have to be concerned with heterogeneous schemas and data.

A typical system consists of a server component, an integrator, one or more live catalog objects, and many client applications. The constituent objects are components that confirm to CORBA specification and may be distributed across networks. In addition, we factor a coarse-grained controller into live catalog components, a server component, and an integrator that may run on different machines. Thus, we can distribute the load among several nodes and provide fault tolerance by running multiple instances of these components. This architecture is scalable because not one coarse-grained server but many decomposed servers provide functions related to catalogs and CORBA makes it easier to add new objects to the system.

## 3.2 Description of System Usage

In this subsection, we describe the behavior of CatalogStop using a sequence diagram. Figure 7 illustrates typical interactions among components. The diagram is read as follows:

1. When users log into the system, the server component finds (or creates) the default live catalog and sends its reference to the client applications. Then, users can navigate the full hierarchy that the live catalog provides and find useful information they want.
2. If the user wants to register his/her product catalog as a catalog provider, the client application sends the message Register Catalog to his/her adaptor, which sends the message Advertise Catalog to the live catalog, which forwards the request to the integrator. It stores adaptor-provided advertisements of coverage in its database.
3. Users can send queries to the live catalog to get information on the product they want to purchase. The default live catalog processes queries from users with the help of an integrator, which determines which adaptors can support requests, forwards queries to each responding adaptor, and also composes the responses from them. Then, the client applications receive their results in XML and present them visually to users.
4. If the user wants to reduce the search space that the live catalog provides to the more specific space, the client application sends the message Customize View to the live catalog. This message is provided for customizing the current view (i.e. category hierarchy). For example, one user is interested in cars and another in computers. Each of these users can easily be provided with the information of interest.
5. When receiving the message Customize View, the live catalog forwards it to the server component, which coordinates the creation of a live catalog component. After performing some jobs such as checking the load, the server sends the message Create Live Catalog to the integrator, which extracts the customized category hierarchy satisfying the condition given from the user out of the current category hierarchy, and creates the customized live catalog

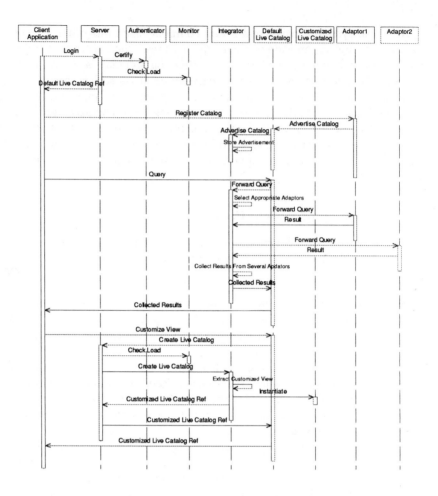

**Fig. 7.** The System Architecture from a Behavioral View

component encapsulating the new hierarchy. Then it returns the reference of the new live catalog to the callee.

The client application receives the reference to the customized live catalog component and can perfrom step 2 through step 5. To delete the customized catalog object, the client application sends the message DeleteView to the live catalog component that created it.

```
// used for binary files such as XML documents or images
typedef sequence<char> ByteStr;

interface LiveCatalog
{
    // The query expression is included in qryArg.
    // It returns product catalogs satisfying the expression in XML.
    void Query(in ByteStr qryArg, out ByteStr result);
    // The condition for customizing the view is included in qryArg.
    // It returns the reference to a new LiveCatalog Object.
    void CustomizeView(in ByteStr qryArg, out LiveCatalog newLiveCat);
    void AdvertiseCatalog(in ByteStr productCatArg, out ByteStr reply);
};

interface Server
{
    void Login(in ByteStr logArg, out ByteStr logInfo, out ByteStr reply);
    void Logout(in ByteStr logInfo, out ByteStr reply);
    void CreateLiveCatalog(in ByteStr qryArg, out LiveCatalog newLiveCat);
};

interface Integrator
{
    void Query(in ByteStr qryArg, out Result result);
    void CreateLiveCatalog (in ByteStr qryArg, out LiveCatalog newLiveCat);
    void AdvertiseCatalog(in ByteStr productCatArg, out ByteStr reply);
};

interface Adaptor
{
    void Query(in ByteStr qryArg, out ByteStr result);
    void RegisterCatalog(in ByteStr productCatArg, out ByteStr reply);
};
```

**Fig. 8.** The Catalog Exchange Protocol

## 3.3 Protocol Beetween Components

The communication language used by components in CatalogStop is Catalog
Exchange Protocol (CEP). CEP describes the nature of actions to be taken.
For example, services such as RegisterCatalog, Query, and customizeView are
included in CEP. CEP is defined in CORBA IDL. The core of CEP is listed
in Figure 8. When a service is processed through an interface in CEP, a client
component passes input in XML and a server output in XML. For example,
when LiveCatalog::Query is processed, the condition and the product catalogs
satisfying it are passed in XML.

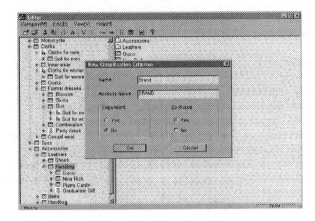

(a) The Category Catalog Manager

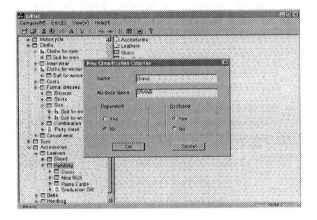

(b) The Product Catalog Manager

**Fig. 9.** The Applications for Live Catalog Management

## 4   Implementation

In this chapter, we describe the implementation of CatalogStop briefly. As explained in an earlier section, CatalogStop has many components such as a server, a live catalog, and an adaptor. The front end of CatalogStop is composed of a Category Catalog Manager and a Product Catalog Manager, which are shown in Figure 9.

The Product Catalog Manager is used for managing the contents of product catalogs. With this, catalog providers can register their product catalogs in CatalogStop and shopping malls can download core catalogs and effectively customize these catalogs to meet their own particular requirements. In addition, this tool can be used to obtain product information with browsing and searching capabilities.

To build category catalogs, the Category Catalog Manger is used. Using this, shopping malls can expand their electronic showcases.

# 5   Discussion

In this chapter, we validate our catalog model and architecture, and present ongoing work.

To validate our catalog model and architecture, we show that CatalogStop can meet the four business scenarios proposed in commerceNet [CommerceNet 1998].

- Scenario 1: Let buyers easily compare similar products offered by competitive suppliers
  CatalogStop allows customers or shopping malls to query multiple catalogs at a time and to receive e-catalogs that are composed of product information satisfying their requests.
- Scenario 2: Present information on a broad range of products offered by a variety of vendors
  Catalogs with listings covering dissimilar items from a range of different suppliers are especially useful for large organizations and for third-party resellers that are focused on specific vertical market opportunities. In CatalogStop, shopping malls can download core catalogs from a number of vendors including manufacturers and other shopping malls, and effectively customize these catalogs to suit their own particular spin, while presenting these catalogs within a look and feel linked to their corporate identity.
- Scenario 3: Incorporate links that let buyers readily obtain information from other catalogs describing items and services that complement or add value to a particular core product
  To provide the means for identifying complementary products, the relatedTo relationship between categories is defined.
- Scenario 4: Provide a consolidated, context-sensitive view of all the items and services pertaining to a particular product
  Because less recognizable brands from small companies can be made just as accessible as the products far more established competitors offer, these larger companies fear that the considerable investments they have already made into building brand identity will suddenly be rendered meaningless. So, interoperable catalog technology should enable a company to provide access to all the information a customer wants to obtain on complementary products and services within the context of its own e-catalog. CatalogStop offers a shopping mall the means for creating category catalogs in which product information drawn from a variety of different sources can be presented without requiring the customer to navigate from its site to another.

We have already implemented a first prototype of CatalogStop that supports the catalog model partially. Some important problems were identified during the development. The following are included in our ongoing work.

First, we need to consider rule optimization so that the performance of our search capability can be improved. For example, the rule of the category, tennis/jogging shoes, is represented as follows:

$$Product\_Family = \text{``}AthleticShoes\text{''} \wedge$$

$$(Purpose = \text{``}Tennis\text{''} \vee Purpose = \text{``}Jogging\text{''}) \ .$$

Suppose that a new category, tennis shoes, is added to the category as a subcategory. The rule of this more specific category can easily be constructed as follows:

$$Product\_Family = \text{``}AthleticShoes\text{''} \wedge$$

$$(Purpose = \text{``}Tennis\text{''} \vee Purpose = \text{``}Jogging\text{''}) \wedge Purpose = \text{``}Tennis\text{''} \ .$$

Though being correct, the rule can be simplified as follows:

$$Product\_Family = \text{``}AthleticShoes\text{''} \wedge Purpose = \text{``}Tennis\text{''} \ .$$

Secondly, to provide an integrator with transparent access to a catalog repository, its apator should maintain mapping data that describe how each attribute in its native schema is mapped to each element in the proposed XML DTD's. While catalog providers are currently responsible for construction such mapping tables, it is desirable to provide a useful tool to automate their routines in the future.

# 6 Conclusion

We proposed an extended catalog model, in which a category is represented as a rule to facilitate the management of the category hierarchy, to resolve problems such as catalog heterogeneity and redundant investment in the making of catalogs. In addition, to realize such a model, we developed a view-integrated architecture, where the Live Catalog is a virtual catalog that can be bound directly to the contents in the catalog repository or to a query that will retrieve the contents from possibly distributed and heterogeneous catalog sources using a standard protocol. Consequently, CatalogStop can play the role of both a shared repository of electronic catalogs in terms of Business to Business and a virtual catalog in terms of Business to Customer.

# References

[CommerceNet 1997] CommerceNet: Catalog for the Digital Marketplace. CommerceNet research report, Mar. 1997, http://www.commerce.net/research/pw/bulletin/97_03_r.pdf

[CommerceNet 1998] CommerceNet: Catalog interoperability study. CommerceNet research report, Feb. 1998, http://www.commerce.net/research/pw/bulletin/98_05_r/98_05_r.pdf

[Gamma et al. 1995] Gamma, E., Helm, R., Johnson, R., and Vlissides, J.: Design pattern: Elements of Reusable Object-Oriented Software. Addison-Wesley, Reading, Mass., 1995.

[Jung et al. 2000] Jihye Jung, Dongkyu Kim, Sang-goo Lee, Chisu Wu, and Kapsoo Kim: EE-Cat: Extended Electronic Catalog for Dynamic and Flexible Electronic Commerce. Proc. of IRMA 2000, May 2000

[Keller 1997] Arthur M. Keller: Smart Catalogs and Virtual Catalogs. in Readings in Electronic Commerce, Ravi Kalakota and Andrew Whinston, eds., Addison-Wesley, 1997

[Lincke et al. 1997] David-Michael Lincke and Beat F. Schmid: Architecture and Business Potential of Mediating Electronic Product Catalogs. Proc. of the Association for Information Systems 1997 Americas Conference (AIS '97), Aug. 1997

[Open Market 1999] Open Market: LiveCommerce Technical Architecture. Open Market Technical White Paper, 1999, http://www.openmarket.com

[Schmid et al. 1998] Schmid, B.F. and Lindemann, M.A.: Elements of a reference model for electronic markets. Proc. of the Thirty-First Hawaii International Conference on System Sciences, 1998

# Digital Divide: Conceptual Discussions and Prospect

Mun-Cho, Kim[1] and Jong-Kil, Kim[2]

[1] Korea University, College of Liberal Arts, Zip Code 136-701
Anam-dong 5-1, Sungbuk-ku, Seoul, Korea
muncho@korea.ac.kr
[2] Duksung Women's University, College of Social Sciences, Zip Code 132-714
Ssangmun-dong 419, Tobong-ku, Seoul, Korea
way21@duksung.ac.kr

**Abstract.** This study begins to examine previous discussions and delineates major dimensions of digital divide. Next, the paper seeks to extend the concept of digital divide to the point to take those issues such as media accessibility, information mobilization and information consciousness into account when we explore ways to solve the problem of widening digital gap. Finally, A suggestion leading to "mature information–based welfare society" by enhancing the right to information access, right to information utilization and right to information reception is proposed.

## 1    Introduction

Some researchers who have tracked the trends of information-based society have said that rapid progress in information technology will accelerate the monopoly or disproportionate distribution of information by a handful of privileged people and thus solidify the existing inequality. Given the notion, digital divide has emerged as one of the challenging problems not only in the U.S. and other developed countries equipped with solid information infrastructure but also in less wired countries which are trying to ride on the information bandwagon. Now, digital divide has become an important issue in the interest of individual countries and international relations as well, as it is being discussed at summit meetings and international conferences.

This paper attempts to lay a logical foundation for coping with digital divide, which is about to challenge the rosy picture of the future society depicted by proponents of information-based society. The paper will outline the future of the information society, examining previous studies about digital divide and analyzing the present states of information gap. It will also attempt to reconstruct the notion of digital divide on the basis of empirical data, and explore ways to solve the problem of widening digital gap. It is hoped that an extensive study on the issue of digital divide and the exploration of policy alternatives will contribute to bridging digital divide in the following ways: 1) Governments will be encouraged to offer a vision of a society where information equality is guaranteed, i.e., "information-based welfare society"; 2) organizations will be inspired to create information-oriented learning process that will narrow digital divide among different classes, generations, sexes, and regions; and 3) individuals will be motivated to enrich their information competence to accept the dynamic changes in their future lives.

## 2    Theoretical Background

Researches examining information inequality in connection with the media began with P. Tichenor and others who formulated the hypothesis of knowledge gap in 1970. Until the early 1980s, studies were widely conducted on the influence of the mass media on unequal distribution of information. But the notion of information gap attracted little attention as a social issue. That is because the notion of the mass media functioning as a cause of information gap became less persuasive by the rapid supply and wide use of radio and TV, although a social gap between the literate and the illiterate has been aggravated by the introduction of newspaper and other printed materials.

Researches in information gap faced a turning point in the late 1980s when the Internet began to be widely used as a result of the integration of computers and communication technologies. Compared with the previous mass media, the Internet was not only entertaining and informative but also expensive and complicated. For the latter reasons, class and regional differences clearly manifested in the use of the new medium, resulting in social and regional gaps in information distribution. In late 1980s, debates over the unequal distribution of the new media became prevalent. Since 1989, when the summer issue of the *Journal of Communication* ran a special article about the information gap created by new communications technology, digital divide came to attract attention as a subject of academic debates.

In Korea, too, where the enthusiasm for information technology is second to none, digital divide has become an important academic and social issue. Despite a wealth of debates, the quality of research findings remains unsatisfactory. Academic circles and research institutions have conducted many studies, but they have focused on information accessibility, ignoring problems related to information inequality and largely indifferent to the need to work out practical strategies or policies for closing the gap.    This is problematic because the information industry—a branch of industry that produces, manufactures, processes, distributes, and utilizes information—has become a driving force of economic development and is making inroads into traditional sectors like agriculture and the manufacturing industry.    Academic circles and policymakers, therefore, will have to assess digital divide comprehensively and produce solutions for heightening people's awareness of the information society and for improving the user-friendliness of information media and information technology.

## 3    Dimensions of Digital Divide

Scholars of the information society are divided over whether social inequality decreases or increase in information-based society. However, they generally agree with the idea that inequality in the information society is fundamentally different from that of industrial society. As informatization progresses in society, the cause and structural nature of social inequality changes as well.

It seems that the information society expands the quantity of information available to the members of a society by revolutionizing the ways of using and exchanging information. But such a view is a superficial analysis based on the quantity of information supplied by various forms of the mass media. A different interpretation is possible when the actual amount of information acquired by the user is taken into account. In fact, the more information flows throughout the entire society, the wider the gap becomes between "information haves" and "information have-nots," leading to digital divide that refers to differential aspects of information-based society.

According to the previous studies, digital divide has been caused by four major elements: class, sex, generation, and region. In terms of class, digital divide exists among different types of workers — knowledge workers, conventional workers, and marginal laborers — and between the upper or middle classes and the lower class. Regarding sex, digital divide exists between men and women. There is also a huge class and generation gap among women themselves. The greatest disparity, however, is between the Net-generation, conversant with personal computers and the Internet, and the older generation, accustomed to an industrial society.

The Net-generation is comfortable with the Internet and other new media, regarding them as indispensable part of life as air. The older generation, on the other hand, finds the new information-related culture and the resulting changes repulsive and burdensome. Regional gap, in terms of information accessibility, occurs between cities and rural areas as well as between big and small cities. Information gap can also occur within a city itself. In addition, international digital divide exists between the developed and the underdeveloped, which is epitomized by the fact that more than 90 percent of Internet servers in the world are located in developed countries and that New York City has more Internet servers than all servers in Africa combined. (Fig. 1)

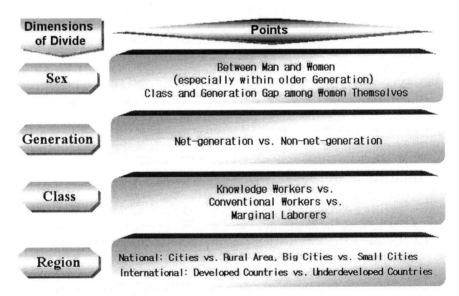

**Fig. 1. Dimensions of Digital Divide**

# 4    Complex Mechanism Producing Digital Divide

Digital divide is created, reproduced, and aggravated through a complex process. Initially, it can be said that economic inequality leads to digital divide, but that does not describe the whole picture. Financial ability does not guarantee the desire to access and use information. Then, what factors influence information access and usage? So far, such key factors as economic power, social status, educational level, and occupation have been mentioned.

In particular, economic power is the most important factor. Because information services that the new media provide are marketed as commercial products, lack of money is the biggest hindrance to accessing information devices and software. That is why economic ability is directly linked to the gap in access to new technology and information. In fact, in an effort to return profit for huge investments in product development, businesses have devised strategies to shorten product life cycles and target rich people. It is noteworthy that economic disparity leads to a gap in access to information and information devices, the initial and most fundamental component of the information society.

Socio-demographic factors are also important. Attitude toward information and Information accessibility and use vary significantly according to social status, occupation, education, and age. These factors change the conditions under which people interact with others and have access to the media. They also change the content of and opportunity for education. And, all of this changes the level of information mindedness.

The "exponential property" of information is another significant element. Generally speaking, information tends to flow toward the information haves. That is because they are more eager than information have-nots to acquire information and more competent to understand information. It is true that people with a higher level of information competency can understand a given message more easily than those with a lower level of information competency. Although a clear explanation of the internal mechanism is not available, a significant correlation does exist between the level of accumulated information and the desire to access new information devices and information. The exponential property of information provides a clear explanation of the obvious advantage of both knowledge leaders and early participants in the information sector.

Another important aspect that has been overlooked in studying digital divide is the multidimensionality or the multiplicity of digital divide. So far, digital divide has been recognized as a comprehensive concept that converges into a single construct. As a result, the multidimensional/multiplex aspects of digital divide have been ignored in researches. However, it is possible to attempt multidimensional analyses for understanding the complexity of digital divide. Digital divide can be categorized into three levels and conditions: access to information devices and information (media accessibility); the ability to utilize information resources (information mobilization); and the eagerness to use information devices and information resources (information consciousness).

Media accessibility: So far, digital divide has focused on the gap in access to information media, which are relatively more expensive and have a shorter lifecycle than ordinary products. Information media accessibility is influenced by economic power, which serves as a major element of digital divide.

Information mobilization: Information mobilization refers to all activities related to using information materials, including the operation of information devices, familiarity with software, and the ability to search information. Users who possess information media or have information accessibility but are not intelligent enough to use them will not be able to fully utilize information resources. On the other hand, if users who have access to information media and are intelligent enough to use them keep gathering useless information, they can be said to be bringing upon themselves information deprivation. In this context, the wide use of the Internet log-in hours as an indicator of informatization leaves much room for reconsideration. The time spent on games and on-line chatting does not constitute the application of useful information services for gaining valuable information resources.

Information consciousness: Information consciousness, often expressed as "information mindedness," refers to the user's ability to judge whether the information in question is good or bad. The mode of utilizing information, which is central to information mobilization, is a matter of the user's habit and practice, while information consciousness is directly linked to the user's subjective life-world, or his reflective power in accordance with the characteristics of the "subculture" to which the user belongs.

But a majority of studies on digital divide have focused on the gap in access to and ability to use the hardware and software of various media, disregarding information consciousness that can be considered a "humanware" as irrelevant. Information consciousness has been discussed only in respect to cultural or ethical aspects of information, out of the realm of digital divide.

This paper, however, views the information consciousness gap as a part of a complex phenomenon. In view of this, the paper will establish various phases or stages of digital divide, and then provide solutions for problems at each phase of digital divide. Recently, personal computers have found their way into many homes, regardless of education and class, increasing information media accessibility as a whole. Nevertheless, a gap in computer usage and information consciousness keeps widening among classes. So it is important to apply multidimensional analyses to understand the full spectrum of digital divide as well as to provide appropriate solutions. (Fig. 2)

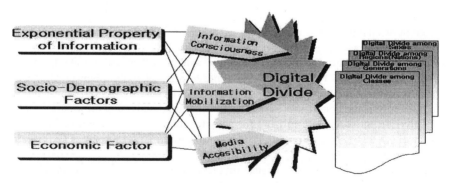

**Fig. 2. Complex Mechanism Producing Digital Divide**

# 5　Stages of Digital Divide

Basically, digital divide is created by socio-economic factors that have influence on access to information devices. Along with computerization process, the core issue of digital divide tends to shift from who has better access to information media or can acquire more information to who makes the right use of the acquired information or what stance a user has on information itself. In other words, the key issue of digital divide is switching from the issue of universal possession to the issue of autonomous reception.

Therefore, on the assumption that digital divide will widen further with the progress of informatization, this paper will examine the current state of digital divide and provide possible solutions by making a tripartite model that consists of the first, second, and third differentiation processes. In the first differentiation process, information accessibility will differentiate users, followed by information utilization in the second, and information receptiveness in the third.

Information accessibility is closely linked to the economic conditions under which users can access information technology. Information utilization is intimately linked to the social environment where users can obtain and process information as well as create added value using information technology. Information receptiveness is about whether users can use information to enrich their own lives intellectually and culturally. Information accessibility and information utilization, both of which are related to the expansion of life chances, and information receptiveness, which pertains to the enrichment of the quality of life, will serve as indicators of the level of individual, organizational, and societal informatization. (Fig. 3)

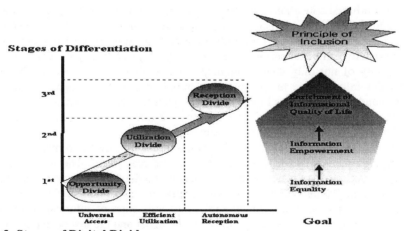

**Fig. 3. Stages of Digital Divide**

## 5.1　The First Differentiation: Information Access

Digital divide is first and foremost evident in the user's access or lack of access to PC, modem, phone lines, and other Internet equipment. Information in the information society is transformed into binary digits, saved as an electronic file, and circulated through information media, such as computers, cellular phones, and the Internet. Information providers gather, treat, and process information in the digital form, and charge fees for information they provide in an effort to return profit for their investment. On the other hand, information users buy computers and modem, and pay fees for access to information. People who are not rich enough to pay fees are most likely to be excluded from the benefits of informatization. In the information society where information users have to pay for both hardware (information devices and machines) and software (data resources), poor people and underdeveloped countries will have a limited opportunity for access to information.

As explained above, digital divide at the first stage can be defined as a sort of "opportunity divide," given the fact that opportunities for access to a medium play an important role in dividing between "the upper and the low" echelons. Furthermore, the disadvantaged group is characterized as being "computer-illiterate". At this stage, whether users have opportunities for access to information depends mainly on their economic resources.

## 5.2    The Second Differentiation: Information Utilization

The primary benefits from the information society go first to people who are rich enough to pay fees for information and are intelligent enough to need and use information. As information technology develops further, people who are excluded from those benefits find it harder to catch up with the early information users. Early adopters of information, who were able to pay for information devices and information-based education, are now enabled to retain an advantage over others in using information. With an increase in the quantity of information, there emerges the demand for enhanced information utilization and for information equipment with a bigger capacity and better performance. The early adopters are rich enough to upgrade the capacity of not only their equipment but also their competence to obtain and understand information. In this process, initial digital divide between the early adopters and non-adopters is highly likely to widen further as information technology continues to make progress, as the quantity of information expands, and as the complexity of information utilization become greater.

Ironically, a gap in the level of information utilization itself is sometimes seen as being symptomatic of economic inequality in the real world. The current upward mobility of venture capitalists or professionals in the digital sector clearly shows that information utilization exerts an important influence on economic power. In the second differentiation process, therefore, a full utilization of information resources plays an important role in dividing between "the upper and the low echelons." In that sense, digital divide at this stage ought to be termed as a "utilization divide." Another required element is "network capital," comprising both personal and physical networks, which is as important as information accessibility for full information utilization.

In this differentiation process, the possession or lack of such network capital divides white-collar workers into either gold-collar workers or routine knowledge workers. And as the framework of the capitalist market undergoes fundamental changes, large corporations will lose their monopoly while some IT businesses armed with the network capital will loom large.

## 5.3    The Third Differentiation: Information Receptiveness

Economic power is considered a prerequisite for accessing information devices and utilizing information, the two key components of digital divide.   It is undeniable that economic power is the primary cause of digital divide, but it is inappropriate to say that economic power determines all dimensions and levels of digital divide. According to studies on technology diffusion theory, non-economic factors like social or cultural needs and information mindedness are as significant as economic factors in accessing information device and utilizing information. In other words, what emerges as a key to bridging digital divide is not access to or utilization of high-tech information devices or facilities but whether the user knows how to use them for the betterment of their quality of life. For example, the same information technology can become either "informative" or totally useless. The door to a mature information society opens only when quantitative increases in information utilization develop into qualitative increases in information content. In many respects, this is not happening in Korea. It is often said that non-economic factors like information consciousness will be converted into economic factor eventually. But when people deal with information, many of them tend to make decisions in favor of non-economic factors, indifferent to their economic interest.

When the information society advances further, the gap in access to the Internet will be narrowed considerably. Then, the focus of debates over digital divide will shift to the question of who will have dominant power under what conditions in the cyberspace. In other words, the focus of studies will move from the issue of unequal access to the cyberspace to the issue of digital divide among participants of the cyberspace.    It is also possible that research interests will shift from economic power to social power and then to cultural power.

In this regard, it would be helpful to look at the interactive communications and behavior patterns of the members of the Usenet groups that are leading the pack of virtual communities. The members of the Usenet groups create and share unequivocal messages in written form to convey physical, emotional, and behavioral signs and meanings. As a form of society based on language, Usenet groups are dependent on symbols, analogies, and metaphors to reconstruct or represent events or behaviors that occur in the real world.

In a networked society like the Usenet groups where a written language plays a dominant role in conveying messages, "the knowledge of language and other cultural elements" is a key factor in discriminating the members. As a result, a good command of language is more valued than in the real world. Consequently, it serves as a new source of power that adds to the actual power that the Usenet group members enjoy in the real world. In other words, the verbal ability to offer a persuasive assertion or to bring up a counterargument will serve as a core source of cultural power (on the assumption that cultural power as such exists) for the members of the cyberspace. So, the members participate in a continuous cycle of statement and reaction to prevent their cultural power from dying out and ceasing to exist.

As suggested by the case of the Usenet groups, the future generation that will spend more time in the cyberspace will see that the popularity of their messages, the number of "hits," persuasive power, quickness to response and reputation will serve as key components that determine their controlling power in the cyberspace. Those competencies, however, are not available to users who spend many hours on on-line games, chatting, on-line shopping, or cyber stock transactions.

To obtain those competencies, it is absolutely necessary to enhance cultural abilities by reading books, engaging in discourse, or experiencing meaningful personal relationships in the real world. In that sense, the elite status in the new cyber society will probably go to "Bobos" who set one foot in the bohemian world in pursuit of cultural creativeness and the other foot in the bourgeois territory filled with ambition and economic success.

As regards the situation in Korea, surveys find that although the spread of information technology has reached the level of economically advanced nations, Koreans read far fewer books than the Japanese and the people of other developed countries. As exemplified by reports that the more hours young students spend on computers, the less hours they spend on books, Korean youths' explosive enthusiasm for the Internet makes it harder for them to find time for reading and contemplating. That seems to serve as a huge obstacle to narrowing digital divide, so we have no choice but to find solutions by offering extensive cultural experiences and expanding discourse opportunities so that young students can exchange their thoughts and feelings in the real world.

In the third differentiation process, what matters is not the universal possession or utilization but the autonomous reception of information. In addition, cultural capital has the dominant influence, since what is important is not the "degree" or the "width," but the "depth" of knowledge. People who find it difficult to access information can become not "computer illiterate" or "Net illiterate" but "cultural illiterate." So, it is necessary to come up with solutions that encompass cognitive, emotional dimensions beyond instrumental, network-based dimensions. (Fig. 4)

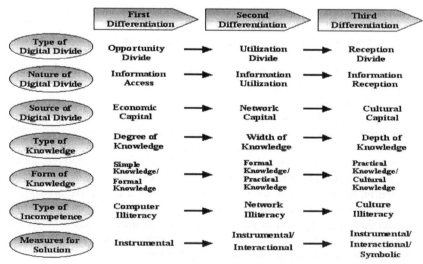

**Fig. 4. Levels and Characteristics of Digital Divide**

In the first differentiation process, short-term investments can help bridge digital divide to some extent. In that sense, digital divide at that stage is characterized by relatively low "gap density." But as digital divide evolves from the second stage to the third, gap density will increase gradually, making it harder to narrow digital divide at later stages. The more stages the divide goes through, the bigger efforts are necessary to close the gap. That is because the narrowing of digital divide can be achieved not through simple increase in investment but through long-term efforts like general, social and cultural learning. In short, with the development of information technology, quantitative digital divide will decline while qualitative divide will emerge as a new problematic. Accordingly, discussion on digital divide is not likely to decrease but rather intensify. (Fig. 5)

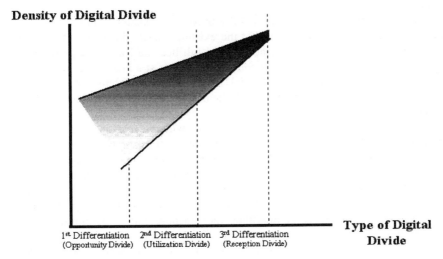

Fig. 5. Density of Digital Divide

## 6 Measures for Narrowing Digital Divide

Digital divide in the information society develops differently according to each stage. So, it is necessary to devise countermeasures for each stage. At the first phase of digital divide, it is of vital importance to enhance the availability of information media. For this, various policies can be applied, like lowering the price of PC and modem, developing cost-effective Internet equipment, and lowering the service fees to a reasonable level through heightened competition among Internet service providers. In the process the public sector, including the related government agencies, can take the initiative in enhancing the availability of information media by assuming the role of a supporter or coordinator. Another important measure is to make it easier to access the Internet by lowering the service fee of high-speed communications networks that are in wide use across the country.

But the availability of information is not a complete cure for bridging digital divide, since digital divide is a complex issue that goes beyond the media availability. Another critical factor that corresponds to the next stage of digital divide is the user's information mobilization power that refers to his or her ability to accomodate information resources.

According to research findings so far, young people in their teens and twenties make the best use of the information media, while older people are less inclined to do so. A chief reason for this seems to be that the formal education of young people included instruction on the use of information media. In terms of competence for information usage, people in their thirties seem to be least apt. However, education programs for enhancing computer and Internet competencies have consistently targeted housewives and elderly citizens, exposing their limitation as a temporary measure. So it is necessary to set up extensive plans to educate more people on a regular basis.

One of the practical options is to fully utilize the existing continuing education infrastructure. It is widely known that the existing social education programs, built under the banner of lifelong education, have fulfilled the learning aspiration of the underprivileged by offering various courses for free or at a low price. So, it will be a cost-effective option to narrow digital divides among different age groups by providing information education through the use of the existing continuing education system.

However, reinforcing information education with the existing social education infrastructure does not guarantee an improved information competence of the underprivileged. As digital divide goes through the second and the third stage, additional efforts are required, for there emerges the need to enhance not only information accessibility but also the ability to utilize comprehensive information resources. The prior conditions for the solution mentioned above are to form a social consensus on the necessity of providing more people with opportunities to access information resources and to create an environment where creativeness and imaginativeness are valued as precious social assets. In short, it is necessary to transform the entire society into "a learning society at large." At the same time, self-controlling measures should be devised to prevent the cyberspace from serving a channel for addictive or hedonistic behaviors. What this means is that efforts to bridge digital divide should be expanded from enhancing merely information media skills to improving the overall ability to mobilize information resources and raising the information consciousness, thereby stimulate social communication.

Human communication has been an integral part of society in any period and place. As informatization progresses even further, communication itself will define and confer meaning to human life. Then, It is impossible to lead a daily life without efficient communication, as information exchanges will shape most of human activities. Communication will become not so much an instrument for conveying messages but a critical factor in enhancing the quality of life. So it is necessary to implement measures to not only increase the media availability but also improve communicative competencies at home and work.

Meanwhile, indicators that are used to determine international digital divide are the number and density of information service providers, number of hosting servers and Internet users, the number of organizations equipped with the networks, the Internet permeation rate, the volume of the Internet content in their own languages, and the usage rate of Internet contents by the major sectors. As of 1999, Finland had more Internet hosting servers than all servers in Latin countries combined, while New York City had more servers than all servers in African countries combined. But now, as informatization has progressed even further, the most critical factor in widening digital divide among countries is language, for English is used in 80 percent of the world's Internet contents. Language is increasingly becoming a determining factor in the widening information media accessibility gap among non-English speaking countries as well as between information-rich countries and information-poor countries. In particular, in the English-dominant Internet, non-English speakers find it hard to use the Internet, however advanced their computer skills may be. Though graphic icons were created to solve that problem, the icons still reflect the English-speaking culture and icon usage is explained in English, making it hard for non-English speaking users to understand. The language used in chatting and message boards in the Internet is resonant with expressions popularized by the young generation, so the older generation has difficulties understanding. It is natural then that the older generation regards the cyberspace as an inaccessible, unknown world, because the language in currency is very much youth-oriented and is strange to the older generation.

To solve this, it is necessary to develop computer terms or online languages that are in accordance with the everyday language. Though languages used in the cyberspace are not always wrong, the current language usage needs to be changed so that everybody feels free to express his or her opinion and communicate with other people in the cyberspace. If the language barrier in the cyberspace estranges users from each other and divides them into groups by age, generation and class, it runs counter to discursive democracy that is the ultimate goal of the information-based welfare society. But lowering the language barrier in the cyberspace is achievable only when users are able to understand their own linguistic culture and socio-culural implications.

At the second or third stage of digital divide, where multidimensional information utilization and autonomous information reception becomes the matter of concern, major factors in digital divide reflect on the user's life-style. So information providers should make efforts to provide information that is useful to daily life of ordinary people. Specifically speaking, computers and the Internet are in wider use among men than women, which seems to result from the fact that information service providers target male users as main customers. The main functions of the computer — a word processor, a database, and a presentation tool — are useful to male workers but not to housewives. The user's occupation is another factor in deciding Internet access. Knowledge workers and students access the Internet and search information more frequently than factory workers and administrative workers. The difference also reflects the importance of the relationship between the Internet content and the user's life-style. Therefore, it is necessary to not only identify what information have-nots need and demand but also to provide them with user-friendly information services.

The essential factor in information receptiveness is information-mindedness. That is because one's receptivity of or apathy to informatization itself can lead to digital divide. Apart from their socio-economic status or other institutional considerations, whether users are information minded or not will affect their ability to utilize information media.

Various approaches are possible to boost information-mindedness. Among others, it is preferable to hold informatization events that target diverse groups in terms of class, sex, generation, and region. So far, "Information Hunting Contests" have been held for the Internet users in an effort to boost interest in information-based society. But they were just shows, targeting information haves who are already armed with the information-mindedness. Those information haves need not be targeted for promotion campaigns, for they have no difficulty in participating in the march to the information society. And yet, the events sponsored by Internet communities and Internet service providers often target information haves and they are the ones who stand out. Even government-sponsored contests tend to target well-educated people who are good at using information media. Those contests may be effective in intensifying the information haves' participation in the informatization process, but are likely to widen the divide between information haves and have-nots, alienating the latter from the information-enhancing process. To overcome that situation, it is absolutely necessary to draw up policies and offer occassions to help the information have-nots. With those policies and occassions, it is possible to cultivate information mindedness as many people as possible and obtain the desired outcomes of narrowing digital divide. Communication is impossible when there is only one party. In that sense, we will say that inviting information have-nots, as the other party, into communication is a way to fulfill Habermasian idea of promoting social rationality in pursuit of ideal speech condition by overcoming oppressive and distorted communication.

## 7    Conclusion

The ultimate goal behind efforts to dismantle the new unequal system created by digital divide is to realize an information-based welfare society. Generally speaking, the welfare society refers to a society where people can fully exhibit their potential and creativeness and where they are evaluated according to their contributions to the collective good. In the information era, all members of society should be guaranteed equal rights to have access to information, obtain useful information, and enjoy information autonomously. In other words, with the progress of the information society, the citizens need to be guaranteed, as civil rights, the rights to information media access, basic information services, better information utilization methods, and information welfare.

With the rise of civil society, the notion of civil rights has surfaced to protect basic human rights, such as personal liberty and freedom of thought, political rights, such as the right to vote, and social rights, such as the right to social participation and the right to welfare. In the information society, on the other hand, the new version of civil rights—the right to information welfare—will have to be guaranteed to protect the rights to information access, information utilization, and information receptiveness. Only when information welfare rights are protected along with civil rights, can we find a fundamental solution for the widening digital divide and leap toward a mature inforamation-based welfare state. (Fig. 6)

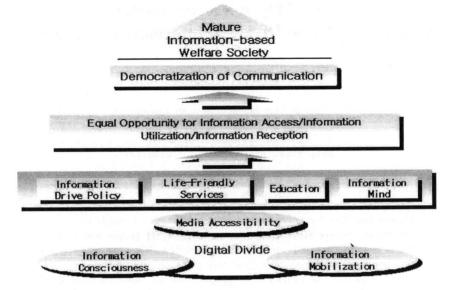

**Fig. 6. Output Image of Information-based Welfare Society**

# Merits of Open-Source Resolution
# to Resolve a Digital Divide in Information Technology

Takayuki Watanabe

Department of Information Science, Shonan Institute of Technology,
1-1-25 Tsujido-NishiKaigan, Fujisawa, Kanagawa, 251-8511, JAPAN
takayuki@la.shonan-it.ac.jp
http://www.sfc.keio.ac.jp/~wata7be/

**Abstract.** The Internet becomes a fundamental infrastructure of the current life. The fundamental technology must be accessible to anyone; otherwise, there arises a digital-divide between the people who can use these technologies and the people who cannot. We must resolve this problem by some means or many people are isolated from the society. To resolve a part of this problem, the author launched Bilingual Emacspeak Project. This open-source project develops a highly capable bilingual speech synthesis system for Japanese visually impaired computer users. In this paper, based on the experiences of Bilingual Emacspeak Project and other projects that concern well-being activities, the prospect, problems, and important points of resolving a digital-divide by open-source project assisted by the Internet is discussed in detail.

## 1 Introduction

The advent of Microsoft Windows and low-cost but powerful hardware spread personal computers to the public. At the same time, the Internet became popular and these personal computers and the Internet produced a so-called the information age. In February of 1999, Japanese company NTT DoCoMo Inc. put an "i-mode" on the market. i-mode is a cellular phone that can seamlessly access the Internet through a wireless telephone network. One to six Japanese, i.e. 20 billion people, have i-mode cellular phones in March of 2001. People can use e-mail and Web anywhere and anytime with these personal network appliances.

When personal computers used MS-DOS as their operating system, it was not difficult for a screen-reader to access the screen to read all the information on a character display. As technology grew more sophisticated, new technologies that made it easier for non-disabled people to use computers often created barriers for people with disabilities. For example, visually impaired (low-vision and blind) users cannot make full use of GUI (Graphical User Interface) of Windows because it is difficult for a screen-reader to transfer 2-dimensional information on a graphic display to an 1-dimensional speech output. Visually impaired people cannot use i-mode to read e-mail because there is no screen-reader for i-mode. Personal computers and personal network appliances become fundamental technology in the current information-age, therefore, these new technologies must be accessible to everyone; otherwise, a digital-divide problem arises. People who are blocked by these technologies cannot benefit from them.

## 2 Bilingual Emacspeak Project

### 2.1 Outline

In late 1990s, T.V. Raman developed a new speech system Emacspeak[1, 2], a self-voicing GNU Emacs. He develops Emacspeak because no speech system fulfilled his demand and he has enough ability to develop a new speech system by himself. He distributed the new system as free software. As there was no useful speech system for Unix, many visually impaired Unix users in the United States started to use Emacspeak. They can use Emacspeak by just downloading the source code and install it to their computers. They can ask a question at an Emacspeak mailing list.

In Japan, a few screen-readers were available for Japanese Windows but some visually impaired computer users wanted to use Emacspeak in Japanese because Emacspeak had unique features not offered by existing Japanese screen-readers. In the fall of 1999, the author and these visually impaired users launched the Bilingual Emacspeak Project (BEP)[3–5]. BEP offers bilingual, Japanese and English, Emacspeak under two operating systems, Linux and Windows. The alpha version of the current system, two bilingual software speech servers for two operating systems and a bilingual extension of Emacspeak lisp package that is common to two operating systems, is distributed as open source at our Web site (http://www.argv.org/bep/).

Bilingual Emacspeak for Windows speaks both Japanese and English according to a language of the text to be spoken. The current project has a plan to extend the bilingual system to multilingual one; especially we want to include Asian languages. Emacs can treat multilingual information simultaneously. Therefore, it is not difficult to make multilingual speech system if 1) text-to-speech engines of that language are available and 2) appropriate functions to process that language are incorporated in the system. As Bilingual Emacspeak is open source, anyone can develop and add these functions to the system.

### 2.2 How open source and the Internet contribute to BEP

BEP modifies Emacspeak to make a bilingual speech system. BEP can use all source code of Emacspeak because Emacspeak is open source (i.e. free software). The bilingual speech server for Windows was not written from scratch but made from G. Bishop's English speech server[6]. This system uses some dictionaries of a Japanese screen-reader developed by J. Ishikawa[7]. Thanks to open source, we can make bilingual Emacspeak without struggling to make the same efforts Raman, Bishop, and Ishikawa had experienced. We can make all modification we want because there is no restriction in modifying a source code of free software.

The development of BEP is carried out through a mailing list and the source code is maintained by a CVS server and distributed on a Web. Users can ask a question and exchange information on a mailing list.

Especially in the field of well-being market, a product not needed by a user sometimes comes out. A manufacturer makes such product because he think it necessary; however, as the needs of people with disabilities are special and diverse, a manufacturer is apt to misinterpret their demands. As BEP is developed by people who want to use it, we can make software that is really needed by users.

## 2.3 Problems

BEP is still under development and we have some problems to release a stable and free bilingual speech system.

1. BEP is developed by people who want to use self-voicing Emacs, who are not professional programmers but write source code at their spare time. We cannot recruit volunteer professional programmers because speech system is special field that does not gather ordinary people's interest.
2. Documentation and support is a time-consuming task and not fully accomplished by the current volunteer members.
3. Text-to-speech engines are necessary for a speech system like fonts are necessary for a display; however, no free Japanese text-to-speech engines are available.

# 3  Other projects to resolve digital divide and their problems

## 3.1  CHASPY

In the fall of 2000, NTT DoCoMo Inc. sold CHASPY, a pocketsize e-mail terminal that uses a cellular phone to connect to a network. CHASPY is unique because it can read e-mail with built-in text-to-speech voices. CHASPY is designed as an enjoyable e-mail terminal that can speak e-mail with various voices, various tunes, and various tones and its target user is a young consumer. CHASPY also considered visually impaired users as its design process to have some tactile marks on the keyboard. Visually impaired users, however, cannot use CHASPY because it lacks some indispensable functions[8]. It lacks these functions because the manufacturer of CHASPY did not carry out a usability testing with visually impaired users. The manufacturer considered a universal design and tried to make it universal, can be used by visually impaired users as well as general consumers, but which failed.

CHASPY should have had at least the following two functions[8]:

1. Voice notification of a screen change: It should speak what screen is displayed when the information on the screen is changed.

2. Voice notification of the selected object: It should speak what item is selected by a cursor.

These two functions can be realized by a slight modification of the software. These functions could be incorporated if the manufacturer noticed that visually impaired user could not use CHASPY without them. Third-party users such as the author, however, cannot carry out these small modifications because CHASPY is a commercial product. Once the first lot was produced and sold on the market, there is no chance to make necessary modification. The only chance is when manufacturer makes updated version of the product. As the number of visually impaired people who uses e-mail is small, the manufacturer does not make modified version for the visually impaired because he cannot make enough profit from this small market.

## 3.2 i-mode

A new type of cellular phone, i-mode, is booming in Japan. There also are some plans that use i-mode as identity authentication device in e-commerce. Visually impaired users, however, cannot use i-mode. J. Ishikawa has a plan to control i-mode from a Braille terminal that is connected to i-mode[9]. He, however, cannot make full use of i-mode if necessary information to control it is not open to public by a manufacturer. In case necessary functions to control i-mode are missing, there seems to be a slight chance to add these functions by a third-party user. Thus, all possibilities depend on the manufacturer.

General people, or people who does not have visual disabilities, do not notice that the current mobile phones like i-mode are difficult to use for visually impaired users. It is hard to imagine the needs of small number of special people.

## 3.3 Linux

As Windows's point-and-click user interface is hard to use for visually impaired, some Japanese visually impaired users still use MS-DOS when they do not need to use Windows applications. Unix is another highly capable, more stable, and network-friendly operating system but there have been no Japanese screen-readers for Unix because the number of users is small. Users who want to or must use Unix have to login a Unix system from a remote terminal that has a speech output.

When personal computers were appeared, a software programmer was a new job opportunity for the visually impaired. With the aid of a screen-reader, they can write Basic and C programs. In 1990s, Microsoft launched visual development tools for Windows. Since then, Windows applications are written with these visual tools, which prevent visually impaired users writing advanced software under Windows.

## 3.4 Screen-readers of various countries

There are useful screen-readers in the United States. In Japan there are some screen-readers but their functions are limited compared to American ones. There seems to be fewer screen-readers for Windows in Korea and China. Generally, a country that has larger number of visually impaired computer users has screen-readers that are more useful. Languages that need multi-byte character encoding schemes are another obstacles because it is not straightforward to localize English software to these languages.

In Japan there are two useful screen-readers for MS-DOS, which were developed by visually impaired Japanese users[10, 7]. These screen readers are useful to many visually disabled users because the developer knows the user's demand well.

Development of screen-readers for Windows is not easy because Windows is complicated and frequently updated operating system. In addition, developers cannot obtain enough information of Windows and cannot make necessary modification to Windows because it is a commercial product. All possibilities are left to a manufacturer, Microsoft. Thus, it is difficult for a country which computer market is small to develop a screen-reader for local Windows.

## 3.5 Open hardware

"iPAQ Pocket PC" is a Windows CE machine sold by Compaq. iPAQ is based on the "Itsy" project (http://research.compaq.com/wrl/projects/itsy/), which was designed as open platform and had flexible interface for adding a custom daughter card. Detailed hardware design specification of iPAQ is disclosed on a Web. Compaq announced its support for the Linux operating system on its iPAQ device. Open hardware like Itsy would be a suitable device to meet requirements of various needs of people with disabilities. Third-party users or developers can make a daughter card or software to fulfill their requirements.

# 4 Discussion

## 4.1 Characteristics of a well-being market

A well-being market has the following features.

1. Small market: number of consumers, people with disabilities, is quite small. A manufacture cannot make enough profits from such a small market and the price of small number of products becomes very expensive.
2. Special and diverse needs: needs of people with disabilities are different from general people and different from each other. Although it is difficult to apply one product to many users, every product must be adapted to each user's demand.
3. Lack of understanding user's demand: sometimes, manufacturers do not understand the needs of people with disabilities well. They, especially in the consumer market, sometimes ignore the needs.

## 4.2 Adapting open source and the Internet to a well-being market

In the world of open software such as GNU free software, everyone can obtain a source code. Everyone can modify source if he conforms to the license (e.g. GNU General Public License), which guarantees a freedom to share and exchange free software. E.S. Raymond showed the importance of a "bazaar model"[11] in software development process and how things work well in a free software world. The bazaar model obtained power when the Internet is available because the Internet prompted frequent and rapid information exchange and share of information by many useful applications such as e-mail, mailing list, Web, ftp, News, BBS, and CVS.

It is quite different from a commercial product. We cannot obtain the source code of Windows. We cannot modify CHASPY or i-mode. A developer of a screen-reader cannot obtain enough information because Windows is not open software. A third-party developer or users cannot make necessary modification to a commercial product, whereas anyone can modify open software if he wants. If Windows is open software, or at least necessary information is open to the public, it will be easier for developers to make useful screen-readers for Windows. If anyone can obtain enough information to control i-mode, it will be easier to control it. If CHASPY is open hardware, a third-party can modify it.

The Internet is more important to the people with disabilities, who are difficult to go outside their home. It offers the way of immediate and worldwide access from home to social activities such as commerce, information, communication, and employment. People with disabilities can order books or food, can read a newspaper, can search a route to their destination, can exchange e-mails with their friends, and can work at home through the Internet staying in their own homes. The Internet shortens the distance between a user and a developer, which helps a developer to know user's demand. It enables every person to send information globally, which makes problems and information to be shared by everyone on the net. People with disabilities suffer from a large gap in information acquisition because they are isolated from the society; however, the Internet prompts everyone's information acquisition.

## 4.3 Important points in adapting open source model in a well-being market

Important points are clear from example projects shown in this paper:

1. Able core developer: As shown in Emacspeak and two Japanese screen-readers for MS-DOS, useful speech systems for the visually impaired was developed by a visually impaired user himself, which shows the importance of user study. As the demands of people with disabilities are special, it is not easy for general people to understand their demands exactly. Thus, we must have people with disabilities who have enough ability to produce accessible technology such as a screen-reader or we must communicate with people with disabilities from an early design process to fully understand and check the user's demand. The Internet helps this communication much.

2. Interesting and useful project: Generally, open source project is started to fulfill a developer's demand. He develops a tool for himself and discloses it as open source software. Another people use this software when it is useful to them. Thus, open source project must produce useful system or no people are interested in the project. If a developed speech system is not useful to anyone, no one will use it. Open source model does not work if the system is not interesting or useful. People want to join and make modification because he wants to use it.

3. Active core team: Open source project generally gathers a lot of people but the number of people who really contributes to the project is very small. Thus, a success of open source project strongly depends on the ability of core members.

4. Adequate budget: Development of software does not need much money but development of hardware needs some budgets. In the field of a well-being market, there are chances to obtain enough budgets from a government.

5. Internationalization: Needs of people with disabilities are almost same in every countries but language of each country is different. The United States is a leading country in the well-being market; therefore, it is strongly recommended to consider internationalization when American software is made.

## 5 Summary

From the experiments of some projects to resolve digital-divide, it is shown that the characteristics of well-being market, i.e. 1) small size, 2) special and diverse needs, and 3) difficulties in understanding user's demand, prevents a developer to make useful products.

Open source and the Internet can be adapted to resolve this problem because 1) they fit into the market of small size and special needs, and 2) they enhance the communication and information exchange.

In adapting these technologies to resolve digital-divide problems in the well-being field, the important points are 1) capable core developer who can make useful core system and understands user's demand well, 2) interesting and useful project, 3) active core team, 4) adequate budget, and 5) internationalization.

## Acknowledgements

The author is grateful to members of Bilingual Emacspeak Project, especially Mr. K. Inoue, for their contributions to the project. Product names shown in this article may be trademarks of their company.

## References

1. Raman, T.V.: Audio system for technical readings. Ph. D thesis, Cornell University (1994)

2. Raman, T.V.: Auditory user interfaces – toward the speaking computer –. Kluwer Academic Publishers (1997)
3. Watanabe, T., Inoue, K., Sakamoto, M., Honda, H., and Kamae, T.: Bilingual Emacspeak for Windows – a self-speaking bilingual Emacs –. Tech. Report of IEICE SP2000, **100**(256) (2000) 29–36, (in Japanese)
4. Watanabe, T., Inoue, K., Sakamoto, M., Kiriake, M., Shirafuji, H., Honda, H., Nishimoto, T., and Kamae, T.: Bilingual Emacspeak and accessibility of Linux for the visually impaired. Proceedings of Linux Conference 2000 Fall, (2000) 246–255, (in Japanese)
5. Watanabe, T., Inoue, K., Sakamoto, M., Kiriake, H., Honda, H., Nishimoto, T., and Kamae. T.: Bilingual Emacspeak Platform – A universal speech interface with GNU Emacs –. Proceedings of the first International Conference in Universal Access in Human-Computer Interaction 2001 (2001), (in print)
6. G. Bishop: English speech server for Windows was written by G. Bishop for personal use and given to us as open source. (1999)
7. Ishikawa, J.: Grass Roots, Screen-reader for MS-DOS. http://www.dinf.ne.jp/doc/software/grsapi.htm (in Japanese)
8. Watanabe, T.: Report of investigating the usability of CHASPY by the visually impaired. http://www.sfc.keio-u.ac.jp/~wata7be/doc/ChaspyReport.html (2001), (in Japanese)
9. Ishikawa, J.: private conversation (2001)
10. Saito, M.: Software Production for the Visually Impaired. Journal of IPSJ, **36**(12) (1995) 1116–1121, (in Japanese)
11. Raymond, E.S.: The Cathedral and the Bazaar. (http://www.tuxedo.org/~esr/writings/cathedral-bazaar/) (1998)

# Emancipatory Learning via the Internet:
# A Model for Reducing Maori Socio-economic Exclusion in Aotearoa/New Zealand

Andy Williamson

Wairua Consulting, PO Box 60-517, Titirangi, Waitakere City, Aotearoa/New Zealand
andy@wairua.co.nz

**Abstract.** Recent debate has suggested that the under-achievement of Maori (and indeed other indigenous or minority groups) is the result of social exclusion based on their socio-economic circumstances. This argument is supported by the over-representation of Maori in most negative socio-economic statistics in Aotearoa/New Zealand. Emancipatory learning is an educational philosophy directed at ending exclusion through learning models created by the community for the community, where learning is developed in a way that enables the learner to understand their own position and, therefore, create the potential for change. The Internet offers a tool that is not only relatively ubiquitous but also economical in terms of media development. The Internet, therefore, presents a potentially suitable platform to develop emancipatory learning solutions and communities of like that can be localised and offer the potential for interaction with similar groups elsewhere.

## 1 Introduction

The colonisation of New Zealand over the last two hundred years has led to an education system based primarily on a Western epistemology and in the devaluation of other models of learning. As a result, many *Maori* have become alienated from education and yet "the power to define knowledge and history gives significant political advantage to those that hold that power" [1, p.26]. Following World War II, New Zealand saw a significant *Maori* migration from rural to urban areas and this has led to alarming levels of socio-economic, educational and health disparity between *Maori* and *Pakeha* [2]. Historically, attempts to correct this imbalance have focused on the *Maori* struggle as one of identity; one of ethnicity and culture.

In this paper I present an argument for *Maori* exclusion being socio-economic, or class-based, [3]. Given its focus on exclusion from a socio-economic perspective, I will explore the application of emancipatory learning principles [4, 5] as a possible solution to these disparities in our society. I will examine the potential for developing a pedagogical framework for adult education that is controlled at a local level but is linked through a technology-based support network of online resources using the Internet as a way of creating a networked community of like within the context of empowering the dispossessed within *Maoridom*.

I am aware that, since I am not *Maori*, there is an inherent risk that I am inappropriately overlaying westernised views onto a framework that I am not fully immersed in nor fully understand [6]. Therefore, this paper does not attempt to be prescriptive but rather attempts to approach the issues objectively from the viewpoint of an English-born Celt.

## 2 Emancipatory learning

Before looking at the issues affecting *Maori* in Aotearoa/New Zealand, I will review the philosophy that underpins emancipatory learning, as defined in the seminal work of Brazilian educationalist Paulo Freire [4]. Emancipatory learning is closely aligned with the philosophies of critical pedagogy [Habermas cited in 7] and transformative learning [Mezirow cited in 7]. These philosophies place a dual focus on education and culture, believing that the former must exist in a context that is appropriate to the latter. Empowering individuals to understand the nature and causation of their circumstances in order that they can develop strategies that enable change to occur is a fundamental premise of emancipatory learning [8].

Freire [4, p. 46] challenged the "banking model" of education, which he argued promoted a prescriptive dissemination of the knowledge of the dominant culture in such a way that "knowledge is a gift bestowed by those who consider themselves knowledgeable upon those who they consider to know nothing". Instead, Freire proposed a liberatory, or emancipatory, model that was based on leveling the power imbalance between teacher and learner, critical thinking and social transformation [9]. In this model, the teacher becomes a facilitator who, together with the students, forms a cultural circle where the emphasis is shifted from the didactic to a delivery mechanism whereby content is seen as relevant to the group [4].

Freire's work is grounded in the context of critical social theory, a philosophy originating in the 1920s at Germany's Frankfurt School and which attempts to promote processes of inquiry that led to social transformation via emancipation from oppression through the critique of ideological domination [10]. These theories were born out Freire's work with the poor and disposed of Brazil, Uruguay and Chile, where he attempted to introduce educational practices that enabled those who were disposed and excluded from society to find their own voice in order to be able to articulate and understand their circumstances, ultimately becoming sufficiently empowered to bring about change [11]. It is Freire's argument that all human beings are able to think critically and, if they can be liberated through the educational process, can transform their own oppressive situations [10].

Freire's work is imbued with the micro-level daily lives of individuals, whether those experiences were oppressive or not, and then situated in a macro-level narrative that contextualises the experiences within a larger societal picture [11]. These theories, however, are not for the most part new; rather Freire brought together the theoretical perspectives of many before him, including such diverse sources as Socrates, Marx, Sartre, Husserl, Guevara and the Bible [9]. Freire's influence in the field of adult education comes from his combining the ideas of these and many others into a single and original formulation that he expresses in the form of emancipatory learning. In doing so, Freire "articulated a language of critique and a language of possibility at a time when it was most needed" [9, p.2].

An important concept of Freire's early work is *conscientisation*, or the ability to critically perceive the causes of ones own reality. The use of this term is cautioned since it is not a original to Freire, having its origins in France, and was abandoned by him in 1972 as the term became popularised, coming into common educational parlance as a way of appearing revolutionary whilst in fact maintaining the status quo [9].

Having identified emancipatory learning as an appropriate pedagogical strategy for empowering those who are marginalised and oppressed within society, I will now look at the socio-economic context of *Maori* in order to determine how emancipatory learning could be appropriate in this context.

## 3 Maori

*Maori* are the Indigenous people of Aotearoa/New Zealand, whose relationship with *Pakeha* and other non-*Maori* is defined in *Te Tiriti O Waitangi*/The Treaty of Waitangi, a document of international legal standing that was signed in 1840 by the Crown and *Maori* Chiefs [12]. As Du Plessis and Alice observed, *Te Tiriti* forms the basis for biculturalism, which Sullivan [13] defined as:

1. Equal partnership between two groups.
2. *Maori* are acknowledged as *tangata whenua*.
3. The *Maori* translation of *Te Tiriti O Waitangi* is acknowledged as the founding document of Aotearoa/New Zealand.
4. Concerned with addressing past injustices and re-empowering indigenous people.

### 3.1 Population and Demographics

In 1996, people of *Maori* ancestry accounted for 16 percent of the population, with approximately 80 percent living in urban areas [14]. The *Maori* population is younger than the non-*Maori* population: In 1996, 45.7 percent were aged 15 to 29, compared to 24 percent of the total population [14]. The rapid post-war urban drift described by Statistics New Zealand [14] has led to a dislocation from traditional *iwi* structures for many [2], raising the question of representation for these *Maori* who, as James [15] observed, cannot locate or choose not to claim a connection to *iwi*.

## 3.2 Education and Employment

Unemployment became a major social issue in Aotearoa/New Zealand from the 1970s with *Maori* the group most vulnerable to this economic dislocation [16]. Traditionally, *Maori* had been employed in agriculture, forestry, at the freezing works or on the railways, all industries that suffered severe contractions in employment. Keefe et al. reported that *Maori* unemployment in 1984 was 22.4 percent, comparing unfavourably with the general rate at the time of 9.4 percent, and that this was further compounded because *Maori* were not only more likely to be unemployed but were also more likely to remain unemployed. Moving forward, the unemployment rate for *Maori* in 1999 was 19 percent, compared to only 6 percent for non-*Maori*. In 1997 *Maori* represented 40 percent of those who remained unemployed for two years or more [17]. *Maori* unemployment shows regional and demographic variations, with the rates being highest in the rural areas of Northland and the Bay of Plenty/Gisborne and amongst the young: 18 percent of all unemployed *Maori* are aged under nineteen and 32 percent of *Maori* aged fifteen to nineteen are unemployed [17].

*Maori* are over-represented in most negative socio-economic statistics and major disparities exist in housing, health, employment and education [2]. Although Durie noted that some educational disparities have been removed, *Maori* remain under-represented in the tertiary education sector [18] and are less likely to have formal qualifications than non-*Maori* [19]. *Maori* who are degree-qualified are significantly more likely to be in employment, with an unemployment rate amongst this group of 5 percent in 1996 [17]. *Maori* participation in the tertiary sector is shown in the table below:

Table 1. *Maori* and the education system (1994)

|  | *Maori* | Non-*Maori* |
|---|---|---|
| Percentage school leavers with no qualifications | 34.6 | 12.1 |
| Percentage enrolments in tertiary sector |  |  |
| University | 9 | 91 |
| Polytechnic | 12 | 88 |
| College of education | 12 | 88 |
| *Wananga* | 94 | 6 |

[Source: Ministry of Education cited in 2, p.87]

## 3.3 Indigenous Knowledge

Despite the renaissance in *Maori* culture and an increased awareness of *Te Tiriti*, little value has been placed on indigenous knowledge in Aotearoa/New Zealand. This is evidenced by a government strategic paper on the future of Research, Science and Technology [cited in 20], which described *Maori* knowledge as "other kinds of knowledge". Cunningham observed that this is unfortunate since *Maori* knowledge has equal status within the concept of partnership and should never be judged as 'other'. Nor should *Maori* knowledge be ascribed to 'tradition', since this implies that it is outdated. Gorjestani [21] observed that the community, not the individual, holds indigenous knowledge and Durie [2] supported this in the context of *Maori*. Such knowledge is often tacit and, therefore, difficult to codify in terms of Western ways of thinking [21]. The New Zealand education system has, in general, failed to embrace *Maori* concepts of knowledge and learning [cited in 20]. Even education for *Maori* by *Maori* is still to a large degree bound by western paradigms and such initiatives are seen as having only limited success [22].

The Ministry of Education and Ministry of *Maori* Affairs [cited in 22, p.92] stated that "education is a key to personal, social and economic issues", yet because of the failure of the education system to embrace other ways of learning, many *Maori* feel marginalised. Many *Maori* returning to adult education later in life report disillusionment with their earlier educational experiences and some do not understand the benefits that education has to offer [23].

### 3.4  Kaupapa Maori

An ontology that encapsulates the *Maori* world-view is described by the term *kaupapa Maori*, which in turn can be seen as both a theory and a transformative praxis [Smith cited in 24]. Despite the lack of present day value placed on indigenous knowledge, *Maori* had developed complex ways of knowing, philosophies and ethical models that underpinned their society prior to European arrival [1]. As Henry [24] noted, colonisation eroded these practices, forcing what remained to become aligned within a cognitive framework understood by the coloniser. Despite this erosion, *Maori* culture has proven resilient and this is manifested in the retention of many traditional structures [22, 24]. This resilience is seen in the success of *kohanga reo*, or *Maori* early childhood education centres [2].

Before the arrival of Europeans, *Maori* society was tribal and based on a system of kinship that was founded on humanism, obligatory reciprocity and gift giving. Henry [24, p.7] observed that *Maori* society was "underpinned by an economy of affection," and that this was in direct contrast to the European capitalist "economy of exploitation".

*Kaupapa Maori* embraces the *tikanga* of *Maori*, recognising a connection with the spiritual and sacred and with the reciprocity that is inherent in human relationships [24]. *Maori* knowledge exists in a context of *whakapapa* [25] and, according to Penetito [22], is grounded in a concept of "place", encapsulating *turangawaewae*, *papakainga*, *whenua matua*, *kainga* and *mana whenua*.

Cram [cited in 24] observed that whilst *Pakeha* view knowledge as cumulative, *Maori* embrace the acquisition and construction of knowledge in order to uphold the *mana* of the community. However, as Henry noted, *Maori* knowledge was not universal since it was considered *tapu* and protocols existed to ensure that its oral transmission was both appropriate and accurate. This *tapu* is seen today within *Maori* communities, where protocols establish research as *taonga tuku iho*, literally, treasures passed down from the ancients [24]. The different philosophies of sharing knowledge between *Maori* and Western cultures is strikingly described in 'w*aka rorohiko*', a poem by Robert Sullivan [26, p.59]:

> I heard it at Awataha Marae
> in te reo – waka rorohiko –
> 'computer waka', about a database
> containing whakapapa. About tapu
> information, not for publication.
> A dilemma for library culture
> of access for all, no matter who, how,
> why. A big Western principle stressing
> egalitarianism. My respects.
> However, Maori knowledge brings many
> together to share their passed down wisdom
> in person to verify their inheritance;
> without this unity our collective knowledge
> dissipates into cults of personality

### 3.5 Locating Emancipatory Learning in a Maori Context

Although emancipatory learning is derived from Western paradigms it has relevance for *Maori*; Bishop [cited in 24] advocated that *Maori* research must be founded on self-determination, legitimacy, authority and empowerment. One of the core tenets of critical pedagogies is that they are built around the knowledge and experience of the learner [27], therefore allowing learning to take place in a culturally appropriate way, grounded in *Maori tikanga*. Freire's [4] discussion of the anti-dialogical actions of the coloniser and the internalisation amongst the colonised of the myths that promote the veracity of the coloniser whilst promulgating the inferiority of the colonised reflects *Maori* experience in post-colonial New Zealand [22]. Therefore, it appears reasonable to conclude that strategies promoting the establishment of true dialogue that led *Maori* to create "an encounter amongst men in order to name the world" [4, p.18] are worthy of further exploration.

## 4 Exclusion and Class

Underlying much of the work of Freire and other critical and transformative models is the concept of exclusion [28]. Post-modernists, such as Foucault, argue that knowledge, power and language are inter-connected. Giddings [10, p.13] explained this concept as follows:

> Knowledge and power are intertwined (the power/knowledge nexus); knowledge shapes the social context; power and knowledge are exercised in

relation to a resistance; and meanings are historically situated, constructed and deconstructed through language.

Bhalla and Lapeyre [28] described the effect of exclusion from this process as economic marginalisation, which in turn creates political marginalisation and polarisation and ultimately social marginalisation as networks and opportunities for participation in society are lost.

Class is itself a subset of this process, caught up in the dual dialectics of privilege and marginalisation, both of which can occur for reasons of class but also as a result of gender, ethnicity, age, religion, ableness or sexual identity [10]. Bourdieu [cited in 29] developed a definition of class that goes beyond the purely economic concepts of Marx [30], marrying these with Weber's concept of class as being a group sharing common interests, life style and prestige [31]. In doing so, Bourdieu identified two primary types of symbolic capital, "economic capital" and "habitus" as being determinants of class [32]. Bourdieu's concept of habitus is particularly relevant to this paper. As Croteau [29] argued, Bourdieu created a definition of class based on a common set of identifiable conditions that produce a common conditioning. Lawley [32, p.4] agreed, stating that cultural capital "also functions as a major factor in class definition." This can be directly related to the concept of lived experience, which is fundamental to critical social theory, to the concept of emancipatory learning and also to the values inherent to *kaupapa Maori*.

## 4.1 Class in New Zealand

It has been a long held belief that New Zealand is a "classless society" [31]. As recently as 1969, Jackson and Harre [cited in 31] stated that New Zealand had no poor and, therefore, no class struggle. However, it is clear that major inter-generational socio-economic disparities and exclusion exist amongst *Maori* [2] and that this needs to be addressed. Since this disparity aligns comfortably within the definition of class given above [3], it seems acceptable to describe this situation in the context of a class struggle and to conclude that both class and poverty do exist in New Zealand and that Jackson and Harre were wrong or, at best, victims of the Eurocentric scientific paradigm in which they operated.

## 4.2 Maori and Class

Although solutions to *Maori* alienation and under-achievement in society are often linked to ethnicity, which is a legitimate factor leading to exclusion and oppression [10], not all *Maori* are poor, not all *Maori* are academic under-achievers and not all *Maori* are unemployed. Therefore, any policy that targets "*Maori*" is not focused directly on those in most need of help [3]. Furthermore, *Maori* are not a homogenous group; differences exist between *iwi* and between the rural and urban *Maori* populations [2, 22]. According to Chapple, *Maori* over-representation in negative statistics results from the over-representation of *Maori* amongst the lower socio-economic classes. This, according to Penetito [22, p.101], is a direct result of exclusion and alienation from society through "two hundred years of intensive colonial imposition" and a failure of the majority Westernised culture in New Zealand to ascribe value to traditional ways. This is a process mirrored in the antidialogical practices of the oppressor described by Freire [4] and the cycle of economic, political and social marginalisation defined by Bhalla and Lapeyre [28].

## 5 The Internet

Having first defined the philosophy of emancipatory learning and placed the socio-economic disparity of *Maori* into an historical and political context within New Zealand society, I then considered the causes and nature of this exclusion and promoted a class-based approach linked to emancipatory learning and *kaupapa Maori* as a potential solution to *Maori* exclusion. I will now focus on the potential of the Internet as a tool for supporting such an environment, describing the history and growth of the Internet and its potential as a tool for social and educational change.

### 5.1 Historical Development and Growth

The Internet is a network of networks [33], where computers are connected together using a standard protocol that allows them to communicate. The primary difference between the public Internet and a private network is that the Internet is not owned or managed by a single entity, although its component networks are. Choi et al [33] stated that the Internet has become a dominant infrastructure not because it is unique but because it offers distributed computing and openness.

Although the Internet originated at UCLA in 1969 [34], it was the development of usable browser software to take advantage of the World Wide Web that has led to today's Internet explosion [35]. As of September 2000, Nua Ltd [36] estimated over 377 million users of the Internet worldwide, accounting for approximately five percent of the world's population. In New Zealand, a recent International Data Corporation (IDC) survey [37] reported regular Internet usage at 34 percent of the population. The availability of distance learning provided through the Internet has also increased dramatically: In the United States, it increased by 72% between 1995 and 1998, with 1,680 institutions offering 54,000 online courses [27].

Access to the Internet is unevenly biased in favour of developed countries and, within those, the urban centres [38]. Barriers to access for many, as Arnum [38] observed, include cost, particularly the cost of the associated telephone call, and both the quality and capacity of the telecommunications network and infrastructure.

### 5.2 The Internet as a Network for Change

Whilst Castells [39, p.1] argued that technology does not in itself determine social process, he suggested that it is:

A mediating factor in the complex matrix of interaction between social structures, social actors and their socially constructed tools.

However, because information and communication are at the core of human action the rapid development of new technology-based tools of knowledge generation and information processing have major implications and, where society is exposed to such technology, it is now being fundamentally changed by new information and communication technologies (ICT). Research indicates that ICT can be used to improve learning in schools but this research also tends to be qualified in terms of a strong correlation between success and the pedagogical strategies employed in the place of learning. Therefore, the issue is not technology per se but the appropriate application of that technology [39].

Since the Internet is not controlled or managed, it offers the potential to develop community and to itself be developed and used in ways that are appropriate to the needs of a community. Castells [39] described the Internet as an appropriate tool for social and grass-roots mobilisation that can support the exercise of democracy. Hall [27] argued that success in the network economy depends on learning how to learn and, if this is true, then it has the potential to increase rather than decrease the digital divide. Increased access to quality education is recognised as essential to the future of the developing world; however, this must be done in ways that are pedagogically sound and not just for the sake of employing new technology. Despite this, little research has been carried out on the pedagogical implications of online learning [27].

Since knowledge of and access to ICT opens up access to the information economy, such learning can potentially be used to increase opportunities for work and employment. However, Castells [39] observed that traditional sources of exclusion are duplicated on the Internet. The challenge, therefore, for an alternative education network is that it is able to provide access to learning that takes advantage of the new possibilities of the Internet whilst at the same time tackling the consequences of marginalisation and underdevelopment [27]. This raises a number of key issues which are at the heart of the philosophy of emancipatory learning and critical pedagogy and which appear to have been overlooked in the rush towards the virtual classroom [27]. For example, Castells [39] argued that sociability on the Internet is both weak and strong, depending on the people, content and relationships. He argued that the electronic world does not exist in a vacuum and that it requires some reference to the physical and social worlds of its participants. In the context of online learning, it is important that the "knowledge is created through the transformation of experience" [Kolb cited in 27, p.8] and that, for learning to be effective, it must value the learner's prior knowledge, world view and experience and must incorporate reflection, which Dewey [cited in 27, p.8] described as "the postponement of immediate action allowing observation and judgement to intervene."

### 5.3 Maori in the Information Age

Graeme Everton, a claimant in the recent Waitangi Tribunal claim for *Maori* ownership of the radio spectrum, argued that whilst *Maori* have the content they lack the knowledge or guidance on how to tell the story online. This is an issue that is still to be addressed other than by a few individuals. Everton believes that *Maori* need to look at creating national and international networks that support the culture and that they must look at using technology to support decision making at *iwi*, *hapu* and *whanau* levels. Through this process the Internet will become a virtual network delivering services to *Maoridom* [40].

Present solutions are being driven by the bureaucrats and the politicians, not by *Maori* and certainly not at a grass-roots level. There are no telecommunications policies that address *Maori* needs and, although, the New Zealand Government's recent report on the Knowledge Economy [41] identified *Maori* culture as a unique feature of New Zealand, it made no attempt to address *Maori* involvement in the new economy. The question for Graeme Everton was clear: How do *Maori* take advantage of the information economy instead of being taken advantage of? He cited the example of tourism, which today is run by *Maori* as opposed to twenty years ago when *Maori* were merely actors in a *Pakeha* business [40].

## 6 The Importance of Literacy

In the information society, education and specifically literacy become critical. This is a society based on the production of knowledge, not of physical goods [27], where the network itself becomes the social structure and the Internet is the central technology [Castells cited in 42]. Tangaere [43] observed that research indicates socialisation of the young within a cultural context is considerably improved by the development of that child's own language. Rules exist for acquiring and using language but also for acquiring and using cultural values. Tangaere, therefore, concluded that as the child at *Kohanga Reo* learns *Maori*, they also learn to socialise within their own culture. Aspin [44] argeed, describing language as an essential component for the development and understanding of one's own identity.

Penetito [22] described a praxis for being that is built upon a theory for knowing and a theory for doing. The traditional education system in New Zealand has consistently failed *Maori* students because those aspects of school life that are designed to help one understand the interplay of passions, emotions, rationality and intellect can also cause the student to lose their way if they are unable give meaning to them [22]. The Western education system places a strong value on learning to know through the prepositional knowledge of the formal curriculum, learning to do is about an exploration of place and the discovery of personal meaning.

New Zealand, like many other Western countries, has begun developing policy initiatives that aim to raise levels of literacy but which also place an emphasis on the integration of ICT into the curriculum [45]. However, in 1990 New Zealand reported the widest gap between its highest and lowest rates of literacy of any developed country [45]. Yet, research indicates that *Maori* who are schooled in *te reo Maori* through the *kura kaupapa Maori* system and are therefore bilingual can achieve higher results than *Maori* schooled in the English-only schools system [44].

## 7  Physical and Virtual Community

In order to develop an Internet based learning environment that supports *Maori* needs, it is necessary to encompass the development of localised solutions, where the experiences of the learner are used to create the experience of learning, where language and culture are key elements of such a development and the learning environment is immersed in the culture of the community that it serves.

A key issue to clarify when exploring the potential for class-based emancipatory learning via the Internet is whether a pre-existing community can be transformed, at least in part, into an online community and, if so, what constitutes such a community. It is interesting to note that Rheingold's [46] discussion of what constitutes a virtual community, is not dissimilar to Bourdieu's definition of a physical community [32]. However, Rheingold goes on to explore how community can exist beyond time and space, based on a common agenda or set of beliefs. It is this removal of the constraints of physicality and time that both Castells [39] and Rheingold have observed that makes the Internet a powerful tool not only for building a localised community network but also for creating a network of individuals and communities based on common interests regardless of their location. In the context of emancipatory learning, this presents an opportunity for localised grass-roots projects to be empowered and supported, whether by way of resources, mentoring or other forms of support by similar groups either within *Maoridom* or from indigenous communities elsewhere who face similar issues.

## 8  Conclusion

Many *Maori* face significant social and economic disadvantage as a result of their historical circumstances and current marginalisation within New Zealand society. This pattern is historical, becoming cyclical as the next generation, often failing to thrive in the westernised education system, are forced to fall back on low paying, low skilled and increasingly hard to find manual jobs [2]. If the key to success is education then, in the information society, the ultimate key is literacy of the media that drives this age [27].

*Maori* ontology is as valid today as it was prior to colonisation and the imposition of a Western epistemology. However, for *kaupapa Maori* to be effective *Maori* networks require the social entrepreneurs at grass roots level to build emancipatory solutions within the community so that the learner is the one defining the learning.

The Internet offers a relative low cost technology that can bring together disparate and dispersed communities through the sharing of common resources and knowledge. Such a network offers the potential for support from other *Maori* communities within Aotearoa/New Zealand and by sharing knowledge and resources appropriately with other indigenous peoples. In building a networked community from the ground up that is based on an epistemology of *kaupapa Maori* and grounded in *tikanga*, it should be possible to create an educational platform that can increase *Maori* participation in the economic base of this country, whilst at the same time protecting and promoting *Maori* culture and cultural values, placing these on an equal footing with their westernised counterpart.

# References

1. McMurchy-Pilkington, C., *Ina te mahi he Rangatira*, in *He paepae kōrero: Research perspectives in Māori education*, B. Webber, Editor. 1996, New Zealand Council for Educational Research: Welllington.
2. Durie, M., *Te mana, te kāwanatanga: The politics of Māori self-determination*. 1998, Auckland: Oxford University Press.
3. Chapple, S., *Maori socio-economic disparity*, . 2000, Labour Market Policy Group, Department of Labour: Wellington.
4. Freire, P., *Pedagogy of the oppressed*. 1972, Harmondsworth: Penguin.
5. Freire, P. and I. Shor, *A pedagogy for liberation: Dialogues on transforming education*. 1987, London: MacMillan.
6. Paulin, K., *Putting Pakeha in the picture: Analysing lesbian/bi-sexual politics in Aotearoa/New Zealand*, in *Representing the other: A feminism and psychology reader*, S. Wilkinson and C. Kitzinger, Editors. 1996, Sage: London.
7. Roberts, G.M.O.B., *Action researching my practice as a facilitator of experiential learning with pastoralist farmers in Central West Queensland*, in *The School of Agriculture and Rural Development*. 1997, University of Western Sydney: Richmond, NSW.
8. National Institute for Adult Continuing Education, *Emancipatory learning*. 2000: National Institute for Adult Continuing Education. See www.niace.org.uk/Information/Briefing_sheets/Emancipatorylearningmar00
9. Schugurensky, D., *1968: Paolo Freire publishes Pedagogy of the Oppressed*. Undated: University of Toronto. See fcis.oise.utoronto.ca/~danial_schugurensky/assignment1/1968pedofopp
10. Giddings, L., *In/visibility in nursing: Stories from the margins*, in *Faculty of the Graduate School*. 1997, University of Colorado: Denver, CO.
11. Heaney, T., *Adult education for social change: From center stage to the wings and back again*. 1995: ERIC Digest. See nlu.nl.edu/ace/Resources/Documents/ERIC1.html
12. Du Plessis, R. and L. Alice, *Feminisms, connections and differences*, in *Feminist thought in Aotearoa New Zealand*, R. Du Plessis and L. Alice, Editors. 1998, Oxford Unversity Press: Auckland.
13. Sullivan, K., *Bicultural education in Aotearoa/New Zealand*, in *New Zealand annual review of education/Te arotake a tau o te ao o te mataurangi i Aotearoa*, H. Manson, Editor. 1994, Victoria University: Wellington, NZ.
14. Statistics New Zealand, *Maori population*. 1999: Statistics New Zealand. See www.stats.govt.nz/domino/external/PASfull/PASfull.nsf/7cbdaf9dea00c1b94c2563ea001a 5289/3e787d00458326594c2567d60079a014?OpenDocument

15. James, P., *Case study: Sealord and treaty settlement*, in *Changing places: New Zealand in the nineties*, R. Le Heron and E. Pawson, Editors. 1996, Longman Paul: Auckland.

16. Keefe, V., *et al. Mauri mahi, mauri ora, mauri noho, mauri mate: Health effects of unemployment portfolio*. in *Te Oru Rangahau: Maori Research and Development Conference*. 1998. Massey University, Palmerston North: Massey University.

17. Te Puni Kokiri, *Maori unemployment*, . 1999, Te Puni Kokiri/Ministry of Maori Affairs: Wellington, NZ.

18. Nga korero o te wa, *Nga korero: Business*, in *Nga korero o te wa*. 1999.

19. Statistics New Zealand, *Maori*. 1999: Statistics New Zealand. See www.stats.govt.nz/domino/external/pas/pascs96.nsf/9ba8dae140673e414c25643700043c54 /698dc3471796eb624c25666c000077581?OpenDocument

20. Cunningham, C. *A framework for addressing Maori knowledge in research, science and technology*. in *Te Oru Rangahau: Maori Research and Development Conference*. 1998. Massey University, Palmerston North: Massey University.

21. Gorjestani, N. *Indigenous knowledge for development*. in *First international conference on rural telecommunications*. 1998. Valletta, Malta: International Telecommunications Union.

22. Penetito, W. *'He haeata tiaho': Straetgic planning for whanau, hapu and iwi education*. in *Te Oru Rangahau: Maori Research and Development Conference*. 1998. Massey University, Palmerston North: Massey University.

23. Jeffries, R. *Maori participation in tertiary education - Barriers and strategies to overcome them*. in *Te Oru Rangahau: Maori Research and Development Conference*. 1998. Massey University, Palmerston North: Massey University.

24. Henry, E. *Kaupapa Maori: Locating indigenous ontology, epistemology and methodology in the academy*. in *Building the research capacity within Maori communities*. 1999. Wellington: New Zealand Council for Educational Research.

25. Pere, R.R. *Different ways of knowing*. in *Building the research capacity within Maori communities*. 1999. Wellington: New Zealand Council for Educational Research.

26. Sullivan, R., *Star waka*. 1999, Auckland, N.Z.: Auckland University Press.

27. Hall, M., *Realizing the virtual hamburger: Education and the margins of the network society*. 2000: University of Cape Town. See www.chet.org.za/debates/MartinHall.html

28. Bhalla, A.S. and F. Lapeyre, *Poverty and exclusion in a global world*. 1999, Basingstoke: Macmillan.

29. Croteau, D., *Politics and the class divide: Working people and the middle class left*. Labour and social change, ed. P. Rayman and C. Sirianni. 1999, Philadelphia, PA: Temple University Press.

30. Marx, K., *Capital*. 1981, London: Penguin.

31. Pitt, D., *Are there social classes in New Zealand*, in *Social class in New Zealand*, D. Pitt, Editor. 1977, Longman Paul: Auckland, N.Z.

32. Lawley, E.L., *The sociology of culture in computer-mediated communication: An initial exploration*. 1994: Elizabeth Lawley. See www.itcs.com/elawley/bourdieu.html

33. Choi, S.-Y., D.O. Stahl, and A.B. Whinston, *The economics of electronic commerce*. 1997, Indianapolis, IN: Macmillan Technical Publishing.

34. Sterling, B., *Short History of the Internet*. 1993: University of Chicago. See w3.aces.uiuc.edu/AIM/scale/nethistory.html

35. CERN, *The World Wide Web*. 1998: CERN. See public.web.cern.ch/Public/ACHIEVEMENTS/web.html

36. Nua Ltd, *How many online?* 2000: Nua Ltd. See http://www.nua.ie/surveys/how_many_online/index.html

37. IDC, *New Zealand Most Wired Country in Asia Pacific*, . 2000, International Data Corporation: New York.

38. Arnum, E., *Internet topology and connectivity in the Americas*, . 1999, Inter-American Biodiversity Information Network.: Brasília, Brazil.

39. Castells, M., *The social implications of information and communication technologies*, in *World social science report*, UNESCO, Editor. 1999, UNESCO: New York.
40. Everton, G., *Telephone conversation with the author*, . 2000.
41. Information Technology Advisory Group, *The Knowledge Economy*, . 1999, Information Technology Advisory Group.: Wellington, N.Z.
42. Nee, E., *Interview with Manual Castells*, in *Fortune*. 2000. p. 114.
43. Tangaere, A.R., *Maori human development learning theory*, in *He paepae kōrero: Research perspectives in Māori education*, B. Webber, Editor. 1996, New Zealand Council for Educational Research: Welllington.
44. Aspin, C., *Learning mathematics in Maori*, in *He paepae kōrero: Research perspectives in Māori education*, B. Webber, Editor. 1996, New Zealand Council for Educational Research: Welllington.
45. Leu, D.J. and C.K. Kinzer, *The convergence of literacy instruction with networked technologies for information and communication.* Reading Research Quarterly, 2000. 35(1): p. 108-127.
46. Rheingold, H., *The virtual community.* 1994, London: Minerva.

## Glossary of Maori Terms

| | |
|---|---|
| *Hapu* | Sub-tribe |
| *Iwi* | Tribe |
| *Kainga* | Home |
| *Kaupapa Maori* | The philosophy of Maori knowledge and learning |
| *Kohanga reo* | Maori-language early childhood centre, literally a language nest |
| *Kura kaupapa Maori* | Maori language schools |
| *Mana* | Power |
| *Mana whenua* | Lore of authority and control related to land. |
| *Maori* | The indigenous people of Aotearoa/New Zealand |
| *Pakeha* | Europeans and other non-Maori |
| *Papakainga* | Home village or marae |
| *Tanagata whenua* | Maori, literally, the people of the land |
| *Taonga tuku iho* | The treasures passed down from the ancients |
| *Tapu* | Sacred, to be treated with respect, a restriction, being with potentiality for power, integrity |
| *Te reo [Maori]* | The Maori language |
| *Tikanga* | Customs, values, beliefs and attitude |
| *Turangawaewae* | A place to stand |
| *Wananga* | Maori tertiary institution |
| *Whakapapa* | Genealogy |
| *Whanau* | Extended family |
| *Whenua matua* | Homeland |

# Analysis of Internet Reference Behaviors in the Korean Education Network

Hyokyung Bahn, Yong H. Shin, and Kern Koh

School of Computer Science and Engineering, Seoul National University
56-1, Shillim-Dong, Kwanak-Ku, Seoul, 151-742, Korea
{hyokyung,yhshin,kernkoh}@oslab.snu.ac.kr

**Abstract.** Due to the recent popularity of the Internet over the world, the Internet now becomes one of the most important communication channels for human societies in Korea. In this paper, we present a comprehensive analysis on Internet reference behaviors in the Korean Education Network (KREN), which is one of the main Internet service networks in Korea. The purpose of this paper is to present a contents analysis of Internet references as well as a formal analysis of workload characteristics. We use the proxy server logs at KREN to characterize the Internet reference behaviors. The analysis consists of three steps: 1) Web document based analysis, 2) Web server based analysis, and 3) International link based analysis. In each step of analysis, we present the distribution and top ranking subjects of references, and analyze the areas of interests that are frequently referenced by KREN users.

## 1  Introduction

With the explosive increase in usage of the Internet around the world, the Internet has recently become one of the most important communication channels for human societies in Korea. There exist 0.5 million Internet hosts and about 16 million Internet users in Korea. This implies that about 1/3 of all Koreans use the Internet nowadays.

In this paper, we present a comprehensive analysis of the Internet reference behaviors in the Korean Education Network (KREN), which is one of the main Internet service networks in Korea. There have been a number of workload characterization studies for Internet references [1-10]. Most of these studies have focused on the formal analysis of workload characteristics. This paper, however, presents a characterization study focused on the contents analysis of Internet references rather than the external analysis of workload characteristics.

We use the proxy server logs at KREN to characterize the Internet reference behaviors in Korea. We first present the ranking and distribution of *Web documents* and show the characteristics of popular URLs. Then, the same analysis is done for *Web server* ranking and distribution to show the characteristics of popular Web sites. Finally, we present the usage of international links of KREN and analyze the characteristics of international Web accesses. The purpose of this paper is to present a workload characterization study of the Internet references in Korea and show the areas of interests that are frequently referenced through the Internet.

## 1.1 Topology of KREN

KREN is the Internet service network for universities, schools, and educational organizations in Korea. The root of KREN is located at Seoul National University and downlinks are connected with other universities (45Mbps) and 140 regional centers in Korea. The root of KREN is connected with other top links in Korea: the National Computerization Agency (155Mbps), DACOM (155Mbps), Korea Telecom (90Mbps), ThruNet (100Mbps), Nowcom (45Mbps), etc. International links of KREN are connected with Sprint in the US (45Mbps) and TeleGlobe in Canada (45Mbps). Fig. 1 shows the network topology of KREN [11].

## 1.2 The Remainder of the Paper

The remainder of the paper is organized as follows. Section 2 explains some related studies of Internet reference analysis. In Section 3, we show the analysis of reference behaviors at KREN. The section consists of three parts. First, we show the ranking and distribution of Internet references based on Web documents, and analyze the results. Second, we show the ranking and distribution of Web servers, and analyze the characteristics of popular Web servers. Third, we show the usage of international link of KREN and discuss the popular international sites. We conclude the paper in Section 4.

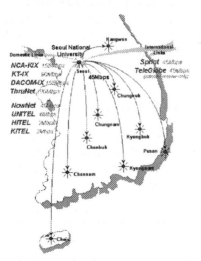

**Fig. 1.** Network topology of KREN.

## 2. Related Works

To date, there have been a number of efforts that attempt to characterize the workload of Internet references. The characterization can be done from various viewpoints such as from the Web client side and the Web server side.

In the case of Web server side studies, Arlitt and Williamson present a workload characterization study for Internet Web servers [1, 2]. They show some invariants from their workload characterization, such as the successive connection rate, file type distributions, file size distribution, inter-reference time distribution, etc. Almeida et al. propose models for temporal locality and spatial locality of reference in streams of requests arriving at Web servers [3]. They show that temporal locality can be characterized by the marginal distribution of the stack distance model and spatial locality in a reference stream can be characterized using the notion of self-similarity. Some studies present the workload characteristics of specific Web servers. In [4], Arlitt and Jin show a workload characterization study of the 1998 world cup Web site. Menasce et al. characterize the workload of E-commerce sites [5].

In the case of Web client side studies, Nagarajan and Raghavan characterize the behavior of Web clients and design a prefetching engine that exploits the characterization [6]. Web proxy server side analysis shows more generalized characteristics of the client side behaviors. Breslau et al. present the distributions of Web request streams seen at proxy servers [7]. They show that the Web document request distribution seen by Web proxy caches follows a Zipf-like distribution. They also show the correlation between the reference frequency of a Web document and its size, and the correlation between the reference frequency and its rate of change. Jin and Bestavros show that temporal locality of Web reference streams seen at proxy servers emerges from two sources, i.e., the long-term popularity of Web documents and the short-term temporal correlations of references [8]. Arlitt et al. characterize the workload of a Web proxy in a cable modem environment [9]. Pitkow summarizes the Web workload characterizations from three points of view: the client side, the Web server side, and the proxy server side [10].

## 3. Analysis of Reference Behaviors at KREN

We use the proxy server logs of KREN to analyze the Internet reference behaviors. Proxy servers act as agents on behalf of clients to send HTTP requests to Web servers and are often used to manage the local copies of Web documents. Table 1 summarizes the characteristics of the log.

**Table 1.** Characteristics of the KREN proxy log used.

| Total Period | 6 days |
|---|---|
| Total Requests | 5,704,851 |
| Total distinct Web documents | 1,308,730 |
| Total distinct Web servers | 988,036 |

## 3.1 Web Document Ranking and Distribution

Our first analysis focuses on the frequency of reference for different Web documents. Clearly, not all Web documents are equally popular. Fig. 2 shows the number of times that a Web document has been referenced versus the ranking of the document, where ranking 1 is the most frequently referenced document. Note that both axes in the figure are in log scale.

The curve in the figure shows that references are excessively biased to some hot documents. The curve is almost a straight line, which means that the reference frequency of the $i$-th popular document (i.e., ranking $i$) is proportional to $1/i^b$, where $b$ is the slope of the line. This type of distribution is called a Zipf-like distribution [12].

In Fig. 3, we illustrate the cumulative frequency of references versus the fraction of the total Web documents referenced. Note that the Web documents shown in the $x$-axis are sorted into a decreasing order based on the reference counts. The figure shows that 10% of the distinct documents are responsible for about 70% of all references and 30% of documents are responsible for 80% of all references. This also shows the evidence for the skewed popularity of Web documents.

The next step in our analysis is to classify Web documents by URL type. Classification is based on the suffix used in the URL (for example, GIF, HTML, CGI, MPG, etc). Table 2 shows the distribution of URL types. As shown in the table, 75.2% of the total Web references are made to image files such as GIF and JPG. This is because Web pages often contain many image files such as banners, logos, icons, and buttons. Since these images are often small, the total sizes of the images are only 48.4% of the total object sizes. HTML documents are responsible for 13.6% of the total references and 8.3% of the total sizes. Multimedia data such as audio and video are responsible for only 0.3% of the total reference counts, but for 11.3% of the total sizes. This implies that even though multimedia data are not frequently referenced via the Internet when compared with other data types, the size of the multimedia data accounts for quite a large portion in Internet traffic.

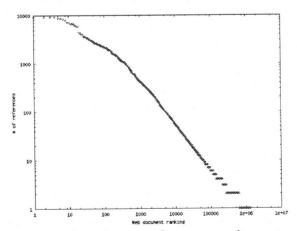

**Fig. 2.** Frequency of Web document references versus document ranking.

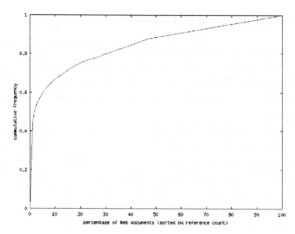

**Fig. 3.** Cumulative distribution of Web documents.

Fig. 4 shows the top 50 URLs in KREN proxy logs. There are many URLs which belong to the same Web server. This is because the distribution of Web servers is also heavily skewed. (Detailed discussion on Web server distributions will be provided in the next subsection.) The most parts of the top 50 URLs are GIF files (38 out of the top 50 URLs). There are three CGIs, three ASPs, and only two HTMLs. The two HTMLs are the homepage of Netscape, and the Simmany site, which is one of the most popular search engine sites in Korea. The Netscape site is frequently referenced because the Netscape Web browser sets the default Web page as the Netscape site.

### 3.2 Web Server Ranking and Distribution

Subsection 3.1 presented the analysis of Internet reference behaviors based on Web documents. The results showed that references for Web documents are excessively biased to some hot documents, which can be characterized as a Zipf-like distribution. In this subsection, we present the same analysis on Web servers. Since Web documents are formatted with hyperlink structures, the origins of skewed popularity may be not only human-originated preferences, but also structure-based effects. For example, the main page of a Web server can be frequently referenced while the leaf page of the same server may rarely be referenced due to the different arrangement of hyperlink structures. However, this factor is less influential in the case of Web servers, and hence we can see the human-originated reference behaviors more accurately by server-based analysis.

Fig. 5 shows the number of times that a Web server has been referenced versus the ranking of the server, where ranking 1 is the most frequently referenced site. Note that both axes in the figure are in log scale. Like the Web document case, references are excessively biased to some hot servers. The distribution is again characterized as a Zipf-like distribution. This implies that most of the skewed references are originated from the human preferences and not from the structural effect of Web formats.

| Ranking | URL | Reference count |
|---|---|---|
| 1 | http://www.joongang.co.kr/cdf/img/joongang16.ico | 18021 |
| 2 | http://www.nownuri.net/channel/i_fol.gif | 9168 |
| 3 | http://news.joongang.co.kr/online_news/image/background_new.gif | 9125 |
| 4 | http://news.joongang.co.kr/online_news/icon/icon_contents.gif | 9125 |
| 5 | http://news.joongang.co.kr/online_news/image/dot_g.gif | 9121 |
| 6 | http://news.joongang.co.kr/adv/ad_common_01.gif | 8767 |
| 7 | http://news.joongang.co.kr/online_news/icon/logo_s.gif | 8603 |
| 8 | http://www.nownuri.net/channel/i_subnow.gif | 8261 |
| 9 | http://news.joongang.co.kr/online_news/image/pixel_w.gif | 7839 |
| 10 | http://news.joongang.co.kr/cgi-bin | 7123 |
| 11 | http://news.joongang.co.kr/online_news/icon/newlogo.gif | 7091 |
| 12 | http://news.joongang.co.kr/online_news/icon/right_menu_sec.gif | 6727 |
| 13 | http://news.joongang.co.kr/online_news/icon/left_menu_main.gif | 6682 |
| 14 | http://simmany.hnc.net/cgi-bin/search.cgi | 6646 |
| 15 | http://news.joongang.co.kr/online_news/icon/left_menu_sec.gif | 6619 |
| 16 | http://www.sbs.co.kr/channel/sbs3.gif | 6212 |
| 17 | http://www.chosun.com/w20_images/pattern.gif | 6033 |
| 18 | http://www.chosun.com/w20_images/ball.gif | 5914 |
| 19 | http://www2.dongailbo.co.kr/tbin/chatting1_1.cgi | 5808 |
| 20 | http://203.255.99.1/w21_images/etc.gif | 4488 |
| 21 | http://blue.nowcom.co.kr/~womantnk/cgi10/guest3.pl | 4357 |
| 22 | http://news21.hani.co.kr/HAN/tickerFrame.asp | 4326 |
| 23 | http://news.joongang.co.kr/adv/ad_hot_02.gif | 4123 |
| 24 | http://home.netscape.com/ | 4017 |
| 25 | http://news.joongang.co.kr/icon/listicon.gif | 3990 |
| 26 | http://ads.web.aol.com/content/B0/0/qW9O30WF_IT69xZimje5h | 3954 |
| 27 | http://www.chosun.com/images/camera.gif | 3621 |
| 28 | http://www.chosun.com/w20_images/line4.gif | 3613 |
| 29 | http://ps.sbswebvision.com/channel/sbs3.gif | 3597 |
| 30 | http://simmany.hnc.net/ | 3580 |
| 31 | http://www.chosun.com/w20_images/gohome.gif | 3481 |
| 32 | http://www.chosun.com/w20_images/secmenu.gif | 3446 |
| 33 | http://news.joongang.co.kr/online_news/icon/icon_new_top.gif | 3405 |
| 34 | http://news.joongang.co.kr/online_news/icon/icon_new_l.gif | 3390 |
| 35 | http://news.joongang.co.kr/online_news/icon/icon_old_l.gif | 3381 |
| 36 | http://www.chosun.com/ad_sponcer/sec_adinfo.gif | 3241 |
| 37 | http://simmany.hnc.net/picts/help.gif | 3110 |
| 38 | http://www.nownuri.net/channel/bbs/img/bar_r.gif | 3107 |
| 39 | http://www.nownuri.net/channel/bbs/img/titlecircle.gif | 3021 |
| 40 | http://news.joongang.co.kr/online_news/icon/pol/icon_cyberpol.gif | 2898 |
| 41 | http://www.chosun.com/w21_images/etcmenu2.gif | 2895 |
| 42 | http://www.joongang.co.kr/cdf/img/folder.ico | 2887 |
| 43 | http://home.netscape.com/images/banners/netscape_c0.gif | 2698 |
| 44 | http://home.netscape.com/images/footer_new.gif | 2664 |
| 45 | http://news.joongang.co.kr/adv/ad_hot_01.gif | 2628 |
| 46 | http://news.joongang.co.kr/online_news/image/title_hot.gif | 2608 |
| 47 | http://www.nownuri.net/channel/bbs/gamebb.asp | 2587 |
| 48 | http://home.netscape.com/imagehs/netcent.gif | 2500 |
| 49 | http://www.nownuri.net/channel/bbs/leports.asp | 2484 |
| 50 | http://www.chosun.com/feature/copyright.gif | 2386 |

**Fig. 4.** Top 50 URLs.

**Table 2.** Distribution of URL types.

| Data type | Total count | Total Mbytes |
|---|---|---|
| Image | 2627982 (75.2%) | 14134.1 (48.4%) |
| HTML | 475182 (13.6%) | 2404.4 (8.3%) |
| Application | 24925 (0.7%) | 1942.2 (6.6%) |
| Multimedia | 8700 (0.3%) | 3290.2 (11.3%) |
| Others | 357659 (10.2%) | 7433.3 (25.4%) |

In Fig. 7, we illustrate the cumulative frequency of references versus the fraction of the total Web servers referenced. Note that the Web servers shown in the $x$-axis are sorted into decreasing order based on the reference counts. The figure shows that 10% of the Web servers are responsible for 80% of all references and 30% of servers for 90% of all references. This again shows the evidence for human preferences for some popular Web sites.

Fig. 6 shows the top 100 sites. We visited these sites and classified into nine groups based on the contents provided by the sites: *news, portal, ISP, business, organization, entertainment, Web hosting, program,* and *others*. Each group is defined as follows.

- *news*: daily news sites, newspaper homepages, and homepages of broadcasting company,
- *portal*: portal sites and search engine sites,
- *ISP*: Internet Service Providers and online service sites,
- *business*: servers of companies, e-businesses, and advertisements,
- *organization*: nonprofit corporation and universities,
- *entertainment*: sites for entertainment such as sports, game, and adult,
- *Web hosting*: Web hosting sites,
- *program*: homepages for computer program and program download sites, and
- *others*: unknown or vanished sites.

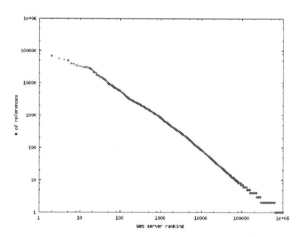

**Fig. 5.** Number of references to Web servers versus server ranking.

| Ranking | Site (group) | Reference count | Ranking | Site (group) | Reference count |
|---|---|---|---|---|---|
| 1 | news.joongang.co.kr (news) | 191510 | 51 | www.kbs.co.kr (news) | 9540 |
| 2 | www.chosun.com (news) | 106693 | 52 | soback.kornet.nm.kr (ISP) | 8921 |
| 3 | www.nownuri.net (ISP) | 67990 | 53 | www.altavista.digital.com (portal) | 8553 |
| 4 | www.joongang.co.kr (news) | 55909 | 54 | www.samsung.com (business) | 8495 |
| 5 | www.dongailbo.co.kr (news) | 52366 | 55 | search.hnc.net (portal) | 8459 |
| 6 | home.netscape.com (program) | 49600 | 56 | lion.netcenter.co.kr (others) | 8419 |
| 7 | 203.255.99.1 (others) | 39562 | 57 | www.hanmail.net (portal) | 8166 |
| 8 | www.munhwa.co.kr (news) | 38674 | 58 | www.jring.inter.net (others) | 7765 |
| 9 | www.mbc.co.kr (news) | 35018 | 59 | www.yahoo.com (portal) | 7758 |
| 10 | www.hani.co.kr (news) | 33564 | 60 | www.m2000.co.kr (news) | 7605 |
| 11 | www.samsung.co.kr (business) | 32315 | 61 | home.microsoft.com (program) | 7268 |
| 12 | www.chollian.net (ISP) | 32069 | 62 | 203.249.157.50 (others) | 7089 |
| 13 | simmany.hnc.net (portal) | 30841 | 63 | bora.dacom.co.kr (ISP) | 7039 |
| 14 | www.seoul.co.kr (news) | 30594 | 64 | solarsnet.snu.ac.kr (organ) | 7033 |
| 15 | www.microsoft.com (program) | 30162 | 65 | plaza1.snu.ac.kr (organ) | 7029 |
| 16 | www.bekkoame.or.jp (portal) | 29864 | 66 | 210.124.99.3 (others) | 6827 |
| 17 | www.snu.ac.kr (organ) | 29355 | 67 | www.cityscape.co.kr (portal) | 6736 |
| 18 | www1.hitel.net (ISP) | 28683 | 68 | www.adexpo.co.kr (company) | 6685 |
| 19 | www.cherry.inter.net (others) | 27732 | 69 | news.hani.co.kr (news) | 6344 |
| 20 | iie.joongang.co.kr (news) | 26746 | 70 | artmedia.cyso.net (others) | 6222 |
| 21 | channel.etnews.co.kr (news) | 24171 | 71 | www.kpi.or.kr (organ) | 6205 |
| 22 | www.geocities.com (Web host) | 23179 | 72 | goldbank.co.kr (entertain) | 6192 |
| 23 | www2.dongailbo.co.kr (news) | 21311 | 73 | www.chosun.co.kr (news) | 6063 |
| 24 | www.shinbiro.com (Web host) | 20885 | 74 | www.elim.net (ISP) | 6015 |
| 25 | ps.sbswebvision.com (news) | 20315 | 75 | www.intel.com (business) | 5965 |
| 26 | www.khan.co.kr (news) | 19926 | 76 | www.eduland.com (business) | 5958 |
| 27 | www.web114.co.kr (entertain) | 17502 | 77 | rose0.kyungpook.ac.kr (organ) | 5882 |
| 28 | puzzle.nownuri.net (ISP) | 17294 | 78 | www.hei.co.kr (business) | 5881 |
| 29 | ad.doubleclick.net (business) | 16596 | 79 | edunet.nmc.nm.kr (business) | 5875 |
| 30 | www.netsgo.com (ISP) | 16057 | 80 | www.nba.com (entertain) | 5827 |
| 31 | gic.kyungpook.ac.kr (organ) | 15457 | 81 | www.lg.co.kr (business) | 5796 |
| 32 | www.etnews.co.kr (news) | 15201 | 82 | blue.nowcom.co.kr (ISP) | 5545 |
| 33 | www.kyungpook.ac.kr (organ) | 15161 | 83 | 203.252.3.14 (others) | 5493 |
| 34 | www.kntl.co.kr (business) | 14974 | 84 | altavista.digital.com (portal) | 5427 |
| 35 | www.korealink.co.kr (news) | 14598 | 85 | us.yimg.com (portal) | 5349 |
| 36 | www.ladyasia.com (entertain) | 14513 | 86 | www.pusan.ac.kr (organ) | 5335 |
| 37 | biz.nownuri.net (ISP) | 13518 | 87 | www.maeilbiznews.co.kr (news) | 5295 |
| 38 | www.sbs.co.kr (news) | 13309 | 88 | www.infoseek.com (portal) | 5216 |
| 39 | www.iworld.net (Web host) | 13239 | 89 | www.donga.com (news) | 5187 |
| 40 | www.interpia.net (entertain) | 12983 | 90 | www.kepri.re.kr (organ) | 5162 |
| 41 | members.iworld.net (Web host) | 12832 | 91 | www.kornet.nm.kr (ISP) | 5062 |
| 42 | channel.cnn.com (news) | 12641 | 92 | images.yahoo.com (portal) | 4932 |
| 43 | www.msnbc.com (news) | 12114 | 93 | 207.221.59.58 (others) | 4894 |
| 44 | www.goldbank.co.kr (entertain) | 11783 | 94 | members.aol.com (Web host) | 4889 |
| 45 | 209.1.112.251 (others) | 11271 | 95 | www.real.com (program) | 4706 |
| 46 | www.dynamix.net (entertain) | 10876 | 96 | news21.hani.co.kr (news) | 4663 |
| 47 | home.taegu.net (organ) | 10539 | 97 | www.myst.inter.net (others) | 4593 |
| 48 | www.unitel.co.kr (ISP) | 10375 | 98 | www.mbcnewsdesk.com (news) | 4553 |
| 49 | uplanet.ik.co.kr (others) | 9933 | 99 | inote.com (others) | 4411 |
| 50 | www.yahoo.co.kr (portal) | 9587 | 100 | klepc17.seri.re.kr (organ) | 2715 |

**Fig. 6.** Top 100 sites.

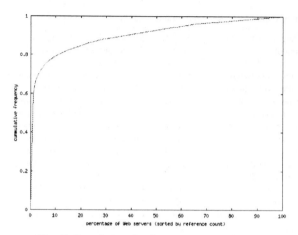

**Fig. 7.** Cumulative distribution of Web servers.

Fig. 8 shows the percentage of references made to each group of sites. The figure shows that *news* sites are responsible for the majority of references (44% of the total references), and all of the other categories are responsible for less than 10% of the total references except for the *ISP* (12.5%). There are six *news* sites out of the top 10 sites, including Joongang (ranking 1), Chosun (ranking 2), and Donga (ranking 5) which are three major newspaper publishing companies in Korea. From this result, we can conclude that *news* is the most frequently referenced information through the Internet by KREN users.

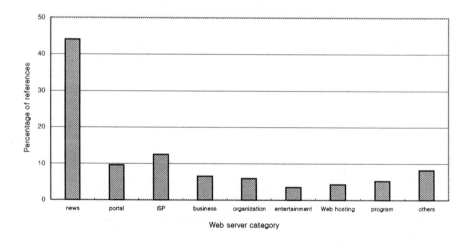

**Fig. 8.** Percentage of references made to each group of sites.

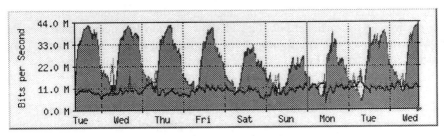

**Fig. 9.** Usage of international links.

## 3.3 Usage of International Links

In this subsection, we analyze the usage of international links of KREN. The purpose of this study is to extract some peculiarities of international references. As explained previously, the international link of KREN is connected with Sprint in the United States (45Mbps). Fig. 9 shows the usage of the link for a week. The curve in the upper position represents the usage of the incoming link (from Sprint to KREN) and the curve in the lower position represents the usage of the outgoing link (from KREN to Sprint). As shown in the figure, the usage of the incoming link is larger than that of the outgoing link. Note that the incoming part of the international link has often been the bottleneck point of KREN and has recently been extended several times to relieve network congestion.

The usage of the incoming link increases and decreases periodically and the cycle is one day. This is due to the human life cycle of the 24-hour pattern. The peak time is during the office hours (12:00-15:00) and the idle time is the midnight or dawn (3:00-6:00).

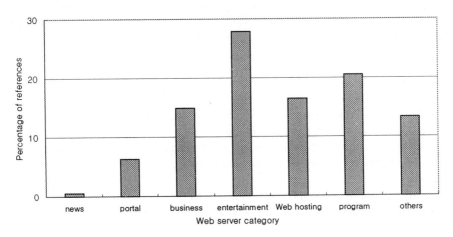

**Fig. 10.** Percentage of international references made to each group of sites.

To see the reference behaviors in the international link, we gathered all the HTTP data passing the international link. Fig. 11 shows the top 100 international sites that are most frequently referenced through the international link by KREN users. (Note that reference counts in Fig. 11 are not consistent with the counts in Fig. 6 because these counts show all references passing the international link while Fig. 6 shows the counts of references made only by the proxy users.)

We classified these sites into categories as done in the previous subsection. Fig. 10 shows the percentage of references made to each group of sites. The figure is obviously different from the case when domestic references are included. *Entertainment* sites are responsible for almost 30% of the total international references. Specifically, *adult* sites occupy 90% of the total *entertainment* sites and 38 out of the top 100 international sites are adult sites. Note that no domestic adult site was found in the top 100 servers in the previous subsection. We think that this is because adult sites in Korea are controlled and regulated by Korean domestic laws. *Program* sites are responsible for more than 20% of the total international references. These sites include the homepages of Microsoft, Netscape, Realplayer, etc. One major reason for this phenomenon is that most Web browsers and PC softwares often set the program to connect their download sites automatically. Note that the rankings of the Microsoft and Netscape in the top 100 international sites are 1 and 6, respectively. Another interesting result is that *news* sites occupy only 0.5% of international references (only one site, CNN exists in the top 100 international sites). This implies that most of the *news* sites visited by KREN users are domestic sites, that are written in Korean.

## 4. Summary

The Internet now becomes one of the most important communication channels for human societies in Korea. In this paper, we presented a comprehensive analysis on Internet reference behaviors in the Korean Education Network, specifically focused on the contents analysis. From this analysis, the following observations are made:

### Distribution of Web documents

- References to Web documents are excessively biased to some hot documents and can be modeled as a Zipf-like distribution.
- The top 10% of popular documents are responsible for 70% of all references.
- 75.2% of Web references are made to small image files such as banners, logos, and icons.
- HTML documents are responsible for 13.6% of the total references.
- Multimedia data are responsible for only 0.3% of the total reference counts, but for 11.3% of the total sizes.

| Ranking | Site (group) | Reference count | Ranking | Site (group) | Reference count |
|---|---|---|---|---|---|
| 1 | www.microsoft.com (program) | 398346 | 51 | www.fortunecity.com (Web host) | 27126 |
| 2 | www.nettaxi.com (others) | 230638 | 52 | stats.hitbox.com (program) | 26891 |
| 3 | www.geocities.com (Web host) | 207917 | 53 | adex3.flycast.com (others) | 26693 |
| 4 | ad.doubleclick.net (business) | 170414 | 54 | www.adultland.com (entertain) | 26455 |
| 5 | members.tripod.com (Web host) | 163407 | 55 | infoseek.go.com (portal) | 26386 |
| 6 | home.netscape.com (program) | 147566 | 56 | snatches.porncity.net (entertain) | 26376 |
| 7 | members.theglobe.com (Web host) | 146835 | 57 | fastcounter.linkexchange.net (program) | 25794 |
| 8 | members.xoom.com (Web host) | 146663 | 58 | images.blizzard.com (entertain) | 25707 |
| 9 | adforce.imgis.com (business) | 121624 | 59 | banners.porncity.net (entertain) | 25537 |
| 10 | us.yimg.com (portal) | 109939 | 60 | www.macromedia.com (program) | 25052 |
| 11 | chat.caltech.net (entertain) | 109589 | 61 | www.cnn.com (news) | 24891 |
| 12 | home.microsoft.com (program) | 98683 | 62 | 207.82.250.251 (others) | 24811 |
| 13 | graphics1.sextracker.com (entertain) | 85426 | 63 | asian.sexhound.net (entertain) | 24481 |
| 14 | lezvill.porncity.net (entertain) | 79212 | 64 | www.18x.com (entertain) | 24314 |
| 15 | 216.49.12.200 (others) | 75571 | 65 | www.minju.com (others) | 24191 |
| 16 | www.dynamix.net (entertain) | 63574 | 66 | www.amazon.com (business) | 23846 |
| 17 | www.altavista.com (portal) | 61026 | 67 | www.playboy.com (entertain) | 23797 |
| 18 | imageserv1.imgis.com (business) | 58382 | 68 | w11.hitbox.com (program) | 23296 |
| 19 | 209.185.130.251 (others) | 54132 | 69 | www.clublove.com (entertain) | 22896 |
| 20 | www.neoqst.com (business) | 51893 | 70 | www.purejapan.com (entertain) | 22647 |
| 21 | lovers-lane.porncity.net (entertain) | 50478 | 71 | leader.linkexchange.com (program) | 22020 |
| 22 | www.remarq.com (business) | 48470 | 72 | 209.90.128.55 (others) | 21893 |
| 23 | www.real.com (program) | 45766 | 73 | www.angelfire.com (portal) | 21336 |
| 24 | www.asiannudes.com (entertain) | 44227 | 74 | www.exit69.com (entertain) | 21040 |
| 25 | counter14.sextracker.com (entertain) | 44096 | 75 | w22.hitbox.com (program) | 20955 |
| 26 | www.c4cash.com (business) | 43435 | 76 | www.yahoo.com (portal) | 20911 |
| 27 | home.kr.netscape.com (program) | 43118 | 77 | members.teensteam.com (entertain) | 20871 |
| 28 | pic.geocities.com (Web host) | 42617 | 78 | d1.ex.remarq.com (business) | 20783 |
| 29 | www.korean-babes.com (entertain) | 41928 | 79 | media.xoom.com (entertain) | 20609 |
| 30 | artemis.porntrack.com (entertain) | 40083 | 80 | pimp-hill.porncity.net (entertain) | 20550 |
| 31 | freehosting.at.webjump.com(Web host) | 29763 | 81 | aphrodite.porntrack.com (entertain) | 20174 |
| 32 | grph.theglobe.com (others) | 39828 | 82 | m.doubleclick.net (business) | 20148 |
| 33 | www.datais.com (business) | 39618 | 83 | home.fiberia.com (Web host) | 19891 |
| 34 | kor.kuki.co.jp (entertain) | 39305 | 84 | www.asiansexygirl.com (entertain) | 19761 |
| 35 | busty-hills.porncity.net (entertain) | 39123 | 85 | www.smutland.com (entertain) | 19745 |
| 36 | www.pornographysex.com (entertain) | 36106 | 86 | www1.cafeflesh.com (entertain) | 19480 |
| 37 | web100.co.kr (entertain) | 34771 | 87 | www.sexteens.com (entertain) | 18989 |
| 38 | channels.real.com (program) | 34646 | 88 | www.king50.com (entertain) | 18931 |
| 39 | www.kgirls.org (entertain) | 33785 | 89 | www.bubblegumtv.com (entertain) | 18402 |
| 40 | www.jgirls.com (entertain) | 33491 | 90 | nt17.nettaxi.com (others) | 18376 |
| 41 | www.scscwarez.com (others) | 32613 | 91 | my.netscape.com (program) | 18294 |
| 42 | images.real.com (program) | 31326 | 92 | image.linkexchange.com (business) | 18284 |
| 43 | www.uh-oh.com (others) | 30692 | 93 | www.pridesites.com (entertain) | 17762 |
| 44 | www.saram.net (portal | 30512 | 94 | www.jade.dti.ne.jp (business) | 17678 |
| 45 | image.click2net.com (business) | 29011 | 95 | www.intel.com (business) | 17534 |
| 46 | www.teleway.ne.jp (others) | 28804 | 96 | windowsupdate.microsoft.com (program) | 15219 |
| 47 | creampuff-park.porncity.net (entertain) | 25967 | 97 | adult.sexhound.net (entertain) | 17201 |
| 48 | me.doubleclick.net (business) | 28188 | 98 | kor.kukinet.or.jp (entertain) | 17169 |
| 49 | 209.1.112.251 (others) | 27709 | 99 | www.unfaithful.com (entertain) | 17131 |
| 50 | www.bekkoame.ne.jp (portal) | 27151 | 100 | www.privategold.com (entertain) | 16678 |

**Fig. 11.** Top 100 international sites.

## Distribution of Web servers

* References to Web servers are excessively biased to some hot sites and can be modeled as a Zipf-like distribution.
* The top 10% of popular sites account for 80% of all references.
* News sites are responsible for the majority of references (44% of total references in the top 100 sites).

## Usage of International Links

* The traffic of international link changes periodically according to the human life cycle.
* International references are obviously different from domestic references.
* Adult sites account for the majority of references (about 30% of total references in the top 100 international sites).
* Program sites are responsible for 20% of total references due to the default setting of program homepages (e.g., Netscape Navigator and Internet Explorer).

We believe that the characterization and analysis study presented in this paper can be helpful to government policy makers and e-business people, as well as researchers related to the Internet technologies. For example, e-advertisers may be interested in the popularity of Web sites and researchers may be interested in the distribution of the Internet references. Our future research includes the Web caching technologies for efficient services of Internet contents by exploiting the results of this study.

# References

1. M. F. Arlitt and C. L. Williamson: Web Server Workload Characterization: The Search for Invariants. Proceedings of the ACM SIGMETRICS '96 Conference, Philadelphia, PA (1996)
2. M. F. Arlitt and C. L. Williamson: Internet Web Servers: Workload Characterization and Performance Implications. IEEE/ACM Transactions on Networking, Vol. 5, No. 5 (1997) 631-645
3. V. Almeida, A. Bestavros, M. Crovella, and A. Oliveira: Characterizing Reference Locality in the WWW. Proceedings of the IEEE Conference on Parallel and Distributed Information Systems, Miami Beach, FL (1996)
4. M. Arlitt and T. Jin: A Workload Characterization Study of the 1998 World Cup Web Site. IEEE Network (2000)
5. D. A. Menasce, V. Almeida, R. Fonseca, and M.A. Mendes: A Methodology for Workload Characterization of E-commerce Sites. Proceedings of the ACM Conference on Electronic Commerce, Denver, CO (1999)

6. S. Nagarajan and S. V. Raghavan: Intelligent Prefetch in WWW Using Client Behavior Characterization. Proceedings of the International Symposium on Modeling, Analysis and Simulation of Computer and Telecommunication Systems (MASCOTS'00), San Francisco, CA (2000)

7. L. Breslau, P. Cao, L. Fan, G. Phillips, and S. Shenker: Web Caching and Zipf-like Distributions: Evidence and Implications. Proceedings of IEEE Infocom '99, New York, NY (1999) 126-134

8. S. Jin and A. Bestavros: Characterizing Two Sources of Temporal Locality in Web Request Streams. Proceedings of the IEEE International Symposium on Modeling, Analysis and Simulation of Computer and Telecommunication Systems (MASCOTS'00), San Francisco, CA (2000)

9. M. Arlitt, R. Friedrich, and T. Jin: Workload Characterization of a Web Proxy in a Cable Modem Environment. ACM Performance Evaluation Review, Vol. 27, No. 2 (1999) 25-36

10. J. E. Pitkow: Summary of WWW Characterizations. Proceedings of the Seventh International World Wide Web Conference, Brisbane, Australia (1998)

11. Korean Education Network (KREN), http://www.kren.ne.kr.

12. G. K. Zipf: Human Behavior and the Principle of Least Effort: An Introduction to Human Ecology, Addison Wesley Press (1949)

# Load Balancing Studies on an H.323 Gatekeeper Prototype

Cheng-Yue Chang and Ming-Syan Chen *

Department of Electrical Engineering
National Taiwan University
Taipei, Taiwan, ROC
E-mail: mschen@cc.ee.ntu.edu.tw

**Abstract.** Internet telephony or VoIP, in recent years, has been deemed a very important application on the Internet. A significant number of architectures are proposed to provide telephony services over packet-based networks. Among others, ITU-T Rec. H.323 is the primary standard for the Internet telephony. While the H.323 is continuously revised, there are, however, still many important issues needed to be further discussed. Among others, the call routing method among gatekeepers has not yet been well designed in the H.323, and the primitive method in the current version may cause the loads of the gatekeepers unbalanced. To resolve this problem, we devise in this paper an enhanced call routing method to deal with the load balancing problem among the gatekeepers. This method for load balancing is based on "Multiple-Registration with Multicasted LRQ". The simulation results show that the *Call Blocking Rate* and *Channel Utilization* are significantly improved by the proposed load-balancing method.

## 1    Introduction

Internet telephony or VoIP, in recent years, has been deemed a very important application on the Internet [7][18]. A significant number of architectures are proposed to provide telephony services over packet-based networks, such as [2][8][16][20]. The main reason for the increasing popularity of Internet telephony is that it has the potential to significantly reduce the cost of long distance voice communication [5]. To provide the interoperability between various telephony products and services from multiple vendors, ITU-T first started the standardization process in 1996 and resulted in ITU-T Rec. H.323 [14][17]. The H.323 specifies the technical requirements for audio, video, and data communications across IP-based networks. In essence, H.323 is an umbrella recommendation, and includes the system components (i.e., terminals, gateways, gatekeepers and multipoint control units), audio/video codecs [4][9][12][13], call signaling/control protocols [11][15], and network interface [10]. Currently, the H.323 has become the primary standard for the Internet telephony.

---

* The corresponding author of this paper.

While the H.323 is continuously revised, there are, however, still many important issues needed to be further discussed [19]. Among others, the call routing method among gatekeepers has not yet been addressed in the H.323. The primitive method of the current version in the H.323 is by sending the LRQ (Location Request) message to a specific *Gatekeeper's RAS Channel TSAP Identifier*, or by multicasting the GRQ message to the gatekeeper's well-known discovery multicast address. The gatekeeper with which the requested endpoint is registered shall respond with the Location Confirmation (LCF) message containing the contact information of the endpoint or the endpoint's gatekeeper. Such a routing method suffers from some drawbacks. The most important drawback is that it may cause the loads of the gatekeepers unbalanced, and, thus, significantly affect the system performance in terms of *Call Blocking Rate* and *Channel Utilization*. To eliminate this problem, we have designed an enhanced call routing method in this paper and incorporated it into the gatekeeper prototype in [6]. The enhanced call routing method for load balancing is based on "Multiple-Registration with Multicasted LRQ". We will describe the design principles later. In addition, to evaluate the performance improvements by our load-balancing method, we designed an event-driven simulator and conducted some experiments on it. We focus on two performance metrics, *Call Blocking Rate* and *Channel Utilization*, which are both sensitive to the condition of load distribution. The experimental results show that the *Call Blocking Rate* and *Channel Utilization* can be significantly improved by the proposed load-balancing method. It is also observed from our empirical results that the *Call Blocking Rate* is more sensitive to the traffic load whereas the *Channel Utilization* is more sensitive to the duration of a call. The fast growing of IP-based applications justifies the timeliness and importance of this study.

The rest of this paper is organized as follows. The preliminaries are introduced in Section 2. In Section 3, we explain the design principles of the improved call routing mechanism to deal with the load balancing problem among gatekeepers. The performance of the improved gatekeeper prototype is evaluated and analyzed in Section 4. We conclude this paper with Section 5.

## 2 Preliminaries

To facilitate our later discussions on the enhanced call routing mechanism, we describe the RAS (Registration, Admission and Status) and call routing functions of an H.323 gatekeeper in Section 2.1 and Section 2.2 respectively. The details of other mandatory functions can be found in [14].

### 2.1 RAS (Registration, Admission and Status)

RAS messages are used in the H.323 to exchange information between H.323 gatekeepers and other endpoints (i.e., terminals, gateways and multipoint control units). An H.323 gatekeeper utilizes RAS messages to provide mandatory functions, such as endpoint registration and call admission. First, the H.323 gatekeeper provides services for the endpoints which have registered at it. Explicitly, an endpoint has to register at a gatekeeper before it is able to take advantages of the services provided. To determine which gatekeeper to register with, an endpoint should run gatekeeper discovery process first. After the gatekeeper discovery process, the endpoint knows which gatekeeper to be associated with, and then sends RRQ (Registration Request) to that gatekeeper. The gatekeeper shall wait for incoming RAS messages by listening to a well-known transport address. Upon receiving the RRQ from the endpoints, the gatekeeper shall authorize the registration based on some authorization rules. For example, the gatekeeper may limit the vendors or manufacturers of the endpoints to the trusted ones.

In addition, the H.323 endpoints shall get the admission from the registered gatekeeper before they initiate or answer the calls. The admission procedure is critical for the gatekeeper to manage the resources (including the network bandwidth, CPU time, memory and etc.) owned by it. Thus, the gatekeeper administrator shall customized the admission mechanism to facilitate the management of the resources owned by the gatekeeper. For example, administrators can make the H.323 gatekeeper to work with other mechanisms (such as bandwidth management or call management module). Note that the H.323 allows three kinds of addressing methods for the calling party to initiate a call. They are the E.164 [3] address, the H.323 ID and the transport address. To establish a call with E.164 addresses or H.323 IDs, the H.323 gatekeeper shall additionally provide the address translation of these alias addresses to the transport addresses when performing call admission. If the address translation fails, the gatekeeper shall response the endpoint with ARJ (Admission Reject).

## 2.2 H.323 Call Routing

In the H.323, a call can be established directly between the endpoints or routed via the H.323 gatekeepers. In the latter case, the H.323 gatekeeper shall provide the routing service for the endpoints as depicted in Figure 1. However, the endpoints may or may not have registered at the gatekeepers. In addition, it is possible that the calling and called parties either register at the same gatekeeper or register at different gatekeepers. Thus, there are several call routing scenarios defined in the H.323.

Nevertheless, the call routing method among gatekeepers has not yet been well designed in the H.323. The primitive method of the current version in the H.323 is by sending the LRQ (Location Request) message to a specific *Gatekeeper's RAS Channel TSAP Identifier*, or by multicasting the GRQ message to the gatekeeper's well-known discovery multicast address. The gatekeeper with which the requested endpoint is registered shall respond with the Location Confirmation (LCF) message containing the contact information of the endpoint or the endpoint's gatekeeper. Such a routing method suffers from some drawbacks. Most importantly, it may cause the loads of the gatekeepers unbalanced, and thus, significantly degrade the performance in terms of *Call Blocking Rate* and *Channel Utilization*. To eliminate this problem, we have designed an enhanced

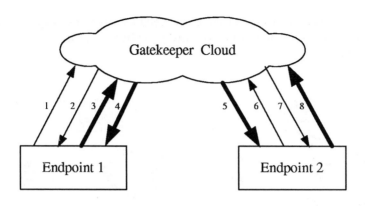

**Fig. 1.** gatekeeper routed call signaling

call routing method and incorporated it into the gatekeeper prototype devised in our prior work [6] where more details can be found for interested readers.

## 3  Improved H.323 Call Routing Methods

As pointed out, the primitive method of call routing in the current version of the H.323 may cause the loads of the gatekeeper unbalanced. To resolve this, we extended our gatekeeper to deal with the load balancing problem among gatekeepers by adding a improved call routing mechanism into the gatekeeper prototype. This method for load balancing is based on "Multiple-Registration with Multicasted LRQ".

Conventionally, each terminal always registers to "one" gatekeeper after the gatekeeper discovery process in the H.323. In our method, we design our terminal program to allow it to register to more than one gatekeeper. When a terminal start to initiate a call, it has to launch the "Admission" process in the beginning to request for the admission to set up a call. In the stage of "Admission", a calling terminal sends "ARQ" messages to all the registered gatekeepers. The calling gatekeepers will then check the destination information (i.e., information for the called endpoint), including endpoint addresses or alias names received from the terminal. First, the gatekeepers will search the destination information in their local database. If the destination terminal has registered at these gatekeeper, it will know the exact transport address of the destination terminal and proceed finishing the remaining call setup procedure. If the called endpoint did not register at these gatekeepers, the gatekeepers will issue "LRQ" messages on the specific multicast address and look for help from other gatekeepers which know the information of the called endpoints. This process is illustrated in Figure 2(a). Terminal 1 has registered to GK11 and GK12, and wants to make a call to terminal 2. It first sends "ARQ" messages to GK11 and GK2 for call admission and address translation. Then, GK11 and GK2 notice that Terminal

2 does not register to them, and multicast LRQ to other gatekeeprs for address translation (e.g., GK11 multicasts the LRQ to GK12, ..., GK1n, GK21, GK22, ...and GK2n).

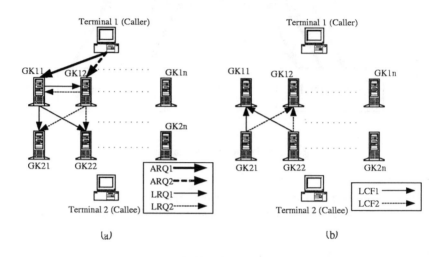

**Fig. 2.** (a) the process of admission request and location request; (b) the process of location confirm.

In order to achieve the goal of load balancing, if the called endpoint does not register to the same gatekeepers as the calling endpoint, our gatekeepers will send "LRQ" messages to other gatekeepers no matter what kind of address the calling endpoint provides. Explicitly, even the calling endpoint calls the destination endpoint by transport address, we still send "LRQ" messages to other gatekeepers. In this case, the gatekeeper will stuff specific information in the "cmRASParamNonStandard" parameter which is reserved by H.323 protocol stack for the use of protocol extension [1]. When a gatekeeper receives "LRQ" messages, it will check this parameter first. If the "cmRASParamNonStandard" parameter is stuffed by this specific information, our gatekeeper will know that this "LRQ" message is used not only for address translation but also for load condition request. If the called endpoint is registered to our gatekeeper, it will then stuff its load data into the "cmRASParamNonStandard" parameter and return with an "LCF" message. The process is illustrated in Figure 2(b). Following the example in Figure 2(a), after receiving the "LRQ" messages, GK21 and GK22 notice that Terminal 2 has registered to them. Thus, GK21 and GK22 return "LCF" messages with load information stuffed to GK11 and GK12.

Note that because each terminal registers to more than one gatekeeper in the stage of "Registration", more than one gatekeeper will respond the "LRQ" messages. During this period, we stuff the load information of each gatekeeper in the returning "LCF" messages if they confirm the location request messages.

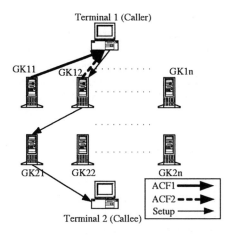

**Fig. 3.** the process of admission confirm and call setup.

When the gatekeeper which issued the "LRQ" message receives the returning "LCF" messages, it will know which gatekeepers the destination endpoint has registered and the load information of each of them. Then the calling gatekeepers decide which gatekeeper to use for routing the call according to the load information and reply to the "ARQ" messages with "ACF" messages if there is any gatekeeper which can provide the call routing services. Note that we also stuff the load information of the calling gatekeepers in the returning "ACF" messages. After the calling endpoint receives the returning "ACF" messages, it decides which gatekeeper to use, and starts the call setup procedure. This process is illustrated in Figure 3. Following the above example, GK11 and GK2 have received "LCF" messages from GK21 and GK22. Assume that the load of GK21 is lighter than GK22, so GK11 and GK12 select GK21 as the called gatekeeper to route this call, and return "ACF" messages to Terminal 1. Again, assume that the load of GK12 is lighter than GK11, so Terminal 1 selects GK12 as the calling gatekeeper to setup this call. Thus, the call setup path goes from Terminal 1 through GK12, GK21 to Terminal 2.

   With the help of the load-balancing method described in this section, we can obtain better performance than the circumstance without using them. First, the multiple-registration technique allows a terminal of registering to more than one gatekeeper for future processing. The potential benefit of this feature is that a terminal will be served by the gatekeeper with the lightest load and thus gain better quality of service. The extra cost for this technique is only on slightly increased storage capacity for more registration entries. The extra cost is deemed negligible in view of the huge capacity of current hard drives. Second, we stuff load data of each gatekeeper in the "ACF" and "LCF" messages, and this allows the calling endpoint of choosing a calling gatekeeper with the lightest load to set up a call and allows the calling gatekeeper of choosing a called gatekeeper with the lightest load to route the call. Clearly, this feature is able to achieve load-balancing among gatekeepers and accommodate more users to initiate video-conferences (will be shown in the Section 4). Note that the extra data in an "ACF" and "LCF" message takes only 4 bytes, resulting in very small overhead. In addition, we use the non-standard parameter reserved by H.323 protocol stack, meaning that no incompatibility is incurred to achieve the goal of load balancing.

## 4 Performance Analysis

In this section, we experimentally compare the performance of an H.323 gate-keeper under the circumstances with and without the proposed load-balancing method. We will introduce the system simulation model in Section 4.1. The experimental results will be discussed and analyzed in Section 4.2.

### 4.1 System Simulation Model

In order to evaluate the performance of the proposed load-balancing methods described in Section 3, we design a system simulation model as depicted in Figure 4. This model is designed to reflect the load-balancing problem among gatekeepers. Without loss of generality, we assume that the number of available gatekeepers in the calling and called party side are both $m$. That is, there are total $2m$ gatekeepers in our model. Without load-balancing methods, the calling party randomly selects a certain GK in the calling party side to set up the Internet telephony call, and the selected GK then also randomly selects a certain GK in the called party side to route this call. With the help of our load balancing methods, the gatekeeper with the lightest load is always selected in the calling and called party side to initiate and route the call.

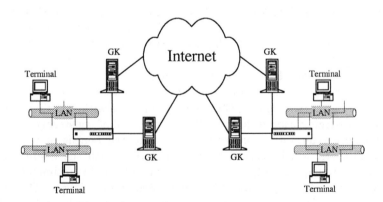

**Fig. 4.** System simulation model

**Table 1.** Parameters of the system model

| System Parameters | Value (default) |
|---|---|
| Total number of call setup attempts | 10000 |
| Number of GKs ($2m$) | 2 in each side |
| Number of channels each GK admits ($c$) | 10 |
| Interarrival time of call setup attempts ($t$) | Exp. ($\mu = 5$ sec.) |
| Duration of each call ($d$) | 100 sec. |

In addition, we assume that each gatekeeper can admit at most $c$ full-duplex channels, i.e., allows at most $c$ Internet telephony calls to be established simultaneously. The interarrival time of two consecutive call setup attempts follows the exponential distribution with the mean value of $t$. The mean duration of each call is assumed to be $d$. Table 1 provides a summary of the parameters and default values used in the system simulation model.

## 4.2 Experimental Results

Based on the system simulation model designed, we implement a simulator using Microsoft Visual C++ package. We focus on two performance metrics, *Call Blocking Rate* and *Channel Utilization*, which are both sensitive to the condition of load distribution. The main objective of our simulations is to show the impact of our load-balancing methods on the *Call Blocking Rate* with the aim to minimize it, and also the impact on *Channel Utilization* with the aim to maximize it. Each value is the result of 10,000 inputs of call setup attempts.

In the first set of experiments, we compare the *Call Blocking Rates* under the circumstances with and without load-balancing methods. First, we fix the mean duration of each call to 100 seconds, and examine the *Call Blocking Rates* when the value of the mean interarrival time of two consecutive call setup attempts increases. The *Call Blocking Rate* in the experiments is calculated as

$$Call\ Blocking\ Rate = \frac{Number\ of\ call\ setup\ rejects}{Number\ of\ call\ setup\ attempts}.$$

Figure 5(a) shows the *Call Blocking Rate* as the value of the mean interarrival time of two consecutive call setup attempts varies. We observe that the *Call Blocking Rate* under the circumstance with load-balancing methods is in general smaller for different values of the mean interarrival time of two consecutive call setup attempts. The reason is that without load-balancing methods, the probability of which the overall load will be rivetted on some gatekeepers raises as the overall traffic increases. It will, in turn, increase the *Call Blocking Rate*. However, with our load-balancing methods, the overall load will be equally distributed to each gatekeeper while the overall traffic increases. Thus, the *Call Blocking Rate* can be decreased. Note that as the traffic load increases to some level, the *Call Blocking Rates* are high in both cases.

Next, we fix the mean interarrival time of two consecutive call setup attempts to 5 seconds, and increase the mean duration of each call to examine the variation of the *Call Blocking Rate*. Figure 5(b) shows the *Call Blocking Rate* against the mean duration of each call. We can find that the *Call Blocking Rate* is minimized with proposed load-balancing methods when the mean duration of each call increases. This is also due to the fact that the overall load is fairly distributed to all gatekeepers. Note that the increasing slopes of the unbalanced and balanced load are similar to each other. It is because the *Call Blocking Rate* is more sensitive to the traffic load (as shown in Figure 5(a)) rather than to the mean duration of each call (as shown in Figure 5(b)).

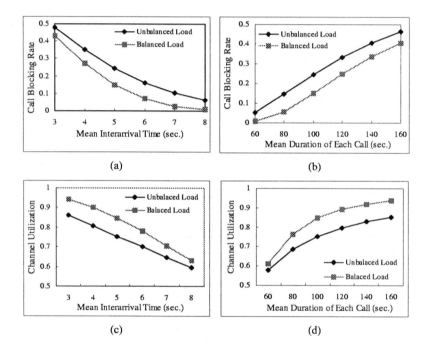

**Fig. 5.** call blocking rates against (a) mean interarrival time and (b) mean duration of each call; channel utilizations against (c) mean interarrival time and (d) mean duration of each call.

In the second set of experiments, we evaluate the effect on the *Channel Utilization* under the circumstances with load-balancing methods. Similar to the first set of experiments, we first fix the mean duration of each call to 100 seconds, and examine the *Channel Utilization* when the value of the mean interarrival time of two consecutive call setup attempts increases. The *Channel Utilization* in the experiments is calculated as

$$ChannelUtilization = \frac{Mean\ number\ of\ channels\ occupied}{Total\ number\ of\ available\ channels}.$$

Figure 5(c) shows the *Channel Utilization* against the mean interarrival time of two consecutive call setup attempts. It can be seen that *Channel Utilization* performs better with our load-balancing methods especially when the traffic load is high (i.e., the mean interarrival time of two consecutive call setup attempts is short). The reason is that the *Call Blocking Rate* is minimized by our load-balancing methods, so the *Channel Utilization* is, in turn, increased.

Then, we fix the mean interarrival time of two consecutive call setup attempts to 5 seconds, and increase the mean duration of each call to examine the variation of the *Channel Utilization*. Figure 5(d) shows the *Channel Utilization* against the mean duration of each call. The result also reveals that the *Channel Utilization* performs better under the effect of our load-balancing methods on minimizing the *Call Blocking Rate*. It is noted that the *Channel Utilization* raises more sharply under the circumstance with load-balancing methods when the mean duration of each call increases. The reason is that the *Channel Utilization* is more sensitive to the mean duration of each call than the traffic load.

## 5 Conclusions

In this paper, we designed a new method to deal with the load balancing problem among the gatekeepers. This method is based on "Multiple-Registration with Multicasted LRQ". To evaluate the performance improvement achieved, we conducted some event-driven simulations. The experimental results showed that the *Call Blocking Rate* and *Channel Utilization* can be significantly improved by the proposed load-balancing method. It was also observed from our empirical results that the *Call Blocking Rate* is more sensitive to the traffic load whereas the *Channel Utilization* is more sensitive to the duration of a call.

## 6 Acknowledgment

The authors are supported in part by the National Science Council, Project No. NSC 89-2219-E-002-007 and NSC 89-2213-E-002-032, Taiwan, Republic of China.

## References

1. *User's Manual: Radvision H.323 Protocol Stack: Programmer's Guide.* Radvision Corporation, 1998.
2. N. Anerousis, R. Gopalakrishnan, C. R. Kalmanek, A. E. Kaplan, W. T. Marshall, P. P. Mishra, P. Z. Onufryk, K. K. Ramakrishanan, and C. J. Sreenan. TOPS: An Architecture for Telephony over Packet Networks. *IEEE Journal on Selected Area in Communications, Vol.17(1)*, pages 91–108, January 1999.

3. CCITT/ITU-T. Recommendation E.164: Telephone Network and ISDN Operation, Numbering, Routing and Mobile Service.

4. CCITT/ITU-T. Recommendation G.711: Pulse Code Modulation of Voice Frequencies.

5. C.-Y. Chang and M.-S. Chen. On Building an Internet Gateway for Internet Telephony. In *Proc. of the IEEE International Conference on Multimedia and Expo*, August 2000.

6. C.-Y. Chang, P.-H. Huang, and M.-S. Chen. Design and Implementation of an H.323 Gatekeeper Prototype. In *Proc. of the IEEE International Conference on Multimedia and Expo*, August 2001.

7. M. Hassan, A. Nayandoro, and M. Atiquzzaman. Internet Telephony: Services, Technical Challenges, and Products. *IEEE Communications Magazine, Vol.38(4)*, pages 96–103, April 2000.

8. C. Huitema, J. Cameron, P. Mouchtaris, and D. Smyk. An Architecture for Residential Internet Telephony Service. *IEEE Network, Vol.13*, pages 50–56, May-June 1999.

9. ITU-T. Recommendation G.723: Dual Rate Speech Coder for Multimedia Communications Transmitting at 5.3 and 6.3 Kbps Using Low-delay Code Excited Linear Prediction.

10. ITU-T. Recommendation H.225: Media Stream Packetization and Synchronization on Non-Guaranteed Quality of Service LANs.

11. ITU-T. Recommendation H.245: Control Protocol for Multimedia Conferencing.

12. ITU-T. Recommendation H.261: Video Codec for Audiovisual Services at p x 64 Kbps.

13. ITU-T. Recommendation H.263: Video Coding for Low Bit Rate Communication.

14. ITU-T. Recommendation H.323: Visual Telephone Systems and Equipment for Local Area Networks which Provide a Non-guaranteed Quality of Services.

15. ITU-T. Recommendation Q.931: ISDN User-Network Interface Layer 3 Specification for Basic Call Control.

16. C. R. Kalmanek, W. T. Marshall, P. P. Mishra, D. M. Nartz, and K. K. Ramakrishnan. DOSA: An Architecture for Providing a Robust IP Telephony Service. In *Proc. of INFOCOM 2000.*, 2000.

17. S. Okubo, S. dunstan, G. Morrison, M. Nilsson, H. Radha, D. L. Skran, and G. Thom. ITU Standardization of Audiovisual Communication Systems in ATM and LAN Environment. *IEEE Journal on Selected Area in Communications, Vol.15(6)*, pages 965–982, August 1997.

18. C. A. Polyzois, K. H. Purdy, P. F. Yang, D. Shrader, H. Sinnreich, F. Mard, and H. Schulzrinne. From POTS to PANS - A Commentary on the Evolution to Internet Telephony. *IEEE Network, vol. 3*, May/June 1999.

19. D. Rizzetto and C. Catania. A Voice over IP Service Architecture for Integrated Communications. *IEEE Internet Computing*, May/June:53–62, 1999.

20. H. Schulzrinne and J. Rosenberg. Internet Telephony: Architecture and Protocols - an IETF Perspective. *Computer Networks and ISDN Systems vol.31*, pages 237–255, Feb. 1999.

# Framework for Building
# Mobile Context-Aware Applications

Sei-Ie Jang[1], Joong-Han Kim[2], R.S.Ramakrishna[2]

[1] Formally P&G Lab., [2] P&G Lab. Department of Information and Communication, K-JIST,
1-BunGi, Oryong-Dong Buk-Gu, KwangJu, Korea
{[1]darkblue [2]jini, [2]rsr}@kjist.ac.kr

**Abstract.** Computers are no match to humans in deducing situational information from their environment and in using it in their interactions. The advent of Context-aware applications seems to offer a way out to the computer that is not context-sensitive. Context-aware applications sense context information and modify their behavior accordingly without explicit user intervention, thereby providing human-centric services. Currently available context-aware application development environments are not user friendly, not to speak of the difficulty in sensing context. Many frameworks for context-aware applications have been devised in this regard. Most frameworks help develop context-aware applications, but none of them provides the generic kernel that can be adapted to different kinds of context-aware application in the mobile and Internet computing environments. This paper proposes a general, conceptual framework. It attempts to incorporate all the features of earlier framework architectures in a non-redundant manner. Also, the proposal is being tried on the OASIS(Office Application Service for Intelligent Systems being developed by the authors) system that is based on Jini and Internet technologies. The conceptual framework appears to be an efficient and adequate mechanism for mobile context-aware applications.

## 1  Introduction

Humans interact with other fellow beings and the surrounding environment at a high conversational bandwidth by implicitly drawing on the situational information, or context. That is, they can intuitively deduce and interpret the context of the current situation and react appropriately. For example, a person automatically observes the body language and voice tone of the other conversing party and reacts in the expected way. This is due to many factors : the richness of the shared language, a general comprehension of how the world works and an implicit understanding of everyday situations.

Computers cannot easily take advantage of such information in a transparent way. Situational information will have to be provided in an explicit and unambiguous manner. That is a challenge for investigators in human computer interaction studies. Current user interfaces can seldom provide services and information according to location and activity. There are many ways for using context information to make computer systems and applications more user-friendly, flexible, and adaptable. The use of context information is especially important in a mobile and context-aware computing environment, where the environment of interaction, execution, and usage change rapidly and unexpectedly. Context includes information that is part of an application's operating environment. It can be sensed by the application. This typically includes the location, identity, activity and state of people, groups and objects. Context-aware applications sense context information and modify their behavior accordingly without explicit user intervention[1].

Easy availability of commercial, off-the-shelf sensing technologies is making it feasible to sense context in a variety of environments. Mobile computing permits enormous (human) mobility. The prevalence of powerful, networked computers allow the distribution of context over multiple applications.

A major problem has been the lack of uniform support for building and executing these types of application. The onerous task of bridging the gap between sensing and interpretation techniques on the one hand and applications on the other is mostly addressed with ad hoc techniques. The lack of generic infrastructure forces developers to rely on custom solutions for handling context. This discourages the development of new applications. The idea is to try to simplify the development of context-aware applications. Of particular interest is the provision of support infrastructure that makes it easier to develop context-aware applications in the mobile Internet environment. Exploiting the facilities provided by Jini, a Java-based dynamic discovery protocol from Sun Microsystems[2] seems quite natural in this context. The efficacy of the approach is being tested on OASIS(Office Application Service for Intelligent System), a context-aware application framework being developed by the authors.

Related work and the attendant problems are discussed below. The current status of computing environments is reported thereafter. A general conceptual framework for context aware application is proposed next. OASIS system overview and implementation follow this proposal. Suggestions for future work conclude the paper.

## 2 Related Work

The advantages and disadvantages of extant systems are gathered here. The discussion will not enter into specifics of any system, though. Systems that permit fairly general usage without major changes will be considered. Many frameworks and applications for context-aware mobile computing have been devised. They have their own particular architectures and their own specific implementations, thereby barring widespread commercial distribution. Fully developed infrastructure for context aware computing (ex. mobile communication, internet) was not on hand a few years ago. However, many new technologies have been created in the recent past. Further, the cost of network infrastructure and mobile and handheld computer devices has nosedived. It is widely believed that Internet is the best killing application. Many systems have tried to make their services available to users at any place and any time through just the web browser. All legacy applications have been ported to web-based applications, and newly created applications are based on the Web. It is felt that the time for context-aware mobile computing has arrived. Some of the earlier context-aware systems were not really mobile and could not be used easily.

## Pervasive Computing

IBM researchers investigate context-aware computing under what they call "pervasive computing[3]". They are building systems with devices (PDAs, mobile phones, office PCs and home entertainment systems) that can access any information and work together in one seamless, integrated manner. Their research target is to provide infrastructure to help manage information quickly, efficiently, and effortlessly. They introduced the concept of a universal information appliance(UIA)[4]. This way it is possible for most physical user interfaces to electronic systems to be tailored to the greatest common denominator of human experience. Human interfaces are dynamically adapted to an individual's needs and context.

The UIA has three main features: (1) A user interface to the digital domain (2) A wireless infrastructure and (3) Communicating middleware connecting the UIA to services and information. New technologies or methods for implementing UIA framework have been developed by IBM. The main components in this regard are : MoDAL(Mobile Document Application Language)[5], UIA Engine, and TSpaces[6].

Mobile devices can communicate with each other using TSpaces regardless of their own protocols. Portability and flexibility of mobile context-aware applications are promoted through an application representation language and communication buffer mechanism.

## Situated Computing

Researchers at the Hewlett Packard Laboratories worked on a framework for context-aware applications in 1997[7]. They called it "an environment for situational computing". The idea was to have a so-called Situated Computing(SitComp) server that had a set of services for interpreting sensor data into useful events. The services are responsible for retrieving information from the sensors and abstracting that information for applications. However, the work was at a conceptual level and it is difficult to apply it in real computing environments. Only one prototype was constructed incorporating the concept, using active tag detectors as a single sensor type.

## Context Toolkit

Georgia Tech's FCE (Future Computing Environment) group proposed an architecture to support context-aware applications and the infrastructure for smart environment based on Context ToolKit[8]. They argued that context handling mechanisms should have features similar to those found in input handling widgets. They also proposed the architecture for building context-aware applications. The main components of the system are: a context widget, an interpreter and a server(aggregator). Using the context toolkit, context can be shared and reused seamlessly and easily. Some strong points of the approach are: lightweight integration, usage simplicity and openness to new contexts. Classroom 2000, a context-aware application for education was developed by them using the context toolkit[9]. Classroom 2000 captures contexts and all communication between students and lecturer and uses them for better education. All the resources about lectures can be accessed with context-aware web applications.

## Context Framework

The MIT media lab has been active in this area[10]. Three models have been described in this regard: task models, user models, system models. Task models are the acts that a person performs to accomplish a task with a system. User models consist of task-relevant background information about the user. System models refer to the capabilities of the computer system-its structure and ability to accomplish an existing task.

## iRoom(Interactive Workspace)

The Interactive Workspaces(iRoom) Project at Stanford[11] explores new possibilities for people to work together in technology-rich spaces with computing and interaction devices on many different scales. Multidevice, multiuser environments based on novel architectures that permit easy creation and addition of new display and input devices, movement of work of different kinds from one computing device to another and interactions among groups have been experimented with. Research areas in the Interactive Room(iRoom) architecture  include : graphics, human-computer interaction(HCI), networking, and context-aware computing.

There are some outstanding features of iRoom project. First, different mobile devices and network protocols have been employed in the experiments. They can, therefore, be used in any real environment without any major changes. Second, a new architectural concept and primary software abstraction, called an event heap, enhance the generality of the approach. Event heap facilitates multiple entities subscription, automatic garbage-collection of events and self-describing features of events. The implementation is based on TSpaces. People in iRoom can access devices and information appliances with web browsers or some desktop applications compliant with the iRoom architecture. They argued that web-based approach for information appliances and event heap based model make a reasonable conceptual model and easy-to-use, robust environment.

There are some related context-aware and mobile systems. Gerd and his colleagues[12] at the University of Oregon built context-aware wearable computers and interactive interfaces for intelligent environments. The HMD of a mobile user with a wearable computer shows the available services related to the current task. A user can detail any service in the current context or environment without having to set any configuration or perform search. They propose a service binding mechanism and web-based interaction in their work.

Couderc and Kermarrec[13] proposed an architecture and a framework for general context-aware computing environments. They introduced the concept of "contextual object(CO)" for context management. Their context-aware framework consists of an Information Server, an Adaptive Layer, and a Notification Layer that uses the contextual object.

The above systems are not, however, sufficiently general in their scope. Their lack of sweeping scope hampers their use in real world applications. In particular, a portable framework that can be employed in real life applications is needed. Prohibitive cost is another problem with some of these systems. Some systems, in addition, demand highly skilled personnel to efficiently use them.
A general, portable framework for mobile context-aware applications is proposed in the next section.

## 3 A Conceptual Framework

### 3.1 The Problems With Earlier Systems

It is well known that it can be very difficult to obtain and process context-aware information. It is desirable that applications that use context information and context-sensors be interoperable, which means that there is a need for a standardized infrastructure for context-information. Several investigators have proposed and prototyped general frameworks to support context-aware applications. Most of the existing applications are prototypes developed in research labs and universities. There do not yet exist many commercially viable solutions. But the computing environment has dynamically been changing into context-aware application. These changes in computing environment for context-aware applications are outlined below.

### 3.2 The Current Status Of Computing Environments

Many technologies for enabling context-aware computing have been around for some time. Moreover, communication infrastructure for mobile and nomadic users has been developed and implemented. They are economically highly viable. The outstanding changes in computing environments related to context-aware computing and support framework are categorized below.

## Internet related Technologies

There is no doubt that the best killing application is the Internet. Since its birth, web and web-based applications have become indispensable in computing environments. Without supports for web-based applications and interfaces, viable systems are unthinkable. Web applications are user-friendly. Moreover, almost all platforms support web-based infrastructure and applications. It is felt that the Internet and its related technologies should be exploited to the maximum due to their portability and user friendliness.

## Mobile Communication and Devices

Mobile technology is one of the major innovations in recent times. Mobile network infrastructure was either non-existent or imperfectly implemented earlier. Things have changed for the better. Many people routinely use mobile phones or wireless network services, because of the availability of the required infrastructure at low cost. Mobile phone related technologies (GSM, CDMA, etc) can be used for long distance communication, and HomeRF, Wireless LAN(IEEE 802.11), Bluetooth, etc., can be used in short distance communication environments. Context-aware computing makes use of mobile technology to support nomadic users without any barriers of place, thereby permitting increased user mobility.

## Information Appliance related Technologies

"Information Appliance" is the current buzzword. It encompasses the rapidly evolving area of computer-related fields. Information appliances take computing off the desktop and into the everyday world. Unlike traditional appliances, information appliances have some outstanding features: network-awareness and intelligence. They can communicate with each other and other devices or users with some level of 'intelligence'. An additional feature is invisibility. Some information appliances are embedded in walls or other devices. They serve the user without being seen. All the devices and machines in a context-aware computing environment provide services in an unconditional manner. The advent of information appliances enables context-aware computing to be exploited in real life.

## 3.3 A New Conceptual Framework For Mobile And Context-Aware Applications

A new conceptual framework for context-aware applications in current mobile and Internet environments is proposed in this section. As was pointed out above, there are many technologies and infrastructures that enable context-aware computing to be exploited in real life. The proposed system can be adapted to any situation under varying conditions without having to modify the framework itself. A system that is implemented around this conceptual framework, it is hoped, becomes a full-fledged context-aware framework for mobile and Internet context-aware environments. The framework has three parts: the context management part, the service management part and the adaptive user interface part **Fig. 1.**

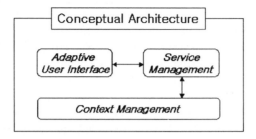

**Fig. 1.** Conceptual architecture for mobile context-aware application

All the three parts cooperate with each other in order to offer the best possible support to users in the development of context-aware applications. The context management part plays a major role in getting sensed data, aggregating it and managing the set of context groups. The service management part selects the appropriate services with context information from context management part, and returns the services to adaptive user interface part. It also manages event solicitation and notification of services related to contexts. The adaptive user interface part provides users with the adaptive and web-based user interface with selected services. Users can work on their jobs with service browsers in their favorite environments.

**Context Management**

It is responsible for sensing the changes in the environment, collecting context and managing it. The basic idea is drawn from the context toolkit of Georgia Tech[14]. **Fig. 2** shows the details of the context management component.

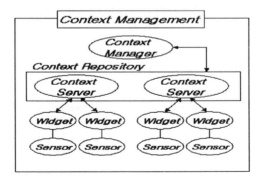

**Fig. 2.** Context Management Component

Context widget has in common with the interface, attributes and callbacks. Attributes are pieces of context that are made available to the context server via polling or subscription. Callbacks represent the types of event that the widget can use to notify to the subscribing context server. Context server can query the widget's attributes and callbacks. It does not have to know the capabilities of the widget at design time. Context widget supports both the polling and notification mechanisms to allow context servers to retrieve current context information from sensors. A widget designer has to specify the widget's attributes and callbacks and develop software to facilitate communication with the sensor in use. The time when new data from the sensor is available must also be specified. The context server collects all the contexts about a particular entity, such as a person, for example. It is created in order primarily to facilitate a service to utilize the context information. Instead of being forced to subscribe to every widget that could provide information about a person of interest, the service can simply communicate with a single object, that person's context server. It is responsible for subscribing to every widget of interest by querying the widget's attributes and callbacks. A context server exists constantly in a local area because of service locality. On change of location, new services that are different from the previous ones will be available.

The context manager manages the context servers in the repository. It can create a context server for a service, or remove a context server from the repository. It communicates with the service management component. When the adaptive layer of service management requires context information, the context manager returns the requested context information by choosing the appropriate context server.

**Service Management**

The service management part plays a role in selecting the appropriate services with context information from the context management part, and returns the services to the adaptive user interface part. It not only connects between the context management part and the adaptive user interface part, but also manages services that can be exploited by users. It also implicitly does some useful work for the users. The architecture of the service management part is shown in **Fig. 3**.

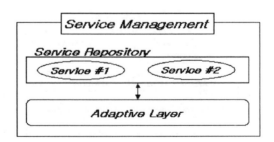

**Fig. 3.** Service Management Component

There is a service repository that contains and maintains the services. The incoming context information reaches the adaptive layer of the service management part. The adaptive layer selects some services related to the context information by querying the services at the service repository. After getting the requested services, the service management part returns them to the users.

**Adaptive User Interface**

This is one of the most important parts in the proposed framework. In order to accommodate non-expert users, an adaptive user interface associated with the services returned from the service management part must be provided. The adaptive user interface is shown in **Fig. 4**. The service browser shows the available services returned from the service management part. When the services are executed in the service browser, the latter sends the request to the service management part. As shown in [Figure 4], there are two paths between the service browser and the service management part. High end machines can accommodate the returned services. In that case, they may be executed without any problem. However, the mobile user's computing devices are not powerful enough to accommodate the returned services. A middle layer that manages returned services for mobile devices is needed in that case. This is the 'Service Proxy'. The job of the service proxy is to store the returned services and execute them between the service browser and the selection part.

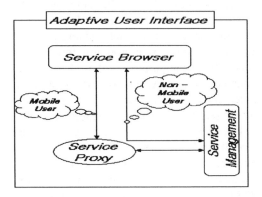

**Fig. 4.** Adaptive User Interface Component

# 4 OASIS(Office Application Server for Intelligent Services)

The OASIS system is being devised with a view to evaluate the proposed conceptual framework. It is based on Jini and will be in place soon. It is a system that manages and selects services for mobile users with context information – location, temperature, user profile etc. Mobile users can get local services of an office, i.e., air conditioner, printer, scanner, light system etc., and use or control the services with web-based user interfaces in OASIS. The architecture of the OASIS system is shown in **Fig. 5**.

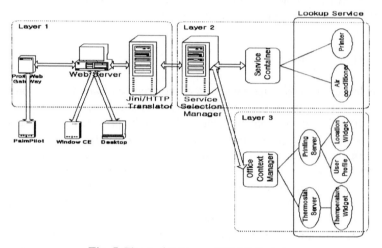

**Fig. 5.** The Architecture of OASIS System

There are three layers in the system. Each layer corresponds to a part in the proposed conceptual framework. Layer 1 plays the same role as the adaptive user interface part in the conceptual framework. The Jini/HTTP translation layer implemented by Servlet/Jsp, allows Jini services to be displayed and used in web-based browsers. As PalmPilot does not support direct web-browsing, the ProxyWeb gateway has been included. Layer 2 serves the same purpose as that of the service management part. The Jini lookup service is used as service repository in the service management part. Services can be implemented as Jini services (i.e., printer service, air conditioner service, etc.) The service selection manager is mapped on to the adaptive layer of the conceptual framework. Layer 3 corresponds to the context management part of the conceptual framework. It performs the same functions (eg. context sensing, context managing, and context reporting). All components in Layer 3 are implemented as Jini services. Moreover, context is sent to the service selection manager using Jini event mechanism. **Table. 1** shows a scenario example of the OASIS system.

**Table 1.** The Scenario Example of OASIS System

| |
|---|
| John is a staff in the marketing part in a company. He often moves in his office to other offices, because he needs to handle and manage his job with some colleagues. The scenario is like this: John goes to Mary's office with his printed documents, but he notices that he has missed some documents. He opens his PDA, and logs on to OASIS application management panel. The application management panel shows him the list of available printers nearby and some other services. He just selects the appropriate printer and prints the missed documents. |

# 5 Conclusion

When humans interact with other humans and the surrounding environment, the situational information or context is implicitly made use of thereby increasing the conversational bandwidth. Computers are far behind humans in deducing situational information from their environment and in using it in their interactions. The concept of context-aware applications appears to solve the problem of the computer that is not context-sensitive. Context-aware applications sense context information and modify their behavior accordingly without explicit user intervention, thus providing human-centric services. However, context-aware applications have their own problems. Many frameworks for context-aware applications have been developed to address or mitigate these problems. Most of the frameworks have limitations in general situations, especially changing ones.

A general, conceptual framework that includes all the features of extant framework architectures has been proposed in the paper. The OASIS system based on Jini and Internet technologies is being built around the framework in order to evaluate its strengths and weaknesses as a model for mobile context-aware applications. A knowledge-based system represents contexts precisely, regardless of specific situations.

# 6 Reference

1. Daniel Salber, Gregory D. Abowd,: The Design and Use of a Generic Context Server, In the Proceedings of the Perceptual User Interfaces Workshop (PUI '98), San Francisco, CA, November 5-6 (1998) 63-66.
2. J. Waldo,: The Jini Architecture for Network-Centric Computing, Communications of the ACM, 42(7), July (1999) 76-82,.
3. IBM Pervasive Computing Site, http://www-3.ibm.com/pvc/index.shtml
4. K.F. Eustice, et, al.,: A universal information appliance, IBM System Journal Vol 38, No. 4 - Pervasive Computing
5. A.Morales, M.Guillen,: The MoDAL Language Specification, IBM Working Document
6. P.Wyckoff, et. al.,: TSpaces, IBM System Journal 37, No. 3, (1998) 454-474
7. Hull, R., et, al.,: Towards Situated Computing, 1st International Symposium on Wearable Computers, San Francisco, California, 18-19 October (1999) 73-78
8. Anind K. Dey, Gregory D.Abowd, Daniel Salber,: A Context-Based Infrastructure for Smart Environments, In the proceedings of the 1st International Workshop on Managing Interactions in Smart Environments(MANSE '99), Dublin, Ireland, December 13-14, (1999) 114-128
9. Gregory D. Abowd,: Classroom 2000: An Experiment with the Instrumentation of a Living Educational Environment, IBM Systems Journal, Special issue on Pervasive Computing, Volume 38, Number 4, October (1999) 508-530.
10. Ted and Win Burleson's paper, :Context-Aware Design, for the IBM Systems Journal, Vol. 39, Nos. 3 & 4 - MIT Media Laboratory
11. Armando Fox, et. al.,: Integrating Information Appliances into an Interactive Workspace, IEEE Computer Graphics and Applications, May/June 2000

12. Gerd Kortuem, et, al.,: Context-Aware, Adaptive Wearable Computers as Remote Interfaces to 'Intelligent' Environments, $2^{nd}$ International Symposium on Wearable Computers, 19-20 October, 1998

13. Couderc, Kermarrec,: Improving level of service for mobile users using context-awareness, Reliable Distributed Systems, 1999. Proceedings of the 18th IEEE Symposium on (1999 ) 24-33

14 Anind K. Dey, Daniel Salber, :An Architecture To Support Context-Aware Applications, Masayasu Futakawa and Gregory D. Abowd. GVU Technical Report GIT-GVU-99-23. June 1999.

# Personal Information Market ••
# - Toward a Secure and Efficient Trade of Privacy -

Takuya Otsuka          Akira Onozawa

{otsuka,onoz}@aecl.ntt.co.jp
NTT Lifestyle and Environmental Technology Laboratories
3-1 Morinosato Wakamiya, Atsugi-shi Kanagawa Pref.,243-0198 Japan
Keywords: privacy control, information sharing, e-commerce, security protocol

**Abstract.** As the Internet becomes more and more indispensable in our society, the issue of personal information handling between consumers and businesses is recognized as a critical one in building a secure and efficient social system on the Internet. In handling personal information, consumers generally want their privacy to be protected, but businesses need reliable personal information and an access channel to consumers for e-commerce. Clearly these demands must be satisfied to establish sound e-commerce. However, most existing approaches for personal information handling can not satisfy all of them. This paper proposes the idea of the Personal Information Market (PIM), which can satisfy all of these demands. A protocol that supports the PIM and an implementation in the form of personalized advertisement service are described.

## 1. Introduction

Today, many businesses provide customized services to their customers by utilizing customer preference information and/or behavioral information. Various web sites can collect each web user's browsing log and display personalized pages for them by installing and collecting Cookies. For instance, Amazon adopts a sophisticated collaborative filtering [ 1 ] to create personalized recommendation service.

These customized services certainly make our life more convenient. Therefore, it is reasonable to allow a business to provide such services. Whether a business is successful or not often depends it on having more information about its consumers than competitors do. This means a business has to gather as much information about consumers as possible, which increases the possibility of unintentional, or intentional, infringement of consumers' privacy. Continued abuses of consumers' privacy makes consumers very uneasy about sharing their personal information with businesses. We have to remember that human society on the Internet will thrive only if the privacy rights of individuals are balanced with the benefits associated with the flow of personal information.

Here, we define the notion of privacy control as the right of a consumer to control the process of the disclosure of her personal information. We believe that this definition can be widely accepted in our society. It means that users can specify what information should be disclosed to whom, when it should be disclosed, and for what purpose, and that they are guaranteed the information will be treated so.

In general, the explicit demands from consumers and businesses regarding commerce based on the consumers' personal information are as follows. Consumers want to be able to control their privacy perfectly while getting the best personalized service available from business. Businesses need reliable and various consumer personal information and an access channel to bring the service to the appropriate consumer. The above discussions can be summarized in the form of three requirements for sound commerce based on personal information:

**1. Privacy Control**: Consumers should be provided with a means to decide when, what and for what purpose their personal information is used. Anonymous transaction technology is one of the most powerful tools for controlling privacy, as we will describe in the next section.

**2. Data Reliability**: Businesses should be provided with a means to obtain reliable consumer information.

**3. Consumer Accessibility**: Businesses should be provided with a means to access targeted consumers directly.

As we will see in the next section, the existing approaches only partially satisfy the above requirements. We propose the Personal Information Market ( PIM ), which meets all the above requirements. In the PIM, it is assumed that consumers' personal information consists of two categories: the Identifier and Payload. The Identifier is a part of the personal information with which the consumer can be identified, such as an e-mail address, phone number, etc., while the Payload is other personal information with which its holder cannot be identified. The framework of the PIM is constructed by using cryptography in a way that none of the entities except the consumer can have both, which satisfies the requirement for the Privacy Control. Also, as consumers don't have to tell lies to control their privacy, business can trust the PIM as a reliable personal information source. Furthermore, the business can access targeted consumers whose Identifier is unknown to the business.

The rest of the paper is organized as follows. Section 2 reviews the existing approaches for personal information handling. The proposed framework for the PIM is explained in Section 3, while Section 4 describes its current implementation. We conclude our paper in Section 5.

## 2. Existing approaches

In this section, we compare the existing approaches for personal information handling, from the point of view of the three requirements described in the previous section. The result of the comparison is summarized in Table 1. As shown, none of the existing approaches is satisfactory.

| Approach | Requirement | | |
|---|---|---|---|
| | Privacy Control | Data Reliability | Consumer Accessibility |
| P3P | Low | High | High |
| Pseudonym | High | Low | N.A. |
| Attribute Certificate | Medium | High | N.A. |
| *PIM* | High | High | High |

Table 1  Comparison of Existing Approach

## 2-1. Platform for Privacy Preferences Project (P3P)

As both consumers and businesses become more aware of online privacy, some web sites have begun to show a so-called privacy policy statement by which they declare what they will do with the collected personal information. In this statement they declare the possibility of the user's personal information being used for commercial purposes and/or transferred to a third organization.

For better communication of privacy policies on the Internet, the Platform for Privacy Preferences Project (P3P) [ 2 ] was undertaken by the W3C. The P3P procedure is quite simple. First, a user sets a generic privacy policy, which is encoded in XML, upon which his browser automatically acts. Web sites also set their privacy policy upon which they treat the collected user's personal information. When the user visits the web sites, the web sites' privacy policies are checked to see if they meet user's privacy policy. Then the user's personal information is transferred, including behavioral and identifiable information. When a user encounters a web site with "exceptional" policies outside his generic privacy policy, he is asked if he wishes to consent to these policies. This scenario can be provided by using privacy management tools, such as SmartSense and Orby privacy plus [ 3 ] developed by YOUPowered.

By following the above procedure, the personal information cannot be transferred automatically unless the consumer's policy matches the business's policy. On the surface, it looks like the privacy can be controlled. However, in reality, consumers cannot control their privacy using this procedure alone. Consumers are too often asked to give up their privacy for personalized services that are indispensable for a convenient life. The FTC report [ 4 ] released in 2000 well describes the problem regarding P3P.

So P3P technical implementations have to be accompanied by law enforcement against businesses and self-regulation efforts attempted by BBBOnline [ 5 ] and TRUSTe [ 6 ] by utilizing seal programs. This punitive law enforcement and self-regulation might work as a preventive measure against privacy infringement to some extent, but monitoring all the privacy data that have to be shared among associated companies or that are held by small businesses is infeasible. Furthermore, considering the possibility of mergers, acquisitions and/or corporate bankruptcies, users can hardly expect a corporation to treat their personal information according to their privacy policy.

Overall, the P3P approach effectively provides businesses with users' personal information and accessibility to users, but fails in privacy control by users (see Table 1). The eXtensible Name Service [ 7 ] by XNSORG takes a similar approach, utilizing "privacy contract" and "XNS agent", which is not completely enough for the privacy control, neither.

## 2.2 Pseudonym with anonymous transactions

Meanwhile, many technologies for privacy protection are available on the Internet. Most of them make it possible to browse the net anonymously without leaving personally identifiable information on web sites. One of those technologies is the Lucent Personalized Web Assistant (LPWA)[ 8 ], developed by Bell Labs. It enables web users to create a pseudonym consisting of a pseudo name, pseudo e-mail address, and other information required on web sites that protects their identities online. A similar approach was taken by Zero-Knowledge Systems, Inc. in its privacy protection software called Freedom [ 9 ].

Such privacy protection client software must come with proxy services or anonymous transaction technologies, for which Crowds [ 10 ] or Onion Routing[ 11 ] are examples, that provide anonymity of information sources. In the case of proxy services, a "proxy machine" run by a trusted organization provides anonymity of identity information such as an IP address. On the other hand, in the case of anonymous transaction technologies, such as Crowds and Onion Routing, the collected web users group cooperatively provides the group member's anonymity.

It seems that these methods are the perfect tools for giving users complete control over their privacy on the Internet. But, considering the business-side perspective, those anonymous transaction technologies would result in thousands of bogus customers. This would clearly discourage businesses from making use of Internet resources. While this approach successfully provides privacy control for consumers, it cannot provide businesses with reliable consumer personal information and accessibility to appropriate consumers. See Table 1 for a summary.

## 2.3 Attribute Certificate by SPKI

Another type of technology to control a user's privacy has been proposed. Users can anonymously show their attributes, such as gender or age, by using an authorization certificate linked with a corresponding public key. This is one application of access control by SPKI (Simple Public Key Infrastructure)[ 12 ].

This works as follows. First, the user registers the personal information that he wants to show web sites to a trusted third party (TTP). After the TTP checks the validity of the registered data,' it issues an authorization certificate linked with user's private key, which represents the user's attribute and contains no identifiable information. The user sends the set of the certificates corresponding to the attributes he wants to present to the web site. An important point of this approach is that user never sends his identity information, but only his attributes, to web sites. Therefore, the information that web sites get is useful only at the time of the user's access to them; It will be meaningless later.

This framework seems to allow users to control the privacy. But it has some problems in terms of its feasibility. First, the user has to prepare and manage all certificates corresponding to each attribute of his personal information that he has to register to the TTP beforehand. This means the TTP would be quite knowledgeable about an individual's private life. Second, the user has to frequently update his public key, otherwise he could be tracked with the public key, because the public key itself can be an identifier. This means TTP has to issue certificates again and again.

As a whole, this approach successfully provides web sites with reliable consumer's personal information by the help of a TTP. But the TTP will know many details of an individual's private life. Therefore, we need another scheme to keep the TTP trustworthy. Besides, this approach does not provide accessibility to the consumers by businesses. This is summarized in Table 1.

In summary, from the viewpoint of privacy control of users, the pseudonym approach is successful, while the P3P approach actually fails. From the viewpoint of the reliability of available data, the attribute certification approach seems to be successful, while the pseudonym approach cannot meet this requirement. On the other hand, most existing approaches except P3P do not take into consideration the importance of accessibility to consumers, although it is crucial for the market place.

# 3. Platform for Personal Information Market

From the above discussion, it is clear that none of the above-mentioned approaches fulfills all the requirements for personal information handling. In this paper, we propose the Personal Information Market (PIM), which is a carefully designed personal information sharing framework that satisfies all the requirements in Table 1. In the PIM, people trade their own behavioral information with others. In most cases, businesses buy the information from consumers. Not to mention, consumers can control the use of their personal information.

### 3.1 An overview of The Personal Information Market

The PIM framework consists of four entities: Sender, who provides his personal information; Receiver, who collects it, exploits it, and provides services to Sender; Broker, who intermediates between Sender and Receiver; and Deliverer, who delivers the services from Receiver to Sender. In the typical case, Senders are consumers, Receivers are businesses or other consumers.

The Sender splits his own personal information into the Identifier, such as addresses or phone numbers that can identify individuals, and the Payload, which contains individual's attributes such as gender, age, and history of behavior like purchase records or diaries. The Payload consists of set of categorized behavioral data. The PIM is so organized that Entities who hold only the Payload cannot know from whom

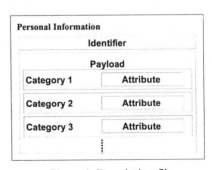

Figure 1 Description file

it comes, while entities who hold only the Identifier cannot know its accompanying Payload. The Sender holds his personal information as the structured format shown in Fig. 1, which we call a description file.

The Receiver can know only the Sender's Payload but not the Identifier. The Broker and Deliverer can know the Identifier but not the Payload. The PIM framework guarantees a one-time opportunity to access the Sender by the Receiver without knowing the Sender's Identifier. As a whole, the Sender can anonymously provide the Receiver with the Sender's Payload, while the Sender leaves no Payload for the Broker and Deliverer. Therefore the Sender can control the flow of his personal information.

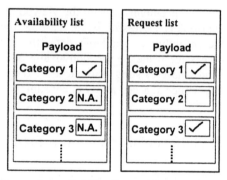

Figure 2 Availability list and Request list

The sender agent installed on the sender's computing device keeps obtaining a record of the Sender's behavior and makes a description file of the Payload as shown in Fig.1. The Sender makes an availability list, which is a list of categories containing the information that the Sender allows to be exploited by Receivers, and registers it to the Broker. Then the Receiver makes a "request list", which is a list of categories that contain the information he wants to see (See Fig. 2 ).

The Receiver tries to find an appropriate Sender, or targeted consumer, by sending a request list to the Broker. The Broker mediates between the Sender and the Receiver according to the availability list and request list. A negotiation between the Sender and Receiver starts, where the Receiver is not allowed to see Sender's Identifier. When an agreement has been reached, the Receiver gets the set of attributes from the Sender's Payload and sends the services back via the Deliverer.

By following the protocol described below, neither the Broker nor Deliverer is allowed to have the Sender's Payload. Figure 3 illustrates the framework.

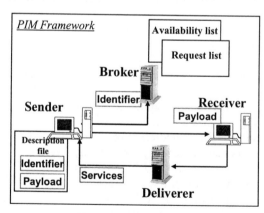

Figure 3  PIM framework

## 3.2 The PIM Protocol

All entities have a public key signed by a certification authority (CA). Transactions between the entities are secured by encrypted messages with authentication. The protocol is outlined in Fig. 4. We call it the PIM protocol.

### Step#1. Registration of "availability list"
The Sender (S) makes an availability list and registers it to the Broker (B). B stores all of availability list registered by S.

### Step#2. Mediation between the Sender and the Receiver
The Receiver (R) sends a request list (Lr) to B. B searches all the stored availability lists to find better matching ones. Then B makes a pseudonym ID (IDpseu) that corresponds to the S's identifiers (IDs), and sends back the IDpseu and the corresponding availability list (Ls) to R. Note that nobody except the Broker can know the correspondence between IDpseu and IDs at this point.

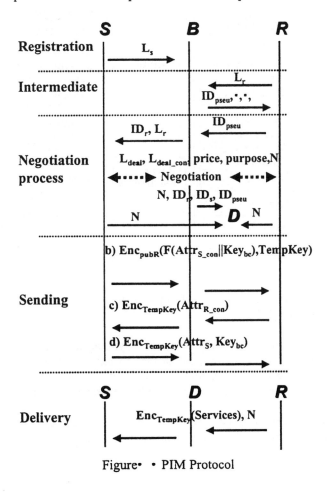

Figure• • PIM Protocol

The Receiver receives the IDpseu and the corresponding Ls, and stores them as a candidate list.

### Step#3. Negotiation

R selects the IDpseu from the candidate list, with whom he wants to negotiate, and sends it to B. B calls S corresponding to the IDpseu, by sending the Receiver's ID (IDr) and his Lr. This is followed by a negotiation process. B mediates the negotiation process, during which S and R negotiate over the deal ( the price of the information, the purpose of its use, the list of categories that they will trade (Ldeal), and the list of categories containing the attributes for which R has a particular requirement (Ldeal_con). Note that Ldeal_con • Ldeal • • (Lr • • Ls). Figure 5 illustrates the relationship among Ldeal_con and Ldeal and Lr and Ls.

Once an agreement is reached, B sends the negotiation number (N), the IDr, and the correspondence table (IDs, IDpseu) to the Deliverer (D). B sends N to S and R. Both the S and the R send N as an acknowledgment to D.

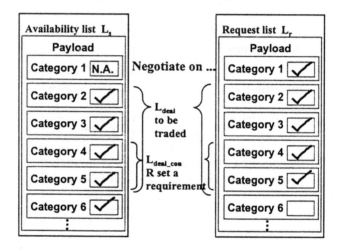

Figure 5   Negotiation on Ldeal_con and Ldeal

### Step4. Sending

To minimize the unnecessary flow of personal information, S and R exploit the bit commitment scheme [ 13 ].

**a)** S makes a secret key (TempKey) for symmetric cryptography and a bit commitment F(AttrS_con || Keybc) out of the attribute which S's Ldeal_con contain, where F( ) is a one-way hash function with input of the concatenation of S's attribute (AttrS_con) in Ldeal_con and the randomly generated key for bit commitment (Keybc).
**b)** S encrypts both the TempKey and the F(AttrS_con || Keybc) with R's public key, i.e., EncpubR(F(AttrS_con || Keybc),TempKey). The encrypted message is sent to R via B.

**c)** R encrypts the prerequisite attribute (AttrR_con), which is the attribute targeted by R, with TempKey, i.e., EncTempKey (AttrR_con). The encrypted message is sent to S via B.

**d)** When S compares and identifies AttrR_con with S's attribute (AttrS_con), he encrypts all of the attributes (AttrS) contained in Ldeal and Keybc with Tempkey, i.e., EncTempKey (AttrS, Keybc). S sends it to R via B.

Figure 6 illustrates relationship among AttrS and AttrS_con and AttrR_con

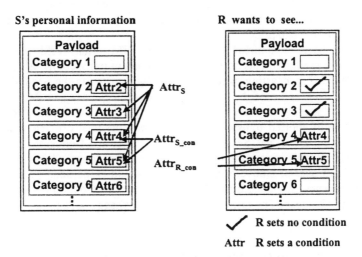

Figure 6   Bit Commitment of AttrS_con

### Step5. Delivering the services

R verifies F(AttrS_con || Keybc) with Keybc and AttrS_con. R sends N and services, encrypted with Tempkey if necessary, to S via D.

### 3.3 Discussions

In this subsection, we show that the PIM protocol can satisfy the three requirements for personal information handling, which are Privacy Control, Data Reliability and Consumer Accessibility. And also we point out the other features of PIM.

*(1) Privacy Control:*

By following the PIM protocol, the Receiver (business) can exploit the Payload without knowing the Sender's (consumer's) Identifier. The Broker and the Deliverer can obtain only the Sender's Identifier, not the Payload. The Receiver can have a one-time communication channel to the Sender. As a whole, it can be said that the Sender can control his privacy.

*(2) Data Reliability:*
The use of the bit commitment scheme in sending the Payload clearly helps increase data reliability, because the Sender can not lie about her attributes. In addition to this, having the Deliverer in the PIM, the Broker can not make bogus Senders.
*(3) Consumer Accessibility:*
It is clear that the Receiver can access the Sender without identifying him / her.

As a whole, we can state that PIM successfully fulfills all the requirements in Table1 .

In the PIM framework, the broker knows what categories of personal information are traded, and how much they cost. So he may play a role as a market organizer and help to establish the market price of personal information by announcing its average price.

We have to address two issues in PIM. First, PIM meets the three aforementioned requirements at the cost of redundant transactions. Although the PIM protocol avoids broadcasting query messages by registering the Sender's *availability list* to the broker, some of the transactions between Sender and Receiver would be aborted at the *sending step* due to the result of the bit commitment scheme. Since an accumulation of aborted transactions might erode the total efficiency, techniques to reduce them are necessary. Second, since the Broker and Deliverer internally have a correspondence table containing the identifier and pseudonym identifier, a conspiracy between the Broker or Deliverer and Receiver would erode Sender's privacy control. As a consequence, someone other than the Sender could obtain both of the Sender's Identifier and Payload. The resolution of these drawbacks remains as future work.

# 4. Implementation for personalized advertisement service

By looking at personalized advertisement service as an application working on the PIM one can better understand the aforementioned procedure. In this scenario the business M wants to find consumers who bought book A, and plans to send customized advertisement depending on what TV programs the consumer watches. In the trial implementation we used JDK 1.2, IAIK-JCE 2.61, JSSE 1.0.2, OpenSSL 0.9.5a, and xerces-J-tools 1.2.3 for RMI agents, data encryption, secure SSL transactions, Certificate Authority, and the XML parser, respectively.

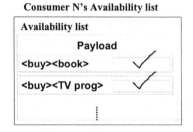

Figure 7 Description file    Figure 8  Availability list

## Making behavioral description file

All participants share the identical description format of consumer's behavior in XML, which is a list of tagged categories. And consumers have the description file of their personal information. For instance, in the case consumer N has purchased a book titled A and has watched TV program B, her agent puts "book A" in the category field tagged <buy><book> and puts "program B" in the category field tagged <buy><TV program>. (Fig. 7)

### Step#1. Making availability list

Consumer N makes her availability list, which has the same format as the description file. When consumer N allows businesses to exploit her behavioral information, i.e., that she bought "book A" and watched "program B", she checks the categories tagged <buy><book> and <buy><TV program>. Then, Consumer N registers it to the Broker (Fig. 8).

### Step#2. Mediation

In this scenario, Business M wants to know what TV programs are watched by consumers who bought book A. Business M makes his request list (Lr), in which she checks the categories <buy><book> and <buy><TV program> (Fig. 9). Then, Business M asks the Broker for the candidate list. In this case, the Broker sends back the pseudonym ID (IDpseu) for the consumer N and her availability list (Ls).

**Business M's request list**

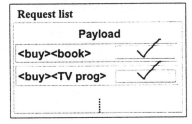

Figure•• 9 Request list

### Step#3. Negotiation

Business M selects a pseudonym ID for consumer N from the candidate list (We assume•• that consumer N is the only one on the candidate list in this scenario), and gets into the negotiation process. They reach an agreement on the price for the information, the purpose of usage, the categories <buy><book> and <buy><TV program> (Ldeal) and the category <buy><book> (Ldeal_con). Note that Business M has particular requirement for category <buy><book> , but has not disclosed yet that the requirement is book A ( Fig. 10 ).

### Step#4. Sending

Consumer N makes a bit commitment out of the attribute, that is book A, set in the category

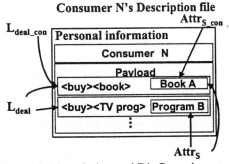

Figure 10 Negotiation and Bit Commitment

<buy><book> (AttrS_con), and sends it to business M via the Broker. Business M sends back the prerequisite attribute, that is book A for the category <buy><book> (AttrR_con). Consumer N identifies her attribute with business M's requirement and sends all the attributes (AttrS), book A and program B, for the category <buy><book> and the category <buy><TV program> respectively.

**Step#5. Delivery**

Now business M can access the consumer who bought book A and also knows that the consumer watched TV program B. Then, business M can make a customized advertisement and can send it to the consumer, without knowing that it is consumer B, via the Deliverer.

We have shown this simple personalized advertisement service scenario so one can see how the PIM works. Figure 11 shows the display of a consumer's PC. However, the PIM is a platform on which many kinds of applications can work. We are planning the development of more applications on the PIM.

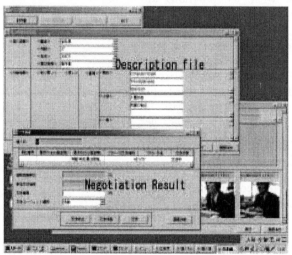

Figure 11  An Example of Consumer's Display

# 5. Conclusion

We have proposed a framework called the Personal Information Market (PIM) for secure and efficient personal information handling in the commerce. In the PIM, businesses can obtain reliable personal information and access consumers while consumers can control their privacy. In other words, the PIM can satisfy three indispensable requirements for the personal data handling, which are Privacy Control, Data Reliability, and Consumer Accessibility, by using the proposed protocol. The existing approaches for personal information handling can only satisfy them partially.

In the PIM framework, the Broker and Deliverer internally have a correspondence table containing the identifier and pseudonym identifier. Therefore, conspiracy between the Broker or Deliverer and the Receiver could erode the Sender's privacy control. One future work is to build a framework on which no entity has the correspondence table. And, as an accumulation of redundant transactions might erode total efficiency, another future work is to design a protocol with fewer redundant transactions.

## 6. Acknowledgement

The authors thank Drs. Takeshi Ogura, Hitoshi Kitazawa and Hisao Nojima for their helpful discussions and continuous encouragement.

## References

[ 1 ] D. Goldberg, D. Nichols, B. M. Oki and D. Terry: "Using Collaborative Filtering to Weave an Information Tapestry", Communications of ACM, Vol.35, No.12, pp.61-70, 1992.
[ 2 ] http://www.w3.org/P3P/
[ 3 ] http://www.youpowered.com/
[ 4 ] http://www.ftc.gov/reports/privacy2000/privacy2000.pdf
[ 5 ] http://www.bbbonline.org/
[ 6 ] http://www.etrust.org/
[ 7 ] http://www.ksg.harvard.edu/iip/stp305/Fall2000/delaney.PDF
[ 8 ] http://www.lpwa.com/
[ 9 ] http://www.freedom.net/
[ 10 ] M. K. Reiter and A. D. Rubin: "Crowds: Anonumity for Web transactions", ACM Trans. Info. Sysyt. Security Vol. 1, No. 1, pp.66-92, 1998.
[ 11 ] M. Reed, P. Syverson, and D. Goldschlag: "Anonymous conections and Onion Routing", IEEE J.Selected Areas in Communications. Vol. 16, No. 4, pp.482-494. 1998
[ 12 ] T.Saito, K.Umesawa, and H.G.Okuno: "Privacy Enhanced Access Control by SPKI", Proc. of the Seventh International Conference on Parallel and Distributed Systems : International Workshop on Next Generaration Internet Technologies and Applications, pp.301-306. 2000
[ 13 ] R. S. Douglas: "CryptoGraphy Theory and Practice", CRCPress 1995

# Security Enhancement on Mobile Commerce

Eun-Kyeong Kwon[1], Yong-Gu Cho[2], Ki-Joon Chae[3]

[1] Kaywon School of Art and Design, Department of Information Network & Communication, San 125, Naeson-dong, Euiwang-shi, Kyunggi-do, 437-712 Korea
ekkwon@kaywon.ac.kr
[2] Youngdong University, Department of Computer Engineering, San 12-1, Seolgye-ri, Youngdong, Chungbuk, 370-800 Korea
ygcho@youngdong.ac.kr
[3] Ewha Womans University, Department of Computer Science and Engineering, 11-1 Daehyun-dong, Seodaemun-gu, Seoul, 120-750 Korea
kjchae@ewha.ac.kr

**Abstract.** Mobile commerce is more than a mobile and wireless extension of the Web-based e-commerce. It is being spurred by the mobile phone industry's widespread support of the Wireless Application Protocol. WTLS (Wireless Transport Layer Security) is based on the industry-standard TLS protocol, is optimised for use over narrow-band communication channels and is used with the WAP transport protocols. Since mobile commerce differs to "fixed" commerce in instantaneous delivery, micro payment and mobile context, a user-friendly payment scheme and user authentication is required. But poor power and memory of mobile terminals must be taken into account when cryptographic algorithms are chosen. Through mobile application survey, we found that the security levels of request and response data are different and request data is more important. In order to upgrade both total security level and performance, we proposed a security enhancement mechanism, in which security parameters of request and response data are processed separately. We made algorithms code value changed with meaningful most left two bits in WTLS handshake.

## 1 Introduction

Mobile commerce is an electronic commerce brought to mobile users via mobile devices such as palmtops, PDAs or most dominantly mobile phones. Mobile commerce is more than a mobile and wireless extension of the Web-based e-commerce. It is an entirely new sales and promotion channel, and is the enabler for a whole range of new services such as buy a Coke, pay for parking, buy train ticket, etc. via mobile phones. In fact, the essence of commerce is to be able to satisfy the demands of the users. It is important not only to be able to offer whatever the user wants but also whenever he wants. Mobile commerce can also be customised such it fits the preferences of the user in combination with time and location. Another important aspect of mobile commerce is the ability to mix electronic media with other media such as newspaper, TV, radio, natural communication in any of the commerce phases i.e. presentation, selection, ordering, payment, delivery and obtain the location of the closest shop.

In order to deliver these mobile services and applications over the Internet in a secure, scalable and manageable way, new architectures and protocols are being designed. The WAP (Wireless Application Protocol) is a result of continuous work to define an industry-wide specification. Mobile commerce is being spurred by the mobile phone industry's widespread support of the Wireless Application Protocol. The protocol stack defined in WAP 1.0 optimizes standard TCP/IP/HTTP/HTML protocols, for use under the low bandwidth, high latency conditions often found in wireless networks. The improvements made in the WAP protocol stack lead to significant savings in wireless bandwidth [1].

As more subscribers demand WAP services, the need for wireless Internet security will continue to grow. By 1998, the security infrastructure with TLS (Transport Layer Security) and encryption was in place, triggering a dramatic increase in electronic commerce transactions [2]. WTLS (Wireless Transport Layer Security) is based on the industry-standard TLS protocol, is optimised for use over narrow-band communication channels and is used with the WAP transport protocols. WTLS processes security algorithms faster by minimizing protocol overhead and enables more data compression than traditional TLS solutions.

At first glance, mobile commerce may appear to be identical to "fixed" commerce extended with mobile wireless access and the solutions used in Web commerce, e.g. Web shopping, Web banking can be applied directly to mobile commerce. However, mobile commerce differs to "fixed" commerce in the following respects: Instantaneous delivery, Micro payment, and Mobile context. The payment scheme of Web shopping where the user has to enter his personal data and his credit card number is hence not appropriate for the mobile user. A user-friendly payment scheme and user authentication is required. But the processing power of many mobile terminals is quite limited and their memory capacity is very modest. This must be taken into account when cryptographic algorithms are chosen. In this paper, we proposed security enhancement mechanism on mobile commerce, in order to upgrade total security level and decrease processing load of mobile terminals at the same time. It means revised WTLS with minimal change of standard WTLS.

In chapter 2, security requirements in electronic commerce are listed and web shopping and banking procedure are described to show how to solve the security requirements. In chapter 3, ideal mobile shopping procedure and the limitation of mobile phones are followed. In chapter 4, the result of mobile applications survey is extracted and we show the main idea and design principle of our proposal. In chapter 5, we prove the relationship of the security level and performance according to various types and in chapter 6 our conclusion is placed.

## 2 Security Issues on Electronic Commerce

In electronic commerce where the consumer and the merchant communicate indirectly via software entities and the Internet, trust must be somehow established between the two parties. In order to achieve trust the following security functions must be performed [3]:

- Authentication: Each party needs to be able to authenticate its counterpart, i.e. to make sure that the counterpart is the one he claimed to be.
- Integrity: Each party needs to make sure that the received messages are not altered or fabricated by other than their counterpart.
- Confidentiality: Each party wants to keep the content of their communication secret
- Message authentication: Each party wants to make sure that the received messages do really come from his counterpart.
- Non-repudiation: Each party wants to prevent that the counterpart later on denies the agreements that he has approved earlier.

Since our intention is not to give a deep presentation about web-based electronic commerce but only an elucidation necessary for the explanation of mobile commerce later on, only simplified views of web shopping and web banking are described.

### 2.1 Web Shopping

Web shopping is getting more and more popular, especially for books, music, films, etc. The procedure varies slightly depending on the visited web site but can be summarised as follows:

- A user visits a web site of a merchant. He browses among the offers. Up to this point, no security measure is needed since everything is public.
- He wants to order goods or services.
- The web server asserts its site identity by signing its server certificate and sending it to the browser. In this case the server must be a secure server, i.e. having a server certificate and enabled for security. The browser uses the server's public key (from the server's certificate) to verify that the owner of the certificate is the same one who signed it.
- The browser checks if the issuing CA is one that it accepts. The trusted CAs is specified in the list of so-called trusted root-certificates
- The user manually (visually) authenticates that a trusted third party for the exact site the user is visiting issued the site's certificate.
- The browser generates a session key, encrypts this key with the server public key and sends it securely back to the server.
- A secure channel is established, with the session key generated by the browser.
- The user will be asked to enter his personal data, i.e. name, address, email.
- The user will be asked to enter his credit card number that will be charged for the purchase.

- The server issues a receipt to the user or sends it back via email.
- The merchant validates the credit card number and if valid ships the purchased goods to the user.
- The transaction can be closed at this stage.

## 2.2 Web Banking

Many banks in Europe have realized that by providing banking services such as paying bills, money transfer, balance check, etc. on the Web they can reduce costs at the same time as better services can be offered to customers. However, they are very concerned about security and do not find the procedure used in web shopping secure enough since no client authentication is performed. In order to remedy the situation, the banks have adopted different authentication schemes.

- Authentication using a set of numerated passcodes: The user receives from the bank by post a plastic card where a series of numbered passcodes are printed on. When the user visits the Bank's site, a secure communication is first established between the user's computer and the bank's server. Then, the user is asked to enter his username. The server will then ask him to enter for example passcode number n. The user consults his plastic card and enters the value of the passcode number n. If the passcode is correct, the user is authenticated.
- Authentication using a passcode calculator: The user receives from the bank by post a calculator, which is capable of generating a one-time code. The calculator is secured by PIN code chosen by the user at initialisation. This is same as the previous one except the passcode is generated by the calculator. This method requires a synchronisation between the two calculators.
- Authentication using software: Instead of a physical calculator the calculation function is delivered to the user as software in diskette or cd-rom. The user installs it in his PC. Alternatively, the calculation function can be provided in a smart card but in this case the user must have a card reader and associated software. The authentication is carried out by the user's client program (browser) and the merchant's server without intervention of the user.

## 3 Limitations on Mobile Commerce

There are two kinds of limitations relating to security: procedural and environmental. The former extracts ideal mobile commerce system, the latter is mobile terminals problems as follows.

## 3.1 Ideal Mobile Commerce System

At first glance, mobile commerce may appear to be identical to "fixed" commerce extended with mobile wireless access and the solutions used in Web commerce, e.g. Web shopping, Web banking can be applied directly to mobile commerce. However, mobile commerce differs to "fixed" commerce in the following respects:

- Instantaneous delivery: The mobile user is of course interested in having service like web shopping where the delivery of non-electronic goods is carried out later. But in addition he may want to have the goods delivered to him immediately or in a short delay. For example, after paying for a Coke via his mobile phone he expects the can to run out from the Coke automat.
- Micro payment: For mobile users it is also to be able to buy small things and to pay small amount of money. The fees for such payments must be small compared to the payments.
- Mobile context: The mobile user in many situations must be able to operate the services with only one hand. The user may be in environments that are distracting, e.g. crowded, noisy and interactions with the electronic commerce services must both simple and small in numbers.

The payment scheme of Web shopping described earlier where the user has to enter his personal data and his credit card number is hence not appropriate for the mobile user. A user-friendly payment scheme is required. An ideal mobile commerce should support the following:

- User authentication
- Merchant authentication
- Secure channel
- User friendly payment scheme supporting micro payment
- Receipt delivery
- Simple user interface

## 3.2 Limitations of Mobile Phones

To understand the attribute of mobile phones is important, since mobile phones dominantly are used in mobile commerce. Like the following table 1, mobile phones have many limitations of screen size, input utility, processing power and memory. Especially, the processing power of many mobile terminals is quite limited. This must be taken into account when cryptographic algorithms are chosen. Their memory capacity is very modest. Therefore, the number of cryptographic algorithms must be minimised and small-sized algorithms must be chosen. And the RAM requirements must be as low as possible.

**Table 1.** Comparison between wired and wireless Internet

|  | Wired Internet | Wireless Internet |
| --- | --- | --- |
| Rate | 56Kbps – 1Mbps | 14.4Kbps – 56Kbps |
| Screen | Over 640 * 480 pixels | 4*16 Chars, |

| Interface | Keyboard, Mouse, Pen, Monitor, Printer | 8*16 Chars(smart phone) LCD screen, soft button |
|---|---|---|
| Communication error rate | Low | High |
| Storage | Large | Small |
| Duration time | Long | Short (1-2 sites access) |
| Payment will | No | Yes |

# 4 The Idea and Design for Security Enhancement

According to previous chapter 3, we got to know that there is need to enforce client authentication comparing to "fixed" commerce and since mobile phones have many limitation in processing power and memory, overhead from security have to be minimised. In order to upgrade both total security level and performance, security enhancement mechanism is required. At first, we need to analyse the application attribute on mobile commerce.

## 4.1 Application Analysis on Mobile Commerce

There are five mobile telephone companies in Korea; they have already opened wireless Internet service as table 2.

**Table 2.** Wireless Internet service in Korea

| Company | SK 011 | Sinsegi 017 | KT 016 | KT 018 | LG 019 |
|---|---|---|---|---|---|
| Service name | n.Top | i-touch017 | persnet | M-Life | EZ-I |
| Browser | WAP (Errisson) | WAP (Phone.com) | ME (MS) | ME (MS) | WAP (Phone.com) |
| Contents | WML | HDML | mHTML | mHTML | HDML |
| Service open | 99.12 (first) 00.2(second) | 99.12 | 99.9 | 99.2(first) 99.2(second) | 99.5 |

Until now, wireless Internet contents can be divided into the following four areas. Among those, commerce service is on the initial stage, many wireless contents providers are preparing their services.
- Personal information management: email, schedule, address book, memo
- **Commerce service: mobile banking, ticket reservation, trading, auction, shopping**
- General information supporting: yellow book, weather, travel, recruit, news, location search in current position
- Entertainment: chatting, circles, quiz, game

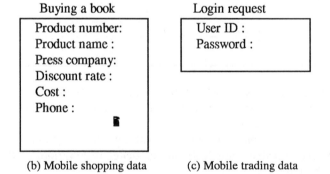

---

**Request data**

Login request

```
ID :
Password :
```

money transfer request

```
Withdraw account :
Account password:
Deposit bank :
Deposit account :
Deposit account holder:
Remittance amount :
Remittance date :
```

Card amount inquiry request

```
Card number :
Card password :
Inquiry term :
```

---

**Response Data**

amount inquiry response

```
Account :
Total amount :
```

transaction inquiry response

```
Transaction Date :
Deposit/withdraw :
Transaction amount :
Total amount :
```

Card status inquiry response

```
Address :
Phone number :
Card type :
Card number :
Expire date :
Service limitation :
Availability :
```

(a) Mobile banking request/ response data

Buying a book

```
Product number:
Product name :
Press company:
Discount rate :
Cost :
Phone :
```

Login request

```
User ID :
Password :
```

(b) Mobile shopping data          (c) Mobile trading data

**Fig. 1.** Mobile application request/ response data

When we surveyed existing wireless commerce services, we found that shopping doesn't include payment procedure, just give phone number or support automatic calling to helpdesk. In banking and trading, "login request" is used to authenticate a client. As a result, we found that request data – especially gray color elements in figure 1 – is more important, because a faker can reuse the request data to counterfeit and response data brings just privacy problem. The analysis of request/response data is showed in figure 1. Mobile bank data of figure 1 is customized from demo program of one bank, which is preparing his service open.

According to this result, to process security parameters of request and receive data separately seems to be efficient and it's the main idea of our proposal. To maintain request/response security parameters separately, four types are defined as follows. Especially this proposal will be effective in case of decrease of receive data decryption load because of longer bytes of receive data than request data. At the next section, existing security parameter handshake procedure is described.

- Type1: secure send/receive, same security level
- Type2: secure send, open receive
- Type3: open send, secure receive (no meaning)
- Type4: secure send/receive, different security level

## 4.2 Security Parameter Analysis

The cryptographic parameters of the secure session are produced by the WTLS handshake protocol, which operates on top of the WTLS record layer. When a WTLS client and server first start communicating, they agree on a protocol version, select cryptographic algorithms, optionally authenticate each other, and use public-key encryption techniques to generate a shared secret. The WTLS handshake protocol includes following steps, figure 2 is one of three handshake types. After the negotiations, both communicative parties have a uniform secure state, which contains the security parameter [4][5].

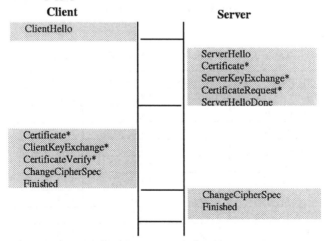

**Fig. 2.** WTLS full handshake procedure

- Exchange hello messages to agree on algorithms, exchange random values.
- Exchange the necessary cryptographic parameters to allow the client and server to agree on a pre-master secret.
- Exchange certificates and cryptographic information to allow the client and server to authenticate themselves.
- Generate a master secret from the pre-master secret and exchanged random values.
- Provide security parameter to the record layer.
- Allow the client and server to verify that their peer has calculated the same security parameter and that the handshake occurred without tampering by an attacker.

## 4.3 Design

To cover existing WTLS standard and minimize the change, we made algorithms code value changed like table 3, 4. The principle to arrange the code value is using the most left two bits. Like figure 3, if two bits are 01, the code is used for request data (client) and if 10, used for response data (server).

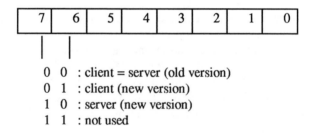

| 7 | 6 | 5 | 4 | 3 | 2 | 1 | 0 |

0 0 : client = server (old version)
0 1 : client (new version)
1 0 : server (new version)
1 1 : not used

**Fig. 3.** Algorithms code byte

**Table 3.** The new bulk encryption algorithms code

| Algorithm | Old version | For client | For server |
|---|---|---|---|
| NULL | 0 | 64 | 128 |
| RC5_CBC_40 | 1 | 65 | 129 |
| RC5_CBC_56 | 2 | 66 | 130 |
| RC5_CBC | 3 | 67 | 131 |
| DES_CBC | 5 | 68 | 132 |
| 3DES_CBC_EDE | 6 | 69 | 133 |
| IDEA_CBC_40 | 7 | 70 | 134 |
| IDEA_CBC_56 | 8 | 71 | 135 |
| IDEA_CBC | 9 | 72 | 136 |

**Table 4.** The new keyed MAC algorithms code[6]

| Algorithm | Old version | For client | For server |
|---|---|---|---|
| SHA_0 | 0 | 64 | 128 |
| SHA_40 | 1 | 65 | 129 |
| SHA_80 | 2 | 66 | 130 |
| SHA | 3 | 67 | 131 |
| SHA_XOR_40 | 5 | 68 | 132 |
| MD5_40 | 6 | 69 | 133 |
| MD5_80 | 7 | 70 | 134 |
| MD5 | 8 | 71 | 135 |

There is no syntax change in ClientHello. Just remind that type4 must have two cipher suits at least. But cipher suite of ServerHello has to be changed to array structure in order to cover type4.

ClientHello
    Client_version
    Random_number
    Session_id
    Client_key_ids $[0..2^{16} -1]$ (Key_exchange_suite, Parameter_specifier, Identifier)
    Trusted_key_ids
    **Cipher_suites $[2..2^{8} -1]$ (bulk_cipher_algorithm, mac_algorithm)**
        **type1 : old-version**
        **type2 : several things for only the client**
        **type3 : several things for only the server (no meaning)**
        **type4 : several things for both the client and the server**
    Compression_methods
    Sequence_number
    Key_refresh

ServerHello
    Server_version
    Random_number
    Session_id
    Client_key_id (Key_exchange_suite, Parameter_specifier, Identifier)
    **Cipher_suite [0..1] (bulk_cipher_algorithm, mac_algorithm)**
        **type1 : select one (old-version )**
        **type2 : select one for only the client**
        **type3 : select one for only the server (no meaning)**
        **type4 : select two for both the client and the server**
    Compression_method
    Sequence_number
    Key_refresh

In record layer, new security parameter is as follows. Bold character elements have to be changed to array structure in which 0-index means a client and 1-index does a server.

| Old Security Parameter | New Security Parameter |
|---|---|
| Entity | Entity |
| **Bulk_cipher_algorithm** | **Bulk_cipher_algorithm[0..1]** |
| **Cyper_type** | **(0:client, 1:server)** |
| **Key_size** | **Cyper_type[0..1]** |
| **Iv_size** | **Key_size[0..1]** |
| **Key_material_size** | **Iv_size[0..1]** |
| **Is_exportable** | **Key_material_size[0..1]** |
| **Mac_algorithm** | **Is_exportable[0..1]** |
| **Mac_key_size** | **Mac_algorithm[0..1]** |
| **Mac_size** | **Mac_key_size[0..1]** |
| Compression_algorithm | **Mac_size[0..1]** |
| Master_secret(20) | Compression_algorithm |
| Client_random(16) | Master_secret(20) |
| Server_random(16) | Client_random(16) |
| Sequence_number_mode | Server_random(16) |
| Key_refresh | Sequence_number_mode |
| | Key_refresh |

New connection-state variables have to use new security parameter, so that, client key results from index-0, server key results from index-1.

Client write MAC secret[SecurityParameters.mac_key_size[0]]
Client write Key secret[SecurityParameters.key_material_length[0]]
Client write IV secret[SecurityParameters.IV_size[0]]
Server write MAC secret[SecurityParameters.mac_key_size[1]]
Server write Key secret[SecurityParameters.key_material_length[1]]
Server write IV secret[SecurityParameters.IV_size[1]]

# 5 Analysis

For reference table 5 gives a picture of the average time estimates for a hardware brute-force attacks. The figures are based on the estimates made in 1995. According to the Moore's Law, nowadays the time estimates can be divided by 10 [7]. In the WTLS, the most useful encryption algorithms for ciphering the communication channel will be the RC5_CBC with 40- and 56-bit keys and DES_CBC with a 40-bit key. Needless to say, 40 or 56 bits are not enough. There are no technical restrictions for using longer keys, even the current CPU resources and the available bandwidth would be adequate for a stronger encryption. In our proposal, it is possible to use separate key lengths for a client and a server, for example, RC5_CBC_40 is used for a server, and RC5_CBC_56 is used for a client. But to use separate algorithms is not recommended because of increase of the number of algorithms to be selected.

**Table 5.** Average time estimates for a hardware brute-force attack in 1995[8]

| Cost [$] | Length of key in bits | | | | | |
|----------|------|-------|------|---------|--------|--------|
|          | 40   | 56    | 64   | 80      | 112    | 128    |
| 100 K    | 2 s  | 35 h  | 1 a  | 70 000 a| 10xE14 | 10xE19 |
| 1 M      | 0.2 s| 3.5 h | 37 d | 700e0 a | 10xE13 | 10xE18 |
| 10 M     | 0.02 s| 21 min| 4 d | 700 a   | 10xE12 | 10xE17 |
| 100 M    | 2 ms | 2 min | 9 h  | 70 a    | 10xE11 | 10xE16 |
| 1 G      | 0.02 ms| 13 s | 1 h | 7 a     | 10xE10 | 10xE15 |

Of course, as the key lengths are longer, more secure session is guaranteed, but it takes longer time to encrypt and decrypt. As a result, we can predict the situation as following figure 4. Since type2 has only secure request channel, total security level is decreased but better performance is guaranteed than type1. In case of no security-critical of response data, type2 is a good solution with reasonable performance. Type4 has more secure request channel and less secure response channel, not only total security level upgrade but also better performance are guaranteed if proper security parameters are selected because it takes longer time to decrypt receive data which is longer than request data in many times.

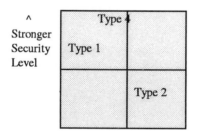

Fig. 4. Security & performance analysis

# 6 Conclusion

Now the industry is poised to take its next big leap forward into the wireless world. In this paper a security enhancement mechanism is presented. The proposed solution can give a guideline to perform in a more secure and faster way any mobile commerce services such as doing bank transaction, buys goods or services, from mobile phones. But our proposal is not perfect and some issues remain to be done such as combination of proper parameters, preferred security level for each data. Since it is not implemented now, it is difficult to know how much it is enforced numerically. We will continue to refine this proposal including implementation and performance analysis.

# References

1. WAP Forum : Wireless Application Protocol Architecture Specification, version 1.2, WAP Forum (1998)
2. T. Dierks, C. Allen : The TLS Protocol Version 1.0, RFC2246 (1999)
3. Understanding Security on the Wireless Internet, Phone.com (2000)
4. WAP Forum : Wireless Transport Layer Security Specification, version 1.2 (1999)
5. Martin Christinat, Markus Lsler : WTLS – The security layer in the WAP stack, keyon (2000)
6. H. Krawczyk , M. Bellare , R. Canetti : HMAC: Keyed-Hashing for Message Authentication, RFC2104 (1997)
7. D. Stinson : Cryptography Theory and Practice, CRC Press, Boca Raton (1995)
8. B. Schneier : Applied Cryptography, $2^{nd}$ ed., Wiley, New York (1995)

# The Innovation of E-marketing Combination Tactics

Qin Qiuli [1]    Xizhao[2]    Chen Jingyan[1]

[1] Economy and Management College, Northern China jiaotong University, Beijing, China,
xzqql@263.net
[2] Technology & Quality Dept., Beijing  ShouGang Co. Ltd.
xzqql@263.net

**Abstract**  Marketing, which is a way and function to communicate enterprise and external circumstance changes with the environment development. E-marketing under the Internet environment changes the base of traditional marketing tactics and expands the concept of marketing. The paper expounds the innovation of E-marketing combination tactics from four aspects: product tactics innovation, price tactics innovation, marketing channel innovation and promotion tactics innovation.

## 1   Introduction

In traditional marketing tactics, because of the confinement of the material base and  technology means , the product price, sales channel, place of the producer and promotion tatics have become the critical content of market analysis and management tactics of the enterprise. This is 4P's combination of the marketing, namely product, price, place and promotion.[1] But in the E-marketing, this kind of marketing tactics is changed. The marketing tactics need be thought over some new questions.For example, how to do owner's page well and build the network marketing system in order to make things convenient for consumer to express purchase desire and requirement? How to satisfy the consumer's purchase desire and the cost? And how to make consumer establish the convenient, prompt and friendly communication?[2]

## 2  The innovation of product tactics

During the marketing combination, the product tactics are important parts. The proportion that the information factor occupied in E-marketing is more and more. The traditional product tactics begin slant and gradually become the marketing tactics of satisfying the consumer's requirement.

## 2.1 The change of the product

As a new kind of medium, Internet can carry on market surveying in the scope of the whole world. And by way of gaining feedback information about product concept and the advertisement effect, it also can test the different requirements of customer, thus it can easily track the consumer's action method and special fondness. Mostly the product of traditional meaning is one kind of concept of physics, namely practical thing. But the product concept of E-marketing has changed, it is evolved a concept of synthetical service and satisfying requirement from material. That is to say, what sold out in the enterprise not only is some products of material model , but also is one kind of synthesis service. It includes : various kind of product and commodity in direct consumption market or production market; the after-sale service or invisible product; product image, product civilization and the standard serialize of follow-up product; the new product development tactics around consumer's requirement. So the enterprise can strengthen customer service online, and the customer can reflect or ask about the question at any time and quickly get the key that comes from the various places in world by way of the network. At the same time , the company can get the information feedback immediately.

It would be better to say that enterprise provides the "settlement scheme" to the customer other than the product in E-marketing. In the famous BABI company of the United States, the customer orders its product on the net, and the customer design by himself the baby's height, colour of skin, eyebrows and eyes, even the very slight part. The company has provided the big and powerful data base material , and customer can make up the baby that he likes from the interior. The company comes to arrange to produce according to the requirement of customer completely , and Agile Manufacture just looks to be more important.

## 2.2 The change of product life period

The life of traditional product is divided into in period five stages: start period, growth period, mature period, saturation period and decline period. The middle has one course from low to high.    Because the fact that the companies do not come into contact with the consumer under traditional environment, so it is difficult for the enterprise to grasp the correct direction of the product development. Moreover the grasp of product saturation period and decline period is always stagnant.

But the situation changes under Internet circumstance, the concept of product life period just can be desalinated step by step. Moreover the enterprise can directly understand the consumer's suggection on the net, so it knows the improvement direction from the product thrown in the market. When the old product still is in mature period, the enterprise just has been in progress next generation's product research and development. The introduction of series product has replaced the saturation period and decline period of original product, which makes the product be full of youthful spitit forever and vigorous. Thus the product is seem to grow up forever.

# 3 The innovation of price tactics

## 3.1 The tactics of fixing the price

Changes of two factors which influences the tactics of fixing a price tactics are: the monopoly of market is reducing; and the mentality characteristic of purchase person is hastened in reason. E-marketing makes consumer increase many chances to select , and they are very easy to compare the product overall on the net, and the non-price factor of product will be taken the more and more important effect .

If certain price standard of product is not unified or is frequently changed, customer can know this kind of price difference by way of the Internet very fast, therefore it probably will lead to the discontent of customer. So relatively with the various mediums at present, the advanced browse and service of Internet can make the indefinite and diferrent price standard be same. This will give rise to the huge shock to the company whose retail seller is overseas and adopts different price. The difference of price discount can make the Internet user of world and business which made by retail seller or does not need discount be affected. Agency who searchs for the special product on Internet will realize the price difference, thus it will aggravate the unfavorable influence on the price discriminated. This is a serious question for the company of differenceization price tactics.

E-marketing is a management course of customer's requirement, that is how to grasp the customer by enterprise's own Web Site, how to analyze the customer and meet his requirement. This need the close cooperation of enterprise outside information system and internal information system, that is the cooperation of understanding requirement of customer's and the disicion of customer information. The connection of  internal and the outside is Web Site , so the Web Site should lay stress on the management of customer's requirement information.

## 3.2 Fix the price by antiauction

One kind of new fixing a price situation on E-marketing is Antiauction. Sellinging off goods by auction on the net is one kind of common form, and the anti-auction of new situation has unfoldd one kind of requirement of customer's by way of the network. For example, customer shows that he has a hundred thousand kilograms of requirements of pork by way of the network, and puts forward the lower price of condition requirement , this kind of requirement of customer's will be reasonably selected by way of network, and it directly aggravate the competition of the suppliers. This kind of method leads to not only the competing but the cooperation. For example, when customer puts forward a big requirement, a supplier can not satisfy this kind of requirement, and it can ask partner to come to accomplish jointly the requirement. The anti-auction sales model on the net is directed  by requirement. When raises the requirement, the best prce and quality are needed.

### 3.3 Fix a price according to the brand

With the development of internet, consumer becomes more and more reasonably. Only reduce the prices blindly can make E-marketing sink into the confusion state. But relying on the brand to fix a price can not appear this kind of circumstances, customer has a mentality price. If the difference is not too big, the customer can not too haggle over price, but pay attention the prestige degree of the company. For example, on a web site(www.ra tingwonders.com), visitor can find some policy for returning the product, the way of payment and secret businesses. And consumer even can put up the buying experience on the network.

### 4 The innovation of marketing channel

Marketing theory thinks the relations between the market main body is decided by his actual strength and superiority. The actual strength embodies not only the function, price and after-sale service of the product, but also the construction of channel. As an important invisible capital, the channel is paid attention by the producer. Under the E-marketing condition , the sales channel of traditional marketing can not satisfy the low cost and diversity requirement of producer. The sale channel length has reduced the middle level of business and made the wide channel marketing realize a qualitative leap.[3]

### 4.1 The comparison of traditional marketing channel and new marketing channel

Narrowly speaking , the channel here is only the commodity one-sided circulation and the material transformationfrom producer to consumer. Its function is to realize the effective distribution from the firm to customer and achieve the profit maxmium of rational producer and effectiveness maxmiun of rational consumer. The emergence of middle trade is a major source of realizing economic benefit. Shown in figure 1.

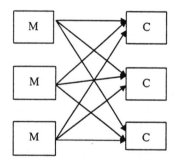 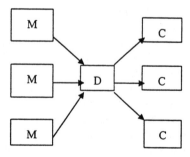

(a) Business times: M×C=3×3=9          (b) Business times: M+C=6
M=Producer  C=Customer  D=Devided sales trader

**Fig.1.** The traditional business

Part (a) has shown three producers , and every producer all uses directly marketing to contact with three customers respectively. This system asks for contaction for 9 times. Part ( b ) has shown three producers contact with three customers by the same agancy. This system asks for contaction for six times. Thus the agency has lessoned the work load that must be in progress, and has reduced the business cost at the same time. This is the existed basic cause of agency.

Shown in figure2. Under the E-marketing, though the business times is 9, the customer and producer can accomplish the business without going out. It has reduced the business cost and makes the direct marketing become possibile.

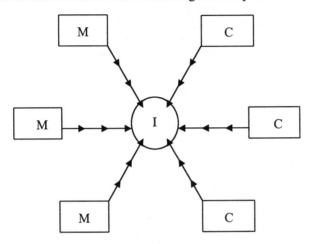

Business times: 3×3=9次
M=Producer   C=Customer  D=Devided sales trader  I=Internet
**Fig.2.**   The business under the Internet

The figure 3 and figure 4 show the difference of traditional marketing channel and E-marketing channel.

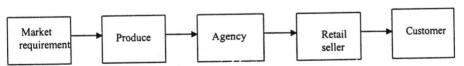

**Fig. 3.**  Taditional marketing channel

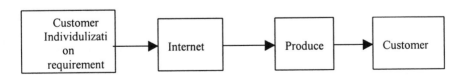

**Fig.4.**  E-marketing  channel

## 4.2 E-marketing channel integration

Integration is that making the entire function occur qualitative leap by the optimization conformity to the system related factor. The nucleus of integration tactics is using the view of system integration to direct the marketing channel's construction, raising the rapid penetration and competition strength of channel by way of compensation and blend of every resource factors, and promoting the effectiveness , coordination and continuity of marketing activity. The elements of different marketing channel system have different distribution and formation, but the function elements are same. They can be concluded roughly: product R&D, supplier's interest and tactics, the interest and tactics of logistic organisation, logistic organization and its running rule, the specialization character of logistic organization, the customer's requirement, recognization and satisfaction. The integration tactics are made of below three mutually additional and mutual coordinated mechanisms:

### 4.2.1 The whole optimization

To make every factor of the channel system synthetically run, realize great coupling change, and give rise to the magnifying effect of function and superiority, the first importance operating mechanism should be the whole optimization. At present, the effect of the active essential factor whose nucleus is knowledge should be noticed. And drives the improvement of other essential factor function with this.

### 4.2.2 The cooperation alliance

The cooperation alliance is popular, but as a channel construction running mechanium, it has deeper intension. By way of superiority compensation, the cooperation alliance builds the integration effct and strengthens the channel competition at vertical and deep aspects. At the same time it is a dynamic engineering which can greatly promote the channel superiority. By way of coordinating in many waysand giving play to the resources superiority each other to realize the purpose of prolonging the antenna in market, scattering the market risk and enlarging the superiority scope, and achieve the effect of intergrowth and interhonor.

### 4.2.3 The high efficiency communication

The information communication includes idea, knowledge, civilization and commercial affairs.      In the integration strategy , in order to realize the high efficiency communication, the enterprise should pay attention to the following aspects: idea modernization; civilization completization; information numeralization.

# 5 The innovation of promotion tactics

## 5.1 The information propagation under the network environment

### 5.1.1 The difference dissemination medium.

Internet possesses the characters of striding time, space and the region, covering whole world, conveying information with the two-way of multi-medium form, and the renewed information immediately. Compared with Internet, the traditional propagation has apparent region and monotonous nature.

### 5.1.2 The difference marketing quality

The birth of Internet not only has created one kind of completely new propagation means for people, but also becomes a vigorous market. The market of E-marketing possesses suitable invented nature. What the customer saw is not the material object, but the description of product by producer. The possibility of striking a bargain is decided by the product description and credit degree of producer. But customer of traditional market has a perception impression to the commodity by way of the sense organ of visual sense , tactile sense and smell sense, and buy the commodity by synthetical factor.

## 5.2 The innovation of the network advertisement

The advertisement is the important promotion means of marketing methods. The traditional advertisement promotion looks thin and can not popularize under the internet circumstance. The network advertisement is one kind of new advertisement form whose medium is Internet. The difference between the mutual and accurate network and traditional medium is bigger and bigger. The internet advertisement has changed the shortcomings of single direct circulation, isolation and time difference during the information transmits and feedbacks. It makes the receiver and sender realize communicate each other. The sender can adjust the information according the change of receiver requirement and meet the requirement better. With the deep unfold of revelance, the two-way communication between enterprise and customer becomes deeper, the dependence becomes stronger, and the market barrier of entering becomes higher, at last the "one to one" marketing relation between enterprise and customer is established.

The internet advertisement has changed the method of " pushing " in traditional advertisement communication. It makes the customer can select according to own wish. This kind of communication method of receiver asking for the special information from the sender is " pulling " method..

Under the joint effects, which are large network information space, low price, and information requirement from the objective custiomer, the mechanism of the advertisement convincing the customer to act has changed. The basic information requirement of objective customer is not only an impression.

## 5.3 The innovation of public relations on the network

The public relations is another kind important promotion method. The enterprise is not only concerned with consumer, supplier and agency, but also concerned with batch of other interest public.      Men such as editor , reporter and director etc act as the role of goalkeeper, they can decide whether the news of your enterprise to see on the newspaper, and they still decide the show style of this news even the implied content at the same time. Alao the timeliness can not be pledged yet in the tradition public relations. The network gives the public relations activity of enterprise more chances. The network makes it possible that the enterprise is directly faced with the consumer to issue news without the medium. And this is a very important revolution. The enterprise on the network directly issue enterprise news by way of network forum, BBS, news group, E-mail and other methods. The specific timely and relevance property of E-mail makes that the public relations on the network also possess the superority of "one to one" relation between the enterprise and customer.

# 6 Conclusion

Internet environment and E-marketing has changed the foundation of traditional marketing tactics and has greatly expanded the concept of original marketing. Under the Internet economy times in the 21 century, with the development of E-commerce, E-marketing theory will be more perfect.

# References

[1]Fillip • Ketle.Marketing (Asia edition), Beijing: Chinese People University Press, 1997
[2]Huang Hengxue,Marketing Innovation, Beijing:Tsinghua University Press,1998
[3]Zhang Xianfeng, Rebuild the agency sales channel. E-commerce in China.2000.7

# Online Branding:
# An Antipodean Experience

Jack Yan[1]

[1] CEO, Jack Yan & Associates, PO Box 14-368, Wellington 6041, New Zealand
jack.yan@jyanet.com

**Abstract.** Australia and New Zealand enjoy high per-capita internet usage and have a small group of organizations that have succeeded globally on the web despite less capitalization and fewer resources. The author, a web pioneer and identity expert, examines how they have instead leveraged brands and intellectual capital, and looks at implications for all firms wishing to incorporate a web element to their marketing.

## 1   The theory of identity and branding

### 1.1   Introduction

The web has impacted on developed nations and the way we conduct business. The structure of commerce has changed significantly with the rise of infomediaries [1] and portals but one constant has been the need for the branding of goods and services in online and cross-media[1] firms. Many web business failures are tied in with poor branding and as more of the world goes online, this area seems even more important to organizations. With the increased reach of the web, companies are finding proper branding more vital for international dealing. Similarly, branding has become more important in ensuring value for marketing dollars with numerous high-profile ebusiness failures [2] and the end of the late-1990s' online gold rush.

'Wired' consumers have been the target of these branding efforts. Since the mid-1990s, traditional firms going on to the web and web-only enterprises have tried to woo them using traditional and emerging branding models. In some cases, novelty, rather than long-term branding considerations, were the initial and only attraction. This paper looks at what has made successful, global brands in Australia and New Zealand. It further addresses how they could win future consumers using the internet and other media.

---

[1]   The author uses this term to mean organizations that have online (web) and offline (bricks-and-mortar, print, TV) presences, adapting from the publishing industry.

## 1.2 What is branding?

With more practitioners in branding, the offline phenomenon of experts disagreeing on the definition of the word has made its way online. [3] One authority is Wally Olins, chairman and co-founder of identity consultancy Wolff Olins, who states that the brand began as "the emanation of the company's products as far as one audience was concerned ... the customer." [4, 5] But the company (or the non-profit organization, or even the nation) [6] is now becoming a brand, representing an "attitude". The "totality of the corporate whole" is represented by the brand. [5]

In other words, the brand has an outward focus, i.e. it is a representation of an organization's vision. It is part of a larger framework of "identity", or:

the explicit management of all the ways in which the organization presents itself through experiences and perceptions to all of its audiences. [7]

Identity begins with a vision or a corporate *raison d'être*. Some organizations use a mission statement, but research by the author [8] shows that a slogan is equally powerful, such as Saturn's "A different kind of company. A different kind of car," and Caltex's "We're pumping," the latter used in New Zealand in the late 1990s for relaunching that company's brand. The important aspects are:

(a)   the uniqueness of the statement relative to other entrants in the market-place;
(b)   the ability to summarize an 'attitude' of the organization.

These elements are then linked with other aspects of the brand, such as its symbol or logotype (or the proprietary brand assets). Audiences, including internal audiences based on Olins's latest thinking on branding, come to learn the association between the attitude and the symbol through a careful communications' campaign.

Semiotics are key. [9] Symbols, logos, etc., signify certain things that form mental pictures in our mind when we interpret them. The campaign ensures that the correct pictures are formed and that incorrect or earlier ones are replaced. [10] Repeated exposures reinforce meaning, which is why consistency in branding is important.

This leads to brand equity [11] – the added value which a brand endows a product – divided into the associations and proprietary assets mentioned, plus brand loyalty, perceived quality and brand awareness. [12] As audiences – whether they are shareholders, future customers, students or any other group – select or think of the brand more frequently, they ultimately contribute to the organization's business performance in economic or strategic terms. [13, 14]

Given all these activities involve the brand, it is hard to pinpoint exactly what "branding" is. "Identity", as defined, must include every element from vision through to image because these are ways the organization presents itself. Some authors like to include the entire process for branding, but that would be contrary to the established usage of "identity". In the literal sense, of branding animals, it comes with the labelling. Its origins began in the nineteenth century with the bestowing of names for common products, usually commodities, while advertising allowed companies to speak to consumers directly. [15] Therefore, branding is restricted to exercises which communicate the identity to audiences. It is the realization of the explicit management in Olins's quote, therefore:

the methods in which the organization communicates, symbolizes and differentiates itself to audiences. [16]

The brand may be thought of as "an inclusive term which refers to a product or service. It includes its trademark, its name, its reputation and the sensual and emotional buttons surrounding it, most often created by advertising." [17]

## 1.3 The modern wired consumer

Today's web has parallels to the advent of television in that organizations do not yet know the ideal method of reaching audiences. Olins forecasts that "these teething troubles are going to last for a long time." [5] However, the consumer psychological process remains largely the same. [10] The principal difference is that more experienced audience members often seek information online and are not exposed to it 'unexpectedly', with the exception of online advertising. Some younger internet users, having grown up with advertising and computers, take the web's presence for granted and browse with tightly defined criteria. The question is how an organization ensures its brand is at the top of the user's consideration set and, on a related note, how it can appear in search engines and portals prominently. As stated by Ries, "Internet brands are invisible until you input the brand name into the keyboard. If you don't know the brand name and how to spell it, no sale can happen. Therefore, online, name recognition is paramount." [18]

Organizations must find ways of reaching consumers and becoming their preferred or only source if their online ventures are to be successful. Even if there were agreed definitions on branding, there is still the issue of practice.

There is an additional challenge. Brands have become so high profile that the public is fascinated by the organizations behind them. Corporate citizenship has become important. The flip side of branding is that companies that employ sweatshop labour and other unethical practices are more easily targeted. Modern consumers fight establishment brands, preferring niche players partly because of increased segmentation, as sales leaders Nike and Levi's found in the late-1990s. [19, 20] This suggests that organizations must not risk appearing too overwhelming and retain an entrepreneurial style.

## 1.4 Australia and New Zealand

The author focuses on Australia and New Zealand. These two countries are developed and economically free, [21] although the combined population is only roughly 20 million. However, Australia's area is equal to that of the United States. Some organizations from Australasia wishing to compete online cannot realistically focus on a domestic market if they wish to have sufficient viewer numbers or customers. Sources of capital are also expectedly fewer. Currency differences, not least the drop in the value of the Australian and New Zealand dollars against the US dollar and other major currencies over 2000, mean that organizations have had to get more value from their earnings, especially if they relied on infrastructure in the United States. To provide them with reach, they have had to adopt careful branding strategies, cultivating their presences online against much larger players.

This is typical of countries that do not have a ready access to capital, despite its mobility. [22] The successful organizations there have to leverage their intangible assets, in this case, their brands, and, by definition, part of their intellectual property. If intangibles are the "scarce resource" of the twenty-first century, [22] then there are many lessons to be learned from this part of the world.

Relative to the United States, the Australasian web has been quieter. Despite contemporaneous availability, the smaller population meant there were fewer taking advantage of it. Although there is a very high per capita internet use, the numbers do not match that of Silicon Valley. Differing government policies meant that Australia and New Zealand did not duplicate the degree of innovation seen in Sweden, that resulted in many popular sites visited by international audiences. Flotations of dot coms barely registered in the news.

## 1.5 Structure

The following section features an analysis of the players, detailing specific efforts and how they have affected the internet public. The paper concludes with the lessons they provide for future branding for businesses.

## 2 The practice

### 2.1 The identity and branding model

The identity and branding model was developed after a full analysis of the literature and research into branding practice (see Fig. 1 overleaf). [23] This model links vision, research, exposition and image with business performance. Image is the consequence of branding activity and deals with how audiences have reacted. Each of these elements is analysed qualitatively here.

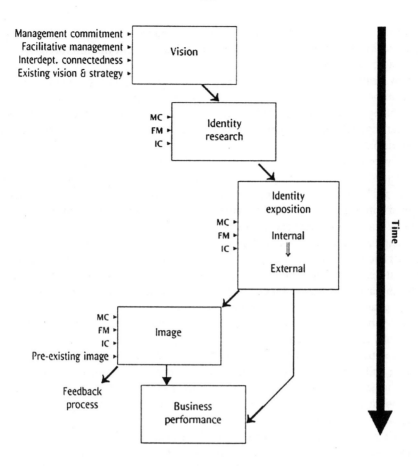

**Fig. 1.** The identity and branding model, from JY&A Consulting: JY&A Consulting Profile. JY&A Consulting, Wellington (2000). The model blends the author's identity research with the principles of market orientation

## 2.2 Vision

Vision is crucial, according to earlier literature. [7, 24] However, the author found in an earlier study of offline firms that it only provides a foundation for branding activity. [5] Its effect on the other branding stages is not as strong as once thought. This seems to make sense for online firms where having a narrowly defined vision restricts potential development. A loosely defined vision that can give rise to an 'attitude' suits the organization more.

Online companies did not have visions that tied them down to product categories or geographical markets. They had a main philosophy but the interpretation of that into strategy was flexible.

New Zealand's Jenniferann.com, the world's leading online lingerie store, has a vision of being a "strong brand" and a "women's super-store", says CEO Jenny Hannah. [25] It eventually etailed homeware and gifts as well. Although its homeware and gifts' diversification happened earlier than planned, it was still accommodated for in her vision.

nzgirl.co.nz defined itself by an attitude ("building self-esteem, self-awareness and confidence"). [26] Technically not a dot com, nzgirl's reputation is global and has been approached by international concerns interested in syndicating its distinctive teenage-targeted content. nzgirl's Jenene Crossan-Nicholls says that her business operates "flexibly" to take on "unexpected turns."

Lucire, Australasia's most widely read fashion title, is one of the very few online entrants allowed into New York Fashion Week (the other noticeable player is Condé Nast's style.com). Arriving later (1997) than its principal competitors except for harpersbazaar.com, Lucire had to differentiate, being independent and showcasing emerging talent alongside established players. It is a highly recognized brand. [27, 28] It was flexible: originally the magazine was regional but became global, when some projections did not eventuate.

The author has called his company "organic", [29] saying that an organization working online has to change with necessity and acquire competences as it develops. Lucire has gradually brought more of its skills in-house, as has Australia's Hippies, a well-known fashion brand, that began with an off-site ecommerce store and now incorporates it under its own domain.

None felt they had stepped away from their principal visions.

The founders were in their 20s. All said that their organizations reflect their personalities, as might be expected with a 'first-generation' firm.[2] There was no evident positioning statement–tagline as with Saturn or Caltex, with the exception of Lucire, which uses "The global fashion magazine". However, that fails to sum up its 'attitude'.

The small sample suggests that taglines or vision statements are less important than the actions demonstrating commitment, attitude and positioning. Site content is stronger for a web-savvy public tired of the commercialism of slogans.

## 2.3  Researching the venture

In the author's earlier study, the Narver and Slater market orientation dimensions of management commitment, facilitative management and interdepartmental connected-ness [30] impact on subsequent branding stages. Proper research is vital.

Larger organizations research their visions and their suitability because the personality of the organization is not the creation of the CEO alone. Fekete & Com-

---

[2]  A firm where the founder is still the managing director, owner or chief executive.

pany of Columbus, Ohio, has found that "79 per cent of the CEOs selected a different personality type [for their companies] than did their team of key executives." [31] For the smaller organizations examined, all of whom had more limited resources, research was more ad hoc and the danger of differing personalities not as great. Greater 'tightness' within the team became more important.

Generally, research was not as deep as in offline corporations, compensated for by speed, low cost and a willingness to try, since there was little existing wisdom on how to brand online then. All were active in ensuring that the research's findings would be carried through to the product, strengthening their validity.

Hannah said, "I base a lot of my business decisions on 'gut feel'. Of course, I researched my competitors and the whole internet industry. However, I am a strong believer in ... getting on with it." This reflected Lucire's gestation: research in 1996 gave indications but the product differed in execution.

As a result, there is management commitment because the CEO is the centre of the network and the champion of the vision, often using email as the first medium for contact.

**Low cost.** There is an emphasis on low cost. Hannah brought on team members on an as-needed basis, something shared with Lucire. Hippies' Vanessa Palmer kept her core web team to three although her whole staff's input is sought at meetings when changes are being made. [32] JY&A Fonts, Australasia's leading font software company, relies on others' ecommerce operations to take care of order fulfilment and credit card processing, paying a relatively low commission compared with its offline retailers.

**Close relationships.** They allow people from across the organization to have input into the venture, demonstrating facilitative management. Openness is encouraged – Hannah calling it "crucial" to her company's success.

Close relationships are important. As there are no formal departments, "interdepartmental connectedness" is inapplicable. Palmer says there is 'no formal structure' at Hippies. "Everyone has their own roles and responsibilities, but if someone needs help in another area, you just get in and do it."

Because they are able to find like-minded individuals more easily online, or because they rely on friends, a shared vision is quickly understood. This leads to "fun" – a word commonly found in responses – indicating tightly knit groups.

Crossan-Nicholls "surrounded myself with people that also believed in what we're doing." Lucire reports the same, beginning with its first correspondent, Sidney Morningstar, and later its fashion editor (now editor-in-chief) Simone Knol and photo editor Rebecca Thorpe. [29] As Knol, Thorpe and others emigrated, the venture changed to accommodate them while keeping its principles. Diversifying into television production, the Lucire team has ensured that the original values are retained under its New York-based creative producer Monica Parente. nzgirl is planning its own cross-media move, a strategy which will allow it to get additional readers.

There was no agreement on whether face-to-face meetings were necessary: physical and virtual techniques were employed.

The function of departments is largely replaced by the ability to use technology. Palmer began videoconferencing in late 2000 to keep in touch with her American office. This suggests that intangibles, such as intellectual property and professional skills, in addition to brands, are valued more online than scale. The challenge will be for the organizations to retain an entrepreneurial spirit as they grow, but technology, such as videoconferencing, is aiding that.

## 2.4 Branding the venture

In online business, Olins may be right in using a more inclusive 'attitude' approach, where independent contractors, freelance workers and virtual team members are literally external to management. They take on more of the behaviours of channel members who need to be sold on the venture but are not full-time employees.

Offline, the most important aspect is facilitative management. The provision of sufficient branding material (e.g. graphics, stationery) and other resources (e.g. funding), and cooperation between management and team members, ensured strong brands. It was reflected online, concerning brand use consistency.

For the organization that has accepted a vision encompassing offline and online ventures, there are issues of:

(a) whether a brand should be built from scratch for the online medium or adapted from an offline concern and the cost of doing either;

(b) whether to adopt a different brand for the online arm; [18]

(c) how great a focus the online venture will have relative to other (offline) ones, if they exist;

(d) whether to have a different (usually global) target audience for the online venture (which leads to concerns of how high-tech the site can be), if an offline venture already exists;

(e) whether to mask its national origins through a dot com domain name;

(f) whether the brand itself is strong enough to remain online-only or whether additional media support is required (not just PR and advertising, but extending the brand into different media).

Those beginning offline adopted existing brands. Bloom Cosmetics, Evolu, Karen Walker and Zambesi ensured commonality across print and web media, furthering the belief that brands created specifically for the web that differ from their online counterparts do not contribute to brand equity.[3] These organizations saw the online presence as more secondary to existing branding methods.

Online ventures had to create brands and predictably placed a greater focus on them. Unlike Amazon.com, they did not change the logo or symbol after going online.

---

[3] Notable exceptions, such as ninemsn.com.au, the Australian portal developed by Nine Network and Microsoft, and stuff.co.nz, owned by Independent Newspapers Ltd., half-owned by News Corp., had cross-media support coupled with substantial financing. However, they target domestic audiences although their resources exceed the independent firms aiming globally.

The brand equity associated with the original manifestation of the brand exists today.[4] Lucire intentionally went with its sans serif masthead to contrast established players such as Elle, Vogue and the now-defunct Lumière.[5] Careful positioning at the beginning ensured they did not have to change.

Consistency in the domain name was important. Those examined did not have a separate web brand.[6] Doing so would have burdened them with the greater cost of pushing what would have effectively been two brands, diluting them both, and using funds that were scarce.

**Think global, act global.** Recognizing the largest market would be the United States, all stayed clear of pushing a stereotypically antipodean image. "We don't hide the fact that we are a New Zealand company," says Hannah, "however, we certainly don't promote it." Her site even adopts American spellings and like all the etailers here, quotes in US dollars. Lucire believes that the use of a New Zealand image is disadvantageous, when many believe it is rural, rather than high-tech. Hippies launched in the United States and Australia simultaneously, using common campaigns for both nations, preventing the use of an overtly Australian image.

All indicated that offline, they did not target a different audience but accepted that events and print media coverage brought them additional awareness outside their core demographics.

For them, national branding is unimportant. Their decisions point to a global society. Competing for its share of mind requires strong, internationally biased brand strategies. These businesses succeeded against traditional players because they do not rely on production techniques, capital or labour, but on brand equity and networks.[7]

In the case of Jenniferann.com, Evolu, Karen Walker, Lucire and men's interest site eMale, the founders had prior expertise in visual communications or marketing, meaning that branding advice could be implemented without delay, reliance on outside parties and expense.

**Cross-media importance.** Each used a unique strategy to expose the brand, having secured internal buy-in through management commitment. Hannah went as far as changing the name of her home town, Pokeno, to Jenniferann.com for 12 months. This move attracted media, including a film crew from Japan.

Hippies enters web site awards. Such events are important to bring a human face to the ventures.

---

4 Only Lucire reported difficulties in controlling how others used its brand. Approved parties that linked to Lucire online did not cause any problems, but unexpected links meant the logotype had been incorrectly displayed. The company regularly 'ego surfs' and provides correct graphics for the parties who linked without permission.

5 Though still online, Lumière's content has not been updated since January 1999.

6 Examples of these extra brands include Moët & Chandon's champagne.com, Odimo's diamond.com and La Perla's glamonweb.com.

7 The exception here is that Jenniferann.com finds that shipping from New Zealand raises its cost, although this will be remedied when Jenny Hannah opens warehouses and offices in Australia and the United States.

They use standard methods for online promotion, including link exchanges, seeking press coverage, syndication and banner advertising. Links help positioning in search engines, which in turn help users find the sites when performing a specific search.

All try to appear in non-web media – whether through getting covered by others or starting ventures in other media – to increase potential audiences and raise their brands' profile, while retaining a team feel through careful and constant internal communication of their philosophy. Generally, few believed that an online-only presence would work.

## 2.5 Image

External audiences (in the traditional sense, *viz.* people who do not come under the organization's brand) must view top management as standing behind the organization's claims. This is critical when it comes to order fulfilment, overcoming normally offline or late-adopting customers' fears about credit card use on the web and returning goods. The other limbs are important, too, with facilitative management interpreted as advertising support or acquiring links for the venture.

Interdepartmental connectedness is traditionally the most important element to image, because every member of the team must live up to the ideal. [5] A variant of it – perhaps more accurately described as ensuring buy-in across the team – is reflected online.

Brand equity is built as part of the venture's image. Brand associations, proprietary brand assets, brand loyalty, perceived quality and brand awareness are all consequences [33] of the branding effort. These lead to purchases, repeated visits, registrations, recommendations (e.g. through viral email marketing[8]), bookmarking,[9] linking,[10] syndicating (whether formally[11] or through a DIY portal page such as My

---

[8] The encouragement of the forwarding of email messages from the venture by registered subscribers to their friends.

[9] Including the addition of Active Channels on Microsoft Internet Explorer, where a user may include a small file that details the latest from a selected site and load its contents for later offline browsing.

[10] Including link-back programmes where users are permitted to take certain graphics or banner advertisements and link exchanges.

[11] For instance, sites such as Lucire and nzgirl.co.nz provide their content to others through paid and unpaid syndication arrangements.

Netscape[12]), having parties join an affiliate programme,[13] and other activities that help strengthen and propagate[14] the brand.

Audiences are motivated by the need to trust the organizations they deal with, and give loyalty to them. The brand equity elements do not change online: audiences require assurance that real people, especially the founder, stand behind the product or service.

As none of the companies match large American and European groups budget-wise for promotion, getting into a typical internet user's consideration set means emphasis on below-the-line promotion. Press coverage was perfect for Hippies, producing a unique product. Domestic and American press has been "phenomenal". nzgirl differentiates on content and, in Crossan-Nicholls's words, utilizes marketing along-side events and word-of-mouth. Lucire uses alliances with related, though not supple-mentary, ventures such as Y2G.com, a hip-hop fashion and entertainment site which syndicates its video footage, iWon.com and Yahoo!, and has used viral email market-ing, encouraging users to forward Lucire update emails to friends, who then sign up as registered readers.

Table 1. A selection of Lucire partner sites. Lucire has used link exchanges and closer partner-ships to help its standing. It has not pursued sites that have an identical psycho- and demo-graphic but those with related audiences that it otherwise would not have reached. A small listing of partner organizations is below.

| Site | Niche |
|------|-------|
| BrideSave.com | Bridal etailing |
| eMale | Men's interest and fashion |
| ID Models | Modelling |
| iWon.com | General audiences |
| NYSALE.com | Sales in tri-state area |
| Sirenne | New women's interest magazine from JY&A Media, summer 2001 launch |

[12] My Netscape allows users to select "channels" to add to a customized homepage.

[13] Essentially an online sales-commission programme where individuals set up "shops" on their own sites that sell the venture's goods, using coding and branding provided by the venture. The most successful example is Amazon.com's affiliate programme, duplicated by its UK and German subsidiaries.

[14] Some users will (usually illegally) take a site's logo and use it for linking to the site from their own pages. This phenomenon means that organizations need to keep a careful watch over how their brands are used. Not only can the user's pages provide improper associations (such as online adult magazines) but they can misuse the logo or symbol through cropping, resizing and other techniques. Some companies, such as the author's, regularly "ego-surf" (check for their own names through search engines) to patrol and enforce trademark use.

Although none directly addressed the issue, they have been careful not to appear too large as modern consumers react against corporations perceived to be exploitative.[15] This has a negative effect internally, too. Online ventures risk losing team spirit, the very thing that helped their growth.

The "attitude" referred to by Olins is apparent. Although no external audiences were researched, respondents said that they believed they conveyed a fun or supportive image. These were elements of their attitudes. Other elements, like morality or justice, play their part. Respondents appear keen to counter the dishonesty that audiences perceive of large corporations, a trend that began in the 1990s and offline.

Therefore, nzgirl aims to be its audience's "'best friend' … they can come and be anonymous, yet get advice, make friends, be entertained, gain information, not be threatened or made to feel bad. … They can rely on us to be here 24–7." Lucire ensures timely replies to readers' queries and has a policy of helping enquiring students with their research.

The trend toward caring brands will continue – and there is evidence to show that consumers' preference for them is nothing new. [10, 34] What has changed is access to information that help consumers make informed decisions in an increasingly global society. Every respondent understands that the image must be backed up by substance. As the ventures can remain small using technology as a bridge, CEOs will be able to respond directly to their audiences and understand how they are doing image-wise, continuing the environmental scanning required to focus or reposition their brands without added expense. Additionally, this allows them to keep in touch with changing trends and constantly acquire knowledge about their operations. It is a variant of the traditional notions of market orientation, [30] stripping out research intermediaries so that top management has first-hand contact with audiences.

Unless there is a change in their corporate structure, such as acquisition or merger, these antipodean online ventures should be able to continue their growth by being small, moving quickly, and thinking globally. They are typical of the organizations that can survive alongside large, merged corporations because of careful branding, specialization, and managerial responsibility and responsiveness.

## 2.6 Performance

Since numerous online ventures do not post a profit (e.g. Amazon.com), performance cannot always be measured in strict financial terms. With smaller privately held companies, financial data are not available. In subjective or strategic terms, visitor numbers, rankings *vis-à-vis* its competitors, number of registered users and reputation in the industry (judged by links to the site, number of parties syndicating content or

---

[15] At the time of writing, an email attacking Nike's alleged use of sweatshop labour is being circulated. Other urban myths are reported as fact – one 'cookie recipe' blames Neiman-Marcus for overcharging. Because inaccurate news like this can travel quickly, no organization wishes to be the target of fictions.

entering into affiliate programmes, or by the view from independent industry observers) are valuable indicators.

Respondents were pleased with their ventures. Jenniferann.com has met Hannah's expectations "insomuch as we enjoy a steady rate of growth, exceptionally good feedback and overwhelming support from our suppliers." Crossan-Nicholls says that nzgirl is "so much more than we could have ever hoped for." In strategic terms, there was good feedback.

Web rankings for the sites examined [35] are shown below in bold. These are slightly more objective, yet they must be interpreted relative to their industry and their starting dates.

"Links in" indicates the number of links to the site. Some better-capitalized US and European competitors selected by the author are listed below each for comparison. Domestically targeted sites are also listed where applicable.

The table does show that despite generally later starts, less capitalization and fewer resources, antipodean sites have fared well and better than those targeted domestically, with few exceptions. The importance of differentiation and cross-media presence is highlighted.

**Table 2.** Rankings of sites, according to Alexa Internet, 26 April 2001

| Site | Date online at current URL | Links in [34] | Alexa ranking |
|------|------|------|------|
| **Bloom Cosmetics** | | 3 | 328,684 |
| Stila Cosmetics | April 1998 | 37 | 166,919 |
| | | | |
| **eMale** | | | 346,575 |
| *Breaka* (XM, AU) | | | 521,592 |
| *GQ* UK (XM) | April 1998 | 378 | 24,638 |
| *Razor* (XM) | | 1 | 17,424 |
| SharpMan (OO) | August 1998 | 100 | 175,114 |
| *FHM* Australia (XM, AU) | | | 86,121 |
| | | | |
| **Evolu** | **December 1998**[16] | | **4,681,028\*\*** |
| | | | |
| **Hippies** | **March 1998** | 86 | 608,952 |
| Hanes Hosiery | October 1995 | 74 | 297,831 |
| Wolford | January 1997 | 170 | 54,335 |
| | | | |
| **Jenniferann.com** | **June 1999** | 85 | 325,978 |
| Glam on Web (La Perla) | | | 48,172 |
| ·No Regrets | | | 95,393 |

---

[16] Network Solutions Whois record domain registration date, not when the web site was launched.

| | | | |
|---|---|---|---|
| IM Imports (AU) | | | 575,635 |
| | | | |
| **JY&A Fonts** | **March 1997** | 818 | 134,669* |
| Agfa Monotype | | 3,801 | 269,266 |
| Font Bureau | September 1995 | 436 | 192,982 |
| International Typeface Corp. | April 1997 | 1,675 | 132,967 |
| Hoefler Type Foundry | January 1996 | 101 | 866,662 |
| | | | |
| **Karen Walker** | **February 2000**[17] | | 1,311,824** |
| Anna Sui October 1996 | | | 438,325** |
| | | | |
| *Lucire* | **December 1998** | 816 | 36,533 |
| Elle.com (XM) | April 1996 | 4,937 | 5,248 |
| *Fashion Live* (OO) | November 1997 | 72 | 34,082 |
| *Hint* (OO) | October 1997 | 1,039 | 48,425 |
| style.com (Condé Nast, XM) | April 2000 | 97 | 3,869 |
| Fashion New Zealand (NZ) | 1998–9 | | 105,095 |
| | | | |
| **nzgirl** | **December 1999** [35] | | 508,642 |
| gURL (OO) | December 1997 | 35,222 | 5,182 |
| Teenmag.com (XM) | January 1996 | 1,793 | 4,671 |
| Teen-net (OO) | July 1996 | 1,108 | 361,836 |
| girl.com.au (AU) | | | 518,508 |
| | | | |
| **Zambesi** | | | 1,226,760** |

*Key*
XM = cross-media
OO = online-only
NZ = domestically targeted, New Zealand
AU = domestically targeted, Australia

* This figure is inaccurate for comparison purposes as it has been boosted by JY&A's Consulting and Media divisions. Comparison to the International Typeface Corp. site may be fairer considering both JY&A and ITC store online magazines under their domains.

** Intended as brand support and brochureware rather than the main communications channel with audiences, hence the low ranking.

---

[17] Ibid.

## 3   Conclusions

The organizations examined indicate that the practice of identity and branding online has not changed drastically from its offline progenitor. It continues to revolve around differentiation and trust, as it always has. Consumers depend on both. Technology has become an intermediary linking the CEO and the vision to the public, with fewer distractions arising internally, and vice versa.

Larger, traditional organizations have trouble communicating the vision because the message can be lost through the number of staff and the expense required to communicate to them. Management tends to be distant from consumers and their impression of the organization.

Antipodean organizations are excellent examples because there are national traditions of innovation and independence. [37] The purity of this concept has been carried through more strongly online. The do-it-yourself nature of Australasians seems particularly suited to the medium. Visions must be strong, but organizations must exhibit flexibility and acquire competences as technology changes increasingly more quickly.[18]

They have each tapped in to an increasing cynicism against big business. In many cases, they were part of their own demographic, using their own needs to form strategy. [38] The brands they created stand independently and have an entrepreneurial image. They generally place little emphasis on taglines, another differentiating factor against larger, traditional enterprises. Instead, there is a reliance upon a brand attitude.

Skilful branding was imperative given the limits to expenditure. Costs are kept very low while management structures are organic and flat.

As the organizations grow, the entrepreneurial spirit can be retained by technology. Tools such as videoconferencing and the lower prices of telephone calls allow them to keep a team spirit without adding on additional personnel who risk diluting or misunderstanding the vision.

Consistency is paramount. There must be no difference in the way the organization is perceived on- and offline, hence the establishment of online-only brands has been avoided by all the respondents. All recognize the emergence of a global consumer society.

### 3.1   Implications

Cross-media presence was considered important. However, implications arise here. Large corporations can afford cross-media promotions. These organizations tend to be based in a single country so offline promotions will be domestic and below-the-line, unless they can create events of international interest, such as Hannah's town-renaming or Lucire's use of Yahoo! Full Coverage to generate hits. The study shows that these are rare although they cement the case for strong brand foundations as well as

---

[18] This must be tempered by the need to reach emerging economies, whose telecommunications infrastructures and computers may not be able to handle high-bandwidth transmissions.

the belief that intellectual capital is the driving resource. They have certainly created reputations for themselves as visionaries. To continue this, the antipodean organization must be prepared to use ingenuity to create global interest, otherwise it risks being lost amongst organizations whose promotional budgets alone rival its capital. This issue aalso brings the possibility of mergers, acquisitions and alliances.

If "fun" is a critical part of these brands, then there is a possibility that they are visited because they provide entertainment. [39] Those that are not already providing media services such as nzgirl, eMale and Lucire may find that this is a possible route to generate consumer interest.

A bimodal distribution of organizations, where there are large conglomerates and boutique players, but no mid-size firms, looks set to continue for the foreseeable future, with one difference: the boutique players, which the Australian and New Zealand firms are in resource terms, must think globally and reach the same potential audience. This will be done through coordinated marketing and responsiveness, but most importantly, their ability to communicate brand values to publics – including the media – and shift more quickly than the larger corporations. As Table 2 showed, the entrepreneurs have been able to compete, largely because the CEOs remained aware of changes.

A further issue lies with the change from the first to the second generation. Although there is nothing to suggest that the respondents will leave their companies, succession must play on their minds. While they are sure that their creations will continue, they have become intertwined with their brand. The face of Jenniferann.com is Jenny Hannah. Vanessa Palmer appears in her own promotions. Since they were the ones who showed management commitment, will team members who may have only had email contact be prepared for the change? And will the brand need to change?

If there is such cynicism amongst the public about businesses, will the internet remain an effective tool? As mentioned, some web surfers go online with tightly defined criteria. They do not have the same fascination for the new medium as the 20-something originators of the successful antipodean brands. Capturing the hearts of today's teen audience to ensure continued web patronage is an issue for all but nzgirl, which already targets that age group.

The study shows that the online public has the same concerns as the offline one about corporate citizenship and trust. The companies' moves to cross-media presences indicate that they see a merging of the 'wired' and 'unwired'. Both must be reached with strong, branded campaigns. They also cater for a global audience, but none have branched into non-English sites, which needs to be remedied with a new set of competences, while ensuring the brand philosophies 'translate' into another culture.

Thus, the 'think global, act global' stance could have an Achilles' heel. However, it has enabled the organizations to recognize the potential of global markets and forces such as harmonization and a borderless internet. Table 2 indicates that locally targeted sites cannot realize visitor numbers if the web is their primary medium. 'Thinking local' should be the realm of organizations that are inherently local, such as city councils or groups that depend on physical location.

The attraction of analysing the antipodean firm is the small size of the region and high per capita internet usage. Australasians have also been immune to the cynicism that set in when some likened the internet gold rush to tulipomania. Despite their later adoption, there are lessons for all organizations wishing to work commercially on the web or field coordinated marketing campaigns that recognize the growing internet public.

# References

1.  Hagel, J. and Singer, M.: Unbundling the Corporation. McKinsey Quarterly, No. 3 (2000) 148–161
2.  Yan, J.: Boo.com Boo Hoo. CAP Online (19 May 2000) http://jyanet.com/cap/2000/0518ob0.shtml; Emmott, B. (ed.): Business This Week. The Economist (27 January 2001); Klein, A.: Disney Red-Lights Go.com Site. The Washington Post (30 January 2001) E12. Cf. King, C.: Walt Disney Internet Group Shows Financial Gain. InternetNews.com (9 November 2000) http://www.internetnews.com/fina-news/article/0,,5_507471,00.html; Lambeth, J.: Surviving the Big Squeeze. Electronic Telegraph (19 October 2000) http://www.telegraph.co.uk
3.  Frankel, R. (ed.): I-Branding Digest, No. 8 (16 January 2001) http://list.audettemedia.com/archives/archives.html
4.  Interview by the author with Wally Olins (19 June 2000)
5.  Yan, J.: The Attitude of Identity. Desktop (October 2000) 26–31
6.  Olins, W.: Trading Identities: Why Countries and Companies Are Taking on Each Other's Role. The Foreign Policy Centre, London (1999)
7.  Olins, W.: The New Guide to Identity. Gower Publishing, Aldershot (1995)
8.  Yan, J.: Corporate Identity: Its Effects on Business Performance—a Thesis Submitted for the Master of Commerce and Administration Degree. Victoria University, Wellington (1999)
9.  White, I.: Learn to Read the Sign Language. Desktop (September 1999) 66–69
10. Engel, J., Blackwell, R. and Miniard, P.: Consumer Behavior, 6th edn. Dryden Press, Chicago (1990); q.v. Barkow, T.: The New New Ecommerce. Webreview.com (26 January 2001) http://www.webreview.com/soapbox/2001/01_26_01.shtml
11. Farquhar, P. H.: Managing Brand Equity. J. Ad. Res. (August–September 1990) RC-7–12
12. Aaker, D.: Building Strong Brands. Free Press, New York (1991)
13. Cavusgil, S. T. and Zou, S.: Marketing Strategy–Performance Relationship: an Investigation of the Empirical Link in Export Market Ventures. J. Mktg., 58 (1994) 1–21
14. Dau, R. and Thirkell, P.: The Relationship Between Marketing Orientation and Export Performance: Further Empirical Evidence. Proceedings of the 1996 Australia–New Zealand Marketing Educators' Conference. Wellington (1996) 369–386
15. Klein, N.: No Logo: Taking Aim at the Brand Bullies. Picador, New York (2000)
16. Combining Olins, W.: The New Guide, op. cit.; and after Littler, D.: Editorial. Int. Marketing R., Vol. 12, No. 2 (1995) 4–8, referencing Kim: A Perspective on Brands, J. Consumer Marketing, Vol. 7, No. 4 (1990) 63–7; and American Marketing Association: Marketing Definitions: a Glossary of Marketing Terms in Kotler, P.: Marketing Management: Analysis, Planning, Implementation and Control. 6th edn. Prentice Hall, Englewood Cliffs and London (1988)

17. Cahalan, A., as quoted in Yan: The Attitude of Identity, op. cit.

18. Rochman: Marketing Guru Al Ries Talks about the Web. Webreview.com (28 July 2000) http://www.webreview.com/2000/07_28/strategists/07_28_00_3.shtml

19. Nike Ten-Year Financial History. Nike Inc., Beaverton (2000) http://nikebiz.com/invest/ar_00/financials/10_year_history.pdf

20. Levi Strauss & Co.: 2000 Annual Report. Levi Strauss & Co., San Francisco (2000); Branded. BBC Television, London (1996); Terpstra, V. and Sarathy, R.: International Marketing, 5th edn. Dryden Press, Chicago (199) 488–489

21. Gwartney, J. and Lawson, R.: Economic Freedom of the World: 1997 Annual Report. The Fraser Institute, Vancouver (1997)

22. Bryan, L. and Fraser, J.: Getting to Global. McKinsey Quarterly, No. 4 (1999) 68–81

23. JY&A Consulting: JY&A Consulting Profile. JY&A Consulting, Wellington (2000)

24. Margulies, W.: Making the Most of Your Corporate Identity. Harvard Bus Rev, Vol. 55, No. 4 (1977) 66–72

25. Email interview with Jenny Hannah, CEO, Jenniferann.com (26 February 2001)

26. Email interview with Jenene Crossan-Nicholls, Publisher, nzgirl.co.nz (12 February 2001)

27. Ptasznik, J. (ed.): Fashion Websites: the Year of Truth. Visual Arts Trends, Electronic Edition, No. eS20 (2001) http://www.visualartstrends.com/Ea/Ea6/eS20-fashion.html

28. For example, Galaxy.com: Galaxy.com Fashion Report. Galaxy.com, Franklin (2000); Wiley, L.: The A-List. Access (29 April 2001); Vidal, J.: The Web that Jack Built. Flair Supplement, The Evening Post (5 December 2000) 8

29. Martinkus, A.: An Open Mind and a Global Company. Desktop (September 1999) 46–47

30. Narver J. and Slater, S.: The Effect of a Market Orientation on Business Profitability. J. Mktg. 54 (October 1990) 20–35

31. Fekete & Co.: Companies Are People, Too. Fekete & Co., Columbus (1997)

32. Email interview with Vanessa Palmer and Rhiannon Davies of Hippies (26 February 2001)

33. Cadogan, J. and Diamantopoulos, A.: Narver and Slater, Kohli and Jaworski and the Market Orientation Construct: Integration and Internationalization. J. Strategic Mktg. 3 (1995) 41–60; Jaworski, B. and Kohli, A.: Market Orientation: Antecedents and Consequences. J Mktg. 57 (July 1993) 53–70

34. Yan, J.: The Moral Globalist: Making Globalization Work. CAP Online (2 May 2001) http://jyanet.com/cap/2001/0502fe0.shtml

35. Alexa Internet Rankings. Alexa Internet, San Francisco (26 April 2001) http://www.alexa.com

36. Knol, S. (ed.): Teen Portal nzgirl Gets New Look. Lucire (8 February 2001) http://lucire.com/news.html

37. Ministry of Commerce: Bright Future. Ministry of Commerce, Wellington (1999)

38. Bhide, A.: How Entrepreneurs Craft Strategies that Work. Harvard Bus. Rev., Vol. 73, No. 2 (1994) 150–161

39. Yan, J.: Range on the Home. Visual Arts Trends, No. 3S (December 2000) 63–65

# Staying Put But Going Far: Empowering Online Rural Communities in Malaysia

*Weng-Kin Lai, Chandran Elamvazuthi & Normaziah Abdul Aziz*

MIMOS Berhad,
Technology Park Malaysia,
57000 Kuala Lumpur,
MALAYSIA

lai@mimos.my

**Abstract**

> *Currently, equity of and access to information and communication technologies (ICTs) is a burning issue in many countries around the world. Malaysia, as a nation of about 22 million inhabitants, has taken some strong strides in recent times to bridge the access and equity gaps through appropriate strategic national programmes as well as policies. One such initiative has recently been submitted to the government for consideration to be funded for the next five years under the national developmental budget. This paper will look at some of the key elements of this programme and identify some of the major challenges that it hopes to resolve.*

> **Keywords** : *Information Communication Technologies (ICTs), Digital Divide, Internet, Telecommunications, Personal Computers, Malaysia.*

## 1 Introduction

Malaysia, located within the southeastern part of Asia, occupies an area of about 330,113 square kilometers[1]. It is made up of two distinctive parts, with Peninsular Malaysia in the west and the two states of Sabah and Sarawak (inclusive of the second Federal Territory of Labuan), on Borneo Island in the east. With a population of about 22 million, it is blessed with abundant natural resources in the form of oil reserves, natural gas, tropical timber, rubber, and oil palm. Since achieving independence from England some 44 years ago, agriculture and mining have played a very significant role in the development of the nation's economy. It is only in recent times that manufacturing (production) has overtaken agriculture as the main economic driver of the nation's wealth.

With the advent of the information and knowledge era in the last ten years, knowledge has become the key wealth creator, and this has given rise to what is commonly known as the Knowledge- or *K-economy*. To meet the expected challenges, Malaysia has embarked on a drive to intensify knowledge used in all sectors of the economy, which includes both the traditional as well as the new. This will entail the concerted effort of all the various stakeholders in the Malaysian economy to *acquire and generate bodies of knowledge*[2]. In order to fulfill the nation's aspirations and objectives, the necessary ICT infrastructures must be developed to the extent that access to information is on par with the access to basic amenities like clean water and electricity. A nation's ICT infrastructure is a very vital ingredient for the dissemination and consumption of knowledge[2].

Many countries around the world have already put in place the necessary infrastructure that may be used to facilitate global communications and commerce. While Malaysia's readiness in this area may already be at an adequate level, we may be lagging behind some of our Asian neighbours like South Korea, Singapore, Hong Kong and Taiwan.

As a Government Corporation involved in research and development, *MIMOS* plays a pivotal role in developing the country's capabilities in ICT and microelectronics. The role is further strengthened since MIMOS is also the Secretariat to the highest ICT think-thank in the nation – the *National Information Technology Council* (NITC). This is the organization that advises the Government on matters pertaining to the development of ICT in the country. To reinforce the commitment and importance of the NITC's role in the nation, the council is chaired by the Hon. Prime Minister of Malaysia, with the Deputy Prime Minister as its Deputy Chairman.

One of the long-term national development programs is a five-year development plan. Every five years the Malaysian Federal Government will invite fresh applications from the various Government departments and agencies to submit proposals for national developmental programmes. We have just come to the end of the fifth year of the seventh of such programmes and the Government has already commenced reviewing proposals for the *Eighth Malaysian Plan* that will take the nation forward for the next five years to 2005. Along with several other developmental programmes for the nation, MIMOS has submitted a proposal to the Government to better prepare the nation for the challenges of the new economy ahead. The programme, known *as Desa Digital (Digital Village)* in the Malay language, will seek to develop and expand the existing ICT infostructure[3,4] throughout the nation so as to sustain economic prosperity in the face of greater global competition. This is especially relevant for those who are on the economically marginalised side of the divide. However, as we will show later on, the challenges here are much more than merely installing telecommunication infrastructures throughout the nation.

In the next section, we will examine some of the important indices that will give an indication of the country's ability to migrate to this new economy. We will then describe some of the fundamental issues and challenges that contribute towards the digital divide within the Malaysian context. Finally, a summary of the major elements of *Desa Digital* will be presented in section 8.

# 2 Migrating towards the new economy

Access to the vast electronic storehouse of information, commonly known as the Internet has been deemed especially crucial if Malaysia's stated objective of becoming a developed nation by 2020 is to become a reality. Unfortunately, as in any new technology, there is usually one group who has managed to successfully embrace it ahead of others. This is especially true when this has been left to the natural market forces alone, without any strategic intervention and assistance from the Government. While this may be of no major or urgent concern in the past, the current scenario has significantly shifted to the extent that this will greatly affect and harm the economic health of the nation if the Government does not act fast enough. Malaysia's economic growth in the past has been largely dependent on a Production- or *P-economy,* which essentially is based on our natural resources in the agriculture and mining sectors. However, this has changed in recent times. Due to the rapid global changes taking place and the ushering in of the *K-economy,* this dependence on the P-economy must be re-looked into within the Malaysian context so that the nation will not be left behind in the race towards owning a piece of the global K-economy cake. Therefore it may not be surprising for the Government to declare that the nation must prepare itself to be a part of this global K-economy. Although there has been some progress made here, indications are that there are many more challenges that the nation has to face and the pace of progress may not be what the Government would like it to be. And this is where the problem lies. As a result of this slower pace of progress, it has contributed to a significant gulf between the *"information-haves"* and the *"information-have-nots"* in the country. Fundamentally, this is the chasm that divides those with access to the new technologies and those without. Furthermore, because to its implications and strategic importance, this digital chasm has also become an economic as well as a civil rights issue. Even though some of those on the other (weaker) side of the divide may not be aware of it, they must be convinced that they just cannot afford to be left behind in this global phenomenon that is affecting the world today. They have to be a part of this. What then are the major challenges that have hindered the closing of the divide? Even though these challenges for Malaysia may not be exactly the same as in other parts of the world, it can be seen that they do belong to the same set. *Danowitz et al.* studied this for five North African countries and came to the realization that the major barriers come from low income levels, lack of telecommunication infrastructure, language, and cultural differences[5]. This may be summarized into three broad areas, viz.

- affordability (financial),
- access (language,etc.),
- the mind set.

## 2.1 The Malaysian Context

In Malaysia, even though there has been a growing realization that knowledge, and mastery of ICT are vital to the country's economic survival, the pace and depth of their progress have not been very satisfactory. According to a press release by the *Malaysian Energy, Communications and Multimedia Ministry* a year ago, there are some 900,000 Internet subscribers in Malaysia[6], which unfortunately, only accounts for 4.2 % of the total population as a whole. Even though this may be much higher than many of Malaysia's neighbouring countries, we are far behind when compared with the more advanced nations of the world. The latest figures are summarized in Table 1 below.

**Table 1**: Number of Internet subscribers for a selected number of countries

| Country | *Internet Subscribers* | % of population |
|---------|------------------------|-----------------|
| United States of America | *153,840,000* | 55.83% |
| Hong Kong SAR | *3,460,000* | 48.69% |
| Singapore | *1,850,000* | 44.58% |
| Australia | *8,420,000* | 43.94% |
| New Zealand | *1,490,000* | 39.03% |
| South Korea | *16,400,000* | 34.55% |
| United Kingdom | *19,980,000* | 33.58% |
| Japan | *38,640,000* | 30.53% |
| Taiwan | *6,400,000* | 28.84% |
| Malaysia | *1,500,000* | 6.88% |
| Thailand | *1,000,000* | 1.65% |
| China | *16,900,000* | 1.34% |
| Phillipines | *500,000* | 0.62% |
| India | *4,500,000* | 0.45% |
| Indonesia | *400,000* | 0.18% |

**Source** : http://www.nua.com/surveys/how_many_online/index.html

## 2.1.1    PC Ownership

Fundamental to this issue of access is the question of the access devices themselves. Currently, the most common and popular means of getting accessibility or connection to the Internet is through a personal computer (PC). However, the current landscape may change somewhat when wireless access gains popularity with WAP-enabled devices (e.g hand-phones, palm-tops, etc.), but for the time being, personal computers remain the firm favourite. Unfortunately, separate studies have indicated there are not enough Malaysians who own a PC compared to the size of the population in the country. This is especially obvious when we compare with some of the more developed nations of the world (Table 2) Malaysia, with a rate of 46.1, is ranked ninth in this study, after the U.S.A., Singapore, Australia, New Zealand, U.K., Hong Kong, Japan, and South Korea. It is obvious the number of people who own such devices in Malaysia is significantly smaller when compared with those from the more developed countries around the world. The nation would need to increase this considerably and quickly too, if it wishes to significantly increase the number of Malaysians on the Net. The PC is currently still the main doorway to this digital world.

**Table 2**: PC Ownership

| Country | PC Ownership (per 1,000 people) |
|---|---|
| United States of America | 406.7 |
| Singapore | 399.5 |
| Australia | 362.2 |
| New Zealand | 263.9 |
| United Kingdom | 242.4 |
| Hong Kong SAR | 230.8 |
| Japan | 202.4 |
| South Korea | 150.7 |
| Malaysia | 46.1 |
| Thailand | 19.8 |
| Phillipines | 13.6 |
| Indonesia | 8.0 |
| China | 6.0 |
| India | 2.1 |
| Taiwan | *- not available -* |

**Source** : *World Development Report, 1999/2000*

While the PCs were more commonly found in institutions of higher learning or computer organisations in the past, the user-friendliness of such machines plus the advent of the Internet have made them useful and popular in the homes as well. In Malaysia, one can get the very basic Internet-ready PC for about RM2,500 (USD 657.9). However, this does not include the cost of Internet access. Even though the Internet charges in Malaysia may not be the lowest in the region, they are comparable to that of a neighbouring Asian country like Singapore. This is shown in table 3.

## 2.1.2    Network Access Charges

The data shown in Table 3 is based on a 40 hour off-peak rate per month.

**Table 3** : Comparative cost of Internet access

| Country | ISP Charge* (USD) |
|---------|-------------------|
| Japan | 84.80 |
| Indonesia | 41.74 |
| New Zealand | 36.80 |
| United States of America | 36.80 |
| Australia | 35.20 |
| United Kingdom | 31.20 |
| South Korea | 28.80 |
| **Malaysia** | 22.15 |
| Singapore | 15.52 |

*based on a 40 hour off-peak rate per month.*

It may seem logical that with such low costs, a large portion of the Malaysian public should be able to afford such access. The cost of Internet access in South Korea is USD28.80, and their Internet population is estimated to be 34.55% of their total population. As a comparison, even though the cost of access in Malaysia is marginally lower than that of South Korea's it only has 6.88% of the population on the Internet. We would have expected this penetration to be at a higher rate. Next, we examine the case for Singapore. The number of Singaporean Internet subscribers is significantly higher than both Malaysia and South Korea, even though they pay a total of USD15.52 for 40 hours of off-peak access. Note that their cost of access is the lowest among the list of countries shown here. However, this may be just a simple analysis based on the data shown here. Obviously, whether one has enough disposable income for such an activity, which some may still perceive as a luxury item, plays a very important role here. This may involve a mindset change.

Consequently, to complete the picture, we would also have to look at the wealth of the country as well. The cost of Internet access as a percentage of the *Gross Domestic Product* (GDP) per capita of the country is shown in table 4.

**Table 4** : Comparative cost of Internet access as a percentage of the *GDP per capita*

| Country | ISP Charge* % of GDP per capita |
|---------|--------------------------------|
| Indonesia | 1.47 |
| Japan | 0.37 |
| Malaysia | 0.24 |
| South Korea | 0.23 |
| New Zealand | 0.22 |
| Australia | 0.17 |
| United Kingdom | 0.15 |
| United States of America | 0.12 |
| Singapore | 0.06 |

Although Malaysians are only paying an equivalent of *USD22.15* for 40 hours of off-peak Internet access, this comes to a total of 0.24% of Malaysia's GDP per capita. With the exception of Japan and Indonesia, all of the other countries in this list have shown a value less than this.

Clearly, for those countries with a large Internet subscriber base, the relative cost of Internet charges as a percentage of their GDP per capita is comparatively low. When such regular payments do not make a big dent in the household disposal income, one may assume many more would come forward to be a part of the Internet phenomena. As an indication, the disposal income for both the rural and urban sectors in Malaysia is shown in the table 5. Note the impact that the cost of this access (**USD** *22.15*) makes on the disposable income for each group

**Table 5** : Household expenses and incomes for the rural and urban sectors in Malaysia

| Household  (monthly) | Urban *(USD)* | Rural *(USD)* |
|---|---|---|
| *Expenses* | 511 | 334 |
| *Income* | 843 | 413 |
| *Disposal Income* | 332 | 79 |

**Source** : *Malaysia Yearbook of Statistics, 1998 & 2000*

Owning a PC so that one can access the Internet and the vast storehouse of information that comes with it at one's leisure would probably be the first step towards building a nation of ICT-savvy citizens. As in any household purchase, the cost of the PC would play a very important role. Unfortunately, for the past several years, there has not been any noticeable sharp falls in their retail prices which we believe if left to the current market forces and constraints, will either migrate to a lower price – *slowly,* or at worst, not at all. However, this is only one part of the big equation. Initiatives of any kind to lower the prices are always most welcomed, but it is not just this alone that will bring about the elimination of the gulf that currently exists between the information *"haves"* and *"have-nots"*. Training and awareness activities to influence the mindset of a large proportion of the society are also needed urgently.

# 3    Strategic Intervention

The adoption of ICT across the population, in particular, the Internet, will probably not improve, if this is left to the market forces alone. In such a situation, only the rich will benefit. ICT adoption needs to be addressed from several aspects. It is just not about having more of the population signing up with the friendly neighbourhood Internet Service Provider (ISP). Neither is it just about buying a PC for home use as well. Other important elements of the infostructure, for example, appropriate software & applications, standards & protocols, etc. have to be quickly put in place too.

An obvious indicator of the state of the telecommunications infrastructure of a nation is the number of telephone subscribers in the country. This is shown in table 6 for several countries. For a technologically advanced country like Japan, there are 64 million telephone subscribers, and if we take into account the size of the Japanese population, the ratio of the population to telephones is about 2:1. This ratio is about the same for the United Kingdom, but is much higher than that of the United States. Within some of the member states of *the Association of South-East Nations* (ASEAN), this ratio is significantly higher for some of these countries. For example, for a highly populated country like Indonesia, that has a population of 206 million, the ratio of people to a phone is 162. This is a far cry from that of the more developed countries of the world, where this ratio is just under two per phone. However, one must also appreciate that geographically, Indonesia is quite dispersed. Setting up an adequate telecommunication infrastructure to cover all of its 17,508 islands[7] is a very challenging task, not to mention, an expensive one indeed.

**Table 6**: Number of telephone subscribers

| Country | Telephone Subscribers | Ratio (# Pop. per Phone) |
|---|---|---|
| Australia | 8,700,000 | 2.1 |
| China | 105,000,000 | 12.0 |
| Hong Kong SAR | 4,470,000 | 1.5 |
| India | 12,000,000 | 81.9 |
| Indonesia | 1,276,600 | 161.6 |
| Japan | 64,000,000 | 2.0 |
| Malaysia | 4,154,193 | 5.0 |
| New Zealand | 1,700,000 | 2.2 |
| Phillipines | 1,900,000 | 38.4 |
| Singapore | 1,400,000 | 2.5 |
| South Korea | 16,600,000 | 2.8 |
| Taiwan | 11,526,000 | 1.9 |
| Thailand | 1,553,200 | 38.8 |
| United Kingdom | 29,500,000 | 2.0 |
| United States of America | 182,558,000 | 1.5 |

Compared to many of the countries in the region, Malaysia may have a significantly large number of homes with telephone access and a much higher Internet penetration as well. However, this penetration rate is still far behind that of the more advanced countries in the world. Evidently, having a good telecommunication infrastructure is just not enough. A closer examination at some of those countries that are already significantly advanced in this field suggests that there should also be concerted efforts in other areas (mindsets, cultural differences, etc.) as well.

Table 7 shows the ratio of the number of PCs to the number of Internet subscribers. The United Kingdom, with about 20 million registered Internet subscribers and 242.2 PCs per 1,000 of their population, has a ratio of PCs to Internet subscribers of 1:1.137. The United States has shown a slightly lower value at 1:1.048. For Malaysia, with a total population of 22 million people, the ratio (1:1.108) is quite similar to these two countries. None of the 15 countries studied here has shown a ratio of less than one. We believe the optimal value would be one, i.e. one access device (which may not necessarily be a PC) per registered Internet user for several reasons. Firstly, with the proliferation of the Internet, one may be able to afford *not to share* such access devices with anyone else. Moreover, they may need to gain access at any time from anywhere. The network access devices has become personalised in nature – just like a wristwatch. Secondly, if efforts to quickly lower the cost of such devices are successful, there may not be any need to share them. In such a scenario, the ratio may even be higher, i.e. maybe two or even three of these access devices to one Internet account. Such a scenario may already be unfolding in those richer countries in this list (table 7).

**Table 7**: Internet Absorption

| Country | PCs to Subscriber ratio |
|---|---|
| Australia | 1.220 |
| China | 1.884 |
| Hong Kong SAR | 1.808 |
| India | 2.578 |
| Indonesia | 20.634 |
| Japan | 2.531 |
| Malaysia | 1.108 |
| New Zealand | 1.786 |
| Phillipines | 3.100 |
| Singapore | 2.777 |
| South Korea | 1.737 |
| Taiwan | *not available* |
| Thailand | 9.114 |
| United Kingdom | 1.137 |
| United States of America | 1.048 |

With about 1.5 million Internet subscribers in the country, and over 4 million fixed line residential subscribers[8], Malaysia may have sufficient fixed line network infrastructure to cater for any immediate and huge increase in the number of Internet subscribers without the need of having to expand the infrastructure aspects at this point in time. Additionally, with the emergence of the *Wireless Application Protocol* (WAP) in recent years, wireless access will gain more acceptance and popularity. Consequently, access to the Internet will no longer be dependent on the fixed line communication networks anymore. The network infrastructure will not be the major concern in the near future. What the Government needs to do is to encourage lowering the cost of personal computers quickly enough so that they are more affordable. With the ongoing efforts to increase the performance of these computing devices, such as improved manufacturing processes, etc. the relative cost of computing is already coming down. Such efficiencies would, ultimately, be passed on to the consumers, driving the overall cost of computing further down. On the software side, strong interests in making useful and reliable software available with minimal or no charge, in the form of the freeware movement will also bring about considerable savings in the cost of PC ownership. For example, the Star Office freeware, running on the *Linux* operating system (another freeware) has the looks and feel of the popular Microsoft Office suit, but is distributed free of charge! Although it is not receiving the wide appeal or popularity which we believe it deserves, eventual wide spread acceptance in pre-loading it in new home PCs can drive the prices down further. We feel that technically, in no way are these products inferior to their more popular cousins.

**Figure 1**: Average Annual Household Income (in USD)

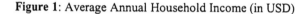

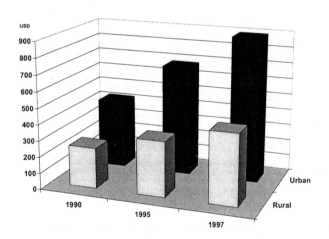

Figure 1 shows the disparity between the average annual income of rural and urban areas for a period of over 17 years in Malaysia. Even though the income for the rural inhabitants has increased in the period shown, the actual amount is still lagging behind those living in the urban areas. Equally important, notice the gulf between the two has increased over the period. This widening income inequality in the country was brought about mainly by the difference in the rates of growth of the rural and urban economies. The agriculture sector, which was the mainstay of the rural economy grew at only 2.0 % per annum, compared with the double-digit growth rates of the manufacturing sector. As a consequent of this slowing down in the agriculture sector, there was a movement of workers to more remunerative jobs in the manufacturing and service sectors. Not surprisingly, these two sectors are mainly located in the urban areas.

It would be grossly unfair and incorrect if the conclusion from the data presented in the preceding paragraphs is that the Malaysian Government has been sitting idly watching from the sidelines and not doing anything to stem this widening rift between the two main sectors of the population. In the *Seventh Malaysian Plan*, the Malaysian Government has clearly identified seven key strategies to narrow the economic differences between those in the rural with those in the urban areas[8]. Increasing the number of Internet subscribers alone but neglecting the PC ownership issue may not be sufficient to bridge the digital divide for Malaysia. Programmes to address this and other issues that we have described in the previous sections which are related to the Malaysian Digital Divide must be put in place quickly. Such programmes will accelerate the penetration of ICT to the whole nation so that the people can begin to exploit the economic benefits associated with it. In addition, such programmes may also address some of the challenges that the country is facing as a result of globalisation.

Unfortunately, such initiatives when left on their own and either through private or even commercial efforts, will not gain enough support to create the much needed critical mass to make a difference. Many of these initiatives would need initial strategic interventions from the Government. In addition, legal as well as economic rules may have to be redefined to promote the acceptance of new technologies, regardless of whether this is towards the lowering of import duties of key computer components or otherwise. The Government, with all its immense resources at its disposal, can initiate massive programmes throughout the country to gain the attention, interest and commitment from the public in order to make it a success. Such initiatives would be in addition to other economic or financial incentives that the Government can offer through the relevant Ministries to the private sector. One such initiative is the Universal Services Provision (USP) Fund which will help finance projects to expand ICT infrastructures that may otherwise be uneconomic for the service providers to invest[9]

In the next few sections we will look closely at some of the solutions that may address several key aspects of the digital divide.

## 4    Cost of Access

One obvious solution to address some aspects of the challenges described in the previous sections would be to lower the price of the access devices. Encouraging increased competition within the PC industry may be one way in which the price of PCs may come down quickly enough. Moreover, our local PC industry will also have to broaden their markets, to target not only the local markets, but global ones as well. The anticipated sales volume within the country may not be enough for them to enjoy the associated economies of scale to lower their selling prices further. Government intervention to support such initiatives should be encouraged, as such price reductions will be vital in making these information access devices more affordable. Furthermore, in many of the advanced Western nations, there are usually several Internet Service Providers, and the competition they provide may promote the cost of access to be competitive. Within Malaysia, the Government has already granted licenses to several more operators to manage such services. Licenses to operate such services should be increased, not decreased. However, this is only one part of the solution. On a broader perspective, such solutions may involve various alternatives. Lower prices, leasing arrangements, and even free computer deals may bridge the digital gap and make the cost of access affordable for many.

## 5  Expanding Community Access Centers

Even though prices of computing devices and Internet access fee may drop, it is unlikely they will fall to a point where most homes will have computers and Internet access quickly enough so that the people may enjoy the advantages and not be left behind in the current transition to a new economy. Therefore, some solutions to address these gaps should also be provided. An interim solution may lie in providing Internet access at community access centers for those who cannot afford to have such access in the comfort of their homes or work place. These are usually the minorities, for example, people earning lower incomes, those with lower education levels, and the unemployed, etc.

Alternatively, the wealthy companies in the country should be encouraged to donate computers, appropriate software or maybe even set up such community centers for these purposes. The Government should actively promote such schemes by providing sufficient financial incentives to attract more corporations to participate, e.g. allowing hefty corporate tax deductions, etc. Some Asian countries are already adopting such a strategy.

## 6  Building Awareness

Many may have already embraced ICT. Yet, there are many more who may not have. This latter group probably does not realize that this technology is crucial and relevant to their lives. Initiatives should also be started to reach out to such groups and let them know why it is important that they should become involved -- how ICT and the related technologies can open new opportunities, and make a difference for them and their children.

On the other hand, bringing new technology to the population is one thing, but getting them to embrace this wholeheartedly is another, as there may be other real concerns that can prove to be major barriers. For instance, valid concerns have been raised about children's safety while using the Internet and issues like this have to be tackled before the Government can introduce the Internet to more homes. While there are currently software systems that can bar minors from visiting pornographic sites, for example, many may not be aware of them. Significant pogress has also been made in other areas that are of major concerns to many families. For example, web sites that provide guidance to the parents and teachers in selecting what is culturally acceptable, in the local languages have also been developed (see http://www.bijak.net.my).

# 7  Lowering language and cultural barriers

As we have outlined in the earlier sections, issues related to the infrastructure is only just one from a list of contributing factors. There are also language and cultural barriers that would have to be addressed, as the Internet today is predominantly Western and Anglophone. What is acceptable to the Western society may not be to another society, and in a population where English is not our Mother tongue, accepting and understanding the contents of web pages in this language can sometimes prove to be a tremendous challenge. The latter issue is even more pertinent in many other parts of Asia. Education or training programmes should also be provided for those who may have missed the opportunity, but remain keen to learn. The older segments of society who have not been exposed to these new technologies should also be encouraged to undergo such assimilation programmes. Minority segments of the society or those who are disadvantaged should also be encouraged to pick up sufficient ICT skills. For example, within the Malaysian context, the percentage of women who are computer literate is still low compared to the men [10]. Moreover, the literacy rate in Malaysia is in the region of 73% to 80% [11]. Fundamentally, this means that three out of four Malaysians are able to read and write. However, this need not necessarily be in the current language of the Internet – English. Suitable educational programmes will also have to be developed to help them assimilate into the Internet society. Content development in any of the local Asian languages in the country should be encouraged too.

# 8  Desa Digital

"Desa Digital" (Digital Villages) is a nation-wide programme that will encourage the application of ICT to all segments of the rural community. It emphasizes the innovative use of ICT to enable and sustain economic growth and prosperity for those who have been sidelined by the global information tidal wave that is currently sweeping through the world. Elements within this programme basically address many of the major challenges of the digital divide that are of great concern to the country. Such a programme may accelerate the penetration of ICT within the Malaysia so that the nation can be better prepared and equipped to move into the K-economy. In addition, it is also expected to help develop and strengthen the electronic community of entrepreneurs so that they can create employment for the surrounding communities. That is not all. Desa Digital will attempt to overcome the issues related to access and affordability of ICT for all segments of the Malaysian society, regardless of their race, creed or physical location. This programme is also expected to promote and facilitate a wider acceptance of teleworking. Through the setting up of a network of *digital centers* throughout the country, it is hoped that there will be a reduction of social problems facing the youth of the country whereby their energies may be harnessed for better and more productive use.

Generally, people migrate to the cities because of the better economic opportunities found in such areas. Unfortunately, the quantum and speed of this migration has placed a considerable strain on the physical as well as social infrastructures of the major towns and cities. Insufficient housing, traffic congestion, waste disposal, insufficient clean water supply, etc. are just some examples of the consequence of this. With the centers set up, and better opportunities for employment, either through actual work at the centers or through teleworking, there may no longer be a need for them to migrate from the rural areas to the urban areas anymore.

**Table 8** : *Rural population as* a percentage of the total population in Malaysia

|  | 1970 | 1980 | 1991 |
|---|---|---|---|
| **Rural Population** | 73.2 % | 65.6 % | 49.0 % |

Table 8 gives some indication of the trend in the migration of the rural population over a period of about 20 years. There may be a host of reasons why this is happening, but in search for a better livelihood by being at the center of better economic opportunities is at the top of the list [8].

To ensure the success of the *Desa Digital* programme, MIMOS will be working closely with government agencies, non-governmental organisations, as well as the other appropriate partners. The programme is divided into two major components. In the first part, the appropriate physical infrastructures will have to be put into place where none exists or is grossly insufficient. Under the proposal, it is anticipated that there will be a total of 42 such centers developed within the period of five years. Such digital centers will serve their surrounding communities within a radius of 2 to 10 kilometers. In addition to providing the basic Internet access, these centers will also provide facilities for teleworking, distance learning, community center, application development, content aggregation as well as a public service outlet. With the expected influence of these centers on the surrounding areas, we expect some 210,000 people would directly benefit from this programme and become active participants in the digital economy by 2005. Under the second part of this programme, and moving in tandem, will be the development of various contents or applications that will encourage the assimilation of ICT into the very social fabrics of the community. However, it is obvious that MIMOS will have to work with the content experts to co-develop these applications quickly and efficiently.

Mimos submitted this *Desa Digital* programme to the Malaysian Government for funding towards the end of last year. We are now awaiting for the relevant Ministry to make the final decision.

# 9 Conclusions

When the Internet first began in the early Eighties, in this country, many would have thought that this was just another of those *"techie"* fads that would quickly fade into oblivion - just like *bell-bottoms and hoopla-hoops*. However, as time has shown, not only has it become firmly entrenched in the technical arena, but it has also become a vital ingredient for the economic survival of a country. With its ease of use and extensive reach, no one should be left behind in learning how to use it for personal gain - be it economically or otherwise. This will be especially crucial as Malaysia advances into the 21st Century and the K-economy, where having access to computers and the Internet may be the key to unleashing the inherent potential in each and every one of us so that we can become more productive and successful members of society. A local writer[11] aptly summed this up with the following quotation,

> Give a man a fish and you feed him for a day,
> Teach him how to fish and you feed him for life.
> Teach a man how to tap the Net and cast it wide,
> And you'll teach him how to create wealth.

As we have illustrated in the preceding sections, there are several important contributing factors to the Digital Divide, viz.

✓ the wealth of the nation,
✓ the technical infostructure,
✓ the (computer) literacy rate and/or mindset of the population.

In addition to this set of challenges, Malaysia, as a small Asian country does have additional and unique ones to overcome. Ours is a multiracial and multi-religious society and although each community shares similar core values, there are significant differences. In addition, while many Malaysians can communicate in English, the national language that unites the various races is Malay.

PC adoption and usage among Malaysians is growing and the challenge is to increase this rate. To be on par with the rest of the developed world, we will need to expand our computer density to 7.7 million PCs - an additional growth of 5.2 million PCs over the next few years[13]. Within the country and in many places around the world too, various initiatives are in already in progress to come up with a more affordable computer, without sacrificing any of the main functionalities. Furthermore, we believe that such initiatives should not only be targeted towards the PC alone, but to extend this to all the essential peripherals as well. Generally, a PC alone may be insufficient to cover even the most basic of computing needs, for the users would need access to printers, scanners, modems, as well as some of the more essential software. All these can add up to a very hefty sum of money.

Secondly, a low computer literacy rate level will only lead to an equally worrisome low level of PC ownership, for the computer illiterate would not be aware of the advantages and benefits of owning one. However, solutions to reverse this trend could be more challenging, for they may have to involve significant curriculum changes in the schools. Basic computing courses may have to be introduced at all the schools to equip the younger generation with basic computing skills and knowledge. Various initiatives by either the private or public sectors to address this issue are already operating on the ground, e.g. the Government sponsored National Smart Schools programme, the MIMOS driven Smart Learning Environment, etc. However, there is much more that the Malaysian Government will need to address with much vigor.

Malaysia may already have sufficient financial resources as well as the necessary infrastructure (fixed telecommunication network) [9] in place to fuel any further growth in the number of people connected to the Internet. However, there will need to be stronger commitment and support from both the Government and the Malaysian public for this to succeed. Appropriate development plans must be quickly put into place to address these challenges as the nation cannot afford to be left behind in the race to be remain competitive enough to face the many economic challenges in the new world order. Perhaps more importantly, the Government must also realize that there may be other viable alternatives that may not necessarily require huge financial investments. Malaysia must continuously strive to increase the tele-densities and improve the service levels, even though these may be at adequate levels. Although the game has started, we will need to maintain and even increase the nation's pace so that we remain competitive in the lead pack.

## Acknowledgements

The authors would like to thank Dr. *Mohamed Awang Lah* for his invaluable comments and suggestions in helping us to refine this paper.

## Disclaimer

The opinions expressed here only reflect those of the authors and cannot be assumed to reflect those of their employer, or any of her subsidiaries, etc.

# References

1. Yearbook of Statistics, Malaysia 2000.

2. *"Dr M: Pursue knowledge vigorously'"*, New Straits Times, page 2, August 22nd 2000.

3. *"Infostructure: A Key Concept in the Information Society"*, Alfons Cornella.
   http://www.infonomics.net/cornella/ainfoang.pdf

4. *"Alberta's Information Technology and Telecommunications Infrastructure: Building on Our Strengths,"* Marshall M. Williams.
   *http://www.gov.ab.ca/sra/publicdocs/itt/itrpt_to.html*

5. *"CyberSpace across the Sahara: Computing in North Africa"*, A. Danowitz, Y. Nassef, and S. E. Goodman, Communications of the ACM 38(12), page 23-28, 1995.

6. *"Cheaper Internet access rates being considered"*, New Straits Times, page 7, January 23rd 2000.

7. http://www.tourismindonesia.com/

8. Seventh Malaysian Plan.

9. *Local e-readiness at a high level"*, Computimes, March 1st. 2001, pp 10.

10. *Women told to pick up IT Skills'"*, New Straits Times, page 16, August 22nd 2000.

11. *thnologue: Languages of the World*, Thirteenth Edition, Editor Barbara F. Grimes, 1999.

12. *A Kampung Gets IT"*, SH Lim.
    http://itmy.newscom-asia.com/jan1m20/foc1.htm

13. http://www.pcoc.com.my/why.html

# Enterprise Alliance and Virtue Enterprise: A Systematic Analysis and Theoretical Explanation

Tao Meng[1]    Ning Ding[2]

[1]Industrial Economics, Dongbei University of Finance & Economics, Dalian, P.R. China

mengtao@mba-edu.net

[2]Industrial Economics, Dongbei University of Finance & Economics, Dalian, P.R. China

emilyding@mba-edu.net

**Abstract.** Internet enterprise organization ("EO") with representation of enterprise alliance ("EA") and virtue enterprise (VE) is now a prevailing form of organization in developed countries. This paper attempts to put EA and VE together in a systematic analysis way. We first explain some basic problems on EA and VE as two forms of Internet organization in Internet Economy, such as their concepts, forms and differences, then, we discuss how EA and VE come into beings with the theory of transaction cost, we finally draw a conclusion and further develop the effects on them in China.

## 1    Systematic Analysis

The revolution of Information Technology ("IT") and the integration of global economy make the EO forms in great change since 1980s, on the background that EA and VE as new prevailing forms in developed countries, take increasing attention in both theory and business circles. EA is a kind of loose combination in advantage compensation and division cooperation by two or above enterprises for the purpose of common interest, cooperation, risk-sharing, the main forms of which are joint-ventures, cooperative development, brand production and franchise, whilst VE is a kind of enterprises featured function specialization, cooperated operation, structure decentralization by way of transferring hard and non-efficient production and service to other enterprises and only conserving the most functional of its own in order to best develop the advantages of scared resources. There are two major forms: one is virtue function, which the function of technology development, production and sales is in charge of other enterprises, the other is virtue form, which breaks its original organization form and wholly relies on Internet, such as virtue banks and virtue shops. The spirit of EA and VE are EO forms in re-adjusting resource advantages, that is to say, by constructing EA and VE, the enterprises can re-adjust external resource advantages, break tangible EO borders, shrink EO structure so that the sights of management are widened and super-development are achieved.

Currently, there are no general and clear knowledge on EA and VE. Some learners consider EA as VE with equality, while others think EA is a form of VE. In this paper, we set EA and VE under Internet economy environment in a systematic way. In a keen market competition and fast developing IT age, as Internet-style information structure devastates traditional pyramid-style organization structure, enterprise has to be full of flexibility with the environment changes. On the on hand, flexibility requires spread and fast internal communication ability and self-construction by setting up groups in every department, on the other hand, it also demands external cooperative relationships to apply to environment changes at any time and obtains capability from the external. It therefore, results in the occurrence of Internet EO. According to the two respects of EO flexibility, the contains of the Internet include internal and external internet respectively, in which the internal is centered by internal department, members as Internet nodes in the main form of matrix structure, multi-dimension structure and work-team, while the external is shaped into the relationship among enterprises on the base of the Internet node of other enterprises and itself with the form of EA and VE.

The common characteristics of both EA and VA are multi-cooperation, loose relation, flexibility mechanism, variable form and high efficient operation. However, there exist differences:

I.    Different perspectives of analysis. EA and VA are two sides of a coin. EA refers to organic of many enterprises and it mainly describes the alliance of many enterprises, while VE means an enterprise which does virtue operation and it focuses on how a single enterprise conducts virtue operation.

II.   Different degree of form shown. Though both EA and VE are by way of external resources, degree of using resources are different. EA can only transfer the non self-fulfill or not high efficient tasks to other enterprises and preserve its core competition power, whilst VE in general deliver all the basic business functions to other enterprises and conserve the tasks on communication and re-adjustment. That is to say, VE depends more on computer web than that of EA, so it is just a "hulk".

III.  Different causes of occurrence. EA is formed by organized market, while VE comes into power by marketed enterprise. The next part of this paper will give a detailed demonstration about the following charts.

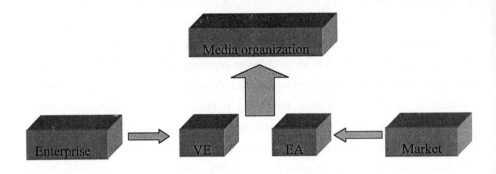

Chart 1. The relationship between EA and VE

## 2  Theoretical Explanation

Generally speaking, market is a free trade under price mechanism in classic economics, whilst enterprise can come to trade completely through executive order, the relationship on which is little discussion. The one that put market and enterprise closely together is transaction cost concept. It described precisely that market and enterprise are two substitutive mechanisms of resource allocation, between which the boarders is determined by the comparative results of marginal enterprise organization cost and marginal market transaction cost. However, it is illustrated in The Nature of The Firm (R.H.Coase, 1937) that an enterprise is only a classic concept with the ownership and control rights united and it still uses "the one into two approach" to market and enterprise. As the time goes by, the simple approach has failed to detail the complicated economic organizations in modern world; even Coase himself is committed to the media organization between market and enterprise. He has ever said as a substitute of price mechanism, vertical integration is in great difference among different industries and different enterprises (R.H.Coase, 1991). Therefore, market and enterprise transactions each are only two special examples of all kinds, among which a great deal are in form of media organizations. Though, it did not catch one's eye, western economists called it "the third organization form" or "media organization", the basic features on which are dual, that is visible hand and invisible hand on behalf of executive plan control and market price mechanism respectively. Furthermore, media organization can play an important roll in resource allocation for enterprise itself and between enterprises and consumers----market in enterprise, as enterprise in market----media organization is shaped in the course of their transferring, shown as organized market and marketed enterprise. Organized Market is converted market transaction into intra-enterprise business with the market relationship into intra-enterprise governance relationship, though it comes to no enterprise in the end, it is only a organizational market on the basis of market relationship, to the contrary, enterprise-marketing means introducing market mechanism into enterprise and external enterprising transaction into market transaction.

The theory of media organization open a new perspective on complicated economic organization, thus we have a new knowledge about EA and VE. EA is a loose combination of many enterprises with the essence of long-time contracts between enterprises. The two parties of EA require a long-run cooperative relationship burdened by contracts. The single enterprise in EA is undependable and keeps self-operating rights. It belongs to media organization. While VE is somehow another kind EO. It increases the independence of its departments through internalizing market mechanism, makes the original executive relationship into market relationship, further transfer non-efficient production and service to other enterprises in the result that enterprise itself has no such function.

The corollary of EA and VE can also be stated by media organization theory. As a media organization, EA and VE not only save transaction costs, but also avoid more organization costs. EA is such a non-competitive system that simplified transaction costs, lowered market risks by way of sharing information, channels and members. Since an enterprise fully depended on executive order in resource allocation can also come up with such problems as non-efficient management system, asymmetric information and higher organization costs, VE can benefit more to some extent.

## 3　Conclusions

As the above-mentioned, EA and VE as a media organization, play a key roll in modern society. They show a guidance of management idea, organization form and operation patterns for modern enterprises in new centuries. It also exhibits a gentile and united Internet function on EO in a center of information technology. Furthermore, they have special meanings for China in macro respects. They perfect market economic system, provide an idea of re-organization of industry structure, push the reform of medium-small size enterprises, promote the develop of enterprise groups, increase the international competition. All in all, EA and VE break the pure borders between market and enterprise, re-adjust the external resources, destroy tangible boarders of EO, weaken the initial organization structure and widen the enterprise management. EA and VE are big tendency of global enterprise organization in the 21$^{st}$ centuries.

## References

R.H. Coase, 1937 : *"The Nature of The Firm"*, " *Property Rights and Institutional Change"*, etc.

# Challenges in Building Design and the Construction Industry: The Future of Design and Construction in the Internet Age

Sanghyun Lee

Ewha Womans University, 11-1 Daehyun-dong, Seodaemun-gu, Seoul, 120-750, Korea
sanglee@mm.ewha.ac.kr

**Abstract.** This paper aims at reviewing the changes in building design and the construction industry brought by the Internet and also addressing the challenges for the future of design and construction in the Internet age. A review on the industry reveals that there were a number of remarkable changes in building design and the construction industry in terms of its organizational structure and knowledge representation. The former includes facilitation of horizontal and virtual business organizations, and shortened value chain while the latter is about the change in means of communications. These changes provide a good opportunity for those in the construction industry to meet clients' demands for consistency in quality, standardized process management and effective control of time and other resources.

## 1  Introduction

The Internet, whose growth stemmed from the necessity to efficiently share study results among research institutions, has expanded into new realms such as e-commerce and public service, i.e., on-line government. Its influence has brought great changes upon building design and the construction industry as well. The construction industry has a unique organizational structure and business value chain unlike those seen in other forms of commerce or the public sector; it is a structure that requires seamlessly integrated collaboration of multiple expert groups that are in charge of the various sub-processes that comprise the whole process. Therefore, the Internet was welcomed as a useful tool to facilitate communication among expert groups that comprise the whole process.

While it is true that the Internet is a useful tool for the construction industry, currently the rate of Internet usage in this field lags behind that of other business activities or even public sector service. The reason behind the slow progress in the spread of Internet usage in the construction realm is due to the fact that, unlike other business sectors or even public service, no consensus has been formed regarding the means of representation of knowledge. In other words, each expert group in a construction project employs its own unique way of communicating information. Therefore, human intervention is necessary whenever a piece of information is transferred from one group to another, in order for the receiving party to truly comprehend that information. Another reason behind such lack of progress in making full use of the Internet in the construction business stems from the fact that it is a process of creative activity and its operation is different from, say, a manufacturing industry producing pre-determined goods in a pre-determined way. This characteristic of the construction industry makes it difficult to define its production system.

In this study, we will observe the key features of the construction industry before the arrival of the Internet, from two perspectives: its organizational structure and means of information communication. Then we will move on to discuss the changes occurring in this realm with the Internet and the subsequent means of communication. Lastly, we will focus on the direction of future change that the Internet poses.

# 2 The Construction Industry -- before the Internet

## 2.1 Fragmentation of the Business Value Chain

The construction process is comprised of a group of multiple sub-processes, or various phases: feasibility study, architectural programming, conceptual design, design development, bidding, construction, and facilities management. Each individual process requires collaboration of multiple consulting groups that comprise the process. In particular, the collaboration of many consultants is necessary in the design development phase. For instance, the structural engineer, mechanical engineer, electrical engineer, and experts of other specialized facilities need to cooperate for successful development of a design.

The construction industry features various forms or organizations depending on how the sub-processes interact. The needs of each specific construction project and the strategy of the company determine what form or shape the organization takes. Traditionally, the industry has exhibited one of two forms of organization. The first occurs when collaborating expert groups comprise each process inside a large organization. This is an organization where detailed processes and expert groups are vertically integrated. The other most widely observed form of organization is one in which individual companies in charge of the sub-processes jointly execute the project.

In both types of organizations, the overall construction process is severely fragmented, which is why coordination is a major factor that determines the success of a construction project. A vertically integrated organization upon closer inspection is actually comprised of small-sized and locally independent businesses. Since these vertically integrated businesses take up only a small portion of the overall construction industry, the fragmentation issue is a crucial problem. This is well illustrated in the fact that the top ten U.S. construction firms' share of total revenues in the sector is less than 5% as of 1996.[1]

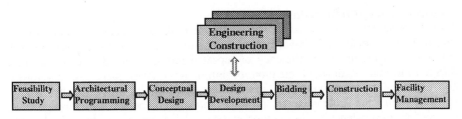

**Fig. 1.** The Processes of Building Design in the Construction Industry

## 2.2    Islands of Automation

The fragmented industrial structure can be seen in the use of information technology as well. The construction industry is one of the areas where information technology was adopted and effectively employed. In structural engineering, software for structural analysis has been in use for some time; capacity analysis and HVAC design software is available in facilities planning; documentation and visual presentation software for architectural design; and specialized software for construction. Therefore, it can be safely said that no sub-process exists in construction that does not employ software based on information and telecommunication technology.

However, since each software was developed with the exclusive goal of meeting its purpose only, each reflects its own chosen method of knowledge representation, thereby lacking interoperability. To describe it otherwise, each software is effective in processing information within its own domain, but an additional task of modification and processing is required in order for the same information to be understood and processed by other software that supports other sub-processes in a collaborative setting. Spiro Pollalis calls this state of non-compatibility among different realms "islands of automation.[2]"

Thus, collaboration in and among the sub-processes is inefficient, since project information is often transferred from paper to computer, back to paper, and finally back to a paper again it travels among firms.

## 2.3    Problems in Traditional Collaboration

### (1) The Need for Timely Information Exchange

In collaboration among the complicated and intricately linked sub-processes of construction, it is difficult to provide the right information to each sub-process in a timely manner. Users of the information are multifaceted and it is not easy to gain access to necessary information in the right format inside the fragmented organizational structure. Fragmentation of the business value chain and islands of automation undermine the efficiency of collaboration among sub-processes. Without timely access to information, delays in tasks ensue, as well as execution of erroneous or unnecessary tasks, thereby causing loss of labor and time, not to mention the diminished quality of the final product.

## (2) Redundancy of Information

Another issue faced by the construction process is the redundancy of unnecessary information. As discussed above, lack of compatibility in the software used in each sub-process leads to the inefficiency of repeated reproduction of information in a different format. Redundant creation of information takes place in two forms: conversion of information into a new format that can be processed by another software, and the guarantee to promote human comprehension through data conversion. Redundancy of information in different formats creates loss of labor and time resources in having to recreate the same information, and the errors that take place in the conversion process can lead to compromising the quality of the design and construction project and failure of the project, in worst cases.

## (3) Loss of Semantics

As was discussed earlier, the construction industry is an area where the ingenuity of the designer is a highly crucial element that determines the success of the project. Frequent conversion and processing of information created in one phase for use in the next phase has the potential to disrupt seamless transfer of the originality of the design and the ideas behind it.

# 3 The Demand of the Buyers and the Introduction of the Internet

## 3.1 The Demand of the Buyers

The clients of a construction project demand the same standards of quality from architects. They also call for standard criteria in cost and construction period. Chris Castle summarizes the demands of the client as follows[3]: "A recent survey of the top 400 building owners in the United States revealed that owners are increasingly asking for greater focus on quality. A senior project engineer for Eli Lilly explained that they expect their suppliers(architects) to meet the standard Eli Lilly uses to measure its own internal processes. Eli Lilly's Economic Value Added metric is a combination of initial capital cost, operating costs, and accelerated time to market...the new emphasis on process improvement and reduction in cycle time have construction industry leaders turning to information technology for new capability. The increasing technical complexity of buildings, sophistication of customers, and time pressure in the construction industry are creating a demand for an efficient, economical means of inter-organizational communication."

## 3.2 Introduction of the Internet

What will be the economic means of communication among sub-processes? How can the fragmented construction processes be dynamically integrated? In addressing this pressing need, we find a potential for resolution in the Internet. There also arises the need to address the issue of overcoming the islands of automation.

This study will illustrate the features of the Internet as a communications tool that can be used effectively to integrate the construction process, as well as some of the current discussions on ways to overcome the quandary of islands of automation.

## (1) Existing Means for Communication in Building Design and the Construction Industry

<Table 1> is a depiction of the communications tools traditionally employed by the construction industry.

**Table 1.** Communication Means used in Building Design and the Construction Industry [4]

|  | On-site | Remote |
|---|---|---|
| Synchronous | Face-to-face | Telephone |
| Asynchronous | Memos | Fax, letters, voice messages, Internet |

The face-to-face meetings where the parties gather at one site for discussion at a given time can be categorized as an on-site synchronous method of communication. Although this method is the most effective means of communication, it entails cost in execution since it requires the presence of all necessary parties at one location at a certain time. Dana Cuff's research shows that how much time is useless spent on preparing the face-to-face meetings.[5] Therefore, it is becoming a general trend to avoid such face-to-face interaction as a means of communication in light of the loss of time.

A good example of communication on a synchronous basis from remote locations is use of the telephone, which is still widely used as an effective means of communication. However, it also comes with the inconvenience of having to arrange the time for the telephone call, which is keenly experienced in the case of international collaboration, where members of the project are geographically dispersed, and frequently are calling in from different time zones. Memos are often used by members of the same construction office to communicate when they are working in different time slots, a good example of on-site asynchronous means of communication.

As seen in <Table 1> remote asynchronous communication tools are fax, letters, and answering machines. The Internet is another example, but it has different characteristics from those of other remote asynchronous communication tools, which are described below.

**(2) Characteristics of the Internet as an Advanced Means of Communication among Different Expert Groups**

*1) Demand-oriented Communication*
The overriding feature of the Internet that differentiates it from other types of remote asynchronous communication tools is that it is demand-oriented. In other words, other means of remote asynchronous communication tools, such as letters, voice messages and facsimile are supply-oriented, where the information user unilaterally sends information regardless of when the information will be used. In comparison, Internet communication allows the user to receive information when it is needed. Therefore, while letters and faxes are an information sender-oriented tool, the Internet is a user demand-oriented tool. This alternative provides timely information exchange, which was a major concern of the construction industry in the pre-Internet age.

*2) Interactive Communication*
Another aspect of the Internet is the supply of interactive information. It is rarely the case to receive accurate and adequate information through one exchange or communication of the need for information. The Internet enables interactive provision of information through various trials and errors on the part of the user.

*3) Multi-User-Involved Communication*
Another advantage of using the Internet in communication in the construction process is the simultaneous sharing of information by multiple users. Parties that need to collaborate can have access to information being exchanged by others in the same time frame. In effect, information transaction among relevant parties takes place simultaneously and not consecutively, enabling a faster and accurate decision-making process.

# 4    The Construction Industry – after the arrival of the Internet

The advantages of the Internet discussed above have brought major changes in the way collaboration takes place in the construction industry. Traditional face-to-face meetings are slowly being replaced by remote asynchronous communication as a means of collaboration. This trend is creating changes in the organizational structure of the industry, and efforts are underway to standardize inter-organizational communication means.

## 4.1    Changes in the Organizational Structure

### (1) Changes in the Inter-Organizational Structure

*1) From Physical Integration to Virtual Integration Centering on the Standardized Building Data Model: from Vertical Integration to Horizontal Integration*

The traditional structure of the construction industry was one in which a large organization controlled all sub-processes of the construction project in a single corporate structure. In most cases, the entire process from feasibility study to construction programming, basic design, engineering consultation and construction all took place inside a large corporate entity, which is a single organization. As discussed above, another structure in the construction industry takes place as a lax temporary union of completely independent sub-processes.

The advent of the Internet has brought fundamental changes to such industrial structure. Communication via the Internet and other types of information technology has led to virtual integration of individual units and groups into a corporation-like entity, since it is no longer necessary to have one organization or corporation in charge of independent groups that implement each process. The sophistication of information technology has enabled collaboration that transcends the boundaries of individual companies (and their sub-processes), leading to gains in work efficiency and productivity.[6] Such changes in the way construction companies operate has brought on two economic benefits: the creation of a strong link in the value chain, which maximizes the strength of vertical integration offered by the traditional organization, as well as the competitive edge of individual groups.

## 2) Changes in the Value Chain: the broker becomes obsolete

The Internet renders the information broker obsolete. Traditionally, the role of the information broker in the construction industry was vital in the discovery of adequate sub-processes and procurement of construction material. The broker was the agent of the building client in facilitating all procedures necessary for construction, but the Internet has now made this role unnecessary. However, this is not to say that information brokerage itself is no longer relevant. The need for information brokerage subsists; the traditional broker that served as a go-between for the client and the construction company is being replaced by direct contact between the client and the construction organization.

## 3) Globalization

Remote asynchronous collaboration using the Internet is leading to globalization of the construction organization. Groups that were traditionally located in geographical vicinity, if not the same location, in order to hold meetings in a short time span, are now stepping out of the boundaries of time and space to collaborate widely on a global basis. This was possible due to the breakdown of the time-space barrier through remote-asynchronous collaboration.

## 4) The Architect as an Information Manager

The Internet and information technology is influencing the role of the architect as never before. The architect before the arrival of the Internet was in charge of tasks related to the construction design itself as a part of the overall organization, whereas the architect that uses the Internet is often the information manager that oversees the flow of information inside the collaborative organization. This change stems from the necessity for efficient communication, since it is now beneficial for the success of the project that the architect promotes and controls the exchange of information as a focal point in the process. This is clearly stated by Barrow et al.: "With introducing this information manager to the value chain, communication amongst the team members throughout the design process is greatly simplified. This method generates a more efficient overall design and construction process in what is traditionally a very fragmented group.[7]"

## (2) Changes in the Intra-Organizational Structure

The Internet has changed the inner structure of the sub-processes that form the total construction process. One of the most noticeable changes that are taking place in the individual organizations is the simplification of layers of work division. Traditionally, tasks inside a work group were divided into three layers: trivial information processing, problem-solving and design and management.

However, increased efficiency in communication with the use of the Internet as well as automated computer applications used by each group has diminished the need for the lower layer, where information was manually converted for processing. The designers that form the middle layer of the organization are increasingly solving problems in design, as well as processing and converting information, such as creating layouts and specifications. The workload of project managers that traditionally oversaw communication with clients and inside the organization as well as making decisions is fundamentally decreasing. As the designer takes charge of the communication process inside the team and even with the client, the designer who was until now the middle layer is now expanding to the realm of project management. The role of the project manager, accordingly, now includes participation in the design process itself.

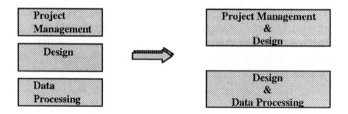

**Fig. 2.** Changes in the Intra-Organizational Structure

In essence, the organization of individual group is shifting from a three-layered structure to a two-layered structure as shown in fig 2.

## 4.2 Changes in Knowledge Representation

## (1) Standardization of Building Representation through Use of the Product Model

Standardization of knowledge representation is a vital precondition for effective remote asynchronous collaboration, since it is necessary to convey information to every member of the project in a way as to allow clear comprehension and not require a face-to-face interaction with a relevant expert or the writer of the information for explanation. Standardization of knowledge representation is an important precondition for enhancing compatibility among computer applications used in each sub-process. Since computers were actively introduced in the construction industry and applications evolved in each sub-process as islands of automation without any viable link, many researchers have explored the issue of interoperability in building representation; RATAS, STEP(ISO 1992), Combine, and IFC, to name a few.[8]

**(2) Integration of Building Design and Construction Processes**
Development of communications tools in the construction industry is in line with standardization, and active study has been taking place to develop means of representing geometric and non-geometric information in an integrated form, as well as comprehensive representation of relevant knowledge. Many proposals have been placed on the table regarding the means of integration, but the most widely considered alternative is the product model. Among the various forms the product model can take, the most favored answer is the core-aspect model approach, shown in <Fig 3,> which is integration of certain aspect models that fit the necessity of each expert involved in a construction process.

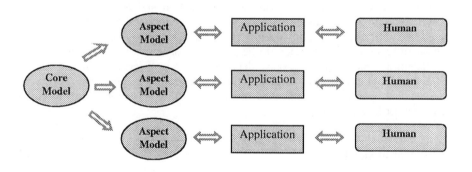

**Fig. 3.** Integration of Building Design and Construction Processes with the Product Model as the focal center(the Core-Aspect Approach)

In the core-aspect model, each expert is able to use only the information that is required (through abstraction) from the core model.
 By using this method, data and knowledge is integrated so as to minimize the need for direct human interaction among involved parties and increase the efficiency of remote asynchronous collaboration.

**(3) Problems that Need to be Addressed in Knowledge Representation**
Efforts are underway to standardize communication means in order to maximize the efficiency of Internet communications, but nonetheless some issues still demand attention.

*1) Transferring Unstructured Information*
The most urgent issue in standardization and integration of communication means lies in the question of how to deliver unstructured information. As was discussed above, the construction industry consists of a series of specialized processes that demand the ingenuity of the designer. In such a creative process, a large part of the generated information is by nature difficult to convey through use of standardized methodology only. Information on form, structure, function and performance can be relatively easy to represent in a standardized format, since such information is usually of a quantitative nature and can be systematically well-defined. However, the task becomes trickier with unstructured information such as the design intent, since it is by definition difficult to define systematically. Development of methodology for effective delivery of non-standardized information such as the designer's intentions is a pressing need at this time.

*2) Passive Database vs. Argumentative Database*
Another concern posed by the collaborative model that is suggested currently is the passive utilization of information and knowledge embedded in the product model that doubles as a database and visual representation of information. An expert involved in the process is unable to recognize the issues that stemmed from his/her decision until he/she actively searches for the necessary information and evaluates his/her own decision. The current databases in use are very passive in that they do not operate on such a scale until a request for evaluation is placed. Thus arises the need to revise the database and its operational system to be more argumentative in nature. Simply put, the collaborative model needs to make decisions on its own regarding if and when to intervene, without having to receive an evaluation request from a human expert. Some of the scholars who have spearheaded research into this new domain are Raymond McCall and Erik Johnson.[9]

## 4.3   Potential Side Effects

Not everything about the introduction of the Internet and the widespread usage of information technology brings positive influences on the construction industry. Thus we will explore some potential side effects that the Internet and information technology can bring to this industry.

### (1) Collapse of Regionalism
The remote asynchronous collaboration model entails standardization of production of construction products. With the elimination of barriers posed by time and space, international collaboration has emerged as a general trend. This has led to the erosion of the foundation for construction that reflects the unique traits of indigenous regions and cultures. This lack of regard for regional characteristics in construction began with the spread of globalization of rational architecture, or internationalism. Internationalism has provided the theoretical and philosophical basis for undermining the values of regional architecture, while the use of standardized construction representation models and remote collaboration led to globalization that could potentially obliterate regional construction. It is a valid and grave concern indeed that the Internet could provide the momentum to internationalism that denies regional identity and render all regional construction one and the same.

## (2) Constraints on Creativity

Standardization of communication through the use of a set of criteria on architectural representation can limit the scope of creativity enjoyed by the architect. History abounds with examples of how differences in architectural representation affected the way an architect exercised creative powers. Perspective, discovered in the Renaissance age, helped further the concept of depth in space in the architectural realm, while a school of architects called The Style refused to adopt the illusionary effects of perspective and steadfastly adhered to axonometric drawings. Both schools of thought created their unique architectural touch. Standardization of communication methods and architectural representation is a double-sided sword: it can help make full use of the Internet while carrying the risk of undermining creative development of architecture.

## 5   Conclusion

The construction industry is going through a major change with the arrival of the Internet. One of the main factors that led to this medium's prevailing influence on this industry lies in the fact that it enables effective asynchronous collaboration from remote locations. Changes in work methodology brought about by the Internet affected the value chain of the construction industry, while influencing the internal structure of sub-processes that form the process as a whole. Such changes can be summarized into two aspects; facilitation of horizontal and virtual business organizations, and shortened value chain.

The Internet is not only affecting the structural aspects of a company, but also the means of communication employed inside that organization. It was a change made to support the new communication tool. Changes in communication means as well as in organizational structures provide a good opportunity for those in the construction industry to meet clients' demands for consistency in quality, standardized process management and effective control of time and other resources.

However, the Internet is a blessing in disguise: it enables creation of new values as well as posing potentially negative side effects. Automation based on the Internet, standardized communication channels, and computer applications can be a threat to regional architecture and the creativity of the architect, which are the unique values of the construction industry. The construction industry will do well to bear in mind that the Internet is an enabling source of power that should be harnessed for effective use and control.

## Reference

1. Reina, Peter and Gary Tulacz. 1997. "The Top 225 Global Contractors," ENR Engineering News Record, August 25. pp. 67-74.
2. Pollalis, S.N., "Beyond Islands of Automation," BOSS, No 4, April 1997, pp 28-29, Bouwkunde, TU-Delft, The Netherlands.)
3. Castle, Christopher nd Pollalis, Spiro. 1998. "On-line Networks for Construction Projects," Harvard Design School.
4. Mitchell, William. 1995. "City of Bits," MIT Press: Cambridge

5. Cuff, Dana. 1992. "Architecture: The Story of Practice," MIT Press
6. Magretta, Joan. 1998. "The Power of Virtual Integration: An Interview with Dell Computer's Michael Dell" in Harvard Business Review pp. 72-85. March-April 1998.
7. Barrow, Larry., Savvides, Andreas., Hou, June-Hao., and Cacace, Katie. 1999. "Margulies & Associates, Inc," Harvard Design School
8. Lee, Sanghyun. 1999. "Internet-based Collaborative Design Evaluation," Doctoral Thesis, Harvard Design School.
9. McCall, Raymond and Johnson, Erik. 1997. "Using argumentative agents to catalyze and support collaboration in design," in Automation in Construction 6(1997), ELSEVIER.

# Towards Policy-Based Management QoS in Multicommunicative Education

Oscar Díaz-Alcántara[1], Dermot McCluskey[2]

[1]Department of Computing, Imperial College, 180 Queen's Gate, London SW7 2BZ
oda@doc.ic.ac.uk
[2] Universidad Anáhuac del Sur, Ave. Torres 131, 01780, México City
dermot@ds.uas.mx

**Abstract.** This project begins with introductory comments on the need for models that maximise the benefits of e-Education for regions and persons that are not directly benefited at this time. The project also describes the Multicommunicative Education at Universidad Anáhuac del Sur in Mexico and show how Quality of Service Management Policies, specified using the Ponder policy language developed at Imperial College in London can be applied in this environment.

## 1    Introduction

The Internet is the technology that never sleeps. It is constantly being used worldwide and also never stops being developed. So far there are multiple areas where Internet is involved e.g. communications, business, military, education and so on. The Third Millennium is opening with a revolution in higher education. Technology is altering and enhancing the way courses are offered in traditional colleges and universities and in so doing is enabling a whole new educational paradigm. Worldwide we find ourselves in a period of transition.

Research studies have been quite consistent in finding that distance learning classrooms report similar effectiveness results as reported under traditional instruction methods. In addition, research studies often point out that student attitudes about distance learning are generally positive. [1]

This project involves two big ongoing projects, first at Imperial College London and second at Universidad Anáhuac del Sur (UAS) Mexico. Imperial College is contributing to provide quality of service on the Internet to users and Institutions participating in the Multicommunicative Education project (ME) pertaining to UAS.

The structure of the paper is as follows. In section 2 we present some barriers and challenges for an electronic education paradigm. In section 3 we briefly describe both projects: Ponder as a policy specification language and ME the multicommunicative education model. In section 4 we introduce some of the ideas to deploy QoS in the multicommunicative education paradigm and show some examples to accomplish this QoS. We finish the paper with the summary and future work.

# 2 Barriers and Challenges for a Real and Fair e-Education

Most of the universities, colleges and public and private institutions involved on distance learning or e-Education are concerned about the rapid change and development of the education at the beginning of our new millennium. Virtually all of them are looking for strategies to provide effective and reliable education in order to survive to this change that technology is provoking all around the world.

For profit institutions already respond to an important demand for life-long learning and for retraining of people as they go through life and from one employment to another. It is well known that many universities and colleges join for-profit learning venture projects to develop better technologies that provide qualitative education, but how many of them are really prepared for the future Internet applications? The use of Internet among Universities has been on the rise [2], e-Education has to launch courses across major disciplines including Social Studies, Medicine, Science and Information Technology by providing extensive training, offering seminars covering every aspect associated with the design and implementation of online learning programs for students. Unfortunately, costs can be excessive, leaving smaller institutions and countries, where expensive technologies are not still accessible, unable to join these ventures. It is also clear that the benefit of e-Learning is not equal across ages and genders.

In the ME we are exploring some ways to minimize the disadvantages and differences among countries and institutions, ages and genders. In this section we present some of the barriers and challenges that still exist in e-Education and that ME is looking forward to solving. ME thus seeks to provide guidance to students, teachers and educationalists at a particular moment when the accelerated technology development is decreasing the working markets in traditional sectors. But there is also the creation of new sectors, and in synthesis, a change in the qualifications needed on those students in order to enter the market.

Historically technology development has been associated to countries of four regions [3] Northern America, Europe, Japan and Oceania. These countries have very well developed e-networks and the human capital needed to make them effective and as always it would seem that opportunity follows wealth and existing assets. Professor Quah of the LSE [4] has made interesting observations about the way in which growth is related to e-networks and shows how important it is to invest in knowledge network infrastructures. Can Internet and its strategic use by historically disadvantages regions provide a solution and allow many countries to leapfrog to development or at least, minimize differences in all regions around the World? Projects like ME are supporting the minimization of difference of development among countries by delivering and exchanging education over a distance.

A fundamental aim of an e-Education would be spreading out rapid adaptation to the learning community by providing knowledge and resources through available financial programs and solid knowledge foundation that readies students to participate in a knowledge-based economy around the world. To achieve this it will be necessary to find the best way of using the resources of Internet for these countries and within the terms of reference of their cultures and learning modes. It will be necessary to create a new style of learning and of teaching, understanding that the Internet is a network that has the potential for enriching existing teaching in many ways.

Another barrier that projects as ME have to face is the differences between the various cohorts of ages with their young and adults and between genders. Any successful project will have to identify different segments of population according to their attitudes relating e-Education. Key questions that e-Education must answer include; How are people from different ages and gender affected by Internet in different countries? How do they perceive the new technologies, particularly Internet, telecommunications and convergence process among telephone, mobile and computer? Do they see in them new and attainable learning opportunities? A summary review of the literature shows that there are in fact great differences in the level of access and the ability to take advantage of e-Education as it stands at the moment.

Teaching strategies based on computer applications are emerging on the e-Education paradigm, yet they have to provide the solutions to these differences. ME seeks precisely to develop strategies that can have the widest possible benefit and that are comfortable with multiple channels or media and thus are ready to use electronic networks but with an important focus on new paradigms for teachers and learners and on a new style of learning community which will be cheaper to implement but may build on the undoubted communicative skills of many of the countries or groups that are in danger of not benefiting the new technologies.

An Internet that serves education can also benefit the community at large. In rural areas, especially, telecommunications systems and services are tied increasingly to economic development and community survival. New uses for distance learning include the application of information and educational resources for students, adults, local governments, organisations and businesses. ME gives priority to equity of access to information and opportunities and believes that its model can dramatically decrease the costs and inconveniences associated with maintaining a well-trained work force.

## 3    Multicommunicative Education Project at UAS

Multicommunicative education (ME) is a term used in this project to characterise what happens in all education or learning, where multiple channels are used to create, strengthen and direct the learning community as well as providing the means to deliver knowledge and develop mental and other skills.

The general objective of this characterisation is to find ways of improving the structure and use of diverse communication channels so as to give the greatest scope to the learning community in its endeavor. It does so by examining the multichannel communication process in successful learning communities to identify methodological constructs that may aid educational practitioners, learners and curriculum and developers of educational offerings. This reflection is called ME analysis and planning. ME analysis asks itself the general question as to what may be the expert rules that successful designers and conductors of multichannel education use? Then asks how these rules may be translated into measurable and understandable criteria.

Many currently and historically successful candidates come to mind for ME analysis. Currently there are very interesting cases in media based education, virtual education, computer mediated learning, asynchronous learning systems and so forth. Outstanding is the current success of universities such as Phoenix in the USA[5]. The systems for developing a community of learning for navy servicemen in the US have been largely successful with the support of institutions such as the University of Maryland [6]. States such as Oregon [7] and the various provinces of Canada [8, 9] have long traditions, as does the UK with projects such as the Open University [10].

ME analysis initially looks for common criteria in the area of finance, curriculum definition, channel selection, teacher training, training for learning, methods of community building, empowerment and approaches towards various types of content. It asks how ME creates space for diversity in learning styles times and educational background. It takes special interest in new contexts and new types of communities such as that formed by people scattered in space and time. It is not a technology based study but rather a way of understanding how technologies as diverse as the letters of St. Paul and the transmissions of the Open University have succeeded. It is as happy discussing a correspondence course as it is reflecting on Internet learning and tries to establish common and useful keys to understanding them.

In the area of finance and economy the factors of supply and demand, availability of technology and cluster theory are important. The choices on what quality to expect and how much to spend on technology requires consideration.

Channel selection takes into account the extent to which the system must build a community or is working within a well developed community. Communities built on principles of autonomous learners seem to have greater need of self access, although to fewer channels and therefore require well developed searching systems.

Teacher training seems successful when teachers are involved in the setting up of the system and/or it translates fairly well into the type of learning that they expect. An eminent example of the latter is the success of correspondence courses and of the former the many undergraduate ME projects that exist at colleges.

Learner training is complex as communicative principles tell us that the use of communicative systems tends to stabilise in people and therefore they may find it difficult to use a complex system such as the Internet to learn and study in a structured way. All successful projects seem to have teachers who are naturally aware of this aspect and devise specific approaches for students to avoid errors in their use of media. Learners also need to learn behaviour and communication etiquette, "how to", new writing skills, etc.

### 3.1   ME Model

Figure 1 outlines the Multicommunicative Education model and the multidisciplinary groups that collaborate on it to provide a multi channel way of Education in a worldwide perspective.

ME is an approach that allows for the improvement of learning and therefore the success of multicultural projects over a multinational scope and transfer studies insofar as it allows us to build larger and more diverse communities, creating a living node in a network of learning.

ME is richly constituted by a multidisciplinary group as is shown in figure 1. It is outlined the groups interacting to create and update the programs and objectives of ME. Here we briefly describe each of those groups, which are formed by members of every country where ME is deployed.

*The Multicommunicative Design Group* is involved in designing technology-pedagogy interfaces that facilitate as much as possible the understanding of the material developed by ME at any level of knowledge.

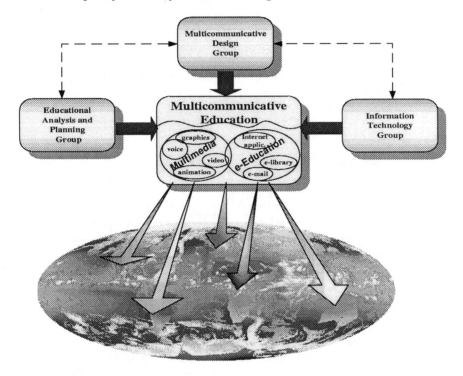

**Fig. 1.** Multicommunicative Education Model.

*The Educational Analysis and Planning Group* is looking at how to migrate from traditional classroom pedagogy to an online format. Although content based curriculum are supposedly a thing of the past, the consideration of the match between channels structure and content continues to occupy the minds of successful members of this group who are clever at technology and quick at using it. In addition, this group is concerned with issues about the pedagogy of future ways of learning.

*The Information Technology Group* is concerned with technical and technological research and evaluation issues. This group also looks at clusters of technology and success, cultural changes and the problem of quality. At a deeper level it proposes to look at the communication and thinking structures that are strengthened by multicommunicative education just as the printed press in its day caused profound changes.

# 4 Ponder a Policy Language

Ponder [11] is a language for specifying security and management policies for distributed systems. This is a research work carried out at Imperial College Department of Computing.

In Ponder, a policy is a rule that can be used to change the behaviour of a system. Separating policies from the managers that interpret them allows the behaviour and strategy of the management system to be changed without re-coding the managers. The management system can then adapt to changing requirements by disabling policies or replacing old policies with new ones without shutting down the system.

At the moment Ponder can be used to specify security policies with role-based access control, as well as general-purpose management policies, but is intended to be extensible to cater for future types of policies, i.e. Quality of Service policies.

Ponder supports the following kinds of policies:

**Table 1.** Ponder Policies

| Basic policies | Composite policies | Other |
|---|---|---|
| Positive Authorisation policy | Group | Meta-policy |
| Negative Authorisation policy | Role | |
| Obligation policy | Relationship | |
| Refrain Policy | Management Structure | |
| Positive Delegation policy | | |
| Negative Delegation policy | | |

*Authorisation Policies:* Positive (Auth+) or negative (Auth-), define what activities a member of the subject domain is allowed or forbidden to perform on the set of objects in the target domain. Are essentially security policies related to access-control. They are designed to protect target objects.

*Obligation Policies:* Specify what activities a subject must do to a target domain and are essentially events-condition-action rules which provide the ability to respond to changing circumstances. Events can be simple, i.e. internal timer event, or an external event notified by monitoring service components, e.g. a component failing.

*Refrain Policies:* These are similar to negative authorisation policies and specify what a subject must refrain from doing. They could be used when the subject is permitted to perform an action but prevented until certain conditions are met.

*Delegation Policies:* These policies specify which actions of the authorisation policies, subjects are allowed to delegate to others. A delegation policy permits subjects to grant privileges, which they posses, to grantees to perform an action on their behalf, e.g. passing read rights to a printer spooler in order to print a file.

*Groups:* Group related policies together for the purposes of policy organisation and reusability. A reason for using groups is that policies may relate to the same departments or apply to the same application.

*Roles:* Roles provide a semantic grouping of policies with a common subject, generally pertaining to a position within an organisation such as department manager, project manager or designer.

*Relationships:* Managers acting in organisational positions (roles) interact with each other. A relationship groups the policies defining the rights and duties of roles toward each other. It can also include policies related to resources that are shared by the roles within the relationship.

*Management Structures:* Ponder supports the notion of management structures to define a configuration in terms of instances of roles, relationships and nested management structures relating to organisational units. For example a management structure would be used to define a department in a university or a country.

## 4.1 Mapping Ponder to the IETF Policy Information Model

This is an ongoing project to address a general-purpose deployment model for policies [12]. Policies express business rules, and policies in distributed systems, define how resources in the network are accessed, configured and used. Policy selection is the mechanism that determines what policies should be applied to a given operation [13]. There might be a set of policies governing network bandwidth reservations, another set that determines access to documents and services, a set controlling router configurations, a set for setting up secure Internet connections, and so on.

Each of these policies applies to particular subjects and targets, in the context of particular operations. Evaluating all policies for all operations is expensive in terms of time and inefficiency. A given policy usually applies to a narrow set of circumstances and is meaningless outside of that set. As an example, desktop policies never apply to router configuration.

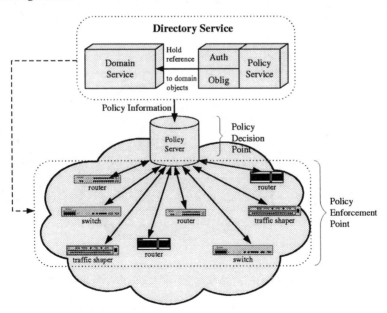

**Fig. 2.** QoS policy deployment model

When using Ponder to map the (Internet Engineering Task Force) IETF Policy Information Model, one is able to store information essential to create and manage QoS on the network in a scalable, secure directory service that presents a logically centralised view of physically distributed information, as it is outlined in Figure 2. Ponder becomes an Internet application that will take advantage of future developments of IETF [14, 15] based-policy decision points and policy enforcement points. For instance, Ponder will be used as a high-level application language for generating the IETF syntax about QoS.

So far we have talked about policies and quality of service but what it does mean?. QoS can be defined as the ability of a network element (an application, host or router) to have some level of assurance that its traffic and service requirements can be satisfied. Quality of Service means a measurement of how well a network behaves. When a network provides "Quality of Service" then it delivers data in a reliable manner.

There are many reasons to deploy QoS on the Internet some of them are listed below [13]

- Mission critical applications need QoS to ensure delivery that won't be impacted when misbehaving or bandwidth-intensive applications are using the network
- Internet service providers change for guaranteeing a minimum bandwidth, during periods when the network is congested.
- Real-time traffic generated by multimedia applications like video or voice needs QoS to guarantee latency, jitter and a specified level of packet loss.

Essentially there are two approaches to supporting QoS in the Internet, Integrated Services(IntServ) [16], and Differentiated Services (DiffServ) [17]. In addition, some different QoS mechanisms as admission control, congestion management, congestion avoidance, traffic shaping whereas priority queuing is the simplest one.

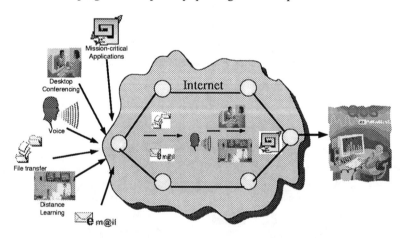

**Fig. 3.** QoS on the Internet in Terms of the Priority Giving to the Applications

Network managers can use concepts such as relative priority, classes of service, transmission rate and admission control to deploy QoS solution. The policy network manager system is responsible for mapping those policies into enforcement on network resources.

The mechanisms above mentioned are beyond the scope of this paper and further information can be found in [18, 19], but are mentioned here to give an idea about what mechanism are possible to implement on the Internet to provide quality of service. Figure 3 shows the QoS in terms of priority given to Internet applications.

## 5 QoS Deployment in Multicommunicative Education, Breaking Barriers and Distributing Fairness

This section is focused on the Information Technology Group scope, since it describes some features developed in the area of IT as that of QoS Policy Management specification. We present here some typical policies applied to a process of e-Education that provide QoS to the users or ME.

As we mentioned in section 2 and 3, the multidisciplinary group in ME is working on the distribution of fairness for people regardless of country, economic condition, age, gender or position. In this paper we are proposing Policy-based management QoS as a mean for users of ME to experiment better quality of services than the best effort paradigm that we receive so far on the Internet.

By allowing QoS on the Internet we want to accomplish some of the challenges described in section 2, finding better ways of using Internet resources and allow students and clients of ME enriching their own learning or teaching understanding and by exchanging distance experiences and knowledge. The following section will show some QoS policy specified in Ponder.

### 5.1 Policy Samples Applied to Multicommunicative Education

This section intends to exemplify the QoS policy applied to a process of e-Education by describing policies specified in Ponder language and the interpretation giving in English. Consider a scenario where a student from Central America admitted to an undergraduate program wants to establish a connection with UAS to read and copy material pertaining to a subject and then he wants to open a pre-recorded multimedia file about a lecture offered at UAS. We show several Authorisation policies, as we believe that security issues are related to Quality of Service as well. We also show an example for a Videoconference application where we establish a policy to manage QoS. Notice that examples could be express in a more complicate way but we wanted to express them simpler for understandable purpose. Also notice that isolated QoS policy examples are presented here but we are aware that for a real policy-base management of QoS, a combination of the QoS mechanism mentioned in section 4 is needed.

**Example 1** Authorising access to Undergraduate students
  **auth+** CACountries {

    **subject** countries/centralAmerica
    **target** ME/Files/HighEducationFiles
    **action** read(), copy()
    **when** time.between(1400,2000) }

This policy can be interpreted as any user from Central America is allowed to Access (read and copy) Files corresponding to Higher Education any day between 14:00 and 20:00 hours.

**Example 2** Authorisation to read media files constraining time

**auth+** openMultimedia {
    **subject** countries/centralAmerica
    **target** ME/Files/lectures
    **action** read()
    **when** time.between(1800,2000)

This policy is interpreted as any user from Central America is allowed to read any multimedia file about pre-stored lectures in the domain ME/Files/lectures, but only during 18:00 and 20:00 hours.

**Example 3** Obligation policy for priority QoS

**oblig** priorityQoS {
    **subject** ME/routers/edgeRouters /centralAmerica
    **on** access(lectureMath1)
    **target** edgeRouters/outInterface
    **action** priority=6
    **when** time.between(1800,2000)

This QoS policy is concerned with high priority mechanism. This policy is deployed to the edge routers and configuring them with priority = 6. The application lectureMath1 traffic between users from Central America and UAS gets high priority on the forwarding queue mechanism at specific time of the day (18:00 and 20:00 hours).

**Example 4** Obligation policy for Committed Rate QoS

**Oblig** committedBw{
    **subject** ME/trafficshaper/UAS + ME/Trafficshaper/CostaRica +
        ME/Trafficshaper/Panama
    **on** Videoconference
    **target** ME/trafficshaper/outboundInterface
    **action** committedRate(800 kpbs)
    **when** time.between(1500,1600)

Committed rate policy type allows constructing QoS policies that define a committed rate for a class of application flows. Traffic shapers and some edge routers support committed rates for aggregated flows. This policy could be deployed to traffic shapers at UAS, Costa Rica and Panama in order to assure bandwidth for the videoconference application.

This policy aggregates flows outbound to the clients into 800 kbps. This example assumes other server applications exist but that the Videoconference application flows get the majority of available bandwidth between 3:00 and 4:00 p.m.

**Example 5** Denying access. Negative authorisation policy

**auth-** otherMaterial {
    **subject** countries/centralAmerica/undergraduate
    **target** ME/Files/Primary + ME/Files/Secondary + ME/Files/HigSchool
    **action** read(), write()

This negative authorisation policy has been defined for two reasons, first because a Student from higher educations is not allowed to read information from a different program than the one he/she is admitted but mainly because we want the students concentrate in the material they have to access and not wasting their time surfing in different ME domains. The policy means that students from undergraduate studies cannot read or write files on primary, secondary and high school domains.

# 6 Summary and future work

In this paper we have presented ME an e-Education model currently being developed at Universidad Anahuac del Sur, Mexico and the groups conforming it. We presented some of the barriers and challenges that nowadays still exist around the e-Education and distance learning paradigms.

We wanted to move forward in the quality of service management debate, especially in this moment when there is so much to be lost or gained for those clients of the e-Education by having the right approach.

We showed the concern of the IT group about the policy management of QoS, as a mean of contributing to break barriers related to the e-Education paradigms and distribute fairness around Internet users.

QoS is an extended issue and there are different schemas that represent the task of managing Quality of Service as the one presented here, the IETF Policy information Model. We are currently researching on the map of Ponder to IETF policy LDAP (Lightweight Directory Access Protocol) schema to represent QoS policy and to let interoperability among different implementations and vendors.

# Acknowledgement

We gratefully acknowledge to Prof. Morris Sloman from Imperial College for his comments about this paper, especially in the Ponder policy specification examples.

# References

1. USDLA, *USDLA*, 2001, see www.usdla.org.
2. Shan, A. and D. Bruin, Internet use among Universities rises, see http://www.studentadvantage.com/article/0,1075,c4-i8-t0-a11687,00.html, UCLA.
3. Statistics Division, U.N., Composition of macro geographical regions, see http://www.un.org/Depts/unsd/methods/m49regin.htm. December 2000.
4. Quah, D., *Cross-Country Growth comparison: Theory to Empirics*, January 2000, LSE Economics Department, see http://cep.lse.ac.uk/papers/discussion/download/dp0442.pdf.
5. University of Phoenix, Online home, see http://online.uophx.edu/.
6. Navy College Program, U. Maryland U.C., see http://www.umuc.edu/navy/ncpp.html
7. Oregon Network Education, see http://oregonone.org/.
8. Canadian Virtual University, see http://www.cvu-uvc.ca .
9. Canada's Open University, see http://www.athabascau.ca .
10. The Open University, see http://www.open.ac.uk/frames.html.
11. Damianou, N., et al. The Ponder Policy Specification Language. In Policies for Distributed Systems and Networks. 2001. Bristol, UK: Springer.
12. Diaz-Alcantara, O., Mapping Ponder to IETF Policy Schema, Case Study, 2001.
13. TechNet, M., *Implementing Directory Enabled Networks Using Windows 2000 Technology.* 2000, see http://www.microsoft.com/technet/win2000/win2ksrv/technote/denuse.asp.
14. Moore, B., E. Ellesson, and J. Strassner, *Policy Core Information Model, Version 1 Specification*, 2000, IETF [PCIM], draft-ietf-policy-core-model-08.txt.
15. Snir, Y., et al., *Policy Framework QoS Information Model.* 2000, IETF, draft-ietf-policy-qos-info-model-02.txt, work in progress.
16. Braden, R. and S. Shenker, *Integrated Service in the Internet Architecture: an Overview*, 1994, IETF, see http://www.eitf.org/rfc/rfc1633.txt.
17. Blaek, S., et al., *An Architecture for Differentiated Services*, 1998, IETF, see ftp://ftp.isi.edu/in-notes/rfc2475.txt.
18. Strassner, J., *Directory Enabled Networks*. Technology Series, ed. M.T. Publishing. 1999, Indianapolis USA: MacMillan Technical Publishing. 726.
19. Strassner, J., et al., Information Model for Describing Network Device QoS Mechanisms for Differentiated Services, 2000, IETF, draft-ietf-policy-qos-device-info-model-02.txt.

# Challenges and Promises in the Cyber World with Young Children

Eunhye Park

Department of Early Childhood Education
Ewha Womans University
Seoul 120-750, Korea
ehparkh@ewha.ac.kr

## 1 Introduction

Each time a new technology is introduced into the classroom, there are those who claim that it will revolutionize the way teachers teach, the way students learn, and in general, the way we conduct education. In the 50s it was film; in the 60s it was broadcast educational television, slides; in the 70s it was video and computer assisted instruction, and in the 80s it was videodisc. As we heading toward a new millennium, the new player on the scene is clearly the Internet. Matrix Information and Directory Services [26] estimated that the total number of worldwide users will grow to 707 million by the 2001. According to a research by [22], over 90 percent of parents and 80percent of teachers believe that young children can use computers and are ready for multimedia technology. A strong and pervasive faith makes younger and younger children at home and at school expose to the cyber world. Will web-based activities be valuable to the growth and development of young children, especially those under the age of eight? Currently, researchers and educators offer conflicting advice on whether children should be encouraged to surf the web. Regardless of the debate, many young children are now using computers and will continue to do so. Where in our curriculum do we help children navigate this new world? How will schools keep up with the pace of change? How will early childhood educators ensure equitable access to everyone? How will we deal with information complexity and quantity? What about standards for quality? In order to answer the above questions, this paper will examine the difficulties of using networks successfully in early childhood education. Several issues to overcome these barriers will be addressed.

## 2 Challenges in using the Internet with young children

### 2.1 Developmentally appropriate practices and technology

The collection of principles and activities that guide effective and educational practice in the field of early childhood education is called developmentally appropriate practices [5]. DAP results from the process of professionals making decisions about the well-being and education of children based on at least three important kinds of information or knowledge: what is known about child development and learning(age appropriate); what is known about the strengths, interests, and needs of each individual child in the group(individually appropriate); and knowledge of the social and cultural contexts in which children live(culturally appropriate). While theoretical debates proceed regarding DAP [24], there is little controversy over what is the best practices for young children.

Are young children developmentally ready for web-based experiences? The answer from research with young children is not clear. DAP recommends that the beneficial experiences for young children are to be active, naturally engaging, and concrete. Research is contradictory as to whether technology provides concrete experiences to young children, because the definition of concrete varies. For some, concrete may be the same as relevant and vivid. Clements and his collegues [6] feel that what is concrete to the child may have more to do with meaningful and manipulable than with physical characteristics. In other words, if the computer program is relevant and children can explore and experiment throughout the program, the computer program provides young children a concrete experience. For others, concrete experiences must be physical with tactile manipulative. In addition, Harbeck and Sherman [16] raise two more concerns regarding young children's developmental level dealing with the Internet. First, young children respond in a very limited way to most stimuli. One widely acknowledged asset of the Internet is access to massive amounts of information. Expose young children to stimuli should be controlled so as to avoid overburdening children's receptive capabilities. The dominance of visually mediated messages causes another concern. The pervasive influence of television on young children is well documented [2]. The web has the same potential to over stimulate young children with negative outcome parallel to television, particularly with web sites that make commercial appeals and present violence. Internet, once a haven for noncommercial collaboration, has become a medium for advertising and pay-per-view information, including pornography. Early childhood educators should listen to what research consistently warns three problems associated with heavy viewing of television violence: children may become less sensitive to the pain and suffering of others; they may become more fearful of the world around them; and they may be more likely to behave aggressive or harmful ways toward others [35] [34]. The same problems could be applied to the heavy use of the Internet.

## 2.2   Not enough infrastructure and lack of standardization

There are three hardware related barriers associated with the success of technology usage in educational environment. A first is infrastructure, which includes wiring, modems or high-speed connections, and other peripheral. Current estimates are that only 11percent of Korea's kindergarten classrooms are connected to the Internet, while 63 percent of the nation's classrooms are connected to the Internet in the U.S.A [19] [27]. A number of studies indicate that it is important for teachers to have the Internet access in their own classrooms [21]. Second is the additional budget for repairs, maintenance, upgrades, and operational training. The rapid changes in technology have resulted in many schools dealing with obsolete, broken, or unused equipment. How will schools keep up with the pace of rapid change in technology without allocated budget? Final barrier is the standardization of hardware. The widespread adoption of any information technology depends upon a base of off-the-shelf software and upon easy exchange of programs among users in various locations [14]. When a number of incompatible standards are released on the market, most of them will be abandoned. More elaborate web pages rely on specific browser or plug-ins to work properly. And interactive multimedia still suffer from a lack of standardization in computer sound cards, file formats, screen displays etc. In order to enjoy wide use of Internet web pages, users should be able to find appropriate playback hardware virtually anywhere.

## 2.3 Separation of technology from curriculum

As was the case almost two decades ago when television was adopted in schools, computers have been purchased and the Internet has been connected largely without a clear indication of how to be used in day-to-day activities. Instructors are presenting more and more traditional educational material on the Internet, with little consideration of the Internet's many unique features. Internet has three key features that characterize its usage and usefulness: presentation, communication, and dynamic interaction [10]. Typical web sites which contain pages of text and graphics are examples of where the Internet is being used as a presentation medium. The Internet allows many different types of communication. Types of Internet communications are: one-way communication(e.g., web pages); Two-way communication(e.g., e-mails), one-to-many communication(e.g., list-servs, discussion groups); Many-to-many communication. Dynamic Interaction is the most under-utilized feature of the Internet and potentially the most important. It is unique to the Internet, as no other medium or technology has identical capabilities. Currently, the Internet is being used to publish information in a static way-the style of the vast majority of web activities for young children are no different in principle form of drill-and- practice worksheets. Parents and teachers can easily find activities such as coloring, worksheets, arcade games, etc. on the Internet sites(for example, http://www.aidul.com, http://www.kidsi.net/). Any program using new media to simply re-package existing content and designs into some new box fails to engage children in meaningful learning [14]. Early childhood educators need to truly understand what innovative modalities are afforded by new media and design learning systems to make appropriate use of them.

## 2.4 Unprepared teachers

One of the challenges to the appropriate use of technology with young children is the discomfort that some teachers feel as a result of their own lack of skill in using it. Teachers' attitudes toward computers in the classroom range from complete acceptance to utter fear. While some comfortably accept computers as an effective instructional tool, others distance themselves and resist the opportunities technology provides. Many teachers are simply not willing to alter their teaching style to one that will adopt new technology in their classroom. According to Naisbitt [30], when a new technology enter into the classroom, it pass through three stages and in the first stage, the new technology follows the line of least resistance, into a ready market. Some educators are fearful of computers due to their own lack of experience with them [23]. Hakkinen [15] categorized anxiety into a state anxiety or a trait anxiety. Whereas state anxiety may fade away with changes in the conditions that caused it, trait anxiety is more persistent and may become a constituent of the individual's psychological status. According to researchers, the most common type of computer anxiety is mutable state anxiety resulting from psychological stress during a period of time, which could be diminished with more computing experience and training [37]. Determining the quality of a computer-based experience and how it supports children's learning is difficult for the teacher if she cannot get beyond the anxiety of accessing the keyboard. When almost 4,000 school district computer budgets were examined, 55percent of the money was designated for hardware, 30percent for software, and only 15 % for teacher training([25]). These data suggest that professional development opportunities for teachers are often overlooked. Even in the age of technology, it is through relationships with others-through joint activities, language, and shared feelings with other human beings-that children grasp meaning. This fact emphasizes the importance of human mediators of technology experiences and preparation of teachers for the role.

## 2.5  Digital divide

Recent research confirms serious differences in how girls and boys use technology in schools. Researchers have discovered that attitudes toward computer technology, and perceived competency with it, differ by sex. A study showed the result that girls of all ethnicities consistently rated themselves significantly lower than boys on computer ability and were less likely than boys to think computers help them do better in schools [1]. The findings are consistent with earlier data: A meta-analysis of 81studies from 1973 to 1992 found that boys exhibited greater sex-role stereotyping of computer use and deeper confidence with technology [39]. Research on equity among different racial and SES group indicates that children from minority and lower SES populations have fewer computers at home and use more drill software [40]. Teachers, while concerned about equity, believed that better-behaved children deserved more computer time and that the primary benefit of computers for low-achieving students was mastery of basic skills [36]. Digital divides in early childhood settings reverberate into K-12, postsecondary education, and finally the job market. Since in our technology-driven society, educational inequities can lead to economic ones, educators should fine a way to reduce these gaps [38].

## 2.6 Business oriented market

In the 90s, media technologies have become controlled by big business and have largely become commercialized, rather than being the tools of researchers and teachers. We have observed many projects that corporations attempted to make instruction more effective and efficient by using new technologies. ACOT(Apple Classroom of Tomorrow) is one of them. The project began in 1986 by donating two computers for each participating students and teachers from seven classrooms across the country. After nearly eight years of studying the computer's effects on classroom, ACOT researchers claim that they have observed profound changes in the nature of instruction, learning, assessment, and the school culture itself [11]. Noble [31] claims that it is market fantasies and intense competition that typically drives corporate decisions in educational technology. According to him, computer based education is more about using the education market in the service of technological product development than it is about using technology in the service of education. Technology adoption often led by vendors and directors rather than teachers. Because of this, hardware may be sold to users who are unprepared to design effective programs or who lack the appropriate information to use it well. Information highway is but the latest, and potentially the most costly, bill of goods sold to the schools. Increasing number of commercial web sites, which claim an educational purpose and target young children, are being developed.

## 3 New directions for the future

As young children's use of technology becomes more widespread, early childhood educators must take responsibility to influence events that are transforming the daily lives of children and families. Reflecting this concern, several issues related to use of the Internet with young children should be addressed

### 3.1 In any given situation, specific use of technology should be age appropriate, individually appropriate, and culturally appropriate

A professional in the field of early childhood education should take the essential role in determining appropriate uses of technology. All materials can be well used or misused. To ensure that computer use supports a developmentally appropriate program, Davidson and Wright [8] suggest that educators need to have the following attitudes and assumptions: (1) computer use is a social activity; (2) computer use is a child-initiated and child-directed activity; (3) computer software allows children to explore, experiment, and problem solve; (4) computers offer new learning opportunities when unexpected things happen; (5) computers are one of many materials in a developmentally appropriate classroom. These guidelines can provide a firm foundation for the design and implementation of the Internet in the early childhood curriculum. Harbeck and Sherman [16] suggested seven principles of designing developmentally appropriate web sites for young children:(1) children's web sites should be concrete, provide clear and simple navigation, have simple page design, and use large icons; (2) children interacting with the Internet should be guided by an adult; (3) web sites should be progressive and individualized in that the content and design of the site changes appropriately as a child matures; (4) web activities should have relevance to real world situations and provide integrated experiences; (5) web activities should cover a variety of content areas; (6) web sites should provide active and enjoyable experiences to ensure a positive and affective response; (7) web sites should be exploratory and provide predictable action.

## 3.2 Technology should enhance the development of the whole child

Not only should web based activities involve and relate as many content areas as possible, they should also combine physical, cognitive, emotional, and social experiences. When used appropriately, the positive effects of technology in children's learning and development, both cognitive and social, could occur. Researches have consistently observed that children engage in high levels of spoken communication and cooperation at the computer [6]. In fact, in order to use Internet successfully, work should take place in heterogeneous, collaborative groups [28]. Placing computer along with developmentally appropriate software in kindergarten's classrooms for several months significantly increases reading readiness skills, problem-solving, and creative activities [6]. Technology with the potential of access to the Internet provides access to the riches of the world. Through virtual field trips in real time or via diskette, children are able to share different cultural and environmental experiences. Children in remote rural locations can reach the Library of Congress, classes in Korea can visit the Louvre, and go to virtual field trips to Central American rain forest. Networks also have made new forms of local and worldwide collaborative learning possible. E-mail can facilitate direct communication and promote social interactions previously limited by the physical location of participating learners. For example, four classrooms interacted with each other using e-mail while they write letters, compose stories, create poems about a virtual monster(http://www.2cyberlinks.com/monster.html). Internet also allows children and teachers to draw from many fields, not just education and share their findings with the world at large. Two examples are

Ask Dr. Math (http://forum.swarthmore.edu/dr.math/)

Ask an Astronaut (http://www.nss.org/askastro/home.html).

## 3.3 Technology should be integrated into early childhood curriculum

Early studies showed that teachers were occupied with ideas such as the dehumanizing effect of computers in society and in the classroom when computers were just beginning to enter the field of education at the school level. At that time little reference to the impact of computer use on the regular curriculum was made, because teachers were overwhelmed by the potential of the technology itself. The research of the late 1980s and early 1990s started to denote teachers' concerns regarding the use of computers in the classrooms [3], [15]. In order to accommodate integration of the Internet into early childhood practices, teachers should locate computers in the classroom, rather than in a separate computer lab [7]. Pulling children out of the group into a computer lab demands rigid scheduling and takes away the other rich options from which children may choose. When teachers view computer utilization in the classroom as a simple supplement to the existing curriculum, rather than an integral part of it, teachers fail to take advantage of the computer's full capabilities [13]. In early childhood settings, if computers are used, they should be one of many classroom activity choices. Early childhood curriculum consists of several themes that are interesting to children, relate to their communities and broad enough to be broken into subtopics that encourage cross-disciplinary work. New technology can support a unit on three levels: specific software or Internet site can provide unit-related information; tool software can be used to create unit-related products; web-based activities can be designed to support the unit theme. The teacher implementing the unit 'animals', for example, might have children use on-line encyclopedias to gather data on animals (http://www.encarta.msn.com), visit 'San Diego Zoo' home page (http://www.sandiegozoo.com) to search animals in the zoo. A virtual trip to the zoo will give children opportunities to see pictures, hear animal sounds, and view movies of animals exploring their natural habitats. Teachers could get animal pictures from "http://www.kidsfarm.com" to make instructional materials for a group time.

### 3.4 Early childhood educators should look for educationally sound Internet sites

Today's world wide web is disorganized, of uneven quality, and overrun with commercial advertising. Special attention should be paid to eliminating children's exposure to violence or sex on the Internet. Just like movies and television today, children's software, video games downloaded from Internet sites are often violent and much of it explicit and brutally graphic. Sometimes, these sites can contain biases toward certain groups of people. One of the key features of the Internet is that it can be reached to anybody including children under the age of eight. Simply making the Internet available in classrooms is not enough. Teachers should ask themselves how is material on the Internet judged and refereed? How can we trust the information we receive? How can we protect children from receiving harmful information? Teachers should be aware that some developmentally appropriate sites and many terrible sites reside side by side. There are several useful sites that guide teachers and parents to choose good Internet sites. Teacher might visit some of the sites on the Internet that have posted site validation checklists, including Kathy Schrock's guide for educators: Critical evaluation surveys (http://www.capecod.net/schrockguide/ eval.htm), Evaluating Internet resources: A checklist (http://infopeople.berkeley. edu:8000/bkmk/select.html), and how to find a good site (http://www.childrenssoftware.com: CSR). Among these sites CSR(Children's Software Revue) is a relatively new publication founded by Warren Buckleitner, formerly of High/Scope. CSR is based upon a philosophy of children being active learners who construct knowledge. CSR identified factors as being most important to good quality Internet sites:

- Ease of Use. No matter how strong the content, a site needs to be easy to use
- Educational. Eight key points to consider about content
- Entertaining. These factors can help determine a site's fun value
- Design Features. Good sites stand up to a wide range of users
- Safety and Responsibility. Good sites take care of children.

There are also several sites that provide information on how to protect children from receiving harmful information. Those are:

American Library Association(http:// www.ala.org)

Cyber Angels (http://www.cyberangels.org)

FreeZone (http://www.freezone.com/safety.kfrag.html)

NetNany (http://www.netnanny.com)

Parents place (http://www.parentsplace.com)

Net Parents (http://www.netparents.org)

## 3.5 Early childhood educators should ensure equitable and universal access to technology for all children

According to researchers [36], preschool-age boys and girls show equal interests in computers, but as they grow older girls begin to spend less time with computers than boys. Early childhood educators must find ways to preserve equity of access and minimize or even reverse these trends. Considering girl's interests and interaction styles when selecting software or the Internet site for classroom use could be one possible solution. Offering special times designated for girls only could be another thing that teachers can try [9]. Efforts should be made to ensure access to appropriate technology for children with special needs, too. The computer can meet both cognitive and socio-emotional needs of children with disabilities, given the appropriate level of assistance [20]. Early childhood educators must match the technology to each child's unique special needs, learning styles, and individual preferences. How could this happen? Studies suggested that the solutions could be found in ensuring that sufficient numbers of computers are available in schools. Where the ratio of computers to students reach 1:1 in and out of school settings, it is more likely that girls, children from low SES families, minorities are using computers as often as their counterparts. The research findings and explanations also indicate that attitudes of family, school, and the larger culture toward this group influence their access to and use of computers [18].

## 3.6 Early childhood educators should give special attention to professional development

Goals for staff development in technology should be on the reducing teachers' technophobia and creating a simultaneous focus on technology and curriculum. As a predominantly female population, teachers have been charged with a technophobic resistance to computers in the classroom. When the teacher is comfortable with technology, she can offer the computer as a meaningful tool. Feelings of technological inadequacy seriously limit a teachers' creativity in designing and implementing connections between the internet and other classroom activities. Teacher training in the past tended to take the form of an introduction to the mechanics of the equipment, rather than how to incorporate it to do teaching jobs more effectively. Teachers will still need computer literacy skills, but they must go beyond the paradigm of simply responding to information one of transforming information. Teachers need to become technologically competent to create a multidimensional learning environment in which computers are an integral component of the curriculum rather than a supplement. Within this environment, students are challenged to learn by solving meaningful problems with a variety of resource and the computer becomes the process of constructing knowledge. Knowledge construction will be enhanced and enabled by the technologically competent teacher who designs, facilitates, and manages a student-centered multidimensional learning environment that embeds the use of technology into the instruction. Given the need for staff development to support integration of technology in early childhood education practice, Epstein [12] identifies practical experience, workshops, models and mentors, and supervisory follow-up as critical elements of effective staff development for early childhood educators. The appropriate use of the Internet also has many implications for early childhood professional development. Internet can enable teachers to obtain information and new ideas from around the world and to interact with distant experts and peers [17]. Early childhood educators can incorporate principles of cooperative learning as they assist distant peers in acquiring new skills; share curriculum ideas and resources; exchange advice. With a responsive on-line system, mentors can assist novices in becoming more technology competent [4], [29].

## 3.7 Early childhood educators should initiate a major program of experimental research

The Panel on Educational Technology that was part of the U.S. President's Committee of Advisors on Science and Technology made recommendation that many research on the impact of technology on children's learning should be conducted [32]. Meanwhile, commercial interests frequently develop their products without investing sufficiently in substantive research or evaluation, school administrators and others often make major educational technology purchase decisions without reference to current research findings [33]. Every time new technology was introduced into the classroom, many educators and researchers said "we still don't have a clear concept of the uniqueness of the media and how to use them". To-day we could equally say about the Internet-based learning experience and the Internet as a medium. It is now time to find out how best to utilize the Internet as an (inter)active learning technology [10]. Educators need not keep abreast of every innovation for fear of losing ground or falling behind. While researchers conduct studies the rest of us, with renewed integrity, should follow our own sense of sound educational practice, using proven technologies when applicable. There is no need to join the mad rush into the future or to gamble with our children's education [31].

# 4 Conclusion

There are the most important needs and characteristics required for the peo-ple who will work in the 21st century: greater ability for capturing knowledge and collaboration; desire to foster attitudes and behaviors of empowerment, self-directedness, and critical thinking; more emphasis on team work and collabo-ration; flexible intelligence; and lifelong ability to learn new ways of solving problems. Constructivist emphasizes the fact that learning is a social process and should take place within authentic situations, and an authentic task should be the starting point. Technology should provide meaningful real-world con-texts for learning, and connections to outside expert's visualization and analysis tools. This vision endorses teaching children to be active users of technology rather than mere reactors to it, a vision wherein technology does not simply entail putting the same old thing inside a box rather than on a piece of paper, a blackboard, or a slate but is a tool for their thinking. Significant educational improvements are more likely to stem from changes in the message(i.e., content and pedagogy) than merely switching to another medium [33].

According to Naisbitt [30], new technologies pass through three states. In the first stage, the new technology follows the line of least resistance, into a ready market. At the second stage, users improve or replace previous technologies with the new technology. Finally, in the third stage, users discover new functions for the technology, based on its potentials. In the educational use of modern elec-tronic technologies, we are just entering this third stage. For some time now, early childhood educators have been using computers at stage two: creating puzzles, delivering instruction, assessing children's progress, and producing reports. Ed-ucators who have moved to stage three are asking, "How for a paradigm shift, not just a way to squeeze technological tools between the existing bricks of yes-terday's educational practices?" Despite of the promises and predictions made by researchers in the early 1980s, computers have not revolutionized education yet. Through experience, we have learned that it is not the technology itself, but the teacher who implement computer use in their classrooms. While evidence is slowly mounting about technology's positive impact in schools, it is already clear that digital technologies are well on the way to becoming a permanent part of the educational arena at all levels and in countries around the world. Without proper integration of computers into curriculum, appropriate financial and administrative support, and adequate teacher training, the benefits of the technology to foster children's learning cannot be fully achieved.

# References

1. AAUW Educational Foundation(1998). Gender gaps: Where schools still fail our children. Washington, DC: Authors.
2. Aidman, A. (1997). Television violence: Content, context, and consequences. (ERIC Document Reproduction Service No. ED 414 078).
3. Ayersman, D. (1996). Effects of computer instruction, learning style, gender, and experience on computer anxiety. Computers in the Schools, 12(4), 15-30.
4. Bliss, T., Mazur, J. (1996). Common thread case project: Developing associations of experience and novice educators through technology. Journal of Teacher Education, 47(3), 185-190.
5. Bredekamp,S., Coople, C. (1997). Developmentally appropriate practice in early childhood programs serving children from birth through age8(Rev. eds). Washington, DC: National Association for Education of Young Children.
6. Clements, D. H., Nastasi, B. K., Swaminathan, S. (1993). Young children and computers: Crossroads and directions from research. Young Children, 48(2), 56-64.
7. Davis, B. C., Shade, D. D. (1994). Integrate, don't isolate!-Computers in the early childhood curriculum. ERIC Digest(December). No. EDO-PS-94-17.
8. Davidson, J., Wright, J. L. (1994). The potential of the microcomputer in the early childhood classroom. In J. L. Wright and D. D. Shade(eds.). Young Children: Active learners in a technological age. (pp. 77-92). Washington, DC: NAEYC.
9. Derman-Sparks, L., the A.B.C. Task Force(1989). Anti-bias curriculum: Tools for empowering young children. Washington, DC: National Association for the Education of Young Children.
10. Doherty, A.(1998). The Internet: Destined to become a passive surfing technology? Educational Technology, 38(5), 61-63.
11. Dwyer, D. (1994). Apple classrooms of tomorrow: What we've learned. Educational Leadership, 52(2), 4-10.
12. Epstein, A. (1993). Training for quality. Ypsilanti, MI: High/Scope Press.
13. Evans-Andris, M. (1995). An examination of computing styles of teachers in elementary schools. Educational Technology Research and Development, 43, 15-30.
14. Gayeski, D. M. (1997). Predicting the success of new media for organizational learing: How can we avoid costly mistakes? Educational Technology, 37, 5-12.
15. Hakkinen, P. (1994). Changes in computer anxiety in a required computer course. Journal of Research on Computing Education, 27(2), 141-143.
16. Harbeck, J. D., Sherman, T. M (1999). Seven principles for designing developmentally appropriate web sites for young children. Educational Technology, 39(4), 39-44.
17. Hawkes, M. (1999). Exploring network-based communication in teacher professional development. Educational Technology, 39(4), 45-52.
18. Kirkpatrick, H., Cuban, L. (1998). Should we be worried: What the research says about gender differences in access, use, attitudes, and achievement with computers. Educational Technology, 38(4), 56-58.
19. Lee, K., Lee, Y. (2000). The statistics and prospects of children's computer education in Korea.

20. Lesar, S. (1998). Use of assistive technology with young children with disabilities: Current status and training needs. Journal of Early Intervention, 21(2), 146-159.
21. Levin, S. R. (1995). Teachers using technology: Barriers and breakthroughs. International Journal of Educational Telecommunications, 1(1), 53-70.
22. Liu, M. (1996). An exploratory study of how pre-kindergarten children use the interactive multimedia technology: Implications for multimedia software design. (ERIC Reproduction Document Service No. ED 396 713.)
23. Lowther, D. L., Bassoppo-Moyo, T., Mossison, G. R. (1998). Moving from computer literate to technologically competent: The next educational reform. Computers in Human Behavior, 14(1), 93-109.
24. Mallory, B. L., New, R. S. (1994)(eds.) Diversity and developmentally appropriate practices: Challenges for early childhood education. New York: Teachers College Press.
25. Market Data Retrieval. (1992). The survey of microcomputers in schools[Report]. Shelton, CT: Market Data Retrieval, Inc. (ERIC Document Reproduction Service No. ED 352-930).
26. Matrix Information and Directory Services(1999). [online] http://www.mids.org/mmq/501/pages.html.
27. Means, B. (2000). Technology use in tomorrow's schools. Educational Leadership, 58(4), 57-61.
28. Means, B., Olson, K. (1994). The link between technology and authentic learning. Educational Leadership, 52, 15-18.
29. Merseth, K. K. (1991). Supporting beginning teachers with computer networks. Journal of Teacher Education, 42(2), 140-147.
30. Naisbitt, J. (1982). Megatrends. New York: Warner Books.
31. Noble, D. (1996). Mad rushes into the future: The overselling of educational technology. Educational Leadership, 54(3), 18-23.
32. President's Committee of Advisors on Science and Technology. (1997, March). Report on the use of technology to strengthen K-12 education in the United States. [online] http://www.whitehouse.gov/ WH/EOP/OSTP/ NSTC/PCAST/ k-12ed.html).
33. Reeves, T. C. (1998). 'Future Schlock,' 'The computer delusion,' and The end of education': Responding to critics of educational technology. Educational Technology, 38(5), 49-53.
34. Rule, B., Ferguson, T. (1986). The effects of media violence on attitudes, emotions and cognition. Journal of Social Issues, 42, 29-50.
35. Singer, J. L., Singer, D. G (1986). Family experiences and television viewing as predictors of children's imagination, restlessness, and aggression. Journal of Social Issues, 42, 107-124.
36. Thouvenelle, S., Borunda, M., McDowell, C. (1994). Replicating inequities: Are we doing it again? In J. L. Wright and D. D. Shade(eds.). Young Children: Active learners in a technological age. (pp. 151-66). Washington, DC: NAEYC.
37. Yaghi, H. M., Abu-Saba, M. B. (1998). Teachers' computer anxiety: An international perspective. Computers in Human Behavior, 14(2), 321-336. .
38. Weinman, J., Haag, P. (1999). Gender equity in cyberspace. Educational Leadership, 56(5), 44-49.
39. Whitley, Jr., B. E. (1997). Gender differences in computer-related attitude and behavior: A meta-analysis. Computing in Human Behavior, 13(1), 1-2.
40. Wright, J. L., Shade, D. D. (1994)(eds.). Young children: Active learners in a technological age. Washington, DC: NAEYC.

# A Vision for Improving Mathematics Education in the Internet-Based Society

Sunsook Noh

Department of Mathematics Education
Ewha Womans University
Seoul 120-750, Korea
noh@ewha.ac.kr

**Abstract.** The development of the Internet has brought new opportunities for education. As more and more education related web sites appear daily, there is a need to determine the framework with which the Internet could be best used for education. One vision for the framework based on experiences with mathematics education is the following. First, use the Internet to help teachers to become better teachers. Second, develop web-based instruction contents that are coordinated with the curriculum and the textbook for teachers to use in the classroom. Finally, support more research to determine the best ways of developing web-based contents that show clear improvement in learning. The vision is based on the assumption that teachers, especially in the $K$-12 grade levels, will continue to be the most important part of the educational process for students even in the Internet-based society.

## 1 Introduction

The rapid growth of the Internet worldwide and advancements in Internet technology have brought on what could be described as a start of a revolutionary change in education around the world. The tradition of learning from books and teachers in the classroom during a specified time of the day is slowly being supplemented with wide ranging Internet-based educational opportunities for students of all grade levels from kindergarten to post graduate education and beyond. The ability to freely access information from almost anywhere in the world at anytime of the day coupled with advanced multimedia communication capabilities has opened up new and exciting opportunities to fundamentally change the way people learn and to change the way people view the educational process. In fact, the explosion of information that is available through the Internet has coined the phrase the "knowledge based society" to describe the future.

Along with information revolution comes additional educational opportunities. The additional educational opportunities provided by the Internet today vary widely from simply finding information through the Internet to taking a graduate course on-line. Today, even a grade school student can use the variety of user friendly search engines on the Internet to find many types of information that may not have been easily accessible even from the local library. The

Internet provides a continuously updating and expanding source of information for anyone who is looking for information. And conversely, the Internet provides an easy outlet for anyone who is trying to make information available to anyone who might be interested in the information.

More and more schools around the world are offering distance education courses that use the Internet as the communication channel between students and teachers. The traditional classrooms are replaced with virtual classrooms. Students and teacher could choose to meet in the virtual classroom at a designated time through the use of Internet feature such as real time chat. The advanced state of technology offers a wide range of communication capability over the Internet from simple text based chat to video conferencing depending on the need. Conversely, the teacher can choose to manage the on-line course with asynchronous communication where all discussion and flow of information occur by the use of electronic mail and bulletin board system. This means that students and teachers do not communicate in real time. The benefit of the on-line course is the flexibility of time management and the elimination of spatial distance as a barrier to education. The on-line course provides new opportunities for many students who could not attend traditional schools for various reasons. The flexibility of the cyber education also provides a practical way for many people to continue their education after traditional schooling is finished.

In addition to cyber education based distance learning, many other educational use of the Internet is appearing daily. For example, the Internet can be used to carry out educational projects with students from different parts of the world. Students can collaborate with other students to share and exchange information and ideas. Students benefit by learning to work in a group and learn to communicate with others. The opportunity to work with students from anywhere around the world can provide an invaluable experience for the students. Another example is an interactive lesson site that runs specific lesson units. Variety of topics from virtual dissection of a frog to visualizing chaos theory can be found on the Internet. Some Internet sites provide test questions to help practice taking tests and other sites provide textbook type of information for students. The variety of educational application on the Internet is limited only by the creativity of the authors who create the sites. As the technology of the Internet continues to improve, educators will have even more ways of utilizing the Internet for education.

One of the educational areas where the Internet could make a significant contribution in improving education is mathematics education for the K-12 grade levels. Many students have difficulties in learning mathematics and many teachers have difficulties in teaching mathematics. The current reform movement in mathematics tries to improve mathematics education by incorporating technology when it is possible to enhance the learning process. At first glance, the Internet may not provide any significant benefit in teaching and learning that could not be obtained from multimedia textbooks and lesson-based computer software. In fact, multimedia textbook CD-ROMs and special educational computer software would be easier and faster to use on the local personal computer.

Using the Internet requires another level of hardware and software requirement that makes the use of the technology more complicated. The benefit of using the Internet is that the Internet can provide a common basis for all information for teachers and students everywhere.

One of the promises of the Internet for education use is that the Internet will help to bring equity in education. Students everywhere should not be limited in their educational opportunity by their immediate learning environment. A student with limited learning resources due to geographic location or economic status should have the same opportunity for learning as any other student. The Internet can provide the equity in opportunity for learning by making the same resources available to all students at once. The only requirement will be that the access to the Internet is available to all students equally. Without equal access to the Internet, equity in educational opportunity cannot be achieved. Instead, a new problem of digital divide can occur where students with access to the Internet will have a greater learning opportunity than students without access.

In this paper, a vision of how the Internet could be used to improve mathematics education is described where the emphasis of using the Internet is placed around supporting the mathematics teachers instead of the student. There are two main ways in which the Internet can be used in instruction in a school setting. One is a complete instruction package for students to use in a distance education type of situation and the other is a partial instruction unit for use by the teacher in traditional classrooms. In mathematics education at the K-12 grade levels, the use of the Internet to support the traditional classroom appears to be the best choice. The assumption here is that learning mathematics requires a level of guidance and interaction with the teacher that cannot be obtained by using technology alone. The role of the Internet is then to be a resource for making sure that teachers everywhere are providing the best possible instruction to students. The Internet can provide an invaluable resource for mathematics teachers to share and obtain information about teaching in addition to being a source for standardized lessons that are specifically developed for the curriculum.

## 2 The Need for Technology in Mathematics Education

In recent years, mathematics education has received more and more attention around the world because a technology-based society requires higher competency in mathematics. Mathematics is not only used to develop the technology for our modern society but a certain level of understanding of mathematics is required for everyone to make the most effective use of technology. It is generally agreed that competency in mathematics is directly related to the economical success of individuals and countries.

The recognition of the importance of mathematics education in today's society and the difficulties faced by educators in teaching mathematics prompted the National Council of Teachers of Mathematics in the United States to develop and release the NCTM Curriculum and Evaluation Standards for School Mathematics in 1989 [16]. In 2000, the updated Principles and Standards for

School Mathematics [17] was released. The Standards is a comprehensive set of guidelines that suggests how mathematics should be viewed and taught by the teachers of mathematics. The main goal was to shift the emphasis of mathematics learning from memorization of algorithms to developing critical problem solving skills. The use of available technology such as computers and the Internet is enthusiastically supported as a way of engaging students in learning mathematics. The students could use the technology to explore and experiment with mathematical ideas instead of just memorizing solving problem steps. Using graphing programs on the computer to visualize and compare mathematical functions is an example of the use of technology. The underlying belief of the NCTM Standards is that students will learn more mathematics if they are allowed to explore mathematics to construct their own knowledge.

The strong motivation to reform mathematics education for U.S. educators came from the data that the students in the U.S. typically performed poorly in international mathematics assessments. The recent Third International Mathematics and Science Study (TIMSS) in 1995 showed that U.S. was far behind many countries in mathematics assessment ([1], [12], [14], [29]). The 1999 repeated assessment for the 8th grade level (TIMSS-R) showed that U.S. had not made much progress in improving mathematics performance for the 8th grade students [15] as shown in Table 1.

**Table 1.** Distribution of Mathematics Achievement in the Eighth Grade($Max = 800$)

| Country | 1995 | 1999 |
|---|---|---|
| Singapore | 643 | 604 |
| Korea | 581 | 587 |
| Japan | 581 | 579 |
| U. S. | 492 | 502 |
| International Average | 519 | 521 |

Source: IEA's TIMSS-R, 1999

The TIMSS results showed that U.S. lagged far behind many countries in mathematics achievement and had average scores below the international average for both 1995 and 1999 assessments. The study also showed that Singapore was the best in both assessments. Korea and Japan also performed well in mathematics assessment, which were well above the international average. This result could be interpreted as a proof that mathematics education in Korea is very effective but most educators in Korea would disagree with this interpretation. The reason for the disagreement can also be seen in the TIMSS survey result of students shown in Table 2. While the achievement scores are high for Korea, the attitude of the students and students belief about the reason for studying mathematics do not align with the high scores.

**Table 2.** Percentage of students at high level of index of positive attitudes towards mathematics(%)

| Country | 1995 | 1999 |
|---|---|---|
| Singapore | 45 | 45 |
| Korea | 12 | 9 |
| Japan | 10 | 9 |
| U. S. | 35 | 35 |
| International Average | 30 | 30 |

Source: IEA's TIMSS-R, 1999

The percent of students with positive attitudes towards mathematics is much lower than the international average for both Korea and Japan as shown in Table 2. Singapore and the U.S. have higher than the international average. Generally, one would assume that positive attitude should correlate with higher performance. Only Singapore showed high achievement scores and higher positive attitudes towards mathematics than the international average. Korea and Japan showed high scores with negative attitudes towards mathematics than the international average. The U.S. showed low scores with higher positive attitudes towards mathematics than Korea and Japan.

**Table 3.** Percentage of students who responded to agree or strongly agree to the question why they need to do well in mathematics(%)

| Country | For job | For college entrance |
|---|---|---|
| Singapore | 86 | 95 |
| Korea | 44 | 85 |
| Japan | 51 | 88 |
| U. S. | 81 | 94 |
| International Average | 81 | 87 |

Source: IEA's TIMSS-R, 1999

The percent of students who believe that they need to do well in mathematics for entrance to college was universally high for all countries as shown in Table 3. Almost every student in every country knew that mathematics achievement was important for college entrance. The interesting data from TIMSS is how the students responded to the same question about jobs. Majority of U.S. and Singapore students (over 80%) agreed that doing well in mathematics was important also for getting a job. Only half of the students in Japan and Korea agreed that mathematics was important for getting a job. The data suggests that the high achievement for students in Japan and Korea is driven by college entrance without much connection to jobs and the real world. This appears to also explain the strong negative attitudes toward mathematics for students in Korea and Japan.

The reason for the high scores for Korea and Japan can be explained by the fact that many of the students take after school classes that are designed specifically for college entrance examination. A recent survey of 694 students by the Curriculum Research Project at Ewha University showed that about 70% of the students in the primary, middle and high school students in Korea attend after school classes in Hakwon or get private tutoring [2]. In addition, the survey also showed that about 70% of the students surveyed in K-12 schools thought that the lessons that they received from after school classes were more effective than the lessons that they received from regular schools [2]. This trend was not conveyed accurately in the TIMSS survey. The TIMSS survey showed that students in Korea actually spent less time after school studying mathematics than U.S. students. The reason for the discrepancy in the TIMSS survey is not clear but students in Korea clearly attend many hours of after school classes studying mathematics.

The disconnection between attitude and performance is a serious one for mathematics educators because the high assessment scores may not truly represent the level of mathematical understanding or the development of critical problem solving skills that are needed in the knowledge-based society. Therefore, the NCTM's mathematics reform movement with its emphasis on technology to enhance the learning process is viewed as an important step in improving mathematics education. The NCTM's offers a series of exemplary mathematics less plans on the Internet written by various mathematics teachers in which the Internet is used as a necessary tool in changing the way mathematics is taught [24].

In Korea, the Ministry of Education has also highly recommended the integration of information technology in school mathematics to promote in addition to computational skills, also conceptual understanding and problem solving abilities [13]. The current 7th national curriculum that went into practice since the year 2000 parallels many of the reform concepts that were described in the NCTM Standards [25], [26], [27].

## 3    Using the Internet to Support Teachers

One simple but an effective way to use the Internet to improve mathematics education is to use the Internet as the base for continuing teacher education. Already, there are many resource sites and organizations with information and communication channels over the Internet to help mathematics teachers. Teachers could use the Internet to exchange ideas, lesson plans and keep up to date on the latest information. One of the problems for teachers in implementing the use of technology into daily teaching is that they are not prepared to use the technology. Technology is constantly being changed and updated including the Internet. New applications and methods for using computers and Internet are being created daily by educators around the world. Teachers can not be expected to keep up to date on all the new advancements and ideas in applying technology to teaching.

A recent research project that was carried out at Ewha University in 1999 showed that most mathematics teachers were not prepared to use computers and the Internet to help them teach mathematics [5], [9]. In the research project, a central Internet resource web site for mathematics teachers was developed. The Internet provides a convenient network for teachers to share and get information ([10], [11], [20]). The web site [23] (http://ermt.ewha.ac.kr) used a simple database program to allow teachers to upload and download instructional materials. The purpose was to make available a central bank for instructional material that teachers could use freely and teachers could contribute freely. The biggest problem with the use of the web site by mathematics teachers was that most teachers were not familiar with using the Internet at the time of the research. A survey of mathematics teachers showed that most of the teachers were eager and willing to spend time to learn but many did not have the opportunity [5]. Therefore, the web site only saw uses from teachers who were comfortable using the Internet and recent graduates who learned to use the site during school. Only 6% of the 555 mathematics teachers in the country replied that they had computers in the classroom with Internet access and only 22% of the teachers had experience to use Internet for instructional preparation [9]. After one year, another project that was carried out at Ewha University in 2000 showed more than half of the surveyed 528 mathematics teachers in Korea were using the Internet occasionally to very frequently [7]. And the Internet resource was the third material that they mostly refer for class preparation after textbooks and reference books. Those teachers also replied that they refer textbooks [6]. The most recent survey that was just carried out on 36 mathematics teachers from Seoul and Kyonggi-do area showed that all teachers use Internet on daily basis for 1-3 hours as a major resource for class preparation [19].

While the use of the Internet by teachers increased dramatically in the past three years, the hardware infrastructure to support Internet based teaching and learning in the schools is still deficient. The Internet access is available in every school but there are not enough computers for students to use it as a regular part of their instruction. One of the problems is that the technology is changing rapidly to provide more advanced capabilities but the infrastructure in the schools are lagging behind. Even at the university level, a computer lab with brand new up to date computers become slow and difficult to use in just a couple of years because new softwares demand faster machines. Therefore, without the proper support to maintain and update both the hardware and software, the use of technology becomes difficult. This means that instead of technology becoming an equalizer for education, it becomes a dividing factor that separates educational opportunities for students. Students with better hardware, software and faster Internet connection will be able to benefit more from advances in educational technology versus students who do not have the access. Ideally, it is hoped that all students will be able to have equal access to technology at the school. Today, the situation is far from the ideal setting. This is one reason why effort should be made to help the teachers.

The key idea in making an effort to help teachers is that teachers will still need to be the central piece of the puzzle in education. The Internet and new technologies can provide new and exciting ways for students to enhance their learning, but teachers will be needed to provide guidance, organization and feedback to the students. For students in the $K$-12 levels, an integrated approach to teaching using available technologies should be used. Even the best technology can not provide the same type of personal attention and interaction that a teacher can give to a student.

## 4 Developing Effective Web-based Instruction

The Internet can provide many ways of enhancing education. The students can use multimedia lessons with hyper-links to navigate the text freely or use interactive programs to experiment. Another way of using the Internet is to enhance communication by providing a way for students to ask questions.

One of the initial research topics for investigating the use of the Internet as an educational tool for high school mathematics was to see if a new communication channel for students would allow the students to participate more actively in their own learning by asking questions ([4], [8]). A class of high school students were asked to participate in an after school session using computers and the Internet to access lessons on a web page that was designed specifically for the study. The students were taught to use the bulletin board system on the web page to ask questions as they studied the materials on the web page. When the questions were posted on the bulletin board, students were given immediate feedback on their questions by teachers monitoring the bulletin board at the university. Analysis of the bulletin board usage showed that students asked about 12.5 times more questions about the lessons compared to typical classroom instruction [4]. And, the students also asked meaningful questions about the subject matter. The study showed that one simple way of using the Internet for mathematics education would be to provide a resource for students to ask questions that they could not typically ask in the classroom.

The project showed that students used the opportunity to communicate more freely using the Internet, but the lesson materials which were essentially transferred from text books to the web site did not provide any additional interest for the students [8]. Initially, the students were interested and excited about using the computer and the Internet for learning, but the novelty quickly dissipated. The students showed that unless the web-based instruction material is truly engaging, it will not succeed as a replacement for textbooks.

What is needed for web-based instruction is high quality lesson units which are closely coordinated with the curriculum and the textbooks. The web-based material should supplement the classroom teaching where it is appropriate rather than becoming the main focus of the teaching. The instruction material should not be placed on the web for the sake of placing it on the web. Careful consideration and planning should be used to determine appropriate contents and use that will maximize the educational potential of the Internet. For example, collaborative projects using the Internet would be one way of using the Internet. Another way would be to provide detailed explanations about solutions to homework problems that can be accessed by the students at anytime. Graphical explanation and exploratory functions would be another area for web-based instruction. The emphasis on developing web-based instruction material should be on adding value to the lesson topic which is being taught by the teacher.

## 5  The Need for More Research in Web-based Instruction

Using the Internet to teach and developing web-based instruction material is still a very new process. Although many educators and researchers are working on developing better ways of using the Internet to distribute learning materials, there is a lack of research on determining the effectiveness of web-based instruction. The recently published report of the Web-Based Education Commission to the President and the Congress of the United States ([21], [22]) states that while web-based education has extraordinary possibilities, there are key barriers that are preventing the realization of the full potential. The barriers range from hardware access to privacy issues for the users. Based on the identification of the barriers, the following key recommendations were made by the commission.

- work to make Internet infrastructure available to everyone for equal access to the Internet
- provide continuous training and support for educators and administrators
- develop research framework for studying how students learn in the Internet age
- develop effective online educational content that meets the need of learners
- revise regulations that impede Internet use for education
- protect online learners and their privacy
- provide funding to support all the above items

The true potential of the Internet for education is that it can provide equity in education. This means that students anywhere can have the opportunity to receive the best possible education without any geographic barriers or time constraints. This can only happen if the infrastructure to provide easy and convenient access to the Internet is available for all students.

Once the infrastructure is in place, proper content has to be provided to the students to make web-based instruction succeed. A recent review of the contemporary research on the effectiveness of web-based education in higher learning published by the Institute for Higher Education Policy found that much of current research efforts have shortcomings which make the conclusions inconclusive [3]. So far, most of the conclusions were positive about the impact of distance learning. Clearly, more work is needed to understand the true impact of web-based instruction and to develop new teaching pedagogy to optimize web-based instruction.

# 6 Conclusion

In a very short time, the Internet has become a valuable resource for education. Undoubtedly, the Internet will become even more valuable for education in the future as computers and infrastructure for high speed access become more widely available and the technology to deliver high quality interactive multimedia content becomes faster, easier and more economical. The potential of the Internet as an educational resource appears to be unlimited at this point. But, as with all valuable natural resources such as trees, water and crude oil, careful planning and management of the Internet resource are needed to maximize the benefit and to minimize any negative consequences. As more and more education related web sites appear on the Internet, there is an increasing need for educators to develop a coherent framework for incorporating the Internet into everyday education. The vision described in this paper is one suggestion on how the Internet could be used to improve the overall educational process. The following vision for using the Internet to improve mathematics education is a simple one that could also be applicable to other areas of education.

First, consider the teacher first when developing educational contents, policies and communication channels on the Internet. The interactivity provided by the Internet is an excellent way for students to receive information and feedback but it can not surpass the interactivity that can be provided by the teacher. The teachers are on the front line of education and they bear the responsibility of teaching and assessing the effectiveness of the teaching material. The Internet should be used to its fullest potential to provide as much help as possible to the teachers.

Secondly, educational contents developed for the Internet should be closely coordinated with the curriculum and the textbooks so that teachers and students can use the Internet content as an integral part of everyday school material. Teachers should have the option to use the Internet-based material when necessary to enhance the teaching process. The students should have the freedom to access the Internet-based material as an integral or supplementary material to get additional help in understanding the topic.

Finally, more research should be carried out to determine the best ways of developing educational materials for the Internet. The lesson materials developed for the curriculum should be researched and tested to make sure that concrete benefit is found for the material.

The goal of education is clear and the importance of education in today's technology driven society cannot be denied. Every student should be given the same opportunity for the best education that is possible and the Internet is the tool that has the best chance today of providing that opportunity.

*Acknowledgement.* This work was supported by Korea Research Foundation Grant: KRF-99-005-c00051.

# References

1. Beaton, A. E., Mullis, I. V. S., Martin, M. O., Gonzalez, E. J., Kelly, D. L., Smith, T. A.: Mathematics Achievement in the Middle School Years: IEA's Third International Mathematics and Science Study (TIMSS). TIMSS International Study Center, Chestnut Hill, MA: Center for the Study of Testing, Evaluation, and Education Policy, Boston College (1996).
2. Cho, K. W., Kim, K., Noh, S. et al.: Survey for the curriculum development research in the knowledge-based society, Journal of Educational Studies (of Ewha Educational Research Institute) **31**(2) (2000) 1-505.
3. Institute for Higher Education Policy: What's the Difference? A review of contemporary research on the effectiveness of distance learning in higher education (1999).
4. Kim, M. K., Noh, S.: An analysis of contents and usage of a Web Bulletin Board System: A case study of an Internet-based mathematics instruction, Journal of Educational Technology (of The Korean Society for Educational Technology) **15**(1) (1999) 219-239.
5. Kim, M. K., Noh, S.: A study on the development of an interactive Web-based resource center for K-12 mathematics teachers, Journal of the Korea Society of Mathematical Education **39**(1) (2000) 71-80.
6. Kim, M. K., Noh, S.: A survey of teachers, students, parents towards instructional media in math education, Journal of the Korea Society of Mathematical Education **40** (2001), to appear.
7. Kim, M. K., Noh, S.: Use of computers in mathematics education, School Mathematics (of The Korea Society of Educational Studies in Mathematics) **3**(1) (2001), to appear.
8. Kim, M. K., Noh, S., Lee, J.: Effectiveness of using a Web-site for two-way communication in mathematics education. Journal of Educational Technology (of The Korean Society for Educational Technology) **14**(3) (1998) 81-104.
9. Kim, M. K., Noh, S., Lee, J.: Internet usage of school mathematics, Journal of the Korea Society of Educational Information Science **5**(2) (2001), to appear.
10. Lieberman, A.: Networks as learning communities: Shaping the future of teacher development, J. Teacher Education **51**(3) (2000) 221-227.
11. Lieberman, A.: Transforming teaching and schooling in the twenty-first century, The 1st Emma Lecture, Ewha Womans University, Seoul, Korea (2000).
12. Martin, M. O., Mullis, I. V. S., Gonzalez, E. J., Kelly, D. L., Smith, T. A.: School Contexts for Learning and Instruction: IEA's Third International Mathematics and Science Study (TIMSS). TIMSS International Study Center, Chestnut Hill, MA: Center for the Study of Testing, Evaluation, and Education Policy, Boston College (1999).
13. Ministry of Education (of Korea): The 7th National Mathematics Curriculum Standards. MOE (1997).
14. Mullis, I. V. S., Martin, M. O., Beaton, A. E., Gonzalez, E. J., Kelly, D. L., Smith, T. A.: Mathematics Achievement in the Primary School Years: IEA's Third International Mathematics and Science Study (TIMSS). TIMSS International Study Center, Chestnut Hill, MA: Center for the Study of Testing, Evaluation, and Education Policy, Boston College (1997).
15. Mullis, I. V. S., Martin, M. O., Gonzalez, E. J., Gregory, K. D., Garden, R. A., O'Conner, K. M., Chrostowski, S. J., Smith, T. A.: TIMSS 1999 International Mathematics Report: Findings from IEA's Repeat of the The International Mathematics and Science Study at the Eight Grade. The International Asssociation for the Evaluation of Educational Achievement (2000).

16. National Council of Teachers of Mathematics: Curriculum and Evaluation Standards for School Mathematics. Reston, VA: Author (1989).

17. National Council of Teachers of Mathematics: Principles and Standards for School Mathematics. Reston, VA: Author (2000).

18. Noh, S.: Utilizing the Internet as a knowledge base system resource for teachers. Journal of the Research Institute of Curriculum Instruction (of Ewha W. University), 3(2) (1999) 133–146.

19. Noh, S.: Teaching with technology and mathematics teachers, in preparation.

20. Selwyn, N.: Creating a "connected" community? Teachers' use of an electronic discussion group. Teachers College Record 102(4) (2000) 750–778.

21. Web-based Education Commission: Report of the Web-Based Education Commission to the President and the Congress of the United States (2000).

22. Web-Based Education Commission: The Power of the Internet for Learning: moving from promise to practice, Washington D.C. (2000).

23. http://ermt.ewha.ac.kr

24. http://illuminations.nctm.org

25. http://www.edunet4u.net

26. http://www.keris.re.kr

27. http://www.moe.go.kr

28. http://www.nctm.org

29. http://www.timss.org

# Leapfrogging from Traditional Government to e-Government

Seang-Tae Kim[1]

[1]Department of Public Administration, Sungkyunkwan Univeristy, 53, 3-Ga Myonguyun-Dong Seoul 110-745
kimst@yurim.skku.ac.kr

**Abstract**. This research project begins with question of the reason why we faces the difficulty of realizing e-government. The research evaluated the current situation of e-government. Based on this evaluation, the research extracts and explains the critical success factors, which have effects on the construction of e-government. As well, this research shows the co-relation among factors. As a result, the government should approach realizing e-government on systematic and aggregate strategy and policy

# 1 Introduction

## 1.1 Current Background and Purpose

Recently perception about contribution of Information Technology(hereby after IT) to improvement of productivity and the public service in local government has led to investment on IT especially e-government. Actually, IT is absorbing an ever-increasing proportion of the resources of local governments, both in terms of limited budget and human resources, with many projects of IT utilization

Before 1990, IT had been generally applied to the citizen registration services, real estate management services, and car registration services as the projects of computerization of public administration in local governments. These projects have been driven by the central government through top-down approach.

Since Kwangju Metropolitan City set up 'Integrated Urban Information System' to utilizing GIS in 1990, a new era of independent information policy by local governments has been opened. Since 1993, several local governments such as Kyungki, Taejon, Kangwon, Chungbuk, established the informatization plan. Since 1996, local governments utilized Internet as the means of various information projects including public administration, industry, citizen life etc. Almost every local government operates web sites and applies them to the non-stop services in civil affairs.

There have been much efforts to make "new government" by using IT like e-government in information society. However, this transformation to e-government still lags behind the rapid change. Therefore, it is important to find out how to deal with IT in and on the government for getting better government and public service. For this reason, many traditional governments are seeking the best way to transform into e-government.

The purpose of this research is to evaluate the current situation of e-government and tasks of utilizing IT in local governments in Korea. For that purpose, first, this research based on the theoretical discussion shows evaluation indicators. Second, the research identifies the critical success factors by assessing the current situation of e-government and tasks of utilizing IT on evaluation indicators.

## 1.2 Research Methodolgy

In the research, to evaluate the present situation and tasks of e-government in local governments, several methods including interview with CIO and public employees, on-the-spot survey, and survey with e-mail, etc., were applied, given those evaluation indicators

## 2 Theoretical Reviews and Framework

The goal of adopting IT is changing the traditional role of the government into that of Electronic Government. The ultimate ideology of electronic government is to secure a democracy and public welfare by increasing transparency as well as efficiency in public administration and enhancing competitiveness of public services.

Based on the definition of e-government, the research review many components of e-government for making evaluative indicators. According to the literatures, the components of electronic government, which can fulfill its goal and ideology, are as follows: managerial aspects, information resource management (IRM) aspects, opening public information aspects, organizational aspects IT and environmental aspects, etc.

At first, realization of electronic government will be possible by simplifying the process of public affairs by introducing BPR in public management, and electronic document flow system is one aspect of the fundamental components of the electronic government.

Second, many experts argue that Information Resource Management is key way to secure the success of e-government. Successful electronic government can come true based on the IRM. The precondition for IRM introduces standardization of information related system and database (DB) linkage system between inter and intra-organization. As well, in order to maximize the role of electronic government, the overall IRM systems should be introduced. In the IRM systems, basic guidelines and principles on the IT, manpower, budget, facilities etc., should be included.

Information opening system and network infrastructure would be indispensable for successful electronic government. The accessibility from citizens should be enhanced by providing public information through the Internet with every homepages in public organizations.

As another important component of e-government, organizational aspects include CIO System and Enhancing Information Literacy and Capability.

CIO System would be indispensable for reforming the government based on the IT. The major role of CIO is in charge of IRM including introduction of IT and it's strategic utilization based on the BPR. The level of public employee's information literacy and capability would be important factors, which determine the successful electronic government. Thus education systems and training strategies to enhance the level of public employee's information related ability should be well organized and prepared.

At last, IT and Environmental Aspects, being an infrastructure, Intranet/Extranet system is one of the most important components of electronic government.

Based on of the components of electronic government, this research evaluate the current situation and tasks of e-government in local governments in Korea.

# 3. Evaluation of e-Government

## 3.1 Overall Description

According to on-the-spot survey, it is believed that the successful e-government depends on the strong leadership at the highest level, because the level of IT applications in local government might be directly related with the level of concern and strong will of governors or mayors. They would influence on the information policy related organization and information policy related budget. As a result, the budget influences on the information infrastructure.

In a case of street level or lower level of public employees, the desire and ability to utilizing the IT to their works are very high. However, the management level of bureaucrats would not be well utilize them, compared with the street or lower level. These evaluations surveyed on the informatization related satisfaction level of public servants in local governments, following results are reported: 10-70 percentage of public employees responded on "Blow Average" for information planning. In terms of an allocation in budget, manpower, and IT resources, 10-50 percentages of respondents expressed the dissatisfaction on "Not Adequate". On this survey, reportedly, 10-40 percentage of public servants believed their opinions have not been reflected in the process of setting up information policy. At last, 20 percentages of respondents evaluated the leadership and ability of CEO and CIO to promote information policy as "Low".

The following table 1 indicates the overall evaluation results, which come from the interview with CIO and Public employees, on-the-spot survey, and survey with e-mail.

The overall evaluation results show that the average of metropolitan and provincial government records C. The level of category in the Information Infrastructure and Public Service belongs to B and D. In terms of Information Infrastructure, the level of inner telecommunication network in local government is lower than that of the outer telecommunication network. In assessing the public service, local governments have not built enough homepages to provide information. Even though the great advantage of IT is the dissemination of information in economic way, local governments do not seem to recognize this advantage.

Table 1 Overall Evaluation Results

| Grade | A | B | C | D | E |
|---|---|---|---|---|---|
| Information Planning and Mind of Leader's | 2 | 5 | 8 | 1 | 0 |
| Information Infrastructure | 0 | 5 | 0 | 0 | 1 |
| Information Utilization | 0 | 0 | 4 | 9 | 3 |
| Public Service | 0 | 3 | 8 | 4 | 1 |
| Projects for Local Government | 3 | 5 | 5 | 3 | 0 |
| Total Average | 0 | 5 | 5 | 6 | 0 |

Note 1) The figure in the table is the number of local government.

Even though lacking the recognition of the benefits, local governments have initiated some pilot-projects, which relate to regional economy development as well as other projects such as Urban Information System (UIS) and Geographic Information System (GIS).

## 3.2 The System of CIO as Driving Force of e-Government

It revealed that the degree of authority and status of CIO influence much of the level of e-government in the organization.

Local governments in Korea have three types of CIO system. The first one is that the director in charge of department of planning and management holds another additional post of CIO. The second system is that the secretary of chief hold another additional post of CIO. The third one is CIO from the external recruitment.

The advantages of the first type of CIO system are, in case that the CIO has strong will for e-government policy implementation, the IT related budget can be supported as well as the e-government projects of each department can be coordinated. In addition, the information policy can be efficiently promoted. However, this system has an important limitation, that is, a lack of professionalism due to the bureaucratic background of the chief of planning and management. Furthermore, they do not have enough time to consider the e-government policy implementation sufficiently.

In a case of the third type of CIO system, the advantage is that CIO has the professionalism and strong will for e-government policy implementation. However, the limitation of this system is the CIO from outside would not have a power to control the overall organization. In order to overcome this kind of limitation, the CIO should have a budget control power and personnel related power. As a natural result, the effectiveness of this kind of system depends on the will of the Governor or Mayor of the corresponding local government.

The analyses of the data related with CIO in local governments are as follows: first, the status of CIO varies from 1st grade to 4th according to each local government, because political fad among local governments brings about establishing the position of CIO. It directly means that local government does not clearly account for what the roles and responsibilities of CIO are in legislating. In a real case, one local government puts a position of CIO as the status of professional. The CIO would impossibly implement e-government over a budget and make IT investment strategy. Second, on the survey of tenure of an office, it reveals that CIO in 7 local governments has not yet worked longer than a year. 4 local governments have CIO position just before 3 month. The tenure of last 4 CIO is under 6 month. At last, the academic background of CIO is almost public administration (8). However, 2 CIO's background came from computer science, due to people's mind that CIO should know and handle the computer system. Other major of CIO is the economics(2) and law (2).

### 3.3 e-Government Policy

In evaluating e-government policy of local governments, many aspects should be examined such as the consistency between a long-term and mid-term developing planning and policy, the feasibility of e-government policy, and an adequacy of its sub-area. The following table 2 is showing the results of evaluation.

Table 2 Selected Evaluation Results of Information Planning

| Grade | A | B | C | D | E |
|---|---|---|---|---|---|
| Information Policy Adequacy | 6 | 5 | 3 | 2 | 0 |
| Organization Adequacy | 4 | 10 | 1 | 1 | 0 |
| CEO Mind | 2 | 7 | 5 | 1 | 1 |
| CIO Mind | 4 | 6 | 5 | 1 | 0 |
| The rate of Informatization Budget | 1 | 0 | 7 | 6 | 2 |
| Increasing rate of informatization budget | 2 | 2 | 4 | 5 | 3 |
| Total Average | 2 | 5 | 8 | 1 | 0 |

Note 1) The figure in the table is the number of local government.

Currently, most of local governments belong to B and C grade. As you can be seen from table 2, the overall level of e-government policy and organization adequacy in local governments is highly recorded. The statistics of CEO and CIO Mind indicate that high policy-decision makers recognize the e-government as an important tool of developing their regions and capacity of government. However, as a difficult factor for implementing successful e-government, the proportion of e-government budget in local government's revenue indicates the low level. In addition, the rate of e-government budget over a year before is not highly increased.

The general problems of e-government in local governments are as follows: First, the information planning should provide the guide-lines of establishing strategies for IT projects and also provide a criteria for allocation of information related resources. In these aspects, it appears that almost all of the local governments fail to have a direct relationship between them. Second, there are few cases that a local government adjusts the information plan related with the level of budget and implementation. In order to overcome these problems, the e-government policy should be modified annually as a rolling plan system and action plan which reflects the present budget level and situations of local governments, should be prepared.

### 3.4 Information Infrastructures and Its Utilization

The level of information infrastructure is directly related with the fiscal situation of local governments. The evaluation results reveal that the local governments have some difficulty to build with building the information infrastructure due to the lack of budget. Owing to this limitation, it is clear that the level of information infrastructure situation and its utilization has been a critical stepping-stone to make an efficient e-government. The evaluation results of information infrastructure situation are shown in the following table 3.

Table 3 Selected Evaluation Results of Information Infrastructure in Local Governments

| Grade | | A | B | C | D | E |
|---|---|---|---|---|---|---|
| Telecommunication | Outer Telecommunication Network | 4 | 11 | 0 | 0 | 1 |
| | Inner Telecommunication Network | 3 | 0 | 6 | 5 | 2 |
| Hard-Ware | PC connected with LAN per person | 2 | 6 | 4 | 4 | 0 |
| | PC per person | 1 | 0 | 9 | 5 | 1 |
| | PC connected with a printer | 4 | 1 | 8 | 1 | 2 |
| Soft-Ware | Word Processor per each PC | 1 | 2 | 4 | 8 | 0 |
| | Soft Ware in legal | 1 | 10 | 5 | 0 | 0 |
| The Adequacy of Network Security System | | 5 | 4 | 4 | 3 | 0 |
| Informatization Education Facilities | | 2 | 9 | 2 | 2 | 0 |
| Informatization Education Actual Results | | 2 | 5 | 7 | 2 | 0 |
| Owners of IT related Certificate | | 2 | 4 | 6 | 2 | 2 |
| Total Average | | 0 | 5 | 10 | 0 | 1 |

Note 1) The figure in the table is the number of local government.

The results on the evaluation of telecommunication infrastructure indicate that the outer telecommunication network has been almost installed. However, the inner telecommunication network is not still enough to intercommunicate between outside and inside. As can be seen in the table 3, the inner communication network marks C and D. Furthermore, the evaluation of hardware situation records C to D. As a result, local government could not effectively utilize the outer telecommunication infrastructure, even though this outer environment has been improved and successfully built. This fact is closely related to the utilization of information infrastructure. The evaluation of its utilization in the table 4 shows the productivity of utilizing IT in local governments has not been improved in local governments.

Table 4 Selected Evaluation Results of Information Infrastructure Utilization

| Grade | A | B | C | D | E |
|---|---|---|---|---|---|
| Ability of utilizing PC and the Internet | 3 | 9 | 3 | 1 | 0 |
| Electronic Document Interchange (EDI) | 3 | 6 | 2 | 3 | 2 |
| Utilizing Electronic BBS | 1 | 10 | 3 | 2 | 0 |
| Average hour of using the Internet per a day | 3 | 9 | 4 | 0 | 0 |
| Providing E-mail and ID | 5 | 5 | 1 | 2 | 3 |
| Improving productivity by using IT | 0 | 0 | 0 | 9 | 7 |
| Total Average | 0 | 0 | 4 | 9 | 3 |

Note 1) The figure in the table is the number of local government.

The overall level of utilizing IT in local government results in C and D. In this survey, the ability of utilizing PC and the Internet as an evaluation indicator, which shows the public employees, have a good IT literacy. The public employees of local governments in Korea utilize PC 1-3 hour in average. The purpose of the utilizing PC is as follows: word processing, information searching, electronic data interchange, etc. However, 4-20% of them answered that introducing IT to public affairs failed to promote morale of public servants. As a result of the high level of public employees using IT, the utilization degree of Electronic Document Interchange(EDI), electronic BBS, E-mail, recorded high scores. Even though public employees have used the information-related equipment, this situation does not contribute to improve productivity in local governments. Therefore, local governments should investigate the way to improve productivity by using IT as much as it has invested its budget on IT. In a case of EDI, most of the local government in Korea operates EDI and flow system as a pilot project: the organization utilizes that system in relatively lower level. The major problem of this system results from the fact that BPR has not been introduced before adopting electronic document interchange and flow system

Almost all the local governments are confronted with the problems which arise from the inadequate allocation of budget in the field of e-government policy and this in turn results in a lack of efficient utilization of information, related equipment. The main reason for that is a lack of understanding on the information resource management (IRM) and lack of professionalism in its implementing organization including CIO system.

## 3.5 Pubic Service

Local Government has not utilized IT for providing public service efficiently. The main evaluation indicator in the Public Service is the Homepage in which people could access, whenever as well as wherever they want to get some information. However, most municipal and provincial governments have not built their Web sites on the view of the public service adequately.

Table 5 Selected Evaluation Results of Public Service

| Grade | A | B | C | D | E |
|---|---|---|---|---|---|
| Homepage | 0 | 4 | 7 | 3 | 2 |
| Internet Public Service on Civil Affair | 6 | 5 | 5 | 0 | 0 |
| Informatization Event and Education for Citizen | 0 | 0 | 7 | 8 | 1 |
| Regional Information Industry Supporting | 0 | 3 | 10 | 2 | 1 |
| Total Average | 0 | 3 | 8 | 4 | 1 |

Note: The figure in the table is the number of local government.

## 3.6 Regional e-Government Project

As a regional e-government project UIS(Urban Information System) and GIS (Geographic Information System) are the most frequent typologies in local governments. It is expected that UIS and GIS projects would influence strongly on the citizen's daily-life by improving public services in the long run. However, those projects expect much more investment are needed and it takes much more time to get enough effects. Therefore, the priority of investment should be examined carefully. In case of that every local government promotes UIS and GIS projects independently, the issue of nationwide information sharing for them would be very important. This is the reason coordinating among the regions and standardization issue should be emphasized and well prepared.

Many local governments introduce electronic commerce as a regional e-government pilot project. The main reason for adopting this system is to vitalize the local economy.

For that purpose, most of those systems contain specialties and products of regional firms as service targets. However, according to the evaluation of that system, even if the systems are successfully developed in technical sense, it fails to achieve the major purpose. The main reason for that kind of result comes from the fact that a local government cannot be the adequate major operator due to their lack of their professional marketing abilities.

## 4. Correlation Analysis: Identifying Critical Success Factors of e-Government

The results of correlation analysis with each evaluation indicator variables of 16 metropolitan municipalities and provincial government are as follows.

There is a significant positive association between 'Information Policy related Organization' and 'Information Policy' ($r=.496$, $p<.05$). This can be interpreted that well operation of CIO and information promoting committee would influence on the level of quality of the basic information planning.

The level of 'Information Mind of Leader's' has a significant positive correlation to 'Information Policy related Organization' ($r=.575$, $p<.001$). This fact means that the level of Governor or Mayor's information mind and concern influence on the effective operation of CIO system and information promoting council.

Surprisingly, there is significant negative relationship between 'Information Policy and Productivity and System Satisfaction', while there are significant positive relationship between 'Information Policy' and the level of 'Homepage and Citizen's accessibility'. This can be interpreted that the Information planning cannot be implemented successfully to support the promotion of the organizational productivity.

The Information related Investment has a moderate positive correlation with information related organization and manpower ($r=.660$, $p<.005$). However, there is no significant relationship with other important variables including the variable, organizational productivity.

The level of 'Telecommunication Network' shows strong positive relationship to the level of Hardware system ($r=.828$, $p<.000$). And it shows a moderate relationship to the degree of PC/Internet Utilization. ($r=.530$, $p<.05$) However, the relationships between 'Telecommunication Network' and 'Information Education Facilities and Activities' as well as 'Information related Manpower' are not significant. These facts imply that information policy in localities would not be systematic as well as Information Resource Management would not be introduced and applied successfully in localities.

Information Education Facilities and Activities have significant positive relationship with EDI/Intranet utilization. ($r=.603$, $p<.01$) And it has also positive relationship with Projects for local informatization. ($r=.610$, $p<.001$) These facts imply that Information Education Facilities and Activities influence much on enhancing the level of information literacy and ability of public employees in local government, which however cannot be linked with the enhancement of the organizational productivity.

The overall analysis shows that there are no relationships between organizational productivity and many important variables such as Information Policy, Information related Investment, and Information Infrastructure (Network, H/W, S/W etc.). From this, it can be interpreted as the information policy in local government can not be appropriately set up and implemented successfully based on the concept of IRM as well as BPR in terms of long term perspective. Thus, the local governments failed to promote organizational productivity by adopting IT, which means that CIO systems would not operate well.

Table 6 Correlation Matrices

|       | IP     | IPO    | IML    | IRI    | TN     | HWS    | SWS    | ISS    | IEFC   |
|-------|--------|--------|--------|--------|--------|--------|--------|--------|--------|
| IP1   | 1.000  | .496*  | .190   | .036   | .212   | .143   | .268   | -.204  | -.034  |
| IPO   | .496*  | 1.000  | .575*  | .370   | -.001  | .148   | .314   | .156   | -.115  |
| IML   | .190   | .575*  | 1.000  | .078   | .107   | .106   | .064   | .022   | .337   |
| IRI   | .036   | .370   | .078   | 1.000  | .174   | .266   | .425   | .154   | -.180  |
| TN    | .212   | -.001  | .107   | .174   | 1.000  | .828** | -.070  | -.466  | .207   |
| HWS   | .143   | .148   | .106   | .266   | .828** | 1.000  | -.136  | -.467  | .009   |
| SWS   | .268   | .314   | .064   | .425   | -.070  | -.136  | 1.000  | .457   | .030   |
| ISS   | -.204  | .156   | .022   | .154   | -.466  | -.467  | .457   | 1.000  | -.306  |
| IEFC  | -.034  | -.115  | .337   | -.180  | .207   | .009   | .030   | -.306  | 1.000  |
| IM    | .399   | .469   | .039   | .660** | .206   | .189   | .378   | .240   | -.109  |
| PCU   | .031   | -.008  | .307   | .268   | .530*  | .423   | -.029  | -.146  | .368   |
| EDIU  | .144   | -.044  | .306   | .109   | .433   | .056   | .298   | -.026  | .603*  |
| IU    | -.039  | -.388  | -.498* | .113   | .102   | .137   | -.407  | -.168  | -.027  |
| PSS   | -.497* | -.259  | .018   | .233   | .140   | .116   | .113   | .430   | .064   |
| HP    | .511*  | .285   | .208   | .186   | .172   | .133   | .405   | -.215  | .014   |
| SCE   | .228   | .206   | .319   | .105   | .161   | .242   | .068   | -.421  | .484*  |
| IEEC  | -.137  | .007   | .103   | .066   | -.153  | -.488* | .436   | .642** | .239   |
| PLI   | -.072  | .053   | .546*  | -.323  | .097   | .020   | .050   | .199   | .610** |

Notes: *Correlation is significant at the 0.05 level, **Correlation is significant at the 0.001 level

---

[1] The abbreviation of each indicator used as a name of variables in the correlation analyses. The full name of each variable is as follows: **Information Planning & Information Mind of Leader's** Information Policy (IP: 40), Information Policy related Organization (IPO: 20), Information Mind of Leader's (IML: 100), Information related Investment (IRI: 40), **Information Infrastructure** Telecommunication Network (TN: 30), Hardware Systems (HWS: 50), Software Systems (SWS: 20), Information Security Systems (ISS: 20), Information Education Facilities and Actual Results (IEFA: 30), Information related Manpower (IM: 30), **Information Utilization** PC Utilization (PCU: 30), Electronic Document and Intranet Utilization (EDIU: 80), Internet Utilization (IU: 30), Productivity and System Satisfaction (PSS: 60), **Public Services** Home-pages (HP: 230), Services for Civil Affairs (SCA: 20), Information related Education events for citizen (IEEC: 50), **Projects for Local Informatization** Projects for Local Informatization (PLI: 100)

# 5. Conclusion

The analyses in this research show that the overall IT related environment has been developed rapidly in terms of information infrastructure (h/w, network, etc) in local governments. However, almost all the local governments are confronted with the problems, which arise from the inadequate allocation of budget in the field of e-government policy and this in turn results in a lack of efficient utilization of information, related equipment. The main reason for that is a lack of understanding on the information resource management (IRM) and lack of professionalism in its implementing organization including CIO system.

The study has examined a perception about the contribution of leadership to successful e-government. Some results validated that strong will of mayor or governor has not always an effect on overall informatization except information policy related organization.

It can be concluded that the e-government budget has not been invested effectively, considering that this investment has not contributed to productivity improvement in local government. This problem is due to the failure to apply the information resource management. Furthermore, most of local government introduced hardware system and software system including Electronic Document Flow System without analyzing workload and process for adopting IT on management. Consequently, the amount of investment has not realized the advantage of adopting IT such as productivity improvement, efficiency.

'Information Education Facilities and Activities' influence much on enhancing the level of information literacy and ability of public employee in local government, which however cannot be linked to the enhancement of the organizational productivity.

The overall analysis shows that there are no relationship between 'organizational productivity' and many important variables such as 'information policy', 'information related investment', and 'information infrastructure'. From these facts, it can be concluded that the information policy in local government cannot be set up and implemented appropriately based on the concept of IRM as well as BPR in terms of the long-term perspective. Thus, the local governments failed to promote organizational productivity by adopting IT, which means that CIO systems would not operate well. These are the major urgent tasks, which should be overcome, for introducing the information technology in local governments in Korea.

# References

Andersen, David F. and Sharon S. Dawes. (1991). *Government information management A Primer and Casebook.* New Jersey, Prentice-Hall.

Boddy, David and Nicky Gunson. (1996). *Organizations in the network age.* London, Routledge

Cabinet Office. (2000. 4) *e-government: A strategic framework for public services in the information age*

Cabinet Office. (2000. 5) *Successful IT: Modernizing Government in Action*

CITU. (2000). *Information Age Government: Benchmarking Electronic Service Delivery.* <Http://www.citu.gov.uk/iform-rep.doc>

CITU. (1999). *Intelligent Form - A Case Study of Successful Electronic Government.* <Http://www.citu.gov.uk/iform-close.htm>

CITU. (2000.4). *Implementing e-government: Guidelines for local Government* London

Clinton, J. W. (1999). *Memorandum for the Heads of Executive Department and Agencies*

Currid, C. & Company (1994). *Computing Strategies for Reengineering Your Organization.* Rocklin, CA. Prima Publishing

Heeks, Richard. (1999). *Reinventing Government in the Information Age: International practice in IT-enabled public sector reform.* London, Routledge

KickStart Initiative. (1993) *Connecting America's Communities to the Information Superhighway.*
<http://www.benton.org/KickStart/kick.home.html. ftp//cdnet.com /Benton/KickStart.>

Minoli, Daniel. (1995). *Analizing Outsourcing: Reengineering Information and Communication Systems.* New York, McGraw-Hill

O'Riordan, P. (1987) "The CIO: MIS Makes its Move into the Executive Suite" *Journal of Information Systems Management,* Vol.4,
No.3, pp.54-56

Toregas, Costis (ed.) (1985). *Managing New Technologies: The Information Revolution in Local Government,* Washington D.C. ICMA.

Strassmann, Paul A., (1995). *The Politics of Information Management: Policy Guidelines.* New Canaan, Connecticut, The Information Economic Press.

# Towards Cyber-democracy: True Representation

Craig Carter[1], Kay Fielden[2]

[1]Royal New Zealand Navy
[2]Associate Professor, Information Systems and Computing
School of Information Systems and Computing

**Abstract.** True elector representation in democratic processes can be achieved in a safe and secure environment using the Internet as the electoral vehicle. Clift(2000) maintains that democracy is run by the people who show up, and states that the Internet will bring people closer to the democratic processes of government. This paper describes a qualitative research study conducted by Carter (2001) in which both the barriers and opportunities for electronic voting in New Zealand were explored. The aim was to seek an understanding of the relationship between evoting and electoral improvement. Primary data was collected from voters using a multiple case-study methodology involving the use of an evoting prototype. Secondary data was obtained from an extensive literature review. Analysis of the results showed that there was strong support for the evoting prototype. Further research is required to identify the acceptability level by the New Zealand voting population.

## Keywords

Cyber-governance, Electronic Voting, Elector Participation, Web development

## Introduction

Cyber-governance includes online participation in decision-making processes, access to public information and to government services online. Democratic participation by ordinary citizens in government decision-making requires that the integrity and validity of the system that permits such participation be beyond reproach. Furthermore, appropriate levels must be set for system fairness, system access and the degree of acceptability. These are the very issues that have prevented electronic voting (evoting) from being used in electoral systems.

Electronic commerce technology enables business to be done on-line over the Internet from anywhere, at anytime and in an instant. But evoting remains a glaring omission from the information superhighway, and the ballot box is one of the last bastions of the pre-digital information era.

This paper discusses the results of a recent New Zealand evoting study. The study provides a basis for understanding the issues that must be addressed before the evoting taboo can be broken. Once broken, it is not only elections, but also governance, in the form of on-line democratic participation in government decision-making, that stand to benefit from the information technology revolution.

To obtain a perspective on the background to the situation it is useful to examine what other commentators have said about evoting. Carey (1998) believes that electronic voting "appears to be an information age taboo" because of concerns about voter fraud, privacy, and hackers who might "stuff electronic ballot boxes". Carey states that there have been few responses to such concerns. Similar sentiments were expressed a decade earlier over computerized election systems and questions were raised about security, verification, adherence to election rules, error correction and public response of such systems (Kassicieh, et al, 1988).

The issues surrounding evoting and cyber-governance reside within the divide that exists between present electoral systems and the prophecy that Internet voting will produce globally based democracies with voters no longer aggregated on any geographical basis. This paper examines the issues that lie between these two extremes, and focuses on how evoting can be used to improve the electoral system in New Zealand. In particular the results of a study that examined voter perceptions in detail are summarised. The research is unique in that it investigates the issues of voter acceptance, accessibility, and familiarity with computers and the Internet in the specific contextual setting of an evoting system. It also investigates voter perceptions surrounding security and privacy. While it appears that most of the concerns over the possible risks of evoting have their origins within conventional voting systems, the biggest issues that people focus on are voter fraud and system security.

## Voter Fraud

Voter fraud has always been a concern. In the 1960's in Chicago USA, it was claimed that one-third of the people who died in a given year nonetheless managed to vote in the next election (Carey, 1998). In the past, prosecutions for dual or multiple voting instances in NZ have occurred, but are few in number and have never caused any change in the election result (Hunn and Smith, 2000: pg42). During a trial of evoting in the 2000 US Presidential Election, fraud was rumored to have surfaced in the form of 'vote-swapping', the use or potential use of the Internet for people to trade votes tactically between states. More alarmingly, a site was set up called Voteauction.com purporting to help people auction their votes to the highest bidder: this was shut down by a Chicago judge, although its owner later claimed the exercise had been satirical.

## System Security

Security has been a long held concern. With current systems, the accuracy of the vote count is not absolute. Vote recounts often return a different result from the original count. Validity of votes has also always been an issue. But with evoting, there are many more ways to check the identity of electronic voters such as passwords, smart cards, thumb print scanning, retina scanning, and voice recognition. If electronic security methods were not reliable, banks would not permit hundreds of billions of dollars to move through banking systems around the world electronically every day. There is also much confidence in today's encryption technology, and with it, evoting could be used to reduce fraud as well as ensure privacy.

## Election Legislation

The electoral legislation that exists in most democracies, including New Zealand, has not been written with the technological solutions that are available today in mind. While such legislation has not been written explicitly to exclude electronic voting, in most cases the advent of evoting is not provided for. Just as with e-commerce, the legislature is struggling to keep up with the pace of developments in evoting and in fact the digital economy as a whole. Legislative support for evoting in democratic elections seems to lag well behind. Laws governing the layout and content of ballot papers may, albeit unintentionally, prohibit the use of a computer screen to display it. Some countries are providing legislative support for evoting. Radical new measures that will help modernise voting and registration procedures for UK elections became law on 9 March 2000. A few states in the US have already approved the use of electronic voting systems, but not all state lawmakers are convinced that evoting is the way ahead.

## Barriers to the Adoption of Evoting

Online voting has come under fire from several different sources, some of whom claim that the system does not offer enough security and privacy, or provide a truly reliable way of insuring that voters do not participate in an election multiple times. In the US, there is a project called The Voting Integrity Project which has used the digital divide argument to come out against Internet voting, suggesting that it discriminates against poorer citizens who would be unlikely to have home Internet connections (MacMillan, 2000).

## Familiarity, Acceptability, and Accessibility

In a discussion paper for New Zealand local authorities on proposed local government legislation, it is stated that "Issues of familiarity, acceptability, and accessibility for voters are of fundamental importance to the adoption of new voting technologies. (The Electoral Way Forward, Discussion Paper for Local Authorities On Proposed Local Government Election Legislation, September 1999, http://www.localgovt.co.nz). This statement raises two main issues. The first is the issue of legislation allowing for new voting technologies. The second is the issue of appropriateness (familiarity, acceptability, accessibility) of the technology.

Familiarity, acceptability and accessibility, which are all barriers to evoting, are examined in the survey results reported below.

## Unique Identifiers

In some cases it is believed that the lack of a national ID card presents the biggest barrier to evoting. A national ID smart card is seen as part of a solution to the identification problem by some commentators. The issue of access to the Internet and lack of necessary skills is also seen as a primary issue. Many believe that, for evoting to occur, the creation of a unique identifier for each citizen would be needed.

## Soft Infrastructure

Some commentaries say that it is not technological issues that present a problem. Rather, it is the 'soft' infrastructure consisting of the people and the work culture, and in particular the degree of trust in the evoting system, that may present the biggest hurdles.

## Fraud and Abuse

Some believe election fraud is low because the existing systems are so decentralized and cumbersome. It is considered by some that centralized and computerized data would be a tempting target for hackers, subversives and perhaps foreign governments. Citing such fears, Mr Lewis from the US Electoral Center is quoted as saying "Everyone wants instant Internet gratification. We've been conditioned to expect this now. The truth is we're not going to have instantaneous Internet voting. We're not going to be doing this in 'Internet time'" (Chapman, 2000).

## E-Security Perceptions

The California secretary of state's task force on Internet voting recommended against remote online voting earlier this year. David Jefferson, the technical director of the California Internet Voting Task Force and a researcher at Compaq Systems Research Center in Palo Alto said "We have to understand that the security problems for allowing that are so severe that we can't recommend that solution at all. These problems are inherent in the architecture of the personal computer," (Chapman, 2000). There are signs though that the tide may turn on past barriers to the introduction of evoting. In the US, in the wake of the 7 November 2000 Presidential Election, Cathy Cox, the Georgia secretary of state, said that "the Florida voting fiasco has advanced the cause of electronic voting like nothing we could have imagined". Cox agrees that ultimately the US will have the option of voting online from personal computers at home, but that security and other problems "may push that day years away" (Holsendolph, 2000).

## Safety and Fairness

According to Strausman(2000), the two most common criticisms of Internet voting are that it's not safe and not fair (The Teledemocracy Revolution That Never Was, E-Government Bulletin, Newsletter On Electronic Government, UK And Worldwide. Issue 93, November 2000). He believes that Internet voting "won't actually have much effect on the operation of the political process or the distribution of power in advanced societies". He states that it "will make voting easier and more convenient for those voters who already vote". Beyond that, Strausman believes, there will be "little to distinguish the political landscape of a jurisdiction using remote Internet voting from one using any of the legacy systems now in place". "Letting people vote for their favorite candidate on the Net instead of at the traditional polling place just doesn't make any difference". However Strausman does qualify his viewpoint as he goes on to state "this isn't to say that the Internet is not capable of mediating the political process in ways that would give citizens more choices, that would significantly reduce the influence of money in the process, and that would give them more control over the outcome of disputes over issues". Strausman believes that what is required to bring about genuine reforms is actually the legal recognition of a citizens' right to have an impact online as well as the practical means to accomplish it. He believes that, although letting people pay their taxes, apply for licenses, or find out about government services online is very good (since it saves government money and makes the lives of citizens easier), it is not electronic democracy. It is not using the Internet as it could be used to make government 'more democratic' instead of just 'more responsive.' He says "Making government more democratic by means of the Internet means changing the laws and institutional arrangements we have now to include the active, daily participation of regular citizens in the formulation, discussion, and enactment of the laws by which society is governed. It means letting us govern ourselves with the best tools available, including especially the Internet".

## Computer Access and Computer Literacy

Online voting presents the problem of equal voter access to computers and computer literacy. Most experts agree, however, that as our society becomes increasingly more computer literate, the access issue will eventually be eliminated (Zaino, 2000).

# Politics

In the past the introduction of evoting has been prevented because of disagreement between political parties. For example, in India efforts were made to introduce evoting into the conduct and management of government elections, originally in 1990. The Indian Electoral Commission procured over 5,000 electronic voting machines for large-scale use in general elections. However, with political parties not agreeing to their introduction, these machines were still lying unused eight years later (Anonymous, CMC puts EC on the Net, Businessline, Islamabad, 2 October 1998).

# The Research Method

For the purposes of investigating how evoting could be used improve the New Zealand electoral system, the research set out to determine why and how is it better to capture a voter's decision in digital form rather than on paper. Specifically the researcher sought answers to the following questions:

− How can evoting be used to reduce the time taken (and hence the cost) to count votes?
− How can evoting be used to improve the accuracy of the vote count?
− How can evoting be used to prevent voter fraud?

However, seeking answers to these questions creates a problem: Evoting is not an established method of electing a government, indeed we are yet to see any country elect its government through voters casting digital votes on-line. To progress the research it was therefore necessary to triangulate evidence from multiple sources. Those multiple sources included multiple case studies of democratic entities that have used on-line voting, together with primary data obtained from simulated evoting trials conducted by the researcher. The research was in the form of a qualitative dominant multiple case study seeking to investigate how people make sense of evoting in the context of their experiences and the environment. This involved the design and development of an evoting prototype with an accompanying evoting survey.

The prototype and the survey investigated issues surrounding the 'Six Lessons of Teledemocracy' as proposed by Larsen, 1999):

1. Habits Matter - voters may be expected to react negatively to any deviation from the service to which they are accustomed.
2. Simplicity Matters. When designing voting systems, it is important to understand that the user population is not the same as the mainly self-selected population using PCs at home and at work. The voter population will include people with little or no computer experience.
3. Privacy Matters. Voters will expect any technological solution connected to elections or teledemocracy to maintain their privacy. Any real or perceived threat to a voter's privacy will probably lead to extensive negative publicity.
4. Failure Sensitivity. Evoting is very sensitive in terms of failures. Even sub percentage failure rates may affect the votes of thousands of people, and are

unacceptable. Such errors may, in addition to receiving much attention from the press, leave potential voters disillusioned about their role in our democracy.

5. Power and Change. In our democratic system, many people have become powerful players by understanding and working within the current system. Any significant change in the system is likely to affect the power-base of the current players, thereby leading some powerful players and stakeholder groups to resist the introduction of a teledemocracy.

6. High Visibility. When the technology driving teledemocracy fails, it is hard or impossible to cover it up. Such failures are likely to be widely publicized.

The fears frequently associated with evoting have their origins in conventional systems and this creates a barrier to the use of information processing technology to solve long-standing problems. Evoting promises to fix the ills of the past in a way that is more comprehensive than previously possible. Refer to Table 1 for a summary of the solutions that evoting offers. From the table it can be seen that evoting has the potential to solve existing problems but one problem that will always exist with any type of system is the possibility of losing votes. The solution is to minimize the possibility of loss.

**Table 1.** Comparison of Existing System Problems to Evoting Solutions

| Current System Problem | Impact of Evoting Solution |
|---|---|
| Counting and balancing votes takes too long | Counting is automated and the need for separately balancing the count is eliminated. Time is significantly reduced |
| Split votes take longer to count and balance | Split votes have zero impact on time. It takes no longer to count a split vote than a non-split vote |
| Time taken to complete final count is measured in days | Time taken to complete final count is measured in hours or minutes |
| Insufficient Polling Booths and staff, long queues | Internet evoting allows voters to vote from any Internet connected PC. This significantly reduces the need for polling booths and staff |
| Huge amount of paper | Need for paper is eliminated |
| Loss of votes | No paper votes to lose but introduces risk of e-votes being lost or becoming inaccessible |
| Voter cannot check and correct their vote | Voter has facility to check and correct their vote |
| Significant number of disallowed votes due to forms being incorrectly filled out | Voter cannot fill out form incorrectly. (e.g. system will not permit voter to select more than one candidate or more than one party) |
| High overall cost of running the election | Cost is significantly reduced |
| Fraudulent voting difficult to detect and successful detecting is time consuming. Most instances are found to be human administrative errors. | Voter can only vote once. System will not permit the same voter to register more than one vote. System eliminates human error |

# Data Collection

Collection of secondary data involved examining published accounts of small-scale evoting trials as well as elections that did not contain evoting. The cases involving evoting gave insight into the contribution that evoting can make to the democratic processes, while the cases excluding evoting provided documentary evidence of the problem domain to which evoting can be applied. The case studies themselves contained predominantly qualitative data. Although the primary research instrument itself (the survey) was predominantly qualitative, its design enabled most responses to be quantified.

The survey was designed to capture data about voter perceptions and preferences. In particular the design of the survey and the prototype enabled data to be collected about the usefulness of evoting to the voter, the simplicity of the prototype, the degree of voter acceptance of, and trust in, an evoting system. The design enabled data to be collected specifically about voter perceptions, evote accessibility, familiarity, ease of use, privacy, and security. The actual voter responses, although from a statistically insignificant sample (just 0.014 of 1% of the entire voting population) are unique in that they were captured in the actual evoting domain rather than the paper-voting domain. This was only made possible by the development of the evote prototype. The prototype enabled participants to experience evoting and to compare it to their previous election experiences. The prototype also demonstrated the speed with which a 100% correct election result could be returned. While the sample size is too small to say that the results are representative of the voting population, the action of giving the evote experience to all the voters who participated in the research ensured the validity of the application of the conclusions drawn from the data analysis to the evote domain. All participants were registered on the electoral roll and voted using the prototype. On conclusion of voting, election results were revealed.

# Data Analysis

The categorisation of data has been driven by the themes that emerged during data collection. Through patterns extracted from the interviews an explanation of the causal links between the voter opinions and voter profiles has been established. Although the data obtained from the evoting prototype survey is qualitative, links between the researcher's interpretation and the underlying data are traceable because the verbal responses recorded have been categorised according to whether they are positive, negative, or neutral. This strategy provides the reliability and internal validity needed for the study. Analysis of data first involved the comparison of the sample demographics to population demographics. All comparisons are based on 1996 census figures. Statistics were collected on ethnicity, education, employment status, and income of the sample group. This allowed for the possibility that patterns in the data were attributable to those factors.

# The Results from this Study

The participation of voters in elections was investigated and it was found that 49% of the participants considered that the aspect of the election experience that makes them feel they are participating in a democratic process is the fact that they can vote, whether they exercise that choice or not. Only 6% considered that going to a polling booth to vote was an important part of the democratic process.

Support for evoting over paper voting was overwhelming. A staggering 92% considered evoting was easier to use, 93% said it was quicker to use, 89% said it was the most accurate, and 78% considered it the most secure. 89% of all respondents said that, if the government offered evoting in the next General Election, that they would consider using it. Support for evoting in the survey was highest among ages 18 to 35, 100% of whom supported evoting. Even in the 55 plus age group, support was high at 81%. 100% of respondents earning NZ$100,000 supported evoting, but it was still high in lower income groups with 85% of those earning NZ$30,000 or less supporting it. Of the 89% who said they would consider using evoting in a general election, the biggest percentage (52%) indicated a preference for using it from a computer at home. For the timing of voting, the biggest proportion (46%) considered that an evote should be cast on election day, 33% considered that an evote should be cast up to two weeks prior to election day, while 21% had no preference either way. One feature of the prototype's electronic ballot paper is that the voter's name actually appears on the screen at the top of the ballot paper. The survey contained the surprising result that voters like to see their name on the e-ballot page: "it assured that the system knows its me, and that my vote has been counted". Prior to the survey the concern was that this feature might give voters the feeling that their privacy was being compromised in some way. However this was not the case, and 80% considered that having their name appear on the ballot was a positive and reassuring feature. Only 12% considered it a negative feature. 88% made positive comments about the layout of the ballot paper itself.

# Fears and Failures

Evoting is its own nemesis. Evoting promises to fix the ills of the past in a way that is more comprehensive than previously possible. It promises what eludes modern democracies: a faultless election in which everyone votes, no matter where they happen to be, an election in which the integrity of the individual vote is assured and the result is able to be validated. This promise escalates expectations, which in turn imposes barriers to implementation. Evoting should be Internet based, as this will aid its acceptance. But the Internet is instant, and this also heightens expectations. Evoting will be compared to on-line shopping and banking and it will not be judged by comparison to the current voting system. The fear of electronic failure looms large. Countries that have experienced evoting failures in the past experience set backs measured in decades not years.

Larsen (1999) describes two different attempts at teledemocracy, both of which ended in failure. The first case describes the technical problems encountered by

Pennsylvania's Montgomery County in moving from mechanical to electronic voting machines. The second case describes a Norwegian effort to implement a fully automated voting system in Oslo County, and how technical problems led to a parliamentary crisis. Because of this experience, there are no plans to consider evoting in that country today.

Examples of failures with more traditional systems provide us with some useful lessons. Consider the 7 November 2000 US Presidential election, which was the closest presidential election since the late nineteenth century. It was so close that it turned out that the candidate who received the most votes in Florida was not only the winner of that state, but also the next President of the United States. But unfortunately the debate that raged in the wake of such a close result caused several recounts to occur. At the heart of the debate were issues surrounding the failure of punch card voting machines to return a 100% accurate election result, and the resulting hand recounts that were an attempt obtain an accurate election result. This example has shown that punch card balloting machines can produce an unfortunate number of ballots that are not punched in a clean, complete way by the voter.

Recounting the ballot highlighted another problem with the American voting method of using mechanically punched cards - the problem of 'dimples'. A dimple occurs on a ballot card when a voter's selection is not punched out but merely dented (dimpled). In the end the courts ruled that a dimple could be counted if the voter's intention could be determined with reasonable certainty (Court passes buck over dimples, NZ Herald, 23 November 2000). There was also the issue of whether to count partially punctured ballots. In the end the determination of what constituted a valid vote was left up to the discretion of the counting teams.

Aside from the issues associated with recounting, there was a completely different problem in the 2000 US Presidential election. It was claimed that, in Palm Beach County, Florida, 19,000 votes were not counted at all because voters were confused by the ballot paper and punched two holes instead of one. (http://www.algore.com/briefingroom/releases/pr_111000_Gore_Wins_1.html)

Also in Palm Beach County, two lawsuits were filed that claimed a confusing ballot paper caused thousands of votes (estimates put the figure at 46,000) to be cast mistakenly for the Reform Party candidate, instead of for Al Gore (Forget the votes just pass the salts, NZ Herald, 11-12 November 2000). To obtain a final result took a total of 35 days, which included several recounting rounds accompanied by debate and court action over recount decisions and procedures. The 2000 US presidential election was not the first time that problems with vote counting had been experienced in a presidential election. In 1996 14,872 ballots were invalidated because of double counting. Ironically this was also in Palm Beach County.

The lesson here is that democratic systems that are reliant on human based processes suffer from counting problems: they can neither guarantee the integrity of the individual vote nor validate the actual election result. It is only in very close elections that the absence of these assurances counts. In the absence of such assurances, the possibility of cyber-governance would seem to be light years away. Some would say that that is just as well. Strausman(1999) talks about the global aggregation of like-minded individuals forming global parties and creating a politics that eventually undermines the authority of nation states. Strausman's view is representative of a small body of literature that provides some predictions of what the emergent properties of a direct digital democracy might be. He believes that a more powerful complaint about Internet voting, is simply that "it won't actually have much effect on the operation of the political process or the distribution of power in advanced societies".

## Conclusions

The US 2000 election example shows us that mechanical voting machines do not solve vote-counting problems. Neither do election systems that rely on manual counting; all paper-based systems suffer from counting imprecision to some extent. Evoting is not an observable phenomenon, and information from evoting trials is sparse, conflicting, and in some cases, misleading. The specific improvements that have been examined are vote processing time, accuracy, acceptability, accessibility, familiarity, and security. The explanations of the contribution that evoting has to offer these particular areas have revealed that it is indeed better to capture and process a voter's decision in digital form rather than on paper. Many examples have been given of how such improvements can be achieved. Evoting enables vote checking and validation by the voter, eliminates paper, manual vote sorting and vote counting, and the need for special votes. Evoting also reduces the need for hiring, training and employing vote counting staff. Real problems and faults exist within conventional vote casting and vote counting systems that would never be accepted in an evoting system. It is somewhat ironic that evoting has, in the past, been construed as being part of the problem rather than part of the solution because it has been demonstrated that evoting provides a solution to many recognized but previously unsolvable election system problems. Despite the fact that similar electronic solutions have been successfully applied to similar information processing situations in the business arena, evoting still struggles to establish its rightful place in the information age. Public perceptions of voter privacy and security have long been cited as reasons why evoting has not advanced. However the research results indicate that the NZ voting public has more faith in the privacy and security of an evoting system than the existing system. On the issue of security, some evoting system proponents would have the PIN number invalidated once a vote has been cast to prevent fraud. However, such design is both unnecessary and undesirable. There are other ways to ensure security and the advantage of keeping the PIN intact, is that provision can be made for the voter to re-enter the system and check that their vote has been counted and counted correctly. This was the approach taken in the evote prototype research. Existing election legislation may unintentionally prohibit the use of evoting. In New Zealand election law has not been written with evoting in mind, but some countries are rewriting laws to permit the use of evoting in government elections.

Whilst the introduction of a national ID card/number would likely be useful for evoting, there is little evidence to suggest that measures such as eye or thumb print scanning should be adopted. The existing voter identification system in New Zealand suggests that such identification measures are not required. The use of a password or PIN number known only to the voter, together with a suitable identification number provides sufficient protection, certainly more protection than is offered by the existing system.

Evoting could have prevented the vote counting problems that occurred with the 2000 US election. The deliberations that occurred in the wake of the election determined that a legal vote is "one in which there is a clear indication of the intent of the voter". Even issuing clear instructions to voters will not solve existing voting imprecision. With an evoting system it is simply not possible to become confused about whom a vote is actually cast for. Evoting eliminates the inconsistency endemic in present vote counting processes.

Examples of evoting failures indicate that the cause of failure is not the activities of fraudsters or hackers, the loss of votes, incorrect counts or breeches of security. The cause is more likely to be lack of system availability, which in turn causes voting delays or prevents voters from voting altogether. Indeed the situation that occurred in Norway in 1993 with long queues of voters must be avoided for any system to be a success. System availability can be assured through appropriate design and testing measures, and several examples of small-scale trials do exist. There is only one problem that no system can eliminate entirely: the possibility of vote loss. However, with evoting it is much easier to create duplicate backups and minimize the likelihood of vote loss.

The results of the research survey (Carter, 2001) indicate that support for evoting in New Zealand is likely to be high. Even the majority of voters who do not have Internet access at home support evoting, and if further research can validate this, it would mean that the possibility of involving ordinary citizens in the process of governance is only a mouse click away. Carter showed that support for evoting is likely to be highest in the 18 to 35 age group. This indicates that, as the population ages, support will increase. Although support is highest in high-income groups, it is still high in low-income groups. The survey contained the surprising result that voters like to see their name on the e-ballot page: "it assured that the system knows it's me, and that my vote has been counted".

## Recommendations Emerging from the Study

The results of the study indicate that there is a gap between what voters believe, and what commentators think that voters believe. The use of the evoting prototype has shown that there is also a difference between what type of evote features are necessary, and what commentators think are necessary. A major research survey, using a statistically significant sample of the voting population, in conjunction with an evoting prototype designed to support the investigation of acceptability, accessibility, privacy, security, safety and fairness, is required in order to validate the findings and apply them to the general voting population.

# Future Directions

The changes planned for the 2002 New Zealand elections announced by the government to date are unlikely to have an impact on the technological proficiency of the election. Neither will they reduce the cost of the election. In fact, costs are expected to increase. The US 2000 election example shows us that mechanical voting machines do not solve vote-counting problems. Neither do election systems that rely on manual counting; all such systems suffer from counting imprecision to some extent. The only type of systems that can eliminate imprecision in the vote count are evoting systems, because evoting can allow the voter to check that their vote has been counted correctly, a process which verifies accurate decision capture. On the basis of the Florida experience, and also the 1999 New Zealand election with 80,000 disallowed votes, it seems unwise for any government to introduce any technology that cannot eliminate imprecision in the pursuit of electoral improvement.

However, it would be unwise to apply evoting in a clinical fashion to isolated electoral problems because evoting is sometimes seen as posing a threat to the otherwise familiar and secure, if somewhat laborious, conventional method of running a democratic election.

Perpetrators of fraud could attempt to use the Internet to affect an election. They could set up an illegal site aimed at finding voters who would agree to sell or swap their votes. This is fundamentally no different from setting up a site to trade illegal goods such as drugs, and would require policing to ensure such sites were not established.

Access to the evoting system is an issue. The survey results indicate that most e-voters would prefer to vote from home. Even if computers are provided at polling booths, a situation of unequal access is created, because it will be easier for voters with home Internet connections to vote. If evoting were implemented today, governments would need to decide if such a situation was acceptable. But in the future, the access issue will diminish and perhaps disappear if the home television set becomes an interactive device. Commentators do agree that the access issue will eventually be eliminated.

Any proposal to implement evoting should be cognizant of the fact that evoting is hypersensitive to failure. It is unlikely to survive any actual or perceived threat to privacy or security because evoting errors will never be afforded the same tolerance and acceptance as the errors of present paper-based systems.

More than ever before, the situation is changing in favor of evoting solutions. The Internet, and the growing trust in its application to commerce, may finally provide the opportunity for decision-makers to consider evoting as a serious contender for solving election problems.

Evoting alone does not constitute cyber-governance, whereby the actual decisions of governance are made on-line democratically, but it's implementation promises to create an environment of democratic participation in which the integrity of the individuals decision is assured and the aggregated result of all the individual preferences are able to be validated. It is only from within such an environment that governance can get its ticket into cyberspace and take its rightful place in the information age.

# References

1. Carter,C.W.(2001): Improving Vote Processing Time, Cost and Accuracy for the New Zealand Electoral System Through the use of E-voting. Partial research report for Masters in Information Science, Massey University, Albany, New Zealand.
2. Carey,J.(1998):Electronic Voting: Pros and Cons, Telecommunications, Americas Edition, vol 32 issue 3, March 26,USA
3. Chapman,G.(2000): The Cutting Edge - Focus On Technology - Digital Nation - Online Voting, Even If Secure, Won't Solve Election Troubles. Los Angeles Times, 13 November,USA
4. Clift,S.(2000): Top Ten E-Democracy "To Do List" for Governments Around the World. http://www.publicus.net.
5. Hunn and Smith.(2000): Review of the General Election Process 1999, February, NZ
6. Kaczmarczyk,A.(2000): D-Democracy in e-World. Paper presented on the 2nd Congress on International Direct Democracy, Athens, June 21-25.
7. Larsen,K.(1999): Voting Technological Implementation. Association of Computing Machinery. Communications of the ACM, vol 42 issue 12, pp55-59, USA.
8. MacMillan,R.(2000): Local Government Should Consider E-Voting - Gartner. Newsbytes News Network, 15 November,USA
9. Strausman,M.(1999): Could The Internet Change Everything? The Journal of State Government 72(3), pp22-23, Summer Edition, USA
10. Watson,R.T. & Mundy,B.(2001): A Strategic Perspective of Electronic Democracy. Association of Computing Machinery. Communications of the ACM, vol 42 issue 12, pp27-30, USA.
11. Zaino, J.T.(2000) AAA upgrades its voting capabilities. Advanced telephone and online voting systems now available, Dispute Resolution Journal, New York, Aug-Oct,USA
12. CMC puts EC on the Net(1998), Businessline, Islamabad, 2 October.
13.Court passes buck over dimples(2000), NZ Herald, 23 November.
14. Forget the votes just pass the salts(2000): NZ Herald, 11-12 November.
15. Press Release 111000(2000): http://www.algore.com/briefingroom/releases/pr_111000_Gore_Wins_1.html
16. The Electoral Way Forward(1999): Discussion Paper For Local Authorities On Proposed Local Government Election Legislation, September. http://www.localgovt.co.nz
17. The Teledemocracy Revolution That Never Was (2000): E-Government Bulletin, Newsletter On Electronic Government, UK And Worldwide. Issue 93, November

# Organizational Structure Triangle Stability

Xiaoli Wang[1]    Walter Karten[2]

(1. School of Economic & Management, Tongji University, 200092 Shanghai, P.R.China,

2. Hamburg University, Institute of Insurance Economics, 20146 Hamburg, Germany)

**Abstract**: By case studying, that almost all systems have triangle stability is found. According to the general principle, one 3-dimension hierarchy triangle network structure is designed; its stable binder is also discussed.

**Key words**: organizational stability, triangle structure, and stable binder

## 1. Introduction

Ludwig Von Bertalanffy tried to explore general principles existed in all systems[1]. For example, an exponent function $f(t) = ae^{kt}$, not only describes it system decay process, but also describes system diffuse process. But he didn't find the essence effecting system evolution. F.Y Lin made a research on systems structures[2,3,4], He believed that system structure is core of system and system evolution is decided by its structure. He gave system equilibrium equation and posed one concept of system relation ring which play an important role in system evolution. However, it is only a theory result, he had not given any application background. X.L.Wang[5,6] made a research on macro-economic sectors in China based on system structure theory. He used amount of I/O among sectors and gave the method deciding the relation rings in macro-economic system. Even so, these documents don't touch upon organization management.

In contrast to organization change's absoluteness, organization structure needs a relative ability. Change management is one top topic in organization management at present. Yet, its focus is only on how to predict organizational environment, how to deal with urgent environment and how to adapt organizational environment. Until now, change management does not still make a research on mechanism of organizational stability.

---

This paper is supported by NSFC(79870018) and Alexander von Humboldt Foundation

Organizational stability is under the jurisdiction of organization design. Organizational structure has many similarities to other hard system structures. Because organization system is mainly composed of people, it is an organic system, a varied system and a flexible system. This paper is aimed in organization structure design. By using analogy, it finds that almost all systems have triangles' stability. It further discusses organization systems' stability and development. Under the sharp environment, how is the organization structure adjusted so that it passes dangerous situations and makes operation & development forever? Answer is organization should have 3-dimension hierarchy triangles structure.

## 2. Where do you find the triangles' stability?

### 2.1 General knowledge

In elementary school, we had studied geometry. Triangle' stability is deemed as an axiom. There are many triangles' stability cases in everyday life, for example, sharp-top houses, arc bridges, and so on (see figure 1). Here the mechanical mechanism (mechanical analysis) and mathematical implication (single solution to equation) of triangles' stability are not considered, and supposes it is a well-known fact.

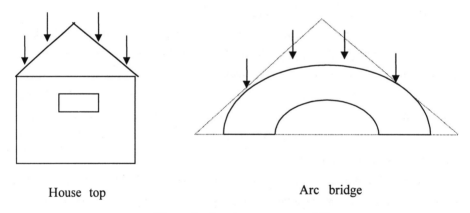

House top                                      Arc bridge

Figure 1 triangle geometry stability

### 2.2 Triangle stability in political organization

Political organization is a power organization. In order to balancing, top-decision making group are composed with add people. For instance, Central Authorities of China consists of seven people. According to the principle of the minority being subordinate to the majority, the important decision will be made. If 3:3 ties appear, then the last vote will play a balance role. But there is a little difference in the president election in America. In America, there are 538 ballots at all, if one of president candidates win at least 270 ballots, he will win the White House. But in case of 269:269 or other uncertainty appear, then Federal Law Court will give last rule. Thus, it forms a triangle structure as follows, which appears in president election 2000 in America. But we don't forget that the Federal Law Court is composed with seven famous judges. These two cases indicate that power balance in political organization and political systems' whole stability are driven by a triangle structure. Because that is a power, its triangle structure has a little fuzzy.

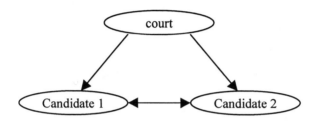

Figure 2 rule of court

## 2.3 Triangle stability in army

Let's recall Anti-Japanese and Liberation Wars in China. One famous military theory is 3-3 system (Lin Biao's military thoughts). This theory is tri-tree principle in army building and developing system (see figure 3). One important application of the theory is when three soldiers march, they often form the march process as follows (see figure 4). In figure 4, we know that triangle structure maintain mini-whole stability and safety in army.

## 2.4 Triangle stability in family

Family is mini-unit of society. Family harmony has a great effect on one's body and mind, sprit and work. Husband and wife are family main roles. The more is their emotion, the more stable is the family. If they have a good emotion, then their children maybe play an important role for family stability. The mentality exists deeply people soul in China. The structure of maintaining family stability can be described as follows (figure 5):

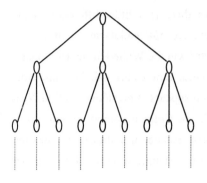

Figure 3 3-3 system in army building

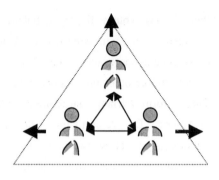

Figure 4  3-3 system's safety

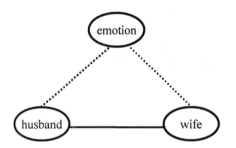

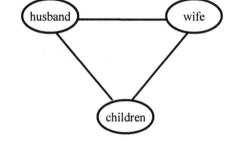

Figure 5  family stability

## 2.5    Sexual love's triangle relationships and social stability

People are complex creatures and their emotions are more complex. Not only have they rational knowledge, but also have they desire. Rational knowledge exists in desire and is often defeated by desire. As stated above, family stability is one common phenomenon. People have many desires. They can do anything for their desires regardless of social stability. Here only using sexual love as a case to make a description and not make further discussion. When sexual life between husband and wife is not harmonious or man and woman need sexual life, there will appear lovers and brothels (see figure 6).

Lovers almost appear among "top people". These top people have power and money, they may have several lovers from whom they obtain sexual satisfaction. But for those people who have not spouse and live social bottom, brothel is only one places to solve their sexual demand. In fact, sexual demands exist deeply between poor people and bottom social classes. Not only are there many single people in China, but also in another countries. Female or male prostitutes maybe one best solution to satisfy theses single people's sexual demand. Lovers and brothels can make sex hungry people to obtain sexual satisfaction, make their psychology to get a calm and to decrease unstable elements risen by their sexual desire. Of course, brothels are not allowed in China, but that they exist everywhere (up or down ground) is one fact. I think brothels, which have had a hundred –thousand –year history, always have their rationality.

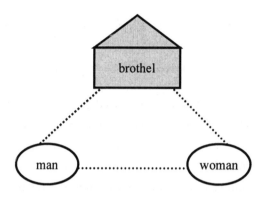

Figure 6  sexual love and social stability

2.6    Binder of stability

We call the elements that maintain organizational stability as binder of stability. Binder of political organizational stability is one power, one view, and one belief controlling people. Binder of military stability (3-3 system) is army stability and soldiers' safety. Family stability relies on yearning and honesty between husband and wife. Sexual love and social stability are built on morality and justice framework and human natural attribute. But what are business organizational stability mechanism and its binder?

## 3. Business organizational triangle stability and its stable binder

From many textbooks, we know that business organizational structures mainly have six forms, they are line structure, staff structure (staff assistant and staff specialist), division structure, functional structure, and committee structure and matrix structure respectively. Because business is a profitability organization, so, its structure design is not separated with its efficiency. As soon as we make a detailed research, we find that these six structures are all triangle structures. These structures appear at different stages of business' life-circle, but their objects are identical------supplying a relative stable inter environment for business organization development (figure 7).

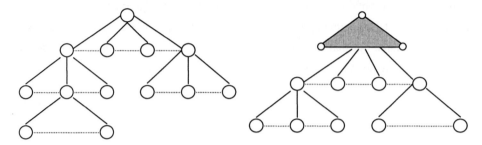

Figure 7 business organizational triangle structure

Why is some business organizations that adopt relevant structures at relevant stages of their life-circle successful and others unsuccessful? An important reason is that there are many differences among managers' viewpoints on organizational triangle structure relationship. Because some managers cannot adjust promptly relationship of organizational structure (for example, the relationship depicted by dashes in figure 7) so that their organizational triangle stability is destroyed. X.L.Wang[7] described how to break organizational boundary and to build organizational order structure, where two measures are important for stabilizing organizational structure.

Triangle structure is business organizational basic structure. Business organizational organism makes it difficult to maintain its structure stability. However, learning organization[8,9] bring us a bright perspective. Vision, mission, strategy, business culture[10] and core value make it possible to build an organizational three-dimension hierarchy triangle network structure. This structure is described as follow (figure 8). It looks like a crystal. Its hierarchy represents business organization power link, three-dimension reflects business organization diversities, and network explains dependent relationship among units in business organization. This organization structure has many similar characteristics as crystal. Not only crystal structure it solid, also is it stable. Thus, the organization structure is very stable. However, if business organization want to develop, to survive, and to expend its size, its organization structure must have a good adaptability to its environment. This asks that business organization should have a relative, dynamic and stable structure. How to make business organization possess the capability? That is what are the crystal organizational structure's stable binders? I think, besides organizational vision, mission, strategy, business culture and core value, organizational learning is the most important stable binder. In order to explore the relationship between organizational structure and behavior, A.Georges L.Romme[11] introduced triple loop learning. He believed that triple loop learning could decrease organizational structure's uncertainties. What do you guess from organizational triangle structure and triple loop learning?

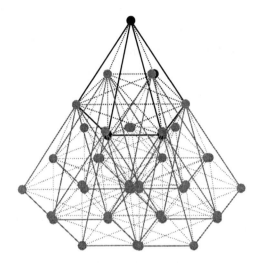

Figure 8  Business organizational three dimension
hierarchy triangle network structure

# 4. Conclusion

This paper started with several cases to demonstrate triangle structure universality. Then it explained triangle stable binders of human organization. At last, one crystal business organizational structure is designed, although its structure functions are not discussed here. I believe that triangle structure is one minimum structure unit in any organizational structure, business organization design should abide by the principle of triangle stability.

# 5. Reference

[1] Ludwig Von Bertalanffy, (1973), General System Theory-Foundation, Development & Application (Revised Edition), George Braziller, Inc.

[2] Lin Fuyong and Wu Jianzhong, (1991), Remarks on The Structure Theory of General Systems, Information and Systems (AMSE 1991), International Academic Publishers, p450-453

[3] Lin Fuyong and Wu Jianzhong, (1992), System Structure and Relation Rings. Journal of Shanghai Jiaotong University, Vol.20, No.5, p20-23

[4] Lin Fuyong and Wu Jianzhong. (1997), General System Structure Theory and Its Application. Journal of Systems Engineering, No.3, p1-10

[5] Xiaoli Wang. (1996), Systems Structure Decomposition Model Based On Relation Degree. Systems Engineering and Market Economy. Nanjing, China, p284-289

[6] Xiaoli Wang, (1997), Research on Structure Decomposition of Economic Sectors and Macro-Economy Policies Making. Proceedings of IFSAM Management Conference '97, Shanghai, China

[7] Xiaoli Wang. (1999), Boundary Infiltration of Organization and Innovation of Organization Structure, Proceedings of 4th Asia Pacific Decision Science Institute Conference, Shanghai, China

[8] Dodgson.M. (1993), Organizational Learning: A Review of Some Literatures. Organization Studies, Vol.14, No.3, p375-394

[9] Senge. P.M. (1990), The Fifth Discipline: The Art and Practice of the Learning Organization, Doubleday, New York

[10] Bonn-Oh Kim, (December 1994), Business Process Reengineering: Building a Cross-Functional Information Architecture. Journal of Systems Management, p30-35

[11] A.Georges L.Romme and Arjen van Witteloostuijn, (1999), Circular Organizing and Triple Loop Learning. Journal of Organizational Change Management, Vol.12, No.5, p439-453

# An Integrated Medical Information System Using XML

Cheolbum Ahn[1], Yunmook Nah[1], Seunghun Park[2], and Jungsun Kim[3]

[1] Department of Computer Engineering, Dankook University, Seoul, Korea
ahn555@dankook.ac.kr, ymnah@dankook.ac.kr,
[2] School of Electronics and Information, Kyung Hee University, Kyunggi-do, Korea
parksh@khu.ac.kr,
[3] School of Electrical Engineering and Computer Engineering, Hanyang University, Kyunggi-do, Korea
jskim@cse.hanyang.ac.kr

**Abstract.** The advanced medical information systems usually consist of loosely-coupled interaction of independent systems, such as HIS, RIS, and PACS. To support easier information exchange between these systems and between hospitals, and to support new types of medical service such as teleradiology, it becomes essential to integrate separated medical information and allow them to be exchanged and retrieved through internet. This paper presents an integrated medical information system using XML. We analyzed HL7 and DICOM standard formats, and designed XML DTDs for HIS, RIS, PACS, and their integration. We extracted information from HL7 messages and DICOM files, and generated XML document instances and XSL stylesheets based on the proposed XML DTDs. We implemented the web interface for the integrated medical information system, which supports data sharing, information exchange and retrieval between two different standard formats. The proposed XML-based integrated medical information system will contribute to solve the problems of current medical information systems, by enabling integration of separated medical informations and by allowing data exchange and sharing through internet.

## 1 Introduction

Currently, more and more medical information is being digitalized. For the electronic transfer of X-ray films within hospitals, DICOM(Digital Imaging and Communication in Medicine) format was proposed and commonly utilized in Picture Archiving and Communication Systems(PACS). Patient and prescription information is being represented in electronic records and handled by Hospital Information Systems(HIS). But, current medical information systems are not fully integrated, thus usually consisted of separated subsystems, such as HIS, Radiology Information Systems(RIS), and PACS[1,2]. Moreover, most of medical information systems are incompatible between hospitals. For the exchange of patient information between hospitals, HL7(Health Level 7) standard was proposed. HIS and RIS are usually based on HL7 standard.

Recent advances of web(WWW; World-Wide Web) enable users to access every information through internet. Since its initial announcement in 1998, XML (eXtensible Markup Language) is rapidly becoming a popular data interchange format. There are efforts to represent HL7 and DICOM information in SGML or XML formats, but most of them are in early stages[4,5,6,7].

This paper is an effort to represent various medical information using XML, thus enabling medical information sharing and exchange through internet. The major contribution of this paper is to show how to utilize XML technology to realize more advanced and open medical information systems. The purpose of this paper is: 1) to provide XML DTDs for HIS, RIS, PACS, and their integration, 2) and to show how effectively medical information sharing and retrieval can be realized. By adopting XML technology into medical domain, we can overcome difficulties in medical information integration and compatibility. Also, by utilizing XML query facility, we can deal with more complex queries on integrated medical information.

The remainder of this paper is organized as follows. Section 2 describes background works. Section 3 analyzes HIS, RIS, and PACS formats and presents XML DTDs for each of them and their integration. In section 4, we describe a system realization scheme of an integrated medical information system. Finally, section 5 summarizes the paper.

## 2   Background

Health Level Seven(HL7) is one of several ANSI-accredited Standards Developing Organization(SDOs) operating in the healthcare arena. "Level Seven" refers to the highest level of the International Standards Organization's (ISO) communications model for Open Systems Interconnection - the application level. HL7 has been actively working with XML technology since the formation of the SGML/XML SIG in 1996. In 1999, HL7 endorsed a recommendation for using XML as an alternative syntax for HL7 V2.3.1 messages[4]. The initial release of Version 3, slated for publication in December 2001, will use only XML encoding. The PRA(Patient Record Architecture) of HL7 V3.0 is written in XML forms based on the "HL7 Document Patient Record Architecture" draft proposed by HL7 SGML/XML SIG in September 1999[6].

Other researches for data exchange between HL7 and DICOM standards are being carried out by HL IMSIG(Image Management SIG) and DICOM WG(Working Group) 20. They also have interests in XML utilization. DICOM WG6 and WG8 studying on DICOM SR(Structured Reporting) are also considering how to utilize XML for DICOM SR[7,10]. But, as we explained earlier, most of these efforts are not finalized yet.

However, it is clear that XML technology will take key roles in representing and exchanging major medical informations for the near future. Figure 1 shows how XML can be utilized as exchange formats between different standards and different hospitals.

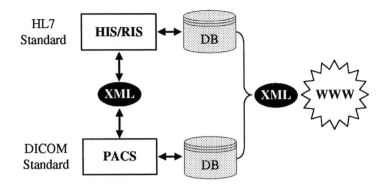

**Fig. 1.** Conceptual architecture of XML based medical information systems

# 3 XML DTDs for medical information

## 3.1 HIS XML DTD

We have used the HL7 Version 2.3 DTD proposed by HL7 SGML/XML SIG[4]. Each HL7 message represents patient-oriented HIS information such as admission, discharge, and transfer. To generate the HIS DTD, we first extract HL7 message table from HL7 standard. All the messages, segments, fields, and data types in this table are then transformed into XML elements according to the appropriate DTD transformation rules. The detail transformation rules are quite tedious, thus omitted from this paper. Figure 2 shows the outline structure of HIS XML DTD and figure 3 shows only some portion of the final HIS XML DTD.

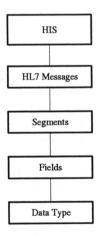

**Fig. 2.** HIS XML DTD Structure

```
<!ELEMENT HIS
(ADT.A01?,ADT.A04?,ACK?,MFK?,MFN.M01?,ORU.RO
1?,QRY.R02?,ORF.R04?)>

<!ELEMENT GRP.1.ADT.A01  (NK1)+>

<!ELEMENT GRP.2.ADT.A01  (DB1)+>

<!ELEMENT GRP.3.ADT.A01  (OBX)+>

<!ELEMENT GRP.4.ADT.A01  (AL1)+>

<!ELEMENT GRP.5.ADT.A01  (DG1)+>

<!ELEMENT GRP.6.ADT.A01  (ROL)+>

<!ELEMENT GRP.7.ADT.A01
(PR1,GRP.6.ADT.A01?)+>

<!ELEMENT GRP.8.ADT.A01  (GT1)+>

<!ELEMENT GRP.9.ADT.A01  (IN1,IN2?,IN3?)+>

<!ELEMENT ADT.A01
(MSH,EVN,PID,PD1?,GRP.1.ADT.A01?,PV1,PV2?,GR
P.2.ADT.A01?,GRP.3.ADT.A01?,GRP.4.ADT.A01?,G
RP.5.ADT.A01?,DRG?,GRP.7.ADT.A01?,GRP.8.ADT.
A01?,GRP.9.ADT.A01?,ACC?,UB1?,UB2?)>

. . . . .

<!ELEMENT VH.1 EMPTY>

<!ATTLIST VH.1  v CDATA #IMPLIED  ty CDATA
#FIXED "ID">

. . . . .
```

**Fig. 3.** HIS.dtd

## 3.2   RIS XML DTD

Some radiology information systems are subsystems of hospital information systems, but sometimes they are operated as stand-alone systems. RIS contains patient demographic, billing information, procedure descriptions, scheduling, diagnostic reports, patient arrival scheduling, film location, movement, and room scheduling. We have designed RIS DTD based on the Radiology Report of HL7 RIM[5,16]. Figure 4 shows the tree structure of RIS XML DTD. The detail descriptions of each elements are as follows.

- RIS element: The RIS element is the root element of RIS XML DTD. It consists of one or more RADIOLOGY.REPORT elements.
- RADIOLOGY.REPORT element: The RADIOLOGY.REPORT element represents diagnostic evaluation reports on DICOM images, which are produced by PACS systems. This element contains attributes such as study.id and study.date. These attributes are utilized as keys to retrieve the related DICOM images. This element consists of HEADER and BODY elements.
- HEADER element: The HEADER element represents the head information of reports. It consists of PATIENT.INFO element and PROCEDURE.INFO elements.
- PATIENT.INFO element: The PATIENT.INFO element represents information on patients. This element contains attributes such as pname(patient name), pid(patient unique id), birthdate, and gender. These attribute values are determined by PID(Patient ID) segments of HIS.

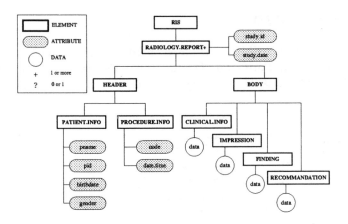

**Fig. 4.** RIS XML DTD structure

- PROCEDURE.INFO element: The PROCEDURE.INFO element represents information on procedures. This element contains code(procedure code) and date.time attributes. These attribute values are determined by PR1(Procedure) segments of HIS.
- BODY element: The BODY element represents information on actual diagnostic evaluation results. It consists of CLINICAL.INFO, IMPRESSION, FINDING, RECOMMENDATION elements. The values of these sub-elements are text data with PCDATA data type.

Figure 5 shows the proposed RIS XML DTD.

```
<!ELEMENT RIS (RADIOLOGY. REPORT)+>
<!ELEMENT RADIOLOGY.REPORT (HEADER, BODY)>
<!ATTLIST RADIOLOGY.REPORT
     study.id CDATA      #REQUIRED
     study.date      CDATA      #REQUIRED>

<!ELEMENT HEADER (PATIENT.INFO, PROCEDURE.INFO)>
<!ELEMENT PATIENT.INFO EMPTY>
<!ATTLIST PATIENT.INFO
     pname      CDATA      #REQUIRED
     pid CDATA      #REQUIRED
     birthdate CDATA      #REQUIRED
     gender      CDATA      #REQUIRED>

<!ELEMENT PROCEDURE.INFO EMPTY>
<!ATTLIST PROCEDURE.INFO
     code CDATA      #REQUIRED
     date.time CDATA      #REQUIRED>

<!ELEMENT BODY (CLINICAL.INFO, FINDING,
IMPRESSION, RECOMMENDATION)>
<!ELEMENT CLINICAL.INFO (#PCDATA)>
<!ELEMENT FINDING (#PCDATA)>
<!ELEMENT IMPRESSION (#PCDATA)>
<!ELEMENT RECOMMENDATION (#PCDATA)>
```

**Fig. 5.** RIS.dtd

## 3.3   PACS XML DTD

We have designed PACS XML DTD based on DICOM Part3(IOD: Informatioin Object Definition) and Part6(Data Dictionary)[7]. Figure 6 shows the tree structure of PACS XML DTD. The detail descriptions of each elements are as follows.

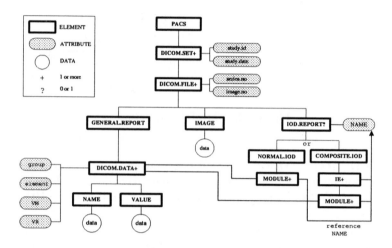

**Fig. 6.** PACS XML DTD structure

- PACS element: The PACS element is the root element of PACS XML DTD. It consists of one or more DICOM.SET elements.
- DICOM.SET element: The DICOM.SET element represents a set of DICOM files. This element contains attributes such as study.id and study.date. The study.id attribute represents the unique shooting number and it is used as a key to identify the appropriate DICOM.SET element. The study.date attribute represents the shoot date. This element consists of DICOM.FILE elements.
- DICOM.FILE element: The DICOM.FILE element represents a physical DICOM file. It contains series.no and image.no attributes. The series.no attribute represents the unique number given by the shooting direction. For a given direction, ten or twenty images are taken usually. The image.no attribute represents the unique number for one of images for the given direction. This element consists of GENERAL.REPORT, IOD.REPORT, and IMAGE elements. The GENERAL.REPORT is mandatory, while IOD.REPORT is optional.
- GENERAL.REPORT element: The GENERAL.REPORT element is used to represent individual DICOM Data Elements extracted from the given DICOM file. Therefore, it consists of one or more DICOM.DATA elements.

- DICOM.DATA element: The DICOM.DATA element represents one of DICOM Data Element of the given DICOM file. It contains attributes such as group, element, VR, and VM. Each attribute represents one of Data Elements of Data Dictionalry of DICOM Part6. This element consists of NAME and VALUE elements.
- NAME and VALUE element: The NAME element represents the name of DICOM Data Element. The VALUE element represents the actual value of the Data Element.
- IOD.REPORT element: The IOD.REPORT element are used to represent DICOM Data Element more hierarchically. This element is based on the DICOM Part3 Data Model. It contains the name attribute. This elements consists of NORMAL.IOD or COMPOSITE.IOD element.
- NORMAL.IOD and COMPOSITE.IOD element: An IOD of DICOM Data Model can be a single object or a composite object, resulting in Normalized IOD or Composited IOD. The NORMAL.IOD element consists of one or more N.MODULE elements. The COMPOSITE.IOD element consists of one or more IE(Information Entity) elements.
- IE element: The IE element contains the name attribute. This element consists of one or more C.MODULE elements.
- N.MODULE and C.MODULE element: These elements contain the name attributes. Both of them consist of one or more DICOM.DATA elements.
- IMAGE element: The IMAGE element represents the image information extracted from DICOM files.

Figure 7 shows the proposed PACS XML DTD.

### 3.4 XML DTD for integration

This section defines an integrated DTD for combining HIS DTD, RIS DTD, and PACS DTD. The generation procedure of this integrated DTD is shown in Figure 8.

The integrated DTD was designed from the viewpoint of patients by combining their related HIS, RIS, and PACS information. The INTEGRATED.REPORT is the root element of this DTD followed by the PATIENT elements. The PATIENT element contains attributes such as pname and pid. These attributes are used as key values for the integrated medical information retrieval. Figure 9 shows the tree structure of the integrated DTD.

The PATIENT element consists of elements, such as HIS, RIS, and PACS elements, which are root elements of HIS, RIS, and PACS DTD defined in the previous sections. Figure 10 shows the top level integrated XML DTD.

```
<!ELEMENT PACS (DICOM.SET)+>
<!ELEMENT DICOM.SET (DICOM.FILE)+>
<!ATTLIST DICOM.SET
    study.id  CDATA#REQUIRED
    study.dateCDATA#REQUIRED>
<!ELEMENT DICOM.FILE (GENERAL.REPORT,IMAGE,IOD.REPORT?)>
<!ATTLIST DICOM.FILE
    series.no CDATA#REQUIRED
    image.no  CDATA#REQUIRED>

<!ELEMENT GENERAL.REPORT (DICOM.DATA)+>

<!ELEMENT DICOM.DATA (NAME,VALUE)+>
<!ATTLIST DICOM.DATA
    groupCDATA#REQUIRED
    element   CDATA#REQUIRED
    VR    CDATA#REQUIRED
    VM    CDATA#REQUIRED>

<!ELEMENT NAME (#PCDATA)>
<!ELEMENT VALUE (#PCDATA)>

<!ENTITY % name "
    name CDATA#REQUIRED">

<!ELEMENT IOD.REPORT (NORMAL.IOD|COMPOSITE.IOD)>
<!ATTLIST IOD.REPORT %name;>

<!ELEMENT NORMAL.IOD (N.MODULE)+>
<!ELEMENT N.MODULE (DICOM.DATA)+>
<!ATTLIST N.MODULE %name;>

<!ELEMENT COMPOSITE.IOD (IE)+>
<!ELEMENT IE (C.MODULE)+>
<!ATTLIST IE %name;>
<!ELEMENT C.MODULE (DICOM.DATA)+>
<!ATTLIST C.MODULE %name;>

<!ELEMENT IMAGE (#PCDATA)>
```

**Fig. 7.** PACS.dtd

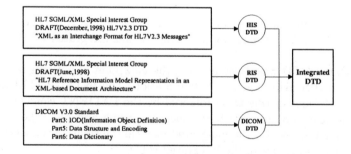

**Fig. 8.** Integrated DTD generation

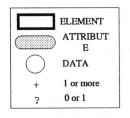

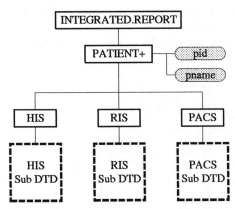

**Fig. 9.** INTEGRATED DTD structure

```
<!ENTITY % HIS-messages PUBLIC
"-//HIS//DTD HIS message definitions//
EN"
"HIS.dtd" >
%HIS-messages;

<!ENTITY % RIS-reports PUBLIC
"-//RIS//DTD RIS report definitions//
EN"
"RIS.dtd" >
%RIS-reports;

<!ENTITY % PACS-images PUBLIC
"-//PACS//DTD PACS image definitions//
EN"
"PACS.dtd" >
%PACS-images;

<!ELEMENT INTEGRATED.REPORT (PATIENT)+>
<!ELEMENT PATIENT (HIS, RIS, PACS)>
<!ATTLIST PATIENT
    pname       CDATA       #REQUIRED
    pid   CDATA       #REQUIRED>
```

**Fig. 10.** INTEGRATED.dtd

# 4   System realization

All the target medical information is extracted from the existing HIS, RIS, and PACS systems. The integrated XML document instances are generated according to the integrated DTD described in the section 3. The proposed XML DTD becomes the XML database schema. The XML instances are stored into XML databases with XSL stylesheets containing the presentation information. We have developed the prototype system using ObjectStore eXcelon and implemented the web interface using ASP(Active Server Page) on Window 2000 Server and IIS 5.0 Web server. The system architecture is shown in Figure 11.

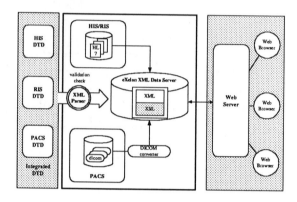

**Fig. 11.** System architecture

## 4.1   Generation of integrated XML documents

Currently, the extraction of medical information from HL7 messages and DICOM files is done manually. The automatic generation of XML instances from HIS, RIS, and PACS systems is one of further research topics. The HIS information is extracted from HL7 standard messages. Based on the extracted information and HIS XML DTD, the HIS XML document instances are generated. Figure 12 shows an example of HIS XML document instance generated from a HL7 ACK message.

In our system, the RIS information was extracted from the diagnostic evaluation reports(1996_RSNA_Reports.txt) for DICOM images provided by RSNA(Radiology Society of North America, Inc.). Based on the extracted information and RIS XML DTD, the RIS XML document instances are generated. Figure 13 shows an example of RIS XML document instance.

A DICOM file is a set of Data Elements having Group, Element, VR, Length, and Value in sequence. The Data Element with Group 0x7FE0 and Element 0x0010 contains the pixel data of the actual binary images[3].

In our system, we extracted each Data Element and image information from bi-

ACK HL7 Message

```
MSH|^~\
&|LAB^foo^bar|767543|ADT|767543|19900314130405||ACK^|XX36
57|P|2.1<CR>
MSA|AA|ZZ9380<CR>
```

HIS XML document

```
<ACK>
<MSH>
      <MSH.1>|</MSH.1>
      <MSH.2>^~\&amp;</MSH.2>
      <MSH.3>
            <HD.1>LAB</HD.1>
            <HD.2>foo</HD.2>
            <HD.3>bar</HD.3>
      </MSH.3>
      <MSH.4><HD.1>767543</HD.1></MSH.4>
      <MSH.5><HD.1>ADT</HD.1></MSH.5>
      <MSH.6><HD.1>767543</HD.1></MSH.6>
      <MSH.7><TS.1>19900314130405</TS.1></MSH.7>
      <MSH.9><MSH.9.CM.1>ACK</MSH.9.CM.1></MSH.9>
      <MSH.10>XX3657</MSH.10>
      <MSH.11><PT.1>P</PT.1></MSH.11>
      <MSH.12>2.3.1</MSH.12>
</MSH>
<MSA>
      <MSA.1>AA</MSA.1>
      <MSA.2>ZZ9380</MSA.2>
</MSA>
</ACK>
```

**Fig. 12.** An example of HIS XML document instance

```
<RIS>
<RADIOLOGY.REPORT>
<HEADER>
<PATIENT.INFO
 pname="Peter" pid="660106115412" birthdate="19660106"
gender="M"/>
<PROCEDURE.INFO code="P5-20000" Date.Time="19980427"/>
</HEADER>
<BODY>
<CLINICAL.INFO>
History of smoking for 32 years.
</CLINICAL.INFORMATION>
<FINDING>
Comparison is made with a chest-x-ray done 6 months ago.
The 1cm nodule previously noted in the right lower lobe is
larger,
approximately 1.8 cm. The nodule is round, with no
calcification.
There is no adenopathy. Heart size and bony structures are
normal.
</FINDING>
<IMPRESSION>
located in the right lower lobe is suggestive of
malignancy.
Compared with a prior CXR from 6 months ago, nodule size
has increased.
</IMPRESSION>
<RECOMMENDATION>
I notified the ordering physician of this finding by
phone.
</RECOMMENDATION>
</BODY>
</RADIOLOGY.REPORT>
```

**Fig. 13.** An example of RIS XML document instance

nary DICOM files by using the DICOM2 converter. Figure14 and 15 show Data Elements and image information extracted from a DICOM file respectively. In figure 14, each row represents one of DICOM Element information. The structure of figure 14 is the same with Part6 Data Dictionary, except for the additional column for Data values.

| Element Description | Group/Element | VM | VR | Data(value) |
|---|---|---|---|---|
| Study Date | (0008,0020) | 1 | DA | [1995.01.19] |
| Modelity | (0008,0060) | 1 | CS | [US] |
| Patient's Name | (0010,0010) | 1 | PN | [NAPPER^MARGRET] |
| Patient's ID | (0010,0020) | 1 | LO | [ACN000001] |
| Patient's Birth Date | (0010,0030) | 1 | DA | [1950.04.20] |
| Performing Physician's Name | (0008,1050) | 1-n | PN | [KLOFAS,EDWARD] |
| ......... | ...... | .. | .. | ......... |

**Fig. 14.** An example of text information from DICOM file

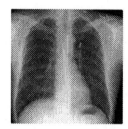

**Fig. 15.** An example of image information from DICOM file (chest.png)

Based on the extracted information and PACS XML DTD, the PACS XML document instances are generated. Figure 16 shows an example of PACS XML document instance.

## 4.2 Storing and retrieving mechanism of integrated XML documents

The resulting XML instances and XSL documents are stored in the XMLStore of ObjectStore eXcelon. The XMLStore parses XML data and supports the indexing mechanism on XML tags. The application programs for the integrated medical information system were developed using ASP. The query data on the web browser is transferred to the web server. The ASP program on the web server generates XQL(XML Query Language) command strings and calls eXcelon API using this XQL command as a parameter.

This call makes Server Extensions(a kind of user defined stored procedures

```
<PACS>
<DICOM.SET study.id="2019" study.date="19980209">
 <DICOM.FILE series.no="1" image.no="1301">
  <GENERAL.REPORT>
      <DICOM.DATA group="0008" element="0016" VR="UI" VM="1">
        <NAME>SOP Class UID</NAME>
        <VALUE>1.2.840.10008.5.1.4.1.1.1</VALUE>
        .........
      <DICOM.DATA group="0028" element="0011" VR="US" VM="1">
        <NAME>Columns</NAME>
        <VALUE>440</VALUE>
      </DICOM.DATA>
  </GENERAL.REPORT>
  <IMAGE>chest.png</IMAGE>
 </DICOM.FILE>
</DICOM.SET>
</PACS>
```

**Fig. 16.** An example of PACS XML document instance

written in Java) to be executed. Finally, the transferred XQL is executed by XMLStore through DOM(Document Object Model). The executed query returns results in XML forms, which are combined with XSL by MS XML, thus finally producing HTML documents for web browsers. Figure 17 summarizes this storing and retrieving mechanism.

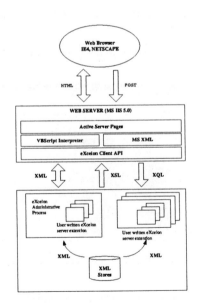

**Fig. 17.** Storing and retrieving mechanism

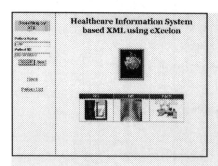

a. Main Screen

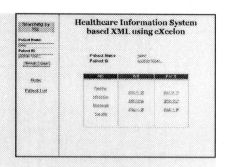

b. Results of integrated retrieval

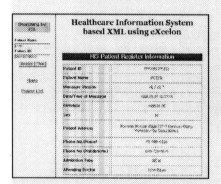

c. Results of HIS information retrieval

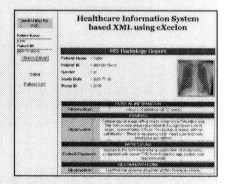

d. Results of RIS information retrieval

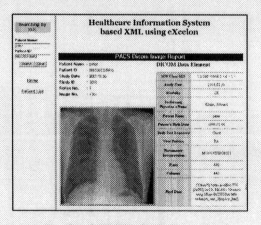

e. Results of PACS information retrieval

**Fig. 18.** Retrieval Examples

## 4.3 Web interface and retrieval examples

When a user logs in, the system shows the main screen. Users provide patient name and ID as query terms(Figure 18.a), and the system shows HIS, RIS, PACS lists for the given patient(Figure 18.b). Each of the lists are linked to the appropriate information. By clicking links, users can retrieve HIS information, PACS images, and diagnostic reports(Figure 18.c, Figure 18.d, Figure 18.e). If users click 'Patient List' link on the left frame in Figure 18.a, the system shows the list of all patients.

The query interface of our system is quite flexible. We can expand the web query interface (like Figure 18.a) by adding more complicated XQL queries and defining appropriate XSL stylesheets for each additional XQL queries. Of course, if users enter XQL directly on the eXcelon query interface, they can retrieve all kinds of information from XML medical databases with more complex query terms.

## 5 Conclusion

In this paper, we focused on the adoption of XML technology into healthcare domain, thus overcoming difficulties in medical information integration and compatibility.

We have analyzed HL7 and DICOM standard formats, and designed XML DTDs for HIS, RIS, PACS, and their integration. We extracted information from HL7 messages and DICOM files, and generated XML document instances and XSL stylesheets based on the proposed XML DTDs. We implemented the web interface for the integrated medical information system, which supports data sharing, information exchange and retrieval between two different standard formats. The proposed XML-based integrated medical information system will contribute to solve the problems of current medical information systems, by enabling integration of separated medical informations and by allowing data exchange and sharing through internet.

There should be further research on automatic generation of XML instances from traditional medical systems. Also, the proposed DTDs should be extended to include ongoing standard efforts, such as HL7 SGML/XML SIG, IMSIG, and DICOM WG20.

## Acknowledgements

This work was supported by the Radiotherapy Medical Instruments Industrialization Technology Development Project of the Ministry of Science and Technology.

# References

1. Lee, D.S., *An Analysis of Medical Image Storage and Transfer System Construction Model using DICOM*, Master Thesis, Yonsei Univ., 1998.
2. Yoon, M.J., *Implementation of MINI-PACS using DICOM converter on the Web*, Master Thesis, Chosun Univ., 1998.
3. Kwon, G.B. and Kim, I.K., "Web-based Medical Information System using DICOM Specification," in Proc. Korean Database Conference 2000, May 2000, pp.215-222.
4. _____, "XML as an Interchange Format for HL7 V2.3 Messages," HL7 SGML/XML SIG, http://www.mcis.duke.edu/standards/HL7/committees/sgml/WhitePapers/hl7v2/hl7xml2.zip, Dec. 1998.
5. _____, "HL7 Reference Information Model Representation in an XML-based Document Architecture," HL7 SGML/XML SIG, http://www.mcis.duke.edu /standards/HL7/committees/sgml/WhitePapers /hl7v2/xml_rim.rtf, June, 1998.
6. _____, "HL7 Document Patient Record Architecture DRAFT-Frame work Document," HL7 SGML/XML SIG, http://www.hl7.org/Special/ Committees/sgml/PRA/HL7_PRA_9_27_1999.rtf, Sept. 1999.
7. _____, "DICOM 1999 - Parts (1-14) - DRAFT VERSION," ACR-NEMA Committee, http://medical .nema.org/dicom/1999.html.
8. _____, "Hospital Information System," http://www.med.usf.edu/CLASS/his.htm.
9. Gum, W. and Kim, I.K., "Design and Implementation of DICOM DB with ATL COM," in Proc. Korean Database Conference 2000, May 2000, pp.243-249.
10. Horiil, S.C., Prior, F.W. and Bidgood, W.D., "DICOM: An Introduction to the Standard," http://www.xray.hmc.psu.edu/dicom/dicom/dicom_intro /DICOMintro.html.
11. _____, *ObjectStore eXcelon User Guide*, Object Design, http://www.odi.com, June, 1999.
12. _____, "Digital Imaging and Communications in Medicine," ACR-NEMA Committee Working Group VIS 255, 1993.
13. Boumphrey, F., et al., *Professional XML Applications*, Information & Culture Press, 1999.
14. _____, "Extensible Stylesheet Language(XSL) Version 1.0," W3C, http://www.w3.org/TR/ 2000/CR-xsl-20001121.
15. _____, "Extensible Markup Language(XML) 1.0(Second Edition)," W3C, http:// www.w3.org/TR/2000/REC-xml-20001006.
16. _____, "HIS/RIS/PACS Interconnection," Korea Radiotherapy Association, http://www.krta.or.kr/guest/pacs/pacs11.htm.
17. Kim, J.H. and Han, M.C., "Integration of Hospital Information System and PACS," http://radhome.snu.ac.kr/Department/Section/pacslab/pacscombine /pacscombine.htm.
18. Chae, J.S. *Producing XML Home Pages*, Hong Pub., 1999.

# Image-Guided Telemedicine System via the Internet

Kyoung-Mi Lee

Department of Computer Science,
The University of Iowa, Iowa City, IA 52242, USA
klee1@cs.uiowa.edu,
WWW home page:http://www.cs.uiowa.edu/~klee1

**Abstract.** This paper presents an Internet software application that is readily available and that can greatly affect practice. Any medical facility with Internet access can use this system to visually diagnose breast fine needle aspirates since the program is implemented as a Java applet and accessed remotely via the World Wide Web. The proposed system automatically indexes objects based on shape and groups them into a set of clusters, or prototypes. Queries are first compared to the set of prototypes and then to the objects in the most similar prototypes. In terms of dissimilarity, each query is performed based on shape, or possibly in combination with other features as size, radius, perimeter, area, smoothness, compactness, concavity, and concave points. Experimental results show that the system achieved satisfactory performance.

## 1 Introduction

As it is revolutionizing society, the Internet can make new computer-based medical technology universally available, both rapidly and inexpensively. For example, a telemedicine application for supporting a decision whether breast cancer cells are benign provides diagnostic and prognostic information that would be otherwise unavailable at most locations. With only a personal computer, an urban medical center or a small-town hospital can now access expertise previously available only at specialized centers.

However, clinicians only recently recognized the potential of content-based retrieval system for medical applications [12]. Content-based image retrieval refers to image retrieval techniques that are based on visual properties of image objects rather than textual annotation. In medicine, the capabilities can be extended to provide valuable teaching, training, and enhanced image interpretation support. Before making a diagnosis, a clinician could retrieve similar cases from the medical archive. Content-based image retrievals would not only yield cases of patients with similar image examinations and similar diagnoses, but also cases of patients with similar image examinations and different diagnoses [9].

In this paper, we present an image-guided telemedicine system accessed via the Internet. The task of the proposed system is to extract, index, retrieve and display cases. The rest of the paper is organized as follows. Section 2 briefly describes the demonstrated application and image database in this paper. In Section 3, an overview of the medical decision support system is presented. Section 4 presents the shape description to represent cells. Section 5 details how we index objects based on shape and Section 6 introduces the dissimilarity metric. The experimental performance of the object-based query system is presented in Section 7. Finally, a conclusion will be presented in Section 8.

## 2 Background

### 2.1 Application

The task of the proposed system is a medical diagnosis for breast cancer. Breast cancer is the major malignancy affecting the female population in industrialized countries: it is estimated that one-third of these patients eventually die because of this disease [11]. There is, however, long-term survival with early detection of the disease, and early detection in turn is enhanced by accurate diagnosis. It has been widely recognized that clinicopathological assessment of several factors enable clinicians to predict individual patient survival and also to choose appropriate modes of treatment.

### 2.2 Image Database

The current image database consists of cytological images from fine-needle biopsies of breast masses, the same images used to train the original Xcyt system. The images are gray-scaled with 640×480 pixel spatial resolution. These images are classified as benign or malignant on a per-sample basis; no classification is available for individual cell nuclei. Therefore in these results we consider all nuclei in benign images to be benign and all nuclei in malignant images to be malignant. This assumption is reasonable but not entirely accurate, making the classification problem particularly difficult due to classification noise caused by some benign cells present in malignant sample.

### 2.3 Problem Definition

Shape-based image retrieval is one of the hardest problems in general image retrieval. This is mainly due to the difficulty of segmenting objects of interest in the images. Consequently, shape retrieval is typically limited to well-distinguished objects in the image [3, 10].

Once the object is detected and located, the next challenge that arises in content-based shape retrieval is that of finding a good measure of 'similarity' between two shapes that is appropriate for the given domain. In medical cell applications, however, it is difficult to objectively validate similarity measures because intuitive similarity may not correspond well with meaningful similarity in the database. Hence we adopt the variance-based distance metric, which takes into account the influence of the scale of each feature using variances.

# 3 Overview of System

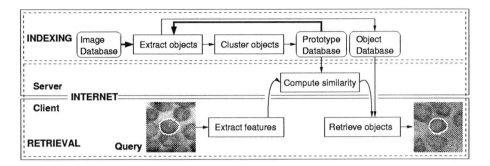

**Fig. 1.** System overview: box = process, rounded box = database, thin arrow = data flow, and thick arrow = queue

Fig. 1 shows the functional overview of the proposed Internet-based telemedicine system which is implemented in Java and is therefore client-server platform-independent. The user at the client can access the object and prototype databases at the server through the Internet.

The user presents a query from a local or remote file system and draws outlines of objects. The client formulates the query, performing feature extraction. The extracted query feature is submitted to the server. Based on the distance metrics, similarities between the query and prototypes are calculated. After sorting the prototypes in terms of similarity, the system returns objects indexed by the prototypes with high similarities.

In the server, shape-based indexing is automatically performed in the background, incorporating two queues which aid indexing of an ever-increasing volume of data. Extracted objects from images are stored both in the object database and the prototype database.

# 4 Shape Description

For effective retrieval, a good representation for the extracted object shape is a necessary requirement. In this paper, we adopt the centroid-radii model to represent a shape by capturing lengths of a shape's radii from its centroid at regular intervals [6, 13]. So the shape can be represented as a vector $\mathbf{v} = (v_1, v_2, \cdots, v_I)$ $= (r_{\theta_1}, r_{\theta_2}, \cdots, r_{\theta_I})$, where $r_{\theta_i}$ is the $i$th radius from the centroid to the boundary of the shape and $\theta_i = \left(\frac{360}{I}\right) i$. This model is invariant to translation through the use of an object-centered coordinate system and to reflection through the use of the reflected shape. Since each representation can be rotated and store scaling factors, only one shape is needed. The lack of the internal information limits to topologically simple shapes with no holes; however, it is suitable to represent cells.

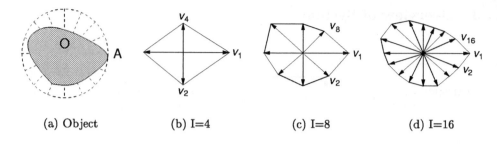

(a) Object          (b) I=4          (c) I=8          (d) I=16

**Fig. 2.** Shape representation

The three representations in Fig. 2 ((b), (c) and (d)) show how this model can facilitate multiresolution representation. This model assumes $I$ is larger than 2. We wish to use only as many points as necessary to adequately model the shape.

## 5 Shape-based Indexing

### 5.1 Detection and Segmentation

For automatic shape-based indexing, the proposed system uses the Generalized Hough Transform (GHT) [2], a standard template-matching algorithm, to detect the boundaries of objects in an image, in the background. GHT requires templates to be predefined and an array of points of the same size as the image, the accumulator, in which each point has a value, $h(x,y)$, specifying the possibility that the reference point of a shape to be detected is located at the point. When the value of the point in the accumulator exceeds a certain threshold, then an object with the desired shape is said to be detected at the location of the point. Further, when the scale and orientation of an input shape are variant and unknown in advance, brute force is usually employed to enumerate all possible scales and orientations of the input shape in the GHT process. There have been several proposals to reduce the huge memory storage capacity and computational time required for GHT [4]. In this paper, we use an iterative approach to GHT (IGHT) proposed in [5,8], for memory efficiency. Then the snakes are initialized using the results of IGHT to segment the object.

If there is a prototype in the prototype queue, the system applies IGHT with the prototype as a template to all images in an image queue. In terms of similarity, if the peak values $h(x,y)$ in an IGHT accumulator are larger than a predefined threshold value, objects whose shapes look like the template are detected and then segmented using snake. Each segmented object is saved into the object database, along with the information on the image. For fast retrieval in Section 6, the distance between the prototype and the segmented object should be stored in the object database, by using $h(x,y)$. Whenever a prototype is updated or added, it is placed the prototype queue, and all images are placed in the image queue. Whenever a new image is added the image database, the indexing procedure places it into the image queue, and all prototypes are placed into the prototype queue. All this processing is done in the background, creating an index of objects that is used for retrieval. Fig. 3 shows examples of cell detection and segmentation.

## 5.2 Incremental Clustering

We adopt an incremental learning method which enables the system to efficiently store and retrieve an ever-increasing volume of data [7]. Mathematically, a given set of $N$ objects, $\mathbf{V} = \{\mathbf{v}^1, \mathbf{v}^2, \cdots, \mathbf{v}^N\}$ will be partitioned into clusters such that data within the same cluster have a high degree of similarity, while shapes belonging to different clusters have a high degree of dissimilarity. Each of these clusters is represented by a prototype $\mathbf{P}^c$. Suppose $N_c$ is the number of objects in the cluster $\mathbf{c}$. The $i$th feature of the prototype, $P_i^c$, can be computed by averaging the features that belong to the cluster $\mathbf{c}$. To measure the spread of a set of data around the center of the data in the cluster, we use the standard deviation ($\sigma$).

Incrementally, whenever a new object is assigned to an existing cluster $\mathbf{c}$, $P_i^c$ and $\sigma_i^c$ are updated by averaging shapes in the cluster. If the new object is not similar to existing prototypes, a new prototype is created with the new object.

## 5.3 Index Tree

With tens of thousand of objects, it is not practical to sequentially compare each object in the database against the query. Since only a small number of objects is likely to match the query, a large number of unnecessary comparisons are being performed. As the comparison is expensive, we use a two-level index tree structure to provide an efficient means to reduce the number of comparisons.

The prototype layer of the tree is a simple filter that reduces the search space quickly, discriminating between the objects based on shape. This structure is easily extensible by adding a new layer to the index structure for a new feature, such as size. If an object is represented by the combination of shape and size features, any path that differs by shape can be pruned away immediately, resulting in a more efficient search. More importantly, using a smaller number of dimensions can avoid performance degeneration that arises for higher-dimensional data.

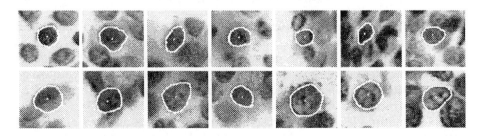

**Fig. 3.** Detection and segmentation of the breast cancer cells. The cells in the upper line are the benign cells and those in the lower line are malignant cells

## 6 Dissimilarity Metric

In this section, we consider the problem of dissimilarity measurement used for indexing and retrieval. The most common measure of dissimilarity between two objects is a linear combination of the distances in each dimension. Since each dimension feature has a different influence, each feature should be rescaled so that all features contribute equally to the distance computation. Thus, for $I$-dimension, the dissimilarity between a prototype $\mathbf{P}^c$ and a given query object $\mathbf{q}$ is computed as

$$\mathbf{d}(\mathbf{q}, \mathbf{P}^c) = \sqrt{\sum_{i=1}^{I} \omega_i^c (q_i - P_i^c)^2}. \tag{1}$$

These weights $\omega_i^c$ enable the distance computation to elongate dissimilar features, and, at the same time, to constrict the closest ones. To capture such scale information as weights, this paper uses the relative distance based on the standard deviation. The weight for a feature $P_i^c$ can be defined as

$$\omega_i^c = \begin{cases} 1 - \exp\left(-\dfrac{|q_i - P_i^c|}{\sigma_i^c}\right), & \text{if } \sigma_i^c \neq 0 \\ 1, & \text{otherwise.} \end{cases} \tag{2}$$

It is evident that $0 \leq \omega_i^c \leq 1$, where $\omega_i^c = 1$ indicates that $q_i$ is too far from $\sigma_i^c$ or $\sigma_i^c$ is 0, and thus $q_i$ isn't similar to $P_i^c$ at all. On the other hand, $\omega_i^c = 0$ indicates that $P_i^c$ and $q_i$ are identical, and so $q_i$ is totally similar to $P_i^c$. Values in between show the degrees of weight that $\mathbf{q}$ exerts at $i$. It reflects the influence of $\mathbf{q}$ on the variation of $\mathbf{P}^c$ at $i$. Note that the technique is shape-based because weights depend on the shape [1].

To avoid simple orientation differences in the shape features, the distance is computed at different rotation angles, and we define the final distance from $\mathbf{q}$ to $\mathbf{P}^c$ as the minimum of these distances. For retrieval, we need two distances: one is between $\mathbf{q}$ and $\mathbf{P}^c$, $\mathbf{d}(\mathbf{q}, \mathbf{P}^c)$, and the other is between $\mathbf{q}$ and a shape $\mathbf{v}$ in $\mathbf{P}^c$ which is similar to $\mathbf{q}$, $\mathbf{d}(\mathbf{q}, \mathbf{v})$. Instead of calculating $\mathbf{d}(\mathbf{q}, \mathbf{v})$ on an on-line retrieval system, we compute as following:

$$\mathbf{d}(\mathbf{q}, \mathbf{v}) = \mathbf{d}(\mathbf{q}, \mathbf{P}^c) + \mathbf{d}(\mathbf{P}^c, \mathbf{v}), \tag{3}$$

where $\mathbf{d}(\mathbf{P}^c, \mathbf{v})$ is the distance between $\mathbf{P}^c$ and $\mathbf{v}$ and is stored in the object database during indexing (Section 5.1). Once $\mathbf{q}$ has been defined by drawing a boundary on a sketch or on an image, the selection of shapes sharing similar characterizing elements begins by comparing $\mathbf{q}$ to the set of prototypes using Eq. (1). If some prototypes are selected as being similar to $\mathbf{q}$, only the shapes in those prototypes calculate the distance with the query using Eq. (3).

If the multiple features are integrated, the combined distance between a query $\mathbf{q}$ and an object $\mathbf{u}$ should be computed. For instance, the Xcyt system was originally designed to diagnose breast tissue as benign or malignant based on derived nuclear features such as area, perimeter, and smoothness [14]. So, the combined distance between **q** and **v** with these nuclear features should be computed. Let $\mathbf{d}_f(\mathbf{q},\mathbf{v})$ is the distance between each nuclear feature of **q** and **v**. The combined distance is defined as

$$\mathbf{D}(\mathbf{q},\mathbf{v}) = \omega_s \mathbf{d}(\mathbf{q},\mathbf{v}) + \sum_f \omega_f \mathbf{d}_f(\mathbf{q},\mathbf{v}), \tag{4}$$

where $\omega_s$ and $\omega_f$ are weight factors of a shape features and nuclear features, respectively.

# 7 Experiments

## 7.1 Experimental setup

We set up the image database, consisting of 12 benign images (600 cells) and 14 malignant images (543 cells). Each cell is represented by a 24-dimensional shape feature and eight nuclear features: size, radius, perimeter, area, compactness, smoothness, concavity, and concave points. For shape-based indexing, the system requires an initial definition of shapes we want to find. In this application, the objects in question are human cell nuclei, which are more or less elliptical in shape. Therefore we can initialize a set of elliptical prototypes with different shapes. Since the algorithm is invariant to size, orientation and reflection, only one prototype with each shape is created. The initial prototypes are created automatically but could easily be drawn by the user or avoided completely, without changing the fundamentals of the algorithm.

After getting the prototypes, the system automatically performs shape-based indexing in the background (Section 5). Each image is first preprocessed to get a good edge image, and then analyzed using IGHT and snake.

The performance in the experiments is evaluated using two measures: precision and recall. Recall is the ratio of relevant images retrieved to the total number in the database; it measures the ability of a system to present all relevant images. Precision is the ratio of relevant images retrieved to the total number of images retrieved; it measures the ability of a system to present only relevant images. For most applications, it is impossible to maximize precision and recall simultaneously, but these values should ideally be as large as possible.

## 7.2 Results

For indexing, the nuclei database was incrementally clustered and 12 prototypes were created. These prototypes are used as a filter of the index tree in Section 5.3. To evaluate indexing effectiveness, we tested some retrieval performance after clustering. Fig. 4 shows how the number of prototypes affects the average performance for 20 queries performed on the database of the 1143 cells. A recall of 1.0 is the case of finding all cases of each class, benign or malignant. Instead of searching and ranking all shapes, the system searches only small set of clusters and ranks cells in the clusters. If some relevant shapes are missed

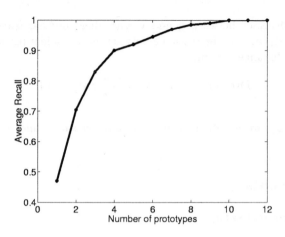

**Fig. 4.** Indexing effectiveness: average retrieval performance vs. number of prototypes

the system searches the next most similar prototypes. With only the one most relevant prototype, cells from the same class were judged as most similar 47% of the time in average. As the number of prototypes reached four, performance achieved 90% and began to exceed 90%.

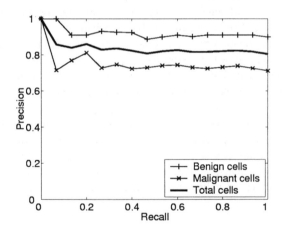

**Fig. 5.** Precision/Recall

The proposed system first finds the most similar prototypes and then ranks shapes in these clusters based on the dissimilarity metric from the queries. Fig. 5 shows the average results of 20 queries. For each query, a recall of 1.0 is the case of finding 15 cases of each class. We achieved 80.95% precision : 89.82% in the 10 benign queries and 71.09% in the 10 malignant queries.

**Table 1.** Confuse matrix corresponding to the first thirty retrievals

| | PREDICTED CLASS | |
|---|---|---|
| TRUE CLASS | BENIGN | MALIGNANT |
| BENIGN | 281 | 19 |
| MALIGNANT | 92 | 208 |

Classification accuracy was also measured on the first thirty retrieval. Table 1 shows the counts for cells using Eq. (4). For 600 cells, we achieved 81.5% as an average classification correctness: 93.67% in the 300 benign cells and 69.33% in the 300 malignant cells.

# 8 Conclusions

This paper presents an image guided telemedicine system that supports medical decisions for breast cancer diagnosis via the Internet. Results of the proposed system showed satisfactory performance. In addition, retrieval is fast, allowing the extension of the current database to thousands of images with no noticeable increase in delay at the end user.

A display capture of the user interface is shown in Fig. 6. The system allows users to analyze their own images via file transfer accomplished with a Common Gateway Interface (CGI) and the query image is top-left. Once the users draw the boundary of the cell to analyze, the resulting feature values can be displayed in the top-middle. The fifteen retrieved images are with class labels (Ben/Mal) at the bottom and thus the users can get cases of similar cells. Further information and the demo of this system is at

> http://dollar.biz.uiowa.edu/~kelly/telemedicine.html.

The following summarizes our contribution in this paper.

– Internet software application: The proposed system is implemented as a Java applet and thus provides operation remotely via the World Wide Web.
– Weighted distance: Since different features may play different degree of importance in the similarity measurement, we use a weighted distance metric based on the clustered database.
– Usage of nuclear features: In addition to shape features for shape-based indexing, this system uses nuclear features which are modeled such that higher values are typically associated with malignancy.

Future work includes:

– Sufficiently better classification method, for example, such as an artificial neural network
– User-friendly interface, for example, incorporation of multimedia such as audio and video
– Other medical application, for example, brain tumor diagnosis

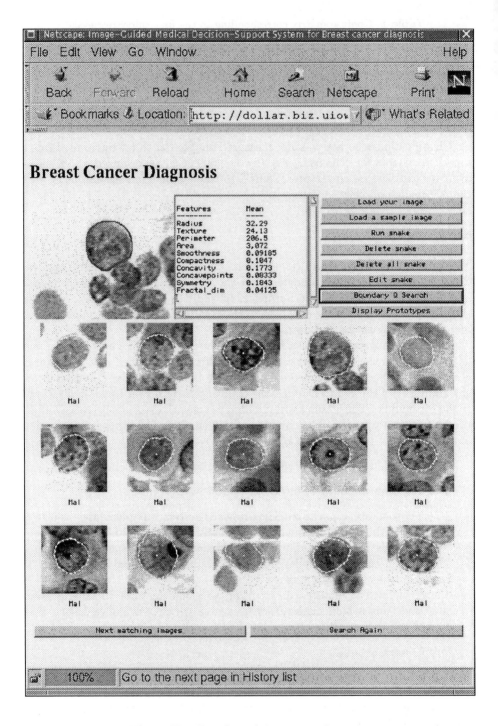

**Fig. 6.** User Interface of the proposed system

# References

1. C. Atkeson, A. W. Moore, and S. Schaal. Locally weighted learning. *AI Review*, 11:11–73, 1997.
2. D. H. Ballard. Generalizing the Hough transform to detect arbitrary shapes. *Pattern Recognition*, 13(2):111–122, 1981.
3. C. Faloutsos, R. Barber, M. Flickner, and J. H. et al. Efficient and effective querying by image content. *Journal of Intelligent Information Systems*, 3:231–262, 1994.
4. A. A. Kassim, T. Tan, and K. H. Tan. A comparative study of efficient generalised Hough transform techniques. *Image and Vision Computing*, 17(10):737–748, 1999.
5. K.-M. Lee and W. N. Street. A fast and robust approach for automated segmentation of breast cancer nuclei. In *Proceedings of the IASTED International Conference on Computer Graphics and Imaging*, pages 42–47, 1999.
6. K.-M. Lee and W. N. Street. Automatic segmentation and classification using on-line shape learning. In *Proceedings of the 5th IEEE Workshop on the Application of Computer Vision*, pages 64–70, 2000.
7. K.-M. Lee and W. N. Street. Dynamic learning of shapes for automatic object recognition. In *Proceedings of the 17th ICML-2000 Workshop on Machine Learning of Spatial Knowledge*, pages 44–49, 2000.
8. K.-M. Lee and W. N. Street. A new approach of generalized Hough transform with flexible templates. In *Proceedings of the 2000 International Conference on Artificial Intelligence*, volume III, pages 1133–1139, 2000.
9. S. C. Orphanoudakis, C. Chronaki, and S. Kostomanolakis. I2C : A system for the indexing, storage, and retrieval of medical images by content. *Journal of Medical Informations*, 19(2):109–122, 1994.
10. A. Pentland, R. W. Picard, and S. Scarloff. Photobook: Tools for content-based manipulation of image databases. In *Proceedings of the SPIE Storage and Retrieval Image and Video Databases II*, volume 185, pages 34–47, 1994.
11. F. Schnorrenberg, N. Tsapatsoulis, C. Pattichis, C. Schizas, S. Kollias, M. Vassiliou, and K. Kyriacou. Modular neural network system for the analysis of nuclei in histopathological sections. *IEEE Engineering in Medicine and Biology*, 19(1):48–63, 2000.
12. H. D. Tagare. Deformable 2-d template matching using othogonal curves. *IEEE Transactions on Medical Imaging*, 16(1):108–116, 1997.
13. K.-L. Tan, B. C. Ooi, and L. F. Thiang. Indexing shapes in image databases using the centroid-radii model. *Data and Knowledge Engineering*, 32(3):271–289, 2000.
14. W. H. Wolberg, W. N. Street, and O. L. Mangasarian. Machine learning techniques to diagnose breast cancer from image-processed nuclear features of fine needle aspirates. *Cancer Letters*, 77:163–171, 1994.

# An Algorithm for Formation and Confirmation of Password for Paid Members on the Internet-Based Telemedicine

Seok-Soo Kim[1], Dae-Joon Hwang[2]

[1] Dept. of Computer Engineering, Dong-yang University, 1 Kyochon-dong, Punggi-eup,
Youngju-city, Kyoungsang North Province, South-Korea, 750-711
sskim@phenix.dyu.ac.kr
[2] School of Electrical and Computer Engineering, Sung-kyun-kwan University, Korea
djhwang@yurim.skku.ac.kr

**Abstract** The password for membership management is made by integrating the information on the paid site, the ID, and the expiration date for the paid period. First, a value of 100 is added to a unique letter from the paid site and to the ASCII code value of the first letter of the ID, and then the ending date is added. Using this method, the passwords for paid members are created and given to the members by mail. This method needs just another password field for paid members added to the previous membership management DB. Even if more sites are formed, it is not necessary to add another field again.

## 1. Introduction

Internet based Telemedicine system has a remote cyber medical examination system (mainly medical consultations), and at the same time, it is run efficiently between doctors and patients by managing the data by being linked to off-line for outpatients. It also has a convenient prescribing-dispensing system between doctors and pharmacists in compliance with "the separation between the prescribing and dispensing functions." That is, i allows medical examinations and consultations on the cyberspace and enables the examinations that are not possible on the Internet to be taken by visiting a doctor off-line.

The examination data (managing each individual's and their family's medical records from on-line and off-line) that are produced from Internet based Telemedicine system can be easily referred by anyone throughout the world. These data are stored semi-permanently, and two different services are provided depending on the type of membership: a doctor service for paid members and other free services for general members. In addition, this system is linked to other medically related sites to build a professional medical web site with a concept of a medical portal system and to provide a variety of services as well as to give benefits to patients, doctors, pharmacists, and health related businesses. This system will offer an opportunity to create a new medical system and business model.

Since the membership is determined by which class (free of charge, fee paid, pharmacist, doctor) the member belongs to, he or she needs to choose the class carefully. The paid members other than free members are required to enter additional information. Also, all the IDs are verified when singing a membership to avoid duplicate IDs. The paid members can consult with a medical professional. When they request for a medical consultation, they need to select a doctor first and then input their requests. After the doctor finishes consulting, the paid member can read the contents. The doctor receives requests, examines them, and then allows the paid members to read the examination results. The paid member takes the examination data to a pharmacy, and a pharmacist dispenses the prescription.[1,2]

## 2. Open Doctor System

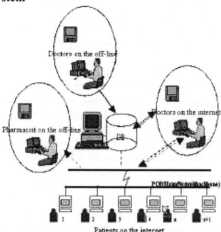

Figure 1. Network Structure of Open Doctor System

In contrast to the previous studies, which are limited to only a part of medical information, this study will build a professional medical web site with a concept of a medical portal system to begin a new medical system that brings benefits as well as a variety of services to patients, doctors, pharmacists and health related businesses. This system has a remote examination and consultation system, and at the same time, it is run efficiently between doctors and patients by managing the data by being linked to off-line for outpatients, and it also has a convenient prescribing-dispensing system between doctors and pharmacists in compliance with "the separation between the prescribing and dispensing functions." Figure 1 describes the overall network structure of this system.[3,4]

### 2.1 Building a web page and a database for private medical information

It allows people to receive medical examinations and medical advices on the Internet and enables the examinations that are not possible on the Internet to be treated after directly contacting the doctor off-line. The medical examinations for all the individuals (their family) can be referred anywhere in the world and are to be stored semi-permanently. This system will have a great influence on national welfare, and its advantages are as follows:

(1) Special member (family doctor service) and general member (free service) method.
    The customers who use the center can have most services free of charge, but some of them are differentiated into special members to have services with better quality. For the members, this method adopts a concept of "home doctor," who does regular check-ups and makes appointments online as well as medical examinations and other services at a hospital (diagnosis,

examination, treatment) off-line. This structure is managed by maintaining a regular membership among the center, the doctor and the patient and having them pay the membership fee.

(2) Management of private medical information

Patients can see their medical examination data, which help them understand their illnesses and take care of themselves. It also allows doctors to give effective treatments and prevent misdiagnosis, based on he past medical history in the data, especially in an emergency or at other hospitals.

(3) Link to other medically related sites

The open doctor system interlinks with many registered doctors (hospitals and clinics), pharmacists (pharmacies) and other health related centers (health centers, health organizations, medical supply stores) and builds cooperative relationships and brings benefits to each of them. That is, patients can do self-care for their health by using a variety of professional medical portal sites. Doctors do free consultation, are seen by patients off-line and can have vast information from cooperative examinations with other doctors. Pharmacists can do business through interactions with registered doctors according to "the separation of prescribing and dispensing functions," which can make great contributions to national welfare. Information on medical supply stores or other health related centers can not only give benefits to patients but also can have various commercial effects when the patients use off-line and on-line (Internet business). [5,6]

## 3. Algorithm for formation and confirmation of password for paid members

Passwords for paid members have been generated through ASP2.0, which is run in IIS4.0, based on Windows NT 4.0. Paid members for specific medical specialty fields (Specialty doctors are also selected) enter their ID and password when they login. They use the ID which they initially enrolled with (used for both free and paid service), but they have to use different passwords for each medical specialty. At this point, a number of database loads might be produced if the members create and check specialty fields in the membership enrollment table. This algorithm simplifies the database, reduces the loads when searching, and allows easy management by providing persistent passwords to the members.

That is, management of paid members generally require the following two basic fields: 1) payment check field to check if the fee has been paid, 2) Expiration date field to check the date that the paid period expires. This method does not have any problems for managing paid members in one site. However, when one customer database is used to share customer information from multiple sites, two fields per site have to be added to check the paid members for each site. In this case, the more the sites that share customer information, the more the fields have to be added to the customer database. If there are more than 10 sites, some fields could be wasted. For remote examinations, there can be a variety number of items (e.g. internal medicine, surgery, urology, plastic surgery, family medicine, ophthalmology) since it is very rare for the users to be paid members of all specialty sites they want. In addition, fields that are not necessary for the record of the customer can be created. The creation of password for membership management has been designed to prevent wasting databases as the above.

The password for membership management is made by integrating the information on the paid site, the ID, and the expiration date for the paid period. First, a value of 100 is added to a unique letter from the paid site and to the ASCII code value of the first letter of the ID, and then the ending date is added. Using this method, the passwords for paid members are created and given to the members by mail. This method needs just another password field for paid members added to the previous membership management DB. Even if more sites are formed, it is not necessary to add another field again.[7,8]

## 4. Formation algorithm

### 4.1 Password formation algorithm

1) Password formation algorithm

Step 1: Obtain an English letter from the requested specialty field.

Step 2: Add a value of 100 in case it comes out more than 2 digits after the ASCII code value and the ending date are added.
- Obtain the ASCII code value of the first digit of the user ID, add 100, and then add today's date.
- Obtain the ASCII code value of the second digit of the user ID, add 100, and then add the expiring year.
- Obtain the ASCII code value of the third digit of the user ID, add 100, and then add the expiring month.

Step 3: Add the produced values from Step 1 and Step 2 as the following:(The ending year, month, and day mean the effective membership period for paid members.)

Specialty field [1 digit]
+ ((The ASCII code value of the first digit of the user ID + 100) + the ending date)[ 3 digits]
+ ((The ASCII code value of the second digit of the user ID + 100) + the ending year)[ 3 digits]
+ ((The ASCII code value of the third digit of the user ID + 100) + the ending month)[ 3 digits]

### 4.2 Confirmation algorithm

1) Password confirmation algorithm

Specialty field [1 digit]
+ (Password 2~4 digits - (the ASCII code value of the first digit of the user ID + 100) = the ending date)
+ (Password 5~7 digits - (the ASCII code value of the second digit of the user ID + 100) = the ending year)
+ (Password 8~10 digits - (the ASCII code value of the third digit of the user ID + 100) = the ending month)

# 5. Testing and verifying the embodied algorithm

Paid members can select many specialty fields, but when the corresponding database is made, it becomes complicated, its speed is decreased, and its management becomes difficult, due to increase in the corresponding tables and felds. To solve these problems, an automatic password formation algorithm has been developed in this system to enhance the efficiency of management and the functions of the database by managing the classification of each paid members and the renewal (or removal) after checking their expiration date. The steps for testing and verifying the algorithm are conducted through the total three steps (raw data presentation step, password formation step, and password confirmation step) as the following:

## 5.1 Raw data input (example data)

1) ID: sskim
2) Medical specialty field: internal department (a)
    (*Surgery is b, OBGYN c, Ophthalmology d, etc.)
3) Fee payment checked date (year, month, day) : March 1, 2001

## 5.2 Password forming process

1) Fee payment checked year: 2001
   Fee payment checked month: 3
   Fee payment checked day: 1

2) The English letter of the first digit of the password => a
   ASCII code value of the first digit of the ID (s:115) + 100 : 215 + Checked day(1) : 216
       ✍✍ English letter + Result : a216
3) Ending year => 1
   ASCII code value of the second digit of the ID (s:115) + 100 : 215 + ending year(01) : 216
       ✍✍ Before result + Current Result : a216216
4) Ending months => 6
   ASCII code value of the third digit of the ID (k:107) + 100
   : 207 + ending month(03+3month=6) : 213
       ✍✍ Before result + Current Result : a216216213
5) Created password   => a216216213

## 5.3 Password confirming process

1) Password recognition

The password can be found from any location of the corresponding field of database, as in the below. That is, the code for the corresponding specialty field can be found by the English letter since the code is unique. (e.g. code for internal department : a)

    < Example on password recognition >

A random password field value 1 => z111111111x222222222a216216213y333333333q444444444
                                                        21
A random password field value 2 => a216216213z555555555x666666666y777777777q888888888
                                    1
A random password field value 3 => z999999999x000000000y555555555t222222222a216216213
                                                                                41

The above example presents 3 random fields for password recognition, and is a method in which each field forms 5 passwords (total 50 letters) including the exact password and the actual password is found in the next 2 steps.

Step 1: Obtain a, the first letter of the password.

Step 2: Find the exact password location in each random field.
- The starting location of the row of letters for the specialty field in random field 1 is 21, and the 10 values from the corresponding location are a216216213.
- The starting location of the row of letters for the specialty field in random field 2 is 1, and the 10 values from the corresponding location are a216216213.
- The starting location of the row of letters for the specialty field in random field 3 is 41, and the 10 values from the corresponding location are a216216213.

Thus, it is concluded that a password in any location, as the above example, can be found (e.g. a216216212).

**2) Expiration date checking process**

Cut the password (e.g. a216216212) by every 3 numbers except for the first digit, that is, the first 3 numbers of the password : 216, the second 3 numbers of the password : 216, and the third 3 numbers of the password : 212. Then, the expiration date (year, month, and day) for the paid members can be obtained. That is, if it is assumed that the joined date is 2001. 03. 01, then that expiration date (Assume the effective period is 3 month) would be 2001. 06. 01.

< Checking expiration date >

- The ending date
 = Password the first digits (216) - (the ASCII code value of the first digit of the user ID (s:115) + 100 = 215) => 01
- The ending year
 = Password second digits (216) - (the ASCII code value of the second digit of the user ID (s:115) + 100 = 215) => 01
- The ending month
 = Password third digits (213) - (the ASCII code value of the third digit of the user ID ((k:107) + 100 = 207) => 6

< Process for removing the post-dated password >

After obtaining the overall length of the row of letters (50) for the password field and finding the beginning and the ending part of the rest of the field except for the password, renew (remove) the database.

## 6. Conclusion

The examination data (managing each individual's and their family's medical records from on-line and off-line) that are produced from Internet based Telemedicine system can be easily referred by anyone throughout the world. These data are stored semi-permanently, and two different services are provided depending on the type of membership: a doctor service for paid members and other free services for general members.

Relation type database is realized by using WinNT 4.0 which is an operation system in order to operate opendoctor site, using IIS 4.0 which is web server program, using SQL and Access 2000 for database of medical examination data with members during web operation, and using ASP language, VBScript, and JavaScript in order to handle DB.

That is, management of paid members generally require the following two basic fields: 1) payment check field to check if the fee has been paid, 2) Expiration date field to check the date that the paid period expires. This method does not have any problems for managing paid members in one site. However, when one customer database is used to share customer information from multiple sites, two fields per site have to be added to check the paid members for each site. In this case, the more the sites that share customer information, the more the fields have to be added to the customer database. If there are more than 10 sites, some fields could be wasted. For remote examinations, there can be a variety number of items (e.g. internal medicine, surgery, urology, plastic surgery, family medicine, ophthalmology) since it is very rare for the users to be paid members of all specialty sites they want. In addition, fields that are not necessary for the record of the customer can be created. The creation of password for membership management has been designed to prevent wasting databases as the above.

## References

1. PACS pages: Eric John Finegan's PACS / Telemedicine Resource page., http://www.dejarnette.com/dfinegan/pacspage.htm
2. T F Gotwald, M Daniaux, A Stoeger, R Knapp and D zur Nedden, "The value of the World Wide Web for tele -education in radiology",Journal of Telemedicine and Telecare,VOLUME 6 NUMBER 1 2000.
3. Elizabeth Krupinski Ph.D.; Phyllis Webster; Mary Dolliver; Ronald S. Weinstein M.D.; Ana Maria Lopez M.D.,M.P.H., "Efficiency Analysis of a Multi-Specialty Telemedicine Service", Telemedicine Journal, Volume 5 Number 3, 1999.
4. D. J. Hwang, Seok. S. Kim "Development of Telemedicine which is a CBM based Collaborative Multimedia System on LAN Environment ", The transactions of the korea information processing society v.4,n.5 pp.1153-1161 May 1997.
5. Kilgore C (Dec 1999) Patients take the wheel with internet health records. Telehealth Magazine 5(7) : 7-8.vol 5, no.7, 2000, Dec.
6. "Telemedicine Coming of Age", The Telemedicine Research Center Home Page, URL: http://trc.telemed.org/, 2000.
7. Hotmail Information, frequently Asked Question, http://lc3.law13. hotmail.passport.com/cgi-bin/dasp/hminfo shell.asp? lang=EN&content=faq.
8. SPEKE: A Strong Password Method http://world.std.com/~dpj/speke.html.

# Agent-Based Approach to e-Learning:
# An Architectural Framework

Elvis Wai Chung LEUNG[1], Qing LI[2]

[1] Hospital Authority, Hong Kong
elvisleung@yahoo.com

[2] Department of Computer Science, City University of Hong Kong
csqli@cityu.edu.hk

**Abstract.** *The World Wide Web (WWW) provides new opportunities for online education on the Internet. With other network tools being applied to the Web, it can create a virtual learning environment to bring together a community of learners for interactive education. Based on the investigation of the use of agent-based approach to e-Learning, this paper shares our views on how to develop an architecture framework to apply the electronic education on the Internet in an effective way.*

**Keywords:** e-learning, agent-based approach, web server, 3-tier architecture, collaborative framework.

## 1 Introduction

With the ability to connect people and information around the world, the Internet is already having a significant impact on the traditional education. Recently, many education providers start to introduce web applications to support teaching. Functions, in general, include downloading course materials, calendar, discussion forum and audio/video tutorial [8,9].

Generally speaking, lectures can be distributed from one site to another by HTML documents that contain graphics, sound and video. The HTML lecture notes, apart from graphics, text, sound, video, animation, simulations and more, can contain links to others HTML documents stored in some servers around the world. It is very common in real lectures that human tutors freely refer to their own previous explanations.

Being treated as a communication tool, the Internet (and particularly the Web) is a good channel to spread information and thus, enhance communication. However, the focus of using web technology in improving traditional education methods might not be the main concern and existing research on Internet-based education is still quite primitive [1,2,3].

Normally, a course is provided with its unique structure. Students are required to complete the course step by step in order to acquire an academic award. There is little facility to help students and teachers to understand the strength and weakness of the students in relation to course subjects and to device the study plan based on individual situation.

Moreover, students are usually only provided with some static paths to retrieve the information. Such systems are therefore rather *passive* in providing course materials. For example, students with different background and knowledge of a given subject are most likely given the same materials. The heart of the problem is the lack of "content/user awareness". These systems are not designed with powerful intelligent knowledge base facilities, such as personal profiles which can help understand students' behavior so as to provide student-specific, content-driven results to different students. The learning and teaching performance is thus inevitably affected by this phenomenon. Thus, an interactive approach for e-Learning becomes a critical issue.

Finally, lack of monitoring and suggesting facilities to students on a timely basis is another fundamental drawback. Based on the e-Learning model, students are not required to go to school. Hence, a practical mechanism for the study assessment becomes indispensable. It is necessary to rely on a robust assessment system to ensure that the students' learning is on the right track.

## 1.1 Paper Objectives and Organization

Through the agent-based approach to e-Learning, we aim to address the following two main issues: (1) How can agent-based approach to e-Learning overcome the limitations of current technologies? (2) How can agent-based approach to e-Learning meet the user needs at present and in the future?

The rest of this paper is organized as follows. Some of the background information about multiagent is revisited in the coming section. The specific features of the architecture framework are detailed in sections 3 and 4, including the three-tier architecture, requirements and functionalities, system architecture and design, and a framework for collaboration. The final section concludes this paper and makes suggestions for further research.

# 2 Background of Research

Intelligent Information Retrieval (IIR) [7] involves content-based access of information, where the meaning and not just the syntax of a query is used to guide and control the retrieval process. Abstractions and models of the data environment and user requirements are used to relate the query to the information so as to facilitate a more pertinent and controlled access to a large array of information repositories.

The abstract models shown in Figure 1 can conceptually capture most of the models for IIR. Figure 1a shows an intelligent information system where an "inference shell" is wrapped around the data repository. We will apply the term *information server* to this combination of an inference engine and a data repository. The inference shell contains the "knowledge" or "domain models" or "abstractions" of the information and serves as an interface through which queries are filtered and recast to associate the task-level content in a query with the information. Although information servers are typically thought of as passive processes, pressed into service for the purpose of satisfying externally generated queries, they may take a much more active role. That is, information servers may seek out and build connections with other servers in the network that contain data related to the information maintained locally. This view treats information servers as intelligent agents with their own goals, adding to both the richness and the complexity of the environment.

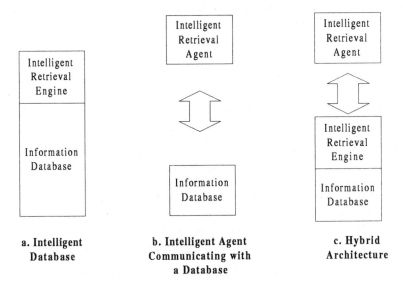

a. Intelligent Database

b. Intelligent Agent Communicating with a Database

c. Hybrid Architecture

Figure 1: Conceptual Models for Intelligent Information Retrieval

Figure 1b shows an intelligent information retrieval agent, carrying user requirements and task-level knowledge, reaching a data repository to extract information from it. The agent formulates a query based on abstractions of the contents of the repository and its own task-level requirements to perform a content-based retrieval.

Figure 1c shows a hybrid model where the intelligent agent carries the user's requirements and, possibly, abstract descriptions of the information sources it can access. The retrieval engine contains a more detailed model of its information database as well as mappings between this model and the abstract descriptions in the agents that can access it. Because both the retrieval engine and the retrieval agent are intelligent, they can engage in a dialog to negotiate the nature of their interaction.

That can be beneficial when access to the information database, which is mediated by the retrieval engine, is costly. The retrieval agent can employ its model of user requirements to determine how to trade off expected completeness, quality and precision of the results of its query based on the retrieval engine's model of the database. In addition, the hybrid view has the advantage of separating the user and the task-level requirements from the conceptual model of the data repository. Therefore, we adopt the hybrid view of IIR (Figure 1c) in our framework.

# 3 Agent-based approach to e-Learning: Design Overview and Functionalities

In this section, we describe our proposed agent-based approach to e-Learning, by providing a design overview and the main functionalities. But first, we start with the specific requirements and objectives of our e-Learning system.

## 3.1 Requirements and Objectives

The specific requirements and objectives are to enable the user to the following tasks: -
- Web-based user interface for learning and teaching.
- Design of case-based program/course plan for individual level.
- Retrieving/storing the course information from/to the central databases for development of course material.
- Constructing the requirement of prerequisite knowledge for the specific course and the possible learning path for individual student at the initial stage.
- Constructing the personal profile for different facets of assessment.
- Monitoring student' learning process and reviewing learning path from time to time.
- Understanding student knowledge through personalized assessment.
- Storing personal data for assessment and future data mining.

## 3.2 System Architecture

In designing the e-Learning system, we adopted a three-tier architecture which is illustrated in Figure 2. As shown in Figure 2, it consists of client, Web server, and database. All three tiers can be on one machine or spread over the network on different machines.

### Client
This client part is responsible for the presentation of data, receiving user events and controlling the user interface. The actual business logic has been moved to an application-server.

## Web Server

The web server handles all communication with the client and handles most of the communication with the database. It implements the business rules and is available to the client-tier. The web server is used to store and process the server-side program such as CGI, ASP, Java JSP, and Servlet. These make up the framework for the entire application, both on the server and on the client.

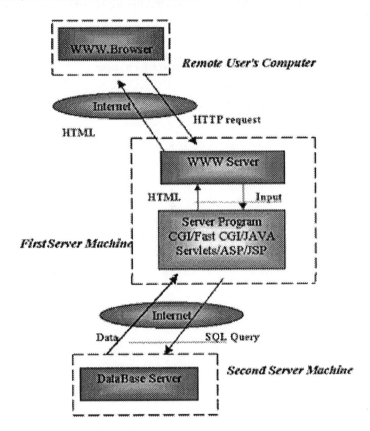

**Figure 2.** The three-tier architecture for e-Learning (all three can be on one machine or spread over the network on different machines as illustrated above).

## Database

This part is responsible for data storage. The database component we proposed to use is Microsoft SQL Server or Oracle database. It supports an Open Database Connectivity (ODBC) interface to the server used to access the database. Open Database Connectivity (ODBC) is a Microsoft established standard that enables software developers to create applications that can work with a number of SQL-based data sources. With ODBC, applications needing data from a data source can generate ODBC calls, and these calls are then translated by an ODBC driver into the native SQL of the data source to be processed. The server uses sever-side program to store and retrieve information from the database.

## 3.3 Server Components and Functionalities

The overall server architecture is given in Figure 3, which contains the six agents such as Home-based Teaching Agent, Personal Profile Agent, Assessment Agent, Dynamic Study plan Agent, Course and Study Material Design Agent and Home-based Learning Agent. A Data Warehouse for Teaching and Learning is used to store data for supporting the e-Learning system and developing possible applications such as data mining.

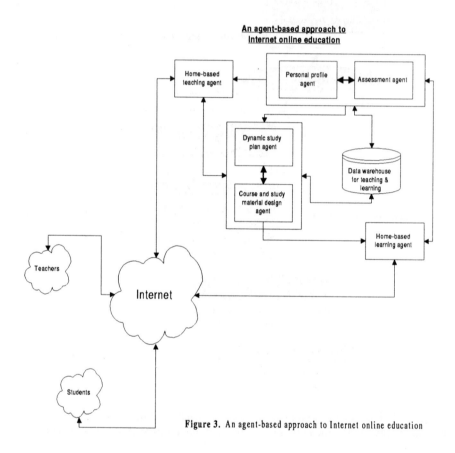

**Figure 3.** An agent-based approach to Internet online education

What follows is a brief description of the functions of the specific agents in our e-Learning system.

- **Home-based Teaching Agent (HTA):** It is a general interface that provides support for the stable interface elements to manage the interaction with the other agents. From a lecturer's point of view, it is a virtual office for the program design and course material development, and it can also retrieve student information from *Personal Profile Agent* and *Assessment Agent* for reviewing study plan of individual student.

- **Personal Profile Agent (PPA):** It is to manage all student information. All agents are required to inform the PPA to retrieve the needed information to ensure the information is kept in a proper manner and to prevent the distribution to other unauthorized places. Normally, the requesters are *Home-based Teaching Agent*, *Dynamic Study Plan Agent* and *Course and Study Material Design Agent*. It also communicates with the *Assessment Agent* to obtain information about the assessment result of each student.

- **Assessment Agent (AA):** For student learning monitoring, the AA is assigned to provide assessment for students. The assessment has two categories:
  1. It provides the assessment to students prior to admission. The level and coverage of the provided assessment is based on the information from PPA.
  2. It provides the ongoing assessments during the studying period. The level and coverage of the given assessment is based on the information from Dynamic Study Plan Agent and Personal Profile Agent.

  Based on the above information, the AA will be responsible for the finding of suitable questions for assessment from the Data Warehouse for Teaching and Learning. The assessment result will then be stored into the Data Warehouse for Teaching and Learning. Also, it will only be requested to provide information to the PPA.

- **Dynamic Study Plan Agent (DSPA):** For initial admission, it will request information from the PPA and AA to perform the task of study plan. It will base on the information and the rules that are collected from Data Warehouse for Teaching and Learning to suggest, among others, the possibility of prerequisite knowledge and learning sequence for the program.

  For ongoing study plan review, it will request information, on timely basis, from PPA and AA and compare with the current study plan. If the students violate the study plan, the DSPA will revise the study plan. Then, warning message will be sent to the HTA to review the revised study plan.

- **Course and Study Material Design Agent (CSMDA):** All course materials and information will be managed by the CSMDA agent. The materials may contain graphics, sound, and video. It will be stored in a central database for future development of course material. For course material development, the CSMDA agent will be responsible to find out some relevant information to the HTA based on the pre-stored rules.

- **Home-based Learning Agent (HLA):** It is a general interface that provides support to the stable interface elements to manage the interaction with other agents. For student's point of view, it is a virtual personal classroom. The lectures will base on the student's personal study plan to deliver. Ideally, lectures will be delivered by HTML documents that can contain graphics, sound and video. Other information relating to study will be distributed through this agent such as course reference, calendar, and so on. Meanwhile, the AA will provide the assessment to students to ensure the learning is in a right track in timely basis.

- **Data Warehouse for Teaching and Learning:** It is a central storage for the teaching and learning such as the course material, student profile, assessment result, student study plan, and knowledge rules. For data exchange among agents, the data will be stored in database or in XML[12] format. For data in XML format, the demand of the database engine will be reduced and the flexibility of data exchange for individual agents will be increased. The respective subjects and performance will be stored for student's assessment and used to plan future course development and data mining.

The overall flows of our server system is exemplified as follows (cf. Figure 4):

1) At the initial stage, the client (a teacher or student), through the browser, makes HTTP request to the Web server.
2) The servlet as a facilitator, located in web server, is waiting for HTTP request. Once the request received, servlet will distribute the request to relevant agent for further action (cf. Section 4.1).
3) Once designated agent receives the request, it will start to provide service. If the existing knowledge is not enough to provide the solution, the agent will make another request to the peer agents.
4) In case the peer agents are also without sufficient knowledge to solve the problem, step 4 will then be repeated.
5) In order to handle the potential infinitive loop for making request to peer agents, the receiver has the right to terminate a duplicate request and inform the requesting agent to leave.
6) Finally, the servlet will send back the result to the client.

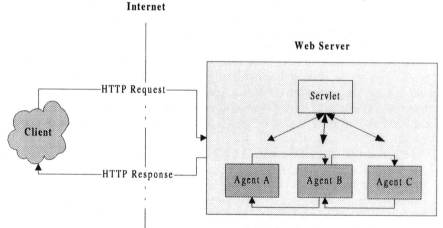

Figure 4. **Overall flows among the server components**

# 4 Framework for Collaboration: Methodology and Development Issues

In this section we advocate a collaborative solution to the e-Learning architecture framework. First, an agent collaboration protocol is described in section 4.1, followed by a discussion of some of the implementation issues and tools in section 4.2.

## 4.1 Agent Collaboration

It is not uncommon that a particular agent may not have any prior knowledge, but there may exist a number of agents belonging to other users who do. Instead of each agent re-learning what other agents have already learned through experience, agents can simply ask for help in such cases. This gives each agent the opportunity of accessing to a potentially vast body of expertise that already exists. Over time each agent builds up a trust relationship with each of its peers analogous to the way we consult different experts for help in particular domains and learn to trust or disregard the opinions of particular individuals.

Through the agent-based approach, the ideas of personalization and interactive learning can also be incorporated more easily. Each agent contains its own functionalities and responsibilities to achieve its own objectives (e.g., the PPA can provide the services of storage based on the students' behavior). Also, an agent can assist other agents when they are in need of help in order to complete the task or request. In this way, the result can be tailor-made for a targeted student under specific situation by the outcome of the best knowledge of different agents.

As the primary task of an agent is to assist its particular user, the protocol for collaboration should be designed to be flexible, efficient and non-binding [4,5,6]. We briefly present such a protocol below.

- Applications can be seen as the combination of several independent agents whose interaction defines the application behavior.
- The applications can serve several users independently accessing the shared environment.
- Several independent applications that run independently can interact. Coordination and communication may happen not just among different modules of a single, complex application, but may arise naturally from independent applications dealing with the same types of information.
- Collaborative communication between agents occurs in the form of *request* and *reply* messages. The types of requests and their associated replies are presented below.
    - **Situation level collaboration**: When a situation occurs for which an agent does not have a good prediction, it sends off a ***Request-for-Prediction*** message to its peers. A prediction request contains all the features of the situation that the agent issuing the request wishes to divulge. An agent receiving a prediction request should provide explanation honestly and distill the information to be returned to the requester properly.
    - **Agent level collaboration**: An agent may send its peers a ***Request-for-Evaluation*** request. An evaluation request is sent when an agent wants to know what some of its peers think about a certain agent in terms of being able to model their users in particular classes of situations.

### 4.1.1 Some Examples

We now present a couple of examples to illustrate the possible collaborations of the various agents, so as to further describe the typical scenarios of our application.

#### (1) Request-for-Prediction

For the teacher making a request of a particular subject's assessment result of a class, the Personal Profile Agent (PPA) is firstly required to provide the information. PPA knows who are in the class and which agent can provide the required assessment result. Then PPA will provide the name list, as Request-for-Prediction, to Assessment Agent (AA) for getting the assessment result of the subject. Once AA collected the related assessment information, it will pass the information to PPA honestly. Finally, PPA will put the information together and send to the teacher.

#### (2) Request-for-Evaluation

For the teacher making a request of collecting the course material of the subject for a particular class, the Course and Study Material Design Agent (CSMDA) is firstly required to provide the information. CSMDA needs to know the number of students in the class, their assessment results, and their study plan. In this case, CSMDA will request the Dynamic Study Plan Agent (DSPA) to provide the study plan of students. Also, CSMDA will send the Request-for-Evaluation to DSPA for obtaining the agents' list that can provide the solution.

### 4.1.2 Advantages of the Collaborative Framework

By structuring a multiagent system, the system will be able to offer the following advantages:

- Speed-up due to concurrent processing.
- Less communication bandwidth requirements because processing is located nearer the source of information.
- More reliability because of the lack of a single point of failure.
- Improved responsiveness due to processing.
- Sensing and effecting being co-located.
- Finally system development becomes easier due to modularity coming from the decomposition into semi-autonomous agents.

### 4.2 Some Development Issues

In developing this application, there are a number of issues/choices pertinent to and/or contributing to the system development, as discussed below.

### 4.2.1 Targeted User Education Level

For maximizing the utilities of this application, the criteria for user selection are purposely set as follows: -

-   High frequency of introducing new subjects and courseware amendment.
-   Students for selection of courses are highly influenced by market need.
-   Generally, users are willing to learn on the Internet.

Thus, in our pilot study, this application is tailor-made to the university students studying in the computer science degree.

### 4.2.2 Tools for Development

#### *Knowledge Management and Reasoning*

Jess [10] will be used for building up the domain knowledge in our system. Jess is a tool for building *Expert System* type of intelligent software. An Expert System is a set of rules that can be repeatedly applied to a collection of facts about the world. Rules that apply are fired, or executed. Jess uses a specific algorithm (ie., Rete [14]) to match the rules to the facts. Rete makes Jess much faster than a simple set of cascading if.. then statements in a loop♥.

#### *User Interface Tier*

In the User Interface Tier where the system interfaces with users, all the applications will be built as web browser-driven applications using Java Server Pages (JSP) and JavaBeans [11]. As JSP pages are intended to focus on presentation but not business logic, it is therefore important that JSP development does not require advanced programming skills in normal cases.

However, some aspects of presentation, such as formatting, can be complex. Java beans are beans that implement a basic business logic step. Their role is to abstract and regularize the computations supported by the business logic of the application.

#### *Application Tier*

On the server-side, servlets are devised to process HTTP requests and to co-ordinate the rest of the application elements. The primary application logic is separated into Java components (command beans) outside the servlet [11] and is independent of the details of HTTP access. This allows these components to be used to support other styles of Web applications such as those based on direct applet to serve communication.

#### *Data Tier*

MS SQLServer2000 [13] will be the database to be used in the Data Tier. Some powerful new features in SQL Server2000 that support XML [12] are listed below:

---

♥ Jess was originally conceived as a Java clone of CLIPS [15], but has many features nowadays that differentiate it from its parent.

- It enables queries to return data in XML format instead of recordset, by using the new key work 'For XML' at the end of the SELECT statement. This will let web service components in middle tier be able to retrieve data in XML format directly from the database.
- Data can be stored in XML format. An XML document can be viewed using OpenXML and then the records in XML can be stored into relational tables.

Based on the above new features, it is suitable for the agents to exchange the information through XML and store the final result into the relevant tables.


# 5 Conclusion

We have described in this paper an agent-based approach to e-Learning, and proposed an architectural framework for developing such an application, which has the following main facilities and "building blocks":

1) An agent-based approach which provides a collaborative approach to apply in e-Learning.
2) Web technology which provides a universal communication and presentation platform.
3) Jess which provide a simple tool to store and execute the knowledge rules.
4) Java technology which provides a powerful language which runs on both client-side and server-side. Also, it facilitates high level co-ordination support for multi-agents.

We remark that the descriptions of our approach to develop an agent-based architecture for e-Learning embodies only one of the possible ways to address a very complex and challenging application. We have shown that combining with Java and agent-based approach, it is feasible to build a flexible, knowledgeable and self-improving system to support e-Learning. Further implementation-oriented research efforts concerning the embedding of coordination models into practical programming are currently being conducted.

For our further research, one of the issues is to develop a methodology for the agents to cope with the dynamic environment change. Adopting a proactive approach for the agent to learn from the interaction process between teachers and students is also an interesting issue to explore, so as to find out some "hot topics" and issues of concern of the e-Learning users. Finally, we also plan to investigate the possible utilization of our system to support other types of applications such as user profiling, and data mining based on the e-Learning data/ knowledge base.

# Reference

[1]     Crane, B. E. (2000), *Teaching with the Internet*, Neal-Schuman Publishers, Inc.

[2]     Wolz, U., McKeown K. R., and Kaiser G.E., (1992), Automated Tutoring in Interactive Environments: A Task-Centered Approach,    in *Intelligent Instruction by Computer, Theory and Practice*, Taylor & Francis New York Inc.

[3]     Regian J. W. and  Shute V. J., Evaluating Intelligent Tutoring Systems, in *Technology Assessment in Education and Training*, Lawrence Erlbaum Associates, Inc.

[4]     Lesser V R (1999), *Cooperative Mutiagent Systems: A Personal View of the State of the Art,* IEEE Transactions on Knowledge and Data Engineering, vol. 11, no.11 Jan –Feb 1999

[5]     Ciancarina, P, Tolksdorf, R, Vitali, F, Rossi, D and Knoche, A (1998), *Coordinating Multiagent Applications on the WWW:A Reference Architecture*, IEEE Transactions on Software Engineering, vol. 24 , no. 5, May 1998

[6]     Lashkari Y, Metral M, Maes P (1994), *Collaborative Interface Agents*, Proceedings of the Twelfth National Conference on Artificial Intelligence

[7]     Oates T, Prasad M V N, Lesser V R, *Cooperative Information Gathering: A Distributed Problem Solving Approach*

[8]     http://www.icdl.open.ac.uk/

[9]     http://www.hull.ac.uk/merlin/

[10]    http://herzberg.ca.sandia.gov/jess/

[11]    http://www.javasoft.com

[12]    http://www.w3.org

[13]    http://www.microsoft.com/sql/

[14]    Forgy, C. L., *Rete: A Fast Algorithm for the Many Pattern/ Many Object Pattern Match Problem,* Artificial Intelligence 19, 17-37, 1982.

[15]    Riley, G., *CLIPS, A Tool for Building Expert Systems.* http://www.ghg.net/clips/CLIPS.html.

# A Design and Implementation of Web-Based Project-Based Learning Support Systems

Hyosook Jung[1], Woochun Jun[2] and Le Gruenwald[3]

[1]Yang-dong Elementary School, Seoul, Korea

E-mail : est0718@chollian.net

[2]Dept of Computer Education, Seoul National Univ. of Education, Seoul, Korea

E-mail : wocjun@ns.seoul-e.ac.kr

[3]School of Computer Science, Univ. of Oklahoma, Norman, OK 73069, USA

E-mail : ggruenwald@ou.edu

*Abstract.* The use of the Web (World Wide Web) has had many positive effects on education. It overcomes time and space limitations in traditional schools. Teachers and students are now using the Web to access vast amounts of information and resources in the cyberspace. Also, learning via the Web enables both synchronous and asynchronous communication. Despite of many benefits of the Web, it may weaken students' motivation due to lack of face-to-face communication. In this paper, we provide a learning model called Web Project Learning, which is based on the principles of contructivism, to provide motivation and collaborative learning for students in the Web environment. The model is based on the Project-Based Learning model and is revised for use on the Web. The model can also encourage the participation of parents as well as students, and be applied to any subject. We implement our model and show that it can be applied for environmental education as an instance.

## 1. Introduction

Recent advances in the Web have rapidly changed our life in various ways. These advances provide new ways for people to communicate on a global scale and assess vast amounts of information. The Web provides educators with opportunities to implement a range of new teaching and learning practices, which redefine classroom-learning experiences. The Web enables a so-called WBI (Web-Based Instruction) system as a teaching aid. The WBI system, which integrates a hypertext information network with communication and collaborative tools, presents two important innovative features: first, it provides specific tools to manipulate the multimedia information contents of the Web pages; second, authorized users can modify the information network in the system [1,2,3].

Despite of many benefits of the Web in the learning process, it may weaken students' motivation in the cyberspace because of lack of face-to-face communication. The lack of student control is also considered one of the drawbacks of WBI unless a teacher keeps the students working towards its goal. As teachers' influence decreases, students may become disengaged. Thus, students are unable to concentrate their thoughts upon their work. It is reported that about 30%-50% of students who have started a distance education course dropped out before the end of the course [4]. To make the learning process effective, we must motivate students to be engaged in the learning activities. A learning experience where the learner must contribute to an activity is called active engagement, while a learning experience where the learner is mainly a recipient of information is called passive engagement [5]. When a form of engagement is engrossed by a learning activity, the learner is focused and attentive, and becomes captured and committed to the task at hand.

Teachers have found that working on projects is an engaging activity with a large potential for facilitating learning [6]. Project work provides a context for taking initiative and assuming responsibility, making decisions and choices, and pursuing interests. The Project-Based Learning Model also can be used to enrich the curriculum, strengthen Internet skills, and provide integrated and thematic learning opportunities [7,8].

In this paper, we present the Web-based Project-Based Learning Model for the Web environment. It is based on the existing Project-Based Learning Model, but it also can motivate students and provide real life contexts for successful collaborative learning in various ways on the Web. Our model also adopts the principles of constructivism so that both collaborative learning and self-learning are emphasized.

We design the model for the Web environment and implement for classroom use. The model can be applied to any subject. We show that the model can be applied for environmental education as an instance.

This paper is organized as follows. In Section 2, we present constructivism and Project-Based Learning on which our model is based. Our proposed Web-Based Project-Based Learning Model is introduced in Section 3. Section 4 describes how the proposed model is implemented. Finally, we give conclusions and further research issues in Section 5.

## 2. Background

### 2.1 Constructivism

Constructivism is an idea that has been embraced by educational researchers and is defined as follows [5]. Each individual must create anything he or she knows using his or her own mind. There are two basic sources of raw material from which new knowledge is created. One is already known thought, and the other is new information available from the senses. New information combined with existing ideas can create modifications to current improvements. On reflection, an idea that we must all create in our own knowledge seems obvious. The value of this idea is in its corollaries. The first of these is that the more one understands, the more readily one can learn new ideas. Or conversely, the less one knows, the harder one can learn new things. The second is that a good learning situation enables us to try out ideas repeatedly, making modifications, seeing what works and what does not, and using this experience to refine our conceptions. The third is that the learner must be an active participant, who is mixing, matching, and trying ideas together. It is not enough to just allow ideas to enter our mind; they must be integrated into existing structures and thought patterns. And this means that for learning to occur, we must be motivated to become engaged in the learning activities.

## 2.2 Project-Based Learning

A project is an in-depth investigation if a topic worth learning more about. The investigation is usually undertaken by a small group of students within a class, sometimes by a whole class, and occasionally by an individual child. The key feature of a project is that it is a research effort deliberately focused on finding answers to questions about a topic posed either by the children, teacher, or the teacher working with the children. The goal of a project is to learn more about the topic rather than to seek the right answers to questions posed by the teacher [7].

Project-Based Learning refers to a set of teaching strategies which enable teachers to guide children through in-depth studies of real-world topics. The Project-Based Learning is not unstructured. There is a complex but flexible framework with features that characterize the teaching-learning interactions. When teachers imp lement Project-Based Learning successfully, students can be highly motivated, feel actively involved in their own learning, and produce work of a high quality [9].

The values of Project-Based Learning include the following:

a). Project-Based Learning is a model for classroom activities that shift away from the traditional classroom practices of short, isolated, teacher-centered lessons, and instead, emphasizes learning activities that are long-term, interdisciplinary, student-centered, and integrated with real-world issues and practices.

b). One immediate benefit of practicing Project-Based Learning is the unique way that can motivate students by engaging them in their own learning. Project-Based Learning provides opportunities for students to pursue their own interests, questions and make decisions about how they will find answers and solve problems.

c). Project-Based Learning also provides opportunities for interdisciplinary learning. Students apply and integrate the content of different subject areas at authentic moments in the production process, instead of in isolation or in an artificial setting. In the classroom, Project-Based Learning provides many unique opportunities for teachers to build relationship with students. Teachers may fill the varied roles of coach, facilitator, and co-learner. Finished products, plans, drafts, and prototypes all make excellent "conversation pieces" around which teachers and students can discuss the learning that is taking place.

d) In the school and beyond, Project-Based Learning also provides opportunities for teachers to build relationships with each other and with those in the larger community. Student' work, which includes documentation of the learning process as well as the students' final projects, can be shared with other teachers, parents, mentors, and the business community who all have a stake in the students' education [10].

## 3. Design of a Web-Based Project-Based Learning Model

### 3.1. Web-Based Project-Based Learning

One of the most promising ways the Internet is being utilized in school is to have students participate in global collaborative Internet projects. In this section, we propose a learning model called the Web-Based Project-Based Learning (hereinafter called 'Web Project Learning') for the Web environment. The Web Project Learning is defined as problem-oriented learning within the framework of a small group, a whole class, or an individual project and using web support for the project activities. The model is based on the Project-Based Learning Model we mentioned earlier in Section 2.2, but it can motivate students to participate in the project voluntarily and actively. It also provides real-life contexts for successful collaborative learning [5].

In teaching, the Web fits very well with the Project-Based Learning Model. The Web can be an organizer, a research tool, a ready source of data, a means for people to communicate with each other, and a repository for artifacts. Because the Web is a part of the real world, and artifacts on the Web can readily be placed in the world beyond school, projects have a scope for authenticity not usually found in the school environment.

The Web Project Learning can motivate both students and teachers as it provides an appealing way for students to gain Internet skills while being engaged in regular classroom activities. Through the projects, students are encouraged to develop a range of skills relating to reading, writing and researching as well as developing their abilities in selecting, presenting and communicating information. When students work on their project, they strengthen research and organization skills while being responsible and self-motivated all skills they will need in the information age. Students feel a sense of engagement because they work with topics that they have chosen for themselves.

## 3.2. Web-Based Project-Based Learning Model

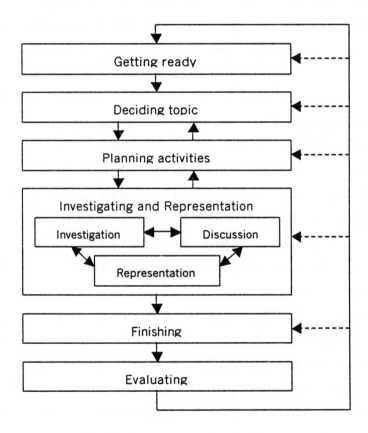

**Fig. 1.** Web Project Learning Model

The Web Project Learning Model is divided into the following six phases instead of only three phases, which are Getting Started, Field Work and Culminating and Debriefing Events, as in the existing Project-Based Learning models [7,8,9].

**1. Getting ready**. First of all, a teacher designs a project outline. The outline's purpose is to provide the information necessary for students to envision their own project within the scope of the outline, and provide resources to help them carry it out. It must provide goals of the whole project for students, and sufficient guidance for students to choose appropriate questions, activities, and products. The outline will be mainly read and used by students. A teacher analyzes and integrates curriculum, lists questions, researches Web sites or resources that can be helpful for students to investigate during the course of the project, and post on the Web.

**2. Deciding topic**. Students read the Web Project outline and search for resources. References to resources consist of URLs to relevant Web materials so that students can be directed immediately to high quality materials that match the project needs. Students recall their own past experiences related to the project, make topic map and exchange their ideas. During preliminary learning, the students decide subtopics of the project for themselves.

**3. Planning activities**. Students work on individual student projects, in-class collaborative projects, or class-to-class projects. They determine the activities and events that will take place at each stage of their subtopics, plan appropriate timelines for all their subtopics, and post on the Web. If they work on a collaborative learning project, each team member must have specific roles and responsibilities. Teachers communicate contents of project planning to parents so that they can help and support their children work on the projects.

**4. Investigating and Representation**. Investigation includes activities such as interviewing experts through e-mail, investigating Web sites, and sharing exchange new experience and knowledge and doing a survey through the Web. In addition, it includes observations, experiments and field trips. Discussion includes both synchronous and asynchronous communication through the chatting or bulletin board system. Representation includes drawing, painting, writing, math diagrams, maps, etc. to represent new learning. Regularly, parents report the children's condition to teachers.

**5.** **Finishing**. Students produce reports, presentations, Web pages, images, pictures, construction, etc. as a result of the activity, share their end products, and celebrate them on the Web. Teachers have students write down their reflections on the project and things to remember for next time.

**6.** **Evaluating**. Teachers evaluate the whole process of the project and arrive at grades based on participation and products.

## 4. Implementation of the Web-Based Project-Based Learning Supporting System

The system is to make teachers and students carry out projects wherever and whenever they may work. It helps teachers and students begin developing an overall plan for managing their project. For Project-Based Learning to be ensured as student-centered learning, the system must give students experience in planning for the project and in working in team or class, and have students create their assignments as form of HTML documents or reports. Normally the environmental education of elementary schools has to be authentic in that it is concerned with a real-world situation or problem because of cognitive development process of students. Our model will be an alternative of environmental education in classroom. As a result, we expect that students will recognize the importance of environmental protection and have motivation to practice environmental conservation.

In this paper, the system is implemented on a Windows NT 4.0 Server and subsequent IIS 4.0. We use database management based on SQL Server 7.0 and the HTML and ASP language for managing information. The overall requirements of hardware and software for the implementation are listed in Table 1. Our system is implemented in **http://203.234.37.75/jung/frame.asp** in Korean. Its English version will be available soon.

**Table 1.** Development environment and tool

| | Elements | Options |
|---|---|---|
| **Hardware** | CPU | Pentium II 333MHz |
| | RAM | 64MB |
| | Secondary storage | 10GB |
| **Software** | Operating System | Windows NT 4.0 |
| | Web Server | IIS 4.0 |
| | Database Server | MS SQL Server 7.0 |
| | Brower | Internet Explorer 5.0 |
| | Programming Language | Active Server Page |

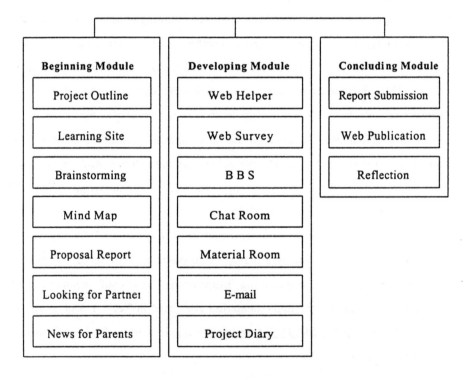

**Fig. 2.** The structure map of the system

## 4.1 Beginning

The "Project outline" explains the project while "Learning site" is connected to useful Web resources within the project. Students explore the Web site in advance, propose what they wish to investigate through brainstorming, and make a mind map. Once a subtopic has been selected, students or small groups of students plan an appropriate timeline and activities for their project and show them to teachers and all their friends on the Web. If necessary, teachers or students can advertise to look for partners on the bulletin board system. Through news for parents, parents can understand the project planning their children will work on. Fig. 3 presents an example of a project outline form. A teacher completes the section of the project outline form and submits it. Information appearing on this form will appear on the Web. So students can read it and understand the central questions of their project, what they are going to do and what products they are going to produce.

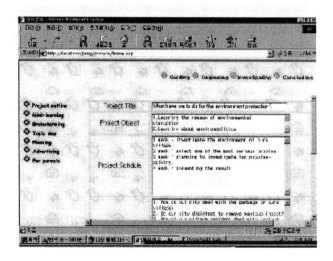

**Fig.3.** An example of a project outline form

## 4.2 Developing Module

Students can use the Web in order to communicate with field experts about experience and knowledge of the topic and use email, chat room, or BBS (Bulletin Board System) to communicate with other people both individually and as a group. Also, they search for information on the Web, do a survey and represent the results, share resource and information on the material room. Project diary is parents' comments on children's work. Parents can appreciate the work in which their children are engaged. They may be able to contribute ideas for field experiences which the teachers may not have thought of, especially when parents can offer practical help in gaining access to a field site or relevant expert. Fig. 4. shows a main picture of the developing module. Two photos show students undertaking learning activities as teamwork.

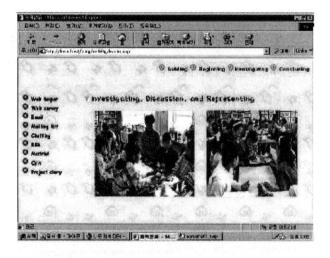

**Fig. 4.** Main picture of the developing module

## 4.3. Concluding Module

Students present reports of results in the form of Web pages, presentations, construction, document files, etc. to the entire class and discuss or write about suggested future improvements. Fig. 5 presents an example of a project report form. Students use this form to report the results of a project.

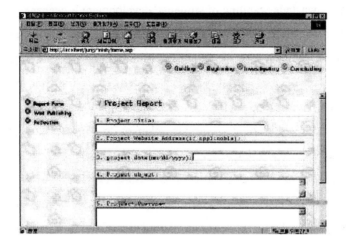

**Fig. 5.** An example of a project report form

## 5. Conclusions and Further Work

In this paper, we proposed a learning model called Web Project Learning to provide motivation and collaborative learning to students in the Web environment. We expect that students are concerned with the problems of their regional environments and investigate them when our learning model is applied to environmental education. Our model also encourages students to interchange their own peculiar environmental characteristics. Using the proposed model, students can strengthen research and organization skills while being responsible and self-motivated. As they gain learning experience for the pure joy of learning, their emotional interest, intrinsic motivation, and hunger for knowledge can also be increased. The students are immersed in an authentic learning environment while undertaking the project. Their activities encourage them to exercise life skills such as problem solving, communication and collaboration, making decisions, and using information technology. Also, parents are concerned about their children's development and thus will participate in and contribute to the project. As teachers examine the students' work and prepare the project, their own understanding of students' development is deepened.

Further research issues are as follows. At first, we need to develop evaluation criteria that we can post it on the Web to let students know how their projects will be evaluated. We will also need to conduct a study comparing the performance of students using our proposed model and that of students following traditional classroom teaching. Currently, various schemes to provide motivation on cyber education are somewhat subjective and depend on psychological effects [11,12,13,14]. As a result, we have to develop the various ways to provide motivation for students. In our earlier work [15], providing motivation on the Web was considered in terms of three categories, Student-to-Course Content relationship, Student-to-Teacher relationship, and Student-to-Student relationship. Currently we are refining the earlier work.

## Reference

[1] Seryn, W. & John, E. (1997), A case Study of communication technology within the elementary school, Australian Journal of Educational Technology, 13(2), 144-164

[2] Giovanni, F. & Rosella, C. (1999), A Web-Based Instruction System to support design activities in Architecture, Paper presented to AusWeb 99, Fifth Australian World Wide Web Conference.

[3] Mason, R. (1991), Moderating Educational Computer Conferencing in DEOSNEWS Vol. 1 No. 19.

[4] Richard, C & Barbara L. M. (1997), The Role of motivation in Web-Based Instruction, Web-Based Instruction, 93-100,

[5] Marv, W. (2000), Learning with the Web, Paper presented to Korea Association of Educational Information & Broadcasting, 2000, November, 7-36

[6]   Katz, L.G. and S.C. Chard. (1989), Engaging children's minds: the project approach, Norwood, NJ: Ablex.

[7]   Katz, L. G. (1994), The Project Approach, ERIC Digest; EDO-PS-94_6, [Online] http://ericps.crc.uiuc.edu/eece/pubs/digests/1994/lk-pro94.html

[8]   http://teacher.scholastic.com/professional/teachtech/usinginternet.htm

[9]   http://www.project-approach.com/definition.htm

[10]  http://pblmm.k12.ca.us/PBLGuide/WhyPBL.html

[11]  P. Duchastel, "A Motivational Framework for Web-based Instruction", in Web Based Instruction, edited by B. H. Khan, Educational Technology Publications, New Jersey, USA, 1997.

[12]  E. Cho, "Distance Instruction", The Journal of KIPS, Vol. 4, No. 3, May 1997, pp. 20 – 28.

[13]  Y. Son and K. Kim, "Evaluating Instructional Web Pages with Web Evaluation Model", Proceedings of the 4th KAIE Winter Conference, 1999, pp. 320 - 328.

[14]  S. Song, Providing Motivation in Web-Based Instruction, in Web-Based Instruction, edited I. Na, Educational Science Press, May 1999, Seoul, Korea.

[15]  W. Jun and L. Gruenwald, "An Evaluation Model for Web-Based Instruction", will appear in IEEE Trans. on Education, May issue, 2001.

# A New Incremental Rerouting for Handoff in Wireless ATM Networks[*]

Hee Yong Youn[1], Hee-Suk Kim[2], Hyunseung Choo[1], and Keecheon Kim[3]

[1] School of Electrical and Computer Engineering
Sungkyunkwan University, Suwon 440-746, Korea
{youn, choo}@ece.skku.ac.kr
[2] Media Communications Dept., Digital Network System Lab.,
LG Electronics, Inc. monet@lge.com
[3] Dept. of Computer Science & Engineering
Konkuk University, Seoul 143-701, Korea
kckim@kkucc.konkuk.ac.kr

**Abstract.** Whenever a handoff occurs in wireless ATM network, the connection for mobile user must be reestablished in the new area. This paper proposes a new path re-routing scheme based on the incremental re-establishment approach, which decides the crossover node by comparing the distances between each node in the existing path and the new location, while traversing the path backward. This scheme allows us to efficiently decide a new path close to the shortest path. In order to realistically evaluate and compare the proposed scheme, we model the distance a mobile user makes for the given mobile speed and call duration statistics and propose a new approach for generating realistic random network. Comprehensive computer simulation for various random networks shows that the proposed scheme outperforms previous schemes in terms of path efficiency and handoff delay. We also obtain path reuse efficiency of more than 80%. The proposed scheme can be implemented by making use of the information in the routing table in the existing network structure.

## 1    Introduction

The demand on high-bandwidth wireless communication services such as video conferencing and E-commerce has been significantly increasing in modern applications of computers and communications. Wireless ATM (WATM) networks aim to supply sufficient multimedia services for the users on move. WATM system consists of WATM terminals, WATM terminal adapters, WATM radio ports (base stations), mobile ATM switches, and standard ATM network [1,2]. Usually, several base stations form a cluster that is managed by a switch.

Various techniques for mobility management have been developed to provide seamless connection services in WATM network. Handoff control is one of the functions needed for dynamically supporting of migration of mobile user. When a mobile user moves to a new cell and thus the signal level of the prior cell degrades, t-

* This work was supported in part by Brain Korea 21 project and grant No. 2000-2-30300-004-3 from the Basic Research Program of Korea Science and Engineering Foundation.

he mobile user's ongoing connection must be reestablished to the new area. To increase the capacity of the mobile system, micro/pico cell structure will be mainly used in the near future. Consequently, handoff requests are expected to be more frequent.

According to [3], handoff schemes can be classified into four types. The *full connection re-establishment scheme* [4] establishes a new connection between two communicating hosts, and thus it requires substantial network resources and setup time. The *path extension schemes* [5-7] establish an additional path from the current base station to the new one without destroying the existing connection. Even though the method is fast, it has long end-to-end delay and possibly a loop. If a loop is detected, it needs to be removed. The *incremental re-establishment schemes* [4,8,9,10], also named as a partial path re-routing, find a crossover node and reestablish a new partial connection from that node to the new base station. This approach can reuse a portion of the existing path from the destination base station to the crossover node. How to discover a crossover node directly affects the speed, efficiency, and the reusability of the existing path in this approach. Hence efficiently finding a crossover node is a critical problem. In the *multicast establishment schemes* [11,12], unlike the point-to-point connection-based schemes above, a set of virtual connections (VCTs) reaching all the cells to which the mobile user may migrate are created when a new call is initiated. Because the network resources are pre-allocated in these schemes, fast handoff is allowed even though enormous resources are consumed. It is generally accepted that, thus, the incremental re-establishment approach is the most practical one.

In this paper we propose a new crossover node discovery scheme based on the incremental re-establishment approach. The proposed scheme decides the crossover node by comparing the distances between each node in the existing path and the new location, while traversing the path backward. This approach allows us to efficiently decide a new path close to the shortest path. In order to realistically evaluate the proposed scheme and compare it with earlier schemes, we model the distance a user travels when the move speed and call duration statistics are given. From this, we find that a typical mobile user causes at most two inter-cluster handoffs. Comprehensive computer simulation for flat-type random networks of various topologies is carried out, and here we propose a new approach for generating realistic random network. The simulation shows that the proposed scheme outperforms previous schemes [9,13] in terms of path efficiency for various mean degrees of random networks. We also obtain path reuse efficiency of more than 80%. By comparing the handoff delays, we find that the proposed scheme is faster than [13] for the processing the handoff operation. The proposed scheme does not require any extra hardware but can be implemented using the existing network structure.

The rest of the paper is organized as follows. In the next section, we review the previous schemes. We present the proposed scheme based on distance factor in Section 3. In Section 4, the scheme is evaluated by computer simulation, and compared with earlier schemes. Finally, we conclude the paper in Section 5.

# 2    Previous Works

In this section we discuss the previous works discovering the crossover node based on the incremental re-establishment approach. Before starting the discussion, we first summarize the basic notation commonly employed in the literature.

## 2.1    Notation

- MH: Mobile host such as portable terminals, cellular phones, etc.
- DH: Destination host communicating with MH, that is mobile or fixed
- BS: Base station providing resources for hosts in its service area
- BS_old/new: The BS serving MH before/after move
- BS_dest: The BS serving DH
- CLS: Cluster switch providing switching support for the BSs in a cluster
- CLS_old/new/dest: The CLS serving BS_old/new/dest
- COS: Crossover switch used for re-routing the connection and releasing the portion of existing path unused

For handoff, there exist basically two approaches, *backward handoff* and *forward handoff*. The backward handoff approach is that MH registers at BS_new via the connectivity of BS_old. With forward handoff, MH directly registers at BS_new, and then BS_new starts the handoff process.

The routing protocol is usually implemented in the network nodes known as switches. Hence each node identifies the next node and the cost for each destination in its routing table. RIP (Routing Information Protocol) and OSPF (Open Shortest Path First) used as Internet routing protocol differ from each other in the routing method, the measure used as the link cost, and the period of exchanging routing information. RIP using distance-vector routing scheme calculates the link cost by counting the hops. OSPF based on link-state routing scheme is designated to calculate the link cost using flexible routing metrics decided according to the type of services. The metrics are, for example, normal hop count, monetary cost, reliability, throughput, and delay[14].

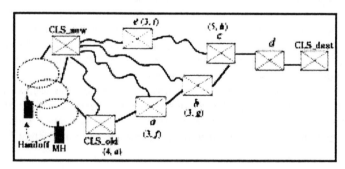

Figure 1. A sample network

Figure 1 depicts that MH moves to a new cell belonging to a different cluster. Here each box represents CLS. In the Figure the solid lines represent direct link between the CLS's, while the curved lines represent paths of one or more links. Note that the information on the path is stored as a tuple in each node, $(D, A)$. Here CLS_new is a destination node, $D$ is the distance from the node to the destination node, and $A$ is the address of the next node. For example, Figure 1 shows that the path from CLS_old to CLS_new has a distance of 4 and the succeeding node from CLS_old is node-$a$. For node-$a$, the path from it to CLS_new has a distance of 3 through node-$f$.

For the evaluation of path re-routing schemes, three measures are usually evaluated – path efficiency, path reuse efficiency, and handoff delay.

$$\text{path efficiency} = \frac{\text{the hop count of optimal path}}{\text{the hop count of new path}} \qquad (1)$$

$$\text{path reuse efficiency} = \frac{\text{the hop count of reuse path}}{\text{the hop count of new path}} \qquad (2)$$

The path efficiency is a measure estimating how much efficient path the handoff allows by comparing the distance with the optimal path. It is obvious that the better the path efficiency, the shorter the end-to-end delay will be. The path reuse efficiency measures the portion of the old path reused. The handoff delay is the time latency required to complete the re-routing process, and it certainly needs to be small. We next discuss three recently proposed schemes discovering a crossover node from which the proposed scheme is motivated.

## 2.2 Nearest Common Node Rerouting (NCNR) [8]

A zone (cluster) managed by a zone manager is a collection of radio ports. The zone manager is actually a CLS and the radio ports are BSs. It is assumed that these zones are connected through the CLS nodes of WATM network. The basic idea of this scheme is to find the nearest common node (NCN) and takes it as COS. An NCN is the node for which the three paths – (from CLS_old to NCN), (from NCN to CLS_dest), and (from NCN to CLS_new) – are edge disjoint. For the example of Figure 1, CLS_old cannot be the NCN since the paths - (from NCN to CLS_dest) and (from NCN to CLS_new) – overlap on the link between NCN and node-$a$. If CLS_old is selected as NCN, the communication between CLS_new and CLS_dest will be

$CLS\_new \rightarrow a \rightarrow CLS\_old \rightarrow a \rightarrow b \rightarrow c \rightarrow d \rightarrow CLS\_dest$. Certainly, CLS_old cannot be NCN but node-$a$ can. Here COS is decided such that the existing path is used as much as possible while any link on it is not traversed more than once.

The detail handoff process is as follows. When a handoff occurs between BS_old and BS_new, CLS_old sends a handoff start message to the succeeding nodes in the original path that includes the addresses of BS_old, BS_new, and DH. The message is relayed by the nodes on the path upto the destination node. In Figure 1, it is sent to node-$a$ first, and then node-$b$, $c$, $d$, and finally to CLS_dest. Each node receiving the message examines whether all the three ATM addresses are routed separately, i.e. on different egress port. If such node is detected, it is considered as NCN. Then, it forwards a reroute message to all the switches located between itself and BS_new. And then BS_new transfers a reroute acknowledge message to BS_old. Upon receiving the message by BS_old, the re-routing process completes. The NCN transfers user data to both BS_old and BS_new in a point-to-multipoint manner. When the new radio link becomes stable, BS_old clears the connection between itself and the NCN by sending a clear connection message to it. One shortcoming of this scheme is that the NCN found may not produce optimal (or suboptimal) re-routing since it was decided based on only the condition of path disjoint excluding the distance factor. Other nodes in the existing path may provide much shorter path than this scheme. In the sense of optimization problem, the NCNR scheme can be said to find a solution locally with a weak constraint. The following scheme improves the shortcoming.

## 2.3    Efficient Rerouting Scheme (ERS) [13]

Compared to [4] where tree-type network is considered, this scheme considers general flat-type network. The handoff control is started at BS_old, and a time is set in which a rerouted path needs to be found. To find COS, CLS_old sends the COS search message to the succeeding switch along the existing path which is relayed until COS is decided. The COS search message contains the identifications of BS_old and CLS_old, and the values of $D\_old$, $D\_back$, and $D\_limit$. Here $D\_old$ is the number of hops from CLS_old to CLS_new, $D\_back$ is the number of hops made so far in the backward trace, and $D\_limit$ is the maximum number of hops allowed for backward trace. The main criteria are whether the number of hops between the candidate COS and CLS_new, $D\_cos$, is smaller than $D\_old + D\_back$ or not, and $D\_back \leq D\_limit$. In any case, the path between the possible COS and CLS_new should not overlap with the existing path as in the NCNR scheme. In ERS, thus, the node which allows a shorter path to CLS_new than the path through CLS_old is selected as COS.

Refer to Figure 1. Here $D\_limit$ is assumed to be 4. When CLS_old is considered as COS, $D\_cos$ (=4) is not less than $D\_old + D\_back$ (=4+0). For node-$a$, the condition $D\_cos$ (=3) $< D\_old + D\_back$ (=4+1) and $D\_back$ (=1) $\leq D\_limit$ (=4) are satisfied. Therefore, node-$a$ is selected as COS. As can be seen from this example, the main motivation of this scheme is to find COS which allows shorter distance than extending the existing path, while the rerouted path does not overlap with the existing path.

Once COS is selected, COS establishes a new path from it to CLS_new. Also a reroute message is sent to BS_new. Then, BS_new sends a connect message back to COS. If BS_new cannot allocate the bandwidth, it sends a response message to COS including the cause of failure. As soon as COS receives the connect message, it sends the user data to both BS_old and BS_new in point-to-multipoint manner. When MH decides to receive the down-link data from BS_new due to the strength of signal power, the process releasing old connection starts. If the path re-routing process fails,

CLS_old decides to assume itself to be COS. Then, path extension is performed. According to [13], this scheme outperforms NCNR [8] and backward tracking [4] in terms of path efficiency. However, this scheme uses a strict condition for COS selection and unfixed value of $D\_limit$, and therefore the path re-routing process may fail. As a result, the overall handoff delay may be large.

## 2.4 Prior-path Knowledge COS Discovery (PKCD) [9]

Here BS_new starts handoff control. That is, COS selection is performed by BS_new. This scheme requires to access the prior information on the nodes in the existing path. The information can be obtained from a connection server which is extra hardware employed in this scheme. Each node in the existing path is taken as the destination of BS_new. The minimum-hop routes from BS_new to these destinations are computed, and the node with the least hop count is selected as COS. If possible COSs have the same minimum-hop count, then the node closest to CLS_old is chosen. In Figure 1, node-*a* and *b* have the minimum hops of three to CLS_new, and node-*a* is selected as COS since it is closer to CLS_old than node-*b*.

This scheme outperforms the others by providing the fastest convergence with shorter resulting paths and higher circuit reuse [9]. The PKCD scheme basically finds COS located at the nearest position from CLS_new in the existing path. However, since it selects COS closest to CLS_old when the hop counts tie which happens very often, the path efficiency is decreased. The most significant overhead of this scheme is, however, the connection server required to be newly employed for supporting the scheme. We next present the proposed scheme allowing high path efficiency with no extra hardware.

## 3 The Proposed Distance Based Rerouting (DBR)

In this section we propose a new partial path re-routing scheme. We first describe the motivation of the proposed COS discovery algorithm, and then present the handoff control procedure.

### 3.1 Motivation

The proposed handoff control scheme is based on the path re-routing approach. In the proposed scheme, we select the hop count from a source to destination as the distance so that we can make use of the information in the routing table for COS search. By traversing the nodes in the old path backward starting from CLS_old, we identify the distance between the node and CLS_new. When the distance of a node starts to increase, the predecessor of the node is determined as COS. Notice from Figure 1 that the distance decreases as the path is traversed backward, but it starts to increase at node-*c*. Thus the proposed scheme selects node-*b* as COS.

Recall that, in ERS, the first node in the backward trace allowing a shorter path than path-extension is selected. Note, however, that the solution is still local as the NCNR scheme even though the constraint is tighter and thus allows better result. For example, assume that the distance from node-*b* to CLS_new is not 3 but 1 in Figure 1. In that case, node-*b* should be able to provide much better result than node-*a*. However, ERS selects node-*a* as COS. This somewhat simple but important notion motivates the proposed scheme where the node in the backward trace is selected whose distance to CLS_new has been confirmed to be a minimum at least locally.

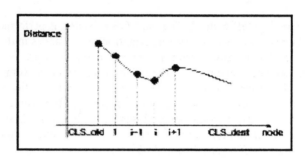

Figure 2. The plot showing distances of the nodes on existing path.

The basic difference between the proposed DBR and ERS is illustrated in Figure 2. Here the distance decreases as the backward trace occurs up to node-*i*, and then grows. Observe that the ERS selects node-1 while the proposed DBR selects node-*i*. Of course, node-*i* is not a global optimum but a local optimum. Note, however, that handoff usually occurs between neighboring clusters, and thus abrupt changes in the distances of the nodes in the existing path are not expected. As a result, the local optimum will be highly likely global optimum (or close to it). Another difference between the ERS and DBR is that the ERS compares the distances of new path and extended path while the DBR scheme compares those of new paths. The following theorem shows that the proposed DBR scheme produces at least as good the same result as ERS.

**Theorem 3.1**: Assume that the distance to CLS_new monotonically decreases as the existing path is traversed backward from CLS_old to CLS_*i* as shown in Figure 2, and then increases. The distance from CLS_*i* to CLS_new is smaller than $D\_old + D\_back$.
**Proof**: Since $D\_1 < D\_old$, $D\_1 < D\_old+1$. Since $D\_2 < D\_1$, $D\_2 < D\_1+1 < D\_old+2$. If continued, $D\_i < D\_old + i$ (= $D\_old + D\_back$). □
As we can see from the proof above, the DBR scheme guarantees the distance from COS is smaller than that of the path extended from the CLS_old, which is the main criterion used by the ERS. The proposed approach will thus be always able to allow equal or better result than the ERS.

## 3.2    Handoff Control Procedure

If MH receives stronger signal from BS_new than from BS_old, it sends a handoff request message to BS_old for migration. The message includes the identifications of BS_new, CLS_new, and user traffic information. BS_old transmits the message to CLS_old. Then CLS_old checks the type of handoff to be processed. In case of intra-cluster handoff where MH moves from a BS coverage area to another under the control of the same CLS, CLS_old changes the channels (radio ports) from BS_old to BS_new. For inter-cluster handoff where MH moves to another BS coverage area under the control of different CLS, handoff control might require re-routing through wired network depending on the location of handoff and topology of the network.

Figure 3 shows the sequence of control messages transmitted when a handoff occurs. In case of inter-cluster handoff, the COS discovery procedure is as follows. CLS_old computes the distance from itself to CLS_new. CLS_old transfers the COS discovery message including the current distance to the next node toward DH in the existing path. That is, the COS discovery message traverses backward the old path hop by hop until COS is found. Each node compares the distance with that of the previous node transmitted along with the COS discovery message. If it is less than or equal to that of previous node, the COS discovery message is continuously transmitted backward. Otherwise, the current node considers its predecessor as COS and informs it. Once COS is decided, it starts to establish a new partial path. When COS establishes a new partial path, it sends down-link data to the two BSs in multicasting manner (see Down-link multicast in Figure 3). MH receives data of the higher signal power. In case of up-link data, MH transfers data to BS_new after it receives the handoff acknowledge message from BS_new (see Up-link data in Figure 3). When COS receives user data through the new path, it checks the order of data. If it is correct, COS starts to release the old path. If not, COS waits for the last user data to arrive along the old path. Then it releases the old partial path, which has just completed its role in handoff.

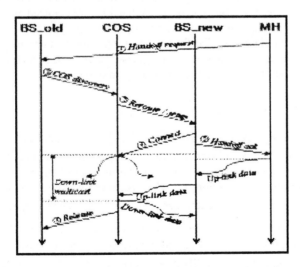

Figure 3. The sequence of control messages involved in handoff.

The six types of the messages involved in handoff are summarized as follows.

Message ①: *Handoff request message* with which MH requests BS_old a handoff for migration.

Message ②: *COS discovery message* which is transmitted from BS_old to COS through CLS_old. This message traverses the current path backward possibly up to CLS_dest to find COS.

Message ③: *Reroute and setup message* which establishes a new partial path from COS to BS_new hop by hop.

Message ④: *Connect message* used as acknowledgement of the setup of partial path which retraverses backward to COS hop by hop.

Message ⑤: *Handoff acknowledge message* sent to MH from BS_new for the partial path establishment.

Message ⑥: *Release message* releasing the partial path between COS and BS_old. We next evaluate the performance of the proposed scheme, and compare it with earlier schemes.

# 4    Performance Evaluation

In this section we first explain the simulation environment employed for the performance evaluation. The performance is then evaluated and compared.

## 4.1    Simulation Environment and Parameters

For the simulation, flat-type random networks with various values of node degree are considered. This is because flat-type network has been recognized as a random graph more closely resembling real network topology than tree-type network. The network has 100 nodes and they are distributed in a random manner over the $x$ and $y$ coordinates so as to give realistic distances between the nodes. In [16], the connectivity between the nodes is determined by an equation below.

$$P_e(x, y) = \frac{k\bar{e}}{n} \beta \exp \left\{ \frac{-d(x, y)}{\alpha L} \right\} \tag{3}$$

where $\bar{e}$ is the mean link degree per node; $d(x, y)$ is the Euclidean distance between the nodes; $\alpha \ (> 0)$ is a parameter controlling the number of links between distant nodes; $\beta \ (\leq 1)$ is another parameter adjusting the number of edges from each node; n is the number of nodes in the graph; L is the maximum possible distance between two nodes; and $\frac{k\bar{e}}{n}$ is a scaling factor ensuring that the mean degree of each node remains constant regardless of the number of nodes. For our 100-node random network, $k$, $\alpha$, and $\beta$ are set to 20, 0.25, and 0.2 respectively as done by others. Unlike in earlier studies, though, we modify the term $d(x, y)$ to $d^2(x, y)$ in Eq. (3). This is because Eq. (3) with $d(x, y)$ results in a totally random graph as shown in [9] while $d^2(x, y)$ allows much more realistic network topology. Refer to Figure 4 obviously,

$d^2(x, y)$ should be the choice for generating realistic random network topology. By using Eq. (3), random networks with mean degree of 2, 3, 4, and 5 are generated.

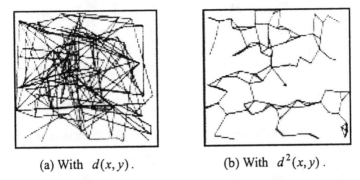

(a) With $d(x, y)$.          (b) With $d^2(x, y)$.

Figure 4. The comparison of the network topologies obtained by Eq. (3).

## 4.2   Performance Comparison

The proposed DBR scheme employs the backward handoff approach while the PKCD scheme does the forward handoff approach requiring a connection server to obtain the information of the nodes in the old path. The ERS also employs the backward handoff approach as ours. We compare the three schemes in terms of path efficiency and path reuse efficiency. Even though the proposed scheme and ERS employ the same backward handoff approach, they are different in the way of finding COS. We thus compare them in terms of handoff delay.

Figure 5 compares the path efficiency of the proposed scheme with others for networks of various mean degrees. In the simulation, mobile users are free to move around for inter-cluster handoff. The number of handoffs is limited to two as identified in the previous subsection. The results shown in Figure 5 are the average values of ten different random graphs. Observe that the proposed scheme shows the best path efficiency in all the cases studied. As the mean degree of the random network increases, however, the path efficiencies of the schemes decrease. This is because there will be much more number of possible paths and thus the probability of selecting near optimal path gets reduced. The path reuse efficiencies of the schemes are very close and they are around 80%.

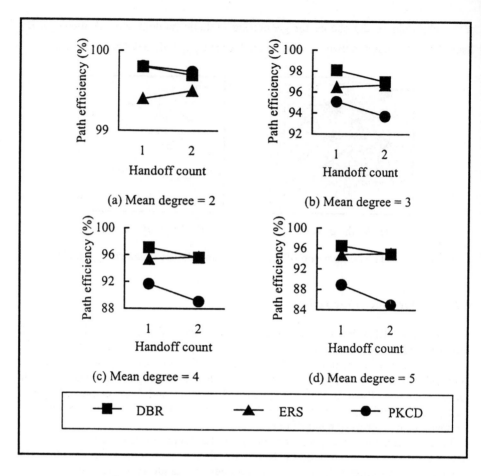

Figure 5. The comparison of the path efficiencies.

We next estimate the handoff delay which is the time taken to complete a handoff. The sequence of control messages involved in the proposed scheme was already shown in Figure 3. We assume that all the control messages are delivered without failure and have the same size and processing time. Table 1 lists the parameters required to be included in the estimation.

Table 1. The network parameters.

| Symbol | Definition | Value |
|--------|------------|-------|
| $BW_{wl}$ | Bandwidth of the wireless link. | 1 Mbps [17] |
| $BW_w'$ | Bandwidth of the wired backbone network. | 1 Gbps [18] |

| $L_{wl}$ | Latency of the wireless link, including data link and network layer processing. | 7 ms [18] |
|---|---|---|
| $L_w$ | Latency of a link in the wired backbone, including data link and network layer processing. | 500 μs [19] |
| $PPT_{fixed}$ | Protocol processing time for control message. | 3 ms |
| $PPT_{adm}$ | Protocol processing time for steps where admission control is to be performed. | 25 ms |
| $S_{ctrl}$ | Upper bound on the size of a control message | 50 bytes |
| $S_{data}$ | Maximum size of a data packet | 8192 bytes |
| $H_{new}$ | Number of hops for a new partial path | Obtained by simulation |
| $H_{search}$ | Number of hops for the COS search | Obtained by simulation |

① Handoff request message: MH requests a handoff to BS_old for migration. The latency needed for this message is the sum of transmission delay of the message on a wireless channel, propagation delay on the wireless link, and fixed protocol processing time on BS_old. The time associated with this message, $T_1$, is

$$T_1 = \left( \frac{S_{ctrl}}{BW_{wl}} \right) + L_{wl} + PPT_{fixed}$$

② COS discovery message: This message is transmitted from BS_old to COS through CLS_old. That is, the message traces backward as many as $(H_{search}+1)$ times. Each switch spends some fixed time for protocol processing required for deciding COS, including the transmission and propagation delay of the message on the wired link.

$$T_2 = \left[ \left( \frac{S_{ctrl}}{BW_w} \right) + L_w + PPT_{fixed} \right] (H_{search} + 1) + \left( \frac{S_{ctrl}}{BW_w} \right) + L_w$$

③ Reroute/setup message: This message establishes a new partial path from COS to BS_new hop by hop. Here time is needed to execute the admission control test in each switch and BS_new in addition to the fixed protocol processing time.

$$T_3 = PPT_{adm} + \left[ \left( \frac{S_{ctrl}}{BW_w} \right) + L_w + PPT_{fixed} + PPT_{adm} \right] (H_{new} + 1)$$

④ Connect message: This is an acknowledgement of establishment of the partial path retracing back to COS hop by hop. The latency includes the time required for transmitting the message from BS_new to COS. As we know, the time for testing the admission control is not necessary.

$$T_4 = \left[\left(\frac{S_{ctrl}}{BW_w}\right) + L_w + PPT_{fixed}\right](H_{new} + 1)$$

⑤ Handoff acknowledge message: BS_new acknowledges the request sent from MH. The latency needed for the message is the sum of transmission and propagation delay of the control message on the wireless channel and fixed protocol processing time on MH.

$$T_5 = \left(\frac{S_{ctrl}}{BW_{wl}}\right) + L_{wl} + PPT_{fixed}$$

⑥ Release message: The latency needed for COS to release an old path is the sum of transmission and propagation delay of the control message and fixed protocol processing time in the nodes of the old path.

$$T_6 = \left[\left(\frac{S_{ctrl}}{BW_w}\right) + L_w + PPT_{fixed}\right](H_{search} + 1)$$

When we compute the handoff delay, we exclude the latency of releasing the old path. For the proposed scheme, the handoff delay is

$T_{delay,DBR} = T_1 + T_2 + T_3 + \left(\frac{S_{ctrl}}{BW_{wl}}\right) + T_5$ . The handoff delay of the ERS includes the

latency of the COS search message [13], $T_2'$ :

$$T_2' = \left[\left(\frac{S_{ctrl}}{BW_w}\right) + L_w + PPT_{fixed}\right](H_{search} + 1)$$

The handoff delay of ERS is then $T_{delay,ERS} = T_1 + T_2' + T_3 + \left(\frac{S_{ctrl}}{BW_{wl}}\right) + T_5$ . From the

simulation, we obtain the hop counts required for a crossover node search and a new partial path setup for both our scheme and the ERS. We then compute the time to handle handoff by using them. Because the PKCD scheme is based on the forward approach and uses extra connection server, we do not include it in the comparison

Table 2 compares the handoff delays of the proposed scheme and ERS. Note that proposed scheme always requires smaller handoff delay than the ERS regardless of mean degree.

Table 2. The comparison of the handoff delays (sec).

| Scheme \ Mean degree | 2 | 3 | 4 | 5 |
|---|---|---|---|---|
| DBR | 0.131 | 0.122 | 0.114 | 0.112 |
| ERS | 0.143 | 0.132 | 0.123 | 0.123 |

# 5    Conclusion

In this paper we have presented a new scheme finding a new path for a mobile user in WATM when a handoff occurs. The proposed crossover node discovery scheme is based on the incremental re-establishment approach. It decides the crossover node by comparing the distances between each node in the existing path and the new location, while traversing the path backward. For realistic evaluation and comparison, we have developed a model of the distance a mobile user makes when the move speed and call duration statistics are given. From this, we have found that a typical mobile user causes at most two inter-cluster handoffs. We have also proposed a new approach for generating realistic random network. Comprehensive computer simulation for flat-type random networks of various topologies was carried out, and it showed that the proposed scheme outperforms previous schemes in terms of path efficiency and handoff delay. We also obtain path reuse efficiency of more than 80%. The proposed scheme can be implemented using the existing network structure.

We have studied the detail of data flow control such as buffering, and sequencing, and multicasting in the consideration of rerouting for a mobile user. In addition to this, we need to reflect the location management issues such as update and page in rerouting. We are currently investigating the relationship among them.

# References

1.  C. K. Toh, "Wireless ATM and Ad-hoc Networks," Kluwer Academic Publisher, (1997)
2.  H. Mitts, H. Hansen, J. Immonen, and S. Veikkolainen, "Lossless handover for wireless ATM," ACM/Balzer Mobile networks and Applications, 1(3), December (1996)
3.  M. A. Marsan, C. F. Chiasserini, R. L. Cigno, M. Munafo, and A. Fumagalli, "Local and global handovers for mobility management in wireless ATM networks," IEEE Personal Communications, (1997) 16 - 24
4.  K. Keeton, B. Mah, S. Seshan, R. Katz, and D. Ferrari, "Providing Connection Oriented Network services To Mobile Hosts," USENIX Symposium on Mobile & Location Independent Computing, (1993)
5.  M. Karol, M. Veeraraghavan, and K. Y. Eng, "Implementation and analysis of handoff procedures in a wireless ATM LAN," Proceeding of GLOBECOM, (1996) 216 - 223
6.  P. P. Mishra and M.B. Srivastava, "Evaluation of virtual circuit Re-routing strategies for Mobility support in ATM Networks," IEEE Intl. Conference on Distributed Computing Systems (ICDCS), Baltimore, Maryland, August (1997)
7.  S. J. Lee and D. K Sung, "A New Fast Handoff Management Scheme in ATM-based Wireless Mobile Networks," Proceedings of GLOBECOM, (1996) 1136 - 1140
8.  B. A. Akyol and D. C. Cox, "Re-routing for Handoff in a Wireless ATM Network," IEEE Personal Communications, October (1996) 26 - 33

9.   C. K. Toh, "Performance Evaluation of Crossover Switch Discovery Algorithms for Wireless ATM LANs," IEEE INFOCOM, (1996) 1380 - 1387

10.  C. K. Toh, "The Design & Implementation of A Hybrid Handover Protocol For Multi-Media Wireless LANs," MOBICOM November (1995)

11.  A. S. Acampora and M. Naghshineh, "An architecture and methodology for mobile executed handoff in cellular ATM networks," IEEE Journal of Selected Areas in Communications, vol. 12, October (1994) 1365 - 1375

12.  O. T. W. Yu and V. C. M. Leung, "Extending B-ISDN to support user terminal mobility over an ATM-based personal communications network," Proceedings of GLOBECOM, (1995) 2289 - 2293

13.  S. M. Choe, Y. S. Mun, and H. Choo, "Re-routing scheme for handoff in Wireless ATM," Electronics Letters, vol. 34, no. 11, (1998) 1076 – 1079

14.  C. Huitema, "Routing in the Internet 2$^{nd}$ Edition," Prentice Hall PTR, (1999)

15.  J. Li, R. Yates, and D. Raychaudhuri, "Mobile ATM: A Generic and Flexible Network Infrastructure for 3G Mobile Services," Journal of Communications and Networks, March (2000)

16.  M. Doar, "Multicast In The ATM Environment," PhD thesis, Cambridge University Computer Laboratory, September (1993)

17.  M. Schroeder, personal communication, Berkeley, CA, October (1992)

18.  R. Brodersen, personal communication, Berkeley, CA, June (1993)

19.  H. Zhang and T. Fisher, "Preliminary Measurement of the RMTP/RTIP", Proc. Third International Workshop on Network and Operating System Support for Digital Audio and Video, San Diego, CA, November (1992)

# A Progressive Image Transmission Scheme Based on Block Truncation Coding

Chin-Chen Chang[1], Hsien-Chu Hsia[1], and Tung-Shou Chen[2]

[1] Department of Computer Science and Information Engineering, National Chung Cheng University, Chia-Yi, Taiwan 621, R. O. C.
[2] Department of Information Management, National Taichung Institute of Technology, Taichung, Taiwan 404, R. O. C.
ccc,hch87@cs.ccu.edu.tw ts.chen@taiwan.com

**Abstract.** In this paper, a new *progressive image transmission* (PIT) method is presented. The proposed method is derived from *block truncation coding* (BTC), which is a simple and fast image compression method in the spatial domain. We add the progressive ability to the traditional BTC method so that it can transmit an image progressively. In this method, we firstly encode an image into a binary tree. The nodes of the binary tree is constructed by BTC and, moreover, in each phase of PIT, we transmit all nodes of the corresponding level of the binary tree to the receiver. The receiver can reconstruct a rough image according to the received messages. This rough image is similar to the original. Moreover, the similarity will be improved phase by phase. In the experiments, we compare the proposed method with the *bit plane method* (BPM) since both BPM and the proposed method belong to the same category of bipartite approach. The results show that the proposed method has the lower bit rate and the higher reconstructed image quality than those of BPM in each phase.

*Keywords:* Block truncation coding, progressive image transmission, bit plane method

## 1 Introduction

*Progressive image transmission* (PIT) is a concept of transmitting a digital image phase by phase. In the first phase, PIT transmits parts of the image to the receiver. The receiver may reconstruct a rough but recognizable image according to the received information. Next, in the following phases, PIT transmits the other parts of the image to the receiver to increase the quality of the received image progressively phase by phase. Note that the receiver can interrupt the transmission before the image has been sent completely. This is an efficient mechanism for saving transmission bandwidth.

A PIT system should obey the following principles: First, the receiver can reconstruct an image by relatively few bits, compared with the size of the original image, in the first several phases (usually phase 1 to phase 3). This reconstructed image should be clear enough for the receiver to decide whether she/he wants it or not. Second, the execution time for coding and reconstructing an image should be short. If the time is almost the same as that needed for transmitting the whole image, we might as well just transmit the original image directly for saving time. We do not need a time-consuming PIT system. Third, the bit rate of each phase should be small. By adding some more bits, we can reconstruct a clearer image phase by phase. It is unacceptable if a PIT system receives a lot of bits with the quality of the reconstructed image scarcely improved. Finally, the receiver should be able to reveal an image which is very similar to the original one in the last phase when the receiver decides to.

In recent years, there have been many literatures concerning PIT ([1]–[4], and [7]). However, most of the methods developed so far either encode images in the frequency domain or employ complex algorithms. And their common property is that they take a lot of time to encode an image. This does not satisfy the second requirement of PIT. One of the fastest and simplest methods for progressive image transmission is the *bit plane method* (BPM) [9]. BPM is an intuitive PIT method in the spatial domain. BPM transmits one bit for each pixel in each phase. Consider a 256 gray-level image with each pixel represented by 8 bits. The image can be transmitted completely in 8 phases in PIT. The priorities of the transmitted bits are of course from the most significant bit to the least significant bit. BPM assumes that the distribution of the pixel values is uniform. Hence BPM applies the bipartite method to divide the pixels into two groups and assume that these two groups have the same size. Therefore, BPM quantizes the original 256 gray-level image by the power of 2. The above process will be repeated in each phase.

As for the receiver, after the first phase, the receiver receives only '0' or '1' for each pixel. The reconstructed image is thus composed of two pixel values only. If the received bit is '1', it means the original pixel value is greater than or equal to 128; if the bit is '0', it means the original pixel value is less than 128. Since the receiver does not know the real pixel values in the first phase, the receiver takes the means of 0 to 127 (i.e., 64) and 128 to 255 (i.e., 192) to reconstruct the image when the received values are '0' and '1', respectively. Similarly, the reconstructed image has four pixel values 32, 96, 160, 244 after the second phase, and so on. However, by using this kind of quantization, the characteristic of an image can not be preserved properly. For example, let $X$ be a $4 \times 4$ image in Figure 1. In the first phase, BPM transmits the first bit of each pixel as illustrated in Figure 2. The receiver reconstructs the image $X'$, which is shown in Figure 3. The reconstructed value is 192 if the received bit is '1', and the reconstructed value is 64 if the received bit is '0'. The *mean squared error* (MSE) between the original image $X$ and the reconstructed image $X'$ is $[(85 - 64)^2 + (81 - 64)^2 + \cdots + (189 - 192)^2]^{1/2} = 762.13$. The quantization method of BPM does not correspond to the pixel values of the original image; as everyone can see, the reconstructed pixel values are always 64 or 192 after the first phase. The same thing goes on in the following phases too. On the contrary, it is of course a better way to quantize an image according to the characteristics of this image.

In this paper, we present a new PIT scheme based on *block truncation coding* (BTC). We call our new scheme the *progressive block truncation coding* (PBTC) method. BTC is a bipartite compression method. It divides an image block into two parts according to the mean of the pixel values in the image block. It can keep more characteristics of the original image than the first phase of BPM. We follow this advantage as we build up the proposed PIT scheme. Thus the PBTC method ought to, as we have mentioned earlier, be better than BPM and, moreover, satisfy the four principles for designing a PIT system.

In the next section, we shall review the traditional BTC method. The proposed PIT method shall be described in Section 3. The experiment results will be given and discussed in Section 4. Finally, we shall present our conclusions in Section 5.

## 2   Block Truncation Coding (BTC)

BTC is a well-known image compression method. It was first introduced in 1979 [5]. This method divides an image into nonoverlapping blocks of $n \times n$ pixels. The block size is usually $4 \times 4$ pixels. Each block is manipulated individually in coding and reconstructing processes. The coding result of each block is composed of one bitmap and two variables.

Consider an image block $X$. Let $x_1$, $x_2$, ..., and $x_{n^2}$ be the pixel values of $X$. We first calculate the mean value $\bar{x}$ of this block by

$$\bar{x} = \frac{1}{n^2} \sum_{i=1}^{n^2} x_i. \tag{1}$$

Next, let $M = \{m_1, m_2, \ldots, m_{n^2}\}$ be a bitmap of size $n \times n$. The value of $m_i$ is produced by the following equation:

$$m_i = \begin{cases} 1 & \text{if } x_i \geq \bar{x}, \\ 0 & \text{otherwise.} \end{cases} \tag{2}$$

Then the block is quantized into two values $a$ and $b$. Let $p$ denote the number of pixel values greater than or equal to the mean $\bar{x}$. Let $q$ denote the number of pixel values less than the mean $\bar{x}$, and $p = n^2 - q$. Then

$$a = \frac{1}{p} \sum_i x_i \text{ for every pixel } x_i \text{ whose corresponding } m_i = 1, \tag{3}$$

and

$$b = \frac{1}{q} \sum_i x_i \text{ for every pixel } x_i \text{ whose corresponding } m_i = 0. \tag{4}$$

We transmit $M$, $a$, and $b$ for each block as the compression code. The receiver decodes the code, i.e., constructs the image block, by using the following function:

$$x_i' = \begin{cases} a & \text{if } m_i = 1 \\ b & \text{otherwise,} \end{cases} \tag{5}$$

where $X' = \{x'_1, x'_2, \ldots, x'_{n^2}\}$ is the reconstructed image block and $x'_i$ is the $i$-th pixel value of $X'$. $X$ and $X'$ are similar but not identical. Hence BTC is a lossy compression method.

Now we show an example to illustrate the BTC method. For example, suppose $X$ is the $4 \times 4$ image block shown in Figure 1. By using Equation (1), we know that the mean $\bar{x}$ of $X$ is 107. According to $\bar{x}$ and Equation (2), since the first pixel of $X$ is 85 and $85 < 107$, the first bit of $M$ is 0. In the same way, we obtain the bitmap $M$, which is shown in Figure 4. The number of the pixel values greater than or equal to $\bar{x}$ is 5 (i.e., $p = 5$), and the number of the pixel values less $\bar{x}$ is 11 (i.e., $q = 11$). Next, according to $X$ and $M$, by Equations (3) and (4), we obtain that the mean of the pixel values greater than or equal to $\bar{x}$ is $164 = (122 + 168 + \cdots + 189)$ and the mean of the pixel values less than $\bar{x}$ is $81 = (85 + 81 + \cdots + 73)/11$. That is, $a = 164$ and $b = 81$. For the receiver, by Equation (5), since the first bit of $M$ is 0, the reconstructed value of the first pixel of $X'$ is equal to $b$ (i.e., 81). In the same way, we can achieve the reconstructed results as illustrated in Figure 5. The MSE between the original image $X$ and the reconstructed image $X'$ is $[(85-81)^2+(81-81)^2+\cdots+(189-164)^2]^{1/2} = 243.06$, which is better than the MSE value of BPM in the first phase. Based on this observation, we see that if we employ this BTC method and go on with the rest of the phases, it may turn out to be a better PIT method than BPM.

## 3  The Proposed Method

In this section, we propose the PBTC method to progressively transmit an image. We add the progressive function to the primitive BTC method and create the new method. The coding and reconstructing processes of PBTC are discussed in the following two subsections.

### 3.1  Coding Process

Suppose we want to transmit a $p \times q$ image $O$ to the receiver. Let $O = \{B_1, B_2, \ldots, B_r\}$, where $B_i$'s, $i = 1, 2, \ldots, r$, are the nonoverlapping blocks of $n \times n$ pixels in $O$ and $r = \frac{p \times q}{n^2}$ is the number of blocks. Each image block is processed individually in the proposed method. The purpose of the coding process is to construct a binary tree for each block. In each progressive transmission phase, we transmit the nodes at one level of the binary tree to the receiver.

Consider an image block $B$. Let $\overline{B}$ be the mean of the pixel values of $B$. According to $\overline{B}$, we have an $n \times n$ bitmap $M$ by Equation (2). With $M$, we compute two mean values, which are the upper mean $a$ and the lower mean $b$, by Equations (3) and (4), respectively. After that, we follow the traditional BTC and obtain $(M, a, b)$. Let $T$ denote the binary tree of $B$. The root of $T$ indicates the whole $B$, and only $(M, a, b)$ is kept in the root. We transmit the root of $T$ to the receiver in phase one of the proposed PIT method.

The detailed procedure for constructing the other nodes of $T$ is shown as follows. Let $P$ be a node of level $j - 1$ of $T$. $L$ and $R$ are the left child node and right child node of $P$, respectively, where $P$ represents a set of pixels which belong to $B$. Assume that $L$ and $R$ are not constructed now. Let $P(M)$, $P(a)$, $P(b)$, $P(p)$, $P(q)$ be the bitmap, the upper mean, the lower mean, the number of 1's in $P(M)$, and the number of 0's in $P(M)$ of node $P$, respectively. Note that, since $P(p)$ and $P(q)$ can be counted from $P(M)$, they are not kept in node $P$. Next, we show the method to construct $L$ and $R$ separately as below.

In PBTC, the left child $L$ denotes the collection of the pixels which belong to $P$, and all of the pixel values of $L$ must not be less than $\overline{P}$, the mean value of the pixel values of $P$. To generate the node $L$, i.e., to apply BTC and encode the pixels of $L$, PBTC needs the messages of $P(M)$, $P(a)$, and $P(p)$. In fact, $P(a)$ is the mean of the pixel values of $L$, and $P(p)$ denotes the number of pixels in $L$. First, according to $P(M)$ and $P(a)$, we construct the bitmap of $L$, i.e., $L(M) = \{Lm_1, Lm_2, \ldots, Lm_{P(p)}\}$, according to the following equation:

$$Lm_k = \begin{cases} 1 & \text{if } B[Pm_{k(=1)}] \geq P(a) \\ 0 & \text{otherwise,} \end{cases} \tag{6}$$

where $Pm_k$ indicates the $k$-th element of $P(m)$, and $Pm_{k(=1)}$ means the $k$-th element of $P(M)$ whose value is 1. As for $B[Pm_{k(=1)}]$, it is the corresponding pixel value of $Pm_{k(=1)}$ in $B$. $B[Pm_{k(=1)}]$ is also a pixel belonging to $L$. Next, from $L(M)$, we compute the upper mean $L(a)$ and the lower mean $L(b)$.

$$L(a) = \frac{1}{L(p)} \sum_{k=1}^{L(p)} B[Lm_{k(=1)}] \tag{7}$$

and

$$L(b) = \frac{P(a) \times P(p) - L(a) \times L(p)}{L(q)}, \tag{8}$$

where $L(p)$ denotes the number of 1's in $L(M)$, and $L(q)$ denotes the number of 0's in $L(M)$. In Equation (8), $P(a) \times P(p)$ means the sum of the pixel values of $L$, and $L(a) \times L(p)$ means the sum of the pixel values of $B[Lm_{k(=1)}]$. Therefore, we can obtain $L(b)$ by the above equation. Finally, we have this $(L(M), L(a))$ for the node $L$.

Similarly, the right child $R$ denotes the collection of the pixels which belong to $P$, and any of the pixel values of $R$ must be less than $\overline{P}$. We need $(P(M), P(b), P(q))$ to generate the node $R$, where $P(q)$ denotes the number of pixels in $R$. First, we construct another bitmap $R(M) = \{Rm_1, Rm_2, \ldots, Rm_{P(q)}\}$ for $R$ according to the following equation:

$$Rm_k = \begin{cases} 1 & \text{if } B[Pm_{k(=0)}] \geq P(b) \\ 0 & \text{otherwise,} \end{cases} \tag{9}$$

where $Pm_{k(=0)}$ means the $k$-th element of $P(M)$ whose value is 0 and $B[Pm_{k(=0)}]$ is the corresponding pixel value of $Pm_{k(=0)}$ in $B$. $B[Pm_{k(=0)}]$ is also a pixel belonging to $R$. Next, from $R(M)$, we compute the upper mean $R(a)$ and the lower mean $R(b)$ as follows.

$$R(a) = \frac{1}{R(p)} \sum_{k=1}^{R(p)} B[Rm_{k(=1)}] \tag{10}$$

and

$$R(b) = \frac{P(b) \times P(q) - R(a) \times R(p)}{R(q)}, \tag{11}$$

where $R(p)$ denotes the number of 1's in $R(M)$, and $R(q)$ denotes the number of 0's in $R(M)$. We can obtain $R(b)$ by $P(b)$, $P(q)$, $R(a)$, $R(p)$, and $R(q)$. Finally, we have this $(R(M), R(a))$ for the node $R$.

In the same way, we can generate every node and construct the binary tree $T$ for each image block. If we have constructed the first level of the binary tree $T$, we can transmit the image $O$ in the first phase. Next, we can transmit the image $O$ in the second phase if the second level of the binary tree $T$ has been constructed, and so on. For each progressive phase $j$, we transmit all nodes of level $j$ of every $T$ to the receiver. Note that, except for the root node, we do not have to transmit the lower mean (i.e., $b$) of each node to the receiver because the receiver can calculate the lower mean by other values of this node and its parent node by Equations (8) or (11). Besides, for reducing the transmission cost of bitmaps, PBTC employs the run–length coding [8] and the arithmetic coding [10] to compress the bitmaps of each phase. This will save a little of transmission cost.

Now we summarize our coding algorithm as follows:
Algorithm: [PBTC Coding]
Input: A $p \times q$ image $O$
Output: A binary tree for each block of $O$

**Step 1:** Divide the image $O$ into $r$ nonoverlapping blocks of $n \times n$ pixels. Let $B_1$, $B_2$, ..., and $B_R$ be these blocks. Process these blocks individually in the subsequent steps.

**Step 2:** Consider each block $B$ and generate its corresponding tree $T$.
Compute the bitmap $M$, the upper mean $a$, and the lower mean $b$ of each block $B$ by Equations (2), (3), and (4), respectively. Let $(M, a, b)$ be the root of $T$.

**Step 3:** For some node $P$ of level $j - 1$, generate its left and right children $L$ and $R$ individually by $P(M)$, $P(a)$, $P(b)$, $P(p)$, and $P(q)$.

    **Step 3.1:** For the left child $L$, according to $P(M)$, $P(a)$, and $P(p)$ of its parent $P$, construct the bitmap $L(M)$, the upper mean $L(a)$, and the lower mean $L(b)$ by Equations (6), (7), and (8), respectively.

    **Step 3.2:** Similarly, for the right child $R$, according to $P(M)$, $P(b)$, and $P(q)$ of its parent $P$, construct the bitmap $R(M)$, the upper mean $R(a)$, and the lower mean $R(b)$ by Equations (9), (10), and (11), respectively.

**Step 4:** Execute Step 3 to generate the binary tree $T$ for each block B repeatedly.

**Step 5:** For each phase $j$, once all nodes of level $j$ have been generated for every binary tree, transmit these nodes to the receiver. Note that we do not transmit the lower mean value (i.e. $b$) of each node to the receiver except for the root node.

Table 1 and Figure 6 demonstrate an example of the proposed method, where the original image $O$ is the same as $X$ in Figure 1. The image size is $4 \times 4$ and the block size is also $4 \times 4$. We use one-dimension representation to represent the bitmaps in each phase. First, the bitmap $M$, the upper mean $a$, and the lower mean $b$ of the root node are generated by Equations (2), (3), (4), respectively. After that, we transmit the root node, i.e., $((0000000100010111)_2, 164, 81)$, to the receiver. Second, let the root node be $P$. We generate the left child $L$ and the right child $R$ of $P$ by Equations (6), (7), (9), and (10), respectively. After that, we transmit these two nodes, i.e., $((01011)_2, 179)$ and $((11010000010)_2, 85)$, to the receiver. By the same token, we can generate the other nodes of the tree $T$. Finally, the structure of the tree $T$ of the image $O$ is illustrated in Figure 6.

### 3.2 Reconstructing Process

After phase $j$, the receiver receives all nodes of the binary trees from level 1 to level $j$ for every image block. The receiver receives the root of the tree for each image block after phase one. By Equation (5), the receiver can reconstruct a rough image for $O$ according to the reconstructing process of BTC. In the subsequent phases, for each non-root node $P$, the receiver first calculates the lower mean $P(b)$ by Equation (8) or Equation (11). Next, for each image block $B$, the receiver reconstructs it by

$$B'[Pm_k] = \begin{cases} P(a) & \text{if } Pm_k = 1 \\ P(b) & \text{otherwise,} \end{cases} \qquad (12)$$

where $B'[Pm_k]$ denotes the corresponding pixel value of $Pm_k$ in $B$. After all nodes of level $j$ are processed, the reconstructed image block after phase $j$ is then finished.

We show the reconstructing process of the above example in Table 2. Assume that the receiver receives the nodes of the binary tree $T$ that are generated in the example of the coding process. Note that we use one-dimension representation to represent the original image and the reconstructed image. After the first phase, the receiver receives $P(P(M), P(a), P(b)) = P((0000000100010111)_2, 164, 81)$ and then substitutes 164 for each '1' and replaces each '0' of $P(M)$ by 81. The reconstructed image is listed in Table 2 with its one-dimension representation. Subsequently, after the second phase, the receiver receives $L(L(M), L(a)) = L((01011)_2, 179)$ and $R(R(M), R(a)) = R((11010000010)_2, 85)$. The receiver first calculates $L(b) = 142$ and $R(b) = 79$ by Equations (8) and (11), respectively. The reconstructed pixel value is 179 if the corresponding values of $P(M)$ and $L(M)$ are both 1; the reconstructed pixel value is 142 if the corresponding $P(M)$ is 1 and the corresponding $L(M)$ is 0. Similarly, the reconstructed pixel value is 85 if the corresponding $P(M)$ is 0 and the corresponding $R(M)$ is 1; the reconstructed pixel value is 79 if both the corresponding values of $P(M)$ and $R(M)$ are 0. The reconstructed image for now is the second phase of Table 2. Going on with this process, the receiver can reconstruct the image phase by phase.

# 4 Experimental Results

In our experiments, we apply BPM and PBTC to the progressive transmission of three test images "Boat", "Lena", and "Zelda" shown in Figure 7. These test images are all $256 \times 256$ images of gray level 256. Each pixel is represented by 8 bits. The experiments are divided into two main parts. In the first part, we compare the quality of the reconstructed images of BPM and PBTC. Then we show the bit rate of BPM and PBTC in the second part of the experiments.

## 4.1 The Quality of the Reconstructed Image

Figures 8 and 9 show the image "Lena" processed by BPM and the proposed PBTC method with $256 \times 256$ block size. This size is equal to that of image. The left images of these two figures are the reconstructed results by PBTC and the right images of these two figures are the reconstructed results by BPM. After the first phase, we roughly see the shape of the reconstructed image "Lena". For the image "Lena", after this phase, the PSNR value of PBTC is 18.80dB and the PSNR value of BPM is 16.82dB. The quality of our method is obviously better than BPM in vision. Our method reconstructs better image than BPM in the first phase. After the second phase, the PSNR value of PBTC is 24.78dB and the PSNR value of BPM is 22.68dB. Therefore, the reconstructed image quality of our method is also better than that of BPM. Then, by transmitting more information of the test image, we get more details and more intensities to represent the reconstructed image. We have to emphasize that, after three phases, the reconstructed image quality of the proposed PBTC method is already visionally acceptable. After five or six phases, the quality of PBTC is very close to the original image. Note that, the PSNR of PBTC is better than BPM in each phase.

The PSNR results of the three test images with several block sizes are illustrated in Table 3. By dividing the original image into nonoverlapping blocks, we can transmit more information to the receiver, and the receiver may reconstruct the image with better image quality in one particular phase. In Figure 10, we can see the results of image "Lena" with three different block sizes.

## 4.2 The Bit Rate of Each Phase

In Table 5, we see the bit rate of each phase of the three test images with the block size $256 \times 256$, $64 \times 64$, and $16 \times 16$, respectively. The bit rate of BPM is always 1 since BPM transmits one bit for each pixel in each phase. If the size of the block is $256 \times 256$, the bit rate of PBTC of the three test images are 0.383, 0.253, and 0.242 in the first phase, respectively. The bit rate performances of

PBTC in the first phase are all better than these of BPM. In fact, as illustrated in Table 5, the bit rate readings of PBTC are always smaller than these of BPM. PBTC transmits less bits than BPM does in each phase. Moreover, as the block size is decreased, the bit rate is increased. However, the decreasing of block size may help the receiver to reconstruct a better image in each phase. This is a trade-off between the reconstructed image quality and the bit rate of each phase. If we want to reconstruct a better image in each phase, we shall employ a smaller block but the bit rate increases. On the other hand, if we want to transmit less bits in one phase, we shall increase the block size, but we will obtain a lower image quality.

## 5 Conclusions

In this paper, we have proposed a new progressive image transmission method by adding progressive function to the original BTC method. We adopt the advantages of BTC method to progressively transmit an image. The experiments show that the quality of the reconstruct image of our method is better than that of BPM. We can reconstruct a much better image than BPM in each phase. Moreover, one thing should be emphasized here that by compressing the bitmaps of each phase, the bit rate can be further condensed.

## References

1. M. Accame and F. Granelli, "Hierarchical Progressive Image Coding Controlled by a Region Based Approach," *IEEE Transactions on Consumer Electronics*, Vol. 45, No. 1, February 1999, pp. 13–20.
2. A. K. Al-Asmari and A. S. Ahmed, "A Low Bit Rate Hybrid Coding Scheme for Progressive Image Transmission," *IEEE Transactions on Consumer Electronics*, Vol. 44, No. 1, February 1998, pp. 226–234.
3. C. C. Chang, J. C. Jau, and T. S. Chen, "A Fast Reconstruction Method for Transmitting Images Progressively," *IEEE Transactions on Consumer Electronics* , Vol. 44, No. 4, November 1998, pp. 1225–1233.
4. T. S. Chen and C. C. Chang, "Progressive Image Transmission Using Side Match Method," *Information Systems ad Technologies for Network Society*, World Scientific Publishing Co. Pte, Ltd., Singapore, 1997, pp. 191–198.
5. E. J. Delp and O. R. Mitchell, "Image Date Compression Using Block Truncation Coding," *IEEE Transactions on Communications*, Vol. COM–27, No. 9, September 1979, pp. 1335–1342.
6. J. In, S. Shirani, and F. Kossentini, "On RD Optimized Progressive Image Coding Using JPEG," *IEEE Transactions on Image Processing*, Vol. 8, No. 11, November 1999, pp. 1630–1638.
7. J. H. Jiang, C. C. Chang, and T. S. Chen, "Selective Progressive Image Transmission Using Diagonal Sampling Technique," *Proceedings of International Symposium on Digital Media Information Base*, Nara, Japan, 1997, pp. 59–67.
8. H. Gharavi, "Conditional Run–length and Variable–length Coding of Digital Pictures," *IEEE Transactions on Communications*, Vol. 35, 1987, pp. 194–203.

9. K. H. Tzou, "Progressive Image Transmission: a Review and Comparison of Techniques," *Optical Engineering*, Vol. 26, No. 7, 1987, pp. 581–589.

10. I. H. Witten, R. M. Neal, and J. G. Cleary, "Arithmetic Coding for Data Compression," *Communications of the ACM*, Vol. 30, No. 6, June 1987, pp. 520–540.

| 85 | 81 | 79 | 92 |
| 80 | 78 | 77 | 122 |
| 79 | 79 | 83 | 168 |
| 73 | 160 | 179 | 189 |

**Fig. 1.** The original image $X$

| 0 | 0 | 0 | 0 |
| 0 | 0 | 0 | 0 |
| 0 | 0 | 0 | 1 |
| 0 | 1 | 1 | 1 |

**Fig. 2.** The bitmap $M$ of the first phase of BPM

| 64 | 64 | 64 | 64 |
| 64 | 64 | 64 | 64 |
| 64 | 64 | 64 | 192 |
| 64 | 192 | 192 | 192 |

**Fig. 3.** The reconstructed image $X'$ after the first phase of BPM

| 0 | 0 | 0 | 0 |
|---|---|---|---|
| 0 | 0 | 0 | 1 |
| 0 | 0 | 0 | 1 |
| 0 | 1 | 1 | 1 |

**Fig. 4.** The bitmap $M$ of BTC

| 81 | 81 | 81 | 81 |
|----|----|----|-----|
| 81 | 81 | 81 | 164 |
| 81 | 81 | 81 | 164 |
| 81 | 164 | 164 | 164 |

**Fig. 5.** The reconstructed image $X'$ of BTC

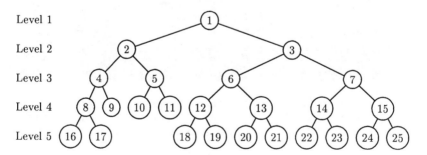

**Fig. 6.** The binary tree $T$ of Table 1

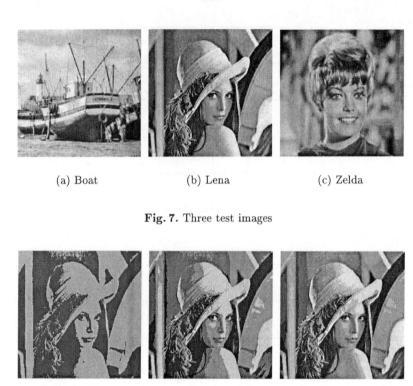

(a) Boat         (b) Lena         (c) Zelda

**Fig. 7.** Three test images

(a) After Phase 1 of PBTC (PSNR=18.80dB)

(b) After Phase 2 of PBTC (PSNR=24.78dB)

(c) After Phase 3 of PBTC (PSNR=31.06dB)

(d) After Phase 1 of BPM (PSNR=16.82dB)

(e) After Phase 2 of BPM (PSNR=22.68dB)

(f) After Phase 3 of BPM (PSNR=28.62dB)

**Fig. 8.** The reconstructed images of phases from one to three.

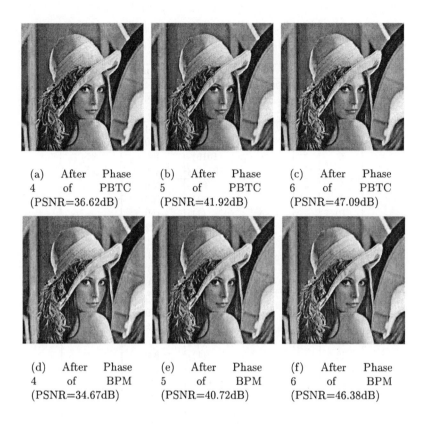

(a) After Phase 4 of PBTC (PSNR=36.62dB)

(b) After Phase 5 of PBTC (PSNR=41.92dB)

(c) After Phase 6 of PBTC (PSNR=47.09dB)

(d) After Phase 4 of BPM (PSNR=34.67dB)

(e) After Phase 5 of BPM (PSNR=40.72dB)

(f) After Phase 6 of BPM (PSNR=46.38dB)

**Fig. 9.** The reconstructed images of phases from four to six.

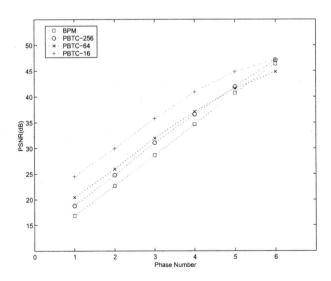

**Fig. 10.** The quality of the reconstructed image "Lena" processed by BPM and PBTC after phases from one to six

**Table 1.** Example of the proposed method from phases 1 to 5

| Node # | level | bitmap | upper mean | lower mean |
|---|---|---|---|---|
| 1 | 1 | $(0000000100010111)_2$ | 164 | 81 |
| 2 | 2 | $(01011)_2$ | 179 | 142 |
| 3 | | $(11010000010)_2$ | 85 | 79 |
| 4 | 3 | $(011)_2$ | 184 | 169 |
| 5 | | $(01)_2$ | 160 | 122 |
| 6 | | $(1010)_2$ | 89 | 81 |
| 7 | | $(1110110)_2$ | 79 | 76 |
| 8 | 4 | $(01)_2$ | 189 | 179 |
| 9 | | $(1)_2$ | 168 | – |
| 10 | | $(1)_2$ | 160 | – |
| 11 | | $(1)_2$ | 122 | – |
| 12 | | $(01)_2$ | 92 | 86 |
| 13 | | $(01)_2$ | 83 | 81 |
| 14 | | $(11011)_2$ | 79 | 79 |
| 15 | | $(10)_2$ | 73 | 77 |
| 16 | 5 | $(1)_2$ | 189 | – |
| 17 | | $(1)_2$ | 179 | – |
| 18 | | $(1)_2$ | 92 | – |
| 19 | | $(1)_2$ | 85 | – |
| 20 | | $(1)_2$ | 83 | – |
| 21 | | $(1)_2$ | 81 | – |
| 22 | | $(1111)_2$ | 79 | – |
| 23 | | $(1)_2$ | 78 | – |
| 24 | | $(1)_2$ | 77 | – |
| 25 | | $(1)_2$ | 73 | – |

**Table 2.** Example of the reconstructing process from phases 1 to 5 when the original image $O = (85, 81, 79, 92, 80, 78, 77, 122, 79, 79, 83, 168, 73, 160, 179, 189)$

| Phase # | Reconstructed Image $O'$ |
|---|---|
| 1 | $(81, 81, 81, 81, 81, 81, 81, 164, 81, 81, 81, 164, 81, 164, 164, 164)$ |
| 2 | $(85, 85, 79, 85, 79, 79, 79, 142, 79, 79, 85, 179, 79, 142, 179, 179)$ |
| 3 | $(89, 81, 79, 89, 79, 79, 76, 122, 79, 79, 81, 169, 76, 160, 184, 184)$ |
| 4 | $(86, 81, 79, 92, 79, 79, 77, 122, 79, 79, 83, 168, 73, 160, 179, 189)$ |
| 5 | $(85, 81, 79, 92, 79, 78, 77, 122, 79, 79, 83, 168, 73, 160, 179, 189)$ |

**Table 3.** The PSNR value of each phase of test images. PBTC-$n$ denotes the PBTC method with block size $n \times n$, where $n = 256$, 64, and 16

| Image | Method | PSNR of each phase | | | | | |
|-------|--------|------|------|------|------|------|------|
|       |        | 1 | 2 | 3 | 4 | 5 | 6 |
| Boat | BPM | 18.11 | 24.26 | 28.84 | 34.63 | 40.73 | 46.39 |
|      | PBTC-256 | 20.00 | 26.09 | 31.11 | 37.05 | 42.66 | 47.65 |
|      | PBTC-64 | 22.45 | 27.46 | 32.95 | 38.26 | 42.52 | 45.29 |
|      | PBTC-16 | 24.55 | 30.23 | 35.80 | 40.86 | 44.85 | 47.19 |
| Lena | BPM | 16.82 | 22.68 | 28.62 | 34.67 | 40.72 | 46.38 |
|      | PBTC-256 | 18.80 | 24.78 | 31.06 | 36.62 | 41.92 | 47.09 |
|      | PBTC-64 | 20.44 | 25.94 | 31.99 | 37.12 | 41.60 | 44.83 |
|      | PBTC-16 | 24.50 | 29.97 | 35.78 | 40.91 | 44.87 | 47.17 |
| Zelda | BPM | 16.32 | 22.85 | 28.86 | 34.87 | 40.74 | 46.39 |
|      | PBTC-256 | 21.69 | 27.35 | 33.03 | 38.59 | 43.83 | 48.58 |
|      | PBTC-64 | 22.76 | 28.50 | 33.99 | 39.18 | 43.14 | 45.54 |
|      | PBTC-16 | 27.03 | 32.56 | 37.88 | 42.58 | 45.69 | 47.33 |

**Table 4.** The bit rate of each phase of test images

| Image | Method | bit rate of each phase | | | | | |
|-------|--------|------|------|------|------|------|------|
|       |        | 1 | 2 | 3 | 4 | 5 | 6 |
| Boat | BPM | 1 | 1 | 1 | 1 | 1 | 1 |
|      | PBTC-256 | 0.383 | 0.542 | 0.690 | 0.820 | 0.949 | 0.988 |
|      | PBTC-64 | 0.462 | 0.728 | 0.846 | 0.955 | 0.977 | 0.764 |
|      | PBTC-16 | 0.742 | 0.918 | 0.970 | 0.921 | 0.767 | 0.594 |
| Lena | BPM | 1 | 1 | 1 | 1 | 1 | 1 |
|      | PBTC-256 | 0.253 | 0.334 | 0.510 | 0.732 | 0.878 | 0.971 |
|      | PBTC-64 | 0.285 | 0.462 | 0.653 | 0.843 | 0.953 | 0.981 |
|      | PBTC-16 | 0.528 | 0.770 | 0.920 | 0.961 | 0.880 | 0.671 |
| Zelda | BPM | 1 | 1 | 1 | 1 | 1 | 1 |
|      | PBTC-256 | 0.242 | 0.364 | 0.538 | 0.742 | 0.905 | 0.978 |
|      | PBTC-64 | 0.298 | 0.432 | 0.641 | 0.835 | 0.953 | 0.980 |
|      | PBTC-16 | 0.484 | 0.707 | 0.902 | 0.974 | 0.916 | 0.741 |

# Reduction of Location Update Traffic UsingVirtual Layer in PCS*

Daewoo Chung, Hyunseung Choo, Hee Yong Youn, and Dong Ryeol Shin

School of Electrical and Computer Engineering
Sungkyunkwan University
Suwon 440-746, Korea
{chung, choo, youn, drshin}@ece.skku.ac.kr

**Abstract.** In mobile wireless network efficient location management for tracking and finding the mobile users is a critical issue. The traffic for location update can be excessive, especially at the base stations that are near to the location area (LA) boundaries. In this paper we propose a new location update scheme which can significantly reduce the signaling traffic for location update. It is based on the virtual layer approach employing SubMSCs. Here the virtual layer is laid upon the original layer of LA's such that the mobile terminals moving around the boundary cells of adjacent LA's become to move within a virtual LA. As a result, the proposed scheme significantly reduces the location update traffic compared to overlapping scheme which is the most recent and efficient location update scheme.

Index terms: location area, mobile terminals, signaling traffic, wireless network, SS7.

## 1   Introduction

Mobile communication has become quite popular over the last few years. Here the users accustomed to the service available from wired networks tend to expect to receive the same quality of services from mobile wireless networks. One of main issues in mobile wireless networks is how to deal with moving terminals. As the movement implies a change of access point, the wireless network must be able to determine the location of moving terminals in order to set-up a connection and route of incoming messages. Location management is concerned with tracking and finding the mobile terminal. Many schemes have been proposed in the literature [1-4] to keep track of the location information of mobile terminals. There exist two standards, IS-41 and GSM, for location management.

Location management that keeps track of the positions of mobile terminals plays an important role for wide area roaming in personal communication systems (PCS) environment. Here two major tasks - *location update* and *paging* are involved. A terminal performs location update whenever it enters a new location area (LA) by transmitting its current location information to the network. This procedure is called location update. Here LA is a service area where several clustered cells are managed by a mobile

* This work was supported in part by Brain Korea 21 project and grant No. 2000-2-30300-004-3 from the Basic Research Program of Korea Science and Engineering Foundation.

switching center (MSC). When a call arrives, the MSC locates the destined terminal by sending a page message to all the cells within its territory. When a terminal responds to the page message, the network sets up a connection to that terminal. This procedure is called paging.

The main problem in location update and paging is that the traffic for location update and paging can be excessive, especially at the base stations that are near to the LA boundaries. We here focus on signaling for location update since its traffic is much heavier than the traffic for paging setup in the boundary cells of LA's. To cope with the problem of excessive traffic due to location update, a number of effective location update schemes have been published. For example, update upon entering another cell [3,4]/new group [5]/a reporting cell, dynamic update scheme based on distance/movement/time, forward pointer strategy [2,3] and overlapping scheme [6] have been proposed. Among the schemes, the recently proposed overlapping scheme is to handle a critical but realistic situation that mobile terminals move back-and-forth repeatedly between two adjacent LA's, which cause frequent location updates. With the overlapping scheme, the location update signaling traffic can be reduced compared to earlier non-overlapping schemes.

In this paper we propose a new location update scheme which further reduces the signaling traffic for location update. It is based on the virtual layer approach employing SubMSCs. Here the virtual layer consists of virtual LA's, each of which is managed by SubMSCs. The layer of virtual LA's is laid upon the original layer of LA's such that each original LA is covered by three virtual LA's. As a result, the mobile terminals moving around the boundary cells of adjacent LA's become to move within a virtual LA. This can greatly save the network resources by eliminating unnecessary location updates. Moreover, the signaling traffic concentrated to some limited number of cells in earlier designs is distributed to several cells in the proposed design. The proposed scheme allows significant reduction of location update traffic compared to the overlapping scheme [6] which is the most recent and efficient scheme.

The rest of the paper is organized as follows. In Section 2, we describe the network architecture of PCS and existing location management techniques. We present the proposed scheme in Section 3. In Section 4, the proposed scheme is evaluated and compared with the overlapping scheme in terms of average location update rate per user. The conclusion and suggestions for future research are given in the last section.

## 2    Background and Previous Works

In this section the PCS is first briefly described. Then the issues related to location update are discussed.

### 2.1    PCS Network

Typically a terminal in a wired network such as telephone network has a fixed location. Therefore, changing the location of a terminal generally involves network administration. Here the incoming calls for a particular terminal are always routed to a fixed location. On the contrary, PCS networks provide wireless communication services to mobile subscribers such that PCS users carrying mobile terminals can communicate with remote terminals regardless of their current location and mobility pattern.

The basic design of PCS network consists of a wired backbone network and wireless mobile units. The current PCS networks adopt a cellular architecture as shown in Figure 1. Here the entire service area is covered with cells, and several cells are grouped into an LA. A cell is serviced by a base station (BS), and several BSs are wired to a base station controller (BSC) which is connected to a mobile switching center (MSC). An MSC provides typical switching functionality, coordinated location registration, and call delivery. It is connected to the backbone wired network such as public switching telephone network (PSTN) and signaling network such as SS7 [7].

In a fixed environment of common telephone network, traffics are routed from a source to a destination having a static address. However, in mobile environment, the endpoint of a connection is unknown by the source. To trace the location of mobile terminals, the network is equipped with location registers that are accessed by relevant network entities. Mobile communication network holds two types of registers. Visit location register (VLR) temporarily stores the service profile and location information of mobile terminals roaming in its area. It is associated with an MSC, which is geographically adjacent to it. Home location register (HLR) permanently stores the information on the mobile terminals currently roaming. In the entire network, only one HLR exist.

The current location management schemes employing the two-type registers are mostly based on a two-level data hierarchy. The location registers are updated for tracking the mobile users when they change the LA's. Figure 2 shows the two operations - Groupfind and Groupupdate - involved in location update. The movement of every mobile unit is recorded in the VLR of the corresponding LA as well as the HLR. For example, IS-41 (AMPS cellular phone system) is a well-defined tool for location update and mobile tracking in wireless system.

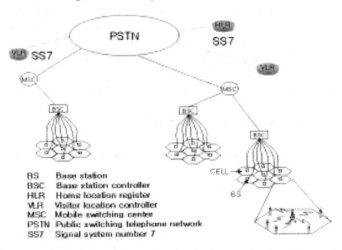

| BS | Base station |
| BSC | Base station controller |
| HLR | Home location register |
| VLR | Visitor location controller |
| MSC | Mobile switching center |
| PSTN | Public switching telephone network |
| SS7 | Signal system number 7 |

Figure 1. The cellular architecture in PCS networks.

```
GroupFind( )
{
Call to PCS user is detected at local switch;
if the called party is the same RA then return;
switch queries called party HLR;
HLR queries called party current VLR, V;
VLR V returns called party location to HLR;
HLR returns location to the calling switch;
If (the called party is found) return;else search the remaining
N-1 cells for the called party;
}

GroupUpdate( )
{
The mobile terminal detects that it is in a new Group;
The mobile terminal sends a registration message to the new VLR;
The new VLR sends a registration message to the user HLR;
The HLR sends a registration cancellation message to old VLR;
The old VLR sends a cancellation confirmation message to the
HLR;
The HLR sends a registration confirmation message to the new
VLR;
}
```

Figure 2. The algorithms involved in location update.

## 2.2 Location Update

In cellular systems handling a large number of subscribers, the traffic required for location update needs to be minimized. In order to solve this problem, several location update schemes have been developed. They are update upon entering another cell or reporting cell, dynamic update based on distance, movement, or time, forward pointer strategy, and overlapping scheme. However, as far as the location update is LA-based, the traffic due to location update is very high at the boundary cells of each LA.

With the "no update" strategy, the location of mobile users is never updated. To detect a specific mobile user, thus, the system must first search the entire network. This strategy involves long call setup delay. The "update upon entering another cell" strategy carries out update task when a mobile user crosses a cell boundary which reduces call setup delay. However, the update cost is high because the update rate for such mobile users is pretty high. The "update upon entering a reporting cell" strategy designates some cells as reporting cells where the mobile users must update the location data upon entering them. Upon arrival of a call, the mobile user is paged in the vicinity of the reporting cell with which it has lastly updated the location. Choosing an optimal set of reporting cells for a general cellular network has been shown to be NP-complete. The three strategies "distance-based update", "movement-based update", and "time-based update" are named by the kind of threshold used to initiate an update, and they are also called as "dynamic update scheme".

Under these schemes, a mobile user updates the location based only on its local activity in the sense that it makes the decision whether to update or not without gathering any global or design specific information about the cell. Under "distance-based update" strategy, the mobile unit is required to track the Euclidean distance from the location of the previous update and initiate a new update if the move distance passes a threshold, $D$. The distance can be specified in terms of the number of cells between the two positions. The "movement-based update" strategy is essentially a way of overestimating the Euclidean distance by the traversed distance, when the distance is measured by the number of cells. Under "time-based update" strategy, the mobile unit sends periodic updates to the system. The period, $T$, can easily be programmed into the mobile unit using a hardware or software timer. However, disadvantage of these strategies is that a network wide searching is still needed.

With the forward pointer strategy, call to user first queries the user's HLR to determine the VLR to which the user registered first, and then follow a chain of forwarding pointers to the user 's current VLR. This strategy is useful for those users who receive calls less frequently than the rate at which they change the registration area. Although this system is low-cost and does not involve searching for a mobile user network wide, redundant setting of forward pointer still occurs. In addition, the longer the pointer chain, the longer is the call setup delay.

The group method divides all the cells into groups, and as a result it saves the update rate to $(4\sqrt{N} - 1)/3N)$ from $N$ of the basic method where $N$ is the number of cells [5]. The group method performs the update task only when a mobile user enters another group. The system has to search for the mobile user only within the group when a mobile user is called. The group method is thus simpler and more effective than the other schemes mentioned above because it does not need to arrange reporting cells while restricting the search scope to a group.

The overlapping scheme [6] prevents a mobile user moving along the border of two LA's from causing increased location update traffic due to short term switching. Overlapping LA's can reduce the traffic as shown in Figure 3. Observe that the two LA's do not overlap in Figure 3(a), while they overlap in Figure 3(b) and (c). Here, $w$ indicates the degree of overlapping which is actually the number of rows of overlapped cells. Without overlapping as in Figure 3(a), everytime a mobile user crosses the LA boundary, the location needs to be updated. If the adjacent LA's are overlapped as in Figure 3(b), only the users crossing the overlapping region cause location update. In other words, a user needs to fully cross a cell to cause location update. Note that it just needs to cross the boundary line to cause location update when the LA's do not overlap but abut against each other. When the overlapping is more significant as in Figure 3(c), the users need to cross several cells (here it is 2) to cause location update. This scheme thus significantly reduces the signaling traffic due to location update compared to non-overlapping scheme. The shortcomings of the overlapping approach are, however, that the cells in an LA are not overlapped uniformly. As a result, managing the location update is complex. Also, since the LA's are overlapped, more number of MSCs (and thus VLRs) are required than with the nonoverlapping scheme. We next present the proposed scheme which can effectively reduce the location update rate without such overhead.

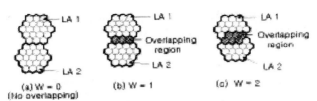

Figure 3. The overlapping scheme.

# 3 The Proposed Scheme

In this section the proposed scheme is presented. First, the basic structure based on virtual layer concept is introduced. Then the detail operation mechanism is explained.

## 3.1 The Basic Structure

In the future microcellular structure is expected to be used for PCS network in order to support high user densities. In such environment the signaling traffic due to location update will be very high since the mobile users can easily cross the LA cell boundaries. In mobile networks, location of a user is identified by the LA it resides. The base stations continuously broadcast the identity of the LA they belong to. When a mobile terminal detects a change in the LA, it sends a location update message to the network. Location update messages generated by many mobile users result in considerable amount of the signaling traffic. As shown in Figure 3, LA's with overlapping regions could reduce the update signaling traffic. Using the virtual layer design proposed in this paper, however, the same objective can be accomplished more effectively.

One of the important facts motivating the proposed design is that the cost of location update for HLR is much higher than that for VLR. This is because the HLR for a user usually locates somewhere far from the user while the VLR is close to the user. Therefore, the traffic required for updating HLR needs to be minimized, and the principle employed in the proposed scheme is to distribute the signaling traffic headed to HLR to VLRs.

The enhanced location management scheme proposed in this paper employs virtual layer as shown in Figure 4. Observe that the entire area is partitioned into seven LA's (LA_2 ~ LA_8) which are marked by bold lines. As afore mentioned, each LA has an associated MSC and VLR. This original layer of LA's is called Layer-1. Also notice that there exist another partition of the area using triplicated lines, which is a virtual layer and we call it Layer-2. Each LA of Layer-2 also has a SubMSC. Note that the Layer-2 partition was decided such that an LA of Layer_1 consists of part of three LA's of Layer-2 of almost equal sizes. In what follows, we denote LA_i, j the LA i of Layer-j. For example, LA_5,1 consists of part of LA_2,2, LA_4,2, and LA_5,2. The MSC of an LA of Layer-1 is connected to three SubMSCs representing the LA's of Layer-2, which partition that LA. For example, MSC_5 is connected to SubMSC_2, 4, and 5. The VLRs are connected to a HLR. The proposed structure effectively avoids the oscillation effect occurring when a mobile user travels along the boundary of two adjacent LA's and distribute the location update signaling traffic over many cells using the virtual layer design as explained next.

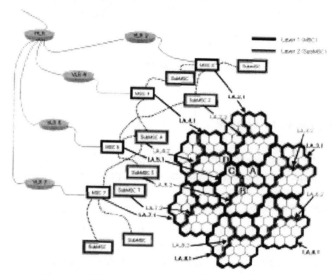

Figure 4. The proposed virtual layer architecture.

## 3.2 Operational Mechanism

We here employ the same environment as in all previous schemes for PCS networks. Each terminal monitors the broadcast message from the base station. If the current LA is different from the LA registered last, then the mobile terminal initiates location update to inform the system about its new LA. When an incoming call arrives for the mobile terminal, the system performs paging operation to locate it. The proposed scheme can be implemented by assigning a unique ID to each LA of Layer-1 and 2. Note that the proposed scheme covers the service area with homogeneous LA's. The original LA's are completely overlapped with the LA's of the virtual layer, and each cell is covered by exactly two different LA's - one of Layer-1 and the other of Layer-2. Even though each cell belongs to two LA's, the mobile user in a cell registers to only one LA at any moment.

The selection is made according to the distance from the cell to the center cells of the two LA's. Among the two, the LA whose distance is smaller is selected. When the distances are same, a random selection is made. For example, a mobile user in Cell-A belongs to both LA_5,1 and LA_2,2, but it registers to LA_2,2 since it is closer to the center cell of LA_2,2 than that of LA_5,1. Similarly, the user in Cell-B registers to LA_5,1. Location update occurs when a user leaves the LA currently registers to, and it always registers to the LA in the different layer from the previous one. Refer to Figure 4. Assume that a user residing in Cell-B (who registered to LA_5,1 belonging to Layer-1) moves to Cell-D through Cell-C, which belongs to both LA_4,1 and LA_4,2. It does not register to LA_4,1 but LA_4,2 belonging to Layer-2. The reason why this approach is taken is to avoid continuous location update due to the users moving around the boundary cells. Assume again that the user arriving in Cell-D registers to LA_4,1 and then soon comes back to Cell-C. It will then require another location update since Cell-C belongs to LA_5,1. Whenever the user moves back and forth between Cell-C and D, location update is necessary. Meanwhile, if it registered to LA_4,2 as suggested in the proposed scheme, no location update is necessary since both Cell-C and D belong to LA_4,2. As we see from this example, the proposed scheme greatly reduces the frequency of location update compared to other schemes including the overlapping scheme.

The functionality of a SubMSC includes switching mobile terminals in the LA of Layer-2. The SubMSCs are simple switches and they do not require a connection to each base station. Each SubMSC is connected to three neighboring MSCs. As an example, SubMSC_4 in Figure 4 is connected to MSC 4, 5, and 7. MSC and SubMSC manage the traffic in the LA's of Layer-1 and Layer-2, respectively. VLR communicates with the MSC connected to three SubMSCs. As far as a mobile user moves within three adjacent LA's managed by a SubMSC, no location update occurs except in few cells. Therefore, the proposed location update with SubMSCs can significantly reduce the traffic to HLR. This is verified by performance evaluation in Section 4. Also the signaling traffic concentrated on the boundary cells of LA's as in the overlapping scheme can be distributed to several cells which is another important benefit of the proposed scheme.

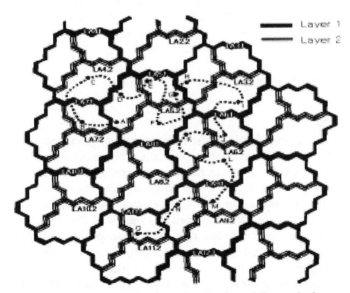

Figure 5. An example of travel path of a mobile terminal.

Table I. The registered LA and updated registers for mobile user of Figure 5.

| Path | Registered LA | Updated register |
|---|---|---|
| A → B | LA_4.2 | VLR |
| B → C | LA_4.2 | None |

| C → D | LA_4.2 | None |
|---|---|---|
| D → E | LA_5.1 | VLR |
| E → F | LA_5.1 | None |
| F → G | LA_5.1 | None |
| G → H | LA_2.2 | VLR |
| H → I | LA_3.1 | HLR, VLR |
| I → J | LA_3.2 | VLR |
| J → K | LA_6.1 | HLR, VLR |
| K → L | LA_6.1 | None |
| L → M | LA_6.2 | VLR |
| M → N | LA_9.1 | HLR, VLR |
| N → O | LA_8.2 | VLR |

Figure 5 shows an example of travel path of a mobile terminal. At first, the mobile terminal is located at A, and thus registers to the VLR of MSC managing LA_5,1 and HLR. When it moves to B, it registers to LA_4,2 managed by a SubMSC. Here only VLR is updated since the MSC is connected to the SubMSC. While it moves from B to D through C, the system does not update either HLR or VLR since the locations are all inside LA_4,2. Upon arriving at E, the VLR is updated for the change made from SubMSC to MSC. Until it reaches G, no update is necessary. Table I lists the movements along with the registered LA and updated register when a mobile user moves from location A to location O. Here 9 VLRs and 3 HLRs were needed to be updated. Note that 7 VLRs and 7 HLRs need to be updated if the proposed virtual layer scheme is not employed.

## 4    Performance Evaluation

### 4.1    Preliminaries

In this paper we assume that PCS network consists of hexagonal cells as shown in Figure 3. Each cell thus has six neighboring cells. This model is suitable for the mobility model in which mobile users can move in any azimuthal direction. An LA denotes a set of cells locating within the update boundary. We employ the concept of rings discussed in [6]. The size of an LA is represented by the number of rings of cells forming the LA, $d$, where the center cell is ring-0 and the outermost ring is ring-$(d-1)$. The average location update rate per user adopts the concept of dwell time. When the dwell time, $T_d$, expires in its current cell, a mobile user moves to one of the neighboring cells with a probability of 1/6. We evaluate the location update rate for a target cell and its six neighboring cells. Assume that the movement of a mobile user is probabilistically independent and statistical equilibrium exists. We develop analytical models of overlapping scheme and the proposed one to compare them. The following are the notations used in the models.

### 4.2    Notations

$K$: The average number of mobile users in a cell.

$d$ : The size of an LA.

$w$: The amount of overlapping ($w < d$) (See Figure 3.)

$T_d$: The average dwell time, while the dwell time is exponentially distributed.

$N$: The total number of mobile users in an LA.

$R_{LA}$: The average location update rate for the given LA.

$R_{MS}$: The average location update rate per user.

$u_{i,j}$: The number of mobile users in cell-$i$ of Layer-$j$ ($j=$ 1, 2).

## 4.3 The Model for the Proposed Scheme

As we can see from Figure 4, MSC 5 and its neighboring SubMSCs_2, 4, and 5 are connected to VLR5. Therefore, location update for the four LA's, LA_5,1, LA_2,2, LA_4,2, and LA_5,2 is handled by VLR5. Since an LA in the proposed scheme has three partitions that are not equal sizes, each cell is assigned a unique number instead of the coordinates. Cells in an LA of the proposed scheme are numbered as shown in Figure 6. Here the upper and lower numbers at each cell represent the cell numbers for Layer-1 and 2, respectively. Also notice that the cells in an LA are numbered row wise starting from the upper left corner cell.

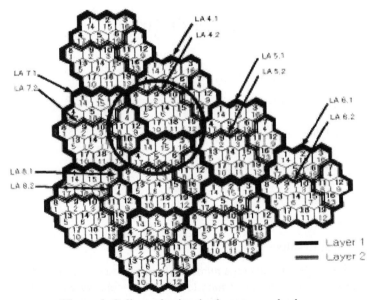

Figure 6. Cell numbering in the proposed scheme.

The number of cells in an LA of $d = 3$ is 19, and thus 19 equations need to be manipulated. It denotes the number of mobile users in a cell. In Figure 6, adding the number of mobile users in cell-7 of LA_4,1 and that of cell-4 of LA_4,2 results in $K$.

$$u_{7,1} + u_{4,2} = K, u_{18,1} + u_{11,2} = K, u_{1,1} + u_{14,2} = K \tag{1}$$

We can apply the same rule for other cells. Refer to the complete report [8].

The number of mobile users in a cell of each layer is represented as follow.

$$u_1 = \frac{1}{6} \cdot \left( u_{3,1} + u_{7,1} + u_{19,1} + u_{2,2} + u_{4,2} + u_{5,2} \right) \tag{2}$$

$$u_5 = \frac{1}{6} \cdot \left( u_{1,2} + u_{2,2} + u_{4,2} + u_{6,2} + u_{9,2} + u_{10,2} + u_{7,1} + u_{12,1} \right)$$

$$u_{16} = \frac{1}{6} \cdot \left( u_{11,2} + u_{12,2} + u_{15,2} + u_{15,2} + u_{19,2} + u_{8,1} + u_{18,1} + u_{19,1} \right)$$

Others are obtained similarly and the complete lists of the equations are in a full report [8].

The average number of mobile terminals in an LA is

$$N = 4 \cdot \sum_{i=1}^{3d^2 - 3d + 1} u_i \cdot \frac{1}{T_d} \tag{3}$$

The average location update rate for a given LA is

$$R_{LA} = \frac{1}{2}(\alpha) + \frac{1}{3}(\beta) + \frac{1}{6}(\gamma) \tag{4}$$

Where, $\alpha = (u_{1,1} + 2 \cdot u_{3,1} + 2 \cdot u_{8,1} + u_{12,1} + u_{17,1} + 2 \cdot u_{19,1})$

$\beta = (u_{1,1} + 2 \cdot u_{2,1} + 2 \cdot u_{4,1} + 2 \cdot u_{7,1} + u_{12,1} + 2 \cdot u_{13,1} + 2 \cdot u_{16,1} + 2 \cdot u_{17,1} + 2 \cdot u_{18,1})$

$\gamma = (u_{1,1} + u_{12,1} + u_{17,1})$

The average location update rate per user is

$$R_{MS} = \frac{R_{LA}}{N} \tag{5}$$

## 4.4 Numerical Results

As done in other papers, the average number of mobile users in a cell is assumed to be 100. To consider various speed of mobile users in a cell, we assume that the dwell time, $T_d$, are 1, 2, 4, and 8 minutes. We compare the proposed scheme with the overlapping scheme in terms of average location update rate per user. Figures 7, 8, and 9 show that the proposed scheme significantly outperforms the overlapping scheme for all the cases studied. Also notice that the rate decreases as the size of LA increases. This is an important fact since the size of LA in typical PCS network is expected to grow as the communication technique and equipment get improved.

In the overlapping scheme, the update rate decreases as overlapping increases. However, the number of MSCs and VLRs are also increased. For example, refer to Figure 7 where d=3 and w=2. In this case, the overlapping scheme needs almost 38 MSCs and VLRs (a double figure of original number) since the overlapping is quite deep. For this condition, the proposed scheme still needs 19 MSCc, VLRs and SubMSCs. Note that SubMSC is a much simpler switch than regular MSCs, and the VLRs and the corresponding connections also require some significant resources. Therefore the overhead of the proposed scheme is much smaller than the overlapping scheme. Moreover, the proposed scheme reduces the traffic at HLR which is very important. Another advantage is that the signaling traffic concentrated on limited number of boundary cells in the overlapping scheme is distributed to many cells in our scheme.

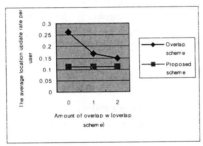

Figure 7. Average location update rate per user when d=3.

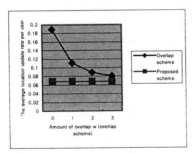

Figure 8. Average location update rate per user when d=4.

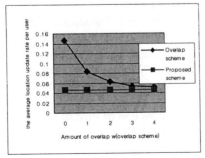

Figure 9. Average location update rate per user when d=5.

# 5    Conclusion

In this paper we have proposed an efficient location update scheme employing SubMSCs to reduce the update signaling traffic in cellular systems. The system has two-layer architecture and is configured by homogenous LA's. Conceptually, the proposed scheme is a combination of grouping, overlapping, and local updating in VLR. This scheme yields a significant performance improvement over the overlapping scheme in terms of the average location update rate per user. Moreover, the new method offers considerable enhancement in utilizing the network resources which otherwise will be wasted by the mobile users causing frequent update in the conventional scheme. The signaling traffic concentrated in boundary cells in the conventional scheme is also distributed to many cells.

In addition to the mobile users at the boundary cells, location update needs to consider other factors such as mobility pattern, dwell time, call to movement ratio, etc. We will investigate the relationship between the factors, and include them in the model of the update rate. This will provide us with a good measure by which efficient location management policy can be derived.

## References

1. A. Bar-Noy and I. Kessler, "Tracking mobile users in wireless communication networks," IEEE Transactions on Information Theory, 39(6) November (1993) 1877-1886
2. Y.-B. Lin and W.-N. Tsai, "Location tracking with distributed HLRs and pointer forwarding," Proc. IEEE Transaction Vehicular Technology., Vol.47. no.1, (1998) 59-64
3. R. Jain, et al., "A forwarding strategy to reduce network impacts of PCS," Proc. INFOCOM'95, (1995) 481-489
4. R. Jain, et al., "A caching strategy to reduce network impacts of PCS," IEEE J. Select. Areas Commun., 12 (8) (1994) 1434-1444
5. C. -M. Weng and P. -W. Huang, "Modified group method for mobility management," Computer Communications 23, (2000) 115-122
6. D. Gu and S.S. Rappaport, "Mobile user registration in cellular systems with overlapping location areas," Proc. VTC '99, May (1999) 802-806
7. Y. B. Lin and S. K. DeVries, "PCS network signaling using SS7," IEEE Personal Commun. Mag., June (1995) 44-55
8. D. Chung, H. Choo, and H. Y. Youn, "Modified Virtual Layer Scheme for Mobility Management in PCS Networks," Technical Report 2000-04-3005, School of Electrical and Computer Engineering, Sungkyunkwan University, Korea, (2001)
9. T. X. Brown and S. Mohan, "Mobility management for personal communication systems," IEEE Transactions on Vehicular Technology, vol.46, no.2, May (1997) 269-278
10. Y. -B. Lin, "Reducing location update cost in a PCS network," IEEE/ACM Trans. Network., Vol.5, no.1, (1997) 25-33

# A Study on Implementation of Evaluation System of Ataxia Using a Tochscreen

Woongjae Lee[1], Jun Hwang[1], Kyung-Moo Lee[2], Inhan Kim[3]

[1] School of Computer Science and Engineering, Seoul Women's University, 126 Nowon-Gu GongReung-Dong Seoul, Korea, 139-774 {wjlee, hjun}@swu.ac.kr

[2] Dept. of Rehabilitation, Chungbuk National University, College of Medicine, HeungDuk-Gu, Gaesin-Dong Chungbuk University Hospital, ChungJu, Korea 361-711, kmlee@med.chungbuk.ac.kr

[3] Department of Internal Medicine, Inha University Hospital, hikim@inha.com

**Abstract.** Dysmetria is a state of decreased ability in controlling motor activity and capability to modulate motor speed and strength which could result in severe disabilities. This study devised a tool that enables researchers to scientifically assess, calculate, and analyze the patients' motor modulating capability. In support, we utilized the Turtle algorithm, which extracts and locates a point on the horizontal and the vertical coordinates on a touchscreen. Based on this model, we proposed and materialized an algorithm that measures ataxia of the patients' upper extremities by analyzing the course and the actual activity of the motor coordination.

## 1 Introduction

Although there are ways to measure fitness aptitude such as measurements of center of gravity with force platform or isokinetic testing, only a little is known for significantly deteriorating ataxia that affects everyday lives of those who suffer. This lack of research data hence yields unavoidable ambiguity in the clinical setting when diagnosing ataxia.

Diagnosing ataxia requires accurate assessment of the mobility of the patients' upper extremities. Although there are finger to finger test, finger to nose test, nose-finger-nose test, alternate pronation supination test, alternate open test, to mention a few of the clinical testing of the ataxia, those tests are not sensitive enough to measure the effectiveness of a certain treatment and the patients' prognosis.

Although there was an attempt to measure dysmetria using a device, such as a digitizer pen, it failed to be useful for the severely impaired patients because they lack the ability to grab the device properly. In order to solve problems like fore-mentioned, this study implemented and performed an algorithm in a drawing test setting using a touchscreen. The reason why our study employed a touchscreen instead of a keyboard, mouse or a digitizer pen is to provide the simplest task as possible for the subjects who might suffer complicated motor deterioration. This method also has an advantage of showing both input and output results on the same screen. Not only that, the subjects have to use their index finger, as in the finger to nose test, which enables the researchers to measure ataxia in most effective and accurate way possible.

## 2    Procedures

Most of the universities, colleges and public and private institutions involved on Most of the universities, colleges and public and private institutions involved on distance learning or e-Education are concerned about the rapid change and development of the education at the beginning of our new millennium. Virtually all of them are looking for strategies to provide effective and reliable education in order to survive to this change that technology is provoking all around the world.

The procedures for the computation of the subjects' motor modulation capability using our device are as follows.

(1) Install the touchscreen to the monitor of a PC.
(2) Situate a subject 40cm away from the monitor.
(3) Display the coordinates as shown in Fig. 1-a.
(4) Instruct the subject to draw a horizontal line and a vertical line that connect two coordinates lying on the same plane as in Fig. 1-b on the touchscreen using his or her index finger.
(5) The horizontal and the vertical drawing test results that need further analysis will be stored separately. Others will be displayed as in real time as we assign x for the horizontal direction, y for the vertical direction, and x for the time.
(6) Analyze the stored line drawing results of a subject to examine ataxia after all the tests were completed. Keep the results as the Microsoft Excel file.

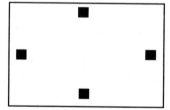

Fig. 1-a Initial Screen

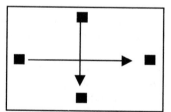

Fig. 1-b Drawing Lines

### 2.1 Measurement Metric

In order to compute ataxia systematically, the following analysis should be followed.

o Movement Path Analysis
- Deviation Area Analysis
- Reverse Movement Analysis
- Discontinuity Analysis
- Beyond Analysis
- Turn-Amplitude Analysis

o Modulation Analysis
- Modulation Speed Analysis
- Modulation Acceleration Analysis

## 2.2 Movement Path Analysis

In order to analyze a path of a movement, the subject first has to have the ability to see the coordinates extracted from the screen. If the subjects try to determine the coordinates as in any other setting, the system might store the results as a straight line only. This false representation will create discrepancies between the real results and the stored results. Our study utilized the Turtle Algorithm to minimize this problem and to provide accurate testing results.

- Tracing of Movement Path

In order to perform fore-mentioned analysis, the system should be able to trace the line drawn by the subject. There are possibly a couple of ways doing that.

Method 1: Fetch the x, y coordinates of the line drawn by the subject from the operating system's touchscreen driver and save them in harddisk. This is done at the same time the test is being processed. The movement path can be identified by the information save in the hard disk.

Method 2: The line drawn by the subject is saved in system's graphic memory as a image. After the test is done, we can identify the movement path by analyzing the image in the graphic memory.

While the first method has the advantage that x and y coordinates can be easily obtained from the touchscreen driver without any complicate procedures, it also has disadvantages that we can't get the data constantly when operating systems are busy for context switching or memory swapping. Rapid changes between the intervals can also not be in effect. We, therefore, used the second method to trace more accurate movement paths. The turtle algorithm was used to get the coordinates of outline of path.

The procedures are shown below;
(1) Find out the color of the object (movement path).
(2) Identify the starting point of object by scanning the screen through x-axis and y-axis. (Fig. 2)

(3) Calculate the coordinate of boundary of line using Turtle algorithm.
(4) By sampling y-axis, find out coordinate of max-y and min-y, also calculate the median of them for each and every x coordinate in unique interval.

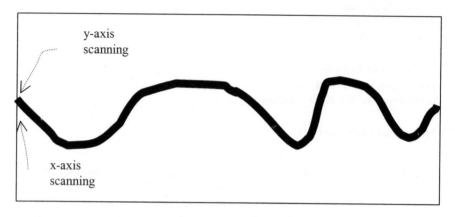

y-axis
scanning

x-axis
scanning

Fig.2 Turtle algorithm for coordinate scanning

## 2.2.1 Deviation Area Analysis

Deviation Area Analysis can be defined as in formula (1), where $\alpha$ stands for median of y coordinate and m stands for the number of x coordinates. It is shown in Fig. 3.

$$\sum_{i=1}^{m} |\ value(y_i) - \alpha\ |, \quad for\ all \quad 1 \leq i \leq m \qquad (1)$$

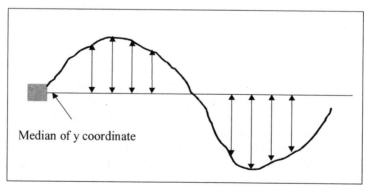

Median of y coordinate

Fig.3. Deviation Area Analysis

## 2.2.2 Reverse Movement Analysis

The reverse movement analysis (Fig. 4) will enable researchers to distinguish the subjects who drew lines in the reverse direction from the instructions given by the instructors. It is important to pay close attention to the followings when analyzing the lines.

(1) Horizontal line originating from left to right: the value of x decreases after its increase and then it increases again

(2) Horizontal line originating from right to left: the value of x increases after its decrease and then it decreases again

(3) Vertical line originating from top to bottom: the value of y increases after its decrease and then it decreases again

(4) Vertical line originating from bottom to top: the value of y decreases after its increase and then it increases again

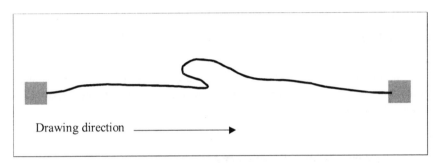

Fig.4. Reverse Movement Analysis

## 2.2.3 Discontinuity Analysis

The discontinuity analysis will show whether a subject drew a line in one attempt without withdrawing a finger. When a subject withdraws the index finger from the screen while being tested, the system computes the number of discontinuities. The computer will automatically connect the line gaps resulted from the discontinuities.

The system traces the line drawn by the subject and identifies discontinuities based on formula (2).

$$
\begin{aligned}
&| value(x_{i-1}) - value(x_i) | \geq 2 \quad or \\
&| value(y_{i-1}) - value(y_i) | \geq 2 \quad for\ all \quad 2 \leq i \leq m
\end{aligned}
\tag{2}
$$

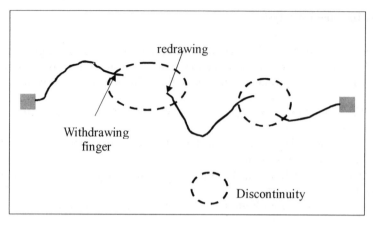

Fig.5 Discontinuity Analysis

## 2.2.4 Beyond Analysis

It is also important to consider the number of out of range attempts by a subject for motor aptitude analysis. If the subject drew a line out of the fixed range of our device, he or she will have to be re-tested (Fig. 6).

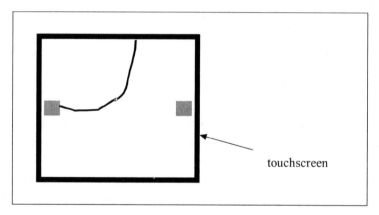

Fig.6. Beyond Analysis

## 2.2.5 Turn-Amplitude Analysis

Turn is defined as turning point in the x-axis in the horizontal test, turning point in the y-axis in the vertical test, while amplitude is defined as the distance between the turns (Fig. 7). The number of turns and magnitude of amplitude are analyzed in the Turn-Amplitude analysis

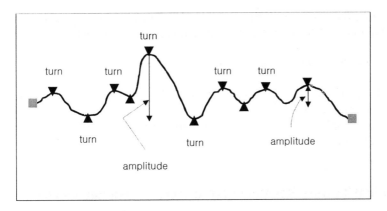

Fig. 7 Turn-Amplitude Analysis

Turn-Amplitude Analysis is defined as follows.

- Drawing Time: The time consumed to draw a line from the beginning point to the end point
- Number of Turns: The total number of turns made from the beginning point to the end point
- Turn/sec: The number of turns made within a fixed time allowance (ex. 1/50sec)
- Average of Amplitude/turn: Average of Amplitude per turn
- Maximum Amplitude: Maximum Amplitude (cm)

## 2.3 Modulation Analysis

The modulation capability of a subject can be measured by analyzing his/her motor speed and the acceleration.

### 2.3.1 Modulation Speed Analysis

Modulation Speed Analysis is done as follows

(1) The velocity function of line in terms of time, V=f(t), can be found by the following formula (3)

$$V = \left\{ \left( \frac{dx}{dt} \right)^2 + \left( \frac{dy}{dt} \right)^2 \right\}^{1/2} \qquad (3)$$

(2) Turn-Amplitude Analysis and Frequency Spectrum Analysis is performed on the velocity function V(t).

### 2.3.2 Modulation Acceleration Analysis

The formula "F = m $\times$ a" tells us that modulation acceleration is directly proportional to the power, since one can assume that the mass of upper extremity is constant. Thus, power control abilities can be identified by modulation acceleration analysis.

The procedures for the modulation acceleration analysis are;

(1) Find out the modulation acceleration curve "a=f(t)" by differentiating the velocity curve "V=f(t)" with respect to time t.
(2) Do the turn-amplitude analysis and frequency spectrum analysis onto the modulation acceleration curve.

# 3    Clinical Testing Results of Dysmetria Measuring Devices

Clinical test implementing a touchscreen method was done in order to evaluate its effectiveness in uniform quantification of dysmetria.

## 3.1    Subject Groups Selection

A sampling group of ten was selected from the external brain damaged patients who visited Chungbuk National University Hospital that showed symptoms of dysmetria. These experimental subjects were chosen on the basis of their ability to comprehend and execute verbal instructions and for their ability to modulate their muscular activities of their upper extremities who could also remain on a chair balanced for a period of time.  The control group was selected from the general population who do not have history of central nervous system disorders

## 3.2    Experiment Procedures

### 3.2.1  Finger to test

We have categorized the subjects into 0,1,2 and 3 based on the severity of their dysmetria symptoms by normal, fair, moderate, and severe respectively incorporating Hore, Swaine and Sullivan's methods.

### 3.2.2  Purdue Test

We have used Purdue Pegboard from Lafayette Instrument Company to evaluate our subjects' upper extremities modulating ability. The Purdue test consists of five particular tests. However, our study performed only the two: right hand and left hand tests. Purdue score was defined as the number of pins put in the hole on top of the Pegboard in 30 seconds as in Tiffin and Asher tests.

### 3.2.3 Drawing test

We defined drawing test as the method we employed to measure dysmetria using a touchscreen. The method of the actual drawing test can be found under procedures of this paper and the measurement metric can also be found under index III in details. The results of the drawing test are to be compared to finger to test and the Purdue test which are more common in clinical studies.

### 3.3 Results Analysis

### 3.3.1 Drawing Test Result

There were no side differences between the results of our study group and the control group in reference to the left hand drawing test (refer to Table 1). The only differences showed were the number of turns, time, area and maximal amplitude-y on the horizontal exercises and the number of turns, area, and number of reverse movements on the vertical exercises of the drawing tests (refer to Table 2). The study group showed less values on the number of turns significantly compared to the control group (p,0.05) (refer to Table 2).

### 3.3.2 Comparative Analysis between the Drawing test and the Clinical Test

In order to further investigate the significance of the drawing test in the clinical field, we have analyzed the results of the horizontal and the vertical drawings with the results derived from the fore-mentioned clinical tests (refer to Table 3,4). We found drawings and in the area of the vertical drawings to the four clinical studies. In addition, we also found correlation of the time of the horizontal drawings to the time of execution and the deviation center. However, there was no correlation found between the number of turns to the dysmetria grade, time of execution, deviation from the center, and the Purdue test on the vertical drawings. We found strong correlation between the time of execution to the vertical drawing test, especially in area and time. We also found another strong correlation between the number of x turns, and the number of y turns on the speed analysis of the vertical drawings ($p < -.001$) Statistically, we found no noticeable patterns to the vertical drawings and the horizontal drawings in terms of speed. Deviation from the center showed correlation to area, time, the number of discontinuities, and the number of reverse movements in the vertical drawing test.

**Table 1.** Results of Drawing Test

(a) Horizontal test

| Variable | | Horizontal test | | | |
|---|---|---|---|---|---|
| | | Right | | Left | |
| | | Controls(n=10) | Patients(n=9) | Controls(n=10) | Patients(n=9) |
| Drawing line | Turn | 2.98 ± 1.87 | 2.51 ± 0.86 | 3.92 ± 2.59 | 1.87 ± 0.75 |
| | Area(cm²) | 11.31 ± 3.86 | 26.00 ± 17.90 | 8.09 ± 2.30 | 16.22 ± 7.46 |
| | Time(sec) | 2.24 ± 1.21 | 4.22 ± 3.30 | 2.03 ± 1.09 | 2.88 ± 0.68 |
| | Disc | 0.22 ± 0.50 | 0.67 ± 0.77 | 0.1 ± 0.11 | 0.20 ± 0.30 |
| | Reverse | 0.02 ± 0.06 | 2.16 ± 5.73 | 0.00 ± 0.00 | 1.00 ± 3.00 |
| Velocity line | Turn-X | 17.68 ± 9.07 | 28.49 ± 24.93 | 18.02 ± 10.32 | 19.98 ± 6.75 |
| | Turn-Y | 15.22 ± 8.68 | 25.89 ± 19.49 | 15.94 ± 8.31 | 17.84 ± 6.69 |
| | Amp/turn-x | 11.73 ± 5.62 | 8.25 ± 9.56 | 13.87* ± 7.06 | 10.17 ± 6.33 |
| | Max amp-x | 24.52 ± 11.51 | 23.12 ± 21.63 | 28.28** ± 12.06 | 30.60* ± 25.65 |
| | Amp/turn-y (cm/sec) | 2.68 ± 3.64 | 6.53 ± 6.32 | 15.94 ± 8.31 | 3.91 ± 3.40 |
| | Max amp-y (cm/sec) | 5.98 ± 7.46 | 19.78 ± 18.26 | 5.67 ± 3.56 | 11.78* ± 10.58 |

Values are given as mean ± S.D

Turn: number of turns, Disc: number of discontinuities, Reverse: number of reverse movements, Turn-x: number of x turns, Turn-y: number of y turns, Amp: amplitude, Max: maximal.

*Significantly different from the right side by Wilcoxon signed rank test($p < 0.05$)

**Significantly different from the right side by Wilcoxon signed rank test ($p < 0.01$)

(b) Vertical test

| Variable | | Vertical test | | | |
|---|---|---|---|---|---|
| | | Right | | Left | |
| | | Controls(n=10) | Patients(n=9) | Controls(n=10) | Patients(n=9) |
| Drawing line | Turn | $1.20 \pm 0.67$ | $1.96 \pm 0.74$ | $1.90 \pm 0.77$ | $2.27 \pm 0.87$ |
| | Area(cm$^2$) | $2.88 \pm 0.84$ | $6.23 \pm 4.20$ | $4.21* \pm 1.83$ | $7.35 \pm 4.81$ |
| | Time(sec) | $1.28 \pm 0.80$ | $1.54 \pm 0.80$ | $1.34 \pm 0.89$ | $1.93 \pm 0.84$ |
| | Disc | $0.1 \pm 0.14$ | $0.22 \pm 0.35$ | $0.10 \pm 0.14$ | $0.29 \pm 0.38$ |
| | Reverse | $0.00 \pm 0.00$ | $0.33 \pm 0.35$ | $0.12 \pm 0.19$ | $0.27 \pm 0.28$ |
| Velocity line | Turn-X | $8.54 \pm 5.12$ | $10.64 \pm 5.38$ | $9.54 \pm 5.93$ | $13.04 \pm 7.27$ |
| | Turn-Y | $10 \pm 6.03$ | $12.02 \pm 5.21$ | $11.2 \pm 7.66$ | $12.07 \pm 7.45$ |
| | Amp/turn-x (cm/sec) | $1.82 \pm 2.07$ | $4.19 \pm 4.81$ | $1.86 \pm 1.80$ | $3.02 \pm 3.19$ |
| | Max amp-x (cm/sec) | $3.30 \pm 4.86$ | $8.32 \pm 8.71$ | $3.65 \pm 4.32$ | $5.09 \pm 5.59$ |
| | Amp/turn-y (cm/sec) | $12.59 \pm 7.78$ | $9.40 \pm 7.74$ | $11.50 \pm 7.53$ | $6.37 \pm 5.33$ |
| | Max amp-y (cm/sec) | $23.33 \pm 12.36$ | $21.45 \pm 17.28$ | $22.76 \pm 12.57$ | $14.65 \pm 12.00$ |

Values are given as mean $\pm$ S.D

Turn: number of turns, Disc: number of discontinuities, Reverse: number of reverse movements, Turn-x: number of x turns, Turn-y: number of y turns, Amp: amplitude, Max: maximal.

*Significantly different from the right side by Wilcoxon signed rank test($p < 0.05$)

**Significantly different from the right side by Wilcoxon signed rank test ($p < 0.01$)

**Table 2** Comparison between the Controls and the Patients Horizontal and Vertical Drawing Test

| Variable | | Horizontal drawing test | | Vertical drawing test | |
|---|---|---|---|---|---|
| | | Controls(n=20) | Patients(n=18) | Controls(n=20) | Patients(n=18) |
| Drawing line | Turn | $3.45 \pm 2.25$ | $2.18 \pm 0.85^*$ | $1.55 \pm 0.79$ | $2.11 \pm 0.80^*$ |
| | Area(cm2) | $9.70 \pm 3.51$ | $21.11 \pm 14.22^{**}$ | $3.55 \pm 1.55$ | $6.79 \pm 4.42^{**}$ |
| | Time(sec) | $2.14 \pm 1.12$ | $3.55 \pm 2.41$ | $1.31 \pm 0.82$ | $1.73 \pm 0.82$ |
| | Disc | $0.16 \pm 0.36$ | $0.43 \pm 0.61$ | $0.10 \pm 0.14$ | $0.26 \pm 0.36$ |
| | Reverse | $0.01 \pm 0.04$ | $1.58 \pm 4.48$ | $0.06 \pm 0.15$ | $0.30 \pm 0.31^{**}$ |
| Velocity line | Turn-x | $17.85 \pm 9.46$ | $24.23 \pm 18.25$ | $9.04 \pm 5.42$ | $11.84 \pm 6.33$ |
| | Turn-y | $15.58 \pm 8.28$ | $21.87 \pm 14.73$ | $10.60 \pm 6.74$ | $12.04 \pm 6.24$ |
| | Amp/turn-x(cm/sec) | $12.80 \pm 6.31$ | $9.21 \pm 7.92$ | $1.84 \pm 1.89$ | $3.60 \pm 4.01$ |
| | Max amp-x(cm/sec) | $26.40 \pm 11.63$ | $26.86 \pm 23.34$ | $3.47 \pm 4.48$ | $7.11 \pm 7.21$ |
| | Amp/turn-y(cm/sec) | $2.70 \pm 2.86$ | $5.22 \pm 5.10$ | $12.05 \pm 7.48$ | $7.88 \pm 6.63$ |
| | Max amp-y(cm/sec) | $5.80 \pm 5.69$ | $15.78 \pm 15.05^*$ | $23.04 \pm 12.14$ | $18.05 \pm 14.85$ |

Values are given as mean $\pm$ S.D

Turn: number of turns, Disc: number of discontinuities, Reverse: number of reverse movements, Turn-x: number of

x turns, Turn-y: number of y turns, Amp: amplitude, Max: maximal.
*Significantly different from the right side by Wilcoxon signed rank test(p 〈 0.05)
**Significantly different from the right side by Wilcoxon signed rank test (p 〈 0.01)

**Table 3.** Correlation Coefficients between the Horizontal Drawing Test
and Evaluations

| Variable | | Finger to nose test | | | Purdue test |
|---|---|---|---|---|---|
| | | Dysmetria grade | Time of execution(sec) | Deviation from center(cm) | |
| Drawing line | Turn | -0.056 | 0.178 | 0.324 | 0.135 |
| | Area(cm2) | 0.471 * | 0.721*** | 0.575* | -0.450* |
| | Time(sec) | 0.163 | 0.900*** | 0.620** | -0.177 |
| | Disc | 0.617 ** | 0.414* | 0.593** | -0.543* |
| | Reverse | 0.656 ** | 0.038 | 0.451* | -0.482* |
| Velocity line | Turn-x | 0.064 | 0.812*** | 0.419* | 0.024 |
| | Turn-y | 0.115 | 0.819*** | 0.362 | 0.027 |
| | Amp/turn-x(cm/sec) | 0.295 | -0.137 | 0.318 | -0.370 |
| | Max amp-x(cm/sec) | 0.433 * | -0.158 | 0.188 | -0.444* |
| | Amp/turn-y(cm/sec) | 0.243 | 0.033 | 0.252 | -0.264 |
| | Max amp-y(cm/sec) | 0.355 | -0.0008 | 0.191 | -0.460* |

Values are given as person and Spearman correlation coefficients .
Turn : number of turns, Disc : number of discontinuities, Reverse : number of reverse movements,
Turn-x : number of x turns, Turn-y : number of y turns, Amp : amplitude, Max : maximal, *p<0.05
**p<0.01 ***p<0.001

**Table 4.** Correlation Coefficients between the Vertical Drawing Test
and Evaluations

| Variable | | Finger to nose test | | | Purdue test |
|---|---|---|---|---|---|
| | | dysmetria grade | Time of execution(sec) | Deviation from center(cm) | |
| Drawing line | Turn | 0.446 * | 0.054 | 0.099 | -0.337 |
| | Area(cm2) | 0.848 *** | 0.658** | 0.409* | -0.549* |
| | Time(sec) | -0.526 * | -0.420* | -0.389 | 0.528* |
| | Disc | 0.437 * | 0.408* | 0.369 | -0.253 |
| | Reverse | 0.531 * | 0.336 | 0.263 | -0.315 |
| Velocity line | Turn-x | -0.449 * | -0.343 | -0.272 | 0.486* |
| | Turn-y | -0.367 | -0.304 | -0.191 | 0.448* |
| | Amp/turn-x(cm/sec) | 0.223 | -0.060 | -0.116 | -0.222 |
| | Max amp-x(cm/sec) | 0.258 | 0.014 | -0.128 | -0.247 |
| | Amp/turn-y(cm/sec) | 0.468 * | 0.367 | 0.495* | -0.374 |
| | Max amp-y(cm/sec) | 0.397 | 0.520* | 0.516* | -0.273 |

Values are given as Pearson and Spearman correlation coefficients .
Turn : number of turns, Disc : number of discontinuities, Reverse : number of reverse movements,
Turn-x : number of x turns, Turn-y : number of y turns, Amp : amplitude, Max : maximal, *p<0.05
**p<0.01 ***p<0.001

# 4    Evaluation

There are finger to nose test, nose-finger-nose test, and finger to finger test that evaluates dysmetria, and there are alternate pronation supination test and alternate open close test that evaluates alternating movement ability to assess patients' upper extremities modulating capability.  Finger to nose test, which is used for diagnosing dysmetria, heavily relies on the subjective observations of the physicians and this causes difficulties for comparative analysis.  This also proves to be a problem for evaluating the effectiveness of a medication after its use.  Not only these, tests like finger to nose test that call for subjective observations usually employ classification. However, this also raises concerns like follows. First, the observation is subjective. Second, the subjectivity causes lack of credibility both on the test itself and among the physicians as Swaine and Sullivan have mentioned.  Third, there exists ambiguity for classifying which in turns cause wrongful categorization of the patients in terms of determining their severity. There are numerous tests that tried to improve these fore-mentioned shortcomings.  Notermans has tried to uniformly quantity the disability by using a clear plastic plate.  He had his subject to put the plate on the tip of the nose and he conducted a finger to nose test.  He then calculated the distance between the point of origin to the point touched by the subject's index finger.  However, this method found to be not effective in quantifying the subjects' disability because the test disregarded the motor activity process calculating only the distance between the point of origin to the destination point.  Compared to the previous test, our drawing test program has an advantage of able to uniformly quantify and to analyze the distance between the point of origin to the destination point by assigning values to each motor activity.  There are also researches measuring the actual time consumed by a subject being tested.  According to Swaine and Sullivan, when the time is concerned, the finger to nose test shows high confidence level of the results and among the physicians themselves.  Desroslers and others' were able to suggest the normal age average points by calculating the numbers of completed cycles made from the tip of the nose and to the destination point within 20 seconds as well. Swaine and Sullivan has compared the results of the finger to nose test performed to the external brain damaged patients and the results of the alternate tests using computers.  They found that the results of the computerized test only support what have already found in the finger to nose test. They also said that it is not proper to compare these two tests, since the finger to nose test is the one to test the dysmetria grad, whereas the computerized test is the one to test the abnormalities in reciprocal movements. This study utilized the quantitative finger to nose test suggested by Notermans and others for clinical testing and it substituted computerized test to the drawing test using a touchscreen. Both of these tests focused on the path of the movement and the speed of its activity, and they both had similar testing conditions and the direction of the movement activity. Our researchers have had experiences with quantifying dysmetria using a digitizer device prior to this test. The current test improved the flaw of the previous test by having the subjects to use their own index finger on the screen, unlike the digitizer pen which cannot be useful for the severely impaired patients. The digitizer test also restricted the movement of the subjects by stabilizing the wrist and the elbow on the table. The touchscreen method enabled the subjects to make movements without fixing of proximal parts just like the finger to nose test. We had experienced difficulties with concluding the movement speed results in terms of the clinical evaluation due to the lack of apparent patterns. The reason could be that it actually shows no relation between the clinical evaluation and the results. But it could also be affected by setting the sampling rate, filtering method and the condition of the turn in the analysis program. This calls for further research in this area. On the vertical drawing test, most of the dysmetria subjects tend to fall their upper extremities involuntarily by the gravity. One can easily see this from time. It had a positive correlation to clinical study in horizontal movement analysis, whereas had a negative correlation in vertical movement analysis. It tells us that subjects with decreased motor controlling abilities have less control capabilities against the gravity in the vertical movement.

We found fairly good correlations in the several fields on the horizontal drawings to the clinical studies. Especially, area turned out to be a typical evaluation field as a index of the upper extremities' delicate modulating capability as well as dysmetria since it shows similar correlation to the all four clinical studies. We also found correlations between area, number of discontinuities, number of reverse movements and dysmetria grad, deviation from center, Purdue test. Thus. it also can be another evaluation field for the upper extremities' controlling capability. The results of the number of reverse movements in the vertical analysis were significant due to the lack of the gravity control.

# 5    Conclusions

Our research has described implementation of system that uniformly quantifies the movement modulating ability, which has a great use in rehabilitation and sports medicine. We have constructed seven major metrical units that analyze the path and the ability of movements. We also proposed the use of the Turtle Algorithm that traces the coordinates of a drawing line. Based on the results of the clinical testing using a touchscreen, which is a dysmetria measuring device, we conclude as follows. 1) Area, the number of discontinuities, the number of reverse movements which all show the degree of deviation in the horizontal drawing test turned out to have significant correlation to what were found in the dysmetria grade, the deviation from the center, and Purdue test. This point signifies its possible use in accurate assessment of dysmetria. 2) The time element of the horizontal drawing test showed another correlation to the time of execution, the deviation from the center elements to the findings of our clinical test. This also signifies its use as a possible measurement device for accurate assessment of this disability. As mentioned before, we have discovered a new way to measure dysmetria using a touchscreen. This method enables physicians to accurately measure and to analyze various aspects multi-dimensionally as well as to provide additional information for the complicated upper extremity movement in space. These all positively indicate the significance of our findings in uniform quantification of dysmetria.

# References

[1] R. Dejong, The Neurologic Examination, 4th ed., 1979, pp. 324-327, pp. 396-401.
[2] Kyoung-Moo Lee, et al., "Quantative Evaluation of Dysmetria," Journal of Korean Academy of Rehabilitation Medicine, Vol. 22, No. 2, 1998, pp. 351-360.
[3] Hansen M, Christensen PB, Sindrup SH, Olsen NK, Kristensen O, Friis ML: Inter-observer variation in the evaluation of neurological signs: patient-related factors. J Neurol 1994; 241(8): 492-496
[4] Hansen M, Sindrup SH, Christensen PB, Olsen NK, Kristensen O, Friis ML: Inter-observer variation in the evaluation of neurological signs: observer dependent factors. Acta Neurol Scand 1994; 90(8): 145-149
[5] Jaewook Kim, Kyoung-Moo Lee , "Evaluation of dysmetria using a digitizer" Journal of Korean Academy of Rehabilitation Medicine, Vol. 19, No. 19, 1995, pp. 890-896.
[6] E. Elble, et al., "Quantification of Tremor with a Digitizing Tablet," Journal of Neurosci Methods, Vol. 32, No. 3, 1990, pp. 193-198.

[7] Jun Hwang, et al., "A study on motion analysis systems", Technical Report, Seoul Women's University, 1998.

[8] I.Pitas, "Digital Image Processing Algorithms", Prentice Hall Inc., New York, 1993

[9] A. Jain, "Fundamentals of Digital Image Processing", Prentice Hall International, Englewood Cliffs, 1989.

**This research was supported by Korea Institute S&T Evaluation Planning.**

# Lossy Compression Tolerant Steganography

Ren-Junn Hwang, Timothy K. Shih, Chuan-Ho Kao and Tsung-Ming Chang

Department of Computer Science and Information Engineering, TamKang University,
Tamsui, Taipei, 251, Taiwan, R.O.C.

**Abstract.** This paper proposes a lossy compression tolerant steganography. Steganography hides the confidential data secretly. The unauthorized people are difficult to detect hidden data. It provides a secure channel to transmit confidential information. Nowadays, it is a very important technique when we are progressively going to computer network age. There are many researchers purposed steganographies, but most of their techniques cannot tolerate the destruction of lossy compression. In this paper, we propose a novel steganography based on the contrastive relation of the grayscale value of neighboring pixels. It is difficult for the human visual system to detect the difference between original image and one that embedded information based on our steganography. Besides, the embedded data can be extracted correctly from the decompressed stego-image. By our technique, the steog-image can be compressed by the lossy JPEG compression process before transmitting or storing it. This feature will speed up the transmission of the stego-image.

## 1. Introduction

With the fast development of Internet technologies, the information and digital age is coming. It is the trend toward each behavior and people must use computer and Internet tools to reduce manpower and raise work efficiency. Moreover, for national defense force, we will be faced with the digital war. The fact that cannot be denied is that all of the information and management, arms system, rear supply system and modernized arms are exchanged with digital mold and transported by the network system. "How to transmit the secret information over the network?" is an important problem. We must prevent peeping, copying and altering the data from conspirators. Of course, using cryptography to encrypt and transmit these data is a good method. However, the cipher texts generated the cryptosystem are meaningless random codes. Transmitting meaningless random codes directly is to tell other people that there are very important messages in it and remind conspirators to cut, hack or break these confused codes. Therefore, the pure encryption technology cannot solve the problem of transmitting secret data completely. Even if transmitting encrypted secret data, we hope the unauthorized people will think it is a meaningful and its means are independent of the confidential data. Only authorized receivers can extract real secret messages from this meaningful data. This technology is so called steganography.

Steganography hides the transmitted data in a meaningful but not related text or image. Those unauthorized receivers are unable to detect the hidden data while transmitting. Thus, we can avoid attackers painstakingly to break and to intercept. In steganography, we randomly select one image (named cover image [7]) and embed data into it. This cover image which embedded with secrete data is named stego-image [7]. The human visual system looks this stego-image similar to cover images. It is difficult to detect the difference between the stego-image and the cover-image by the human visual system. For a conspirator, although the stego-image has important data, he cannot fine it. Therefore, attackers cannot differentiate those that has embedded with secrete data from many of others in the network easily. But for an authorized receiver, he can extract concealed data quickly. In [3][6][9], the authors define the steganography must have the following features:

- Imperceptibly: it is difficult to fine the difference when data embedded in the stego-image.
- Readily Extracted: an authorized receiver can extract concealed data quickly.
- High Capacity: embedding the data into the image as many as possible.
- Resistance Removal: data which be embedded in the stego-image cannot be moved.

In steganography, the most common method is Vector quatization[4][5]. It uses codebook which sender and receiver have to process data embedded. First of all, sender cuts the image in which he wants to embed data and the block size is as the same as the size of codebook block. Next, searching the similar block and obtain its index value. After that, encrypt the index value and embed it in the cover image, then transmit it. When receiver receives the stego-image, it will obtain the index value and decryption. Finally, using the index value and codebook to restore data. This method loses data and stego-image cannot resistant lossy compression. It is not suit to embed text.

The other steganographies use image pixels to embed data. In [8], the authors provide a Fixed Range Equalization method. They divide the gray-level value into sixteen areas: [0~15], [16~31], ..., [240~255]. Depending on index value, their method determines a suitable area of the embedded data and selects one value to replace the embedded data. The selected value cannot repeat. For instance, data value is 25, select one point in area 16 to 31 and exchange its value. The other common steganographies are LSB[2][9]. It embeds the data in lower bit that can reduce the influence on image after embedded data. This method is the simplest and most directly one. Moreover, it has biggest embedded capacity. However, the previous methods cannot tolerate lossy compression, for example JPEG. In this paper, we propose a novel steganography. The stego-image based on our method can satisfy the previous features. Besides, although stego-image is processed by lossy compression, the embedded data still can be extract correctly from the decompressed stego-image. In Section 3, our experimental results show this feature.

## 2. Steganography based on gray-level pixel value contrastive relation

This section will introduce our steganography based on the contrastive relation of gray-level values of the neighbor pixels. In steganography, there are two important data, one is the embedded data and the other is cover image. In accordance with each embed data bit, we select one correspond pixel in the cover image. We use the contrastive relation of gray-level values of the selected pixel and its top, bottom, left and right neighbor pixels to keep this embedded data. Some of the contrastive relations of gray-level values do not destroy after lossy compression and decompression process. We can extract them correctly based on the contrastive relations. In Section 3, our experimental result shows that our method is valid. Without loss of the generality, this paper assumes the cover image C is an m×n gray-level image and the gray-level is 256. The data D, which is embedded in C, we assume it is a g bits stream. We use below expressions to express image C, data D and each pixel separately.

$$C = \{c_{ij} \mid 0 \leq i < m, 0 \leq j < n, c_{ij} \in [0,255] \}, \tag{1}$$

$$D = \{d_i \mid 0 \leq i < g, d_i \in [0,1] \}, \tag{2}$$

We introduce our method in the following two phases:

**[Embedded data Phase]**

    Step-E1 ： Randomly select one number $S$.

    Step-E2 ： Generate $g$ different numbers named $A = \{ a_1, a_2, ..., a_g \}$ based on the seed $S$. Each value $a_i$ ranges between 1 and $m \times n$. For any two different integer numbers $a_i$ and $a_j$ in $A$, their top, bottom, left and right neighbor pixels should be different.

    Step-E3 ： Decide a threshold value $t$. According to the value of each $d_i$ bit, we alter some pixels in $C$ as the following steps. $C'$ is the stego-image embedded the data $D$ in $C$.

        Step-E3-1 ： Compute $k = a_i$ DIV $n$ and $l = a_i$ mod $n$. The "$X$ DIV $Y$" means the quotient of $Y$ dividing $X$, and "$X$ mod $Y$" means remainder of $Y$ dividing $X$.

        Step-E3-2 ： Compute the average value $v$ of the pixel $c_{kl}$ in cover image $C$ and its top, bottom, left and right neighbor pixels' gray-level as $( c_{k-1,l} + c_{k,l-1} + c_{kl} + c_{k,l+1} + c_{k+1,l} ) / 5$ .

        Step-E3-3 ： If $d_i = 0$ ; when $v - c_{kl} \geq t$, keep $c_{kl}$ value, otherwise simultaneously alter $c_{kl}$ value and its top, bottom, left and right neighbor pixels value by the same difference until $v - c_{kl} \geq t$.

            If $d_i = 1$ ; when $v - c_{kl} \leq -t$ ,keep $c_{kl}$ value, otherwise simultaneously alter $c_{kl}$ value and its top, bottom, left and right neighbor pixels value by the same difference until $v - c_{kl} \leq -t$.

    Step-E4: Stego-image $C'$ is the image generated by Step-E3.

    Step-E5: Send the seed $S$ by the secret channel.

〔 **Extract Embedded data Phase** 〕

When receiver receives image $C' = \{ c'_{ij} \mid 0 \leq i < m, \ 0 \leq j < n, \ c'_{ij} \in [0,255] \}$ ，he extracts the embedded data by the following steps.

Step-D1 ： Generate the set $A$ based on the seed $S$ as Step-E3.

Step-D2 ： Extract each bit $d_i$ based on its correspondence value $a_i$ as the following steps.

Step-D2-1 ： Compute $k = a_i$ DIV $n$ and $l = a_i$ mod $n$ .

Step-D2-2 ： Compute the average gray-level value $v$ of the image pixel $c_{kl}$ and its top, bottom, left and right neighbor pixels as $( c'_{k-1,l} + c'_{k,l-1} + c'_{kl} + c'_{k,l+1} + c'_{k+1,l} ) / 5$.

Step-D2-3 ： If $v > c'_{kl}$ then $d'_i = 0$ , otherwise $d'_i = 1$.

Step-D3 ： Integrate all the bits $d'_i$ extracted by Step-D2, and make up the embedded data $D'$.

## 3. Experimental Results and Discussion

This section shows the experimental results of our proposed method. By to this result, we show our method can tolerant JPEG lossy compression and extract the embedded data correctly. Thus, our novel technique not only provides a way to embed secret data which are not easily to be detected while transmitted by the open channel, but also the stego-image can be compressed by the lossy JPEG compression process.

In our experiment, we select the chapter 3 of the Gospel According to Matthw, shown in Figure 1, as the embedded data. It contains 2056 bytes. We select Lena, F16, Baboon, Boat, Pepper, Sailboat and Toys, shown in Figure 2, as the cover images. They are gray-level 512×512 pixels images. In experimental process, we select 15 as the threshold value $t$ in Step-E4.

The stego-images are shown in Figure 3. Clearly, it is hard to recognize embedded data and their location directly from the stego-image by the human visual system. We use the PSNR (Peak Signal to Noise Ratio) value to evaluate the transparency feature of our method. The PSNR is a popular method to evaluate the difference between the decompressed image and its original image. It's defined as following ：

$$ \text{MSE} = (\frac{1}{m \times n})^2 \sum_{i=0}^{i<n} \sum_{j=0}^{j<m} (c'_{ij} - c_{ij})^2 , \tag{3} $$

$$ \text{PSNR} = 10 \log_{10} \frac{255^2}{\text{MSE}} \ \text{dB} , \tag{4} $$

The $c_{ij}$ and $c'_{ij}$ are pixels in $C$ and $C'$ image. The $C$ and $C'$ are $m{\times}n$ size images. Generally speaking, if $C$ and $C'$ 's PSNR value larger than 30dB, the human visual is difficult to recognize the difference between $C$ and $C'$. The first row of Table 1 shows the PSNR values of the stego-image and its cover-image. All of they are larger than 31 dB. Obviously, there are good transparency feature in our proposed method.

To be objectivity and avoid personal subjective conditions, we use the lossy JPEG function of the PhotoShop 5.0 to compress stego-image. The second row of Table 2 shows the compression ratio (image size/compression image size ∶ 1) of the stego-image in which the embedded data can be extract from the decompressed stgo-image correctly. All of the compression ratio is approximately in 2 ∶ 1. It means that we can reduce the half size of the stego-image before transmitting or storing it.

In Step-E2, we generate a seed $S$, it likes a secret-key in traditional encryption. If people cannot obtain $S$, he cannot extract data from stego-image. This shows our method provide a well safety of embedded data. Besides, if we want to intensify the safety of data, the embed secret data can be processed by encryption and digital signature first, then embedded cipher text in cover image. Our steganography can combine with any encryption and decryption technique and digital signature directly.

# 4. Conclusion

In this paper, we propose a steganography based on the contrastive relation of the gray-level values of the neighbor pixels. Some of the contrastive relation among the values of the neighbor pixels does not alter after the JPEG lossy compression process. The proposed steganography does not only contain the features as the other steganography, but also can tolerated JPEG lossy compression. When receiver receives the stego-image, he can decompress stego-image and extract the embedded data correctly from it. The transmissions of lossy compressed stego-images are more efficient than the original stego-image. The proposed steganography is more practical than the other steganography.

# Acknowledgement

This work was supported in part by the National Science Council of the Republic of China under contract NSC89-2218-E-032-027.

# References

[1] The New Testament Revised Standard Version And Chinese Union Version: The Gospel According to Matthew Chapter3, pp. 5-7 (1985)..
[2] E. Adelson (1990), "Digital Signal Encoding and Decoding Apparatus," *U.S. Patent, No.4939515*.
[3] W. Bender, D. Gruhl, N. Morimoto, and A. Lu (1996), "Techniques for Data Hiding," *IBM Systems Journal*, Vol. 35, Nos 3 and 4, pp.313-336.
[4] T. S. Chen, C. C. Chang, and M. S. Hwang (Oct.1998), "Virtual Image Cryptosystem Based upon Vector Quantization," *IEEE Transactions onf Image Processing*, Vol. 7, No. 10, pp.1485-1488.

[5] T. S. Chen, and Y. H. Hsu (1997), "Image Camouflage and Encryption Method Using Vector Quantization," *The Second Conference of Information Management and Its Application in Law Enforcement*, Taipei, R.O.C., pp.97-106.

[6] I. J. Cox, J. Kilian, T. Leighton, and T. Shamoon (September 1996), "Secure Spread Spectrum Watermarking for Images, Audio and Video," *Proceedings of the IEEE International Conference on Image Processing*, Lausanne, Switzerland, ,pp.243-246.

[7] N. F. Johnson and S. Jajodia (Feb. 1998), "Exploring Steganography: Seeing the Unseen," *IEEE Computer Magazine*, Vol. 31, NO. 2, pp.26-34.

[8] M. S. Liaw and L. H. Chen (Nov. 1997), "An Effective Data Hiding Method," *Proceeding of the Sixth National Conference on Science and Technology of National Defense*, Vol. 2, Taoyuan, Taiwan, pp.534-540.

[9] Lisa M. Marvel, Charles T. Retter and Charles G. Boncelet (1998), "Hiding Information in Images," *in Proceedings of ICIP*.

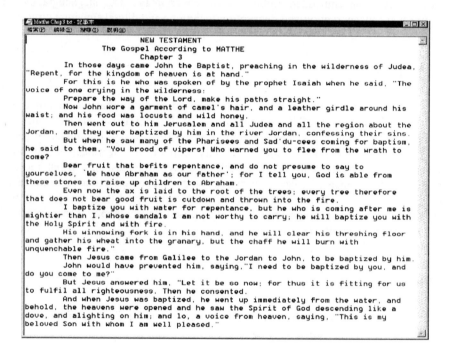

**Fig. 1.** The chapter 3 of the Gospel According to Matthe

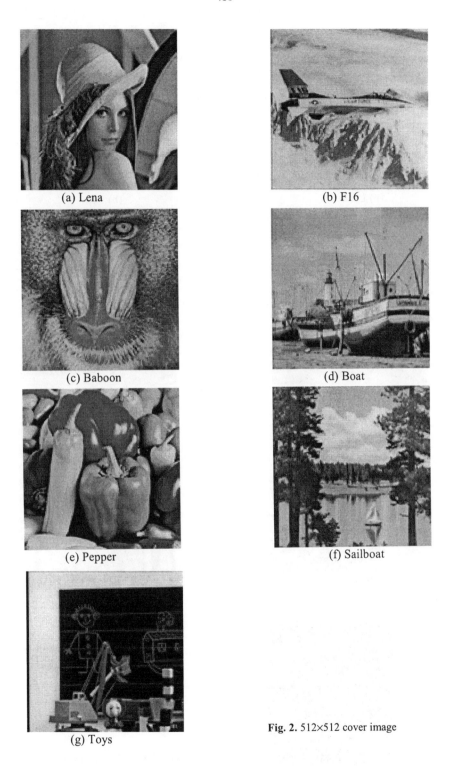

(a) Lena

(b) F16

(c) Baboon

(d) Boat

(e) Pepper

(f) Sailboat

(g) Toys

**Fig. 2.** 512×512 cover image

434

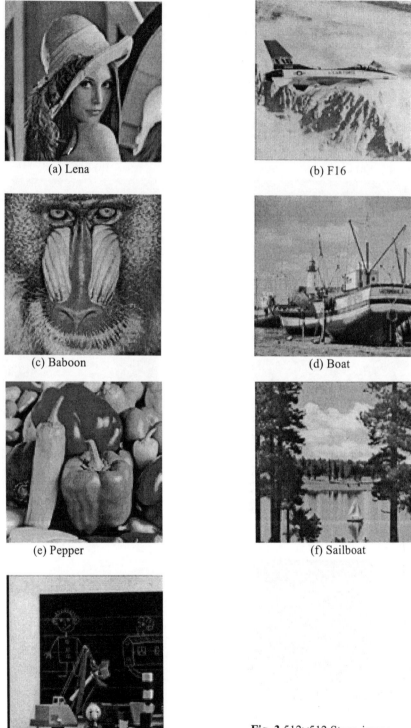

(a) Lena

(b) F16

(c) Baboon

(d) Boat

(e) Pepper

(f) Sailboat

(g) Toys

**Fig. 3** 512×512 Stego-image

**Table 1.** Each image's PSNR value and can extracted 100% compression ratio after embedded Fig. 1 data

|  | Lena | F16 | Baboon | Boat | Sailboat | Toys |
|---|---|---|---|---|---|---|
| PSNR value | 33.07 | 33.03 | 31.72 | 32.84 | 32.71 | 32.93 |
| Compression ratio | 2.42 : 1 | 2.39 : 1 | 2.05 : 1 | 2.31 : 1 | 2.12 : 1 | 2.44 : 1 |

# An Algorithm for Incremental Nearest Neighbor Search in High-Dimensional Data Spaces*

Dong-Ho Lee, Hyung-Dong Lee, Il-Hwan Choi, and Hyoung-Joo Kim

OOPSLA Laboratory,
School of Computer Science and Engineering,
Seoul National University,
Shilim-Dong Gwanak-Gu, Seoul 151-742, KOREA
{dhlee,hdlee,ihchoi,hjk}@oopsla.snu.ac.kr

**Abstract** The SPY-TEC (Spherical Pyramid-Technique) [8] was proposed as a new indexing method for high-dimensional data spaces using a special partitioning strategy that divides a $d$-dimensional data space into $2d$ spherical pyramids. Although the authors of [8] proposed an efficient algorithm for processing hyperspherical range queries, they did not propose an algorithm for processing $k$-nearest neighbor queries that are frequently used in similarity search. In this paper, we propose an efficient algorithm for processing exact nearest neighbor queries on the SPY-TEC by extending the incremental nearest neighbor algorithm proposed in [10]. We also introduce a metric that can be used to guide an ordered best-first traversal when finding nearest neighbors on the SPY-TEC. Finally, we show that our technique significantly outperforms the related techniques in processing $k$-nearest neighbor queries by comparing it to the R*-tree, the X-tree, and the sequential scan through extensive experiments.

**Keywords** : *Similarity Search, High-Dimensional Index Technique, Nearest Neighbor Query, Incremental Nearest Neighbor Algorithm, Approximate Nearest Neighbor Algorithm, SPY-TEC*

## 1 Introduction

Feature-based similarity search has become an important search paradigm for various database applications such as multimedia retrieval, data mining, decision support, and statistical and medical applications. The technique used is to map the data items as points into a high-dimensional feature space. The feature space is usually indexed using a multidimensional index structure. Similarity search then corresponds to a hyperspherical range search, which returns all objects within a threshold level of similarity to the query objects, and a $k$-nearest neighbor search that returns the $k$ most similar objects to the query object. One of the most popular applications using this technique is a content-based image indexing

---

* This research was partially funded by the 1999 BK21 IT area grant of the Ministry of Education in Korea.

and retrieval system [3–5,12] which extracts several features (such as color, texture, shape, etc) from images, indexes the images based on those features, and supports similarity queries based on them. To support efficient similarity search in such a system, robust techniques to index high-dimensional feature spaces need to be developed because the feature vectors used are high-dimensional.

Initially, traditional multidimensional data structures (e.g., R-tree [1], kd-tree [11]), which were designed for indexing low-dimensional spatial data, were used for indexing high-dimensional feature vectors. However, recent research activities [19–21] reported the result that basically none of the querying and indexing techniques which provide good results on low-dimensional data also performs sufficiently well on high-dimensional data. Many researchers have called this problem the *"curse of dimensionality"* [9], and many database-related projects have tried to tackle it. As a result of these research efforts, a variety of new index structures [20, 22], cost models [21] and query processing techniques [18] have been proposed. However, most of the high-dimensional index structures are extensions of the R-tree or the kd-tree adapted to the requirements of high-dimensional indexing. Thus, all of these index structures are limited with respect to data space partitioning and suffer from specific drawbacks of the R-tree or the kd-tree.

For example, most of the R-tree-based index structures, such as the TV-tree [14], X-tree [22], SS-tree [6], and SR-tree [17], tend to have low fanouts and a high degree of overlap between bounding regions in higher dimensions. These degrade the performance of query processing in high-dimensional data spaces. Although the X-tree uses a modified R-tree node splitting algorithm to reduce overlap among the index nodes, it has the overhead of performing disk management operations to create and maintain variable sized nodes (so-called supernodes) produced by this modified splitting algorithm. Also, most of the kd-tree-based index structures, such as the KDB-tree [13], hB-tree [7], and LSDh-tree [2], suffer from such problems as no guaranteed utilization (e.g., KDB-tree) or require storage of redundant information (e.g., hB-tree). In addition to the above drawbacks, these index structures have the well-known drawbacks of multidimensional index structures, such as high costs for insert and delete operations and a poor support of concurrency control and recovery [8].

To overcome these drawbacks, in our earlier work, we proposed a new special space partitioning strategy, the SPY-TEC [8], which is optimized for similarity search in high-dimensional spaces, and proposed the algorithms for processing hyperspherical range queries on the data space partitioned by this strategy. The SPY-TEC first partitions the $d$-dimensional space into $2d$ spherical pyramids having the center point of the space as their top, and the curved $(d-1)$-dimensional surface as their bases, and then cuts each spherical pyramid into several spherical slices. By this partitioning strategy of the SPY-TEC, we were able to transform the given d-dimensional data space into a 1-dimensional value. Thus, we could use a $B^+$-tree to store and access data items, and take advantage of all of the benefits of a $B^+$-tree, such as fast insert, update and delete operations, and good concurrency control and recovery. However, we could not

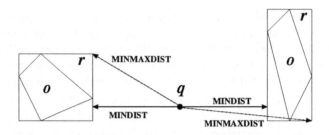

**Fig. 1.** An example of MinDist and MinMaxDist

propose an algorithm for processing nearest neighbor queries efficiently on the SPY-TEC.

In this paper, we introduce a new metric that can be used to guide an ordered best-first traversal when finding nearest neighbors on the SPY-TEC. Based on this new metric, we propose the incremental nearest neighbor algorithm on the SPY-TEC.

The rest of this paper is organized as follows. Section 2 discusses major algorithms related to nearest neighbor queries. Section 3 briefly reviews the structure of the SPY-TEC. Section 4 describes the incremental nearest neighbor algorithm on the SPY-TEC. Section 5 presents the results of an empirical study comparing our technique with the R*-tree, the X-tree and the sequential scan. Finally, we conclude our work and describe our future plans in Section 6.

## 2  Related Work

There are numerous algorithms for answering nearest neighbor or $k$-nearest neighbor queries that are motivated by the importance of these queries in fields including geographical information systems (GIS), document retrieval, pattern recognition, and learning theory [10]. Many of the above algorithms require specialized search structures, but some employ commonly used spatial structures. For example, algorithms exist for the k-d tree, quadtree-related structures, the R-tree, and others. Of these algorithms, there are two major approaches that provide a basis for our work. One was published by Roussopoulos, et al. [18] and we call it the *KNN algorithm* because it was intended for general nearest neighbor or $k$-nearest neighbor queries. The other algorithm was published by Hjaltason and Samet [10]. We call it the *INN algorithm* because it used the incremental nearest neighbor approach. Due to their importance for our work, these algorithms are presented in detail.

In the *KNN algorithm*, the authors proposed an approach for a nearest neighbor search in the R-tree. The key idea of their work is to maintain a global list (*ActiveBranchList*) of the candidate $k$ nearest neighbors as the R-tree is traversed in a depth-first manner. The authors introduced two important distance functions, MinDist and MinMaxDist for ordering nodes that will be visited.

MINDIST is the distance from the query point $q$ to the closest point on the boundary of a bounding rectangle $r$ of node $n$, while MINMAXDIST is the distance from $q$ to the closest corner of $r$ that is "adjacent" to the corner farthest from $q$. Figure 1 shows two examples of the calculation of MINDIST and MINMAXDIST which are shown with a solid and a broken line, respectively. With these distance functions, the authors proposed three strategies for upward and downward pruning. In some sense, the two orderings represent the optimistic (MINDIST) and the pessimistic (MINMAXDIST) ordering choices because experiments reported in [18] showed that ordering the *ActiveBranchList* using MINDIST consistently performed better than using MINMAXDIST. Since MINDIST represents the minimum distance from a query object $q$ to a bounding rectangle $r$, it is the most optimistic ordering choice possible. Thus, it provides a means of pruning nodes from the search, given that a bound on the maximum distance is available. On the other hand, MINMAXDIST is an upper bound on the distance of the object $o$ nearest to $q$. Therefore, it should be clear that MINMAXDIST by itself does not help in pruning the search, as objects closer to $q$ could be found in elements of $n$ at positions with higher MINMAXDIST values [10].

In the *INN algorithm*, the authors proposed the incremental nearest neighbor algorithm that employs what may be termed best-first traversal. When finding $k$ nearest neighbors to the query object using the *KNN algorithm*, $k$ is known prior to the invocation of the algorithm. Thus, if the $(k+1)-th$ neighbor is needed, the $k$-nearest neighbor algorithm needs to be reinvoked for $(k+1)$ neighbors from scratch. To resolve this problem, the authors of the *INN algorithm* proposed the concept of *distance browsing* which is to obtain the neighbors incrementally (i.e., one by one) as they are needed. This operation means browsing through the database on the basis of distance. They showed through various experiments that the *INN algorithm* significantly outperforms the *KNN algorithm* for distance browsing queries and also usually outperforms the *KNN algorithm* when applied to the $k$-nearest neighbor problem for the R-tree. They also showed that the two pruning strategies proposed in [18] are only useful when finding the first nearest neighbor, and the one strategy that does not use MINMAXDIST is sufficient when used in a combination of upward and downward pruning in their algorithm. This implies that MINMAXDIST is not necessary for pruning in the incremental nearest neighbor approach.

To the best of our knowledge, the *INN algorithm* is one of the most efficient algorithms for finding the nearest neighbor or $k$ nearest neighbors. However, this algorithm does not provide good results on high-dimensional data either, as we will show in our experimental evaluation. This is not a problem of the *INN algorithm* itself, but a problem of the spatial index structure (R-tree), which does not support efficient indexing or query processing structurally on a high-dimensional data space.

In this paper, we propose a new metric that can be used to guide an ordered best-first traversal when finding nearest neighbors on the SPY-TEC. We also propose an efficient incremental nearest neighbor algorithm based on this new metric on the SPY-TEC.

# 3 The SPY-TEC

In [20], Berchtold et al. proposed a special partitioning strategy (Pyramid-Technique) that divides the data space first into $2d$ pyramids, and then cuts each pyramid into several slices. They also proposed the algorithms for processing hypercubic range queries on the space partitioned by this strategy. However, the shape of queries used in similarity search is not a hypercube, but a hypersphere [3,5,9,23]. Thus, when processing hyperspherical range queries with the Pyramid-Technique, there is a drawback that exists in all index structures based on the bounding rectangle [8,9].

The main idea of the SPY-TEC is based on the observation that spherical splits will be better than right-angled splits of the Pyramid-Technique for similarity search. This observation is due to the fact that the shape of the queries used in similarity search is not a hypercube, but a hypersphere. Although we

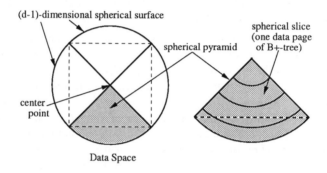

**Fig. 2.** Partitioning strategy of the SPY-TEC

have presented the basic idea and space partitioning strategy of the SPY-TEC in [8], we should explain it again briefly for better understanding of our incremental nearest neighbor algorithm on the SPY-TEC.

The SPY-TEC is to transform $d$-dimensional data points into one-dimensional values and then store and access the values using the $B^+$-tree. Also, we store a $d$-dimensional point *plus* the corresponding one-dimensional key as a record in the leaf nodes of the $B^+$-tree. Therefore, we do not need an inverse mechanism of this transformation. The transformation itself is based on a specific partitioning of the SPY-TEC. To define the transformation, we first explain the data space partitioning strategy of the SPY-TEC.

## 3.1 Data Space Partitioning

The SPY-TEC partitions the data space in two steps: In the first step, we split the $d$-dimensional data space into $2d$ spherical pyramids having the center point of the data space (0.5, 0.5, ..., 0.5) as their top and a (d-1)-dimensional curved

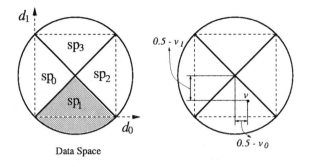

(a) Numbering of Spherical Pyramids

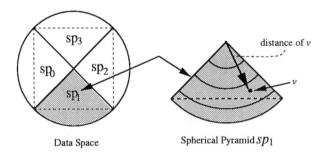

(b) Distance of a Point within its Spherical Pyramid

**Fig. 3.** The SPY-TEC

surface of the data space as their bases. The second step is to divide each of the $2d$ spherical pyramids into several spherical slices, with each slice corresponding to one data page of the $B^+$-tree. Figure 2 shows the data space partitioning of the SPY-TEC in a two-dimensional example. First, the two-dimensional data space has been divided into four spherical pyramids resembling fans. Each of these spherical pyramids has the center point of the data space as its top and one curved line of the data space as its base. In the second step, each of these four spherical pyramids is split again into several data pages which are shaped like the annual rings of a tree. Given a $d$-dimensional space instead of the two-dimensional space, the base of the spherical pyramid is not a 1-dimensional curved line as in the example, but a $(d-1)$-dimensional spherical surface. As a sphere of dimension $d$ has $2d$ $(d-1)$-dimensional spherical surface as a surface, we obviously obtain $2d$ spherical pyramids [8].

Numbering the spherical pyramids is the same as in the Pyramid-Technique. Given a point $v$, we have to find the dimension $i$ having the maximum deviation $|0.5 - v_i|$ from the center to determine the spherical pyramid containing the point *v*. If $v_i$ is greater than or equal to 0.5, then the spherical pyramid containing the point $v$ is $sp_{i+d}$. If it is smaller than 0.5, the spherical pyramid containing the point $v$ is $sp_i$. As depicted in Figure 3(a), the value of $|0.5 - v_1|$ of a point $v$ in two-dimensional space is greater than the value of $|0.5 - v_0|$. Thus, the dimension having the maximum deviation $|0.5 - v_i|$ from the center is $d_1$ and the value of $v_1$ is smaller than 0.5. Therefore, the point $v$ belongs to the spherical pyramid $sp_1$. For example, consider another point $v' = (0.8, 0.4)$. The dimension having the maximum deviation from the center for each dimension of $v'$ is $d_0 (0.3 = |0.5 - v'_0| > |0.5 - v'_1| = 0.1)$. Also, the value of $v'_0$ is greater than 0.5. Therefore, the point $v'$ belongs to the spherical pyramid $sp_{(0+2)}$. Although the formal expression of this procedure was presented in [8], we redefine it formally for better understanding of the partitioning strategy of the SPY-TEC.

**Definition 1. (Spherical pyramid of a point $v$)** A $d$-dimensional point $v$ is defined to be located in a spherical pyramid $sp_i$.

$$i = \begin{cases} j_{max} & \text{if } v_{j_{max}} < 0.5 \\ (j_{max} + d) & \text{if } v_{j_{max}} \geq 0.5 \end{cases}$$

$$j_{max} = (j | (\forall k, 0 \leq (j, k) < d, j \neq k : |0.5 - v_j| \geq |0.5 - v_k|))$$

In Definition 1, $j_{max}$ is the dimension having the maximum deviation $|0.5 - v_i|$ from the center for each dimension of a d-dimensional point $v$ and $i$ is the number of the spherical pyramid containing $v$.

In order to transform $d$-dimensional data into a one-dimensional value, we have to determine the location of a point $v$ within its spherical pyramid. The Pyramid-Technique uses the height of the point within the pyramid as the location of the point. However, we use the distance from the point to the center point of the data space as the location of the point. Figure 3(b) shows the process of determining the distance of the point $v$ as the location within its spherical pyramid. We assume that the distance function is the Euclidean distance which is frequently used for similarity measurement in content-based image retrieval. More formally :

**Definition 2. (Distance of a point $v$)** Given a $d$-dimensional point $v$, the distance $d_v$ of the point $v$ is defined as

$$d_v = \sqrt{\sum_{i=0}^{d-1} (0.5 - v_i)^2}$$

According to Definition 1 and Definition 2, we are able to transform a $d$-dimensional point $v$ into a one-dimensional value $(i \cdot ceil(\sqrt{d}) + d_v)$. In this one-dimensional value, $i$ is the number of the spherical pyramid containing the point $v$, $d$ is the dimension of the point $v$, and $d_v$ is the distance from the point $v$ to the top of its spherical pyramid. More formally :

**Definition 3. (Spherical pyramid value of a point $v$)** Given a $d$-dimensional point $v$, let $i$ be the number of the spherical pyramid containing $v$ according to

Definition 1, and $d_v$ be the distance of $v$ according to Definition 2. Then, the spherical pyramid value $spv_v$ of $v$ is defined as

$$spv_v = (i \cdot ceil(\sqrt{d}) + d_v)$$

Note that $i$ is an integer in the range $[0, 2d]$, $d_v$ is a real number in the range $[0, 0.5\sqrt{d}]$ and $ceil(\sqrt{d})$ is the smallest integer not less than or equal to $\sqrt{d}$. Therefore, every point within a spherical pyramid $sp_i$ has a value in the interval $[i \cdot ceil(\sqrt{d}), (i \cdot ceil(\sqrt{d}) + 0.5\sqrt{d})]$. In order to make the sets of spherical pyramid values covered by any two spherical pyramids $sp_i$ and $sp_j$ be disjunct, we multiply $i$ by $ceil(\sqrt{d})$. Without this multiplication of $i$ by $ceil(\sqrt{d})$, the interval of every point within a spherical pyramid $sp_i$ would be $[i, (i + 0.5\sqrt{d})]$. Thus, there might be intersections in the sets of spherical pyramid values covered by any two spherical pyramids $sp_i$ and $sp_j$ when the dimension is higher than four.

For example, in a 16-dimensional data space, the interval of every point within a spherical pyramid $sp_1$ is $[1, 3]$, and the interval of every point within $sp_2$ is $[2, 4]$. Therefore, these two intervals have an intersection. This intersection may cause the key values of the $B^+$-tree to be redundant. The redundancy of the key values degrades the performance of the $B^+$-tree. In order to avoid this effect, we multiply the spherical pyramid number $i$ by $ceil(\sqrt{d})$. Note further that this transformation is not injective. That is, two points $v$ and $v'$ may have the same spherical pyramid value, but, as mentioned above, we do not need an inverse transformation because we store a $d$-dimensional point *plus* the corresponding one-dimensional key as a record in the leaf nodes of the $B^+$-tree. Therefore, the SPY-TEC does not require a bijective transformation [8].

## 3.2 Index Creation

It is a very simple task to build an index using the SPY-TEC. Given a $d$-dimensional point $v$, we first determine the spherical pyramid value $spv_v$ of the point and then insert the point into a $B^+$-tree using $spv_v$ as a key. Finally, we store the point $v$ and $spv_v$ in the corresponding data page of the $B^+$-tree. Update and delete operations can be done similarly.

The spherical pyramid values of points that all belong to the same spherical pyramid lies in the interval given by the minimum and maximum key values of the data pages. Thus, a single $B^+$-tree data page corresponds to a spherical slice of a spherical pyramid as shown in Figure 2(right). The page regions of the R-tree are (minimum) bounding rectangles, whereas the page regions of the SPY-TEC are spherical slices. Thus, in the rest of the paper, we call the spherical slice the *bounding slice (BS)*.

## 4   Incremental Nearest Neighbor Algorithm on the SPY-TEC

The algorithm proposed in [10] picks the node with the least distance in the set of all nodes that have yet to be visited when deciding what node to traverse

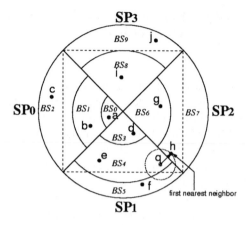

**Fig. 4.** An example of the SPY-TEC for a set of 10 points

next on the R-tree. This means that instead of using a stack or a plain queue to keep track of the nodes to be visited, it uses a priority queue where the distance from the query point is used as a key. In our algorithm, we also use a priority queue where the distance from the query point to the nodes or objects is used as a key.

## 4.1 Metrics for Nearest Neighbor Search

For the incremental nearest neighbor search on the SPY-TEC, we need the minimum possible distance from the query object to a node in the SPY-TEC. Figure 4 shows an example of the SPY-TEC in a two-dimensional data space. For the sake of simplicity, we assume that each bounding slice contains one object. In Figure 4, the query point falls within a bounding slice $BS_4$ in the spherical pyramid $sp_1$. As with most nearest neighbor algorithms, we must first visit the page ($BS_4$ in this example) containing the query point. Then, we visit the next page with the second smallest minimum distance from the query point. To do so, we must calculate the minimum possible distance from the query point to a spherical pyramid or a bounding slice. We first describe the process of calculating the minimum distance between the query point and a spherical pyramid, and then discuss the process of calculating the minimum distance between the query point and a bounding slice.

Lemma 1, which follows, measures the minimum distance MINDIST$(q, sp_i)$ from the query point $q$ to a spherical pyramid $sp_i$. For the sake of simplicity, we focus on the description of the case only for spherical pyramids $sp_i$ where $i < d$. However, this lemma can be extended to all spherical pyramids in a straight-forward manner [8].

**Lemma 1. (Minimum Distance from a Query Point to a Spherical Pyramid)** Given a query point ($q = [q_0, q_1, ..., q_{d-1}]$), let $sp_j$ ($j < d$) be the spherical pyramid containing a query point, and $sp_i$ be the spherical pyramid

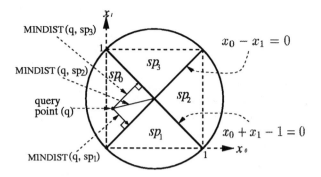

**Fig. 5.** The minimum distance from the query point to a spherical pyramid

that will be examined for the minimum possible distance from $q$. The minimum distance from $q$ to $sp_i$, $\text{MINDIST}(q, sp_i)$, is defined as

$$\text{MINDIST}(q, sp_i) = \begin{cases} 0 & \text{if } i = j \\ d_q & \text{if } |i - j| = d \\ \dfrac{|q_j - q_i|}{\sqrt{2}} & \text{if } i < d \\ \dfrac{|q_j + q_i - 1|}{\sqrt{2}} & \text{if } i > d \end{cases}$$

**Proof :** Given a point $([q_0, q_1, ..., q_{d-1}])$ and a hyperplane $(k_0 x_0 + k_1 x_1 + ... + k_{d-1} x_{d-1} + C = 0)$, the distance from the point to the hyperplane in Euclidean geometry is defined as

$$Distance = \frac{|k_0 q_0 + k_1 q_1 + ... + k_{d-1} q_{d-1} + C|}{\sqrt{k_0^2 + k_1^2 + ... + k_{d-1}^2}} \tag{1}$$

We are able to prove the case $(i > d)$ and the case $(i < d)$ using this formula.
**1.** If $i = j$, $sp_i$ is the spherical pyramid containing the query point $q$. Therefore, $\text{MINDIST}(q, sp_i) = 0$, which is less than or equal to the distance of $q$ from any point in $sp_i$.
**2.** If $|i-j| = d$, $sp_i$ is the spherical pyramid on the opposite side of $sp_j$. Therefore, the minimum distance of q from $sp_i$ is the distance from q to the top of $sp_i$ (the center of the data space). Thus, according to the notation of Definition 2, $\text{MINDIST}(q, sp_i) = d_q$.
**3.** In formula (1), the index $k_n$ and the constant $C$ have discrete values $[-1,0,1]$ because of unit space. If $i < d$, the equation for the closest side plane of a spherical pyramid adjacent to the query point is $k_j x_j + k_i x_i = 0$ as depicted in the 2-dimensional example of Figure 5. This formula can be extended to a $d$-dimensional data space in a straight-forward way. Given a $d$-dimensional space instead of the two-dimensional space, the side plane of a spherical pyramid is not a one-dimensional line as in the example of Figure 5, but a $(d - 1)$-dimensional hyperplane, and the equation for this $(d - 1)$-dimensional hyperplane has the

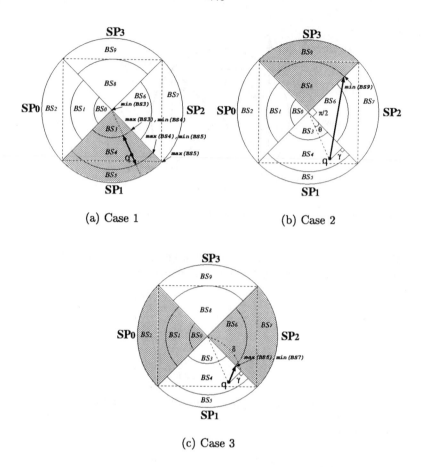

(a) Case 1           (b) Case 2

(c) Case 3

**Fig. 6.** The minimum distance from the query point to a bounding slice

common property that all indices except $k_i$ and $k_j$ are 0. In this case, $k_j = 1$ and $k_i = -1$ because $i < d$. Thus, the minimum distance from the query point to the closest side plane of an adjacent spherical pyramid $sp_i$ is $|q_j - q_i|/\sqrt{2}$. Therefore, $\text{MINDIST}(q, sp_i) = |q_j - q_i|/\sqrt{2}$.

**4.** If $i > d$, the equation for the closest side plane of a spherical pyramid adjacent to the query point is $k_j x_j + k_i x_i - 1 = 0$ (refer to Figure 5). In this case, $k_j = 1$ and $k_i = 1$, because $i > d$. Thus, the minimum distance from the query point to the closest side plane of an adjacent spherical pyramid $sp_i$ is $|q_j + q_i - 1|/\sqrt{2}$. Therefore, $\text{MINDIST}(q, sp_i) = |q_j + q_i - 1|/\sqrt{2}$. □

Calculating the minimum distance from the query point to a bounding slice is more complex than the case of the minimum distance from the query point to a spherical pyramid. However, as depicted in Figure 6 and Lemma 2, we can present it easily by classifying into three cases.

**Lemma 2. (Minimum Distance from a Query Point to a Bounding Slice)** Given a query point ($q$), let $sp_j$ be the spherical pyramid containing a query point, and $BS_l$ be the bounding slice that belongs to a spherical pyramid $sp_i$. The minimum distance from $q$ to a bounding slice $BS_l$, $\text{MINDIST}(q, BS_l)$, is defined as

**Case 1:** ($i = j$ : the case of $BS_l$ belonging to the spherical pyramid that contains $q$.)

$$\text{MINDIST}(q, BS_l) = \begin{cases} |d_q - max(BS_l)| & \text{if } d_q > max(BS_l) \\ 0 & \text{if } min(BS_l) \le d_q \le max(BS_l) \\ |d_q - min(BS_l)| & \text{if } d_q < min(BS_l) \end{cases}$$

**Case 2:** ($|i - j| = d$ : the case of $BS_l$ belonging to the spherical pyramid on the opposite side of $q$.)
Let $\alpha$ be the distance from the closest side plane of a spherical pyramid adjacent to $q$ and $\theta$ ($\le \pi/4$) be the angle of a right-angled triangle which consists of two sides, $\alpha$ and $d_q$ ($sin\theta = \frac{\alpha}{d_q}$),

$$\text{MINDIST}(q, BS_l) = \sqrt{d_q^2 + min(BS_l)^2 - 2d_q min(BS_l)cos(\theta + \tfrac{\pi}{2})}$$

**Case 3:** ($otherwise$ : the case of $BS_l$ belonging to a spherical pyramid adjacent to $q$.)
Let $\delta$ be the length of the base line in a right-angled triangle which consists of two sides, $\alpha$ and $d_q$,

$$\text{MINDIST}(q, BS_l) = \begin{cases} \sqrt{|\delta - max(BS_l)|^2 + \alpha^2} & \text{if } \delta > max(BS_l) \\ \alpha & \text{if } min(BS_l) \le \delta \le max(BS_l) \\ \sqrt{|\delta - min(BS_l)|^2 + \alpha^2} & \text{if } \delta < min(BS_l) \end{cases}$$

where;

$$min(BS_l) = \{d_v \mid (\forall v', v, v' \in BS_l : d_v \le d_{v'})\}$$
$$max(BS_l) = \{d_v \mid (\forall v', v, v' \in BS_l : d_v \ge d_{v'})\}$$

**Proof:** $min(BS_l)$ is $d_v$ of the point $v$ having the smallest value of the points belonging to $BS_l$, while $max(BS_l)$ is $d_v$ of the point $v$ having the largest value. We can prove each case by using $min(BS_l)$ and $max(BS_l)$.

1. If $min(BS_l) \le d_q \le max(BS_l)$, then $q$ is inside $BS_l$. Therefore, $\text{MINDIST}(q, BS_l)$ = 0 because it is less than or equal to the distance of $q$ from any point inside $BS_l$. If $d_q > max(BS_l)$, the distances of all of the points in $BS_l$ from the center of the space are less than the distance of $q$ from the center of the space. Therefore, $\text{MINDIST}(q, BS_l)$ is the difference between $d_q$ and $d_v$, where the point $v$ is in $BS_l$ and is farthest from the center of the space. That is, $\text{MINDIST}(q, BS_l)$ = $|d_q - max(BS_l)|$. Finally, if $d_q < min(BS_l)$, the distance of $q$ from the center is less than the distances of all of the points in $BS_l$ from the center. Therefore, $\text{MINDIST}(q, BS_l)$ is the difference between $d_q$ and $d_v$, where the point $v$ is in $BS_l$ and is closest to the center. That is, $\text{MINDIST}(q, BS_l) = |d_q - min(BS_l)|$. In Figure 6(a), $\text{MINDIST}(q, BS_4)$ is 0 because $q$ is inside $BS_4$. Also, $\text{MINDIST}(q, BS_3)$

is $|d_q - max(BS_3)|$ because the distances of all of the points in $BS_3$ are less than the distance of $q$. Finally, MINDIST$(q, BS_5)$ is $|d_q - min(BS_5)|$ because the distance of $q$ is less than the distances of all of the points in $BS_5$.

**2.** If $|i - j| = d$, $sp_i$ is on the opposite side to the spherical pyramid containing $q$. In this case, the minimum distance from $q$ to $BS_l$ inside $sp_i$ is the length of the base of a triangle which consists of two sides, such as $d_q$ and $min(BS_l)$, and the angle between them as depicted in Figure 6(b). By using the *cosine rule* [15], we can get the length of the base of a triangle. First, the angle of the top of a spherical pyramid is $\pi/2$. Thus, the angle between $d_q$ and $min(BS_l)$ is $(\theta + \pi/2)$ where $\theta = \arcsin(\alpha/d_q)$. Given the lengths of two sides ($b$ and $c$) and the angle ($A$) between them, the cosine rule states : $a^2 = b^2 + c^2 - 2bc \cdot \cos A$. Therefore, by the *cosine rule*, MINDIST$(q, BS_l) = \sqrt{d_q^2 + min(BS_l)^2 - 2d_q min(BS_l) \cdot \cos(\theta + \frac{\pi}{2})}$. Figure 6(b) shows this case in a two-dimensional example. MINDIST$(q, BS_8)$ is $d_q$ because $min(BS_8) = 0$.

**3.** In this case, $sp_i$ is adjacent to $sp_j$ which contains $q$. All sub-cases of this case are similar to those of **Case 1** except that the parameter for classifying each sub-case is not $d_q$, but $\delta$. If $min(BS_l) \leq \delta \leq max(BS_l)$, MINDIST$(q, BS_l)$ is the distance from $q$ to the closest side plane of $sp_i$. That is, MINDIST$(q, BS_l) = \alpha$. This is similar to the sub-case $(min(BS_l) \leq d_q \leq max(BS_l))$ of **Case 1**. If $\delta > max(BS_l)$, MINDIST$(q, BS_l)$ is the length of the hypotenuse in a right-angled triangle which consists of two sides, $\alpha$ and $|\delta - max(BS_l)|$. Therefore, MINDIST$(q, BS_l) = \sqrt{|\delta - max(BS_l)|^2 + \alpha^2}$. Finally, if $\delta < min(BS_l)$, MINDIST$(q, BS_l)$ is the length of the hypotenuse in a right-angled triangle which consists of two sides, $\alpha$ and $|\delta - min(BS_l)|$. Therefore, MINDIST$(q, BS_l) = \sqrt{|\delta - min(BS_l)|^2 + \alpha^2}$. Figure 6(c) shows this case in a two-dimensional example. □

## 4.2 Algorithm Description

Algorithm 1 shows the algorithm for processing the nearest neighbor query. In lines 1~4, the distances of each spherical pyramid from the query point are calculated by using Lemma 1, and then information about each spherical pyramid and its distance are inserted into the priority queue. Since the distance is used as a key in the priority queue, the spherical pyramid closest to the query point is at the head of the queue. The **while**-loop of lines $6 \sim 21$ is the main loop for the algorithm. In line 7, the first element in the head of the queue is dequeued and, according to the type of the element, appropriate operations will be performed. If the type of the element dequeued is a spherical pyramid, as depicted in lines $8 \sim 12$, the distances of each bounding slice in the spherical pyramid from the query point are calculated, and then information of each bounding slice and its distance are inserted into the queue by using Lemma 2. If the type is a bounding slice, as depicted in lines $13 \sim 17$, the distances of each object in the bounding slice from the query point are calculated, and then inserted into the queue. Finally, if the type is an object, it is reported as the next nearest

---

**Algorithm 1** Processing the incremental nearest neighbor query

---
1: **for** $i = 0$ to $2d - 1$ **do**
2:    dist = MINDIST($q, sp_i$); {Using Lemma 1}
3:    ENQUEUE(queue, $sp_i$, dist);
4: **end for**
5:
6: **while** not ISEMPTY(queue) **do**
7:    Element = DEQUEUE(queue);
8:    **if** Element is a spherical pyramid **then**
9:       **for** each bounding slice in a spherical pyramid **do**
10:          dist = MINDIST($q, BS_l$); {Using Lemma 2}
11:          ENQUEUE(queue, $BS_l$, dist);
12:       **end for**
13:    **else if** Element is a bounding slice **then**
14:       **for** each object in a bounding slice **do**
15:          dist = DIST_QUERY_TO_OBJ($q, object$);
16:          ENQUEUE(queue, $object$, dist);
17:       **end for**
18:    **else** {Element is a object}
19:       report element as the next nearest object
20:    **end if**
21: **end while**

---

neighbor object. The first reported object is naturally the nearest neighbor to the query point. If we control the number of reported nearest neighbors in the **while**-loop of Algorithm 1, we can easily process the $k$-nearest neighbor query.

## 4.3  Example

As an example, suppose that we want to find the first nearest neighbor to the query point $q$ in the SPY-TEC given in Figure 4. Below, we show the steps of the algorithm and the contents of the priority queue. Table 1 shows these distances ($SP$ means spherical pyramid and $BS$ means bounding slice). When depicting the contents of the priority queue, the spherical pyramids and bounding slices are listed with their distances from the query point $q$, in order of increasing distance. The objects are denoted in bold letters (e.g., **a**). The algorithm starts by enqueueing $SP_0 \sim SP_3$, after which it executes the following steps:

1. Enqueue $SP_0 \sim SP_3$. Queue : $\{[SP_1,0], [SP_2,4], [SP_0,21], [SP_3,33]\}$
2. Dequeue $SP_1$, enqueue $BS_3, BS_4, BS_5$. Queue : $\{[BS_4,0], [BS_5,2], [SP_2,4], [BS_3,14], [SP_0,21], [SP_3,33]\}$
3. Dequeue $BS_4$, enqueue **e**. Queue : $\{[BS_5,2], [SP_2,4], [BS_3,14], [\mathbf{e},19], [SP_0,21], [SP_3,33]\}$
4. Dequeue $BS_5$, enqueue **f**. Queue : $\{[SP_2,4], [\mathbf{f},12], [BS_3,14], [\mathbf{e},19], [SP_0,21], [SP_3,33]\}$
5. Dequeue $SP_2$, enqueue $BS_6, BS_7$. Queue : $\{[BS_7,4], [BS_6,8], [\mathbf{f},12], [BS_3,14], [\mathbf{e},19], [SP_0,21], [SP_3,33]\}$

| BS | Dist. |
|----|-------|
| $BS_0$ | 21 |
| $BS_1$ | 25 |
| $BS_2$ | 29 |
| $BS_3$ | 14 |
| $BS_4$ | 0 |
| $BS_5$ | 2 |
| $BS_6$ | 8 |
| $BS_7$ | 4 |
| $BS_8$ | 33 |
| $BS_9$ | 42 |

| OBJ | Dist. |
|-----|-------|
| a | 23 |
| b | 27 |
| c | 45 |
| d | 16 |
| e | 19 |
| f | 12 |
| g | 35 |
| h | 6 |
| i | 39 |
| j | 47 |

| SP | Dist. |
|----|-------|
| $SP_0$ | 21 |
| $SP_1$ | 0 |
| $SP_2$ | 4 |
| $SP_3$ | 33 |

**Table 1.** Distances of spherical pyramids and bounding slices from the query point $q$ in the SPY-TEC of Figure 4.

6. Dequeue $BS_7$, enqueue **h**. Queue : {[**h**,6], [$BS_6$,8], [**f**,12], [$BS_3$,14], [**e**,19], [$SP_0$,21], [$SP_3$,33]}
7. Dequeue **h**, report **h** as the first nearest neighbor.

Since the elements in the priority queue are sorted in increasing order of distance, $sp_1$ containing the query point $q$ is at the head of the queue. In line 7 of Algorithm 1, $sp_1$ is dequeued, and then $BS_3$, $BS_4$, and $BS_5$ in $sp_1$ are enqueued in increasing order of their distances from the query point. Now, $BS_4$ is at the head of the queue because it has the smallest distance. $BS_4$ is dequeued, and then the objects in $BS_4$ are enqueued. In this example, since we assume that only one object is contained in a bounding slice, the object **e** in $BS_4$ is enqueued. These operations are repeated until the user finds as many nearest neighbors as desired.

## 5 Experimental Evaluation

We performed various experiments to show the practical impact of the incremental nearest neighbor algorithm on the SPY-TEC and compared it to the R*-tree and the X-tree, as well as the sequential scan.

For clear comparison, we implemented the incremental nearest neighbor algorithm on the R*-tree and the X-tree using the algorithm proposed in [10]. All experiments were performed on a SUN SPARC 20 workstation with 128 MByte main memory and 10 GByte secondary storage. The block size used for our experiments was 4 KBytes. Due to lack of space, we show only the experiment using real data sets, although we performed various experiments using synthetic data sets and real data sets. For a more detailed results of various experiments, you can refer to [16].

The real data consists of Fourier points [22] in 12-dimensional space. We performed 10-nearest neighbor queries with 100 query points that were selected from the real data itself, and varied the database size from 20,000 to 100,000.

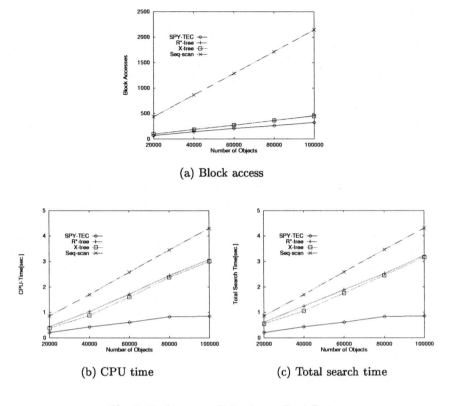

(a) Block access

(b) CPU time

(c) Total search time

**Fig. 7.** Performance Behavior on Real Data

Figure 7 shows the result of the experiment using real data sets. In this experiment, the SPY-TEC, along with the R*-tree or the X-tree significantly outperform the sequential scan regardless of the database size. From this result, we found that the real data consists of well-formed clusters which are meaningful workloads for high-dimensional nearest neighbor queries. The speed-up of the SPY-TEC in the total search time ranges between 2.42 and 3.71 over the X-tree, between 2.85 and 3.78 over the R*-tree, and between 3.90 and 5.04 over the sequential scan. The performance behavior of the number of block accesses and of CPU time are analogous to that of the total search time. The index structures SPY-TEC, X-tree, and R*-tree significantly outperform the sequential scan in all cases, and the SPY-TEC also clearly yields a better performance than do the X-tree and the R*-tree.

## 6 Conclusions

The SPY-TEC is based on a special partitioning strategy which divides the $d$-dimensional data space first into $2d$ spherical pyramids, and then cuts each spherical pyramid into several bounding slices. In this paper, we proposed the incremental nearest neighbor algorithm on the SPY-TEC. We also introduced a metric that can be used to guide an ordered best-first traversal when finding nearest neighbors on the SPY-TEC. The metric (MINDIST), the minimum possible distance of the query point from a spherical pyramid or a bounding slice, produces the most optimistic ordering possible when finding nearest neighbors on the SPY-TEC. We implemented the incremental nearest neighbor algorithm on the SPY-TEC and performed extensive experiments using synthetic data and real data sets to show the practical impacts of these algorithms. Through the experiments, we showed that the incremental algorithm on the SPY-TEC clearly outperforms that of the X-tree, the R*-tree, and the sequential scan.

For highly skewed data distributions or queries, the incremental nearest neighbor algorithm on the SPY-TEC may perform worse than those on other index structures. However, none of the index structure proposed so far can handle highly skewed data or queries efficiently [20]. We plan to address the problem of handling highly skewed data or queries in our future work. We also plan to study the parallel version of the nearest neighbor algorithm on the SPY-TEC using an efficient declustering technique that distributes the data onto the disks so that the data which has to be read when executing a query are distributed as equally as possible among the disks.

# References

1. A. Guttman. "R-trees: a dynamic index structure for spatial searching". *Proc. ACM SIGMOD Int. Conf. on Management of Data*, pages 47–57, June 1984.
2. A. Henrich. "The LSDh-Tree: An Access Structure for Feature Vectors". *Proc. 14th Int. Conf on Data Engineering*, pages 362–369, 1998.
3. C. Faloutsos, R. Barber, M. Flickner, J. Hafner, W. Niblack, D. Petkovic, and W. Equiz. "Efficient and Effective Querying by Image Content". *Journal of Intelligent Information System(JIIS)*, 3(3):231–262, July 1994.
4. B. C. Ooi, K. L. Tan, T. S. Chua, and W. Hsu. "Fast image retrieval using color-spatial information". *The VLDB Journal*, 7(2):115–128, 1998.
5. C. E. Jacobs, A. Finkelstein, and D. H. Salesin. "Fast Multiresolution Image Query". *Proc. of the 1995 ACM SIGGRAPH, New York*, 1995.
6. D. A. White and R. Jain. "Similarity Indexing with the SS-tree". *Proc. 12th Int. Conf on Data Engineering*, pages 516–523, 1996.
7. D. B. Lomet and B. Salzberg. "The hB-Tree: A Multiattribute Indexing Method with Good Guaranteed Performance". *ACM Transaction on Database Systems*, 15(4):625–658, 1990.
8. D. H. Lee and H. J. Kim. "SPY-TEC : An Efficient Indexing Method for Similarity Search in High-Dimensional Data Spaces". *Data & Knowledge Engineering*, 34(1):77–97, 2000.
9. C. Faloutsos. "Fast Searching by Content in Multimedia Databases". *Data Engineering Bulletin*, 18(4), 1995.
10. G. R. Hjaltason and H. Samet. "Distance Browsing in Spatial Databases". *ACM Transaction on Database Systems*, 24(2):265–318, 1999.
11. J. Bentley. "Mutidimensional binary search trees used for associative searching". *Communications of the ACM*, 18(9):509–517, 1975.

12. J. R. Smith and S.-F. Chang. "VisualSEEk: a fully automated content-based image query system". *ACM Multimedia 96, Boston, MA*, 1996.

13. J. T. Robinson. "The K-D-B-tree: a Search Structure for Large Multidimensional Dynamic Indexes". *Proc. ACM SIGMOD, Ann Arbor, USA*, pages 10–18, April 1981.

14. K.-I. Lin, H. V. Jagadish, and C. Faloutsos. "The TV-tree: An Index Structure for High-Dimensional Data". *The VLDB Journal*, 3(4):517–542, 1994.

15. L. Leithold. "Trigonometry". *Addison-Wesley*, 1989.

16. D. H. Lee and H. J. Kim. "An Efficient Nearest Neighbor Search in High-Dimensional Data Spaces". *Seoul National University, CE Technical Report (OOPSLA-TR1028), http://oopsla.snu.ac.kr/~dhlee/OOPSLA-TR1028.ps*, 2000.

17. N. Katayama and S. Satoh. "The SR-tree: An Index Structure for High-Dimensional Nearest Neighbor Queries". *Proc. ACM SIGMOD Int. Conf. on Management of Data*, pages 517–542, May 1997.

18. N. Roussopoulos, S. Kelley, and F. Vincent. "Nearest Neighbor Queries". *Proc. ACM SIGMOD Int. Conf. on Management of Data*, pages 71–79, 1995.

19. K. Beyer, J. Goldstein, R. Ramakrishnan, and U. Shaft. "When Is "Nearest Neighbor" Meaningful ?". *Proc. 7th Int. Conf. on Database Teory*, pages 217–235, January 1999.

20. S. Berchtold, C. Böhm, and H.-P. Kriegel. "The Pyramid-Technique: Towards Breaking the Curse of Dimensionality". *Proc. ACM SIGMOD Int. Conf. on Management of Data*, 1998.

21. S. Berchtold, C. Böhm, D. A. Keim, and H.-P. Kriegel. "A Cost Model For Nearest Neighbor Search in High-Dimensional Data Space". *ACM PODS Symposium on Principles of Database Systems, Tucson, Arizona*, 1997.

22. S. Berchtold, D. A. Keim, and H.-P. Kriegel. "The X-tree: An Indexing Structure for High-Dimensional Data". *Proc. 22nd Int. Conf. on Very Large Database*, pages 28–39, September 1996.

23. P.M. Kelly, T.M. Cannon and D.R. Hush. "Query by image example: the CANDID approach". *Proc. SPIE Storage and Retrieval for Image and Video Databases III*, 2420:238–248, 1995.

# An XML-Based 3-Dimensional Graphic Database System[*]

Jong Ha Hwang[1], Jae Ho Ro[2], Keung Hae Lee[1], Jong Sou Park[1], Soochan Hwang[1]

[1] Department of Computer Engineering, Hankuk Aviation University, Koyang, Korea
{hwangjh, khlee, jspark, schwang}@mail.hangkong.ac.kr

[2] Samsung Data System Information Technology, Seoul, Korea
songod@samsung.co.kr

**Abstract.** Supporting the semantics of 3-D objects and their spatial relations in database systems has been little addressed in the literature. Despite its importance, most 3-D graphic systems lack this capability, mainly focusing on the visualization aspects of 3-D images. We have developed a 3-D graphic data model based on XML that accommodates the semantics of 3-D scenes. This model offers content-based retrievals of scenes containing a particular object or those satisfying certain spatial constraints on them. The model represents scenes as compositions of 3-D graphic objects with associated spatial relations. Complex 3-D objects are modeled using a set of primitive 3-D objects rather than the lines and polygons that are found in traditional graphic systems. This paper presents the data model and its implementation called 3DGML, an XML vocabulary that we developed for modeling 3-D graphic data. This paper also describes a Web-based prototype database system that we developed to support the data model.

## 1. Introduction

As the use of Internet grows popular, the support of multimedia data such as text, graphic, audio, and video has become an active area of research for Web and database systems. Graphic data is one of the most frequently used data types in multimedia applications. The significance of 3-dimensional (3-D) graphic data has been demonstrated in many areas, which include computer simulation, virtual reality, and geographic information system [1,2,9]. Graphic database systems have been recognized to play an important role in providing the feel of reality for the users of many applications.

This paper presents a data model for 3-D graphic images and a 3-D graphic database system based on the data model. The graphic data model defines a set of primitive 3-D objects that are used as building blocks for creating larger 3-D objects by

---

\* This work was supported by grant No. 98-0102-06-01-3 from the Basic Research Program of the Korea Science & Engineering Foundation.

composition as we do with Lego blocks. The database system supports content-based retrievals of 3-D graphic images. In addition, spatial relations may be defined on graphical objects to construct a meaningful 3-D scene together. 3-D scenes are stored in the database as XML documents and retrieved using queries regarding their contents that include 3-D related features.

The content-based retrieval method of our system uses the values that define the 3-D scenes stored in the database. These include the shapes, descriptions and spatial relations of objects contained in a scene. A query on the shape of an object enables retrievals of a scene that contains a particular shape. A query on spatial relations allows scenes to be searched based on spatial relations among objects in the space. Finally, a query can use textual descriptions that include the names, colors, and descriptions of objects.

The 3-D database system presented in this paper was implemented using XML. The 3-D data model proposed in this paper was defined with an XML DTD(Document Type Definition). The database system provides a Web-based user interface. The choice of XML as the description mechanism makes the database system suited to Internet applications requiring database capability. 3-D graphic images are modeled as XML documents, which are validated by an XML parser and stored in the database. The user can pose content-based or spatial relation based queries using a Web browser. A query result is presented to the user through a VRML viewer.

The remainder of this paper is organized as follows. The next chapter discusses previous research related to our work. Chapter 3 introduces the 3-D graphic data model we propose. Chapter 4 presents the XML DTD of our 3-Dimensional Graphical Markup language (3DGML) that supports the 3-D graphic data model. Chapter 5 describes a prototype implementation of the 3-D graphic database system and example queries. Chapter 6 concludes the paper.

## 2. Related Works

The current active research areas of graphic database systems are data modeling, query processing, storage, compression, and visualization [3]. Most of them have been centered around the processing of 2-dimensional graphic data such as images and maps [4,5,8]. Research works on 3-D graphics are mainly concerned about the visualization of data with the goal of providing the user with the experience of its 3-D feel [2,6]. Existing graphic systems represent 3-D data using geometrical objects such as points, lines, and polygons with their properties such as colors and textures. They do not support content-based retrievals or manipulations of 3-D objects.

It is recent that the issues of modeling 3-D images have been addressed in MPEG standards [7,18]. MPEG-4 SNHC(Synthetic, Natural, and Hybrid Coding) has a goal of developing techniques for efficient representations of synthetic images with natural objects. In MPEG-4, 3-D objects are represented by 3-D meshes(surfaces), norm vectors, and their features such as colors, textures, etc. MPEG-7 has targeted describing multimedia contents and enabling search for them. However, MPEG standards have been only considering 3-D objects as a component of video data. Little work has been done in MPEG in modeling 3-D objects as semantic units and supporting spatial relations.

Some systems model the semantics or the spatial relations of objects contained in 3-D scenes. Xiong and Wang [12] described a computer vision based technique, called *geometric hashing*, for similarity search for a chemical application. A 3-D object is represented using points in the Euclidean Space. An object is represented as a 3-D graph consisting of one or more substructures of connected subgraphs. Similarity of two objects is determined by comparing their substructures and edges. Gudivada and Jung [10] proposed an algorithm for retrieving images of relevance based on similarity to user queries. In their image representation scheme called *3-D Spatial Orientation Graph*(SOG), an image is converted to a symbolic/iconic image with human assistance. The symbolic/iconic image is obtained from each domain object by associating a name or an icon with it. The location of a domain object is represented by its centroid coordinate. This method also determines the spatial relation of objects using the connectivity of graphs. While these papers considered geometrical similarity, they did not discuss modeling the semantics of objects or spatial relations on objects in a 3-D scene.

Solving the problems discussed above calls for a new data model that represents 3-D data using semantic units rather than basic geometrical objects. Content-based retrievals for 3-D data require a substantial extension of the techniques used for content-based retrievals of 2-D data. New features for 3-D data should be considered. For example, we need to extend textual descriptions, annotations, colors, textures, objects, and relations on objects used for 2-D problems with 3-D support. A 3-D graphic data modeling requires representations of objects and their spatial relations, which are significantly more complex than those of 2-D.

There are three graphic retrieval methods that are used for 3-D graphic images, namely, feature-based query, similarity query, and spatial relation query [3,8,10,11,12]. The feature-based query relies on the features of graphic objects such as color, texture, shape, and contour. The feature information is provided by the user or generated by the system. It is stored in the database with graphic data and used for retrievals. The similarity query searches for a graphic data in the graphic database using the notion of similarity. The user can specify a graphic data to match or an approximation of the data to search for. Usually, a graphical user interface is offered by the retrieval system. A similarity query typically results in a set of data that are within the similarity distance defined by the system instead of a single item. The spatial relation query allows the user to retrieve a scene based on the specification of a spatial relation among objects that it contains. Other retrieval methods include those based on textual descriptions or annotations of objects.

XML has been widely used for describing complex data types. The openness and the extensibility via the Data Type Definition mechanism make XML an excellent vehicle for defining new languages with a relatively small effort [14]. Several domain specific languages have already been designed with XML before. Examples of such languages are CML(Chemical Markup Language), MathML(Mathematical Markup Language), and MusicML [15]. As their names suggest it, these languages commonly bring the capability to markup and browse complex data types to the user in their targeted application domains.

There are also other types of XML based languages that take advantage of the descriptive power of XML. Synchronized Multimedia Integration Language (SMIL) [20] is an XML-based markup language for authoring multimedia applications that can be presented on the Web browser. SOAP [21] is an XML-based communication protocol that intends to support object messaging across heterogeneous messaging protocols and platforms. MoDAL [19] is an example of user interface description languages intended for mobile PDAs.

While the use of XML is growing in other areas, little work has been reported in the literature that supports modeling 3-D graphic data with XML. We believe that the descriptiveness and the extensibility of XML render it suitable for implementing a flexible 3-D graphic data model.

# 3. 3-D Graphic Data Model

## 3.1 Data Model

A 3-D graphic image has been traditionally modeled using lines and polygons with information on their placements in the space. One problem with this approach is that it prevents the semantic information from being attached to domain objects in the image. The lack of such information makes it difficult to retrieve or manipulate a particular domain object separately from others in the image.

The 3-D graphic data model that we developed offers the capability of modeling complex 3-D images. The model, based on the object-oriented concept, represents 3-D objects using semantic units and their spatial relations. A *3-D scene* is an image consisting of one or more component objects which are meaningful entities in terms of domain semantics. The spatial extent of an object is represented by its location and spatial relation to other objects in a 3-D scene. Each component object is defined using a set of primitive 3-D objects provided by the model rather than lines and polygons that are found in most existing graphic systems. Fig. 3.1 shows the class inheritance hierarchy and the composition hierarchy that are used for constructing 3-D scenes in our model

Basic objects and user defined objects are used as primitive elements for modeling 3-D objects. A *basic object* is a system-defined 3-D object that is used as a building block for representing a 3-D graphic object. Examples of basic objects are cube, cone, sphere, and cylinder. The user can also specify colors and textures for each surface of a basic object. This information is used for retrievals and visualization. A 3-D object that is difficult to model with basic objects only is modeled using user defined objects. A *user defined object* is defined using one or more polygons, each of which may have associated properties as in basic objects. We show an example of a user defined object in Fig. 3.2(a). The 3-D object is modeled as a group of polygons.

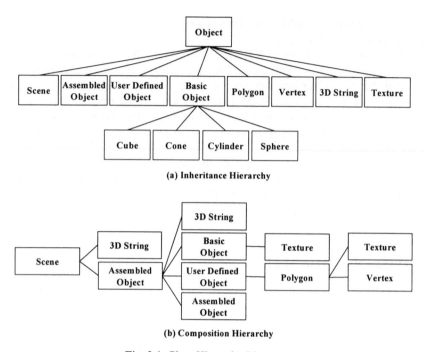

(a) Inheritance Hierarchy

(b) Composition Hierarchy

**Fig. 3.1.** Class Hierarchy Diagrams

More complex 3-D objects are modeled by a composition of basic objects and user defined objects. We call an object composed of more than one object an *assembled object*. An assembled object may be used as components of other assembled objects. In many cases, an assembled object is a semantic unit that has an associated domain semantics such as desk, chair, and table. Fig. 3.2(b) shows an example of an assembled object. The chair in the figure is an assembled object composed of basic objects such as cubes and cylinders.

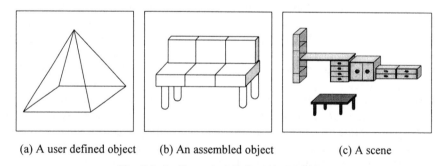

(a) A user defined object      (b) An assembled object      (c) A scene

**Fig. 3.2.** An Example 3-D Graphic Modeling

Fig. 3.2(c) is an example of 3-D scenes that are modeled as assembled objects. Scenes are modeled as a composition of assembled objects and may be associated with domain specific semantics such as office furniture, home furniture, and kitchen furniture.

## 3.2 Modeling spatial relations for the 3-D space

We introduce a *3-D string* technique for expressing spatial relations for 3-D objects. The 3-D string technique is our extension of the 2-D string technique used to express the relations in the 2-D space. A 3-D string can represents the concepts of left-right, above-below, and near-far [16].

The representation of a 3-D string is based on the notion of 1D strings. A 1D string is an encoding of the ordering of positions of objects that are obtained when they are projected on an axis in the rectangular coordinate system. A 1D string is defined by V, the set of objects participating in spatial relations and A, the set of ordering symbols that denote spatial orderings of objects in the space. The ordering symbols for 1D strings are "<" which means near and "=" which means equal. A 3-D string is a 3-tuple (u, v, w), where u, v, and w represent the 1D strings obtained when objects are projected to the X, Y, and Z-axis, respectively.

To see an example of a 3-D string, let's consider objects $a$ and $b$ shown in Fig. 3.3. Object $a$ is located to the left of object $b$ when we project them to the X-axis. From this, we get "$a<b$" as the value of u. As object $a$ is below object $b$, we get "$a<b$" as the value of v when projecting them to the Y-axis. Similarly, we get "$a=b$" as the value of w since object $a$ and object $b$ are located at the same distance from the origin along the Z-axis. Hence the 3-D string that represents the spatial relation on the two objects becomes ($a<b$, $a<b$, $a=b$).

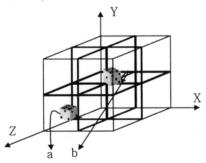

**Fig. 3.3.** Two objects in the 3-D space

# 4. 3DGML

Chapter 4 presents a 3-D graphic object modeling language called 3DGML(3-Dimensional Graphical Markup Language). 3DGML supports the 3-D data model discussed in the previous chapter. We have developed 3DGML as an XML vocabulary by defining an XML DTD for it. In 3DGML, 3-D graphic objects are defined using XML tags and stored in the form of parsed XML documents. We now describe major elements of the 3DGML DTD. The next section provides an example modeling of 3-D scene using 3DGML. The modeling of a furniture set will be discussed.

## 4.1 The DTD for 3DGML

Fig. 4.1 shows the structure of the DTD of 3DGML. We first describe the syntax and semantics of some significant elements of the DTD below, which are used for defining a skeleton structure in a graphic document. Other elements will be discussed in the next section with an example.

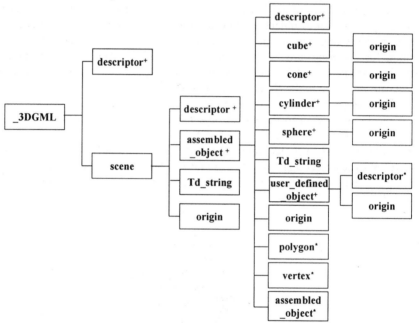

**Fig. 4.1.** The Structure of the 3DGML DTD

A part of 3DGML DTD is shown in Fig. 4.2. The full description of the syntax of the 3DGML DTD is omitted due to the length of the paper.

The root element of the DTD is _3DGML that consists of one or more of descriptors and a scene. A descriptor describes a property associated with its parent element. The scene element, which defines a 3-D graphic scene, consists of one or more descriptors, one or more assembled objects, a 3-D string, and the origin element. The origin denotes the reference point of objects in the 3-D space. A scene must be given an identifier as its attribute. The definition of an assembled_object element includes descriptors and one or more basic objects such as cone, cube, cylinder, sphere, and user defined object. It also includes other assembled objects, a 3-D string, zero or more polygons and vertices. Each assembled object must have an identifier (o_id). The basic objects and the user defined object have their own DTD definition. We will explain them with an example at the next section.

```
<!ELEMENT _3DGML (descriptor+, scene)>

<!ELEMENT scene (descriptor+ , assembled_object+, Td_string, origin)>
        <!ATTLIST scene
              s_id  CDATA  #REQUIRED>

<!ELEMENT assembled_object (descriptor+, (sphere | cylinder | cone | cube |
                    user_defined_object)+, assembled_object*, Td-string,
                    origin, polygon*, vertex*)>
        <!ATTLIST assembled_object
              o_id CDATA   #REQUIRED >

<!ELEMENT Td_string EMPTY>
        <!ATTLIST Td_string
              u       CDATA  #IMPLIED       -- X axis
              v       CDATA  #IMPLIED       -- Y axis
              w       CDATA  #IMPLIED>      -- Z axis
```

**Fig. 4.2.** The Definition of the 3DGML DTD

A 3-D string represents the spatial relations of the objects contained in a scene or within an assembled object. As discussed earlier, the value of a 3-D string depends on the positions of objects in a scene or within an object. An example 3-D string is as follows.

<Td_string u="o1 < o2 = o3 = o4" v="o2 < o3 < o1 < o4" w="o1 < o2 < o3 < o4"/>

According to the value of u in the definition, object o1 is located to the left of o2, while o2, o3, and o4 are at the same position along the X-axis. Similarly, v and w show that o2 is the bottommost object while o1 is the farthest located object.

## 4.2 An Example Modeling of a 3-D Scene

In this section, we discuss modeling a 3-D scene in 3DGML using a more complex example. Fig. 3.2(c) shows a home furniture set consisting of four pieces, viz. a desk with a bookshelf, a cabinet, a chest of drawers, and a tea table. An XML document that models this furniture set using 3DGML is shown Fig. 4.3.

In this description, the furniture set is defined to be a scene composed of four assembled objects in it. The example also shows how the property values of objects are defined as well as the spatial relation of objects contained in the scene. We now take a closer look at the definition.

```
<scene s_id="s1">
    <descriptor name="title" value="home furniture set" type="string" />
    <assembled_object o_id="a1">
        <descriptor name="name" value="tea table" type="string"/>
        <descriptor name="price" value="150000" type="price"/>
        <cube o_id="c1" p_index="p105, p106, p107, p108, p109, p110">
            <origin x="125" y="21" z="100"/>
        </cube>
        <cylinder o_id="cy1" v_tl="109,20,89" v_tr="110,20,89" v_bl="109,0,89"
                            v_br="110, 0, 89" s_texture = "c:\...\t1.tex", ...>
            <origin x="109" y="10" z="89"/>
        </cylinder>
        <!-- . . . other definitions for the table -->
    </assembled_object>
    <assembled_object o_id="a2">
        <descriptor name="name" value="desk" type="string"/>
        <assembled_object o_id="a21">
            <description name="name" value="bookshelf" type="string"/>
            <description name="price" value="100000" type="price"/>
            <!-- . . . definition of the bookshelf object -->
    </assembled_object>
    <assembled_object o_id="a22">
            <descriptor name="name" value="drawer box" type="string"/>
            <!-- . . . definition of the drawer box object -->
    </assembled_object>
    <assembled_object o_id="a23">
            <descriptor name="name" value="top plate" type="string"/>
            <!-- . . . definition of the desk top object -->
    </assembled_object>
    </assembled_object>
    <assembled_object o_id="a3">
            <descriptor name="name" value="cabinet" type="string"/>
            <!-- . . . definition of the cabinet object -->
    </assembled_object>
    <assembled_object o_id="a4">
            <descriptor name="name" value="chest of drawer" type="string"/>
            <!-- . . . definition of the cabinet object -->
    </assembled_object>
    <Td_string u="a2<a1<a3<a4" v="a1=a2=a3=a4" w="a3<a2=a3<a1"/>
    <origin x="90" y="40" z="57.5"/>
</scene>
```

**Fig. 4.3.** A Modeling of the Scene in Fig. 3.2(c) with 3DGML

The XML document defines a scene called a home furniture set. It consists of four assembled objects a1 through a4. The object a2 in turn is composed of three assembled objects a21, a22, and a23, which names the bookshelf, the drawer box, and the top plate, respectively. The spatial relation of the objects is defined by the Td_string element. As shown in the definition, the spatial relation with respect to the X-axis is "a2 < a1 < a3 < a4." This relation, for example, conveys that object a2, desk, is located at the leftmost position in the scene. The descriptor element has three attributes: name, value, and type. In the definition of scene s1, the descriptor of scene, <descriptor name="title" value="home furniture set" type="string" />, represents that the title of the scene is home furniture set and its type is string. The descriptor element plays a role similar to the definition of a field for a database table.

The assembled object a1, tea table, is composed of a cube as a table top and 4 cylinders as legs. The basic object, cube, is defined by a list of polygons, p105 through p110, and its position (125, 21, 100) within the scene. The color and texture information of the cube can be specified by the attributes of its faces (polygons).

A cylinder is defined by four vertices: v_tl, v_tr, v_bl, and v_br. As shown in Fig. 4.4, v_tl and v_tr denotes the center and the rightmost point of the top circle, respectively. Similarly, v_bl and v_br denote the two points for the bottom circle. The color and texture values may be associated with each of the three surfaces of a cylinder. A cone object is defined in a way similar to a cylinder object. It has three vertices and two surfaces such as the bottom and the side surface. The sphere object is simply defined by four attributes consisting of the center point, radius, and color and texture of the surface.

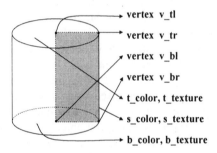

**Fig. 4.4.** Attributes of a Cylinder

# 5. The Implementation of 3-D Graphic Database System

## 5.1 The System Architecture

The implementation of the 3-D graphic database system that we have discussed so far is based on the XML technology. The database system consists of three parts: the user interface, the XML processor, and the database interface. The major components included in each part are shown in Fig. 5.1.

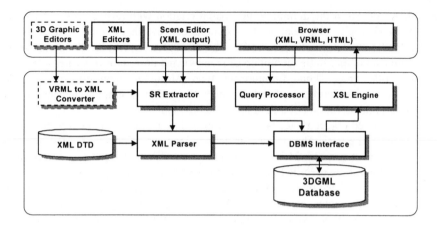

**Fig. 5.1.** An Overview of the 3-D Graphic Database System

The user of the system creates a 3-D scene using a 3-D graphic editor or a 3-D scene editor. The created scene is converted to an XML document by a scene-to-XML converter. SR Extractor is the tool that extracts the spatial relation of the 3-D objects contained in a scene. It generates a 3-D string from XML descriptions of the scene. The resulting XML document is the aggregate of the component objects and the spatial relation defined on them. The document is validated by the 3DGML DTD. If the XML document turns out to be valid, the definitions, attributes, and text of the elements in the document are stored in the database.

The processing of a query is as follows. When the user enters a query condition on the graphical user interface, it is converted to an XML format. 3-D scenes are retrieved from the database using this condition. The query processor supports queries involving descriptors, the existence of a given object in a scene, and spatial relational conditions based on the 3-D string representation. The result of a query is converted to a VRML description using the XSL engine. The VRML description is fed to a VRML viewer, which displays its 3-D image on the Web browser.

For creating 3-D scenes, existing 3-D modeling tools such as 3D Studio and AutoCad can be used. The current prototype system provides a scene editor that we developed to help create valid 3DGML documents. The development of the two modules shown in dotted lines is currently under way. The current prototype has been implemented and runs on the Windows NT platform with IIS(Internet Information Server) of Microsoft. The XML parser was implemented in ASP using DOM API [17]. Parsed XML documents are stored in the MS-SQL server.

## 5.2 The Implementation and Example Retrievals

We now discuss building a sample 3-D database in the current system. Fig. 5.2 shows the screen image and a search dialog of the prototype 3-D graphic database system. The image is part of the furniture catalog provided by an Internet shopping site. It was generated using the data retrieved from the sample database of the electronic commerce site.

The Query Screen shown in Figure 5.2(a) is the interface for the user to enter queries. The user specifies search conditions using descriptors or the shape of the object to be contained in the scene being searched for. When a product is queried using a shape, the user may browse existing shapes using the 3-D scene editor shown in Fig. 5.2(b). If the shape being searched for does not exist in the system yet, the user may first define a new object to use for search. The definition of the new object is converted to an XML document that satisfies the 3DGML DTD. The parsed form of the XML document is stored in the database for future use. A search condition used in a query is converted to an XML. In the example query of Fig. 5.2(a), the user issues a query using four descriptive conditions, viz. product name, usage, manufacturer, and price of the furniture. The user can also create a sample object to be used for searching a scene containing it using the scene editor. Fig. 5.2(b) is a screen shot of the scene editor, where a user creates a drawer box for the search condition. Fig. 5.2(c) shows the result of the query saying "Retrieve the desk which contains the drawer box of the given shape."

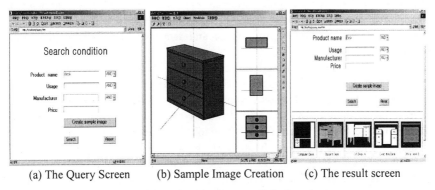

   (a) The Query Screen    (b) Sample Image Creation    (c) The result screen

**Fig. 5.2.** A Sample Query and The Result

The screen shots of Fig. 5.3 show another example of retrieving a 3-D scene using a spatial relation based query. Fig. 5.3(a) shows the search interface where the user specifies the spatial relation for the constituent objects of a scene to satisfy. Fig. 5.3(b) shows a scene that matches the search condition specified by user. The query in this example searched for a desk with two drawers attached to it below the desktop. The condition used for this purpose contains only the v component of (u, v, w) of a 3-D string. The spatial relation for this query expresses the condition *"drawer = drawer < desk"*. We are currently working on the user interface that will allow the user to specify spatial relations through visual interaction with the system on a graphic editor.

(a) A Query Screen        (b) Result Screen

**Fig. 5.3.** An Example of Spatial Relation Query Session

## 6. Conclusion

While XML has become a popular research topic in many application domains, few XML applications are known to support 3-D graphic data. The support of content-based retrievals for 3-D graphic information and data models that enable them are yet to be matured.

We have presented a data model offering the capability of semantic modeling of 3-D graphic objects and a 3-D graphic database system that supports the data model. The descriptiveness of XML allows complex models to be modeled with application semantics in the picture. Modeling the structure of a 3-D object in semantic units is supported by the system. Traditional 3-D graphic tools are based on geometrical objects such as lines and polygons. In contrast, the data model also simplifies modeling of 3-D objects by a set of primitive 3-D objects that can be used in defining complex objects through composition. The concept of 3-D string that we came up with allows the system to formally express spatial relations for the objects in a scene. We explained that these features and the data model described enabled content-based retrievals that involve shapes of object to search and spatial relations among objects. We expect that the 3-D database system described in the paper has a wide applicability for applications that require graphics support.

We are currently developing a user interface that allows the graphic image created on a 3-D graphic editor to be used as input to the database system. For future work, we are planning on providing the support of similarity query based on shapes of objects. Finally, we view that representing spatial relations according to viewpoints is an important issue to be investigated in the future.

# References

1. Menendez, R. G. and J. E. Bernard, "Flight Simulation in Synthetic Environments," IEEE Proceedings of the Digital Avionics Systems Conferences, vol. 1, 2000.
2. Jie, S., "Visualizing 3-D Geographical Data with VRML," IEEE Proceedings of the International on Computer Graphics, pp.108-110, 1998.
3. Bimbo, A. D., *Visual Information Retrieval*, Morgan Kaufmann, 1999.
4. Yining, D., B. S. Manjunath, C. Kenney, M. S. Moore, and S. Hyundoo, "An Efficient Color Representation for image Retrieval," IEEE Transactions on Image Processing, vol. 10, no. 1, pp. 140-147, 2001.
5. Brunelli, R. and O. Mich, "Image Retrieval by Example," IEEE Transactions on Multimedia, vol. 2, no. 3, pp. 164-171, 2000.
6. Weinhaus, F. M. and V. Devarajan, "Texture Mapping 3D Models of Real-World Scenes," ACM Computing Survey, vol. 29, no. 4, pp. 325-368, 1997.
7. Huang, Q., A. Puri, and Z. Liu, "Multimedia Search and Retrieval: New Concepts, System Implementation, and Application," IEEE Transactions on Circuits and System for Video Technology, vol. 10, no. 5, pp. 679-692, 2000.
8. Hung, K. W. and M. A. Yong, "A Content-based Image Retrieval System Integration Color, Shape and Spatial Analysis," IEEE Proceedings of the International Conference on Systems, Man, and Cybernetics, vol. 2, pp. 1484-1488, 2000.
9. Hwang, S., S. Cho, T. Wang, and P. C.-Y. Sheu, "A Fast 3-D Visualization Methodology Using Characteristic Views of Objects," International Journal of Software Engineering and Knowledge Engineering, vol. 8, no. 1, 1998.
10. Gudivada, V. N. and G. S. Jung, "Spatial Knowledge Representation and Retrieval in 3-D Image Database," IEEE Proceedings of the International Conference on Multimedia Computing and Systems, pp. 90-97, 1995.
11. Berretti, S., A. D. Bimbo, and P. Pala, "Retrieval by shape similarity with perceptual distance and effective indexing," IEEE Transactions on Multimedia, vol. 2, no. 4, pp. 225-239, 2000.
12. Xiong, W. and J. T. L. Wang, "Fast Similarity Search in Database of 3D Objects," IEEE International Conference on Tools with Artificial Intelligence, pp.16-23, 1998.
13. Lin, H., T. Risch, and T. Katchaounov, "Object-Oriented Mediator Queries to XML Data," Proceedings of 1st International Conference on Web Information Systems Engineering, vol. 2, 2000.
14. Bray, T., J. Paoli and C. M. Sperberg-McQueen, Extensible Markup Language (XML) 1.0, http://www.w3.org/TR/1998/REC-xml-19980210, 1998.
15. W3 Consortium, Extensible Markup Language(XML) Activity, XML Activity, http://www.w3.org/XML/Activity.html, 1998.
16. Chang, S. K., Q. Y. Shi, and C. W. Yan, "Iconic Indexing by 2-D Strings," IEEE Transactions on Pattern Analysis and Machine Intelligence, vol. 9, no. 3, 1987.
17. W3C Consortium, Document Object Model (DOM), http://www.w3.org/DOM/, 1998.
18. Hunter, J., "MPEG-7 Behind the Scenes", D-Lib Magazine, vol. 5, no. 9, September 1999.
19. Lee, K.H. and T. J. Lehman, MoDAL : An XML Based Dynamic User Interface Description System for Mobile PDAs, Proceedings of the International Conference on Internet Computing, Las Vegas, June 2000.
20. W3 Consortium, Synchronized Multimedia Integration Language (SMIL) 1.0 Specification, http://www.w3.org/TR/REC-smil/, 1998.
21. Microsoft, Simple Object Access Protocol, http://msdn.microsoft.com/soap/, 2000.

# Author Index

# Lecture Notes in Computer Science

For information about Vols. 1–2013
please contact your bookseller or Springer-Verlag

Vol. 2055: M. Margenstern, Y. Rogozhin (Eds.), Machines, Computations, and Universality. Proceedings, 2001. VIII, 321 pages. 2001.

Vol. 2056: E. Stroulia, S. Matwin (Eds.), Advances in Artificial Intelligence. Proceedings, 2001. XII, 366 pages. 2001. (Subseries LNAI).

Vol. 2057: M. Dwyer (Ed.), Model Checking Software. Proceedings, 2001. X, 313 pages. 2001.

Vol. 2059: C. Arcelli, L.P. Cordella, G. Sanniti di Baja (Eds.), Visual Form 2001. Proceedings, 2001. XIV, 799 pages. 2001.

Vol. 2060: T. Böhme, H. Unger (Eds.), Innovative Internet Computing Systems. Proceedings, 2001. VIII, 183 pages. 2001.

Vol. 2062: A. Nareyek, Constraint-Based Agents. XIV, 178 pages. 2001. (Subseries LNAI).

Vol. 2064: J. Blanck, V. Brattka, P. Hertling (Eds.), Computability and Complexity in Analysis. Proceedings, 2000. VIII, 395 pages. 2001.

Vol. 2065: H. Balster, B. de Brock, S. Conrad (Eds.), Database Schema Evolution and Meta-Modeling. Proceedings, 2000. X, 245 pages. 2001.

Vol. 2066: O. Gascuel, M.-F. Sagot (Eds.), Computational Biology. Proceedings, 2000. X, 165 pages. 2001.

Vol. 2068: K.R. Dittrich, A. Geppert, M.C. Norrie (Eds.), Advanced Information Systems Engineering. Proceedings, 2001. XII, 484 pages. 2001.

Vol. 2070: L. Monostori, J. Váncza, M. Ali (Eds.), Engineering of Intelligent Systems. Proceedings, 2001. XVIII, 951 pages. 2001. (Subseries LNAI).

Vol. 2071: R. Harper (Ed.), Types in Compilation. Proceedings, 2000. IX, 207 pages. 2001.

Vol. 2072: J. Lindskov Knudsen (Ed.), ECOOP 2001 – Object-Oriented Programming. Proceedings, 2001. XIII, 429 pages. 2001.

Vol. 2073: V.N. Alexandrov, J.J. Dongarra, B.A. Juliano, R.S. Renner, C.J.K. Tan (Eds.), Computational Science – ICCS 2001. Part I. Proceedings, 2001. XXVIII, 1306 pages. 2001.

Vol. 2074: V.N. Alexandrov, J.J. Dongarra, B.A. Juliano, R.S. Renner, C.J.K. Tan (Eds.), Computational Science – ICCS 2001. Part II. Proceedings, 2001. XXVIII, 1076 pages. 2001.

Vol. 2075: J.-M. Colom, M. Koutny (Eds.), Applications and Theory of Petri Nets 2001. Proceedings, 2001. XII, 403 pages. 2001.

Vol. 2076: F. Orejas, P.G. Spirakis, J. van Leeuwen (Eds.), Automata, Languages and Programming. Proceedings, 2001. XIV, 1083 pages. 2001.

Vol. 2077: V. Ambriola (Ed.), Software Process Technology. Proceedings, 2001. VIII, 247 pages. 2001.

Vol. 2078: R. Reed, J. Reed (Eds.), SDL 2001: Meeting UML. Proceedings, 2001. XI, 439 pages. 2001.

Vol. 2081: K. Aardal, B. Gerards (Eds.), Integer Programming and Combinatorial Optimization. Proceedings, 2001. XI, 423 pages. 2001.

Vol. 2082: M.F. Insana, R.M. Leahy (Eds.), Information Processing in Medical Imaging. Proceedings, 2001. XVI, 537 pages. 2001.

Vol. 2083: R. Goré, A. Leitsch, T. Nipkow (Eds.), Automated Reasoning. Proceedings, 2001. XV, 708 pages. 2001. (Subseries LNAI).

Vol. 2084: J. Mira, A. Prieto (Eds.), Connectionist Models of Neurons, Learning Processes, and Artificial Intelligence. Proceedings, 2001. Part I. XXVII, 836 pages. 2001.

Vol. 2085: J. Mira, A. Prieto (Eds.), Bio-Inspired Applications of Connectionism. Proceedings, 2001. Part II. XXVII, 848 pages. 2001.

Vol. 2086: M. Luck, V. Mařík, O. Štěpánková, R. Trappl (Eds.), Multi-Agent Systems and Applications. Proceedings, 2001. X, 437 pages. 2001. (Subseries LNAI).

Vol. 2089: A. Amir, G.M. Landau (Eds.), Combinatorial Pattern Matching. Proceedings, 2001. VIII, 273 pages. 2001.

Vol. 2091: J. Bigun, F. Smeraldi (Eds.), Audio- and Video-Based Biometric Person Authentication. Proceedings, 2001. XIII, 374 pages. 2001.

Vol. 2092: L. Wolf, D. Hutchison, R. Steinmetz (Eds.), Quality of Service – IWQoS 2001. Proceedings, 2001. XII, 435 pages. 2001.

Vol. 2093: P. Lorenz (Ed.), Networking – ICN 2001. Proceedings, 2001. Part I. XXV, 843 pages. 2001.

Vol. 2094: P. Lorenz (Ed.), Networking – ICN 2001. Proceedings, 2001. Part II. XXV, 899 pages. 2001.

Vol. 2095: B. Schiele, G. Sagerer (Eds.), Computer Vision Systems. Proceedings, 2001. X, 313 pages. 2001.

Vol. 2096: J. Kittler, F. Roli (Eds.), Multiple Classifier Systems. Proceedings, 2001. XII, 456 pages. 2001.

Vol. 2097: B. Read (Ed.), Advances in Databases. Proceedings, 2001. X, 219 pages. 2001.

Vol. 2098: J. Akiyama, M. Kano, M. Urabe (Eds.), Discrete and Computational Geometry. Proceedings, 2000. XI, 381 pages. 2001.

Vol. 2099: P. de Groote, G. Morrill, C. Retoré (Eds.), Logical Aspects of Computational Linguistics. Proceedings, 2001. VIII, 311 pages. 2001. (Subseries LNAI).

Vol. 2105: W. Kim, T.-W. Ling, Y-J. Lee, S.-S. Park (Eds.), The Human Society and the Internet. Proceedings, 2001. XVI, 470 pages. 2001.

Vol. 2106: M. Kerckhove (Ed.), Scale-Space and Morphology in Computer Vision. Proceedings, 2001. XI, 435 pages. 2001.

Vol. 2110: B. Hertzberger, A. Hoekstra, R. Williams (Eds.), High-Performance Computing and Networking. Proceedings, 2001. XVII, 733 pages. 2001.

Vol. 2118: X.S. Wang, G. Yu, H. Lu (Eds.), Advances in Web-Age Information Management. Proceedings, 2001. XV, 418 pages. 2001.

Vol. 2119: V. Varadharajan, Y. Mu (Eds.), Information Security and Privacy. Proceedings, 2001. XI, 522 pages. 2001.

Vol. 2121: C.S. Jensen, M. Schneider, B. Seeger, V.J. Tsotras (Eds.), Advances in Spatial and Temporal Databases. Proceedings, 2001. XI, 543 pages. 2001.

Vol. 2126: P. Cousot (Ed.), Static Analysis. Proceedings, 2001. XI, 439 pages. 2001.